Lecture Notes of the Institute for Computer Sciences, Social Informatics and Telecommunications Engineering 304

More information about this series at http://www.springer.com/series/8197

Songqing Chen · Kim-Kwang Raymond Choo ·
Xinwen Fu · Wenjing Lou ·
Aziz Mohaisen (Eds.)

Security and Privacy in Communication Networks

15th EAI International Conference, SecureComm 2019
Orlando, FL, USA, October 23–25, 2019
Proceedings, Part I

 Springer

Editors
Songqing Chen (iD)
George Mason University
Fairfax, VA, USA

Kim-Kwang Raymond Choo (iD)
The University of Texas at San Antonio
San Antonio, TX, USA

Xinwen Fu (iD)
Boston University
Lowell, MA, USA

Wenjing Lou
Virginia Tech
Blacksburg, VA, USA

Aziz Mohaisen (iD)
University of Central Florida
Orlando, FL, USA

ISSN 1867-8211   ISSN 1867-822X   (electronic)
Lecture Notes of the Institute for Computer Sciences, Social Informatics
and Telecommunications Engineering
ISBN 978-3-030-37227-9   ISBN 978-3-030-37228-6   (eBook)
https://doi.org/10.1007/978-3-030-37228-6

This Springer imprint is published by the registered company Springer Nature Switzerland AG
The registered company address is: Gewerbestrasse 11, 6330 Cham, Switzerland

Preface

The importance of ensuring security and privacy in communications networks is recognized by both the research and practitioner community. This is, for example, evidenced by the establishment of the U.S. Cyber Command as a unified combatant command in May 2018. This is also the focus of the 15th EAI International Conference on Security and Privacy in Communication Networks (SecureComm 2019).

This proceedings contains 56 papers, which were selected from 149 submissions (i.e. acceptance rate of 37.6%) from universities, national laboratories, and the private sector from across the USA as well as other countries in Europe and Asia. All the submissions went through an extensive review process by internationally-recognized experts in cybersecurity.

Any successful conference requires the contributions of different stakeholder groups and individuals, who have selfishly volunteered their time and energy in disseminating the call for papers, submitting their research findings, participating in the peer reviews and discussions, etc. First and foremost, we would like to offer our gratitude to the entire Organizing Committee for guiding the entire process of the conference. We are also deeply grateful to all the Technical Program Committee members for their time and efforts in reading, commenting, debating, and finally selecting the papers. We also thank all the external reviewers for assisting the Technical Program Committee in their particular areas of expertise as well as all the authors, participants, and session chairs for their valuable contributions. Support from the Steering Committee and EAI staff members was also crucial in ensuring the success of the conference. It has been a great privilege to be working with such a large group of dedicated and talented individuals.

We hope that you found the discussions and interactions at SecureComm 2019 intellectually stimulating, as well as enjoyed what Orlando, FL, had to offer. Enjoy the proceedings!

September 2019

Xinwen Fu
Kim-Kwang Raymond Choo
Aziz Mohaisen
Wenjing Lou

Organization

Steering Committee

Imrich Chlamtac   University of Trento, Italy
Guofei Gu   Texas A&M University, USA
Peng Liu   Pennsylvania State University, USA
Sencun Zhu   Pennsylvania State University, USA

Organizing Committee

General Chairs

Xinwen Fu   University of Central Florida, USA
Kim-Kwang Raymond Choo   The University of Texas at San Antonio, USA

TPC Chair and Co-chairs

Aziz Mohaisen   University of Central Florida, USA
Wenjing Lou   Virginia Tech, USA

Sponsorship and Exhibit Chair

Qing Yang   University of North Texas, USA

Local Chairs

Clay Posey   University of Central Florida, USA
Cliff C. Zou   University of Central Florida, USA

Workshops Chairs

Kaiqi Xiong   University of South Florida, USA
Liang Xiao   Xiamen University, China

Publicity and Social Media Chairs

Yao Liu   University of South Florida, USA
Zhen Ling   Southeast University, China

Publications Chairs

Songqing Chen   George Mason University, USA
Houbing Song   Embry-Riddle Aeronautical University, USA

Web Chairs

Bryan Pearson   University of Central Florida, USA
Yue Zhang   University of Central Florida, USA

Panels Chairs

Simon (Xinming) Ou   University of South Florida, USA
Craig A. Shue   Worcester Polytechnic Institute, USA

Demos Chair

Song Han   University of Connecticut, USA

Tutorials Chair

Yong Guan   Iowa State University, USA

Technical Program Committee

Amro Awad   University of Central Florida, USA
Kai Bu   Zhejiang University, China
Yinzhi Cao   Johns Hopkins University, USA
Eric Chan-Tin   Loyola University Chicago, USA
Kai Chen   Chinese Academy of Sciences, China
Yu Chen   Binghamton University - SUNY, USA
Sherman S. M. Chow   The Chinese University of Hong Kong, Hong Kong,
                          China
Jun Dai   California State University, Sacramento, USA
Karim Elish   Florida Polytechnic University, USA
Birhanu Eshete   University of Michigan, USA
Debin Gao   Singapore Management University, Singapore
Le Guan   University of Georgia, USA
Yong Guan   Iowa State University, USA
Yongzhong He   Beijing Jiaotong University, China
Murtuza Jadliwala   The University of Texas at San Antonio, USA
George Kesidis   Pennsylvania State University, USA
Joongheon Kim   Chung-Ang University, South Korea
Hyoungshick Kim   Sungkyunkwan University, South Korea
Gokhan Kul   Delaware State University, USA
Laurent L. Njilla   Air Force Research Laboratory, USA
Yingjiu Li   Singapore Management University, Singapore
Jingqiang Lin   Chinese Academy of Sciences, China
Zhiqiang Lin   The Ohio State University, USA
Yao Liu   University of South Florida, USA
Javier Lopez   UMA, Spain
Wenjing Lou   Virginia Tech, USA
Rongxing Lu   University of New Brunswick, Canada

Contents – Part I

Contents – Part II

Blockchains and IoT

Security and Analytics

Machine Learning, Privately

Better Clouds

ATCS Workshop

Blockchains

Trustless Framework for Iterative Double Auction Based on Blockchain

Truc D. T. Nguyen$^{(\boxtimes)}$ and My T. Thai

Department of Computer and Information Science and Engineering,
University of Florida, Gainesville, FL 32611, USA
truc.nguyen@ufl.edu, mythai@cise.ufl.edu

Abstract. One of the major problems in current implementations of iterative double auction is that they rely on a trusted third party to handle the auction process. This imposes the risk of single point of failures and monopoly. In this paper, we aim to tackle this problem by proposing a novel decentralized and trustless framework for iterative double auction based on blockchain. Our design adopts the smart contract and state channel technologies to enable a double auction process among parties that do not trust each other, while minimizing the blockchain transactions. We provide a formal development of the framework and highlight the security of our design against adversaries.

Keywords: Blockchain · Iterative double auction · Trustless · State channel

1 Introduction

In recent years, following the great success of Bitcoin [1], the *blockchain* technology has emerged as a trending research topic in both academic institutes and industries associations. In a nutshell, blockchain can be seen as a decentralized database or digital ledger that contains append-only data blocks where each block is comprised of valid transactions, timestamp and the cryptographic hash of the previous block. By design, a blockchain system is managed by nodes in a peer-to-peer network and operates efficiently in a decentralized fashion without the need of a central authority. In specific, it enables a trustless network where participants can transact although they do not trust one another. Moreover, a blockchain system may also employ the smart contracts technology to enable a wide range of applications that go beyond financial transactions [2]. In the context of blockchain, *smart contracts* are defined as self-executing and self-enforcing programs that are stored on chain. They are deployed to the blockchain system with publicly visible terms and conditions. Blockchain and smart contracts together have inspired many decentralized applications and stimulated scientific research in diverse domains [3–9].

An auction is a market institution in which traders or parties submit bids that can be an offer to buy or sell at a given price [10]. A market can enable only

© ICST Institute for Computer Sciences, Social Informatics and Telecommunications Engineering 2019
Published by Springer Nature Switzerland AG 2019. All Rights Reserved
S. Chen et al. (Eds.): SecureComm 2019, LNICST 304, pp. 3–22, 2019.
https://doi.org/10.1007/978-3-030-37228-6_1

buyers, only sellers, or both to make offers. In the latter case, it is referred as a two-sided or *double auction*. A double auction process can be one-shot or iterative (repeated). The different between them is that an iterative double auction process has multiple, instead of one, iterations [11]. In each iteration, each party submits a bid illustrating the selling/buying price and supplying/demanding units of resource. This process goes on until the market reaches Nash Equilibrium (NE). In practice, the iterative double auction has been widely used in allocating divisible resources such as energy trading [7,12], mobile data offloading [13], or resource allocation in autonomous networks [14]. However, current implementations of double auction system require a centralized and trusted auctioneer to regulate the auction process. This results in the risk of single point of failures, monopoly, and privacy.

Although many research work has tried to develop a trading system combining the iterative double auction and blockchain [7,15], nonetheless, they still need a trusted third-party to handle the auction process. In this work, we leverage blockchain and smart contracts to propose a general framework for iterative double auction that is completely *decentralized* and *trustless*. Although a naive mechanism to eliminate the trusted third-party is to implement the auctioneer in a blockchain smart contract, this results in high latency and transaction fees. To overcome this problem, we adopt the *state channel* technology [16] that enables the off-chain execution of smart contracts without changing the trust assumption.

Contribution. The key contribution of this work is the formal development of a novel decentralized and trustless framework for iterative double auction based on blockchain. With this framework, we are able to run existing double auction algorithms efficiently on a blockchain network without being suffered from the high latency of on-chain transactions. Specifically, we develop a Universally Composable (UC)-style model [17] for the double auction protocol and prove the security properties of our design using the simulation-based UC framework.

Organization. The remainder of this paper is organized in the following manners. We summarize the related work in Sect. 2. In Sect. 3, we discuss how blockchain and double auction can be combined. We will first present a straw-man design and then provide a high-level view of our framework. Section 4 presents the formal security definitions of our work. Then, we provide a formal specification of our framework in Sect. 5. Finally, Sect. 6 gives the concluding remarks.

2   Related Work

Double Auction Based on Blockchain. As blockchain is an emerging technology, there has been many research work addressing double auction with blockchain. Recently, Thakur et al. [18] published a paper on distributed double auction for peer to peer energy trading. The authors use the McAfee mechanism to process the double auction on smart contracts. In [19], the authors presented BlockCloud which is a service-centric blockchain architecture that supports double auction. The auction model in this work uses a trade-reduction mechanism. However, the double auction mechanism in these work is one-shot and is only applicable to single-unit demands. For applications like energy or wireless spectrum allocation, these models greatly limit users' capability to utilize the products [20].

In [7] and [15], the authors propose blockchain-based energy trading using double auction. The auction mechanism is implemented as an iterative process which can be used for divisible goods. Although the system presented in these papers employ blockchain, the double auction process is still facilitated by a central entity. The blockchain is only used for settling payments. Our work is fundamentally different as we aim to design a framework that can regulate the iterative double auction process in a decentralized and trustless fashion.

State Channel. Although there has been many research effort on payment channels [21,22], the state channel has only emerged in recent years. State channel is a generalization of payment channel in which users can execute complex smart contracts off-chain while still maintains the trustless property. Dziembowski et al. [16] is the first work that present the formal specifications of state channels.

3 Double Auction with Blockchain

3.1 Auction Model

We consider a set of parties that are connected to a blockchain network. We divide the set of parties into a set $\mathcal{B}$ of buyers who require resources from a set $\mathcal{S}$ of sellers. These two sets are disjoint. The demand of a buyer $i \in \mathcal{B}$ is denoted as d_i and the supply of a seller $j \in \mathcal{S}$ is denoted as s_j. In this work, we adopt the auction model proposed in [23], which elicits hidden information about parties in order to maximize social welfare, as a general iterative double auction process that converges to a Nash Equilibrium (NE).

A bid profile of a buyer $i \in \mathcal{B}$ is denoted as $b_i = (\beta_i, x_i)$ where β_i is the buying price per unit of resource and x_i is the amount of resource that i wants to buy. Likewise, a bid profile of a seller $j \in \mathcal{S}$ is denoted as $b_j = (\alpha_j, y_j)$ where α_j is the selling price per unit of resource and y_j is the amount of resource that j wants to supply.

The auction process consists of multiple iterations. At an iteration k, the buyers and sellers submit their bid profiles $b_i^{(k)}$ and $b_j^{(k)}$ to the auctioneer. Then, a double auction algorithm will be used to determine the best response $b_i^{(k+1)}$ and $b_j^{(k+1)}$ for the next iteration. This process goes on until the auction reaches NE, at which the bid demand and supply (x_i, y_j) will converge to an optimal value that maximizes the social welfare. An example of such algorithm can be referred to [23]. The pseudo code for a centralized auctioneer is presented in Algorithm 1.

Algorithm 1

$k \leftarrow 1$
while not NE **do**
    Receive bid profiles $b_i^{(k)}$ and $b_j^{(k)}$ from buyers and sellers
    Compute best responses $b_i^{(k+1)}$ and $b_j^{(k+j)}$ based on [23]
    Send $b_i^{(k+1)}$ and $b_j^{(k+1)}$ back to sellers and buyers
    $k \leftarrow k + 1$
end while

3.2   Straw-Man Design

In this section, we present a design of the trading system. The trading mechanism must meet the following requirements:

(a) Decentralized: the auction process is not facilitated by any central middle-man
(b) Trustless: the parties do not have to trust each other.
(c) Non-Cancellation: parties may attempt to prematurely abort from the protocol to avoid payments. These malicious parties must be financially penalized.

Based on the requirements, we will first show a straw-man design of the system which has some deficiencies in terms of latency and high transaction fee. Then, we will propose a trading system using state channels to address those problems.

In this system, we deploy a smart contract to the blockchain to regulate the trading process. Prior to placing any bid, all parties must make a deposit to the smart contract. If a party tries to cheat by prematurely aborting the trading process, he or she will lose that deposit and the remaining parties will receive compensation. Therefore, the deposit deters parties from cheating. At the end of the trading process, these deposits will be returned to the parties.

In this straw-man design, the auction process will be executed on-chain, that is, the smart contract will act as an auctioneer and thus will execute Algorithm 1. As the auction process consists of multiple iterations, the system will follow the activity diagram in Fig. 1 at each iteration.

At an iteration k, all buyers and sellers submit their bids $b_i^{(k)}$ and $b_j^{(k)}$, respectively, to the smart contract. In order to avoid unresponsiveness, a timeout is set for collecting bids. Should any parties fail to meet this deadline, the system considers that they aborted the process.

The smart contract then determines the best response $b_i^{(k+1)}$ and $b_j^{(k+j)}$ for buyers and sellers, respectively, until the trading system reaches NE. This design works, however, has two main disadvantages:

1. Transaction latency: each message exchanged between parties and the smart contract is treated as a blockchain transaction which takes time to get committed.

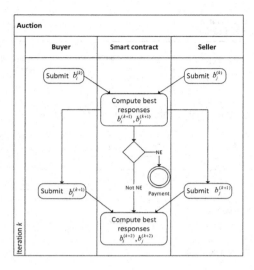

Fig. 1. Auction phase

2. High computational complexity on the smart contract which means that the blockchain will require high transaction fees.

In other words, the buyers and sellers are having the entire blockchain to process their auction.

3.3 Blockchain with State Channels

As the double auction process involves multiple iterations and has a fixed set of participants, state channel [16] is a proper solution to address the deficiencies of the straw-man design. Instead of processing the auction on-chain, the parties will be able to update the states of the auction off-chain. Whenever something goes wrong (e.g., some parties try to cheat), the users always have the option of referring back to the blockchain for the certainty of on-chain transactions.

In the same manner as the straw-man design, the parties deploy a smart contract to the blockchain. However, this smart contract does not regulate the auction process, but instead acts as a judge to resolve disputes. The parties must also make a deposit to this contract prior to the auction. Figure 2 illustrates the overview of the operation in state channel.

After deploying the smart contract, the parties can now begin the auction process in a "state channel". At each iteration k of the auction, we define two operations: (1) collecting bids and (2) determining the best responses. Denoting the set of parties as $\mathcal{P} = \mathcal{B} \cup \mathcal{S} = \{p_1, p_2, ..., p_n\}$, in the first operation, each party broadcasts a blockchain transaction containing its bid $b_{p_i}^{(k)}$ to all other parties. Note that this transaction is a *valid* blockchain transaction and it is only broadcasted locally among the parties. Upon receiving that transaction,

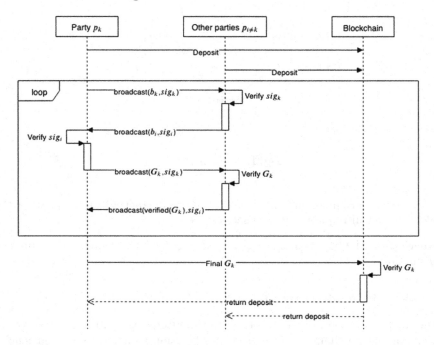

Fig. 2. Double auction state channel

Fig. 3. Sequence diagram of the double auction process.

each party has to verify its signature. After this operation, each party now has the bid profiles of all other parties.

Then we move to the second operation of determining the best response. A party will be chosen to compute the best responses, in fact, it does not matter who will execute this computation because the results will later be verified by other parties. Therefore, this party can be chosen randomly or based on the amount of deposit to the smart contract. Let p_k be the one who carries out the computation at iteration k, G_k be the result that consists of the best response $b_{p_i}^{(k+1)}$ for each party p_i, p_k will broadcast a blockchain transaction containing G_k to all other parties. Upon receiving this transaction, each party has to verify the result G_k, then signs it and broadcasts another transaction containing G_k to all other parties. This action means that the party agrees with G_k. After this step, each party will have G_k together with the signatures of all parties.

When the auction process reaches NE, a party will send the final G_k together with all the signatures to the smart contract. The smart contract then verifies the G_k and if there is no dispute, the state channel is closed. Finally, the payment will be processed on-chain and the smart contract refunds the initial deposit to all parties. The entire process is summarized in the sequence diagram in Fig. 3.

As can be seen, the blockchain is invoked only two times and thus saves tons of transaction fees comparing to the straw-man design. Moreover, as the transactions are not sent to the blockchain, the latency is only limited by the communication network among the parties. We can also see that the bid profiles are only known among the involving parties, not to the entire blockchain, thus enhances the privacy.

4   Formal Definitions and Security Models

In this section, we describe the formal security definitions and models used in the construction of this framework. Before that, we establish some security and privacy goals for our system.

4.1   Security and Privacy Goals

We consider a computationally efficient adversary who can corrupt any subset of parties. By corruption, the attacker can take full control over a party which includes acquiring the internal state and all the messages destined to that party. Moreover, it can send arbitrary messages on the corrupted party's behalf.

With respect to the adversarial model, we define the security and privacy notions of interest as follows:

- Unforgeability: We use the ECDSA signature scheme which is believed to be unforgeable against a chosen message attack [24]. This signature scheme is currently being used in the Ethereum blockchain [2].
- Non-Repudiation: Once a bidder has submitted a bid, they must not be able to repudiate having made the relevant bid.
- Public Verifiability: All parties can be verified as having correctly followed the auction protocol.
- Robustness: The auction process must not be affected by invalid bids nor by participants not following the correct auction protocol.
- Input independence: Each party does not see others' bid before committing to their own.
- Liveness: In an optimistic case when all parties are honest, the computation is processed within a small amount of time (off-chain messages only). When some parties are corrupted, the computation is completed within a predictable amount of time.

4.2   Our Model

The entities in our system are modeled as interactive Turing machines that communicate with each other via a secure and authenticated channel. The system operates in the presence of an adversary $\mathcal{A}$ who, upon corruption of a party p, seizes the internal state of p and all the incoming and outgoing packets of p.

Assumptions and Notation. We denote $\mathcal{P} = \mathcal{B} \cup \mathcal{S} = \{p_1, p_2, ..., p_n\}$ as the set of n parties. We assume that $\mathcal{P}$ is known before opening the state channel and $|\mathcal{P}| \geq 2$. The blockchain is represented as an append-only ledger $\mathcal{L}$ that is managed by a global ideal functionality $\mathcal{F}_{\mathcal{L}}$ (such as [16]). The state of $\mathcal{F}_{\mathcal{L}}$ is defined by the current balance of all accounts and smart contracts' state; and is publicly visible to all parties. $\mathcal{F}_{\mathcal{L}}$ supports the functionalities of adding or subtracting one's balance. We also denote $\mathcal{F}(x)$ as retrieving the current value of the state variable x from an ideal functionality $\mathcal{F}$.

We further assume that any message destined to $\mathcal{F}_{\mathcal{L}}$ can be seen by all parties (in the same manner as blockchain transactions are publicly visible). For simplicity, we assume that all parties have enough fund in their accounts for making deposits to the smart contract. Furthermore, each party and the ideal functionality will automatically discard any messages originated from a party that is not in $\mathcal{P}$ or the message's signature is invalid.

Communication. In this work, we assume a synchronous communication network. We define a *round* as a unit of time corresponding to the maximum delay needed to transmit an off-chain message between a pair of parties. Any modifications on $\mathcal{F}_{\mathcal{L}}$ and smart contracts take at most $\Delta \in \mathbb{N}$ rounds, this Δ reflects the fact that updates on the blockchain are not instant but can be completed within a predictable amount of time. Furthermore, each party can retrieve the current state of $\mathcal{F}_{\mathcal{L}}$ and smart contracts in one round.

5   Double Auction State Channel

In this section, we describe the ideal functionality of our system that defines how a double auction process is operated using the state channel technology. Afterwards, we present the design of our protocol that realizes the ideal functionality.

5.1   Ideal Functionality

First, we define the ledger's ideal functionality $\mathcal{F}_{\mathcal{L}}$. Based on Sect. 4.2, the $\mathcal{F}_{\mathcal{L}}$ supports adding and subtracting one's balance, hence, we give the corresponding definition in Fig. 4.

The formal definition of the ideal functionality $\mathcal{F}_{auction}$ is presented in Fig. 5. As can be seen, it supports the following functionalities:

```
┌─────────────────────────────────────────────────────────────────────────┐
│                          Functionality 𝓕_𝓛                                │
│                                                                           │
│  Store a vector (x₁, x₂, ..., xₙ) that denotes the balance of n parties.  │
│                                                                           │
│  Adding and subtracting balances                                          │
│                                                                           │
│   − On input update(pᵢ, s):                                               │
│      1. If s ≥ 0, set xᵢ = xᵢ + s                                         │
│      2. If s < 0 and xᵢ ≥ −s, set xᵢ = xᵢ + s                             │
│      3. Otherwise, reply with an error() message and stop.                │
│                                                                           │
└─────────────────────────────────────────────────────────────────────────┘
```

Functionality $\mathcal{F}_\mathcal{L}$

Store a vector $(x_1, x_2, ..., x_n)$ that denotes the balance of n parties.

Adding and subtracting balances

- On **input** $update(p_i, s)$:
  1. If $s \geq 0$, set $x_i = x_i + s$
  2. If $s < 0$ and $x_i \geq -s$, set $x_i = x_i + s$
  3. Otherwise, reply with an $error()$ message and stop.

Fig. 4. Ledger's functionality $\mathcal{F}_\mathcal{L}$

- Open channel
- Determine best response
- Revocation
- Close channel

The state channel creation is initiated by receiving a $create()$ message from a party. The functionality then waits for receiving $create()$ from all other parties within $1 + (n - 1)\Delta$ rounds. If this happens then the functionality removes a deposit from each party's balance on the blockchain. Since, all parties have to send the $create()$ message, we achieve the consensus on creation.

Each iteration k of the double auction process starts with receiving the $best\_response(k)$ message from a party. Then all parties must submit a commitment of their bids which is a hash function of the bid and a random nonce. After that, all parties must submit the true bid that matches with the hash they sent before. Any party fails to submit in time or does not submit the true bid will be eliminated from the double auction process. With the commitment step, one party cannot see the other parties' bid which satisfies the *Input independence*.

When one party fails to behave honestly, it will be eliminated from the auction process and will not receive the deposit back. A party can voluntarily abort an auction process by sending a $revoke()$ message and it will receive the deposit back. Then, the auction can continue with the remaining parties. Therefore, the functionality satisfies the *Robustness*. Moreover, a malicious party cannot delay the advancing of the protocol to a great extent, because after timeout, the execution still proceeds. In the best case, when everyone behaves honestly and does not terminate in the middle of the auction process, the computation is processed within $O(1)$ rounds, otherwise, $O(\Delta)$ rounds. Thus, the *Liveness* is satisfied.

In the end, the state channel begins its termination procedure upon receiving a $close()$ message from a party. Next, it awaits obtaining the $close()$ messages from the remaining parties within $1 + (|\mathcal{P}| - 1)\Delta$ rounds. If all the parties are unanimous in closing the state channel, the functionality returns the deposit back to all parties' account.

Functionality $\mathcal{F}_{auction}$

Open channel

- On **input** *create()* from p_i
  1. For each party P_j, $j \neq i$, wait to receive *create()*. If not receiving after $1 + (n-1)\Delta$ rounds then stop.
  2. Otherwise, instruct $\mathcal{F}_{\mathcal{L}}$ to remove a deposit from each of the party's account on the blockchain within Δ rounds.
  3. *channel = created*

Determine best response

- On **input** *best_response(k)* from p_i
  - Commitment:
    1. For each party p_i, wait until receiving $C_i^{(k)} = \mathcal{H}(b_i^{(k)} \| r_i^{(k)})$ from p_i where $b_i^{(k)}$ is the bid and $r_i^{(k)}$ is a random nonce.
    2. If any party p_i fails to submit the commitment within 1 round, remove p_i from $\mathcal{P}$ then stop.
  - Reveal and compute:
    1. For each party P_i, wait until receiving $R_i^{(k)} = (b_i^{(k)} \| r_i^{(k)})$ from p_i.
    2. If any party p_i fails to submit within 1 round or $\mathcal{H}(R_i^{(k)}) \neq C_i^{(k)}$, remove p_i from $\mathcal{P}$ then stop.
    3. Compute best response G_k based on Algorithm 1
    4. Send G_k to all parties in 1 round.

Revocation

- On **input** *revoke()* from p_i: within Δ rounds
  1. remove p_i from $\mathcal{P}$, add the deposit to p_i's balance on the blockchain

Close channel

- On **input** *close()* from p_i: if $p_i \notin \mathcal{P}$ then stop. Otherwise:
  1. Within $1 + (|\mathcal{P}| - 1)\Delta$ rounds, wait for receiving *close()* from $p_j, j \neq i$
  2. If fails to receive then stop.
  3. Else, within Δ rounds, add the deposit to every party p_i's balance on the blockchain, where $p_i \in \mathcal{P}$
  4. *channel = $\perp$*

Fig. 5. Ideal functionality $\mathcal{F}_{auction}$

5.2 Protocol for Double Auction State Channel

In this section, we will discuss in details the double auction protocol based on state channel that realizes the $\mathcal{F}_{auction}$. The protocol includes two main parts: (1) a Judge contact and (2) Off-chain protocol.

Judge Contract. The main functionality of this contract is to regulate the state channel and handle disputes. Every party is able to submit a *state* that everyone has agreed on to this contract. However, the contract only accepts the state with the highest version number. Once a party submits a state G, the contract will wait for some deadline T for other parties to raise disputes. See Fig. 6 for the functionality of the Judge contract. Note that the contract $\mathcal{F}_{Judge}$ has a state variable *channel* which indicates whether the channel is opened or not. If the channel is not opened (*channel* $= \perp$), the three functionalities "State submission", "Revocation", and "Close channel" cannot be executed. In the same manner, if the channel is already opened (*channel* $= created$) then the functionality "Open channel" cannot be executed.

As the contract always maintains the valid state on which all parties have agreed (by verifying all the signatures), we can publicly verify if all parties are following the protocol. When the state channel is closed, the contract is now hold the latest state with the final bids of all the parties, and by the immutability of blockchain, no bidder can deny having made the relevant bid. Therefore, this contract satisfies the *Non-Repudiation* and *Public Verifiability* goals.

Off-chain Protocol π. In this section, we present the off-chain protocol π that operates among parties in a double auction process. In the same manner as $\mathcal{F}_{auction}$, the protocol π consists of four parts: (1) Create state channel, (2) Determine best response, (3) Revocation, and (4) Close state channel.

First, to create a new state channel, the environment sends a message *create()* to one of the parties. Let's denote this initiating party as p_i. The detailed protocol is shown in Fig. 7. p_i will send a *create()* message to the smart contract $\mathcal{F}_{Judge}$ which will take Δ rounds to get confirmed on the blockchain. As this message is visible to the whole network, any $p_{j \neq i}$ can detect this event and also send a *create()* message to $\mathcal{F}_{Judge}$. To detect this event, each p_j needs to retrieve the current state of blockchain which takes 1 round and as there are $n - 1$ parties p_j, thus p_i has to wait $1 + (n - 1)\Delta$ rounds. If all parties agree on creating the state channel, this process will be successful and the channel will be opened. After that, the smart contract will take a deposit from the account of each party.

When parties run into dispute, they will have to resolve on-chain. In specific, the procedure *Submit()* as shown in Fig. 8 allows any party to submit the current state to the smart contract. However, as stated above, $\mathcal{F}_{Judge}$ only considers the valid state that has the highest version number. In this procedure, we also define a *proof* of a state G. Based on the algorithm used for double auction, this *proof* is anything that can verify whether the calculation of G in an iteration is correct or not. For example, *proof* can be all the valid bids in that iteration. When any party submits a state, the $\mathcal{F}_{Judge}$ will raise the state variable $flag = dispute$. Upon detecting this event, other parties can submit their states if they have higher version numbers. After a deadline of T rounds, if none of the parties can submit a newer state, $\mathcal{F}_{Judge}$ will set $flag = \perp$ to conclude the dispute period. Furthermore, we also note that this procedure also supports eliminating any dishonest party that does not follow the protocol by setting the parameter p_r to that party. If a party p_i wants to eliminate a party p_r, it will need other parties, except p_r, to call the *Submit()* procedure to remove p_r from $\mathcal{P}$.

Contract $\mathcal{F}_{Judge}$

Open channel

- On **input** $create()$ from p_i:
    - For each party p_j, $j \neq i$, wait to receive $create()$. If not receiving after Δ rounds then stop.
    - Otherwise:
        * $channel = created$.
        * instruct $\mathcal{F}_{\mathcal{L}}$ to remove a deposit from each of the party's account on the blockchain within Δ rounds.
        * Initialize $bestVersion = -1$, $state = \emptyset$, $flag = \bot$, the set of parties $\mathcal{P}$

State submission

- On **input** $state\_submit(p_r, v, G, proof)$ from p_i
    1. if $p_r \neq \bot$, wait for $(|\mathcal{P}| - 2)\Delta$ rounds. Then, if it receives $state\_submit(p'_r, v', G', proof')$, such that $p'_r = p_r$, from all parties except p_r and p_i then remove p_r from $\mathcal{P}$
    2. if $v \leq bestVersion$ the stop.
    3. Verify the signatures of $\mathcal{P}$ on G and verify the state G using $proof$. If failed then stop
    4. $bestVersion = v$
    5. $state = G$
    6. $flag = dispute$
    7. Set $flag = \bot$ after a deadline of T rounds unless $bestVersion$ is changed.

Revocation

- On **input** $revoke()$ from p_i: within Δ rounds
    1. remove p_i from $\mathcal{P}$, instruct $\mathcal{F}_{\mathcal{L}}$ to add the deposit to p_i's balance on the blockchain

Close channel

- On **input** $close()$ from p_i: if $p_i \notin \mathcal{P}$ then stop. Otherwise:
    1. If $flag = dispute$ then stop.
    2. Within $1 + (|\mathcal{P}| - 1)\Delta$ rounds, wait for receiving $close()$ from $p_j, j \neq i$
    3. If fails to receive then stop.
    4. Else, within Δ rounds, add the deposit to every party p_i's balance on the blockchain, where $p_i \in \mathcal{P}$
    5. $channel = \bot$

Fig. 6. Judge contract

Protocol π: Create state channel

Party p_i: On **input** $create()$ from environment

1. Send $create()$ to $\mathcal{F}_{Judge}$ and wait for $1 + (n-1)\Delta$ rounds.

Party $p_{j \neq i}$: Upon p_i sends $create()$ to $\mathcal{F}_{Judge}$

2. Send $create()$ to $\mathcal{F}_{Judge}$ and wait for $(n-2)\Delta$ rounds.

For each party:

3. If $\mathcal{F}_{Judge}(channel) = created$ then outputs $created()$ to the environment.

Fig. 7. Protocol π: Create state channel

Procedure: $Submit(p_i, p_r, v, G)$

Party p_i

1. If $p_i = \bot$ and $v \leq \mathcal{F}_{judge}(bestVersion)$ then stop.
2. Otherwise, construct $proof$ for G and send $state\_submit(p_r, v, G, proof)$ to $\mathcal{F}_{Judge}$ in Δ rounds.
3. Wait until $\mathcal{F}_{judge}(flag) = \bot$ then stop.

Party $p_{j \neq i}$: On $\mathcal{F}_{judge}(flag) = dispute$

4. If the latest valid state G_k has $k > \mathcal{F}_{judge}(bestVersion)$ then construct $proof$ for G_k and send $state\_submit(\bot, k, G_k, proof)$ to $\mathcal{F}_{Judge}$ in Δ rounds.
5. Wait until $\mathcal{F}_{judge}(flag) = \bot$ then stop.

Fig. 8. Procedure $Submit$

Next, in Fig. 9, we present the protocol for determining the best response which only consists of off-chain messages if all the parties are honest. In each iteration k, this process starts when the environment sends $best\_response(k)$ to a party p_i. Again, this does not violate the trustless property since p_i can be any party chosen at random. First, p_i broadcasts the commitment $C_i^{(k)}$ of its bid which only takes one round since this is an off-chain message. Other parties upon receiving this message will also broadcast their commitments. Then, p_i proceeds to broadcast the reveal $R_i^{(k)}$ of its bid and hence, other parties upon receiving this $R_i^{(k)}$ also broadcast their reveals. If any party refuses to send their bids or sends an invalid bid, other parties will call the $Submit$ procedure to eliminate that dishonest party from the auction process. Thus, that party will lose all the deposit. In practice, one may consider refunding a portion of deposit back to that party. To achieve this, we only need to modify the first line of the functionality "State submission" in $\mathcal{F}_{Judge}$ to return a portion of deposit to p_r.

During the auction process, some parties may want to abort the auction process. In order to avoid losing the deposit, they must use the Revocation protocol described in Fig. 10 to send a $revoke()$ message to $\mathcal{F}_{Judge}$. In this case, they will get the deposit back in full and be removed from the set $\mathcal{P}$. Other parties upon detecting this operation also update their local $\mathcal{P}$ to ensure the consistency.

Finally, Fig. 11 illustrates the protocol for closing the state channel. One technical point in this protocol is that we must check whether there is any ongoing dispute. If so then we must not close the channel. In the same way of opening the channel, a party p_i also initiates the request by sending a message $close()$ to the smart contract. Upon detecting this event, other parties may also send $close()$. If all parties agreed on closing the channel, they will get the deposit back.

5.3   Security and Privacy Analysis

We denote $\text{EXEC}_{\pi,\mathcal{A},\mathcal{E}}$ as the outputs of the environment $\mathcal{E}$ when interacting with the adversary $\mathcal{A}$ and parties running the protocol π. From [17], we have the following definition:

Definition 1 (UC-Security). *A protocol π UC-realizes an ideal functionality $\mathcal{F}$ if for any adversarial $\mathcal{A}$, there exists a simulator $\mathcal{S}$ such that for any environment $\mathcal{E}$ the outputs $\text{EXEC}_{\pi,\mathcal{A},\mathcal{E}}$ and $\text{EXEC}_{\pi,\mathcal{S},\mathcal{E}}$ are computationally indistinguishable.*

In this section, we will prove the following theorem:

Theorem 1. *Under the assumptions given in Sect. 4.2, the protocol π UC-realizes the ideal functionality $\mathcal{F}_{auction}$ in the $(\mathcal{F}_{judge}, \mathcal{F}_{\mathcal{L}})$-hybrid model.*

Proof. The main goal of this analysis is to ensure the consistency of timings, i.e., the environment $\mathcal{E}$ must receive the same message in the same round in both worlds. Furthermore, in any round, the messages exchanged between any entities as well as the internal state of each party must be identical between the two worlds, which will make $\mathcal{E}$ unable to perceive whether it is interacting with the real world or the ideal one.

Per Canneti [17], the proof strategy consists of constructing the simulator $\mathcal{S}$ that handles the corrupted parties and simulates the $(\mathcal{F}_{judge}, \mathcal{F}_{\mathcal{L}})$-hybrid world while interacting with $\mathcal{F}_{auction}$. Hence, the simulator will maintain a copy of the hybrid world internally. We further assume that upon receiving a message from a party, the ideal functionality $\mathcal{F}_{auction}$ will leak that message to the simulator. For simplicity, we omit these operations from the description of the simulator. Since $\mathcal{S}$ locally runs a copy of the hybrid world, $\mathcal{S}$ knows the behavior of the

---

Protocol π: Determine best response

Party p_i: On input _best_response(k)_ from the environment

1. Broadcast $C_i^{(k)} = \mathcal{H}(b_i^{(k)}||r_i^{(k)})$ to other parties and wait for 1 round. Then go to step 4.

> **Party $p_{j \neq i}$: On input $C_i^{(k)}$ from p_i**

2. Broadcast $C_j^{(k)} = \mathcal{H}(b_j^{(k)}||r_j^{(k)})$ to other parties and wait for 1 round.
3. If there exists a party $p_{l \neq j}$ such that it doesn't receive $C_l^{(k)}$ then execute $Submit(p_l, k-1, G_{k-1})$ and stop.

Party p_i

4. If there exists a party p_j such that it doesn't receive $C_j^{(k)}$ then execute $Submit(p_j, k-1, G_{k-1})$ and stop.
5. Broadcast $R_i^{(k)} = (b_i^{(k)}||r_i^{(k)})$ to other parties and wait for 1 round. Then go to step 8.

> **Party $p_{j \neq i}$: On input $R_i^{(k)}$ from p_i**

6. Broadcast $R_j^{(k)} = (b_j^{(k)}||r_j^{(k)})$ to other parties and wait for 1 round.
7. If there exists a party $p_{l \neq j}$ such that it doesn't receive $R_l^{(k)}$ or $\mathcal{H}(R_l^{(k)}) \neq C_l^{(k)}$ then execute $Submit(p_l, k-1, G_{k-1})$ and stop.

Party p_i

8. If there exists a party p_j such that it doesn't receive $R_j^{(k)}$ or $\mathcal{H}(R_j^{(k)}) \neq C_j^{(k)}$ then execute $Submit(p_j, k-1, G_{k-1})$ and stop.
9. Compute best response G_k, $sig_{p_i}^{G_k} = sign_{p_i}(G_k)$ and broadcast $best\_response(G_k, sig_{p_i}^{G_k})$ to other parties. Wait for 1 round then go to step 13.

> **Party $p_{j \neq i}$: On input $best\_response(G_k, sig_{p_i}^{G_k})$ from p_i**

10. Verify G_k
11. If G_k is not correct then execute $Submit(p_i, k-1, G_{k-1})$ and stop.
12. Otherwise, let $sig_{p_j}^{G_k} = sign_{p_j}(G_k)$ and broadcast $verified(G_k, sig_{p_j}^{G_k})$ to other parties. Then wait for 1 round.

For each party:

13. If there exists a party $p_{l \neq i}$ such that it doesn't receive $verified(G_k, sig_{p_l}^{G_k})$ then execute $Submit(p_l, k-1, G_{k-1})$ and stop.

Fig. 9. Protocol π: Determine best response

Protocol π: Revocation

Party p_i: On **input** *revoke()* from the environment

1. Send *revoke()* to $\mathcal{F}_{Judge}$ in Δ rounds then stop.

Party $p_{j \neq i}$: On changes of $\mathcal{F}_{judge}(\mathcal{P})$

2. Update the local $\mathcal{P}$ with $\mathcal{F}_{judge}(\mathcal{P})$

Fig. 10. Protocol π: Revocation

Protocol π: Close state channel

Party p_i: On **input** *close()* from environment

1. If $\mathcal{F}_{Judge}(flag) = dispute$ then stop.
2. Send *close()* to $\mathcal{F}_{Judge}$ and wait for $1 + (|\mathcal{P}| - 1)\Delta$ rounds. Then go to step 4

Party $p_{j \neq i}$: Upon p_i sends *close()* to $\mathcal{F}_{Judge}$

3. Send *close()* to $\mathcal{F}_{Judge}$ and wait for $(|\mathcal{F}_{auction}(\mathcal{P})| - 2)\Delta$ rounds.

For each party:

4. Wait for Δ rounds and check if $\mathcal{F}_{Judge}(channel) = \perp$ then outputs *closed()* to the environment.

Fig. 11. Protocol π: Close state channel

---

corrupted parties and the messages sent from $\mathcal{A}$ to $\mathcal{F}_{Judge}$, therefore, $\mathcal{S}$ can instruct the $\mathcal{F}_{auction}$ to update the ledger $\mathcal{L}$ in the same manner as the hybrid word. We provide the description of $\mathcal{S}$ for each of the functionalities as follows.

Open Channel. Let p_i be the party that initiates the request. We analyze the following cases:

- p_i *is corrupted:* Upon p_i sends *create()* to $\mathcal{F}_{Judge}$
  1. $\mathcal{S}$ waits for Δ rounds
  2. Then sends *create()* to $\mathcal{F}_{auction}$ to make sure that $\mathcal{F}_{auction}$ receives *create()* in the same round as $\mathcal{F}_{Judge}$. Then wait for $1 + (n - 1)\Delta$ rounds
  3. if $\mathcal{F}_{auction}(channel) = created$ then sends *created()* to $\mathcal{E}$ on behalf of p_i.
- $p_{j \neq i}$ *is corrupted:* Upon p_i sends *create()* to $\mathcal{F}_{auction}$
  1. $\mathcal{S}$ waits for Δ rounds

2. If p_j sends $create()$ to $\mathcal{F}_{Judge}$ then $\mathcal{S}$ sends $create()$ to $\mathcal{F}_{auction}$ and wait for $(n-2)\Delta$ rounds
3. if $\mathcal{F}_{auction}(channel) = created$ then sends $created()$ to $\mathcal{E}$ on behalf of p_j.

In all cases above, according to Fig. 7, p_i or p_j will output $created()$ to $\mathcal{E}$ if $\mathcal{F}_{auction}(channel) = created$. Hence, $\mathcal{S}$ also outputs $created()$ in the same round. Therefore, the environment $\mathcal{E}$ receives the same outputs in the same round in both worlds.

Close Channel. Let p_i be the party that initiates the request. We analyze the following cases:

- p_i *is corrupted:* Upon p_i sends $close()$ to $\mathcal{F}_{Judge}$
  1. if $\mathcal{F}_{judge}(flag) = dispute$ then stop. Otherwise, $\mathcal{S}$ waits for Δ rounds
  2. Then sends $close()$ to $\mathcal{F}_{auction}$ to make sure that $\mathcal{F}_{auction}$ receives $close()$ in the same round as $\mathcal{F}_{Judge}$. Then wait for $1+(\mathcal{F}_{auction}(|\mathcal{P}|)-1)\Delta$ rounds
  3. Wait for another Δ round and check if $\mathcal{F}_{auction}(channel) = \perp$ then sends $created()$ to $\mathcal{E}$ on behalf of p_i.
- $p_{j\neq i}$ *is corrupted:* Upon p_i sends $close()$ to $\mathcal{F}_{auction}$
  1. $\mathcal{S}$ waits for Δ rounds
  2. If p_j sends $close()$ to $\mathcal{F}_{Judge}$ then $\mathcal{S}$ sends $close()$ to $\mathcal{F}_{auction}$ and wait for $(|\mathcal{F}_{auction}(\mathcal{P})| - 2)\Delta$ rounds
  3. Wait for another Δ round and check if $\mathcal{F}_{auction}(channel) = \perp$ then sends $closed()$ to $\mathcal{E}$ on behalf of p_j.

The indistinguishability in the view of $\mathcal{E}$ between the two worlds holds in the same manner as *Open channel*.

Revocation. Let p_i be the party that initiates the request. We analyze the following cases:

- p_i *is corrupted:* Upon p_i sends $revoke()$ to $\mathcal{F}_{Judge}$
  1. $\mathcal{S}$ waits for Δ rounds
  2. Then sends $revoke()$ to $\mathcal{F}_{auction}$ to make sure that $\mathcal{F}_{auction}$ receives $revoke()$ in the same round as $\mathcal{F}_{Judge}$.
- $p_{j\neq i}$ *is corrupted:* Upon p_i sends $revoke()$ to $\mathcal{F}_{auction}$
  1. If p_j updates the local $\mathcal{P}$ then $\mathcal{S}$ also updates its $\mathcal{P}$.

In both cases, $\mathcal{S}$ ensures that the messages exchanged between the entities are identical in both worlds. Moreover, since $\mathcal{P}$ is updated according to the real world, thus the internal state of the each party are also identical. Therefore, the view of $\mathcal{E}$ between the two worlds are indistinguishable.

Determine Best Response. We define $S\_Submit()$ as the simulator of the procedure $Submit()$ in the ideal world. Let p_i be the party that calculates the best responses. In each iteration k, we analyze the following cases:

- p_i *is corrupted:* Upon p_i broadcasts $C_i^{(k)}$ to other parties
  1. Send $C_i^{(k)}$ to $\mathcal{F}_{auction}$ and wait for 1 round.
  2. If $\mathcal{F}_{auction}$ removes any party then stop. If p_i executes the $Submit()$ then S also calls the $S\_Submit()$ in the same round.
  3. Otherwise, if p_i broadcasts $R_i^{(k)}$ to other parties then S sends $R_i^{(k)}$ to $\mathcal{F}_{auction}$ and waits for 1 round. Else, stop.
  4. If $\mathcal{F}_{auction}$ removes any party then stop. If p_i executes the $Submit()$ then S also calls the $S\_Submit()$ in the same round. Otherwise, wait for 1 round
  5. Receive G_k from $\mathcal{F}_{auction}$ and wait for 1 round.
  6. If p_i executes the $Submit()$ then S also calls the $S\_Submit()$ in the same round. Otherwise, stop.
- $p_{j \neq i}$ *is corrupted:* Upon p_i sends $best\_response(k)$ to $\mathcal{F}_{auction}$
  1. Wait until p_i sends $C_i^{(k)}$ to $\mathcal{F}_{auction}$, then forwards that $C_i^{(k)}$ to p_j in the same round.
  2. If p_j broadcasts $C_j^{(k)}$ to other parties then S sends $C_j^{(k)}$ to $\mathcal{F}_{auction}$. Else, execute $S\_Submit()$ to eliminate the party that made p_j refuse to broadcast and stop.
  3. Wait for 1 round. If p_i sends $R_i^{(k)}$ to $\mathcal{F}_{auction}$, then forwards that $R_i^{(k)}$ to p_j in the same round. Otherwise, stop.
  4. If p_j broadcasts $R_j^{(k)}$ to other parties then S sends $R_j^{(k)}$ to $\mathcal{F}_{auction}$. Else, execute $S\_Submit()$ to eliminate the party that made p_j refuse to broadcast and stop.
  5. Wait for 1 round, if S doesn't receive G_k from $\mathcal{F}_{auction}$ then stop. Otherwise, S forwards that G_k to p_j.
  6. If p_j executes the $Submit()$ then S also calls the $S\_Submit()$ in the same round. Otherwise, stop.

Since the messages exchanged between any entities are exact in both worlds, the indistinguishability in the view of $\mathcal{E}$ between the two worlds holds.

6   Conclusion

In this paper, we have proposed a novel framework based on blockchain that enables a complete decentralized and trustless iterative double auction. That is, all parties can participate in the auction process without having to rely on an auctioneer and they do not have to trust one another. With the aid of the state channel technology, we were able to reduce the blockchain transactions to avoid high transaction fee and latency. We have provided a formal specification of the framework and our protocol was proven to be secured in the UC model.

Acknowledgment. This paper is partially supported by DTRA HDTRA1-14-1-0055 and NSF CNS-1814614.

References

1. Nakamoto, S.: Bitcoin: a peer-to-peer electronic cash system (2008)
2. Wood, G.: Ethereum: a secure decentralised generalised transaction ledger. Ethereum Proj. Yellow Pap. **151**, 1–32 (2014)
3. Nguyen, L.N., Nguyen, T.D., Dinh, T.N., Thai, M.T.: OptChain: optimal transactions placement for scalable blockchain sharding. In: 2019 IEEE 39th International Conference on Distributed Computing Systems (ICDCS), pp. 525–535. IEEE (2019)
4. Saad, M., Cook, V., Nguyen, L., Thai, M.T., Mohaisen, A.: Partitioning attacks on bitcoin: colliding space, time, and logic. In: 2019 IEEE 39th International Conference on Distributed Computing Systems (ICDCS). IEEE (2019)
5. Azaria, A., Ekblaw, A., Vieira, T., Lippman, A.: MedRec: using blockchain for medical data access and permission management. In: International Conference on Open and Big Data (OBD), pp. 25–30. IEEE (2016)
6. Dinh, T.N., Thai, M.T.: AI and blockchain: a disruptive integration. Computer **51**(9), 48–53 (2018)
7. Kang, J., Yu, R., Huang, X., Maharjan, S., Zhang, Y., Hossain, E.: Enabling localized peer-to-peer electricity trading among plug-in hybrid electric vehicles using consortium blockchains. IEEE Trans. Ind. Inform. **13**(6), 3154–3164 (2017)
8. Aitzhan, N.Z., Svetinovic, D.: Security and privacy in decentralized energy trading through multi-signatures, blockchain and anonymous messaging streams. IEEE Trans. Dependable Secure Comput. **15**(5), 840–852 (2016)
9. Nguyen, T.D.T., Pham, H.-A., Thai, M.T.: Leveraging blockchain to enhance data privacy in IoT-based applications. In: Chen, X., Sen, A., Li, W.W., Thai, M.T. (eds.) CSoNet 2018. LNCS, vol. 11280, pp. 211–221. Springer, Cham (2018). https://doi.org/10.1007/978-3-030-04648-4_18
10. Friedman, D.: The double auction market institution: a survey. Double Auction Market Inst. Theor. Evid. **14**, 3–25 (1993)
11. Parsons, S., Marcinkiewicz, M., Niu, J., Phelps, S.: Everything you wanted to know about double auctions, but were afraid to (bid or) ask (2006)
12. Faqiry, M.N., Das, S.: Double-sided energy auction in microgrid: equilibrium under price anticipation. IEEE Access **4**, 3794–3805 (2016)
13. Iosifidis, G., Gao, L., Huang, J., Tassiulas, L.: An iterative double auction for mobile data offloading. In: 2013 11th International Symposium and Workshops on Modeling and Optimization in Mobile, Ad Hoc and Wireless Networks (WiOpt), pp. 154–161. IEEE (2013)
14. Iosifidis, G., Koutsopoulos, I.: Double auction mechanisms for resource allocation in autonomous networks. IEEE J. Sel. Areas Commun. **28**(1), 95–102 (2010)
15. Wang, J., Wang, Q., Zhou, N.: A decentralized electricity transaction mode of microgrid based on blockchain and continuous double auction. In: 2018 IEEE Power & Energy Society General Meeting (PESGM), pp. 1–5. IEEE (2018)
16. Dziembowski, S., Faust, S., Hostáková, K.: General state channel networks. In: Proceedings of the 2018 ACM SIGSAC Conference on Computer and Communications Security, ser. CCS 2018, pp. 949–966. ACM, New York (2018). https://doi.org/10.1145/3243734.3243856
17. Canetti, R.: Universally composable security: a new paradigm for cryptographic protocols. In: Proceedings 2001 IEEE International Conference on Cluster Computing, pp. 136–145. IEEE (2001)

18. Thakur, S., Hayes, B.P., Breslin, J.G.: Distributed double auction for peer to peer energy trade using blockchains. In: 2018 5th International Symposium on Environment-Friendly Energies and Applications (EFEA), pp. 1–8. IEEE (2018)
19. Ming, Z., et al.: Blockcloud: a blockchain-based service-centric network stack
20. Sun, Y.-E., et al.: SPRITE: a novel strategy-proof multi-unit double auction scheme for spectrum allocation in ubiquitous communications. Pers. Ubiquit. Comput. **18**(4), 939–950 (2014)
21. Malavolta, G., Moreno-Sanchez, P., Kate, A., Maffei, M., Ravi, S.: Concurrency and privacy with payment-channel networks. In: Proceedings of the 2017 ACM SIGSAC Conference on Computer and Communications Security, pp. 455–471. ACM (2017)
22. Miller, A., Bentov, I., Bakshi, S., Kumaresan, R., McCorry, P.: Sprites and state channels: payment networks that go faster than lightning. In: Goldberg, I., Moore, T. (eds.) FC 2019. LNCS, vol. 11598, pp. 508–526. Springer, Cham (2019). https://doi.org/10.1007/978-3-030-32101-7_30
23. Zou, S., Ma, Z., Shao, Y., Ran, L., Liu, X.: Efficient and dynamic double auctions for resource allocation. In: 2016 IEEE 55th Conference on Decision and Control (CDC), pp. 6062–6067. IEEE (2016)
24. Johnson, D., Menezes, A., Vanstone, S.: The elliptic curve digital signature algorithm (ECDSA). Int. J. Inf. Secur. **1**(1), 36–63 (2001)

Towards a Multi-chain Future
of Proof-of-Space

Shuyang Tang[1], Jilai Zheng[1], Yao Deng[1], Ziyu Wang[2], Zhiqiang Liu[1(✉)],
Dawu Gu[1(✉)], Zhen Liu[1], and Yu Long[1]

[1] Department of Computer Science and Engineering, Shanghai Jiao Tong University,
Shanghai, China
{htftsy,zhengjilai,deng19930115}@sjtu.edu.cn
{liu-zq,gu-dw,liuzhen,longyu}@cs.sjtu.edu.cn
[2] School of Cyber Science and Technology, Beihang University, Beijing, China
wangziyu@buaa.edu.cn

Abstract. Proof-of-Space provides an intriguing alternative for consensus protocol of permissionless blockchains due to its recyclable nature and the potential to support multiple chains simultaneously. However, a direct shared proof of the same storage, which was adopted in the existing multi-chain schemes based on Proof-of-Space, could give rise to newborn attack on new chain launching. To fix this gap, we propose an innovative framework of single-chain Proof-of-Space and further present a novel multi-chain scheme which can resist newborn attack effectively by elaborately combining shared proof and chain-specific proof of storage. Moreover, we analyze the security of the multi-chain scheme and prove that it is incentive-compatible. This means that participants in such multi-chain system can achieve their greatest utility with our proposed strategy of storage resource partition.

Keywords: Blockchain · Mechanism design · Consensus ·
Cryptocurrency · Proof-of-Space

1 Introduction

Since the proposal of Bitcoin in 2008 [1], blockchain has been successfully providing a decentralized consensus on a distributive ledger in a permissionless environment through a peer-to-peer network. In a high level, blockchain is a chain of blocks, each containing certain linearly ordered transactions. The consensus of blockchain performs a "leader election" process and a "ledger extension" process for each round. The "leader election" process elects one or few *leaders* from all consensus participants (known as *miners*) according to their computing power, and then these leaders perform a "ledger extension" process via appending their proposed blocks to the rear of the blockchain. Since the specific computing power

The research is supported by the National Natural Science Foundation of China (Grant No. 61672347).

is evaluated by having miners work on finding certain hash functions preimages, such a way of leader election is called *Proof-of-Work* (PoW) [2]. The computing power of conducting PoW is referred to as *hash power*.

PoW consensus scheme suffers from notorious consumption of hash power which turns out to be a waste of natural resource. This circumstances has activated the investigation of alternative consensus schemes which are more energy-efficient. An alternative consensus scheme is *Proof-of-Stake* (PoS) [3–9]. In the "leader election" process of PoS consensus scheme, the leader is randomly selected proportionally to the *stake* that each miner holds, rather than the hash power. Another alternative to PoW is *Proof-of-Space* (aka. *Proof-of-Capacity*, PoC). In PoC consensus, the one-time consumption of hash power is replaced by the holding of the storage resource, namely, recyclable hardware disks. Also, PoC is inherited with a nature of concurrency by providing resource proof for multiple chains simultaneously. With a shared nonce for the *pebbling graph* [10–12] (PG, the building block of most existing PoC-based consensus schemes), the claim on the same storage can be applied to the consensus of more than one PG-based blockchain. With such a shared proof of storage, the same storage contributes to the security of multiple chains – less total resource is required for the same security guarantee globally.

However, a direct shared proof of the same storage brings about *newborn attack*, which makes new chains hard to launch since holders of large storage pools may attack a newly started chain with almost zero-cost (it needs only to duplicate the proof one more time). In this paper, we aim to address this issue by proposing an innovative multi-chain scheme of proof-of-space based on the SpaceMint [13] protocol. This scheme is built on a combination of a shared proof and a chain-specific proof of storage, which makes the same storage source contributes simultaneously to multiple blockchains, and the cost for an adversary to launch a *newborn attack* is enormous. Moreover, we prove that our scheme is incentive-compatible, which means participants can achieve their greatest utility with our desired strategy of storage resource partition.

1.1   Related Works

Two recent works [14,15] both proposed their "Proof-of-Space" protocol. Their main difference is whether the proofs are for transient storage or persistent storage. Proof of transient space (PoTS) by Ateniese et al. [14] enables efficient verification of memory-hard function [16], which is a function that needs a lot of space to compute. In this work, a verifier only needs $O(\text{poly}\log S)$ time and space to verify the claimed space usage of the prover, where S is the amount of storage the prover P wants to dedicate. Proof of persistent space (PoPS) by Dziembowski et al. [15] allows the verifier to repeatedly audit the prover. Only prover who stores the data persistently can pass the repeatedly audit.

Proof of retrievability (PoR) [17] allows a user who outsources some useful data to an untrusted server to repeatedly verify if the data is still existing in the server. The difference between PoPS and PoR is whether a large amount of initial data is transferred from verifier V to prover P.

Previous PoC constructions only differ in the pebbling graphs G. Dziembowski et al. [15] proposed two constructions of PoC schemes in the random oracle model, using Merkle tree and graphs with high "pebbling complexity". One is based on a graph with high pebbling complexity by Paul et al. [18], which is $(\Theta(S/\log S), S/\log S, \infty)$-secure (see definition in Sect. 2.2). Another one combines superconcentrators [19–21], random bipartite expander graphs [22,23] and depth robust graphs [24,25] and is

$$(\Theta(S), \infty, \Theta(S))\text{-secure}$$

The construction of Ren and Devadas [26] uses stacked bipartite expander graphs, which is

$$(\alpha \cdot S, (1-\alpha) \cdot S, \infty)\text{-secure}$$

for any $\alpha \in [0, 0.5]$. The labels of the graph are computed just as in [15], however the prover only stores the labels on top of this stack.

The construction of Krzysztof Pietrzak [27] uses depth-robust graphs from [16] to realize PoC, which is

$$(S \cdot (1 - \epsilon), \infty, S)\text{-secure}$$

This construction has a tight bound, which means it can get security against adversary storing $(1 - \epsilon)$ fraction of the space. Moreover, this construction gets security against parallelism, which implies massive parallelism of oracle queries doesn't benefit the adversary. Besides, this work also introduces and constructs a new type of PoC, which allows the prover to store useful data at the same time.

1.2   Paper Organization

The remainder of this paper is organized as follows. Section 2 introduces notations, building blocks and the background of PoC. Section 3 presents a single-chain PoC scheme built on SpaceMint – one of the most well-known PoC scheme today. Based on this, in Sect. 4, we describe our framework for the multi-chain PoC scheme both by a general functionality and a specific protocol realizing one case of the functionality. Finally, we analyze the incentive compatibility and security of our framework in Sect. 5.

2   Backgrounds

2.1   Notations

For a set S, $|S|$ denotes the number of elements in S. With "$||$" we denote concatenation of strings. More generally, for any two tuples $\boldsymbol{m}_1, \boldsymbol{m}_2$, $\boldsymbol{m}_1 \circ \boldsymbol{m}_2$ is the concatenation of them and for unary tuple $\boldsymbol{m}_1 = (m)$, $\boldsymbol{m}_1 \circ \boldsymbol{m}_2$ is written as $m \circ \boldsymbol{m}_2$ (same to the case of $\boldsymbol{m}_2 = (m)$). We ideally assume N participants and refer to them by either identities $(P_1, P_2, \ldots, P_N)$ or their public keys

$(\mathsf{pk}_1, \mathsf{pk}_2, \ldots, \mathsf{pk}_N)$ interchangeably. The secret key corresponding to a public key pk is denoted as pk^{-1} for simplicity. To further facilitate our description of a high-level framework. We assume a public-key infrastructure (PKI) among all participants, which is described by a functionality $\mathcal{F}_{cert}$. Moreover, to any tuple of messages $(m_0, m_1, \ldots, m_\ell)$, we use $(m_0, m_1, \ldots, m_\ell)_{\mathsf{pk}^{-1}}$ to signify the tuple along with the valid signature on the tuple hash from the participant of public key pk. In later descriptions, we may take the necessity of signing and verifying as granted and avoid redundant descriptions. We assume a hash function $H : \{0, 1\}^* \rightarrow \{0, 1\}^\lambda$ simulating the random oracle [28]. Note that based on H, we can build H_z for any message z as $H_z(\cdot) := H(z||\cdot)$ [29].

2.2 Proof-of-Space

Proof-of-space is an interactive protocol between a prover P and a verifier V that demonstrates the prover P is storing some data of a certain size. The PoC protocol in [15] involves two phases: initialization phase and execution phase.

Initialization is an interactive process between the prover P and the verifier V. It runs on shared inputs (id, S). id is an identifier to assure that the prover P cannot reuse the same disk space to run PoC for different statement. S is the amount of storage the prover P wants to dedicate. After the initialization phase, P stores some data F, whereas V only stores a commitment γ to F.

Execution is an interactive process between the prover P and the verifier V. The prover P runs on data F and the verifier V runs on input γ. Then the verifier V sends challenges to the prover P, obtains back the corresponding openings. At the end V verifies these openings and outputs *accept* or *reject*.

The security of a PoC protocol was formally defined in [15]. Specifically, a (S_0, S_1, T)-adversarial prover $\hat{\mathsf{P}}$ was defined, which means $\hat{\mathsf{P}}$'s storage after the initialization phase is bounded by S_0, while during the execution phase it runs in storage at most S_1 and time at most T. Secure PoC protocols are required to have three properties, which are completeness, soundness and efficiency.

1. Completeness: We say a PoC protocol has completeness if the verifier always outputs *accept* for any honest prover P with probability 1.
2. Soundness: We say a PoC protocol has soundness if the verifier V outputs *accept* with a negligible probability for any (S_0, S_1, T)-adversarial prover $\hat{\mathsf{P}}$.
3. Efficiency: We say a PoC protocol has efficiency if the verifier V can run in time $O(\mathrm{poly} \log S)$.

We say that a PoC protocol is (S_0, S_1, T)-secure if the above three properties are satisfied.

3   Single-Chain Proof-of-Space

In this section, we use SpaceMint protocol as the building block of our multi-chain protocol to be described in the latter section.

3.1   Graph Labeling Game

At first, we introduce the graph labeling game [30, 31].

Definition 1 (Graph Labelling). *We consider a directed acyclic graph (DAG) $G = (V, E)$, which has a vertex set $V = \{0, 1, \ldots, S - 1\}$ and a hash function $H : \{0, 1\}^* \rightarrow \{0, 1\}^\lambda$, the label $l_i \in \{0, 1\}^\lambda$ for each vertex $i \in V$ is recursively computed as $l_i = H(nc, i, l_{p_1}, \ldots, l_{p_t})$ where $l_{p_1}, \ldots, l_{p_t}$ are the parents of vertex i and nc is a unique nonce.*

Graph labeling game is the building block of most PoC protocols. Let $G = (V, E)$ be a directed acyclic graph (DAG) which has S nodes. $H : \{0, 1\}^* \rightarrow \{0, 1\}^\lambda$ is a collision-resistant hash function. For every id, a fresh hash function can be sampled: $H_{id} = H(id||\cdot)$. The PoC protocol based on the graph labeling game is as follows:

1. Initialization: First, P computes the labels on all nodes of G using graph labelling, and commits to them in γ using Merkle-tree Commitment. Then P gets q challenges from V. For each of the challenges $C = (C_1, \ldots, C_q)$, P opens the label on the C_i^{th} node of G, as same as the labels of all its parent nodes. Finally, V checks the openings of all challenge nodes and their parents. V also checks if the challenge nodes are computed correctly from their parents.
2. Execution: V chooses t challenge nodes randomly. Then P sends the opening of these challenge nodes to V. This execution phase can be done repeatedly.

3.2   PoC Definition

Before introducing how to apply any PoC schemes to blockchains, we introduce the formal description of a PoC at first designed to apply between two parties. A PoC scheme built on a hash oracle H is described as $\Pi_{\text{PoC}} = (\text{init}, \text{open}, \text{vrf})$. Specifically,

Space Commitment. $\Pi_{\text{PoC}}.\text{init}^H(S) \rightarrow (\gamma, \widetilde{\gamma})$ inputs the size of the pebbling graph and returns a pair $(\gamma, \widetilde{\gamma})$ after building up the graph where γ is the commitment released to the publicity and $\widetilde{\gamma}$ is a secret to be locally stored.

Commitment Opening. $\Pi_{\text{PoC}}.\text{open}^H(S, \widetilde{\gamma}, C) \rightarrow \tau$ takes as input the graph size, the threshold $\widetilde{\gamma}$, the challenge C and returns a proof τ.

Verification. $\Pi_{\text{PoC}}.\text{vrf}^H(S, \gamma, C, \tau) \rightarrow \{accept, reject\}$ verifies a proof τ for the challenge C to the graph of size S and public commitment γ.

3.3   SpaceMint

In SpaceMint [13], the structure of blocks is identical to Bitcoin blockchain except for containing a space proof instead of a hash solution. Furthermore, the detailed protocol of SpaceMint is similar to any blockchain, in spite that the mining and chain-competition differ from that of PoW-based blockchains. Thereby, it is too redundant to cover every details to introduce the full scheme. To describe SpaceMint, we only need to enumerate all the difference between SpaceMint and the ordinary blockchain.

Fig. 1. Capacity resource partition

Initial Step. For a miner to dedicate λN bits of storage to the blockchain network, it computes and stores the labels of their pebbling graph to get $(\gamma, \widetilde{\gamma}) \leftarrow \Pi_{\mathsf{PoC}}.\mathsf{init}^H(S)$ at the initial stage. Afterwards $sctx = (\mathsf{pk}, \gamma)_{\mathsf{pk}^{-1}}$ is broadcast to the network.

The Mining. Each miner maintains a main chain (the chain branch with the greatest total weight) in its view. We denote the chain as $(A_1, A_2, \ldots, A_{i-1})$ and their corresponding proofs as $\tau^1, \tau^2, \ldots, \tau^{i-1}$ ($i \geq \Delta$). To mine the next block A_i, the miner at first derives the challenge for block i from the proof of block $i - \Delta$, i.e., $C_i = H(\tau_{i-\Delta}) \bmod S$. Thereby, the miner obtains $\tau \leftarrow \Pi_{\mathsf{PoC}}.\mathsf{open}^H(S, \widetilde{\gamma}, C_i)$ and assembles A_i with τ. This differs from PoW.

Block Verification. Different from the nonce verification in the existing blockchain, we in SpaceMint should check the open-up τ of each block by $\Pi_{\mathsf{PoC}}.\mathsf{vrf}^H(S, \gamma, C, \tau)$.

Chain Weight. Assuming a block is followed by m sequential blocks $(A_1, A_2, \ldots, A_m)$, which have valid proofs $\tau^1, \tau^2, \ldots, \tau^m$ respectively, and that the corresponding space contributed by these miners are $S^1, S^2, \ldots, S^m$. The weight of A_i is defined as follows:

$$\mathsf{weight}(A_i) = \left(\frac{H(\tau^i)}{2^\lambda}\right)^{1/S^i}$$

It can be proved that the probability that A_i has the largest weight among these m blocks equals to his fraction of the total space, which is $\frac{S^i}{\sum_{k=1}^m S^k}$. In this way, in a chain competition, the chain branch with the greatest total weight outruns the others. This differs from the existing blockchain where the block weight is atomic (either one or zero).

4   A Multi-chain Scheme

In this section, we introduce our framework for the multi-chain scheme of proof-of-space. To this end, we first describe our high-level functionality and then propose one possible realization of the functionality based on the aforementioned SpaceMint-based single-chain protocol.

4.1   Functionalities

In a high level, as Fig. 1, we expect to have all participants pay half of the total storage for purchasing the upper bound of their admissible storage

---

Functionality $\mathcal{G}_{\text{main}}$

Shared functionality $\mathcal{G}_{\text{main}}$ interacts with all participants $P_1, P_2, \ldots, P_N$, the environment $\mathcal{Z}$, as well as a public-key infrastructure $\mathcal{F}_{cert}$ and a publicly shared global clock functionality $\mathcal{G}_{\text{CLOCK}}$.

This functionality is parameterized by the number of candidates N (this is a variant in the permissionless setting, but we take this notation for the simplicity of descriptions), the number of adversary controlled parties t. A predetermined parameter lsize describes the number of leaders to be elected for a round which varies among different emulations of the functionality. The ledger $\text{ledger}_k := \epsilon$ of each chain $k \in [M]$ is a linearly ordered list of transactions initially set as empty.

Each round (round R) proceeds as follows.

– **Leader Election.**
• Querying each participant P_i for its resource partition $\boldsymbol{s}^i = (s_0^i, s_1^i, \ldots, s_M^i)$.
• For each $i \in [N]$ and $k \in [M]$, calculate $\text{weight}_i^k := w(\boldsymbol{s}^i, \boldsymbol{B}, k)$.
• For each $j \in [\text{lsize}]$ and $k \in [M]$, pick leader_j^k from $\{P_i\}_{i \in [N]}$ randomly such that $\text{leader}_j^k = P_i$ for each participant P_i with the probability proportional to weight_i^k.
– **Ledger Extension.**
• For each chain $k \in [M]$, fetch from the environment $\mathcal{Z}$ a tuple of transactions $\{tx_{R,k}^i\}_{i \in [\ell]}$, sort them into a linear list $\boldsymbol{tx}_{R,k}$.
• For each chain $k \in [M]$, extend the ledger by appending $\boldsymbol{tx}_{R,k}$ into its rear $\text{ledger}_k := \text{ledger}_k \oplus \boldsymbol{tx}_{R,k}$.
– **Reward Issuing.**
• For each chain $k \in [M]$, let $\boldsymbol{tx}_{R,k}^{\text{reward}} := (tx_{\text{leader}_1}^k, tx_{\text{leader}_2}^k, \ldots, tx_{\text{leader}_\text{lsize}}^k)$ where each $tx_{\text{leader}_j}^k$ is a specially formed transaction that allocates $\frac{\text{reward}_R^k + \ell \times \text{fee}}{\text{lsize}}$ to $\text{leader}_{k,j}$.
• For each chain $k \in [M]$, issue rewards and transaction fees to leaders by appending $\boldsymbol{tx}_{R,k}^{\text{reward}}$ to the ledger $\text{ledger}_k := \text{ledger}_k \oplus \boldsymbol{tx}_{R,k}^{\text{reward}}$.
• Pend till the global time clock $\mathcal{G}_{\text{CLOCK}}$ issuing the end of the round $R := R + 1$.

Fig. 2. The main functionality

(the shared proof part, denoted as $\boldsymbol{s}_0$), and allocate the rest half of storage on each supportive chains respectively according to their market weight ($\boldsymbol{s}_i$ for chain i). Specifically, to a chain i with $\beta_i = \frac{B_i}{\|\boldsymbol{B}\|}$ ($\boldsymbol{B}_i$ is the sum of $\boldsymbol{s}_i$ for all participants) fraction of total storage proof, we stimulate the participant to allocate $\boldsymbol{s}_i = \beta_i \boldsymbol{s}_0$ storage on it. To allow for the start-up of new chains, we in actual ask that $\boldsymbol{s}_i \leq (1 + \delta)\beta_i \boldsymbol{s}_0$. Clearly, as an equilibrium of economics, the total storage proof behind a blockchain is proportional to the total market weight of the chain. Therefore, the market weight of each chain is described by the total storage proof behind the chain. Also, we assume that the amount of released coins and transaction fees is the same to all chains for each round and hence the per-coin value is proportional to our defined market weight.

Protocol Π_{main}

Shared protocol Π_{main} is executed by all participants $P_1, P_2, \ldots, P_N$. We assume a public-key infrastructure $\mathcal{F}_{cert}$.

This functionality is parameterized by the number of candidates N (this is a variant in the permissionless setting, but we take this notation for the simplicity of descriptions), the number of adversary controlled parties t. A predetermined parameter lsize describes the number of leaders to be elected for a round which varies among different emulations of the functionality. $H(\cdot) : \{0,1\}^* \to \{0,1\}^\lambda$ is a hash function.

– **System Setup.**

• Each participant from $\mathcal{F}_{cert}$ fetch their key pairs $(\mathsf{pk}_j, \mathsf{sk}_j)$. To facilitate descriptions, we denote $\mathsf{pk}_j^{-1} := \mathsf{sk}_j$.

• Each initially launched chain contains Δ start-up blocks, specifically, A_k^i for chain i and block k.

• Each participant j divides its total resource into $\boldsymbol{s}^j$.

• Each participant j for each chain i generates $(\gamma_i^j, \tilde{\gamma}_i^j) \leftarrow \Pi_{\text{PoC}}.\mathsf{init}^H(\boldsymbol{s}_i^j)$.

• Each participant j issues the resource commitment

$$\mathsf{com}^j := (\mathsf{pk}_j, \boldsymbol{s}^j, \boldsymbol{\gamma}^j = (\gamma_1^j, \gamma_2^j, \ldots, \gamma_M^j))_{\mathsf{pk}_j^{-1}}.$$

• Prepare a set Γ of γ's, initially set as empty. Prepare a map J from public key pk to commitment com.

Each round (round R) proceeds as follows.

– **Block Proposal.**

• Find the current chain branch in view with the greatest total weight $(A_1^i, A_2^i, \ldots, A_{R+\Delta-1}^i)$.

• Calculate the expected market weight of each chain, namely, $\boldsymbol{B}_i := \mu \sum_{k=R}^{R+\Delta-1} \mathsf{weight}(A_k^i)$ for chain i, let $\boldsymbol{\beta} := \frac{\boldsymbol{B}}{\|\boldsymbol{B}\|}$.

• Each participant j for each chain i assembles its own block for the round.

$$\widehat{A_{R+\Delta}^i} := \left(\mathsf{pk}_j, \mathsf{rec}, H(A_{R+\Delta-1}^i), \tau_i^j, \tau_i^j\prime, \mathsf{weight} = \left(\frac{H(\tau_i^j)}{2^\lambda} \right)^{1/\widetilde{\boldsymbol{s}_i^j}}, \mathsf{com}^j \right)_{\mathsf{pk}_j^{-1}},$$

where $\widetilde{\boldsymbol{s}_i^j} := \min\{\boldsymbol{s}_i^j, (1+\delta)\boldsymbol{\beta}_i \boldsymbol{s}_0^j\}$, $\tau_i^j, \tau_i^j\prime$ are two opens $\tau_i^j \leftarrow \Pi_{\text{PoC}}.\mathsf{open}^H\left(\boldsymbol{s}_i^j, \tilde{\gamma}_i^j, H(\tau_{A_R^i})\right)$, $\tau_i^j\prime \leftarrow \Pi_{\text{PoC}}.\mathsf{open}^H\left(\boldsymbol{s}_0^j, \tilde{\gamma}_0^j, H(\tau_{A_R^i})\right)$ and rec has already included all newly appended transactions and the block reward.

Here, for a block $A = (\mathsf{pk}, \mathsf{rec}, \mathsf{hash}, \tau, \mathsf{w}, \mathsf{com})$, $\mathsf{weight}(A) := \mathsf{w}$ and $\tau_A := \tau$.

• After the assembly, $\left(\widehat{A_{R+\Delta}^i}\right)_{\mathsf{pk}_j^{-1}}$ is proposed.

– **Chain Growth.**

• Parse every received block into $\widehat{A_{R+\Delta}^i} \to \left(\mathsf{pk}, \mathsf{rec}, H(A_{R+\Delta-1}^i), \tau_i, \tau_i\prime, \mathsf{weight}, \mathsf{com}\right)$, firstly verify the calculation of weight, integrity of rec, the hash, and the signature. For a block passing the above verification, add it into the current view of block branches if passing through the following verifications:

1. Parse $\mathsf{com} \to \left(\mathsf{pk}', \boldsymbol{s}, \boldsymbol{\gamma} = \{\gamma_i\}_{i \in [M]}\right)$, check $\mathsf{pk}' \stackrel{?}{=} \mathsf{pk}$.
2. Check $\Pi_{\text{PoC}}.\mathsf{vrf}^H\left(s_i, \gamma_i, H(\tau_{A_R^i}), \tau_i\right)$ and $\Pi_{\text{PoC}}.\mathsf{vrf}^H\left(s_0, \gamma_0, H(\tau_{A_R^i}), \tau_i\prime\right)$.
3. Check whether each two elements in Γ are different.
4. Check whether $(\mathsf{pk}, \mathsf{com}) \notin J$ and for each γ_i, it holds $\gamma_i \notin \Gamma$. Reject if the above condition is not satisfied.
5. Update $J := J \uplus \{(\mathsf{pk}, \mathsf{com})\}$ and $\Gamma := \Gamma \uplus \boldsymbol{\gamma}$.

Fig. 3. The main protocol

In all, our system supports M different PoC-based blockchains. Each (j^{th}) of them elects leaders according to s_j^i. Specifically, each miner (i^{th}) has the chance of being the leader of each round by

$$w(s, B, k) := \begin{cases} \frac{s_k}{B_k + s_k}, & s_k \leq (1 + \delta)\beta_k' s_0 \\ \frac{s_k}{B_k + s_k}, & \text{otherwise} \end{cases}$$

where $B_k' := B_k + s_k$, $\beta' := \frac{B'}{\|B'\|}$, and $\widetilde{s_k} := \max_{s_k}\{s_k \leq (1 + \delta)\beta_k' s_0\}$. The exact formula of s_k is easy to uncover by solving a quadratic equation (hence can be described in codes when implemented). However, we remain the current formulation for readability. To facilitate proofs in later sections, we observe that $\psi_{B,k}(s) := w(s, B, k)$ is continuous on $(\mathbb{R}^+)^{M+1}$ and is smooth almost everywhere (a.e.) on $(\mathbb{R}^+)^{M+1}$ except for $\{s \in (\mathbb{R}^+)^{M+1} | s_k = (1 + \delta)\beta_k' s_0\}$ with zero Lebesgue-measure for each $k \in [M]$.

The detailed description of the functionality is shown in Fig. 2, where we aim to provide a framework more general than our specific way of realization so the size of leaders to be elected for each round is parameterized by lsize. In fact, lsize of most existing blockchains and our realization based on SpaceMint is simply 1.

4.2   A Protocol for lsize = 1

To build our realization of the above functionality with lsize = 1 based on our SpaceMint-based single-chain PoC protocol in the previous section, most steps are natural implementations of our building block. However, few issues should be carefully considered alongside. To establish a commonly verifiable computation on the market weight B in a decentralized environment, we assume that the market weight of each chain is proportional to the summed weight of latest Δ consequent blocks by a constant factor μ. To make sure that each space proof is used for only one identity, there should be a pool Γ of space commits locally store in each node. We have put the specific protocol in Fig. 3 since details are not crucial to the roadmap of our paper.

5   Framework Analysis

The realization of our functionality in Fig. 2 should satisfy both safety and liveness. The analysis of basic safety and liveness is specific to the way of realization. In our protocol to realize the functionality with lsize = 1, the basic safety and liveness properties of the realization are inherited from SpaceMint. In this section, we focus on two higher-leveled properties of our general framework for a PoC multi-chain future, namely, incentive compatibility and the system security that a considerable fraction of global storage resource has to be held by an adversary to devastate any chain under the framework, even for newly launched chains or chains with the least market weight.

5.1   Incentive Compatibility

In this part, we prove that our framework is incentive-compatible. Namely, participants achieve their greatest utility (the most expected revenue) with our desired strategy of storage resource partition. Without loss of generality, we consider $\delta = 0$ to simplify our proofs. Also, we assume $\beta' = \beta$ from time to time to simplify proofs. To begin with, we formally describe the partition strategy.

Definition 2 (Capacity Resource Partition). *For each participant with total capacity c, all its admissible resource partitions form the space $\mathscr{D}_c^{M+1} \subset (\mathbb{R}^+)^{M+1}$ that $\sum_{i=0}^{M} s_i = c$ for each $s = (s_0, s_1, \ldots, s_M) \in \mathscr{D}_c^{M+1}$. Furthermore, we introduce $\mathscr{D}^{M+1} := \cup_{c \in \mathbb{R}^+} \mathscr{D}_c^{M+1}$.*

Likewise, we denote $\mathscr{D}_1^M$ as the set of vectors $(\beta_1, \beta_2, \ldots, \beta_M) \subset (\mathbb{R}^+)^M$ of length M that $\sum_{i=0}^{M} \beta_i = 1$.

The utility function is a mapping from a partition strategy to the expected revenue for each round. To define the global utility function, we firstly introduce the chain-specific utility function.

Definition 3 (Chain-Specific Utility Function). *The chain-specific utility function for chain k is*

$$\text{val}(s, B, k) := r \times w(s, B, k) \times \omega B_k.$$

Intuitively, r is a positive constant, $w(s, B, k)$ (proportionally) describes the probability of becoming the leader of each round, and the per-coin value of chain k is proportional to the market weight of the chain (hence is ωB_k for a positive constant ω). Note that we have assume that the minted coins and transaction fees are the same for each chain and for each round, hence it is not a necessity to add in another factor for it in the multiplication.

At a first glance, the formula above seems fit only into the scenario of $\mathsf{lsize} = 1$. Actually, in the multi-leader case, each participant has lsize times the chance to become an leader while each leader has only $\frac{1}{\mathsf{lsize}}$ fraction of total revenue. By $\frac{\mathsf{lsize} \cdot s_k}{B'[k]} \cdot \frac{r}{\mathsf{lsize}} \cdot \omega B'_k = \frac{s_k}{B'_k} \cdot r \cdot \omega B'_k$, the expected revenue remains identical to the one-leader case.

Definition 4 (The Utility Function). *Thereby the final utility function is the sum of all chain-specific utility functions*

$$U(s, B) := \sum_{k=1}^{M} \text{val}(s, B, k).$$

The optimal resource partition strategy is clearly depicted as below.

Definition 5 (Optimal Resource Partition). *To a participant with total storage resource c, its optimal resource partition strategy in the environment where each chain i has market weight B_i is*

$$\widetilde{\text{opt}}(c, B) := \text{argmax}_{s \in \mathscr{D}_c^{M+1}} U(s, B)$$

We aim to show that our desired resource partition strategy optimizes the utility function. That is to have the optimal resource partition equals our desired one.

Theorem 1. *For any $c \in \mathbb{R}^+$ and any $\boldsymbol{B} \in \mathscr{D}_c^M$,*

$$\widetilde{\mathrm{opt}}(c, \boldsymbol{B}) = \frac{c}{2} \circ \frac{c}{2}\beta$$

where $\beta = \frac{B}{||B||}$.

To prove this theorem, we at first introduce two lemmas.

Lemma 1. *For any positive integer n, positive values k, $(\beta_1, \beta_2, \ldots, \beta_n)$ with $\sum_{i=1}^n \beta_i = 1$, function $F(\boldsymbol{x}) := -\sum_{i=1}^n \beta_i \cdot \frac{x_i}{k\beta_i + x_i}$ $(\boldsymbol{x} = (x_0, x_1, \ldots, x_n))$ achieves its minimum in $\hat{\boldsymbol{x}} = (\frac{c}{2}, \frac{\beta_1 c}{2}, \ldots, \frac{\beta_n c}{2})$ subject to*

- $g_i(\boldsymbol{x}) := x_i - \beta_i x_0 \le 0$ *for each* $i \in [n]$,
- $g_{n+i+1}(\boldsymbol{x}) := -x_i \le 0$ *for each* $i \in [n] \cup \{0\}$,
- $h(\boldsymbol{x}) := \sum_{i=0}^n x_i - c = 0$.

Proof. To begin with, we show that F is convex on $(\mathbb{R}^+)^{n+1}$. It is easy to observe that the Hessian matrix of F is diagonal since $\frac{\partial^2 F}{\partial x_i \partial x_j} = 0$ for each $i \ne j$. Each element in the diagonal

$$\frac{\partial^2 F}{\partial x_i^2} = \frac{2\beta_i}{(k\beta_i + x_i)^2}\left(1 - \frac{x_i}{k\beta_i + x_i}\right)$$

is positive so the Hessian matrix is semi-definite and F is convex on $(\mathbb{R}^+)^{n+1}$. Since F and each g_i are convex and h is an affine function, this turns out to be a convex optimization and any minimal value of F is its minimum. According to Karush-Kuhn-Tucker (KKT) conditions, we only need to show that

- $\nabla L(\hat{\boldsymbol{x}}) = \boldsymbol{0}$,
- $\mu_i g_i(\hat{\boldsymbol{x}}) = 0$ for all $i \in [2n+1]$,

where

$$L(\boldsymbol{x}) = F(\boldsymbol{x}) + \sum_{i=1}^{2n+1} \mu_i g_i(\boldsymbol{x}) + \nu h(\boldsymbol{x}) \tag{1}$$

$$= -\sum_{i=1}^n \beta_i \cdot \frac{x_i}{k\beta_i + x_i} + \sum_{i=1}^n \mu_i(x_i - \beta_i x_0) + \nu\left(\sum_{i=0}^n x_i - c\right), \tag{2}$$

$\mu_i = \nu = \frac{k}{c(k+c/2)}$ for each $i \in [n]$. For each natural number $i \le n$, μ_{n+i+1} are set to be zero so $\sum_{i=n+1}^{2n+1} \mu_i g_i(\boldsymbol{x}) = 0$. In fact,

1. From simple derivations,

$$\frac{\partial L(\boldsymbol{x})}{\partial x_0} = \sum_{i=1}^n -\mu_i \beta_i + \nu = \frac{k}{c(k + \frac{c}{2})}\left(1 - \sum_{i=1}^n \beta_i\right) = 0$$

and for each $i \in [n]$,

$$\frac{\partial L(x)}{\partial x_i} = -\beta_i \cdot \frac{k\beta_i}{x_i(k\beta_i + x_i)} + \mu_i + \nu.$$

Thereby,

$$\frac{\partial L(\hat{x})}{\partial x_i} = -\beta_i \cdot \frac{k\beta_i}{\frac{\beta_i c}{2}(k\beta_i + \frac{\beta_i c}{2})} + \frac{2k}{c(k + \frac{c}{2})}$$

$$= -\frac{2k}{c(k + \frac{c}{2})} + \frac{2k}{c(k + \frac{c}{2})} = 0.$$

As a result, we conclude that $\nabla L(\hat{x}) = \mathbf{0}$.

2. The second condition is easy to hold since $g_i(\hat{x}) = 0$ for each $i \leq n$ and $\mu_i = 0$ for each $i > n$.

Therefore, f achieves its minimum in $\hat{x}$.

Intuitively, Lemma 1 alone has proved Theorem 1 since by having $k = ||\mathbf{B}||$,

$$U(s, \mathbf{B}) = -F(s) \times rw||\mathbf{B}||$$

within the boundary in the lemma. Since the Hessian matrix is semi-definite either inside the boundary (shown in the lemma proof) or outside the boundary (easy to verify) and U is obviously continuous everywhere and smooth a.e. except for a subset with zero Lebesgue measure, U is almost convex and the local maximization is actually the global optimization. However, to more strictly prove the theorem, we still require the following lemma.

Lemma 2. *For any space division strategy on n chains, suppose $s^A = (s_0^A, s_1^A, \ldots, s_n^A)$, if $\exists i \in [n] : s_i^A > \beta_i s_0^A$, then there always exists another strategy whose utility is better than s^A.*

Proof. If there exists $i \in [n] : s_i^A > \beta_i s_0^A$, then there must exist a set of index $I^A = \{a_1, a_2, \ldots, a_{exc}\} \subset [n]$ where $\forall i \in I^A, s_i^A > \beta_i s_0^A$ and $\forall i \notin I^A, s_i^A \leq \beta_i s_0^A$ both satisfy. Without loss of generality, we assume

$$\frac{s_{a_1}^A}{\beta_{a_1}} \geq \frac{s_{a_2}^A}{\beta_{a_2}} \geq \ldots \geq \frac{s_{a_{exc}}^A}{\beta_{a_{exc}}} > s_0^A.$$

Consider another strategy $s^{A+} = (s_0^{A+}, s_1^{A+}, \ldots, s_n^{A+})$. When comparing s^{A+} with s^A, the new strategy just subtracts some space division from s_{a_1} and adds it to s_0. In detail, s^{A+} can be formally expressed as

$$s_i^{A+} = \begin{cases} \frac{\beta_{a_1}}{\beta_{a_1}+1}(s_0^A + s_{a_1}^A) & i = a_1 \\ \frac{1}{\beta_{a_1}+1}(s_0^A + s_{a_1}^A) & i = 0 \\ s_i^A & o.w. \end{cases}$$

Notice that if s^A is a valid space division strategy, then s^{A+} is also a valid strategy, as $\sum_{i=0}^{n} s_i^{A+} = \sum_{i=0}^{n} s_i^A = c$.

Now we compare the utility of s_i^A with that of s_i^{A+}. Consider the utility function U for a space division strategy. If we denote the truly effective space division for chain i as seff_i, where

$$\mathsf{seff}_i = \min\{\beta_i s_0, s_i\}.$$

Then, it is obvious that the utility function is monotonic for every seff_i where $i \in [n]$. As a result, if $\forall i \in [n], \mathsf{seff}_i^{A+} \geq \mathsf{seff}_i^A$ and $\exists i \in [n], \mathsf{seff}_i^{A+} > \mathsf{seff}_i^A$, then the utility of strategy s^{A+} is better than that of s^A.

In fact, when $i = a_1$, we have $\mathsf{seff}_i^A = \beta_{a_1} s_0^A$, while $\mathsf{seff}_i^{A+} = s_i^{A+} = \frac{\beta_{a_1}}{\beta_{a_1}+1}(s_0^A + s_{a_1}^A)$. Since $\frac{s_{a_1}^A}{\beta_{a_1}} > s_0^A$, it comes out that $\mathsf{seff}_{a_1}^{A+} > \mathsf{seff}_{a_1}^A$. When $i \in I^A$ and $i \neq a_1$, given that we have assumed $s_i^A > \beta_i s_0^A$, then $\mathsf{seff}_i^A = \beta_i s_0^A$. Since

$$s_0^{A+} = \frac{1}{\beta_{a_1}+1}(s_0^A + s_{a_1}^A) > \frac{1}{\beta_{a_1}+1}(s_0^A + \beta_{a_1} s_0^A) = s_0^A,$$

we have

$$\mathsf{seff}_i^{A+} = \min\{\beta_i s_0^{A+}, s_i^{A+}\} > \beta_i s_0^A = \mathsf{seff}_i^A.$$

When $i \in [n]$ and $i \notin I^A$, it is obvious that $\mathsf{seff}_i^{A+} = s_i^{A+} = s_i^A = \mathsf{seff}_i^A$. And it concludes that the utility of s^{A+} is better than that of s^A.

Now we are allowed to prove Theorem 1.

Proof. We partite $\mathscr{D}_c^{M+1} = D \uplus D'$ into two domains where

$$D = \left\{ s \in \mathscr{D}_c^{M+1} | \forall i \in [M].\ s_i \leq \beta_i s_0 \right\}.$$

Lemma 2 tells that each strategy in D' can be emulated by a strategy in D. Therefore, D includes the optimal partition strategy within $\mathscr{D}_c^{M+1}$. By having $k = ||B||$, $U(s, B) = -F(s) \times rw||B||$ in Lemma 1 within D and so forth the optimal strategy among D is our desired partition.

Based on Theorem 1, we find that the optimization of strategy is indeed independent from the total resource c. Hence we conclude that for any participant, the optimal strategy is to divide half resource for the shared proof and divide the rest part according to the market weight of each chain

$$\mathsf{opt}(\beta) := \frac{1}{c}\widetilde{\mathsf{opt}}(c, B) = \frac{1}{2} \circ \frac{1}{2}\beta.$$

5.2   System Security

In this part, we show the difficulty of devastating a chain (say, i^{th} chain of market weight $B_i = b$) with $\frac{b}{||B||} = \beta$ fraction of total market weight. To devastate chain i, the adversary should occupy the total market weight with total storage resource over αb^1. That is to have $s_i = \alpha(b + s_i)$ and at the same time $(1 + \delta)\beta_i's_0 \geq s_i$ where $\beta_i' = \frac{b+s_i}{||B||+s_i}$. Thereby,

$$s_i = \frac{\alpha}{1 - \alpha}b,$$

and hence

$$
\begin{aligned}
s_0 &\geq \frac{s_i}{(1 + \delta)\beta_i'} = \frac{s_i(||B|| + s_i)}{(1 + \delta)(b + s_i)} \\
&\geq \frac{\frac{\alpha}{1-\alpha}b||B||}{(1 + \delta)(b + \frac{1-\alpha}{\alpha}b)} = \frac{\alpha^2}{(1 + \delta)(1 - \alpha)}||B||.
\end{aligned}
$$

For $\alpha > \frac{1}{3}$ and $\delta = \frac{1}{10}$, $s_0 \geq \frac{5}{33}||B|| > 15\%||B||$. This tells that regardless of the market weight of the chain, the adversary has to devote more than 15% global storage resource (45% to $\alpha > 1/2$) to devastate a chain with even the slightest market weight.

6   Conclusion

In this paper, we have proposed a novel multi-chain scheme from the inherited merit of proof-of-space. With our framework, the same storage source contributes simultaneously to multiple blockchains and newly set up blockchains are hard to be devastated. In the future, we look forward to the flourishing development of PoC-based blockchains and having our framework implemented on them. Also, although we have shown to realize this framework via pebbling graph-styled proof-of-space schemes, we also expect its application on PoC schemes of other styles.

References

1. Nakamoto, S.: Bitcoin: a peer-to-peer electronic cash system (2008)
2. Dwork, C., Naor, M.: Pricing via processing or combatting junk mail. In: Brickell, E.F. (ed.) CRYPTO 1992. LNCS, vol. 740, pp. 139–147. Springer, Heidelberg (1993). https://doi.org/10.1007/3-540-48071-4_10
3. QuantumMechanic et al.: Proof of stake instead of proof of work. Bitcoin Forum (2011). https://bitcointalk.org/index.php?topic=27787.0
4. Bentov, I., Lee, C., Mizrahi, A., Rosenfeld, M.: Proof of activity: extending bitcoin's proof of work via proof of stake [extended abstract]y. SIGMETRICS Perform. Eval. Rev. **42**(3), 34–37 (2014)
5. Bentov, I., Pass, R., Shi, E.: Snow white: provably secure proofs of stake. IACR Cryptology ePrint Archive 2016/919 (2016)
6. Pass, R., Shi, E.: The sleepy model of consensus. In: Takagi, T., Peyrin, T. (eds.) ASIACRYPT 2017. LNCS, vol. 10625, pp. 380–409. Springer, Cham (2017). https://doi.org/10.1007/978-3-319-70697-9_14

---

[1] Most existing systems ask for $\alpha > 1/3$, but we treat α as a tunable parameter to allow flexibility.

7. Kiayias, A., Russell, A., David, B., Oliynykov, R.: Ouroboros: a provably secure proof-of-stake blockchain protocol. In: Katz, J., Shacham, H. (eds.) CRYPTO 2017. LNCS, vol. 10401, pp. 357–388. Springer, Cham (2017). https://doi.org/10.1007/978-3-319-63688-7_12
8. David, B., Gaži, P., Kiayias, A., Russell, A.: Ouroboros praos: an adaptively-secure, semi-synchronous proof-of-stake blockchain. In: Nielsen, J., Rijmen, V. (eds.) EUROCRYPT 2018. LNCS, vol. 10821, pp. 66–98. Springer, Cham (2018). https://doi.org/10.1007/978-3-319-78375-8_3
9. Badertscher, P., Gazi, P., Kiayias, A., Russell, A., Zikas, V.: Ouroboros genesis: composable proof-of-stake blockchains with dynamic availability. In: Proceedings of the 2018 ACM SIGSAC Conference on Computer and Communications Security, CCS 2018, pp. 913–930, Toronto, 15–19 October 2018 (2018)
10. Dwork, C., Naor, M., Wee, H.: Pebbling and proofs of work. In: Shoup, V. (ed.) CRYPTO 2005. LNCS, vol. 3621, pp. 37–54. Springer, Heidelberg (2005). https://doi.org/10.1007/11535218_3
11. Dziembowski, S., Kazana, T., Wichs, D.: Key-evolution schemes resilient to space-bounded leakage. In: Rogaway, P. (ed.) CRYPTO 2011. LNCS, vol. 6841, pp. 335–353. Springer, Heidelberg (2011). https://doi.org/10.1007/978-3-642-22792-9_19
12. Dziembowski, S., Kazana, T., Wichs, D.: One-time computable self-erasing functions. In: Ishai, Y. (ed.) TCC 2011. LNCS, vol. 6597, pp. 125–143. Springer, Heidelberg (2011). https://doi.org/10.1007/978-3-642-19571-6_9
13. Fuchsbauer, G.: Spacemint: a cryptocurrency based on proofs of space. ERCIM News 110, 2017 (2017)
14. Ateniese, G., Bonacina, I., Faonio, A., Galesi, N.: Proofs of space: when space is of the essence. In: Abdalla, M., De Prisco, R. (eds.) SCN 2014. LNCS, vol. 8642, pp. 538–557. Springer, Cham (2014). https://doi.org/10.1007/978-3-319-10879-7_31
15. Dziembowski, S., Faust, S., Kolmogorov, V., Pietrzak, K.: Proofs of space. In: Gennaro, R., Robshaw, M. (eds.) CRYPTO 2015. LNCS, vol. 9216, pp. 585–605. Springer, Heidelberg (2015). https://doi.org/10.1007/978-3-662-48000-7_29
16. Percival, C.: Stronger key derivation via sequential memory-hard functions (2009)
17. Juels, A., Kaliski Jr., B.S.: PORs: proofs of retrievability for large files. In: Proceedings of the 2007 ACM Conference on Computer and Communications Security, CCS 2007, pp. 584–597. Alexandria, 28–31 Oct 2007
18. Paul, W.J., Tarjan, R.E., Celoni, J.R.: Space bounds for a game on graphs. Math. Syst. Theory 10, 239–251 (1977)
19. Alon, N., Capalbo, M.R.: Smaller explicit superconcentrators. Internet Math. 1(2), 151–163 (2003)
20. Schöning, U.: Better expanders and super concentrators by Kolmogorov complexity. In: SIROCCO 1997, 4th International Colloquium on Structural Information and Communication Complexity, pp. 138–150, Ascona, 24–26 July 1997 (1997)
21. Kolmogorov, V., Rolinek, M.: Super concentrators of density. Ars. Comb. 141, 269–304 (2018)
22. Haglin, D.J.: Bipartite expander matching is in NC. Parallel Process. Lett. 5, 413–420 (1995)
23. Thomason, A.: Dense expanders and pseudo-random bipartite graphs. Discret. Math. 75(1–3), 381–386 (1989)
24. Erdoes, P., Graham, R.L., Szemeredi, E.: On sparse graphs with dense long paths. Technical report, Stanford (1975)

25. Alwen, J., Blocki, J., Pietrzak, K.: Depth-robust graphs and their cumulative memory complexity. In: Coron, J.-S., Nielsen, J. (eds.) EUROCRYPT 2017. LNCS, vol. 10212, pp. 3–32. Springer, Cham (2017). https://doi.org/10.1007/978-3-319-56617-7_1
26. Ren, L., Devadas, S.: Proof of space from stacked expanders. In: Hirt, M., Smith, A. (eds.) TCC 2016. LNCS, vol. 9985, pp. 262–285. Springer, Heidelberg (2016). https://doi.org/10.1007/978-3-662-53641-4_11
27. Pietrzak, K.: Proofs of catalytic space. In: 10th Innovations in Theoretical Computer Science Conference, ITCS 2019, pp. 59:1–59:25. San Diego, 10–12 Jan 2019
28. Bellare, M., Rogaway, P.: Random oracles are practical: a paradigm for designing efficient protocols. In: CCS 1993, Proceedings of the 1st ACM Conference on Computer and Communications Security, pp. 62–73. Fairfax, 3–5 November 1993 (1993)
29. Dodis, Y., Guo, S., Katz, J.: Fixing cracks in the concrete: random oracles with auxiliary input, revisited. In: Coron, J.-S., Nielsen, J. (eds.) EUROCRYPT 2017. LNCS, vol. 10211, pp. 473–495. Springer, Cham (2017). https://doi.org/10.1007/978-3-319-56614-6_16
30. Cohen, B., Pietrzak, K.: Simple proofs of sequential work. In: Nielsen, J., Rijmen, V. (eds.) EUROCRYPT 2018. LNCS, vol. 10821, pp. 451–467. Springer, Cham (2018). https://doi.org/10.1007/978-3-319-78375-8_15
31. Savage, J.E.: Models of Computation - Exploring the Power of Computing. Addison-Wesley, Boston (1998)

Secure Consistency Verification for Untrusted Cloud Storage by Public Blockchains

Kai Li[1], Yuzhe Tang[1(✉)], Beom Heyn (Ben) Kim[2], and Jianliang Xu[3]

[1] Syracuse University, New York, USA
ytang100@syr.edu
[2] University of Toronto, Toronto, ON, Canada
[3] Hong Kong Baptist University, Kowloon Tong, Hong Kong

Abstract. This work presents ContractChecker, a Blockchain-based security protocol for verifying the storage consistency between mutually distrusting cloud provider and clients. Unlike existing protocols, the ContractChecker uniquely delegates log auditing to the Blockchain, and has the advantages in reducing client cost and lowering requirements on client availability, lending itself to modern scenarios with mobile and web clients.

The ContractChecker collects the logs from both clients and cloud server, and verifies the consistency by cross-checking the logs. By this means, it does not only detect the attacks from malicious clients and server forging their logs, but also is able to mitigate those attacks and recover the system from them. In addition, we design new attacks against ContractChecker exploiting various limits in real Blockchain systems (e.g., write unavailability, Blockchain forks, contract race conditions). We analyze and harden the security of ContractChecker protocols under these proposed new attacks.

We implement a functional prototype of the ContractChecker on Ethereum/ Solidity. By experiments on private and public Ethereum testnets, we extensively evaluate the cost of the ContractChecker in comparison with that of existing client-based log auditing works. The result shows the ContractChecker can scale to hundreds of clients and save client costs by more than one order of magnitude. The evaluation result verifies our design motivation of delegating log auditing to the Blockchain in ContractChecker.

Keywords: Blockchain applications · Blockchain security · Cloud storage · Storage consistency

1 Introduction

Today, the cloud-storage consistency is a pressingly important security property. With a cloud storage service (e.g., Dropbox [4] and Amazon S3 [1]), the consistency indicates how reads/writes should be ordered and whether a read should reflect the latest write (i.e., freshness). This property is exploitable to a malicious cloud provider and leads to severe security consequences. For instance, when the cloud storage hosts a public-key

S. Chen et al. (Eds.): SecureComm 2019, LNICST 304, pp. 39–62, 2019.
https://doi.org/10.1007/978-3-030-37228-6_3

directory (as in certificate-transparency schemes [2]), a malicious cloud violating storage consistency can return to the user a revoked public key, leading to consequences like impersonation attacks and unauthorized data access. Making a trustworthy assertion about cloud storage consistency is fundamental to supporting information-security infrastructure in the clouds, such as public-key directories, software-update registry, personal device synchronization, etc.

Asserting the storage consistency in a client-server system entails two conceptual steps: W1) establishing a globally consistent view of operation log across clients (i.e., operation log attestation), and W2) auditing the log for checking consistency conditions (i.e., log auditing). To the best of our knowledge, all existing approaches including Caelus [16], CloudProof [20], and Catena [23], assume trusted clients and rely on them to audit the log. More specifically, they make a single party attest to the log of operations (step W1) and send the attested log to individual clients, each of which audits the log against her local operations (W2). In particular, Catena [23] is a novel scheme that makes log attestation based on the Blockchain (W1 on Blockchain), yet still uses clients for log auditing (W2 by clients). These client-based log auditing schemes require high client availability (i.e., all clients have to participate in the protocol execution) and incur high client cost (i.e., a client needs to store the global operation log of all other clients), rendering them ill-suited for applications with a large number of low-end and stateless clients; see Sect. 3.1 for a list of target applications.

We propose ContractChecker, a secure Blockchain-based consistency verification protocol. Distinct from existing works, ContractChecker uniquely delegates both log attestation (W1) and log auditing (W2) to the Blockchain. Concretely, ContractChecker runs a program on the Blockchain (i.e., the so-called smart contracts) to collect log attestations from clients and the server and to audit the log there for making the consistency assertion. Comparing existing works, our approach, by delegating log auditing to Blockchain, has the advantage in lowering client availability requirement (i.e., only active clients who interact with the cloud are required to participate in the protocol) and in minimizing client overhead (i.e., a client only maintains her own operations for a limited period of time).

While it seems straightforward to delegate the log auditing to Blockchain as a trusted third party (TTP), putting this idea into a secure protocol and system raises the following challenges: (1) How to securely collect and audit logs from mutually distrusting clients and server (detailed in Sect. 5.2)? 2) Real-world Blockchain systems are far from an ideal TTP and can be exploited to attack a log-auditing service on Blockchain (detailed in Sect. 5.3). First, a ContractChecker party, be it a client or the server, can be malicious and forge operations in her log attestation in order to trick ContractChecker to make an incorrect assertion about the storage consistency. We propose to cross-check the attestations from both the server and clients to detect any mismatch and log-forging attacks. In addition, in the presence of such attacks, we propose mitigation techniques (in Sect. 5.2) for the ContractChecker to securely attribute the cause of the attacks such that it can make a correct assertion despite of the attacks.

Second, real-world Blockchain systems are known to be limited in terms of E1) write unavailability (i.e., a valid transaction could be dropped by the Blockchain), E2) exploitable smart-contract race conditions (i.e., incorrect contract logic can be triggered by running contract code concurrently), and E3) Blockchain forks (i.e., a Blockchain network or data structure can be forked to multiple instances). We propose attacks against the use of Blockchain in the context of ContractChecker. These new attacks systematically exploit the Blockchain limitations mentioned above, and they are: a selective-omission attack exploiting Blockchain write unavailability (E1), a forking attack exploiting smart-contract race conditions (E2), and another version of forking attack exploiting Blockchain forks (E3).

We propose countermeasures to defend the Blockchain-oriented ContractChecker attacks. To prevent write unavailability (E1), we increase the transaction fee during client attestations to improve the chance of Blockchain accepting a transaction in a certain period of time. To prevent the race conditions on ContractChecker (E2), we define a small critical section in the contract to secure the contract execution yet without losing the support of concurrent server and client attestations. We prevent forking through Blockchain forks (E3) by ensuring all clients and server be aware of the presence of all Blockchain forks.

We build a system prototype of ContractChecker based on Ethereum [5]. The on-chain part runs a smart contract (in Solidity) that collects log attestations from clients and the server, crosschecks them and audits the log with consistency conditions. We envision a novel application of ContractChecker to enforce a consistency-centric service-level agreement (SLA) with cloud providers.

We conduct cost analysis and experimental analysis on our prototype. We evaluate the client cost of the protocol and service under YCSB workloads [13]. Our results show that on Ethereum, ContractChecker results in significant cost saving on the client side, with reasonable Gas cost on running smart contract. We also measure the gas cost of ContractChecker and present the evaluation in technical report [9] (due to space limits). It shows the practicality of ContractChecker to the extent of supporting 613710 operations at the cost of $100 at a real Ether price.

The contributions of this work are:

1. **New use of Blockchain:** This work addresses verifying cloud consistency based on public Blockchain. Unlike existing research, the work delegates log auditing to Blockchain, which has the advantage of reducing client costs and availability requirements. Based on this new use of Blockchain, we propose the ContractChecker consistency-verification protocol (Sects. 2 and 4.1).
2. **Secure protocol design:** We present a secure protocol design for ContractChecker among distrusting clients and cloud provider. The protocol cross-checks logs collected from different parties and then conduct consistency checks. It not only can detect the log-forging attacks from malicious clients and server, but also mitigate those attacks (Sect. 4).
3. **New attacks:** This work presents new security attacks against Blockchain-based log-auditing protocols. These new attacks exploits the limits in real Blockchain systems (e.g., write unavailability, Blockchain forks, contract race conditions). We propose to harden the security of ContractChecker under these proposed new attacks and conduct an extensive security analysis (Sect. 5).

4. **Prototyping and evaluation:** We implement a prototype of the ContractChecker on Ethereum/Solidity. By experiments on private and public Ethereum testnets, we extensively evaluate the client-side cost of the ContractChecker. The result shows the ContractChecker can scale to hundreds of clients and, in this setting, save client costs by more than one order of magnitude when compared with existing client-based log auditing works including Catena. The evaluation on client cost justifies the key design choice in ContractChecker to delegate log auditing to Blockchain (Sect. 6).

2 Preliminary: Secure Consistency Verification Protocols

Suppose there are multiple clients interacting with an untrusted data-storage service. The problem of storage consistency verification is to convince all the clients that the untrusted storage service conforms to a certain storage consistency model. In the existing literature (as will be elaborated on), verifying storage consistency entails two steps: storage log attestation and log auditing. In log attestation, a conceptual trusted party (log attester) makes attestation about the collection of all storage operations and their ordering. The purpose of log attestation is to commit to a globally consistent view about the operation ordering such that the malicious server cannot "fork" different views for different clients (i.e., the forking attack [18]). After a fork-free global log is established, the second step can take place which is to audit the log and check the consistency conditions over the global log of operations.

Existing work specializes the above framework. Specifically, SUNDR [17] does not assume a trusted third party (i.e., no trusted attester) but instead relies on the untrusted server making log attestations to individual clients. Without the trusted attester, SUNDR does not prevent forking attacks, but makes them eventually detectable (i.e., the so-called level of fork consistency [17]). In a sense, SUNDR is a fork-detectable log attestation scheme without trusted third party. Caelus [16] addresses the application scenario with battery-powered clients of a cloud storage service. Caelus rotates (or time-shares) the role of log attester among personal devices to present a virtual and highly-available trusted attester. Log auditing occurs on individual clients and Caelus supports the checking of both strong and weak consistency models. Similarly, CloudProof [20] requires the untrusted server to attest to the operation log and relies on the trusted clients to audit the operation history for a variety of consistency models. Catena [23] is a unique Blockchain-based log attestation scheme, which prevents the server-forking attack by "abusing" the Blockchain security in no double-spending transactions.

All existing consistency-verification schemes including the above rely on trusted clients (or data owners) to audit the operation log and check consistency conditions. In this respect, ContractChecker is the first scheme that delegates log auditing to the Blockchain. The unique design of ContractChecker is depicted in Table 1. Blockchain-oriented log delegation brings benefits in lower client cost and availability requirements as will be elaborated in Sect. 4.1.

Table 1. Distinction of the ContractChecker design: ✗ means the log operation is not supported by Blockchain, but instead by clients.

Solutions	Attestation by Blockchain	Auditing by Blockchain
SUNDR [17], Caelus [16], CloudProof [20]	✗	✗
Catena [23]	✓	✗
ContractChecker	✓	✓

3 Research Formulation

3.1 Target Applications

The target application scenarios of ContractChecker are characterized by the following properties: S1) The clients are of limited capability in computing, storage, and availability. This motivates them to outsource data storage to a more powerful cloud. S2) Violating storage consistency leads to security consequences. S3) The data load is low (e.g., typically lower than tens of operations per second). In particular, the low throughput properties of these typical application scenarios make it amenable for the use of Blockchain, which is known to have limited throughput in ingesting transactions.

In real world, there are many application scenarios that fit the above paradigm. As an example, consider a DockerHub [3] style container registry which distributes software patches for mobile apps. In this scenario, the clients are low-power smart phones (S1). Distributing a stale software image with unfixed security bugs leads to vulnerability on users' phone (S2). In terms of workloads, an IBM report [11] shows that among seven geo-distributed registry deployments, the busiest one serves only 100 requests per minute for more than 80% of time(S3). We believe there are many real-world applications that meet our target scenarios, ranging from Google's certificate-transparency logs [2], iCloud style personal-device synchronization [8], Github-hosted secure software development [7, 24], etc.

3.2 System and Security Model

Our system model consists of three parties: a storage server in the cloud, multiple concurrent clients and the Blockchain. Clients submit storage operations (i.e., data reads and writes) to the storage server. The operations are witnessed by the Blockchain via our ContractChecker protocol.

Clients. Clients are data owners who outsource the data storage to the cloud. They submit operations to the cloud storage to read or update their data. Different clients' operations may occur concurrently, that is, the cloud service may process multiple operations in parallel, with their time intervals overlapped. A client can be active when she has submitted operations recently (we will explain the definition of active clients later) and inactive when she goes offline without any operations on the cloud.

Clients in our model are <u>stateless</u> in the sense that a client does not persist state across active sessions. That is, a client does not need to remember her past operations when she is engaged with a cloud. In addition, among clients, there are no direct communication channels. That is, other than the cloud or Blockchain, clients do not communicate out-of-band. We believe this model reflects low-power clients in many real-world situations, such as smart-phone clients running web browsers. Web clients are stateless and do not directly communicate among themselves.

We assume each ContractChecker client is identified, say by her public key. When the Blockchain needs to identify a client, the client identity can be obtained and verified using client certificates issued by an offline trusted certificate authority (CA). Existing key-transparency systems such as CONIKS [19] can be used here in companion with ContractChecker. More details about client identity management are described in Technical Report [9].

We assume clients share synchronized clocks by running NTP protocols. Synchronized clocks will be useful in our protocol when clients are required to log operations. The accuracy of NTP protocols may affect the precision of our consistency verification results. Existing protocols can achieve highly synchronized clocks and limit clock skews to the level of milliseconds [14], which we believe are sufficient in our system.

A Cloud Storage Service. The cloud service hosts a data store shared among multiple clients. The service accepts clients' requests and processes them concurrently. That is, different operations from clients may be processed in parallel and in an out-of-order fashion.

Under this execution model, we consider strong consistency or linearizability [15]. Linearizability considers independent access to different data records and is sufficiently strong to capture necessary conditions in many security scenarios [16,20]. Weaker consistency that is widely adopted in modern cloud services [21] is commonly less relevant to security-sensitive and critical applications. In this paper, we do not consider database serializability or isolation under multiple keys [12].

We assume the cloud service makes a consistency-centric service-level agreement (SLA) [22] with the clients which states where the cloud service promises to guarantee strong consistency (more specifically, linearizability as will be defined next) over the operations it will serve. An honest server will enforce the promised consistency conditions during operational hours.

A malicious storage server will violate the consistency conditions (as will be elaborated on), by returning a stale result for a read. In addition, a malicious server will not follow our ContractChecker protocol and tries to conceal the operation inconsistency from clients. Consistency violation, if left undetected, can lead to severe security consequences such as impersonation attacks (recall Sect. 3.1).

Moreover, we assume the cloud service is rational. While a malicious cloud server may forge operations to make an inconsistent operation history look like consistent (i.e., concealing the inconsistency), the server will not attempt to make a consistent operation history look like inconsistent. We believe this assumption reflects practical situations with SLA where the cloud server will be charged in case of verified inconsistency, and thus does not have the incentive to forge an inconsistent history.

Consistency Definition: We consider the storage service exposes a standard key-value API, where each data record is a key-value pair and each storage operation accesses the target record by the data key. A storage operation, be it a read or write, is specified by two timestamps, which respectively represent (1) the begin time when the request of the operation is sent by the client, and (2) the end time when the response of the operation is received by the client. Formally, given a key-value pair $\langle K, V \rangle$, a read operation is $V = r_{[t_b, t_e]}(K)$ and $\text{ACK} = w_{[t_b, t_e]}(K, V)$. Here r/w denotes read or write operation. $t_b < t_e$ and they are the begin and end timestamps. If two operations are concurrent, their time intervals $[t_b, t_e]$ may overlap.

An operation history is linearizable if the following two conditions are met: (1) All operations can be mapped to a total-order sequence that is compatible with the real-time intervals of the operations. (2) There is no stale read on the total-order sequence. That is, any read operation should return the record that is fresh on the total-order. This property is also called read freshness.

Any linearizable operation history can be represented by a totally-ordered operation sequence. We denote an operation sequence by operation indices. For instance, in $w_1 w_2 r_3 [w_2]$, the subscription is the operation index in the total-order (described below). Linearizability specifies operations of the same data key; for simplicity, we omit data key in this notation. The square bracket of a read indicates the result record. $r_3[w_2]$ denotes a read operation ordered as the third operation in the total-order sequence and which returns the record written by write w_2.

Network: In this work, we assume a reliable network among clients, the server and Blockchain nodes. When one party sends a message to the network, the network will deliver the message to the receiver with negligible delay (comparing with the period our protocol runs). We do not consider network faults or partition in this work.

Blockchain. The Blockchain in our protocol is a public, permissionless Blockchain running over a large P2P network and supporting smart contract execution. Real-world examples include Ethereum and the latest version of Bitcoin. In this setting, we assume the honest majority among Blockchain miners. We believe this is a reasonable assumption as in practice there are no successful 51% attacks on Bitcoin or Ethereum.

The Blockchain in our protocol is parameterized by the following arguments: block time B, which is the average time to find a block in a Blockchain; and transaction-validation delay P, which is the time between a pending transaction enters the memory pool and when it leaves for transaction validation; and finality delay F, which is the number of blocks needed to be appended after a finalized transaction. That is, a transaction is considered to be finalized in Blockchain when there are at least F blocks included in the Blockchain after the transaction.

The Blockchain supports the execution of smart contracts. The contract is executed across all Blockchain miners. It guarantees the execution integrity and non-stoppability. That is, the Blockchain truthfully executes a smart contract based on the provided arguments, despite of the attacks to subvert the Blockchain (as described below). Once the execution of a contract starts, it is hard to stop the execution or to abort.

Blockchain Write Availability: The Blockchain may drop transactions based on its current load and transaction fee. A transaction with a higher fee will have a lower chance of being dropped [23] and have shorter latency to be included. This assumption will be tested in our evaluation.

Blockchain Attacks: The Blockchain is subject to a series of threats. In this work, we focus on practical Blockchain threats and exclude theoretic threats (e.g., 51% attacks, selfish mining, etc.) and off-chain threats (e.g., stealing wallet coins and secret keys). (1) The Blockchain may be forked permanently due to software update as in the case of Bitcoin cash (Blockchain forks). (2) Smart contracts may contain security bugs that can be exploited by a vector of attacks [6], such as reentrancy attacks, buffer overflow attacks, etc. In practice, the DAO (decentralized autonomous organization) incidents are caused by this attack vector.

3.3   Goals

Security Goals. In our system, there are two main threats: (1) In the case that inconsistency occurs, the malicious server wants to hide the inconsistency from victim clients. (2) In the case that all operations are consistent, a malicious client may want to accuse the benign server of the storage inconsistency that does not occur. We exclude other cases as they are not rational. For instance, we do not consider that a rational server will forge operations such that a consistent operation history will appear inconsistent. We also do not consider that a victim client will want to hide an inconsistent operation history. Due to this reason, we assume clients and the server will not collude to either hide inconsistency or accuse of false consistency.

Our security goals are listed below:

Timely Detection of Inconsistency Against Malicious Server: A malicious server cannot hide the occurrence of inconsistent operations from victim clients. To be concrete, when inconsistency occurs, the protocol will assert there are inconsistent operations in a timely manner, even when a malicious server can forge a seemingly consistent log. In addition to that, the protocol will present a verifiable proof of the inconsistency, so that it can penalize the cloud service for violating the consistency.

No False Accusation of Inconsistency Against Malicious Clients: A malicious client cannot falsely accuse a benign server of inconsistency that does not occur. Given a consistent operation history, the protocol will assert it is consistent, even when there are malicious clients who want to forge inconsistent operations in the log.

Cost Goals.   Client Cost: Clients in our protocol can remain stateless. That is, running the ContractChecker protocol, a client does not need to store her operations indefinitely and can truncate operations after use (i.e., stateless). In addition, the protocol data stored on a client is limited to the client's local operation; a client does not need to store other clients' operations (i.e., local operations). These two requirements make clients lightweight and render the protocol applicable to scenarios with low-power clients.

Non-goals. Data Authenticity: Data authenticity states a malicious cloud service cannot forge a client's data without being detected. We assume an external infrastructure in place that ensures data authenticity, such as MAC or digital signatures. To be more specific, the client who writes a record signs the record, and the signature can be verified to guarantee the data authenticity of the record. Here, clients' public keys are securely distributed by a PKI or a secure communication channel.

Collusion: In ContractChecker, we aim at security guarantees against a malicious cloud server or malicious clients. However, we do not consider the case that a server colludes a client, because this would make it impossible for any third-party to detect the attack. To be concrete, a colluding client can lie about her log (e.g., omitting an operation), and the server can do the same. With the client and server both lying about their operations, any third-party cannot detect the existence of the lie. If an operation can be forged or omitted in a log, the consistency assertion over the log cannot be trusted. For instance, omitting w_2 in $w_1 w_2 r_3 [w_1]$ leads to incorrect consistency assertion. Due to this reason, we exclude from our threat model the collusion among clients and server. In practice, we believe server-client collusion is a rare situation.

4   The Security Protocols

4.1   Design Motivation

The key design in ContractChecker is to use Blockchain to audit the log in a client-server system (recall Table 1). This use of Blockchain is motivated by our observations below:

(1) Low Client Cost: By delegating log audit to the Blockchain, one can significantly relieve the burden from the clients. Existing consistency-verification protocols are based on client-side log auditing [23,25], which requires a client to persist not only her own operations but also operations of all other clients, limiting the system scalability. By delegating log auditing to the Blockchain, a client can be relieved from accessing other clients' operations, and can have a minimal overhead of receiving log-auditing results from the Blockchain.

(2) Freshness with Stateless Clients: Consistency verification needs to access historical operations. With stateless clients who do not communicate, it is impossible to guarantee the freshness of any global state without trusted third party [17,18]. The presence of Blockchain as a trusted third party is necessary and beneficial in guaranteeing the freshness of serving historical operations in the presence of server rollback attack.

(3) Security without Client Availability: Intuitively, Blockchain serves as a highly available[1] trusted third party, and it can be used to support clients with low availability. More specifically, in existing client-based auditing schemes, all clients are assumed to be highly available in the sense that they require inactive clients to participate in log auditing in every epoch. In a world without a highly available third-party, this requirement is necessary because otherwise it is hard to distinguish an inactive client who

---

[1] The condition that Blockchain is highly available is described in Sect. 3.2.

does not report (the benign case), and an active client whose report is suppressed by the malicious server (the attack case). With a Blockchain serving as a reliable broadcast channel among clients,[2] it can afford that an inactive client does not need to participate in the protocol execution. The reliable Blockchain makes it possible to collect all active clients' logs in the presence of untrusted server. (See Sect. 5.1 for a detailed correctness analysis).

In the following, we first present the protocol overview and then justify the design by describing the alternative designs we have explored (and dismissed). After that, we will present the details of our protocol execution.

4.2 Protocol Overview

ContractChecker is a protocol that runs among clients, a storage server and the Blockchain. The purpose of the protocol is to present a trustworthy assertion about the consistency of the operations among clients and the server. At a high level, the protocol works by asking clients and the server to periodically attest to their views of operations to the Blockchain where different views are crosschecked and consistency conditions are verified. The purpose of the crosscheck on Blockchain is to detect and mitigate the attack from a malicious server (or client) who forges her view of the log.

In our protocol, the interaction between the Blockchain and the clients/server off chain can be described by the following three functions. Note that the protocol runs in epochs and here we consider the operations in one epoch.

- $S.\texttt{attestServerLog}(Ops_S, sk_S)$: Server S declares a total-order over the global history of operations in the current epoch (Ops_S). She attests to the declared total-order sequence by signing it with her secret key sk_S.
- $C.\texttt{attestClientLog}(Ops_C, sk_C)$: An active client C attests to her local operations in the current epoch (Ops_C) by signing it with her secret key sk_C. Operations of a single client can also be concurrent and a client does not need to declare a total-order over her own operations. If a client is inactive, meaning she did not submit any operation in the epoch, she does not need to call this function.
- $C.\texttt{consistencyResult}() = \{Y, N\}$: A client C can check consistency of the current operation history. With Blockchain, the checking result is only valid when the attestations are finalized on the chain. This function is blocking until the finality is confirmed. If the attestations are not finalized, it will retry by calling `attestClientLog`.

4.3 Protocol Design Alternatives

No Server Attestation: Our protocol (as presented above) requires to collect the log from both clients and the server. An alternative design is to collect the operation history only from clients. In this scheme, all clients send their local operations to the Blockchain

---

[2] There are situations that consistency verification protocols require client-client communication, such as disseminating the global list of operations for client-based auditing and reporting attack incidents.

without collecting the server log. The union of client logs can reconstruct all operations and their relations in real time (i.e., serial or concurrent with each other). However, there are two limits of this approach. First, the union of client logs does not have the total-order information (among concurrent operations) which is necessary to determine the storage consistency (Recall the consistency definition in Sect. 3.2). Relying on the smart contracts to "solve" the operation total-order, it would be expensive in terms of gas cost. Second, having attestations from both clients and server is helpful to determine which party is lying in the presence of malicious client and server. In particular, without the server attestation, it would be impossible to mitigate attacks from malicious clients. Therefore, our protocol requires the (untrusted) server to declare the operation total-order and send her attestation to the Blockchain.

Synchronizing Public Contract Functions: Our protocol implements log attestation as public contract functions (i.e., `attestServerLog()`, `attestClientLog()`) and implements the log crosschecking and auditing as private contract functions (i.e., `crosscheckLog()`). Our initial design is to implement all three tasks in three public contract functions that can be called from off-chain clients.

However, a problem arises with the order in which these public functions can be executed. The order in which the calls to public contract functions are issued (issuance order) may be different from the order in which the public contract functions are executed on Blockchain miners (execution order). For instance, if a Blockchain client can serially submit functions calls for log attestation, crosscheck and checking, the three functions may be delivered to individual Blockchain miners in a different order, say checking, crosscheck, attestation, which will break the protocol correctness. To fix this, one can rely on clients to synchronize different contract calls, say by requiring a client only calls crosscheck until it confirms the completion (or transaction finality) of the call of log attestation. However, this client-side synchronization is extremely slow and unnecessarily time-consuming.

Therefore, our protocol implements the log crosschecking and auditing by private contract functions that can only be called by another contract on chain. By this means, the serial order is ensured directly by individual miners without expensive client-side finality confirmation.

4.4 The Protocol: Execution and Construction

In this section, we present the protocol in the top-down fashion. We first describe the overall protocol execution flow involving both on-chain and off-chain parties. We then describe the construction of the protocol with the details of the various primitives used in the construction.

Overall Protocol Execution. We present the overall protocol execution. The ContractChecker protocol runs in epochs. Each epoch is of a pre-defined time interval E. During an epoch, clients send read/write requests to the storage server in the cloud. For simplicity, we consider a client runs a single thread.[3] The operations are logged on both

---

[3] In practice, the case of a multi-threaded client can be treated as multiple single-threaded virtual clients.

sides of clients and the server as in Fig. 2). A client logs her own operations while the server logs the operations submitted by all clients. Given an operation, a client logs the start time when the request for the operation is sent and the end time when the response of the operation is received. We assume the NTP protocol in place enables all clients to log operation time with low inaccuracy. Both clients and the server store the logged operations locally.

At the end of the epoch, both clients and the server attest to their operation log. The server calls `attestServerLog(ops_server,`sk_S`)` where she declares a total-order sequence over the operations and signs the log with server key sk_S before sending it the Blockchain. A client calls `attestClientLog(ops_client,` sk_C`)` where she signs the logged operations with secret key sk_C and sends it to the Blockchain. The total-order in the server attestation is necessary for consistency checking (recall the definition in Sect. 3.2).

The smart contract running on the Blockchain receives the calls of `attest-ServerLog(ops_server,`sk_S`)` from the server and `attestClientLog(ops_client,` sk_C`)` from all active clients. After that, it runs log verification, log crosschecking and log auditing which will be elaborated on in Sect. 4.4. The result, namely the assertion of log consistency, is stored on chain for future inquiry. Clients can call `consistencyResult()` to check the consistency result.

The consistency assertion is valid only when two conditions are met: (1) all active clients' transactions `attestClientLog(ops_client,` sk_C`)` are finalized on Blockchain. (2) the consistency assertion (i.e., the result of running `auditLog()`) is finalized on Blockchain. To guarantee the two conditions, all active clients in an epoch are synchronized among themselves and with the Blockchain (see Sect. 4.4 for details).

ContractChecker is parameterized by the duration of an epoch E, which can be set according to application-level requirements in timeliness of consistency assurance (see details in our technical report [9]).

An example is presented in Fig. 1 where the ContractChecker protocol runs one epoch between two clients C_1 and C_2. An epoch can be set to multiple of Blockchain's block time. On Ethereum, it is multiply of 15 s. During the epoch, client C_1 submits two operations to the server, namely w_1 and $r_3[w_1]$. $r_3[w_1]$ represents a read operation that returns write w_1. Client C_2 submits an operation w_2 to the server. All operations are on the same data key, and they are processed by the server in the serial order of $w_1 w_2 r_3[w_1]$. By the end of epoch, it first runs log attestation: C_1 calls `attestClientLog(`w_1, r_3`)` and C_2 calls `attestClientLog(`w_2`)`. The server declares a total-order w_1, w_2, r_3 by calling `attestServerLog(`w_1, w_2, r_3`)`. The smart contract then stores the two client logs and one server log on the Blockchain. After that, it runs two functions: `crosscheckLog(`$\{w_1, r_3\}, \{w_2\}, \{w_1, w_2, r_3\}$`)`, and `auditLog(`$\{w_1, w_2, r_3[w_1]\}$`)`. As a result, the smart contract asserts the log is inconsistent and stores it on chain.

Meanwhile, the clients may call C.`consistencyResult()`. The function call will block until the transaction of C.`attestClientLog()` is finalized on Blockchain. On Ethereum, it takes 25 epochs to finalize a transaction. After 25 epochs, if the transaction is finalized, the consistency assertion stored on chain can be treated

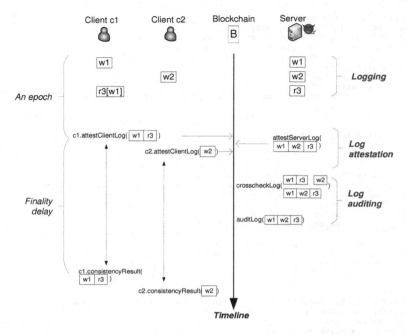

Fig. 1. Running ContractChecker: An example scenario with two clients. Client C_1 sends a write w_1 before a read $r_3[w_1]$ that returns the record written by w_1. Client C_2 sends a write w_2 to the server.

as an immutable statement and be further used by applications. In addition, the client can truncate her local operations in that epoch. If the transaction is not included in the Blockchain, the client will retry `C.attestClientLog()`.

Now we modify the setting of this example that w_1 and w_2 are processed concurrently by the server (i.e., with overlapped time intervals). In this case, a rational server (recall Sect. 3.2) will search and attest to the total-order that is consistent, namely $w_2w_1r_3[w_1]$. Note that the other total-order $w_1w_2r_3[w_1]$ also matches the real-time relation, as w_1 and w_2 are concurrent. But it contains inconsistent read $r_3[w_1]$.

Note that in this example, the ContractChecker clients are stateless (in that client C_1 can discard operations w_1r_3 and truncate the log after client attestation) and store only local operations (in that client C_1 does not need to store the operations of client C_2). This saves the client cost, comparing all existing approaches including Catena and Caelus which require clients to maintain global state without log truncation.

Construction of On-Chain Contracts. The two attestations described in Sect. 4.2 invoke a smart-contract on chain. The smart contract taking as input of log attestations from the server and clients will conduct four operations: verifying client attestations (`verifyClientLog()`), verifying the server attestation (`verifyServerLog()`), crosschecking the logs of clients and server (`crosscheckLog()`), and auditing the checked log to assert consistency (`auditLog()`).

```
 1  contract ContractChecker{
 2    address payable ownerContract;
 3    attestClientLog(Op[] ops_client, signature_client){
 4      if(true == verifyClientLog(ops_client,
 5                    signature_client, pubkey_client)){
 6        lock.acquire();//to prevent race conditions
 7        if(++attested_clients == N
 8            && attested_server = 1){
 9          if(!crosscheckLog(ops_clients, ops_server))
10            throw;
11          if(!auditLog(ops_server)) throw;
12        }
13        lock.release();
14      }
15    }
16
17    attestServerLog(Op[] ops_server, signature_server){
18      if(true == verifyServerLog(ops_server, signature_server, pubkey_server)){
19        lock.acquire();//to prevent race conditions
20        if(attested_clients == N
21            && ++ attested_server = 1){
22          if(!crosscheckLog(ops_clients, ops_server))
23            throw;
24          if(!auditLog(ops_server)) throw;
25        }
26        lock.release();
27      }
28    }
29
30    modifier crosscheckLog(Op[] ops_clients, Op[] ops_server)) returns (false) {...}
31    modifier auditLog(Op[] ops_server)) returns (false) {...}
32    mapping ops_server;
33    mapping ops_clients;
34  }
```

Fig. 2. Smart-contract program of ContractChecker

In `verifyClientLog()`, the contract would verify the client attestation using the client's public key. In `verifyServerLog()`, the contract verifies the server attestation using the server's public key. It is optional that an individual operation can be signed by both the client and server. In this case, both verification functions will verify individual operations as well using both clients' and server's public keys. Once logs are verified, the client logs are union-ed and are crosschecked with the server log to find any inequality (`crosscheckLog()`). Once the logs are successfully cross-checked, it runs log auditing (i.e., `auditLog()`) where strong consistency conditions (e.g., operation ordering and read freshness) are checked over the crosschecked server log.

Finality of Client Attestations. The finality checking is realized by all active clients staying online and confirming the finality of their own attestations. For a client to check the finality of her attestation, she simply checks if there are F blocks on the Blockchain that are ordered after the block where her attestation transaction is stored. Blockchain's immutability guarantees the hardness of altering or omitting the client attestation if its finality is confirmed on the chain. If the transaction is not finalized, the client is responsible for resubmitting `attestClientLog()` until the confirmed finality of the transaction.

A consistency assertion is only valid when all active clients have confirmed the finality of their log attestations. Had one client's log not been confirmed on the Blockchain, a malicious server can launch the selective-omission attack (detailed in Sect. 5.3) that leads to an incorrect assertion. Clients wait until all clients' attestations are finalized on Blockchain (see Sect. 5.3 for a heuristic client-synchronization scheme).

5 Protocol Analysis

In this subsection, we analyze the protocol correctness under both benign and malicious settings. We start with the correctness with benign clients and the server. We consider the case of lowly-available clients. We then focus on the malicious cases, by analyzing protocol security with a malicious server, malicious clients, and unreliable Blockchain.

5.1 Correctness

In ContractChecker, the protocol correctness states that if the protocol is truthfully executed by benign clients and server, a consistent operation history will be asserted as a consistent history, and an inconsistent operation history will be asserted as an inconsistent history. Informally, given any consistent operation history Ops_S and any $\{Ops_C\}$ with $\cup Ops_C = Ops_S$, it holds that $S.\texttt{attestServerLog}(Ops_S)$, $C.\texttt{attestClientLog}(Ops_C)$, $C.\texttt{consistencyResult}() = Y$. For any inconsistency operation history Ops_S and any $\{Ops_C\}$, $S.\texttt{attestServerLog}(Ops_S)$, $C.\texttt{attestClientLog}(Ops_C)$, $C.\texttt{consistencyResult}() = N$.

Analyzing the protocol correctness is straightforward. If the clients and server are benign, the protocol guarantees the authentic copies of client logs and server log are send to the Blockchain as the input of `crosscheckLog()` and `auditLog()`. The computation logic guarantees that a server log with consistency total-order will be asserted as consistency. For an inconsistency log, the server cannot find a total-order without inconsistency and the case of inconsistency will be detected by `auditLog()`.

Correctness with Low Client Availability: In ContractChecker, we consider active clients and inactive clients: Given an epoch, an active client is one that has submitted at least one operation to the cloud. Otherwise, it is an inactive client. ContractChecker requires only active clients in an epoch to be available to participate in the protocol by the end of the epoch. Be more precise, given an inactive client, it does not require its availability for protocol participation.

The protocol correctness without the availability of inactive clients is straightforward. Whether inactive clients send their empty log to the Blockchain, it does not affect either the union of all client operations or the log crosscheck (`crosscheckLog()`). Therefore, an attack is detected by the server-client log inequality, which is irrelevant to the inactive clients' empty logs.

This is in contrast with existing client-based protocols which require the availability of both active and inactive clients. Briefly, the reason that ContractChecker does not require availability of inactive clients while other protocols do is that it cannot distinguish the benign case of an inactive client who is legitimately unavailable from the malicious case of an active client who detects an attack but whose attack report is suppressed by the untrusted server who relays the report among clients. In ContractChecker, it does not rely on the untrusted server to report the case of an attack, but instead by the trusted Blockchain.

5.2   Security Under Server/Client Attacks

In this subsection, we consider the attacks launched by individual malicious clients or server. As reasoned before, our threat model excludes the collusion between a client and server. We leave the Blockchain exploits to the next subsection.

In our threat model, either a client or the server can forge her attestation to the Blockchain. Specifically, she can forge a non-existing operation (A1), omit a valid operation (A2), replays a valid operation multiple times (A3), reorders the serially-executed operations (A4). Recall that our system model considers a rational server who, given concurrent and consistent operations, will not declare a total-order to make it look like an inconsistent log.

A malicious server can exploit the operation forging (A1-A4) to conceal an inconsistent log and to avoid paying the penalty to victim clients. For instance, successfully omitting w_2 in $w_1 w_2 r_3 [w_1]$ may fool the ContractChecker to falsely assert the operation history to be consistent. A malicious client may exploit the operation forging (A1-A4) to forge an inconsistent log and to falsely accuse a benign cloud. For instance, a client can forge an operation (A1) $w_{2.5}$ in a consistent log $w_1 w_2 r_3 [w_2]$ to make it look like inconsistent.

ContractChecker can detect any operation forging (A1, A2) by a mismatch between server attestation and client attestation (in `crosscheckLog()`). Without server-client collusion, if one party, say the server, forge an operation in the server attestation, the forged/omitted operation will be found in the server/client attestation, but not in the client/server attestation. The replay attack (A3) can be detected by multiple identical operations in the server/client log. Reordered operations (A4) can be detected by the condition that the operation order does not match the real-time order (i.e., an operation that occurs later is ordered before an earlier operation).

Security Hardening for Attack Mitigation: ContractChecker is security-hardened to not only detect attacks but also mitigate these attacks. Mitigating the attacks requires attributing an attack to the correct cause and to recover the system from the attack for further processing. The fundamental challenge in the attack attribution is about distinguishing the cause of inconsistency between a malicious client logging a forged operation or a malicious server omitting a valid operation.

To support attack attribution and to overcome this fundamental challenge, we require each online storage operation, when it is being served, needs to be witnessed and doubly signed by both the server and the submitting client. The double signatures can establish a ground truth to distinguish the cause of attacks at the consistency-checking time. For instance, if a doubly-signed operation is found in the server attestation but not in any client attestation, then it is attributed to a malicious client omitting her operation. If a doubly-signed operation is found in a client attestation but not in a server attestation, it is attributed to a malicious server omitting her operation. Note that a malicious client forging an operation can not get away as the forged operation can not be signed by the server. Also note that we don't consider the case of server-client collusion, which presents an impossibility result for attack detection.

By this means, the ContractChecker can distinguish the cause of different attacks (i.e., A1, A2, A3 or A4) and can recover the system from attestation forging. The details of the attack mitigation are presented in Technical Report [9].

5.3 Security Under Blockchain Exploits

Exploiting Blockchain Write Unavailability. Recall that the practical Blockchain systems exhibit low write availability, and may drop valid transactions. Given a faulty Blockchain like this, a malicious server can selectively omit operations in her attestation such that dropped transactions of client attestations correspond to the omitted operations in the server attestation. By this means, the server can omit operations without being detected by ContractChecker, in a way to conceal inconsistency. For instance, in Fig. 1, Client C_2's call of `attestClientLog`(w_2) can be dropped by the Blockchain. The malicious server, observing w_2 is not included in the Blockchain, can selectively omit the operation in her attestation. This will allow the forged log (with omitted operations) to pass the log crosschecking (more specifically, `crosscheckLog`($\{w_1, r_3[w_1]\}, \{w_1, r_3[w_1]\}$)), which further tricks the ContractChecker to assert incorrectly that the operation history (which is actually $w_1, w_2, r_3[w_1]$) is consistent. Because in this attack, the server selectively omit operations based on dropped transactions in Blockchain, we call this attack by selective-omission attack.

Security Hardening Against Blockchain Unavailability: The selective-omission attack can be prevented if the finality of any client's log attestation in Blockchain can be assured of. To prevent the miss of a transaction on Blockchain, a common paradigm is to resubmit the transactions. A naive resubmission policy is to resubmit every F block until the transaction is finalized. With this naive policy, it may lead to an unwanted situation where the resubmitted transaction keeps being declined (e.g., due to low transaction fee).

Enforcing a time bound on transaction finality is crucial to the security of ContractChecker. That is, ContractChecker's security relies on whether a transaction (after resubmission) can be guarantee to succeed before a pre-scribed timeout. Because if both clients and Blockchain are allowed to be unavailable in an arbitrarily long time, it is impossible to distinguish between the benign case of an inactive client where the client does not send a transaction and the malicious case of an unavailable Blockchain under selective-omission attacks.

Therefore, our security hardening technique is to enforce a time bound on the transaction finality. Instead of resubmitting transactions, we require high transaction fee (e.g., based on a heuristic, $20 \cdot 10^9$ Wei in Ethereum transactions) and increase the chance of transaction being accepted in the first place namely in F blocks. The higher transaction fee is, the more likely a transaction is being accepted to be included in the Blockchain. The relationship between Blockchain write availability and transaction fee is evaluated in our technical report [9] With the high transaction fee, all clients wait for F blocks after their transactions.

Analysis of Attack Prevention: If all active ContractChecker clients execute the transaction resubmission policy, the selective-omission attack can be prevented. What follows is the security analysis: Assume the resubmission policy can guarantee the high chance (the evaluation is in our technical report [9]) that all clients' transactions (for `attestClientLog()`) are included in the Blockchain before the timeout of F blocks. The selective-omission attack cannot succeed because any valid operation can be found in the client log attestations and the omission of the operation in the attack can be detected by the mismatch in log crosschecking. In the previous example, by the time w_2 is included in the Blockchain (before F blocks), the ContractChecker can detect the w_2 is absent in the server log as it appears in Client C_2's log. The ContractChecker can identify the attack, recover the server log for making a correct assertion about the operation inconsistency.

Forking Attacks. Preliminary on Forking Attacks: Consider multiple clients share a state hosted on a server. In this setup, a forking attacker is a malicious server who forks the shared state and serves different clients with different (forked) states. In client-based consistency protocols (e.g., Catena and Caelus), the malicious server may fork her log attestations for different auditing clients, such that the forked global logs appear to be consistent from different clients' local views.

In ContractChecker, both clients and server send their attestations to the Blockchain where the crosschecking occurs. The regular forking attack where the server forks her view among clients may not succeed because the Blockchain essentially provides a "gossiping" channel among clients and miners. However, Blockchain provides only an imperfect gossiping channel and there are exploits one can leverage to break the gossiping channel.

The central idea here is that the server can fork the inputs to the `crosscheckLog()` function in smart contract so that the function instances running on different miners take forked inputs (from the server and clients) and falsely accept separately. The forking can be facilitated by exploits such as smart contract races and Blockchain forks.

Exploiting Blockchain forks, the server log is forked by the malicious server and the logs of different clients may be forked due to network partitions. This could effectively lead to a forking attack. Concretely, when the network partition separates the Blockchain network and clients into different partitions and the server is in a position to mount the forking attack and to send different partitions different server views. For instance, consider the server wants to hide a "total-order anomaly" sequence $w_1|w_2, r_3[w_1]|r_4[w_2]$ where w_1 and w_2 are concurrent, r_3 and r_4 are concurrent, and the four operations are submitted from four different clients (respectively C_1, C_2, C_3, C_4). The network partitions clients and Blockchain at the attestation time to two partitions, say P_1 and P_2, where in P_1 clients C_1 and C_3 attest to w_1 and r_3 to the Blockchain, and in P_2 clients C_2 and C_4 attest to w_2 and r_4 to the Blockchain. Then, the server is in a position to launch a forking attack by sending a view of server log ($w_2 w_1 r_3[w_1]$) to Blockchain partition P_1 and another (forked) view of server log ($w_1 w_2 r_4[w_2]$) to Blockchain partition P_2. Because the client attestations are also forked due to network partition, the smart contracts of ContractChecker running in both P_1 and P_2 will (falsely) accept.

To make this attack successful, the key is the Blockchain fork due to the network partition. In practice, however, this type of Blockchain fork is temporary and is resolved when the network reconnects. When the network reconnects, one of the Blockchain forks will be orphaned, which will leave some client attestation omitted eventually. For instance, if the fork in P_1 is chosen and that in P_2 is orphaned, the client attestations from C_2 and C_4 can be permanently lost. In our scheme, this attack is detected by our client-side technique (Sect. 5.3) which will check the finality of transactions after sufficient time.

For other types of Blockchain forks, such as caused by software updates, forking attacks cannot succeed. Because client attestations are not separated, all Blockchain forks will receive the same set of attestations of all clients. To hide an inconsistent anomaly (e.g., stale read), it would require the fresh write operation to be omitted in the Blockchain, which is impossible in the presence of all client attestations. Note that by forking the total-order declaration, it is not sufficient to hide inconsistency anomaly.

Exploiting smart-contract races, the forking server attempts to update the server log in the middle of function execution of `crosscheckLog()` by exploiting race conditions. The goal is to make client logs cross-checked with different (forked) versions of server log. Concretely, consider the function-call sequence S.`serverAttestLog`$(w_1, w_2, r_3[w_1])$, C_1.`clientAttestLog`(w_2), C_2.`clientAttestLog`$(w_1, r_3[w_1])$, S.`serverAttestLog`$(w_2, w_1, r_3[w_1])$. Suppose before S.`serverAttestLog`$(w_2, w_1, r_3[w_1])$ runs, the contract already enters `crosscheckLog()` where the server log $w_1, w_2, r_3[w_1]$ is being crosschecked with client logs w_2 and $w_1, r_3[w_1]$. When S.`serverAttestLog`$(w_2, w_1, r_3[w_1])$ runs, it might happen that the call of S.`serverAttestLog`$(w_2, w_1, r_3[w_1])$ replaces the variable of ops_server <u>during</u> `crosscheckLog()`. This may lead to the unwanted situation that client log w_2 is crosschecked with one version of server log $w_1, w_2, r_3[w_1]$, and client log $w_1, r_3[w_1]$ is crosschecked with another version of server log $w_2, w_1, r_3[w_1]$. In this situation, server log $w_2, w_1, r_3[w_1]$ will survive as the successfully crosschecked version, which will lead to an incorrect consistency. We call this attack by <u>forking-by-races</u> attack.

The ContractChecker prevents the forking-by-races attack by synchronizing the critical functions and avoiding concurrency. Concretely, in ContractChecker, we define a critical section around the functions `crosscheckLog()` and `auditLog()`, such that the execution of these two victim functions needs to be serialized with other functions. To be more specific, in the forking-by-races attack, the attacker (i.e., calling function S.`serverAttestLog`$(w_2, w_1, r_3[w_1])$) and the victim (i.e., running function `crosscheckLog()`) are forced to execute in a serial order. Without concurrent execution of attacking and victim functions, the attack cannot succeed.

5.4 Incentivize DoS Attacks

DoS Attacks: With the policy of high transaction fee, it is tempting to design the following DoS attack: An attacker can (1) join the Blockchain network as an honest miner who mines and executes the smart contract to collect transaction fee, and (2) join the ContractChecker protocol as a client to send transactions and run DoS attacks. The rationale behind the attack is that the attacker can make coins from her "honest miner" role and spend the coins to generate some high-fee transactions sent to the Blockchain. This effect of the high-fee transactions is to race against the transactions sent from honest ContractChecker clients and to prevent them from being included in the Blockchain. The honest clients, in the hope of including their transactions in the Blockchain, would be forced to increase their fee again, which will be collected by the DoS attacker miner and inventive them to launch more DoS attacks.

We believe the above attack is hard to succeed in existing public Blockchain which runs in a large P2P network. The chance of making a perceivable amount of coins (by mining and running smart contract) in today's public Blockchain is slim. A self-sustainable DoS attack would need a large investment (similar to 51% attack) to boot-strap. Without it, any DoS attacker would lose coins and cannot sustain.

6   Evaluation

In this section, we evaluate the client cost in ContractChecker. We first present an analysis of client cost and then present our experimental results.

6.1   Cost Analysis

Cost Model: For a consistency verification protocol, either client-based schemes or ContractChecker, its execution can be modeled by the following: Clients periodically send their log attestations and check the consistency results. In this process, a client's cost is characterized by (1) how many operations the client needs to store, and (2) how long the client needs to maintain an operation. In our cost model, we accredit to one cost unit storing one operation by a client in one epoch. Given a process of T epochs, a client's total cost is the sum of cost units of all operations stored in the client in all epochs. If an operation is stored continuously in a client for T epochs, it is counted as T units.

Based on the above model, we present a cost analysis of client-based auditing schemes and ContractChecker.

Client Cost in Client-Based Auditing: In client-based auditing schemes, a client needs to access operations submitted by all clients in the current epoch, including herself and other clients; these operations may only need to be stored by the clients in one epoch, assuming a trusted third-party attester. For simplicity, we omit the cost of accessing historical operations. Instead, we focus on a low-bound estimate of the client cost in client-based auditing schemes:

$$CCost_{ClientAudit} \geq T \cdot M \cdot N \tag{1}$$

The above equation considers that the protocol is run in T epochs among N clients where each client in one epoch submits M operations on average. The equation reports the total cost. We focus on the "unit" client cost, that is, the client cost per epoch and per operation:

$$CCost_{ClientAudit}^{Avg} = CCost_{ClientAudit}/(T \cdot M) \geq N \tag{2}$$

The above equation considers a client's cost in a process of running client-based auditing scheme in T epochs, with totally N clients where on average each client in one epoch submit M operations.

Client Cost in ContractChecker: In the above setting, a ContractChecker client only needs to store her own operations, that is, M operation per epoch. But the Con-tractChecker client needs to keep an operation for, instead of the current epoch, but an extended period of time denoted by F_t/E epochs. F_t is the average delay for success-fully submitting a client attestation to the Blockchain in ContractChecker. Specifically,

$$F_t = r \cdot (B \cdot F + P) \tag{3}$$

Here r is the average times to resubmit a client attestation, and $F/B/P$ is the finality delay/block time/average wait time for transaction validation. Thus, ContractChecker's client cost is as follows. Note that in ContractChecker, log auditing is fully delegated and clients are relieved from accessing historical operations.

$$CCost^{Avg}_{ContractChecker} = F_t/E \tag{4}$$

Therefore, the cost saving of ContractChecker comparing existing client-based auditing schemes is: $\frac{CCost^{Avg}_{ClientAudit}}{CCost^{Avg}_{ContractChecker}} \geq \frac{E \cdot N}{F_t}$. This formula shows that the cost saving of ContractChecker comparing existing work depends on three factors: the total attestation delay F_t, the maximal number of clients N, and epoch time E. The larger E is, the more costs the ContractChecker saves. Because with a larger E, the client-based schemes have to store an operation for longer time. The larger F_t is, the fewer costs the ContractChecker saves. Because with a larger F_t, an operation needs to be stored on a ContractChecker client for longer time. The more clients there are (a larger N), the more costs the ContractChecker saves. Because with a larger N, the more operations a client needs to store (in client-based auditing schemes).

6.2 Experiments

Client Cost. Based on the cost model above, we design experiments for client cost measurement. Our experiments focus on transaction-validation delay (P) and maximal number of operations ($N \cdot M$), w.r.t. the budgeted amount of Ethers. Based on the results, we compare ContractChecker's client cost with that of client-based auditing schemes.

We design experiments to evaluate the client cost of ContractChecker in compari-son with client-based auditing schemes. From our cost analysis, the unit client cost of ContractChecker is F_t/E (Eq. 4) and that of client-based schemes is proportional to N (Eq. 2). The source of extra cost is that ContractChecker needs to maintain a local operation for extra time and client-based schemes need to replicate a client's operation to all other clients. In this section, we aim at comparing the client costs of these two scheme paradigms using experiments.

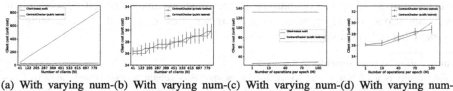

(a) With varying num-ber of clients (b) With varying num-ber of clients (c) With varying num-ber of operations (d) With varying num-ber of operations

Fig. 3. Client costs of ContractChecker

Designing the experiments, we observe there are two factors affecting the cost, the number of clients (i.e., N) and the number of operations per epoch (i.e., M). Increasing N and M, it will saturate the current block ingesting the operations in an epoch and delays the inclusion of all operations to next blocks. We thus design experiments to measure F_t with varying N and M. We consider the setting that E is longer than F_t such that the Blockchain will not permanently drop transactions. To measure F_t, we run N clients to concurrently submit their attestation transactions to the Blockchain. The N clients then proactively check the finality of the transactions. For simplicity, we use the maximal transaction fee to reduce the transaction pending time and exclude the case of dropped transactions. We record the time duration between the first transaction is submitted and the last transaction is finalized on Blockchain.

Experiment Setup: We conduct experiments in a private Ethereum testnet and a public testnet. For the public testnet, we connect our ContractChecker protocol to the Ropsten testnet [10]. For the private testnet, we run four Ethereum miners in an LAN network on campus. The machine specs is Intel 8-core i7-6820HK CPU of 2.70 GHz, 32 GB RAM and 1 TB Disk. The default configuration for Ethereum (e.g., difficulty levels) is used. Note that our target metrics (e.g., transaction fee and Gas) are independent of network scale. We deploy our smart-contract program written in Solidity to the Blockchain, by leveraging an online Python tool[4].

We present the client costs with varying N (number of clients) in Fig. 3a and b. In this experiment, we consider $M = 1$ (each client submits one operation in one epoch) for the maximal scalability. From Fig. 3a, it can be seen that ContractChecker incurs much lower unit client cost than client-based schemes. With increasing number of clients, the client-based schemes incur a linearly increasing cost, while the ContractChecker's cost barely changes (it slightly increases as shown and analyzed in Fig. 3b). The reason behind is that with a new client, the client-based schemes require to replicate a given operation while ContractChecker does not replicate local operations to the new client. With an increasing N, the number of operations per epoch may increase, and that causes ContractChecker's client cost to increase—with more operations in an epoch, it takes more blocks to include the operations, thus longer F_t. This can be seen in Fig. 3b more clearly. More specifically, with the public testnet, it takes one blocks to include all operations produced by up to $N = 200$ clients, takes two blocks by up to 370 clients, etc. The private Blockchain testnet incurs a slightly higher client cost than the public Blockchain[5], and also has lower variance. Note that the increase rate of ContractChecker with N is much slower than that of client-based schemes.

We present the client costs with varying M (the average number of operations per epoch per client) in Fig. 3c. In this experiment, we consider $N = 132$ clients so that we can test up to $M = 100$ operations. The result shows that ContractChecker's client cost is about one fifth of client-based auditing schemes' cost. With the increasing M, ContractChecker's cost slightly increases.

---

[4] https://github.com/ConsenSys/ethjsonrpc.

[5] This result is a bit surprising to us, as the private Blockchain testnet is dedicated to ContractChecker while the public testnet is shared. We verify this is due to that in the private testnet a block can be utilized up to 80% of specified gas limits, while the public testnet a block can be utilized 100%.

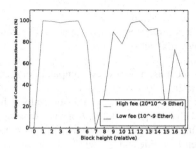

Fig. 4. Blockchain availability under varying transaction fee

Blockchain Availability and Transaction Fee. In this experiment, our goal is to show the relationship between Blockchain write availability and transaction fee. We simultaneously run two Ethereum clients (on two separate machines), each of which drives 1500 transactions to the Ropsten testnet. The two clients respectively use high transaction fee $(20 * 10^{-9}$ Ether) and low fee $(1 * 10^{-9}$ Ether). All transactions are driven to the Blockchain at the time of one block (with the relative block height 0) and we observe how and when transactions of different fees get included in the Blockchain. We repeatedly conduct 10 experiments and present the averaged result in Fig. 4. In this figure, all 1500 transactions with high fee are included in the blocks before (or with smaller block height) the other 1500 transactions with low fee. More specifically, the 1500 transactions of high fee takes about 6 blocks to be included while the 1500 transactions of low fee takes up to 10 blocks to be included. This result shows that with higher transaction fee, transactions get included earlier and it is less likely to drop the transactions with lower fee.

7 Conclusion

This work presents ContractChecker, a lightweight consistency verification protocol based on public Blockchain. It presents a new approach by auditing the storage log on the Blockchain, and has advantages in saving the clients' cost and lower availability requirements. ContractChecker is implemented in a middleware system federating cloud services, clients and the Blockchain.

Acknowledgement. Yuzhe (Richard) Tang's work is supported by National Science Foundation under Grant CNS1815814 and a gift from Intel. Jianliang Xu's work is supported by Hong Kong RGC grants C6030-18GF, C1008-16G, and 12201018. The authors thank Yue Cheng for the discussion of this work in the early stage.

References

1. Amazon s3. https://aws.amazon.com/s3
2. Certificate transparency. https://tools.ietf.org/html/rfc6962
3. Docker hub. https://hub.docker.com/
4. Dropbox. https://www.dropbox.com/

5. Ethereum project. https://www.ethereum.org/
6. Ethereum smart contract best practices: Known attacks. https://consensys.github.io/smart-contract-best-practices/known_attacks/
7. Github. https://github.com/
8. How to fix icloud sync in seconds. https://www.computerworld.com/article/2916476/apple-ios/how-to-fix-icloud-sync-in-seconds.html
9. Secure consistency verification for untrusted cloud storage by public blockchains
10. Testnet ropsten (eth) blockchain explorer. https://ropsten.etherscan.io/
11. Anwar, A., et al.: Improving docker registry design based on production workload analysis. In: 16th USENIX Conference on File and Storage Technologies (FAST 2018), Oakland, CA, pp. 265–278. USENIX Association (2018)
12. Bernstein, P.A., Hadzilacos, V., Goodman, N.: Concurrency Control and Recovery in Database Systems. Addison-Wesley, Reading (1987)
13. Cooper, B.F., Silberstein, A., Tam, E., Ramakrishnan, R., Sears, R.: Benchmarking cloud serving systems with YCSB. In: SoCC, pp. 143–154 (2010)
14. Corbett, J.C., et al.: Spanner: Google's globally distributed database. ACM Trans. Comput. Syst. **31**(3), 8 (2013)
15. Herlihy, M., Wing, J.M.: Linearizability: a correctness condition for concurrent objects. ACM Trans. Program. Lang. Syst. **12**(3), 463–492 (1990)
16. Kim, B.H., Lie, D.: Caelus: verifying the consistency of cloud services with battery-powered devices. In: 2015 IEEE Symposium on Security and Privacy, SP 2015, San Jose, CA, USA, 17–21 May 2015, pp. 880–896. IEEE Computer Society (2015)
17. Li, J., Krohn, M.N., Mazières, D., Shasha, D.: Secure untrusted data repository (SUNDR). In: OSDI, pp. 121–136 (2004)
18. Mazières, D., Shasha, D.: Building secure file systems out of byantine storage. In: Proceedings of the Twenty-First Annual ACM Symposium on Principles of Distributed Computing, PODC 2002, Monterey, California, USA, 21–24 July 2002, pp. 108–117 (2002)
19. Melara, M.S., Blankstein, A., Bonneau, J., Felten, E.W., Freedman, M.J.: CONIKS: bringing key transparency to end users. In: Jung, J., Holz, T. (eds.) 24th USENIX Security Symposium, USENIX Security 2015, Washington, D.C., USA, 12–14 August 2015, pp. 383–398. USENIX Association (2015)
20. Popa, R.A., Lorch, J.R., Molnar, D., Wang, H.J., Zhuang, L.: Enabling security in cloud storage slas with cloudproof. In: Nieh, J., Waldspurger, C.A. (eds.) 2011 USENIX Annual Technical Conference, Portland, OR, USA, 15–17 June 2011. USENIX Association (2011)
21. Terry, D.: Replicated data consistency explained through baseball. Commun. ACM **56**(12), 82–89 (2013)
22. Terry, D.B., Prabhakaran, V., Kotla, R., Balakrishnan, M., Aguilera, M.K., Abu-Libdeh, H.: Consistency-based service level agreements for cloud storage. In: Kaminsky, M., Dahlin, M. (eds.) ACM SIGOPS 24th Symposium on Operating Systems Principles, SOSP 2013, Farmington, PA, USA, 3–6 November 2013, pp. 309–324. ACM (2013)
23. Tomescu, A., Devadas, S.: Catena: efficient non-equivocation via bitcoin. In: 2017 IEEE Symposium on Security and Privacy, SP 2017, San Jose, CA, USA, 22–26 May 2017, pp. 393–409. IEEE Computer Society (2017)
24. Torres-Arias, S., Ammula, A.K., Curtmola, R., Cappos, J.: On omitting commits and committing omissions: preventing git metadata tampering that (re)introduces software vulnerabilities. In: Holz, T., Savage, S. (eds.) 25th USENIX Security Symposium, USENIX Security 2016, Austin, TX, USA, 10–12 August 2016, pp. 379–395. USENIX Association (2016)
25. Zyskind, G., Nathan, O., Pentland, A.: Decentralizing privacy: using blockchain to protect personal data. In: 2015 IEEE Symposium on Security and Privacy Workshops, SPW 2015, San Jose, CA, USA, 21–22 May 2015, pp. 180–184. IEEE Computer Society (2015)

An Enhanced Verifiable Inter-domain Routing Protocol Based on Blockchain

Yaping Liu[1,2], Shuo Zhang[1,2(⊠)], Haojin Zhu[3], Peng-Jun Wan[4],
Lixin Gao[5], and Yaoxue Zhang[6]

[1] Guangzhou University, Guangzhou, China
{ypliu, szhang18}@gzhu.edu.cn
[2] Cyberspace Security Research Center, Peng Cheng Laboratory,
Shenzhen,, China
[3] Shanghai Jiao Tong University, Shanghai, China
zhu-hj@cs.sjtu.edu.cn
[4] Illinois Institute of Technology, Chicago, USA
wan@cs.iit.edu
[5] University of Massachusetts at Amherst, Amherst, USA
lgao@ecs.umass.edu
[6] Tsinghua University, Beijing, China
zyx@csu.edu.cn

Abstract. Promise-violating attack to inter-domain routing protocol is becoming common in recent years, which always causes serious consequences, such as malicious attraction traffic, broken network. To deal with this kind of attack, routing verification is introduced by current research. However, it can only detect attacks against a specific routing policy triggered by one malicious node, and no research has yet been conducted to solve the problem caused by multiple collusion nodes. In this work, we present BRVM, a blockchain-based routing verification model, to address the issue of violating shortest AS Path policy. The main idea of BRVM is to record the route proofs to verify whether a route violates the policy using the blockchain technology. The precondition of avoiding a collusion attack is that the proportion of the malicious verification nodes is lower than the fault tolerance rate of the consensus algorithm used in the blockchain. We theoretically prove the correctness of BRVM, and implement a prototype based on Quagga and Fabric. Our experiments show that BRVM can solve this kind of promise-violating problem caused by multiple collusion nodes, and about 21% faster than SPIDeR [14] in performance.

Keywords: Inter-domain routing · Blockchain · Routing verification · Privacy · Security

1 Introduction

When two Autonomous Systems (ASes) start to establish a connection, they need to negotiate business relationship and routing promises. The negotiation about the provision of routing service and routing promises is very important for network service providers to achieve their contractual goals, such as maintaining traffic ratios. However, in the current Internet, promise-violating events occur often due to misconfiguration or deliberate malicious behaviors [1–5]. Some well-known security events in Internet are

S. Chen et al. (Eds.): SecureComm 2019, LNICST 304, pp. 63–82, 2019.
https://doi.org/10.1007/978-3-030-37228-6_4

caused by policy violation, including the 2004 TTNet route injection event [6], the 2008 Pakistan Telecom hijacking YouTube incident [7], the 2012 Australian network interruption [8], and the 2017 Japanese network interruption by Google's mistake [9]. Sometimes, misconfiguration may cause more damage than attacks, because the AS administrator who violates the promises unintentionally may not prepare for a drastic increase in traffic, result in more serious consequences.

Unfortunately, routing promises are easy to violate, while routing verification is hard to implement in practice. Firstly, promise violations are hard to detect for inter-domain routing protocol. The faked routing information looks the same as the validated route announcements, and the common security methods based on identity authenticity (digital signatures, encryption, etc.) cannot address the issue. Many proposed variants of secure BGP (e.g., S-BGP [11] and So-BGP [12]) can check bogus paths or forged prefixes by path authentication and origin authentication, but they cannot resolve the issue whether the route announcements match the routing contracts between two ASes. Secondly, the privacy of Internet Service Provider (ISP) must be guaranteed during the routing validation. That is, our problem is that for the globally agreed upon BGP best route selection policy, how to verify if a received route is the best one by a route receiver. For security and commercial reasons, it is impossible to expect ISPs to join a centralized management system and share their private information. Theoretically, complete verification can be achieved by revealing all routing tables, but it is unachievable in practice.

It is very difficult to address the upper issue completely satisfying both verifiability and privacy. However, authors in [14] proposes a secure and private inter-domain routing (SPIDeR), which can verify whether the received BGP route meets certain promises (such as shortest AS Path rule) in the route selection process while guaranteeing privacy. Their work enables the network to verify promises collaboratively by breaking every promise into small pieces, which concurrently keeps privacy. However, SPIDeR can only detect promise violations when only one malicious entity exists. It becomes invalid when facing multiple entities collude. The reason is that SPIDeR only performs collaborative multi-party verification based on neighbors of an AS being verified. When a violation occurs, if the neighbor who has announced a better route does not report the fraud, the collusion attack can be successful.

In this paper, we propose a blockchain-based routing verification model (BRVM) to solve the promise-violating issue for the shortest AS Path policy, considering one spurious node or conspiracy of multiple malicious nodes. The main idea of BRVM is to introduce a concept of route proof in the routing verification based on the blockchain. A promise-violating attack can be detected completely when all the verification nodes are honest; if some verification nodes are colluded, the condition for detecting this attack is that the ratio of malicious nodes is lower than the fault tolerance of the blockchain.

The use of blockchain technology in BRVM essentially allows all routing nodes to participate in a multi-party verification system, thereby avoiding the collusion behavior among the routing nodes. The only possibility of collusion attacks occurring in BRVM is that some verification nodes are malicious, resulting in the faked route proofs being put into the block. However, as long as the proportion of the malicious verification nodes is lower than the fault tolerance rate of the consensus algorithm, the violation can still be avoided. For example, the fault tolerance rate of POW is 50%. Considering performance, scalability and fault tolerance, we choose BFT-DPOS as the consensus algorithm with a fault tolerance rate of 33%.

Based on BRVM, we design an enhanced verifiable inter-domain routing protocol (EVIRP). Currently, at least 50K+ ASes are working in the Internet, which is a big challenge for the existing blockchain technology to support this huge scale. Therefore, we implement a practical prototype system based on Quagga BGP and Fabric (using BFT-DPOS as the consensus algorithm), and optimize its performance using a two-tier storage structure. Our work makes two contributions: (1) we are the first to solve this kind of promise-violating problem caused by collusion. (2) analysis and experiments show that the performance of our solution is 21% faster than SPIDeR.

The rest of the paper is organized as follows: In Sect. 2, we introduce some background concepts. We propose BRVM to address the promise-violation issue violating shortest AS Path policy in Sect. 3. A theoretical proof guarantees the correctness of BRVM satisfying privacy and verifiability. We present a verifiable routing protocol in Sect. 4. In Sect. 5, we describe the implementation and experiments. Related work and future work is discussed in Sects. 6 and 7.

2   Background

2.1   Problem Description

2.1.1   Single-Point Attack Scenario
To simplify the explanation, we use name (Alice, Bob, etc.) to represent every AS and edges to represent inter-AS links, and describe the promise-violation problem in Fig. 1. Five ASes are shown here: Bob and his four neighbors Alice, Charlie, Doris and Eliot. The basic process of BGP is described vividly as following: Bob receives three routes to a prefix from Charlie, Doris and Eliot. He chooses one from these routes as its best route according to his promise and decides whether to make this route available to Alice.

A promise of Bob to Alice is a statement that Bob will prefer certain routes over other routes. For example, a promise can be defined as that Bob chooses the shortest AS Path route as the best one and sends to Alice. In the single-point attack scenario of Fig. 1, Charlie announced to Bob a route to prefix 74.125.58.0/24 with AS Path length of 3, Doris announced a route with AS Path length of 4, and Eliot announced a route with AS Path length of 5. According to the promise between Bob and Alice, Bob should announce to Alice the route to prefix 74.125.58.0/24 learnt from Charlie.

However, Bob can easily break his promise and Alice can't verify whether routes from Bob follow the promise between them. For example, Bob intentionally chooses Doris's route to announce out, which is the second-shortest route. Anyway, Alice has to accept this route. The reason is that Bob's incoming routes are not visible to Alice. Figure 1 gives an example that one malicious AS (Bob) breaks its promise.

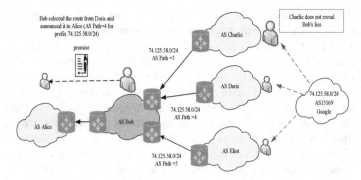

Fig. 1. (1) Single-point attack scenario: Alice receives a route from Bob, but cannot verify if Bob keeps his promise. (2) Multi-point collusion attack scenario: Alice receives a route from Bob, and believes that Bob keeps his promise. In fact, Bob and Charlie deceived Alice jointly.

2.1.2   Multi-point Collusion Attack Scenario

A collusion attack is illustrated as an example in Fig. 1. Bob and Charlie are two spurious ASes, shown with a bigger icon than honest ones. Bob distributes to Alice a route to prefix 74.125.58.0/24 learned from Doris which has the second-shortest AS Path length. In any case, Alice cannot check Bob's incoming routes due to the privacy protection, but she may verify the route, using solutions such as SPIDeR. The situation of using SPIDeR is like this: Alice tells Bob's neighbors that she received from Bob a route with AS Path length of 5. If Bob is the only liar, Charlie will honestly inform Alice that he sent to Bob a route with AS Path length of 3, and Alice can find Bob violated his promise. However, if Charlie is an accomplice of Bob, he obviously has the option of not reporting Bob's cheating. Thus, a collusion attack occurred, and currently few studies can put forward a viable solution for this complex issue.

2.2   Routing Promise

The definition of routing promise in this paper follows the definition in SPIDeR. The routing promise affects the routing decision process, where several routes enter and at most one leaves. A promise does not participate in a single routing process but gives preference information about which route is considered "better" than other routes.

Definition 1: Suppose that $S(A, p)$ is the set of all available routes received by AS A to a prefix p, having a given total order. A promise on $S(A, p)$ defines a partial order $(C, \leq)$, and partitions $S(A, p)$ into several *indifference* classes. We use set C to label various classes of routes, with a partial order, representing the definite preference of one class over another. Every route can be classified to exactly one class in set C. Routes of one class c constitutes a subset S_c that satisfies $S_c \in S(A, p)$ and $S(A, p) = \cup \{S_c\}$ for every $c \in C$. An *indifference* class means that there is no preference among the routes within one class.

In particular, if $c < d$ for $c, d \in C$, then there exists a preference between routes in S_c and S_d: if $r \in S_c$ and $s \in S_d$, then route r is less preferred than route s.

Definition 2: *class of route.* We use $CR(u)$ to represent the class of route u. $CR(u)$ can be defined using a k bit array $[b_1, ..., b_k]$, where $b_j = 1$ iff $u \in S_j$, otherwise $b_j = 0$.

For example, we use AS Path length as the label for various classes of routes, so the set C may contain class with path length 2, class with path length 3, and so on. In addition, a promise is that routes with the shorter AS Path can have a higher priority to be chosen. In Fig. 1, Bob receives three routes from his neighbors, with different AS path length. Hence, the set C can be defined as {'AS path=5', 'AS path=4', 'AS path=3'}, and the route learnt from Charlie is more preferred than routes from Doris and Eliot.

2.3 Verifiability and Privacy

Routing verification is to verify whether an announced route conforms to the routing promise between two ASes. For example, a promise can be defined that any AS chooses the route to a prefix with the shortest AS Path to announce. Then, routing verification is to verify whether the announced route has the shortest AS Path among all possible routes in this AS.

The requirement of privacy is defined the same as that in [14]: (1) any AS cannot infer additional information about routing status or policy of other ASes, beyond what it can already learn via BGP; (2) when a promise violation is detected, it is acceptable to reveal more information to indicate this fact.

3   BRVM: Principle and Model

As we know, route attributes are divided into transitional and non-transitional categories. Some common route attributes, such as Origin, AS-Path and Next-hop, are transitional, while others, such as MED (Multi-Exit-Discriminators), Local-Preference are non-transitional. A non-transitional route attribute only works between two routing nodes, which cannot be verified by our method currently. Our proposed blockchain-based routing verification Model (BRVM) only verifies if a route conforms to the shortest AS Path policy.

3.1   Assumption

We make the following assumptions:

(1) Each AS creates a public-private key pair and uses it in the routing verification process;
(2) No AS can forge the digital signature of any other AS;
(3) Use some security mechanisms to ensure the security of inter-domain routing protocol, including origin authentication and path authentication. Therefore, routes with bogus paths, fake origin or forged prefixes must be discarded by receiver.

3.2   Definition

First, we introduce variable descriptions in Table 1.

Definition 3: *route proof.* We define $RP(u)$ for the route proof of a route u. A route proof is related to exactly one route, and represents this route in the routing verification.

Definition 4: *preceding route proof.* Suppose that AS_t selected a route u learned from AS_u as its best route after a route selection process, then created a route (i.e., route d) and announced route d to AS_d. We define $RP(u)$ as the preceding route proof of route d, denote $PRP(d)$.

According to Definition 1, we get the following expressions.

Expression 1: any route u belongs to one and only one subset $S_x : u \in S_x \Rightarrow u \notin S_y$ (for x, $y \in C$ and $y \neq x$).

Expression 2: if $x < y$ for some x and y in C, then a preference exists between routes in S_x and S_y: for $u \in S_x$ and $w \in S_y$, if $x < y$ (x, $y \in C$), then $CR(u) < CR(w)$.

Table 1. Notations.

Notation	Description
σ_i	private key of AS_i
π_i	public key of AS_i
ID_i	the identification of AS_i, i.e., the hash value of π_i
$OP(u)$	the operation of route u: update or withdraw
$TS(u)$	the timestamp when route u is sent
$Prefix(u)$	the destination prefix of route u
$LSTRP(ID_s, ID_r, p)$	route proof chain of a route to prefix p from AS_s to AS_r

3.3   Blockchain-Based Routing Verification Model

3.3.1   Introduction to the Principle of BRVM

Instead of requiring neighbor ASes to join the collaborative verification, BRVM introduces a distributed routing verification system. Each AS announces a route to its neighbors AS and sends to one node of the routing verification system a route proof corresponding to this route. The route proof is used in the routing verification process; it must be verified and inserted into a block on the blockchain after achieving global consistency through the consensus among the verification nodes which are interconnected in a P2P network. All route proofs for a prefix involved in the route propagation process are organized as a route proof chain.

The route receiver determines whether the received route conforms to the routing promise by querying whether there is a corresponding route proof in the blockchain. The key point of BRVM depends on the correctness and completeness of route proofs recorded on the blockchain. The probability of a promise-violating attack occurring depends on the consensus algorithm used in the blockchain. The routing verification system composes of two parts: *verify module* to verify routes, *proof storage* to store route proofs. *Verify module* consists of verification nodes, and *proof storage* consists of route proofs. Figure 2 shows an example to illustrate the process of BRVM.

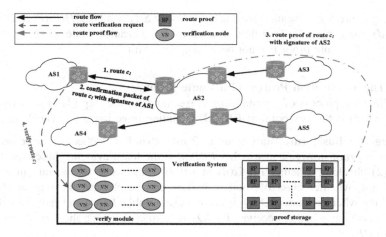

Fig. 2. The process of BRVM.

It includes four steps: (1) AS_t announces a route d with his signature Sig_t and CR (d) to his neighbor AS_d; (2) AS_d signs some information of route d and replies his signature Sig_d to AS_t to indicate that AS_d receives route d. Set $Sig_d = \sigma_d(HASH(ID_t, ID_d, TS(d), Prefix(d), OP(d), CR(d)))$; (3) AS_t constructs a route proof $RP(d)$ with his signature, and sends it to *proof storage* in the verification system, which verifies the received route proofs and stores the verified ones in the blockchain; (4) when receiving route d, AS_d will trigger a request for verifying route d to *verify module* in the verification system, and wait for the response to decide how to deal with route d.

3.3.2 Introduction of Route Proof
The key point of the routing verification system is the design of route proof. A route proof is related to exactly one route.

Suppose that AS_t selected a route u learned from AS_u as its best route after a route selection process, then created a route (i.e., route d) announced route d to AS_d. A route proof $RP(d)$ of route d provided by AS_t has five parts: the preceding route proof PRP (d), the basic information $BIRP(d)$, the identification of route d $IDR(d)$, the signature and public key of receiver$\{Sig_d, \pi_d\}$, and the signature and public key of sender$\{Sig_t, \pi_t\}$. The detail of every part is as below:

- $PRP(d)$ is a pointer to a route proof $RP(u)$ in *proof storage*, which is actually a route proof of route u.
- The basic information $BIRP(d)$ contains six parts: sender ID ID_t, receiver ID ID_d, TS (d), $Prefix(d)$, $OP(d)$, $CR(d)$. For example, we use AS Path as the class of route. If the AS Path of route d is 4 and $k = 8$, then $CR(d) = 00010000$.
- The identification of route d $IDR(d)$, is the unique identification of route d, which can be defined as $HASH(ID_t, ID_d, TS(d), Prefix(d), OP(d))$.
- The signature Sig_d of receiver AS_d can be obtained from a reply that AS_d returns to AS_t; Sig_d is defined in step (2) of the process of BRVM. And public key π_d is used to check the authenticity of the signature of receiver.

- The signature Sig_t of sender AS_t is set as follows: $Sig_t = \sigma_t(HASH(PRP(d), BIRP(d),$ $IDR(d), Sig_d, \pi_d, \pi_t))$. This field is used by a verification node to verify that the content of a route proof has not been tampered with.

3.3.3   The Verification Process of a Route Proof

The verification process of a route proof corresponds to the step (3) in the process of BRVM, which is the key point of BRVM, including three important checking stages:

Checking the Basic Information of a Route Proof. (1) checking whether PRP (d) exists in *proof storage* and whether $PRP(d)$ is the latest evidence based on its time stamp; (2) checking whether $Prefix(d)$ in $RP(d)$ is the same as the one in $PRP(d)$; (3) checking whether class of route $CR(d)$ is consistent with the one in $PRP(d)$; (4) checking whether sender ID ID_s is correct using public key π_t to verify $ID_s = HASH$ (π_t); (5) checking whether receiver ID ID_d is correct using public key π_d to verify $ID_d = HASH(\pi_d)$.

Checking Signatures in a Route Proof. (1) checking if the signature of sender is correct using public key π_t; (2) checking if the signature of receiver is correct using public key π_d.

Optimal Route Checking. In order to check whether route d is the optimal route, the verification system will search for an evidence in *proof storage* to deduce whether the sender AS_t has received a better route than route u. It will retrieval route proofs using receiver ID ID_r as the index under the condition that $ID_r = ID_t$: if there is a route proof satisfying that $CR(w)$ is better than $CR(u)$, this means some AS has sent to AS_t a better route w than the selected route u, but AS_t conceals the route w.

If a route proof passes all the above stages, it can be considered as *verified* and saved into *proof storage*.

3.3.4   The Process for Request of Verifying a Route

Verify module uses $IDR(d)$ as the index to search the match item in *proof storage*. The matching item shows the corresponding route is verified.

3.4   Example

We still use the same examples described in the previous background to explain how BRVM works.

3.4.1   Defend Single-Point Attack

In this scenario, Bob is the only attacker, and he intentionally chooses Doris's route u, which is the second-shortest route (AS Path length is 4), to create a route d and announces route d to Alice.

Bob could conduct a single-point attack in two approaches: (1) sends a faked route proof $RP(d)$ to the verification system, for example, he may announce that AS Path length of the route d is 4, but the actual value is 5; (2) sends a correct route proof RP (d) to the verification system.

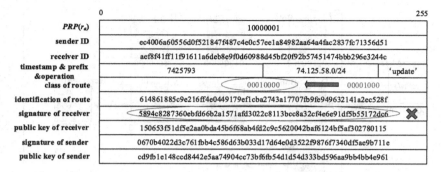

Fig. 3. A faked route proof $RP(d)$ of route d provided by attacker Bob.

For approach (1), Bob provided a faked route proof $RP(d)$ where $CR(d)$ is changed to 00010000 from 00001000 (shown in Fig. 3). This faked route proof $RP(d)$ can be detected in the stage *Checking the signatures in a route proof*, because the signature of Alice is signed for the actual value of $CR(d)$. The content of the faked route proof $RP(d)$ is shown in Fig. 3, where an error is detected when checking the signature of receiver.

For approach (2), route u is leant from Doris, $CR(u)$ is 00010000 and $CR(d)$ is 00001000. Bob has received a route w from Charlie with AS Path length of 3. Since Charlie is honest, he will definitely send a route proof $RP(w)$ to the verification system with $CR(w) = 00100000$. Therefore, $RP(d)$ cannot pass the stage *Optimal route checking*, where $RP(w)$ will always be found because $CR(w)$ is better than $CR(u)$. This process is shown in Fig. 4, where route proofs of all the routes received by Bob are stored in *proof storage*, together with their proceeding route proofs in a route proof chain.

3.4.2 Defend Multi-point Attack Scenario
Bob and Charlie are accomplices. Bob chooses Doris's route u to announce to Alice (a route d is received). The route w learned from Charlie is the best route.

In Fig. 4, AS Path of route w to prefix 74.125.58.0/24 is {Charlie, Green, Henry}. Bob sends a route proof $RP(d)$ of route d to the verification system, and wants to put it in the blockchain. As we know in the former scenario a), $RP(d)$ will be detected wrong when Charlie announced a correct route proof $RP(w)$ to the verification system. The reason is that $CR(w)$ is better than $CR(u)$. Therefore, in order to help Bob pass the verification, Charlie needs to send a faked route proof $RP(w)$ with $CR(w)$ not better than $CR(u)$, e.g., $CR(w) = 00010000$.

Then a problem comes: can this faked $RP(w)$ be accepted by the verification system? It depends on what route proof sent by Green, Charlie's upstream AS. If Green is honest, this faked $RP(w)$ will be detected wrong and collusion attack is over. In order to continue this collusion attack, Green needs to send a faked route proof $RP(v)$ to the verification system.

But the faked $RP(v)$ will not be lucky this time since it meets Henry, a route origin AS, who will not participate in any route proof fraud according to assumption (3).

Therefore, a multi-point attack will always be detected even if most nodes takes part in collusion, because the verification of a route proof will eventually reach the route origin AS.

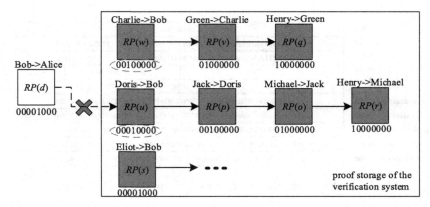

Fig. 4. An example that a route proof is in the verification process.

3.5   Correctness of BRVM

In the following, we will theoretically prove the correctness of our solution BRVM. A promise satisfies the condition: the class of route in a route proof is correct, iff each route proof in the route proof chain is valid and the class of route in each route proof is consistent.

A lemma is introduced to guarantee the correctness of the process of checking the basic information of a route proof. Other two theorems ensure that the promise-violating issue can be solved to meet the needs of verifiability.

Lemma 1. The class of route in route proof of route d, $CR(d)$, is *correct* iff the preceding route proof of route d (i.e., $PRP(d)$) is *correct*, and the class of route in $RP(d)$ *is consistent* with that in $PRP(d)$.

Proof. Suppose that there is n route proofs $RP(d_i)$ ($i = 1, 2, \ldots, n$) in the route proof chain of $RP(d)$, satisfy: $d_n = d$, $PRP(d_i) = RP(d_{i-1})$ for $i = 2, 3, \ldots, n$. We use $MATCH(CR(d_{i-1}), CR(d_i))$ to represent $CR(d_{i-1})$ is consistent with $CR(d_i)$. Proof of Lemma 1 is equivalent to prove the following proposition:

$$P_1 : RP(d_{n-1}) \wedge MATCH(CR(d_{n-1}), CR(d_n)) \Leftrightarrow CR(d_n) \tag{1}$$

The condition that a promise satisfies can be considered as an axiom, which can be described in formula (2).

$$\begin{aligned} & RP(d_1) \wedge RP(d_2) \wedge \cdots \wedge RP(d_{n-1}) \wedge MATCH(CR(d_1), CR(d_2)) \wedge \\ & MATCH(CR(d_2), CR(d_3)) \wedge \cdots \wedge MATCH(CR(d_{n-1}), CR(d_n)) \Leftrightarrow CR(d_n) \end{aligned} \tag{2}$$

We will prove P_1 from two aspects:

(a) prove P_2: $CR(d_n) \Rightarrow RP(d_{n-1}) \wedge MATCH(CR(d_{n-1}), CR(d_n))$.
     According to the Definitions 2, 3 and 4, P_2 is obviously established.
(b) prove P_3: $RP(d_{n-1}) \wedge MATCH(CR(d_{n-1}), CR(d_n)) \Rightarrow CR(d_n)$.

According to the definition of RP, we know $RP(d_{n-1}) \Rightarrow CR(d_{n-1})$. And

$$
\begin{aligned}
CR(d_{n-1}) \Rightarrow & RP(d_1) \wedge RP(d_2) \wedge \cdots \wedge RP(d_{n-2}) \wedge MATCH(CR(d_1), CR(d_2)) \wedge \\
& MATCH(CR(d_2), CR(d_3)) \wedge \cdots \wedge MATCH(CR(d_{n-2}), CR(d_{n-1}))
\end{aligned}
\tag{3}
$$

Therefore, we can get

$$
\begin{aligned}
& RP(d_{n-1}) \wedge MATCH(CR(d_{n-1}), CR(d_n)) \Rightarrow \\
& RP(d_{n-1}) \wedge RP(d_{n-1}) \wedge MATCH(CR(d_{n-1}), CR(d_n)) \Rightarrow RP(d_1) \wedge \\
& RP(d_2) \wedge \cdots \wedge RP(d_{n-2}) \wedge RP(d_{n-1}) \wedge MATCH(CR(d_1), CR(d_2)) \wedge \\
& MATCH(CR(d_2), CR(d_3)) \wedge \cdots \wedge MATCH(CR(d_{n-2}), CR(d_{n-1})) \wedge \\
& MATCH(CR(d_{n-1}), CR(d_n)) \Rightarrow CR(d_n) \qquad \square
\end{aligned}
$$

Theorem 1. *Anti-single point attack:* *If AS_t is the only malicious node in the network, and claims that he announced a route d to AS_d and sent a route proof $RP(d)$ to the verification system later, the verification system can completely verify whether the route d meets the promise made by AS_t.*

Proof. There are only four cases to consider: (1) AS_t announced a non-optimal route u, with a route proof $RP(w)$ for the optimal route w; (2) AS_t announced a non-optimal route u, with a route proof $RP(u)$ for this route u; (3) AS_t announced an optimal route w, with a route proof $RP(u)$ for a non-optimal route u; (4) AS_t announced an optimal route w, with a route proof $RP(w)$ for this optimal route w.

For case (4), it is normal. The route proof $RP(w)$ can be passed the verification process obviously and be put in a block of the blockchain.

For case (1) and (3), they belong to the same kind of the problem that the class of route $CR(u)$ is incorrect. According to step of *Checking the basic information of a route proof* and *Checking the signatures in a route proof*, $CR(u)$ will be detected wrong. According to *Lemma* 1, $CR(u)$ is wrong for inconsistency with that in $PRP(u)$.

For case (2), a promise violation can be detected in step of *Optimal route checking*: there *must* exists a route proof $RP(w)$ satisfies that $CR(w)$ is better than $CR(u)$, because AS_t has received a better route w than route u, and a corresponding route proof $RP(w)$ should be stored in *proof storage* before.

Therefore, it can guarantee that a single point attack can be completely detected in theory, since there is no collusion, and the consensus algorithm provides a certain fault tolerance.

Theorem 2. *Anti-collusion attack:* *If all the verification nodes are honest, the verification system can completely avoid the collusion attacks caused by the routing nodes. If the verification node colludes, the condition for avoiding the promise violation is that the ratio of malicious nodes is lower than the fault tolerance of the consensus algorithm used.*

Proof. For the first part, we prove all the collusion attacks by the routing nodes can be detected.

Similar to Theorem 1, only the same four cases can happen. There is no attack found in case (4), we only consider the first three cases. For case (1) and case (3), the prove process is the same as that in Theorem 1.

In case (2), AS_t announced a route d, which is learnt from a non-optimal route u, and sent a route proof $RP(d)$ to the verification system. Assume AS_t received m routes, and n routes have better AS Path length than route u, marked as $w_1, w_2, \ldots, w_n$, learnt from $AS_{w1}, AS_{w2}, \ldots, AS_{wn}$, respectively.

As long as anyone in $AS_{w1}, AS_{w2}, \ldots, AS_{wn}$ provides a correct route proof, route proof $RP(d)$ cannot pass the verification in step of *Optimal route checking* since there exists a better route proof than $PRP(d)$, i.e., $RP(u)$. Therefore, the precondition that route proof $RP(d)$ can pass the verification is that $AS_{w1}, AS_{w2}, \ldots, AS_{wn}$ all participate in collusion together with AS_t.

We will prove that it can be detected when anyone in $AS_{w1}, AS_{w2}, \ldots, AS_{wn}$ colludes with AS_t. Take AS_{wx} as an example. Assume AS_{wx} sent a route v to AS_t with AS Path length of x, and AS Path of route v is $\{AS_{wx}, AS_{x-1}, \ldots, AS_1\}$.

To support $RP(d)$ to pass the verification, AS_{wx} needs to provide a faked $RP(v)$ with a faked $CR(v)$, which should be no better than $CR(d)$. According to Lemma 1, $CR(v)$ is required to be consistent with its preceding route proof. In order to make this faked CR (v) to become *correct*, it requires all the participants $AS_{x-1}, \ldots, AS_1$ in this route proof chain to provide faked CR value. However, according to assumption (3), a route origin AS is honest, i.e., AS_1 cannot provide a faked route proof.

Therefore, this faked $CR(v)$ cannot be accepted by the verification system because at least one participant in the route proof chain cannot provide a faked CR. So anyone (include AS_{wx}) in $AS_{w1}, AS_{w2}, \ldots, AS_{wn}$ cannot be an accomplice with AS_t to help AS_t to put $RP(d)$ in the verification system.

For the second part, the probability of a collusion attack occurring depends on the consensus algorithm. For example, the fault tolerate rate is 50% for the consensus algorithm, such as POW and POS, while it is 33% for PBFT.

For the second part, the condition for avoiding a collusion attack is that the proportion of the collusion nodes is smaller than the fault tolerate rate of the consensus algorithm, since the working condition of the blockchain usually depends on the fault tolerate rate of the consensus algorithm.

In summary, if all the verification nodes are honest, collusion attack cannot happen. Otherwise, avoiding anti-collusion attack requires that the proportion of collusion nodes does not exceed fault tolerate rate of the consensus algorithm. For example, if POW is used, the collusion attack can be avoided as long as the proportion of malicious verification nodes does not exceed 50%.

According to the mechanism of BRVM, no AS can learn any additional information about the promise of any other AS beyond what it can already learn via BGP. That is, BRVM can satisfy the requirement of privacy in 2.3.

The correctness of route verification depends on the correctness of route proofs. Since the verification node itself can be faked, the correctness of BRVM depends on the consensus algorithm.

4 EVIRP: Mechanism and Protocol

4.1 Protocol Design

Currently at least 50K ASes are working in the Internet and process over 300K routes. Since different ASes do not trust each other, they all want to participate in the verification process of route proofs. Since the default value of MARI (Minimum Route Advertisement Interval) is 30 s, when considering the concurrency, the time required to verify a route should not exceed 0.6 ms (30 s/50K route proofs) theoretically.

EVIRP selects BFT-DPOS as its consensus algorithm, which supports 50K+ nodes and needs 3 s to confirm a block that includes at most 400 route proofs, i.e., the time to confirm a route proof is theoretically 7.5 ms (3 s/400 route proofs). Obviously, the time to verify a route proof cannot meet the performance requirement of EVIRP, so we need to optimize the verification time for EVIRP.

To optimize the verification time, we propose a two-tier verification system, including a local verification system and a global verification system. A node in the local verification system, acts as a node in the blockchain, located in a physical router. It may be a bitcoin core in Bitcoin or an endorser node in Fabric. It does not participate in the consensus process of global verification system, and receives blocks from the global verification system and stores into the cache the index tables of route proofs that it concerns. The communication process is shown in Fig. 5, and involves four entities: a local verifier, a global verifier, a sender of route, and a receiver of route.

When receiving a route proof, a local verifier and a global verifier will check its correctness according to step *the verification process of a route proof* in BRVM. The difference lies in: a local verifier checks the correctness of a route proof locally, while global verifiers will reach a consensus on the correctness of a route proof together. If the verification result for the same route proof is different between a local verifier and global verifiers, only two cases will occur: (1) the local verifier is malicious. Global verifiers will check whether the local verifier is hacked, and ask the route receiver to roll back the incorrect route; (2) the local verifier is honest, but the number of malicious global verifiers exceeds the fault tolerance of the consensus algorithm. EVIRP cannot work in a blockchain with an incorrect status. When receiving a request for verifying a route, a local verifier first searches the route proof of this route locally, and forwards this request to a global verifier if it does not find.

The possible overhead increased is that a local verifier needs to forward the verification request to the global verification system, when it cannot find a corresponding route proof locally. However, a local verifier has a higher probability of storing all the route proofs needed, since it is often closer to the direct neighbors of a receiver. Therefore, it can be inferred that the possible overhead increased is negligible.

4.2 Mechanism

Since the blockchain needs to record a huge number of route proofs, the linear linked list structure of the traditional blockchain will greatly reduce the verification performance. Therefore, due to the irrelevance of route prefixes, multiple route proof

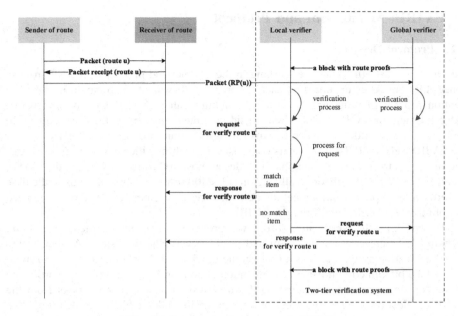

Fig. 5. Communication process in EVIRP

blockchains can be established by route prefix, route senders and route receivers to reduce the number of blocks in a single blockchain.

A single root proof chain $LSTRP(ID_s, ID_r, p)$ is indexed by (ID_s, ID_r, p). It represents a route proof of a route to a prefix p, which is sent by ID_s to ID_r. To locate a route proof chain, we use $ID_s\|ID_r\|p$ as a key. For every AS ID_r as a receiver of route, we retrieval the results for $(*, ID_r, p)$ and save them to accelerate the verification process.

The performance of routing verification mainly depends on the efficiency of local verifiers. Local verifiers mainly perform synchronization, verification and query. Since process of query is simple, we mainly discuss synchronization and verification.

(1) Synchronization blocks with route proofs

In EVIRP, only global verifiers take part in the consensus process and send blocks with route proofs to local verifiers periodically. A local verifier checks the validity of blocks, and put them into its local storage as blockchain does. Besides that, from route proofs received, a local verifier will update its cache that contains index tables and route proofs that it concerns.

(2) Verification of route proofs

The difference in the verification of route proofs in local verifiers and global verifiers is the verification of $CR(u)$. Since a local verifier is located in a physical border router, it can get a route u and calculate its $CR(u)$ directly.

What can be accelerated in a local verifier includes checking whether $PRP(d)$ exists and optimal route checking in a smaller search space. Assume that the storage cost of a route proof is M, the number of different route prefixes is n, the number of ASes is w, the average number of neighbors per AS is b, and the number of changes in each route is c. Then, the space cost for a global verifier is $O(wncM)$, while that cost for a local verifier is $O(bncM)$. We use the key-value form for query, so the cost to locate a root route proof is $O(1)$. Thus, for the verification algorithm, main computation cost is to search if there exists a better preceding root proof, which is $O(b)$.

5 Prototype and Experiment

5.1 Prototype of EVIRP

We implement a prototype of EVIRP, where the verification system is implemented using Fabric [15], and routing system using Quagga [16]. The prototype architecture consists of two parts. The left part is the structure of a local verifier and a global verifier. The modules with dotted line are modified, while the ones with solid line are original. A local verifier, as a node of blockchain, is located in a physical node of the routing system. A routing node runs Quagga/bgpd with some modification, and mainly includes *route receive* routine (bgp_update_receive), *route send* routine (bgp_update) and *an interface to* the local verifier. We add a route verification function in *route receive* routine to deal with incoming routes, and a route proof send function in *route send* routine to send out route proofs. The global verification system is implemented in Fabric, and mainly composes six parts: SDK, chaincode, endorser, committer, orderer and ledger. We mainly modify endorser, chaincode and ledger modules. Route proofs are sent to endorsers to be verified via functions provided in SDK. We implement a new chaincode and modify the endorsement of transaction proposal in endorser nodes to support the routing verification. For the requirements of performance and scalability, we use BFT-DPOS as the consensus algorithm.

5.2 Experiment and Evaluation

Next, we report results from an experimental evaluation of EVIRP. We make experiments to validate that EVIRP is useful to solve the promise-violation issue under two kinds of attacks: one node attack and collude attack. The experiment topology is that: five ASes are deployed in the routing system, the configuration of IP address and AS id of ASes is shown in Table 2. Each node in the experiment is running in a container, such as *Docker*, and runs routing service and blockchain service.

Table 2. Experimental configuration.

AS	AS id	ip addr (one AS may has multiple ip addrs)
AS_1	65531	172.15.0.15, 172.12.0.12
AS_2	65532	172.12.0.21, 172.23.0.23, 172.24.0.24
AS_3	65533	172.23.0.32
AS_4	65534	172.24.0.42
AS_5	65535	172.15.0.51

(1) **One malicious node scenario**

We assume AS_2 is a malicious node, and set the experiment like this: AS_2 receives two routes to prefix 206.223.115.0/24 from AS_3 and AS_4, with AS path length is 3 and 4, respectively. AS_2 sends to AS_1 a route e learnt from AS_4.

According to EVIRP, there exists a route proof in the verification system for route d learnt from AS_3. We can find that there is a route proof for route d from AS_3 to AS_2 that has AS path of 3. So a route proof for route e cannot pass the optimal check in the verification, and is stored in the database for invalid route proofs. The verification mechanism in EVIRP ensures that one malicious node attack cannot be achieved.

(2) **Multiple malicious nodes scenario**

We assume AS_2 and AS_3 are malicious nodes in Fig. 6, and set the experiment like this: AS_2 receives two routes for prefix 206.223.115.0/24 from AS_3 and AS_4, with AS path length is 3 and 4, respectively. AS_2 sends to AS_1 a route e learnt from AS_4.

The experiment result is the same as the case in one malicious node scenario, because *peer*1 can find this error in the optimal check in the verification of route proof for route e. Therefore, the verification mechanism in EVIRP guarantees that collusion attacks caused by multiple malicious nodes are detectable before attacks take effect.

(3) **Performance experiment**

We ran experiments on a cluster of 5 servers connected by a 1 GB Ethernet network. Each server had a 2.1 GHz Intel CPU of 4 cores and 4 GB RAM, and ran Ubuntu 14.04 (Linux 4.4.0).

From the result in Fig. 6, we can find that: the local verification only search the cache to find a match entry or just pass the request to the global verification system, so it is very fast (in milliseconds). For global verification, it costs longer time to wait for a route proof to be stored in a block. Therefore, when the number of routes increases, there is a large probability to wait for the corresponding route proofs. In Fig. 6, the time used for number of routes of 50 is 3.6 s, while the value is 6.2 s with the routes number is 500. A block with 1 MB can contain 400 route proofs, so it takes about 3 s to verify 400 routes in theory. But the actual time is longer than the theoretical value, mainly due to the delay caused by storing blocks, transmission delay, etc.

Similar with the experiment of *SPIDeR*, we also use a 15-minute RouteViews trace the same as *SPIDeR*. Since the experiment server is the similar, we can conduct the performance experiment and compare with *SPIDeR* in two aspects: time used and the storage used to simulation of the trace. The time used to run the experiment is 502.6 s, and used 120.4 MB memory totally, while the value used by *SPIDeR* is 634.5 s, and 94.1 MB, respectively. And the result of compare performance is shown in Fig. 7, with percentage measurement as Y-axis. We can find that though our algorithm uses more storage than *SPIDeR*, but the speed is 21% faster than *SPIDeR*. And *SPIDeR* cannot solve the collude attack, which can be solved in our solution.

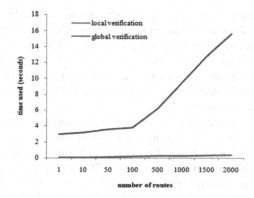

Fig. 6. Performance comparison in local verification and global verification.

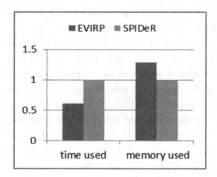

Fig. 7. Performance comparison with SPIDeR.

6 Related Work

The security problem for Internet interdomain routing has been studied for many years. Most previous security related works focus on bogus paths. Butler et al. [17] surveys the current BGP security issues with its solutions such as S-BGP [11], soBGP [12], IRV [18], origin authentication [19], SPV [20] and so on. S-BGP [11] assures the security of information by validating path attributes based on the certificates in the PKI. soBGP [12] can only provide origin authentication, but cannot provide path authentication. IRV is a centralized solution whose operation is independent of routing protocol. It requires that every AS report its link or relationship with other AS to IRV servers. Other solutions can be found, such as signature amortization [21], reference locality [22], psBGP [23], MOAS detection, intrusion detection [24], BPHAS [25], etc. Goldberg et al. [10] pointed out that the existing secure routing protocols only address the security of route announcement semantics, which can only guarantee the paths are topologically valid but fail to ensure the logical trustworthiness. Our work focuses on the issue of the logical trustworthiness.

The secure problems caused by valley paths are the examples of such trustworthiness issues. [1] proposes a mechanism to avoid the valley path by adding a transitive attribute in BGP reflecting the relationships between AS. In fact, this mechanism reveals the business relationships between ASes. SCION [26] is another attempt to provide the valley-free paths. However, it can only guarantee the properties of the valley-free paths in a trust domain (a group of several ASes) without ensuring all the valley-free paths in the whole network.

BorderGuard [27] verified different types of commitments, namely whether the ISP advertises a consistent route using information that is already available to the ISP, so privacy protection is not a problem. NetReview [13] allows routing decisions to be checked without considering privacy protection. SPIDeR performs collaborative verification for inter-domain routing with considering privacy at the same time, which is the most relevant to our work. However, SPIDeR cannot guarantee the detection of promise violation caused by more entities collude. Our solution mainly focused on the promise-violation problem which is caused by collusion of many nodes.

Gupta [28] introduces SMPC (secure multi-party computation) into inter-domain routing, to separate private information into different computing entities, and the results are calculated by multiple entities. Gurney [29] proposes the similar idea with [14]. Chen [30] focuses on privacy protection methods, and to find out how to ensure that the shortest path between two routes with the assumption that two topological nodes are known, without revealing the topology information of the two domains. Sundaresan [31] deals with issue that violates the Gao-Rexford export rule through labeling the valley-path, and the relationship between ASes in the process of route advertisement. Henecka [32] aims to change the principle of route advertisement without revealing the topology structure, and can calculate the shortest path by using the way of backtracking. Hari [33] and Yousef [34] consider the privacy protection issues in blockchain. All of them consider the privacy protection. Muhammad [35] considers improving the security and efficiency of BGP Routing based on blockchain.

7   Future Work

For detecting attacks that violate shortest AS Path policy caused by single node and multiple nodes, we are the first to propose a mechanism based on a blockchain approach. However, we still face many difficult problems to be solved in the future. For example, if a global verifier and a routing node are the same entity, it can infer the detail routing information of others by collecting all routing proofs. The risk of privacy leakage still exists. How to enhance privacy protection is our next research focus. Secondly, the scale of BGP nodes in Internet and the size of routing tables are very large. Our proposed method has still a certain gap from the actual deployment. How to further improve the performance and scalability of the verification system (it only needs 30 seconds for dealing with 300K routes in the real world), and carry out incremental deployment are still challenges we need to consider in the future. Thirdly, the current method is only for one routing. How to find a better method suitable for conformance check of other rules is also a difficult problem to be solved.

Acknowledgements. This work is supported by the National Key Research and Development Program of China under grant No. 2018YFB1003602, and Key Area Research and Development Program of Guangdong Province under grant No. 2019B010137005.

References

1. Qiu, S.Y., McDaniel, P.D., Monrose, F.: Toward valley-free inter-domain routing. In: IEEE ICC 2007, Glasgow, pp. 2009–2016. IEEE (2007)
2. Kalafut, A.J., Shue, C.A., Gupta, M.: Malicious hubs: detecting abnormally malicious autonomous systems. In: IEEE INFOCOM 2010, San Diego, pp. 1–5. IEEE (2010)
3. Mahajan, R., Wetherall, D., Anderson, T.: Understanding BGP misconfiguration. In: ACM SIGCOMM 2002, Pittsburgh, pp. 3–16. ACM (2002)
4. Nordström, O., Dovrolis, C.: Beware of BGP attacks. ACM SIGCOMM Comput. Commun. Rev. **34**(2), 1–8 (2004)
5. Norton, W.B.: Study of 28 Peering Policies. Technical report. http://drpeering.net/whitepapers/Peering-Policies/A-Study-of-28-Peering-Policies.html
6. Rensys Blog, Internet-Wide catastrophe—Last year. http://www.renesys.com/blog/2005/12/internetwide_nearcatastrophela.shtml
7. Rensys Blog, Pakistan hijacks YouTube. http://www.renesys.com/blog/2008/02/pakistan_hijacks_youtube_1.shtml
8. BGPmon Blog, How the Internet in Australia went down under. http://bgpmon.net/blog/?p=554
9. Google made a tiny error and it broke half the internet in Japan. https://thenextweb.com/google/2017/08/28/google-japan-internet-blackout
10. Goldberg, S., Schapira, M., Hummon, P., Rexford, J.: How secure are secure interdomain routing protocols. ACM SIGCOMM Comput. Commun. Rev. **40**(4), 87–98 (2010)
11. Kent, S., Lynn, C., Mikkelson, J., Seo, K.: Secure border gateway protocol (S-BGP). IEEE J. Sel. Areas Commun. **18**, 103–116 (2000)
12. White, R.: Securing BGP through secure origin BGP. Internet Protoc. J. **6**(3), 15–22 (2003)
13. Haeberlen, A., Avramopoulos, I., Rexford, J., Druschel, P.: NetReview: detecting when interdomain routing goes wrong. In: USENIX NSDI 2009, Boston, pp. 437–452. USENIX Association (2009)
14. Zhao, M., Zhou, W., et al.: Private and verifiable interdomain routing decisions. IEEE/ACM Trans. Netw. **24**(2), 1011–1024 (2016)
15. Hyperledger Fabric. https://www.hyperledger.org/projects/fabric
16. Quagga Routing Suite. http://www.nongnu.org/quagga
17. Butler, K.R.B., Farley, T., Mcdaniel, P.D., Rexford, J.: A survey of BGP security issues and solutions. Proc. IEEE **98**(1), 100–122 (2010)
18. Goodell, G., Aiello, W., Griffin, T., et al.: Working around BGP: an incremental approach to improving security and accuracy of interdomain routing. In: NDSS 2003, San Diego (2003)
19. Aiello, W., Ioannidis, J., McDaniel, P.: Origin authentication in interdomain routing. In: ACM CCS 2003, Washington, DC, pp. 165–178. ACM (2003)
20. Hu, Y., Perrig, A., Sirbu, M.A.: SPV: secure path vector routing for securing BGP. In: ACM SIGCOMM 2004, Portland, pp. 179–192. ACM (2004)
21. Smith, S.W., Zhao, M., Nicol, D.M.: Aggregated path authentication for efficient BGP security. In: 12th ACM Conference on Computer and Communications Security, Alexandria, pp. 128–138. ACM (2005)

22. McDaniel, P., Butler, K., Aiello, W.: Optimizing BGP security by exploiting path stability. In: 13th ACM Conference on Computer and Communications Security, Alexandria, pp. 298–310. ACM (2006)
23. Oorschot, P.C.V., Wan, T., Kranakis, E.: On inter-domain routing security and pretty secure BGP (psBGP). ACM (2007)
24. Kruegel, C., Mutz, D., Robertson, W., Valeur, F.: Topology-based detection of anomalous BGP messages. In: Vigna, G., Kruegel, C., Jonsson, E. (eds.) RAID 2003. LNCS, vol. 2820, pp. 17–35. Springer, Heidelberg (2003). https://doi.org/10.1007/978-3-540-45248-5_2
25. Lad, M., Massey, D., Pei, D., et al.: BPHAS: a prefix hijack alert system. In: The 15th USENIX Security Symposium. USENIX Association (2006)
26. Zhang, X., Hsiao, H.C., Hasker, G., et al.: SCION: scalability, control, and isolation on next-generation networks. In: IEEE Symposium on Security and Privacy, Berkeley, pp. 212–227. IEEE (2011)
27. Feamster, N., Mao, Z.M., Rexford, J.: BorderGuard: detecting cold potatoes from peers. In: ACM IMC 2004, Taormina, pp. 213–218. ACM (2004)
28. Gupta, D., Segal, A., Panda, A., Segev, G., et al.: A new approach to interdomain routing based on secure multi-party computation. In: ACM Workshop on Hot Topics in Networks, Seattle, pp. 37–42. ACM (2012)
29. Gurney, A.J.T., Haeberlen, A., Zhou, W., et al.: Having your cake and eating it too: routing security with privacy protections. In: ACM Workshop on Hot Topics in Networks, Cambridge. ACM (2011)
30. Chen, Q., Qian, C., Zhong, S.: Privacy-preserving cross-domain routing optimization - a cryptographic approach. In: IEEE ICNP 2015, San Francisco, pp. 356–365. IEEE (2015)
31. Sundaresan, S., Lychev, R., Valancius, V.: Preventing attacks on BGP policies: one bit is enough. Georgia Institute of Technology (2011)
32. Henecka, W., Roughan, M.: STRIP: privacy-preserving vector-based routing. In: IEEE ICNP 2014, Research Triangle Park, pp. 1–10. IEEE (2014)
33. Hari, A., Lakshman, T.V.: The Internet blockchain: a distributed, tamper-resistant transaction framework for the internet. In: ACM Workshop on Hot Topics in Networks, Atlanta. ACM (2016)
34. Alowayed, Y., Canini, M., Marcos, P., et al.: Picking a partner: a fair blockchain based scoring protocol for autonomous systems. In: ANRW 2018, Montreal. ACM (2018)
35 Saad, M., Anwar, A., Ahmad, A., Alasmary, H., Yukesl, M., Mohaisen, A.: RouteChain: towards blockchain-based secure and efficient BGP routing. In: IEEE International Conference on Blockchain and Cryptocurrency 2019, Seoul. IEEE (2019)

Internet of Things

Edge-Assisted CNN Inference over Encrypted Data for Internet of Things

Yifan Tian[1], Jiawei Yuan[1(✉)], Shucheng Yu[2], Yantian Hou[3],
and Houbing Song[1]

[1] Embry-Riddle Aeronautical University, Daytona Beach, FL 32114, USA
tiany1@my.erau.edu
{yuanj,songh4}@erau.edu
[2] Stevens Institute of Technology, Hoboken, NJ 07030, USA
shucheng.yu@stevens.edu
[3] Boise State University, Boise, ID 83725, USA
yantianhou@boisestate.edu

Abstract. Supporting the inference tasks of convolutional neural network (CNN) on resource-constrained Internet of Things (IoT) devices in a timely manner has been an outstanding challenge for emerging smart systems. To mitigate the burden on IoT devices, one prevalent solution is to offload the CNN inference tasks to the public cloud. However, this "offloading-to-cloud" solution may cause privacy breach since the offloaded data can contain sensitive information. For privacy protection, the research community has resorted to advanced cryptographic primitives to support CNN inference over encrypted data. Nevertheless, these attempts are limited by the real-time performance due to the heavy IoT computational overhead brought by cryptographic primitives.

In this paper, we propose an edge-computing-assisted scheme to boost the efficiency of CNN inference tasks on IoT devices, which also protects the privacy of IoT data to be offloaded. In our scheme, the most time-consuming convolutional and fully-connected layers are offloaded to edge computing devices and the IoT device only performs efficient encryption and decryption on the fly. As a result, our scheme enables IoT devices to securely offload over 99% CNN operations, and edge devices to execute CNN inference over encrypted data as efficiently as on plaintext. Experiments on AlexNet show that our scheme can speed up CNN inference for more than 35× with a 95.56% energy saving for IoT devices.

Keywords: Privacy · Internet of Things · Edge computing · Convolutional neural network · Deep learning

1 Introduction

With the recent advances in artificial intelligence, the integration of deep neural networks and IoT is receiving increasing attention from both academia and

S. Chen et al. (Eds.): SecureComm 2019, LNICST 304, pp. 85–104, 2019.
https://doi.org/10.1007/978-3-030-37228-6_5

industry [1–3]. As the representative of deep neural networks, convolutional neural network (CNN) has been identified as an prevailing structure to enable a spectrum of intelligent IoT applications [4], including visual detection, smart security, audio analytics, health monitoring, infrastructure inspection, etc. In these applications, pre-trained CNN models are deployed on IoT devices, with which the corresponding *CNN inference tasks* can be executed when real-time application requests are initiated. Nevertheless, due to the high computation in the inference tasks, deploying CNNs on resource-constrained IoT devices for time-sensitive services becomes very challenging. For example, popular CNN architectures (e.g., AlexNet [5], FaceNet [6], and ResNet [7]) for visual detection require billions of operations for the execution of a single inference task. Our evaluation results show that a single inference task using AlexNet can cost more than two minutes on an IoT device with comparable computing capability as a Raspberry Pi (Model A).

To soothe IoT devices from heavy computation and energy consumption, offloading CNN inference tasks to public cloud computing platforms has become a popular choice in the literature. However, this type of "cloud-backed" system may raise privacy concerns by sending sensitive data to remote cloud [8]. Moreover, connecting to the cloud can cause additional latency to the system under network congestion and even make the system dysfunction when network is off [9]. While research efforts have been made towards enabling CNN inference over encrypted data using cloud computing [10–18], expensive cryptographic primitives utilized in them (e.g., homomorphic encryption and multi-party secure computation) introduce heavy encryption and communication overhead to IoT devices. Such a performance limitation makes these solutions far away from practical in support of time-sensitive CNN inference tasks on IoT devices, especially for complex CNN architectures. For example, a quad-core Raspberry Pi, which outperforms most resource-constrained IoT devices in terms of computational capability, can perform only four Paillier homomorphic encryption per second [19]. Given a single input of AlexNet which has $227 \times 227 \times 3$ elements, it requires more than 10 h to complete the encryption, which is impractical for most applications in terms of time delay and energy consumption. Besides, these research adopt batch processing to improve their performance, which is more suitable for the "Data Collection and Post-Processing" routine, while differently, real-time processing is desired for IoT devices to fulfill time-sensitive tasks. To the best of our knowledge, enabling real-time execution of complex CNN inference tasks over encrypted data remains as an open problem.

This paper addresses such a challenging problem and proposes an edge-computing-assisted scheme to enable real-time execution of CNN inferences for resource-constrained IoT devices with privacy protection. Different from existing "cloud-backed" designs, our design leverages edge computing to promote the efficiency of offloading IoT data, because it can effectively ameliorate the network latency and availability issue [20]. More importantly, we propose a novel online/offline encryption to assure the real-time CNN inference over encrypted IoT data can be efficiently executed by general edge computing devices (e.g., regular laptop computers), and hence avoid the reliance on powerful cloud servers for computing capabilities. To be specific, since linear operations of CNNs over input data and random noise are linearly separable, decryption of noise can be conveniently computed offline. In practical CNN architectures such as AlexNet and FaceNet, linear operations are dominant due to their vast number. Therefore, it is rewarding to trade offline computation and storage (of random noise) for online computation to assure the real-time performance of CNN inference tasks. As a result, our online/offline encryption allows IoT devices to securely offload over 99% CNN operations to edge devices. In addition, our scheme does not introduce any accuracy loss as compared to CNN inferences over unencrypted data, because it does not utilize any approximation for all required operations. It is also worth to note that our scheme can be customized to support flexible CNN architectures that fulfill the requirements of different applications.

Thorough analysis and extensive experimental evaluation results show the security, efficiency, scalability, and accuracy of our scheme. In particular, we implemented a prototype over the well-known ImageNet [21] dataset using an AlexNet architecture, which involves 2.27 billion operations for each inference task and has comparable complexity with these widely adopted architectures, e.g., FaceNet (1.6 billion operations) and Results (3.6 billion operations). The numerical analysis shows that our scheme can securely offload 99.95% computation from the IoT devices for AlexNet. Correspondingly, our experimental results demonstrate that our scheme is able to speed up 35.63× for the execution of CNN-driven IoT AlexNet tasks using a single laptop as the edge device. Compared with fully executing an AlexNet request on the IoT device, our scheme saves 95.56% energy consumption. In addition, our scheme keeps the high speedup rate as the complexity of CNN layers increases. Therefore, it is promising to be scaled up for more complex CNN architectures.

The rest parts of this paper are organized as follows: In Sect. 2, we introduce the background of CNN, which is followed by the problem formulation in Sect. 3. Section 4 presents the detailed construction of our scheme. We state security analysis and numerical analysis in Sect. 5. We further evaluate the practical performance of our scheme with a prototype evaluation in Sect. 6. We review and discuss related works in Sect. 7 and conclude this paper in Sect. 8.

2   Background of Convolutional Neural Network

A CNN contains a stack of layers that transform input data to outputs with label scores. There are four types of most common layers in CNN architectures, including: *Convolutional Layers, Pooling Layers, Activation Layers*, and *Fully-connected Layers*.

Convolutional layers extract features from input data. Figure 1 depicts an example of convolutional layer that has an input data of size $n \times n \times D$ and H kernels, each of size $k \times k \times D$. The input will be processed into all H kernels independently to extract H different features. Considering the input and each kernel as D levels, where each level of the input and kernel are a $n \times n$ matrix and a $k \times k$ matrix respectively. Each level of a kernel starts scanning the corresponding input level from the top-left corner, and then moves from left to right with s elements, where s is the stride of the convolutional layer. Once the top-right corner is reached, the kernel moves s elements downward and scans from left to right again. This convolution process is repeated until the kernel reaches the bottom-right corner of this input level. For each scan, an output is computed using the dot product between the scanned window of input and the kernel as an example shown in Fig. 1. For each kernel, the output for all D levels will be summed together.

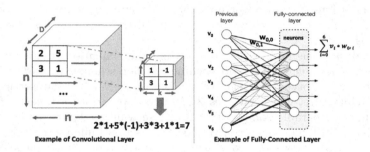

Fig. 1. Examples of a convolutional layer and a fully-connected layer

Pooling layers and activation layers are usually non-linear layers. A pooling layer is periodically inserted between convolutional layers. Pooling layers progressively reduce the spatial size of outputs from convolutional layers, and thus to make data robust against noise and control overfitting. An activation layer utilizes element-wise activation functions to signal distinct identification of their input data. There are a number of popular pooling strategies (e.g., max-pooling and average-pooling) and activation functions (e.g., rectified linear units (ReLUs) and continuous trigger functions), which are computational efficient compared with convolutional layers and fully-connected layers. In our scheme, these two efficient layers will be directly handled on the IoT devices.

Fully-connected layers are usually the final layers of a CNN to output the final results of the network. In case of a fully-connected layer, all neurons in it have full connections to all outputs from the previous layer. As an example shown in Fig. 1, the connection between each neuron and input element has a weight. To obtain the output of a neuron, elements will be multiplied with their weights and then accumulated.

More details about CNN can be found in ref [22].

3   Problem Formulation

In our setting, there are two entities: *IoT Device* and *Edge Computing Device*. The IoT device collects data and needs to perform CNN inference over the data.

The edge device obtains a trained CNN model and contributes its computing capability to the CNN inference task. There are two scenarios for the offloading of CNN inference according to the provider of the trained model: (1) the data holder deploys its own trained model on a computing service platform and later on submits data for inference tasks [10]; (2) the computing service platform offers the trained model and performs inference on data submitted by the data holder, which is known as "machine learning as a service" [15–18]. When privacy is taken into consideration, both scenarios require the protection of data and inference results against the computing service platform, and the second scenario also needs to prevent the data holder from learning the trained model.

In this paper, we focus on the first scenario. To be specific, we wish to design a scheme that the IoT device and edge device engage in, at the end of which the IoT device obtains the CNN inference result over its data, whereas the edge device only assists the computation without learning the data as well as the result.

3.1   Threat Model

We consider the edge device to be "curious-but-honest", i.e., the edge device adheres to the protocol that describes the computation, communication, and storage tasks, but attempts to infer information about the input and output of the IoT device's CNN inference task. Given a CNN inference task, the edge device has access to the trained CNN model (offloaded convolutional layers and fully-connected layers only) as well as the encrypted inputs and outputs of all offloaded layers. The IoT device is considered to be fully trusted and will not be compromised.

We aim at preventing the edge device from learning the IoT devices' inputs and outputs of each offloaded layer. The overall purpose of the inference task is not going to be protected, since the CNN model is known to the edge device. For example, the edge device knows the CNN inference is used for object detection, but shall not learn the input image data and the corresponding detection result. We assume the CNN model is trained by IoT device owner with data in the clear. To prevent privacy leakage of training data from the CNN model, a statistical database can be used for training as discussed in the differential privacy literature [23,24]. The research on privacy-preserving training is orthogonal to this work.

4   Detailed Construction

To assure the real-time performance of CNN inference tasks of an IoT device, we use the online/offline strategy to design our scheme. The online phase refers to the duration when a CNN inference is being executed for the data collected by an IoT device. The offline phase refers to the "no-inference" status of the IoT device and time before the IoT device is deployed. Specifically, the owner of an IoT device pre-computes multiple sets of encryption and decryption keys during the offline phase and loads them into the IoT device. In the online phase, the IoT device uses these pre-computed keys to efficiently encrypt data to be offloaded and decrypt results returned by the edge device. In our system, the IoT device offloads expensive convolutional layers and fully-connected layers to the edge device, and only keeps the compute-efficient layers at local. This is motivated by the fact that convolutional and fully-connected layers occupy majority of computation and parameters storage in typical CNNs [25]. All CNN operations performed by the edge device are over encrypted data.

We now present the detailed construction of our scheme. Important notation is summarized in Table 1.

Table 1. Summary of notations

$n \times n$	The size of each level of a convolutional layer's input
D	The depth of the input of a convolutional layer and kernel
$k \times k$	The size of a convolutional layer's kernel matrix
H	The number of kernels of a convolutional layer
s	The size of stride used for a convolutional layer
p	The size of padding used for a convolutional layer
$\mathcal{R}_{c,d}\ 1 \leq d \leq D$	$n \times n$ random matrices to encrypt the input of a convolutional layer
$\alpha_i\ 1 \leq i \leq H$	$(\frac{n-k+2p}{s} + 1) \times (\frac{n-k+2p}{s} + 1)$ matrices to decrypt a convolutional layer's output from H kernels
m	The size of a fully-connected layer input vector
T	The number of neurons of a fully-connected layer
$\mathcal{R}_f$	A m-dimensional random vector to encrypt the input of a fully-connected layer
β	A T-dimensional decryption vector to decrypt fully-connected layer outputs

4.1 Offline Phase

In the offline phase, the owner generates encryption and decryption keys for all convolutional layers and fully-connected layers in a trained CNN. We consider each element in the input data of convolutional layers and fully-connected layers is γ-bit long, and λ is the security parameter. To ensure the security $\frac{1}{2^{\lambda-\gamma-1}}$ shall be a negligible value in terms of computational secrecy [26], e.g., $< \frac{1}{2^{128}}$. Detailed selection of security parameter is discussed in Sect. 5.1.

As described in Algorithm 1, given a convolutional layer with a $n \times n \times D$ input, stride as s, padding as p, and H kernels ($k \times k$ matrices), the owner generates $\{\mathcal{R}_{c,d}, 1 \leq d \leq D\}$ as the encryption keys and $\{\alpha_i, 1 \leq i \leq H\}$ as its decryption keys, where $\mathcal{R}_{c,d}$ is a $n \times n$ random matrix and α_i is a $(\frac{n-k+2p}{s} + 1) \times (\frac{n-k+2p}{s} + 1)$ matrix. For expression simplicity, we use $\mathbf{Conv}(\mathcal{R}_{c,d}, i_{th})$ to denote the convolution operation for the i_{th} kernel with $\mathcal{R}_{c,d}$ as input.

Given a fully-connected layer with a m-dimensional vector as input and T neurons, the owner first generates a m-dimensional random vector $\mathcal{R}_f$. Then, the owner takes $\mathcal{R}_f$ as the input of the fully-connected layer to output a T-dimensional vector β. $\mathcal{R}_f$ and β are set as the encryption key and decryption key respectively for this layer.

For a CNN with x convolutional layers and y fully-connected layers, x sets of $\{\mathcal{R}_{c,d}, \alpha_i\}_{1 \leq d \leq D_x, 1 \leq i \leq H_x}$ and y sets of $\{\mathcal{R}_f, \beta\}$ are generated by the owner as a final set of keys $\{Enc_{key}, Dec_{key}\}$. **Note that**, *each set of keys is only valid for one CNN request in the later online phase.* Thus, the owner will generate multiple sets of keys according to the necessity of application scenarios as discussed in Sect. 4.3.

Algorithm 1: Offline Preparation of Convolutional Layer

   Input   : Input size $n \times n \times D$, stride s, padding p, H kernels
   Output: Encryption keys $\mathcal{R}_{c,d}, 1 \leq d \leq D$, Decryption keys $\alpha_i, 1 \leq i \leq H$
1 Generate random $n \times n$ matrices $\mathcal{R}_{c,d}, 1 \leq d \leq D$;
2 **for** $1 \leq i \leq H$ **do**
3   **for** $1 \leq d \leq D$ **do**
4   Take $\mathcal{R}_{c,d}$ as input for the i_{th} kernel for convolution and output
            $\mathbf{Conv}(\mathcal{R}_{c,d}, i_{th})$;
5 d++;
6   Set $\alpha_i = \sum_{d=1}^{D} \mathbf{Conv}(\mathcal{R}_{c,d}, i_{th})$;
7 i++;

4.2 Online Phase

During the online phase, the IoT device can efficiently interact with the edge device to conduct CNN inference over encrypted data. The overall process of our online phase is depicted in Algorithm 2. Specifically, the IoT device offloads encrypted data to the edge device for performing compute-intensive convolutional layers and fully-connected layers. Intermediate results are returned back to the IoT device for decryption. Then, these decrypted results are processed with the follow up activation layer and pooling layer (if exist). Outputs are encrypted and offloaded again if the next layer is a convolutional layer or a fully-connected layer. This procedure is conducted iteratively until all CNN layers are executed.

To fulfill these tasks, we designed two privacy-preserving schemes *PPCL* and *PPFL* for convolutional layers and fully-connected layers respectively.

Algorithm 2: Online CNN Inference

Input   : Input Data & Trained CNN
Output: CNN Execution Result
1 **Set** the Layer Input $\mathcal{M}$ = Input Data;
2 **Set** Layers = the collection of all Convolutional Layers and Fully-connected Layers in CNN;
3 **Set** Layer = the first Layer from Layers;
4 **while** *Layer is not null* **do**
5 | **if** *Layer = Convolutional Layer* **then**
6 | | Execute the *PPCL* with $\mathcal{M}$ as input.;
7 | |_ Set $\mathcal{M}$ = output from *PPCL*;
8 | **if** *Layer = Fully-connected Layer* **then**
9 | | Execute the *PPFL* with $\mathcal{M}$ as input.
10 | |_ Set $\mathcal{M}$ = output from *PPFL*;
11 |_ Set Layer = Layers.next();
12 **return** $\mathcal{M}$ as result;

PPCL: Privacy-Preserving Convolutional Layer. In *PPCL*, we consider a general convolutional layer with a $n \times n \times D$ input, stride as s, padding as p, and H kernels with each size of $k \times k \times D$. The d_{th} level of the input is denoted as a $m \times m$ matrix $\mathcal{I}_d$.

Input Encryption: The IoT device encrypts the input using the pre-stored keys $\{\mathcal{R}_{c,d}\}$ for this convolutional layer as

$$Enc(\mathcal{I}_d) = \mathcal{I}_d + \mathcal{R}_{c,d} \tag{1}$$

where $\{Enc(\mathcal{I}_d)\}, 1 \leq d \leq D$ are sent to the edge device.

Privacy-Preserving Execution: The edge device takes each $Enc(\mathcal{I}_d), 1 \leq d \leq D$ as the input of kernels to perform the convolution process. For the i_{th} kernel, the edge device outputs

$$\sum_{d=1}^{D} \mathbf{Conv}(Enc(\mathcal{I}_d), i_{th}) = \sum_{d=1}^{D} \mathbf{Conv}(\mathcal{I}_d, i_{th}) + \sum_{d=1}^{D} \mathbf{Conv}(\mathcal{R}_{c,d}, i_{th})$$

$\sum_{d=1}^{D} \mathbf{Conv}(Enc(\mathcal{I}_d), i_{th}), 1 \leq i \leq H$ are returned back to the IoT device as intermediate results.

Decryption and Preparation for the Next Layer: Given the returned $\sum_{d=1}^{D} \mathbf{Conv}(Enc(\mathcal{I}_d), i_{th}), 1 \leq i \leq H$, the IoT device quickly decrypts them as

$$\sum_{d=1}^{D} \mathbf{Conv}(Enc(\mathcal{I}_d), i_{th}) - \alpha_i = \sum_{d=1}^{D} \mathbf{Conv}(\mathcal{I}_d, i_{th}) \tag{2}$$

where $\{\alpha_i = \sum_{d=1}^{D} \mathbf{Conv}(\mathcal{R}_{c,d}, i_{th})\}, 1 \leq i \leq H$ are the pre-stored decryption keys for this layer. Afterwards, the IoT device performs the activation layer and pooling layer directly over convolutional output, which are compute-efficient. For example, one of the most popular activation layer ReLU only requires translating negative values in the input to 0. The popular max-pooling (or average-pooling) layer simply shrinks the data by taking the max value (or average value respectively) every few values. The output will be encrypted and sent to the edge device using *PPCL* for the next convolutional layer (or *PPFL* respectively for a fully-connected layer).

PPFL: Privacy-Preserving Fully-Connected Layer. In *PPFL*, we consider a general fully-connected layer with T neurons and takes a m-dimensional vector $\mathcal{V}$ as input.

Input Encryption: Given the input, the IoT device encrypts it using the pre-stored encryption key $\mathcal{R}_f$ for this layer as

$$Enc(\mathcal{V}) = \mathcal{V} + \mathcal{R}_f \tag{3}$$

$Enc(\mathcal{V})$ is then sent to the edge device.

Privacy-Preserving Execution: On receiving $Enc(\mathcal{V})$, the edge device takes $Enc(\mathcal{V})$ as the input of the fully-connected layer. Specifically, the encrypted outcome $Enc(\mathcal{O}[j]), 1 \leq j \leq T$ of each neuron is computed as

$$Enc(\mathcal{O}[j]) = \sum_{i=1}^{m} Enc(\mathcal{V})[i] \times w_{i,j} = \mathcal{O}[j] + \beta[j] \tag{4}$$

where $w_{i,j}$ is the weight between the i_{th} element of input vector and the j_{th} neuron. $Enc(\mathcal{O}) = \{Enc(\mathcal{O}[1]), Enc(\mathcal{O}[2]), \cdots, Enc(\mathcal{O}[T])\}$ is sent back to the IoT device as intermediate results.

Decryption and Preparation for the Next Layer: Given the returned $Enc(\mathcal{O})$, the IoT device decrypts each $Enc(\mathcal{O})$ with the pre-stored decryption key β of this layer as

$$\mathcal{O} = Enc(\mathcal{O}) - \beta \tag{5}$$

Then, the IoT device executes the activation layer with $\mathcal{O}$ as input. The output from the activation layer will be encrypted and sent to edge device using *PPFL* if there are any additional fully-connected layers in the CNN.

To this end, the IoT device is able to efficiently handle each layer in a CNN. Compute-intensive convolutional and fully-connected layers are securely offloaded to the edge using *PPCL* and *PPFL*. These compute-efficient layers are directly handled by the IoT device. Since we develop *PPCL* and *PPFL* as independent modules, they can be customized and recursively plugged into any CNN no matter how many different convolutional layers and fully-connected layers it contains.

4.3   Discussion - Storage and Update of Pre-computed Keys

Our scheme considers two major types of resource-constrained IoT devices that run CNN-driven applications.

- Type-1: Mobile IoT devices with limited battery life and computational capability, such as drones.
- Type-2: Static devices with power supply but has limited computational capability, such as security cameras.

The type-1 devices are usually deployed to perform tasks for a period time. Therefore, before each deployment, the device owner can pre-load enough keys to support its CNN tasks. With regards to the type-2 devices, the owner can perform an initial key pre-loading and then use remote update to securely add new offline keys as described in Fig. 2.

Fig. 2. Key update for power connected devices

Our scheme proposes to ensure the timely processing of CNN requests when they are needed on IoT devices. Instead of performing real-time CNN requests on every piece of data collected, resource-constrained IoT devices usually require in-depth analytics using CNN when specific signals are detected. Taking real-time search and monitoring using drones as an example application for type-1 devices, fast local processing will be first performed for data collected to get estimated results [27]. Once suspicious signs are detected in estimated results, CNN based analytics are further conducted for a small set of data (e.g., video frames with the detected suspicious object). Given the high efficiency of our scheme, the performance of such CNN requests will be timely supported when enough pre-computed keys are available. For example, when the average frequency CNN requests is every one per ten seconds for a drone, only 360 sets of pre-computed keys are needed for one-hour deployment, which is longer than most current drones' battery life [28]. Security camera is an example of type-2 devices, which requires CNN-based analytics to extract detailed information only when alarm is triggered by motion or audio sensors of the camera. Similar to the drone case, our scheme can timely support the peak CNN requests when suspicious signs are detected.

Assuming the average frequency of CNN-required alarm in a security camera is one per 10 min, and each alarm requires 5 CNN requests, 720 sets of pre-computed keys are needed for one-day usage. As evaluated in Sect. 5.2, an IoT device with a 32 GB SD card is able to store enough keys to support 1600 requests for AlexNet. Such a result indicates 4.4 deployments and a 2.22-day support for type-1 and type-2 devices respectively when using AlexNet.

Note that, our scheme is designed for low-cost resource-constrained devices that require timely processing of moderate (or low) frequent CNN requests. For application scenarios that involve a large number of constant CNN requests, e.g., security critical surveillance systems, computational powerful devices are suggested to handle CNN requests directly at local.

5   Security and Performance Analysis

5.1   Security Analysis

In this section, we first prove the security of our online/offline encrypted used in *PPCL* and *PPFL*, and then show the security of the overall CNN inference in our setting as described in Sect. 3.1.

Theorem 1. *Given the ciphertext C of a γ-bit random message $\mathcal{M}$ generated using PPCL or PPFL, the probability for a probabilistic polynomial time (PPT) adversary $\mathcal{A}$ to output a correct guess for $\mathcal{M}$ shall have*

$$Pr[(\mathcal{M}^* = \mathcal{M})|\mathcal{C}] - Pr[\mathcal{M}^* = \mathcal{M}] \leq \epsilon \tag{6}$$

where ϵ is a negligible value in terms of computational secrecy [26], $\mathcal{M}^*$ is $\mathcal{A}$'s guess for $\mathcal{M}$, and $Pr[\mathcal{M}^* = \mathcal{M}]$ is the probability $\mathcal{A}$ makes a correct without ciphertext. Specifically, the corresponding ciphertext generated using PPCL or PPFL only introduces negligible additional advantages to $\mathcal{A}$ for making a correct guess of $\mathcal{M}$.

Proof. Given an input matrix $\mathcal{I}_d$ in *PPCL* (input vector $\mathcal{V}$ in *PPFL* respectively), each γ-bit element ($\mathcal{M}$) is encrypted by adding a λ-bit random number from uniform distribution (denoted as R) as shown in Eqs. 1 and 3.

To make a correct guess of $\mathcal{M}$ without the ciphertext, the adversary $\mathcal{A}$ has $Pr[\mathcal{M}^* = \mathcal{M}] = \frac{1}{2^\gamma}$, where $\mathcal{M}^*$ is $\mathcal{A}$'s guess for $\mathcal{M}$. By given the ciphertext $\mathcal{C} = \mathcal{M} + R$, $\mathcal{C} \in [0, 2^\gamma + 2^\lambda]$ there are two cases according to the value of $\mathcal{C}$

1. $2^\gamma \leq \mathcal{C} \leq 2^\lambda$. In this case, we have $Pr[\mathcal{M}^* = \mathcal{M}] = \frac{1}{2^\gamma}$, since $\mathcal{C}$ has the uniform looking as R in the range of $[2^\gamma, 2^\lambda]$.
2. $\mathcal{C} < 2^\gamma$ or $\mathcal{C} > 2^\lambda$. In this case, we have $Pr[\mathcal{M}^* = \mathcal{M}] = \frac{1}{\mathcal{C}}$ or $Pr[\mathcal{M}^* = \mathcal{M}] = \frac{1}{\mathcal{C}-2^\lambda}$, where $Pr[\mathcal{M}^* = \mathcal{M}] > \frac{1}{2^\gamma}$ This is because the distribution of $\mathcal{C}$ is affected by $\mathcal{M}$ and the total possible inputs are now reduced to $\mathcal{C}$ or $\mathcal{C} - 2^\lambda$.

The second case can happen when $R < 2^\gamma$ or $R > 2^\lambda - 2^\gamma$. As $Pr[R < 2^\gamma] = Pr[R > 2^\lambda - 2^\gamma] = \frac{2^\gamma}{2^\lambda}$, we have

$$Pr[R < 2^\gamma \text{ or } R > 2^\lambda - 2^\gamma] = Pr[R < 2^\gamma] + Pr[R > 2^\lambda - 2^\gamma] = \frac{1}{2^{\lambda-\gamma-1}}$$

Thus, to guarantee $\frac{1}{2^{\lambda-\gamma-1}}$ is a negligible probability, such as $\frac{1}{2^{128}}$, our scheme can set the security parameter λ according to size of input message, i.e., $\lambda - \gamma - 1 >$ 128. We now use $\epsilon = \frac{1}{2^{\lambda-\gamma-1}}$ to denote the negligible probability, and get the probability $Pr[(\mathcal{M}^* = \mathcal{M})|\mathcal{C}]$ as

$$Pr[(\mathcal{M}^* = \mathcal{M})|\mathcal{C}] \leq \frac{1}{2^\gamma} * (1 - \epsilon) + 1 * \epsilon = \frac{1}{2^\gamma} + (1 - \frac{1}{2^\gamma})\epsilon$$

where $\frac{1}{2^\gamma} * (1 - \epsilon)$ is the probability for a correct guess for $2^\gamma \leq C \leq 2^\lambda$, and the "1" in $1 * \epsilon$ is best probability for a correct guess $\mathcal{A}$ can have when $\mathcal{C} < 2^\gamma$ or $\mathcal{C} > 2^\lambda$. As a result, we get

$$Pr[(\mathcal{M}^* = \mathcal{M})|\mathcal{C}] - Pr[\mathcal{M}^* = \mathcal{M}] \leq (1 - \frac{1}{2^\gamma})\epsilon < \epsilon$$

As ϵ is negligible value, Theorem 1 is proved.

We now discuss the security of the overall CNN inference. Without loss of generality, we use layer-x to denote a convolutional layer or a fully-connected layer needs to be offloaded, $\mathcal{I}_x$ and $\mathcal{O}_x$ are the input and output of layer-x. With regards to the offloading of layer-x, $\mathcal{I}_x$ is encrypted using our online/offline encryption, which has been proved to be secure as shown in Theorem 1. When moving to the next layer, i.e., layer-(x+1), $\mathcal{O}_x$ is processed through non-linear layers by the IoT device to generate the input of layer-(x+1) as $\mathcal{I}_{(x+1)}$. Before being offloaded, each element $\mathcal{M}$ in $\mathcal{I}_{(x+1)}$ is encrypted by adding a random number R from uniform distribution. By selecting an appropriate security parameter λ, there will be only a negligible probability $\frac{1}{2^{\lambda-\gamma-1}}$ that $\mathcal{M}$ affects the uniform looking of ciphertext $\mathcal{M} + R$ as proved in Theorem 1, where γ is the length of $\mathcal{M}$ in bits. To be specific, by re-encrypting the input of each offloaded layer in our scheme, the negligible additional advantages introduced by each offloaded layer for the adversary to learn its input and output will not be accumulated for later layers in the CNN inference. Therefore, the security of the overall CNN inference is achieved in our scheme with proper selection of λ.

Table 2. Numerical analysis summary

Our scheme	Input size	IoT computation (FLOPs)		Offloaded cost to the edge (FLOPs)	Communication cost (elements)	Storage overhead (elements)
		Input encryption	Results decryption			
Convolutional	$n \times n \times D$	Dn^2	$H(\frac{n-k+2p}{s} + 1)^2$	$2DHk^2 \times (\frac{n-k+2p}{s} + 1)^2$	$Dn^2 + H(\frac{n-k+2p}{s} + 1)^2$	$Dn^2 + H(\frac{n-k+2p}{s} + 1)^2$
Fully-connected	m	m	T	$2mT$	$m + T$	$m + T$
Offloading using plaintext without privacy protection						
Convolutional	$n \times n \times D$	N/A	N/A	$2DHk^2 \times (\frac{n-k+2p}{s} + 1)^2$	$Dn^2 + H(\frac{n-k+2p}{s} + 1)^2$	N/A
Fully-connected	m	N/A	N/A	$2mT$	$m + T$	N/A

In this table: s is the stride, p is the size of padding, H is the number of kernels, $k \times k$ is the size of kernels of a convolutional layer; T is the number of neurons of a fully-connected layer. Each element is 20 Bytes.

5.2 Numerical Analysis

The numerical analysis of our scheme is summarized in Table 2. For expression simplicity, we use one floating point operation (FLOP) to denote an addition or a multiplication. We use an AlexNet [5] model as the study case for analysis.

Computational Cost. In the *Online* phase, the IoT device offloads compute-intensive convolutional layers and fully-connected layers to the edge devices. Given a general convolutional layer, the IoT device only needs to perform D matrix addition with Dn^2 FLOPs for encryption and $H(\frac{n-k+2p}{s}+1)^2$ FLOPs for decryption respectively. Compared with executing the same convolutional layer fully on the IoT device, which takes $2DHk^2(\frac{n-k+2p}{s}+1)^2$ FLOPs, our scheme significantly reduces real-time computation on the IoT device. It is worth to note that the stride s in a convolutional layer is typically a small value (e.g., 1 or 2). For a general fully-connected layer, the IoT device needs to perform m FLOPs for encryption and T FLOPs for decryption as shown in Eqs. 3 and 5 respectively. Differently, if the IoT device executes such a fully-connected layer at local, $2mT$ FLOPs are needed.

Besides the offloading of convolutional layers and fully-connected layers, the IoT device also needs to process non-linear layers locally. These non-linear layers are highly compute-efficient. Taking the widely adopted activation layer - ReLU as an example, it only requires $\frac{1}{2Dk^2}$ of its previous convolutional layer's cost or $\frac{1}{2m}$ of its previous fully-connected layer's cost.

Table 3. Example numerical analysis on AlexNet

	Parameters	Input size	IoT computation (FLOPs)	Offloaded cost (FLOPs)	Offloaded percentage	Communication cost	Storage overhead
Conv-1	$n=227$, $H=96$ $k=11$, $s=4$	227 × 227 ×3	444,987	210,830,400	99.79%	8691.15 KB	8691.15 KB
Conv-2	$n=27$, $H=256$ $k=5$, $s=1$	27 × 27 ×96	256,608	895,795,200	99.97%	5011.88 KB	5011.88 KB
Conv-3	$n=13$, $H=384$ $k=3$, $s=1$	13 × 13 ×256	108,160	299,040,768	99.96%	2112.50 KB	2112.50 KB
Conv-4	$n=13$, $H=384$ $k=3$, $s=1$	13 × 13 ×384	129,792	448,561,152	99.97%	2535.00 KB	2535.00 KB
Conv-5	$n=13$, $H=256$ $k=3$, $s=1$	13 × 13 ×384	108,160	299,040,768	99.96%	2112.50 KB	2112.50 KB
FC-1	$m=9216$, $T=4096$	9216	13,312	75,497,472	99.98%	260.00 KB	260.00 KB
FC-2	$m=4096$, $T=4096$	4096	8,192	33,554,432	99.98%	160.00 KB	160.00 KB
FC-3	$m=4096$, $T=1000$	4096	5,096	8,192,000	99.94%	99.53 KB	99.53 KB
Total Cost	N/A	N/A	1,074,307	2,270,512,192	99.95%	20.49 MB	20.49 MB

Computation for All Activation and Pooling Layers on the IoT: 650,080 FLOPs and 1,102,176 FLOPs

We now discuss the computational cost of our scheme using AlexNet. As shown in Table 3, our scheme can offload over 99.9% computational cost for convolutional layers and fully-connected layers, and only leaves lightweight encryption and decryption on the IoT device. Compared with the offloaded convolutional layers and fully-connected layers, the local execution of all non-linear layers only requires 0.08% operations for AlexNet. This result further affirms our motivation to offload convolutional layers and fully-connected layers.

With regards to the encrypted execution on the edge device, our scheme achieves the same computational cost as that directly using unencrypted data as shown in Table 2. This is because our encryption (Eqs. 1 and 3) in *PPCL* and *PPFL* schemes make the ciphertexts $Enc(\mathcal{I}_d)$ and $Enc(\mathcal{V})$ remain the same dimension as their plaintexts $\mathcal{I}_d$ and $\mathcal{V}$. Such a decent property guarantees real-time computational performance on the edge device.

In the *Offline* phase, the IoT device owner first prepares encryption keys by choosing random matrices for convolutional layers and fully-connected layers that will be offloaded. Meanwhile, the owner will take these encryption keys as inputs for their corresponding convolutional layers or fully-connected layers to obtain results as the decryption keys. In Sect. 6, we show that the offline phase can be efficiently executed using a regular laptop.

Communication Cost. The communication cost of our scheme comes from the transmission of encrypted inputs and outputs of convolutional layers and fully-connected layers. In our implementation, we use 160-bit random numbers (i.e., $\lambda = 160$) during all encryption processes in Eqs. 1 and 3. Thus, each element in the ciphertext (a matrix or a vector) is 20-Byte long. To offload a convolutional layer with a $n \times n \times D$ input, the IoT device first sends its corresponding ciphertext contains D encrypted matrices with Dn^2 elements in total. Then, H encrypted result matrices are received from the edge device with each size of $(\frac{n-k+2p}{s}+1) \times (\frac{n-k+2p}{s}+1)$. With regards to the offloading of a fully-connected layer that takes a m-dimensional vector as input, the IoT device needs to send a m-dimensional vector as encrypted input and receive a T-dimensional vector as encrypted output from the edge device. As shown in Table 3, the communication cost for an offloading of the AlexNet is 20.49MB, which can be efficiently handled under the edge computing environment [29].

Storage Overhead. For the offloading of a convolutional layer with a $n \times n \times D$ input, the IoT device needs to store D random matrices with n^2 elements each as the encryption keys, and H matrices with size of $(\frac{n-k+2p}{s}+1) \times (\frac{n-k+2p}{s}+1)$ as the decryption keys. To offload a fully-connected layer with a m-dimensional vector as input, a m-dimensional vector and a T-dimensional vector need to be pre-stored as the encryption key and decryption key respectively. Table 3 shows the offloading of an AlexNet request needs 20.49 MB storage overhead. With the rise of IoT devices, low-power-consumption SD memory card has become an excellent fit to economically extend the storage of IoT devices [30], which usually have more than 32 GB capacity.

6   Prototype Evaluation

We implemented a prototype of our scheme using Python 2.7. In our implementation, TensorFlow and Keras libraries are adopted to support CNNs. The resource-constrained IoT device is a Raspberry Pi (Model A) with Raspbian Debian 7, which has 700 MHz single-core processor, 256 MB memory, and 32 GB SD card storage. The edge device and the IoT device owner is a Macbook Pro laptop with OS X 10.13.3, 3.1 GHz Intel Core i7 processor, 16 GB memory, and 512 GB SSD. The IoT device and the edge device are connected using WiFi in the same subnet. We use the well-known ImageNet [21] as the dataset for the evaluation of AlexNet. The security parameter λ is set as 160 in our implementation. We also implemented a privacy-preserving AlexNet using CryptoNets [10] for comparison.

Table 4. Experimental evaluation results on AlexNet

	IoT without offloading (second)	Our scheme				
		IoT computation (second)	Edge computation (second)	Communication (second)	Total (second)	Speedup
Conv-1	10.01	0.037	0.0103	0.849	0.896	11.17×
Conv-2	40.68	0.0405	0.0435	0.489	0.573	70.99×
Conv-3	19.93	0.0437	0.013	0.206	0.263	75.78×
Conv-4	29.78	0.0498	0.0184	0.248	0.316	94.24×
Conv-5	19.88	0.0420	0.0127	0.206	0.261	76.17×
FC-1	2.22	0.0013	0.0043	0.025	0.031	71.61×
FC-2	1.08	0.001	0.0025	0.016	0.019	56.84×
FC-3	0.27	0.0008	0.0009	0.01	0.012	22.5×
Non-linear	1.137	1.137	N/A	N/A	1.137	N/A
Total Cost	124.99	1.353	0.106	2.049	3.508	35.63×

Efficiency - Online Phase: We summarize the evaluation results of a real-time AlexNet inference task in Table 4. Compared with executing the entire inference task on the IoT device, our scheme significantly reduces execution time from 124.99 s to 3.508 s, which indicates a 35.63× speedup rate. More importantly, with the increasing complexity of convolutional layers and fully-connected layers, our scheme retains or increases the high speedup rate as shown in the last column of Table 4. Taking AlexNet as an example, the highest speedup rates for them are all achieved with these more complex layers. Therefore, our scheme is promising to be scaled up to support more complex CNN architectures according to practical requirements.

It is noteworthy that the communication occupies 58.4% (2.049 s/3.508 s) cost of an offloaded inference task in our scheme. In our implementation, we use a wireless network with 10 MB/s transmission speed between the IoT device and the edge device. In a real-world scenario, the devices are likely to be connected via wired or cellular connection, which allows a higher transmission speed than our experimental environment. Moreover, the upcoming 5 G era for MEC environment will significantly improve the transmission speed [29] and further optimize the communication performance of our scheme.

Table 5. Comparison between our scheme and cryptonnets in first convolutional layer of AlexNet

	Our scheme (seconds)	A-CryptoNets (seconds)
Encryption	0.012	459.93
Convolution	0.0103	625.86
Decryption	0.025	N/A

6.1   Evaluation Results

Efficiency - Offline Phase: To generate the encryption and decryption keys for the execution of one AlexNet request, our scheme only requires 114 ms for the IoT device owner. While each set of keys will only be used for one request, the owner can efficiently compute more than 2600 sets of keys for AlexNet using 5 min.

To compare our scheme with homomorphic encryption-based solution [10] for CNN inference, we also implemented AlexNet using the CryptoNets scheme proposed in [10], denoted as A-CryptoNets. During our implementation, we use the same linear approximation and YASHE cryptosystem [31] as that in [10]. Table 5 shows the cost of processing the first convolutional layer in our scheme and A-CryptoNets. Due to the large input size required in AlexNet, A-CryptoNets requires 459.93 s for encrypting the input data on the IoT device, and 625.86 s for the convolutional operations on the edge device. This level of computational cost makes CryptoNets become hardly to satisfy time-sensitive tasks with complex CNN inference. As a comparison, our scheme can handle the first convolutional layer using 0.047 s. Even considering the entire AlexNet inference task, our scheme only requires 3.508 s to complete.

Energy Consumption: Compared with fully executing AlexNet inference tasks on the IoT device with high energy consumption, our scheme significantly saves the energy consumption for computation of the IoT device while introducing slight extra energy consumption for communication. In our evaluation, the IoT device (Raspberry Pi Model A) is powered by a 5 V micro-USB adapter. The voltage and current is measured using a Powerjive USB multimeter [32] and the power is calculated by the multiplication of voltage and current. Table 6 shows the average IoT power consumption under different IoT device status.

We observe that the network connection is a major power cost in IoT device. An idle IoT device with network connection can have a comparable power cost (0.78 W) as executing AlexNet locally without network connection (0.81 W). This local AlexNet execution power indicates an energy consumption of 101.24 J when fully executing an inference task on the IoT device in 124.99 s. Differently, our scheme reduces the computation time on the IoT device to 1.353 s (1.59 J energy consumption) with 2.049 s extra communication (2.90 J energy consumption). Therefore, our scheme can save IoT energy consumption by $\frac{101.24-(1.58+2.91)}{101.24} =$ 95.56%.

Table 6. Power and energy consumption evaluation

	IoT local executing AlexNet without network connection	Idle IoT with network connection	Our scheme	
			IoT computation	IoT communication
Power (W)	0.81	0.78	1.17	1.42
Energy (J)	101.24	N/A	1.58	2.91

Accuracy: To validate that there is no accuracy loss in our scheme, we also implemented original AlexNet without privacy protection as baseline. By using the same parameters, we achieve exact the same accuracy (80.1%) as that obtained using original AlexNet [5] without privacy protection. On one hand, no approximation for non-linear layers is required in our scheme. On the other hand, the random noise introduced in our encryption can be perfectly eliminated during the decryption process.

7 Related Work

The problem of privacy-preserving neural network inference (or prediction) has been studied in recent years under the cloud computing environment [10–18]. These works focus on the "machine learning as a service" scenario, wherein the cloud server has a trained neural network model and users submitted encrypted data for predication. One recent line of research uses somewhat or fully homomorphic encryption (HE) to evaluate the neural network model over encrypted inputs after approximating non-linear layers in the neural network [10–12]. Combining multiple secure computation techniques (e.g., HE, Secure multi-party computation (MPC), oblivious transfer (OT)) is another trend to support privacy-preserving neural network inference [13,15,16,18]. The idea behind these mixed protocols is to evaluate scalar products using HE and non-linear activation functions using MPC techniques. In particular, SecureML [13] utilized the mixed-protocol framework proposed in ABY [16], which involves arithmetic sharing, boolean sharing, and Yao's garbled circuits, to implement both privacy-preserving training and inference in a two-party computation setting. In [18], MiniONN is proposed to support privacy-preserving inference by transforming neural networks to the corresponding oblivious version with the Single Instruction Multiple Data (SMID) batch technique. Trusted third-party is invoked in Chameleon [17] and hence greatly reducing the computation and bandwidth cost for a privacy-preserving inference. In [15] GAZELLE is proposed by leveraging lattice-based packed additive homomorphic encryption (PAHE) and two-party secure computation techniques. GAZELLE deploys PAHE in an automorphism manner to achieve fast matrix multiplication/convolution and thus boosting the final run-time efficiency. A multi-sever solution, named SecureNN, is proposed in [14], which greatly improves the privacy-preserving inference performance, i.e., $42.4\times$ faster than MiniONN [18], and $27\times$, $3.68\times$ faster than Chameleon [17] and GAZELLE [15].

While the performance of evaluating neural network over encrypted data for inference keeps being improved, the existing research works only focus on small-scale neural networks. Taking the state-of-the-art SecureNN [14] as an example, the network-A evaluated (also used by [13]) only requires about 1.2 million FLOPs for an inference, which costs 3.1 s with wireless communication in their 3PC setting. As a comparison, the AlexNet evaluated in our scheme contains 2.27 billion FLOPs for one inference, which costs 3.508 s in our scheme with similar wireless transmission speed. It is also worth to note that SecureNN utilizes powerful cloud server (36 vCPU, 132 ECU, 60 GB memory) for evaluation, whereas the edge computing device in this paper is just a regular laptop computer. Scaling up the network size is not a trivial task. For example, compared with the type-A network in [15], its type-C network with $500\times$ multiplication increases the computational cost and communication cost to $430\times$ and $592\times$. Therefore, how to support real-time execution of complex CNN inference tasks over encrypted IoT data remains as an open problem.

8   Conclusion

In this paper, we proposed a novel online/offline scheme that enables resource-constrained IoT devices to efficiently execute CNN requests with privacy protection. Our scheme uniquely designs a lightweight online/offline encryption scheme to provide private, efficient and accurate offloading of CNN inference tasks. By discovering the fact that linear operations in CNNs over input and random noise can be separated, our scheme pre-computes decryption keys to remove random noises and thus boosting the performance of real-time CNN requests. By integrating local edge devices, our scheme ameliorates the network latency and service availability issue. Our scheme also makes the privacy-preserving operation over encrypted data on the edge device as efficient as that over unencrypted data. Moreover, the privacy protection in our scheme does not introduce any accuracy loss to the CNN inference. Thorough security analysis is provided to show that our scheme is secure in the defined threat model. Extensive numerical analysis as well as prototype implementation over the well-known CNN architectures and datasets demonstrate the practical performance of our scheme.

References

1. Verhelst, M., Moons, B.: Embedded deep neural network processing: algorithmic and processor techniques bring deep learning to IoT and edge devices. IEEE Solid-State Circ. Mag. **9**(4), 55–65 (2017)
2. Kodali, S., Hansen, P., Mulholland, N., Whatmough, P., Brooks, D., Wei, G.Y.: Applications of deep neural networks for ultra low power IoT. In 2017 IEEE International Conference on Computer Design (ICCD), pp. 589–592, November 2017
3. Burns, M.: Arm chips with Nvidia AI could change the Internet of Things (2018). https://techcrunch.com/2018/03/27/arm-chips-will-with-nvidia-ai-could-change-the-internet-of-things/. Accessed July 2018
4. Mohammadi, M., Al-Fuqaha, A., Sorour, S., Guizani, M.: Deep learning for IoT big data and streaming analytics: a survey (2017). arXiv:1712.04301
5. Krizhevsky, A., Sutskever, I., Hinton, G.E.: ImageNet classification with deep convolutional neural networks. In: Proceedings of the 25th International Conference on Neural Information Processing Systems NIPS 2012, vol. 1, pp. 1097–1105, Curran Associates Inc., USA (2012)
6. Schroff, F., Kalenichenko, D., Philbin, J.: FaceNet: a unified embedding for face recognition and clustering. In: 2015 IEEE Conference on Computer Vision and Pattern Recognition (CVPR), pp. 815–823, June 2015
7. He, K., Zhang, X., Ren, S., Sun, J.: Deep residual learning for image recognition. In: 2016 IEEE Conference on Computer Vision and Pattern Recognition (CVPR), pp. 770–778, June 2016
8. Zhou, J., Cao, Z., Dong, X., Vasilakos, A.V.: Security and privacy for cloud-based IoT: challenges. IEEE Commun. Mag. **55**(1), 26–33 (2017)
9. Shi, W., Cao, J., Zhang, Q., Li, Y., Xu, L.: Edge computing: vision and challenges. IEEE Internet Things J. **3**(5), 637–646 (2016)
10. Gilad-Bachrach, R., Dowlin, N., Laine, K., Lauter, K.E., Naehrig, M., Wernsing, J.: CryptoNets: applying neural networks to encrypted data with high throughput and accuracy. In: Proceedings of the 33nd International Conference on Machine Learning, ICML 2016, New York City, NY, USA, 19–24 June, pp. 201–210 (2016)
11. Chabanne, H., de Wargny, A., Milgram, J., Morel, C., Prouff, E.: Privacy-preserving classification on deep neural network. IACR Cryptology ePrint Archive 2017/35 (2017)
12. Hesamifard, E., Takabi, H., Ghasemi, M.: CryptoDL: deep neural networks over encrypted data. CoRR, abs/1711.05189 (2017)
13. Mohassel, P., Zhang, Y.: SecureML: a system for scalable privacy-preserving machine learning. In: 2017 IEEE Symposium on Security and Privacy (SP), pp. 19–38, May 2017
14. Wagh, S., Gupta, D., Chandran, N.: SecureNN: efficient and private neural network training. (PETS 2019), February 2019
15. Juvekar, C., Vaikuntanathan, V., Chandrakasan, A.: {GAZELLE}: a low latency framework for secure neural network inference. In: 27th {USENIX} Security Symposium ({USENIX} Security 2018), pp. 1651–1669 (2018)
16. Mohassel, P., Rindal, P.: ABY 3: a mixed protocol framework for machine learning. In: Proceedings of the 2018 ACM SIGSAC Conference on Computer and Communications Security, CCS 2018, pp. 35–52, ACM. New York (2018)
17. Riazi, M.S., Weinert, C., Tkachenko, O., Songhori, E.M., Schneider, T., Koushanfar, F.: Chameleon: a hybrid secure computation framework for machine learning applications. In: Proceedings of the 2018 on Asia Conference on Computer and Communications Security, ASIACCS 2018, pp. 707–721, ACM. New York (2018)

18. Liu, J., Juuti, M., Lu, Y., Asokan, N.: Oblivious neural network predictions via MiniONN transformations. In Proceedings of the 2017 ACM SIGSAC Conference on Computer and Communications Security, CCS 2017, pp. 619–631, ACM. New York (2017)
19. Mario, C., Mathieu, P.: Benchmarking Paillier Encryption (2018). https://medium.com/snips-ai/benchmarking-paillier-encryption-15631a0b5ad8. Accessed July 2018
20. Shi, W., Cao, J., Zhang, Q., Li, Y., Lanyu, X.: Edge computing: vision and challenges. IEEE Internet Things J. 3(5), 637–646 (2016)
21. Deng, J., Dong, W., Socher, R., Li, L.-J., Li, K., Fei-Fei, L.: ImageNet: a large-scale hierarchical image database. In: CVPR 2009 (2009)
22. Wikipedia. Convolutional neural network. https://en.wikipedia.org/wiki/Convolutional_neural_network. Accessed July 2018
23. Phan N.H., Wu, X., Hu, H., Dou, D.: Adaptive laplace mechanism: differential privacy preservation in deep learning. In: Proceedings of the 2017 IEEE International Conference on Data Mining, ICDM 2017. IEEE (2017)
24. Abadi, M., et al.: Deep learning with differential privacy. In: Proceedings of the 2016 ACM SIGSAC Conference on Computer and Communications Security, CCS 2016, pp. 308–318, ACM. New York (2016)
25. Cong, J., Xiao, B.: Minimizing computation in convolutional neural networks. In: Wermter, S., et al. (eds.) ICANN 2014. LNCS, vol. 8681, pp. 281–290. Springer, Cham (2014). https://doi.org/10.1007/978-3-319-11179-7_36
26. Katz, J., Lindell, Y.: Introduction to Modern Cryptography, Chapt. 3.3. Chapman & Hall/CRC (2007)
27. Lee, J., Wang, J., Crandall, D., Šabanović, S., Fox, G.: Real-time, cloud-based object detection for unmanned aerial vehicles. In: 2017 First IEEE International Conference on Robotic Computing (IRC), pp. 36–43, April 2017
28. Airdata UAV. Drone Flight Stats (2018). https://airdata.com/blog/2017/drone-flight-stats-part-1. Accessed July 2018
29. Rimal, B.P., Van, D.P., Maier, M.: Mobile edge computing empowered fiber-wireless access networks in the 5G era. IEEE Commun. Mag. 55(2), 192–200 (2017)
30. Paul, N.: Now trending: SD memory cards (2018). https://www.sdcard.org/press/thoughtleadership/180118_Now_Trending_SD_Memory_Cards.html. Accessed July 2018
31. Bos, J.W., Lauter, K., Loftus, J., Naehrig, M.: Improved security for a ring-based fully homomorphic encryption scheme. In: Stam, M. (ed.) IMACC 2013. LNCS, vol. 8308, pp. 45–64. Springer, Heidelberg (2013). https://doi.org/10.1007/978-3-642-45239-0_4
32. Dramble, R.P.: Power Consumption Benchmarks (2018). http://www.pidramble.com/wiki/benchmarks/power-consumption. Accessed Apr 2019

POKs Based Secure and Energy-Efficient Access Control for Implantable Medical Devices

Chenglong Fu[1]([✉]), Xiaojiang Du[1], Longfei Wu[2], Qiang Zeng[3],
Amr Mohamed[4], and Mohsen Guizani[4]

[1] Temple University, Philadelphia, PA 19122, USA
{chenglong.fu,xjdu}@temple.edu
[2] Fayetteville State University, Fayetteville, NC 28301, USA
lwu@uncfsu.edu
[3] University of South Carolina, Columbia, SC 29208, USA
zeng1@cse.sc.edu
[4] Qatar University, Doha, Qatar
{amrm,mguizani}@ieee.org

Abstract. Implantable medical devices (IMDs), such as pacemakers, implanted cardiac defibrillators and neurostimulators are medical devices implanted into patients' bodies for monitoring physiological signals and performing medical treatments. Many IMDs have built-in wireless communication modules to facilitate data collecting and device reprogramming by external programmers. The wireless communication brings significant conveniences for advanced applications such as real-time and remote monitoring but also introduces the risk of unauthorized wireless access. The absence of effective access control mechanisms exposes patients' life to cyber attacks. In this paper, we present a lightweight and universally applicable access control system for IMDs. By leveraging Physically Obfuscated Keys (POKs) as the hardware root of trust, provable security is achieved based on standard cryptographic primitives while attaining high energy efficiency. In addition, barrier-free IMD access under emergent situations is realized by utilizing the patient's biometrical information. We evaluate our proposed scheme through extensive security analysis and a prototype implementation, which demonstrate our work's superiority on security and energy efficiency.

Keywords: Implantable medical devices · Physical Obfuscation Keys · Access control

1 Introduction

Implantable medical devices (IMDs) are electronic devices that can be either partially or fully implanted into patients' bodies for collecting patients' physiological data and delivering timely treatment. With advantages of providing

S. Chen et al. (Eds.): SecureComm 2019, LNICST 304, pp. 105–125, 2019.
https://doi.org/10.1007/978-3-030-37228-6_6

ongoing diagnosis and treatment, IMDs have been pervasively used for treating chronic medical disorders and are proved to be effective in coping with sudden deaths caused by cardiac arrests and ventricular arrhythmia [33]. Most IMDs are equipped with radio modules for wireless communication with external devices called *programmers* which are used by physicians for data exporting and IMD reprogramming. However, the wireless communication brings attackers extra arsenal to threaten the users' lives with cyber attacks. Jay Radcliffe and Branaby Jack have demonstrated the feasibility to remotely hack the insulin pump in [36] and [1] respectively. Coincidentally, former U.S. Vice President Dick Cheney had the wireless connection of his implanted defibrillator disabled due to the concern of cyber attacks launched by terrorists [18].

Although countermeasures against unauthorized IMD access are critical, the design is challenging due to two technical difficulties. First, requirements for utility and security are conflicting. On the one hand, the scheme must be robust enough to defeat all malicious access. On the other hand, during the emergent situation, first-aiders may need to access or reprogram a patient's IMD immediately without any hindering caused by security mechanisms. Second, the IMD security mechanism must be extremely energy efficient because IMDs are implanted into human's bodies via surgeries and rely on their embedded batteries to operate many years.

To cope with these security problems of medical devices, a series of research works are proposed [22,23,44]. Recent researches tend to address the first difficulty with the *touch-to-access* principle which is based on a reasonable assumption that attackers having physical contact with victims can harm them directly (rather than utilizing IMDs). Following this, many proposed solutions [16,40,46] implement simple access control policies by verifying physical access or proximity for IMD access attempts. However, these proposed works have three drawbacks. (1) Their enforcement of the touch-to-access policy is *not* based on provable security and may be breached by newly-developed attack techniques [39]. (2) They assume IMDs are equipped with special sensing or communication capabilities like ECG measurement and piezo broadcasting. (3) Simple touch-to-access access control policy cannot deal with complicated scenarios like hierarchical privileges.

Our goal is to design an IMD access control solution that provides provable security without high energy consumption. To that end, we present a *Physical Obfuscation Keys* (POKs) based IMD access control system. Leveraging a POKs enabled IC card for secure credential storage, we design a lightweight access control protocol with minimal computation and communication overhead on IMDs. For emergent access, We follow the touch-to-access principle and verify physical contact by requiring the patient's IC card and iris image. Our design is built on standard cryptographic operations to provide provable security and does not need any special sensing or communication capability of the IMD. Moreover, an online *Hospital Authentication Server* (HAS) is integrated in our system to authenticate the programmer's identity and realize the dynamic and fine-grained access control.

In summary, our work has the following contributions:

- *A novel POKs based key agreement scheme:* We innovatively use the POKs enabled IC card to design a secure key agreement scheme for IMDs. In our proposed protocol, computation-intensive operations are offloaded to the IC card and the Hospital Authentication Server to reduce the energy consumption of the IMD.
- *Biometrics based emergent access:* We design a highly secure method that uses the patient's iris for barrier-free emergent access.
- *Real-device implementation:* We implement the IMD's logic on the TelosB sensor mote, analyze the security properties of the design, and evaluate the energy consumption to show our design's advantage of energy efficiency as well as its speed and memory consumption.

The rest of the paper is organized as follows. We first describe some background on POKs and our key generation in Sect. 2. Then we present the system and threat model in Sect. 3. Our access control scheme for normal access and emergent access is described in Sects. 4 and 5, respectively. After that, we analyze the security of our work in Sect. 6 and the results of the overhead consumption evaluation are presented in Sect. 7. The review of the related works is in Sect. 8. Finally, we conclude in Sect. 9.

2 Background and Key Generation

2.1 Background: Physical Obfuscation Keys

Modern crytographic primitives have their security based on the confidentiality of secret credentials. Once the credentials are uncovered, attackers can maliciously impersonate legitimate users or retrieve sensitive information from encrypted communications. Thus, secure secret key storage components such are critical to the security of all kinds of applications. However, recently developed physical tampering attacks such as micro-probing attack and electrical glitching attack have already showed their effectiveness on retrieving secret credentials kept in statical storage devices.

To defeat these physical attacks targeting secret credentials, researches propose the Physical Unclonable Functions (PUFs) [37] as a hardware-based cryptographic component for authentication and secret key storage. PUFs rely on unique physical characteristic variation as the secret challenge-response pattern. When given an input, the PUF responses with a corresponding unpredictable output. These patterns are determined by the PUF's unique and unclonable physical properties such as the integrated circuit's gate propagation delay [30] and SRAM cell initial status [24] which are introduced by uncontrollable variations during the IC fabrication process. Generally, PUFs are divided into two broad categories: strong PUFs and weak PUFs, differing in the number of available Challenge-Response Pairs (CRPs). Typically, strong PUFs can have a large set of CRPs while weak PUFs only support a limited number of CRPs. The Physically Obfuscated Keys (POKs) [15] is an application of weak PUFs that could be considered as a secure key storage technique. The appearance of this technique brings a reliable solution to protect the secret key from being compromised by invasive side-channel attacks. Recent POKs-based secure key generators have reached a bit error rate of less than 1% [26] and require no special processing during the chip fabrication, making it a cost-efficient alternative to expensive secure storage components like EEPROM.

Bringer *et al.* make a further step by proposing POKs compatible cryptographic algorithms [3] to defeat the runtime **memory scanning** attacks which aim to steal the credentials after they are loaded to the memory. They achieve it by splitting scalar product and exclusive OR (XOR), two basic operations used in the linear-feedback shift register (LFSR), into multiple steps. During each step, only part of the secret stored in the POKs are loaded to the memory with all intermediate results *obfuscated*. Based on the specially designed LFSR, secure POKs enabled stream ciphers like Trivium [6] is realized. Therefore, compared with the traditional primitives, POKs enabled cryptographic operations are resilient to memory scanning attacks. Moreover, **invasive tampering attacks** that try to unpack the chip will change physical features the keys rely on and thus destroy the secret inside it permanently. Thus, revealing keys via invasive tampering attacks also fail.

2.2   Key Pair Generator

For multi-party communication, key management (e.g., [10–12, 45]) is important for medical and IoT devices. We design a key generator to synchronously generate temporary keys for each access. As shown in Fig. 1, the key generator has the input of a master key and an initial value fed into a Trivium stream generator. During each access, 256 bits are truncated from the output stream and then be processed by the SHA-256 module to get a 256-bit temporary key. In the system, we have two different long-term master keys Key_1 and Key_2 to derive two temporary keys SA_i and SB_i. Key_1 and Key_2 are stored by the patient's IC card and the HAS (Hospital Authentication Server), respectively, and the IMD stores the two master keys.

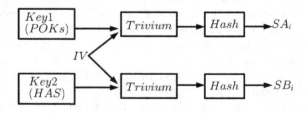

Fig. 1. The key pair generator. SA_i and SB_i are generated by patient's IC card and the hospital authentication server respectively.

On the IC card, we have a POK module to store the master key Key_1 and a POKs-based Trivium generator to generate temporary keys. As illustrated in the Fig. 2, the IC card has the POK module, the Trivium stream generator, and the CPU packed on one chip. The secret stored by the POK module can only be accessed by the Trivium generator which outputs the bitstream directly to the embedded CPU for cryptographic operations. The One-Time Programming (OTP) interface [31] is added to enable one-time access to the secret during the IC card commissioning. After the first access, the OTP interface is physically disabled to prevent any direct access to the master key.

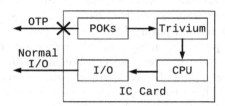

Fig. 2. IC card structure.

The doctor's IC card also has a POK module to store the master key Key_3 that is used for generating 256-bit message authentication code (MAC). The MAC algorithm is based on LFSR as described in [3], which is inherently resistant to memory probe attacks and invasive attacks.

3   System Overview and Threat Model

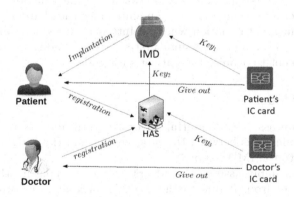

Fig. 3. The enrollment phase.

3.1   System Overview

As shown in Fig. 3, our access control system involves the following components: the IMD, the programmer, the Hospital Authentication Server (HAS), and IC cards for patients and doctors. IC cards are contact cards with embedded POKs modules. The HAS is a centralized authentication server that is expected to be common in modern hospital and e-health systems. Two pre-defined master keys are shared by the patient's IC card and the HAS with the IMD respectively. Each master key is used as the secret seed to generate different temporary keys for each access. Then the programmer authentication and the session key generation are all conducted with the temporary keys.

In our design, the patient's and doctor's IC cards are commissioned as the representation of their identities via the enrollment phase. During the regular access, the doctor firstly plugs his IC card into the programmer to prove his identity to the HAS. Then, the programmer forwards the challenge message received from the IMD to the IC card and the HAS. Finally, the programmer generates the correct response message with the help of the IC card and the HAS and establishes a secure communication channel with the IMD. The HAS enforces fine-grain access control policies according to the doctor's identity and the access operation type.

3.2   Assumptions

For devices, we assume the IMD and IC card are capable of running basic cryptographic operations including SHA-256 and HMAC. While the programmer has Internet access for communicating with the Hospital Authentication Server (HAS). The IC cards are contact cards without wireless communication capability. We can safely assume IC cards are taken with patients and physicians all the time considering its small size easy maintenance (no charging required).

As for the emergent situation when no Internet connection and valid physician's IC card are available, we assume first-aiders can find the patient's IC card have the equipment to acquire the patient's iris code.

3.3   Threat Model

In this paper, we assume a powerful adversary with abilities to eavesdrop all wireless communications between the programmer and the IMD and send arbitrary messages to the IMD remotely.

Also, we reasonably assume the adversary cannot replicate the IC card or retrieve the secret from it due to the POKs's unclonable feature. The secret keys stored in the IMD is also inaccessible because the IMDs are implanted into patients' body and are physically inaccessible. Also, the HAS is considered as secure because the HAS has plenty of resources for enforcing security schemes and is managed by professional security administrators.

4   The Authentication Protocol

In this section, we present our IMD authentication and access control protocol, which is based on the a pair of temporary keys SA_i and SB_i and the doctor's master key Key_3. The protocol is composed of four phases: Enrollment, Service Request, Authorization, and Session Establishment. The following parties are involved: an Implantable Medical Device (IMD), a Hospital authentication Server (HAS), a Programmer (with the doctor's IC card plugged in), and the patient's IC card. Table 1 summarizes all the symbols and notations used in our description. Figures 3 and 4 illustrate the enrollment phase and all the following phases, respectively.

Table 1. Symbols and notations.

Notation	Description
Key_3	Doctor's master key for UMAC
SA_i, SB_i	256-bits temporary key pair
R	32-bits Service Request Code
i	32-bits counter
ID_I, ID_P	32-bits identity for patient and doctor
T_1	32-bits Time stamp
TS	32-bits Time window threshold
T	Current time
$token(i)$	Token for the ith cycle
$S_{key}(i)$	Session key for the ith cycle

4.1   Enrollment

During the enrollment phase, all parties in our protocol are initialized through two independent steps as shown in Fig. 3.

Doctor's Registration. Since we assume the programmer is not bound with the doctor's identity. Hence, registration is required to set up accounts for doctors and link their identities with IC cards.

The doctor's account should contain detailed profile information and the master key Key_3 extracted from the doctor's IC card through the One-time programming (OTP) interface. Aside from this, a corresponding identification number ID_P and password are also configured for login through the programmer. Based on the profile information, HAS can check doctors' privilege of accessing a certain patient's IMD for carrying out dynamic access control. For example, all doctors that are in charge of a certain patient have the permission to export monitoring data from the patient's ICD, but only the chief physician can reconfigure it.

Patient's Registration. Similar to the doctors' registration, patients also need to set up accounts on the HAS which contain their profile information, the initial value (IV) and the master key Key_2.

Before the implantation, the doctor extracts the master key Key_1 from a new IC card through the One-time programming (OTP) interface and then fusing the OTP to prevent further access. After that, two master keys and IV are loaded into the IMD and the cycle counter i is set to 1. Once the implantation is completed, the IC card is delivered to the patient.

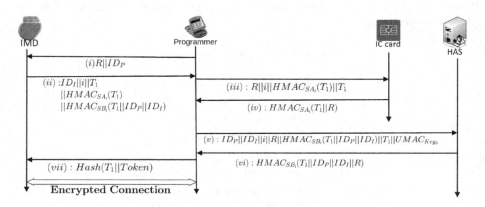

Fig. 4. The authentication workflow.

4.2   Service Request

During normal access circumstances, a patient is conscious, and the wireless connection to the Internet is available. The doctor first inserts his/her IC card into the programmer and the programmer then logs in with his account name and password. Once the doctor's identity is successfully verified, a TLS session between the programmer and HAS is established to protect all communications between them, and the session is tagged by the doctor's identity number ID_P. Thereafter, with the patient's permission, the doctor has the patient's IC card inserted into the programmer.

As shown by step (i) in Fig. 4, the service request is initiated by the programmer sending the request code and the doctor's identity number to the IMD. When the IMD wakes up from periodical hibernation, it first retrieves the cycle counter i and produce the current temporal key pair SA_i and SB_i. Then, a response containing the patient's identity number ID_I, counter i, current timestamp T_1, and two HMACs over these variables are sent back to the programmer (step (ii)) as the challenge message.

4.3   Authorization

When the programmer receives a response from the IMD in step (ii), it forwards the two HMACs to the IC card and HAS respectively, as marked by step (iii) and (v) in Fig. 4. Specifically, for message (v), the programmer makes use of the doctor's IC card to generate a UMAC (a universal hashing based message authentication [2]) for the entire message with the master key Key_3 as a proof of the doctor's identity.

For the patient's IC card, it generate the temporary key SA_i according to the received cycle counter i. With SA_i, it verifies the received HMAC on T_1. If the verification succeeds, the IC card sends back the HMAC on the timestamp T_1 cascaded by request code R and increases its counter i by 1.

Similarly, the HAS generates the temporary key SB_i and verifies the HMAC of concatenated timestamp T_i and two identities: ID_I and ID_P. If the HMAC is valid, the HAS performs following checks:

1. Check the temporal validity indicated by T_1 and time window length TS.
2. Check the doctor's identity by verifying the UMAC with corresponding Key_3.
3. Check the doctor's privilege level of accessing the the IMD with the identity ID_I.

If all checks are successful, the HAS sends back the HMAC of a timestamp, two identity numbers and the request code R as described by the step (vi) in Fig. 4. Finally, HAS's cycle counter i is increased by 1.

4.4   Session Establishment

After the programmer receives the returned HMACs from the patient's IC card and the HAS, the access token is generated by performing XOR operation on the two HMACs as described in (1). Then the programmer sends the hash of timestamp T_1 and the token back to IMD (step (vii)).

$$token(i) = HMAC_{SA_i}(T_1||R)$$
$$\oplus HMAC_{SB_i}(T_1||ID_P||ID_I||R) \tag{1}$$

On receiving the response from the programmer, the IMD first records the current time T and checks whether the response is returned within the time window TS. If the response is timely enough, the IMD generates the token $token'$ (as shown in (1)) by itself independently (the IMD possesses both two master keys to produce both two temporary keys SA_i and SB_i). After that, the IMD compares the received $Hash(T_1||Token)$ with the generated $Hash(T_1||Token')$. If two results match, the programmer is authenticated and authorized to access the IMD, and the cycle counter in the IMD is increased by 1. Otherwise, the IMD discards all completed steps and goes back to listening mode. Once the authentication and authorization is completed, a secret number $SKey(i)$ is generated independently by the IMD and the programmer. The two parties calculate the XOR of two hashed HMACs as described in (2). The secret key can be used as the seed for deriving session keys to encrypt the communication between the programmer and the IMD.

$$SKey(i) = Hash(HMAC_{SA_i}(T_1\|R))$$
$$\oplus Hash(HMAC_{SB_i}(T_1\|ID_P\|ID_I\|R)) \tag{2}$$

5   Enhancement

5.1   Emergent Access

Apart from the normal access control described in Sect. 4, special access mode is necessary for the emergent situation when the patient is unconscious and require emergency care. Under this situation, first aiders may need to access the patient's IMD to measurement the patient's physiological signal and perform timely treatment. However, the response message generated by the HAS may be inaccessible due to the lack of valid privilege or the absence of the Internet connections. To address this problem, we design an offline emergent access control scheme to use the temporal keys SB_i cached inside the patient's IC card as an alternative of the HAS. For the security concern, the cached keys are obfuscated using the patient's iris code.

The HAS can generate patient specified number of temporal keys for future authentication rounds in advance and load them into the patient's IC card during the patient's normal visit to the medical center. With the cached temporal key SB_i, the programmer can independently generate the correct response message as the step (vi) in Fig. 4. When cached temporal keys are invalidated by regular accesses, the patient can easily the cached updated by asking the HAS to generate more.

5.2   Biometric Encryption of the Cached Temporary Key

The drawback of the cached keys is the possible leakage of temporary keys. Since the cache keys are used as a substitution of HAS, disclosure of them would undermine the effectiveness of HAS. For instance, if attackers steal the patient's IC card, they can initiate access to the IMD immediately because both two temporary keys can be obtained from the IC card. Under this situation, the patient has no way to protect himself even he/she realizes the lost and report it to HAS manager. As a result, cached temporal keys must be encrypted to prevent unauthorized accesses. We denote each cache item as

$$cache(i) = i\|En_{C_k}(SB_i)$$

where i is the counter and the C_k is the cache encryption key. The cache encryption key C_k is secured with the biometric encryption where the patient's iris code is exploited to obfuscate the original message as described in [20].

Here, we give some brief retelling about the biometric encryption we use. First, a binary string is derived from an infrared image of patient's iris image by demodulating the phase information with complex-valued 2D Gabor wavelets [5]. The generated reference string, denoted as Θ_{ref}, is acquired in the patient register phase. After that, the HAS generates the cache encryption key C_k and the key is encoded by Hadamard code and Reed-Solomon code. The encoded C_k is then obfuscated by the iris reference Θ_{ref} and the resulted Θ_{lock} is stored in patient's IC card.

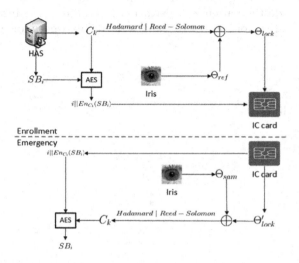

Fig. 5. Iris code assisted emergent access.

During emergent situation, first aiders can use a digital camera (with infrared mode) to capture the patient's iris image and generate the sample binary string Θ_{sam} to decrypt Θ_{lock} with the XOR operation and then acquire C_k by doing Hadamard and Reed-Solomon decoding. After getting the XORed cache encryption key C_k, first aiders are capable of decrypting the temporary key SB_i and access the patient's IMD locally without the HAS's support. The robustness of cache key regeneration is guaranteed by Hadamard and Reed-Solomon code which deals with errors in a binary level and block level respectively (Fig. 5).

5.3   Recovery Mode

To deal with the issue of patients losing their IC cards, we design a recovery mechanism to reset the IMD and pair it with a new IC card. For the security concern of the recovery mode, the patient needs to go to the hospital to report the lost and sign the related documents in person before starting the reset procedure. A programmer operated by the security administrator is granted with the reset permission by the HAS. The recovery mode is triggered by the programmer with a designated service request code. Upon receiving the reset request, the IMD begins to continuously challenge the programmer as shown in Fig. 6. During the challenge process, the IMD asks the programmer to provide the temporary key SB for the cycle counter K. The challenge is conducted continuously for $2 * S$ times where S is the maximum number of cached temporary keys for the emergent access. The reset command is accepted and executed by the IMD if the programmer can provide correct responses to all those challenges with the help of the HAS. When the reset succeeds, the IMD rollback to the registration status to accept the configuration of new master keys Key_1 and Key_2. Thus, the doctor can re-do the patient's registration procedures to pair the IMD with a new IC card, and the old stolen IC card is invalidated permanently.

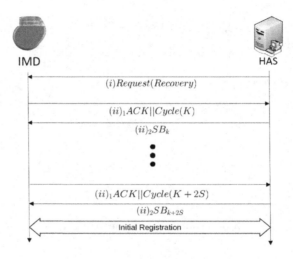

Fig. 6. The recovery process.

6   Security Analysis

6.1   Active Attacks

In active attacks, adversaries intercept the transmission between the IMD and the programmer and then manipulate the message to deceive them. However, the identities of the IMD, the programmer, and the HAS are secured by master keys or kept in the server or the POKs enabled IC card. Even if adversaries can successfully intercept those messages, there is no way to retrieve the valid temporal keys for the current cycle. Without temporal keys, adversaries cannot generate valid HMAC for the tampered message. The reply attack is also not feasible due to the implementation of the time window. The IMD and the programmer would reject all duplicate packets that are outside of the time window.

Another type of active attack is extracting credentials from the IC card through invasive ways. There have been a lot of methods to recover security credentials by tampering IC card circuits [13,32,41]. However, with the master key secured by POKs, any attempt to tamper the circuit would fail and destroy the secret credential permanently.

6.2 Desynchronization Attack

A lot of PUFs-based authentication protocols that rely on synchronization are subject to the desynchronization attack. Normally, the desynchronization attack is achieved by intentional interruptions during normal authentication, which results in the temporary key generator in different components running at malposed cycles. In our work, the desynchronization attack could be avoided by applying one-step cache in the IC card and the HAS for the previous used temporary keys SA_{i-1} and SB_{i-1}. Since the IMD only increases its cycle counter i when authorized by the IC card and the HAS succeeds, the desynchronization condition only happens when the IMD's counter is one step slower than the IC card or the HAS. When the IC card and the HAS receive the counter from the programmer at step (iii) and (v) in Fig. 4, they can easily recover from the desynchronization status with the help of cached keys.

6.3 Identity Impersonation Attack

The adversaries may disguise themselves as legitimate physicians and use a programmer to access patients' IMDs. This kind of identity fraud is prevented in our scheme by the doctor's identity proof at step (v) in Fig. 4. To impersonate a legitimate doctor, the attacker must get the corresponding doctor's identity IC card. Even if the attacker can steal a valid IC card from doctors, the stolen identities are not universally applicable to all IMDs, which restrict the range of damage. Also, this kind of attack cannot bypass the touch-to-access assumption because of requirement of the patient's IC card. It is difficult to use the IC card without the patient's permission. Through physical contacts with the patient, attackers are highly likely to be spotted and recorded by other people or video monitoring systems which greatly undermines the power of attacks.

6.4 Security of the Emergent Access

Many previous attempts introduced additional risk by adding an emergent access mode. For example, cloaker [16] and IMDGuard [46] rely on external devices to secure the IMD. When these external devices are removed, the IMD switches to open access. This can cause potential risk when the external device is stolen or the patient forgets to take it. Instead of trying to let the IMD be aware of the emergent situation, the IMD in our design always runs in the same mode, which means the aforementioned touch-to-access assumption always holds in emergent access since the temporary key SA_i can only be acquired from the patient's IC card. To exploit the emergent access, attackers must get the patient's IC card and iris image. Even if the IC card is obtained by attackers without breaching the touch-to-access assumption (e.g., lost by the patient), the iris image must be captured in front of the patient. Additionally, cached keys in the IC card can be easily invalidated after the patient loses his/her card by rolling the normal access for multiple rounds to override the cached SBs. After that, attackers will not be able to access the patient's IMD even if they get the patient's iris code. The security of the iris code has been extensively discussed and many counterfeit iris detection schemes are proposed in [14,28,43]. However, most of the counterfeit iris attack (e.g., cosmetic lens with texture, printed iris on paper) has the prerequisite of acquiring high resolution of the victim's Iris NIR image. The NIRs that are used to illuminate the iris only has the effective range of 50–70 cm [21]. The successful iris code generation requires a resolution of at least 50 pixels in iris radius for the iris picture [4]. As a result, it is hard for attackers to get the usable iris image without breaching the touch-to-access assumption.

6.5   Security of Trivium

Unlike the block cipher such as AES, there is not a widely recognized secure stream cipher. Trivium has been selected as part of the eSTREAM project [38]. Up to now, no effective analysis attack is proposed that is better than the brute force search. Existing attacks utilizing the side channel like Differential Power attack [27] and Fault Injection attack [34] all require hardware tampering of the cipher IC. This kind of hardware attack is impractical in our design because of the use of tampering-resistant POKs. Once the circuit is tampered, the master key will be destroyed permanently. Moreover, the passive analysis is also not applicable to our design. The output of the Trivium stream generator, the temporary key SA_i, and SB_i are never transmitted directly over the air. Instead, they are only used as keys for HMAC operations.

7   Evaluation

Because commercial IMDs are not opensourced for customization, we implement our design on our own testbed which comprises a TelosB sensor mote, a Raspberry Pi and a Laptop to simulate the IMD, programmer, and HAS respectively. As stated in [46], Telosb sensor mote is built on the similar low-energy platform as commercial IMDs making it a good choice to simulate the overhead of our system on real IMDs. With the prototype implementation, we evaluate the overhead of the consumption of energy, time, memory, and storage for both the computation process and communication.

7.1   Overhead Statistics

To evaluate the overhead, we make statistics about all computing and communicating operations conducted by the IMD during an access cycle as shown in Tables 2 and 3.

Table 2. Computing statistics.

Steps	Operation	Amount	Length (bits)
Service request	HMAC	2	32, 96
Keypair generation	Trivium	2	256, 256
	SHA-256	2	256, 256
Token generation	HMAC	2	32, 128
Session key generation	SHA-256	2	256, 256

Table 3. Communication statistics.

Steps	Operation	Length (bits)
Service request	Receiving	64
	Sending	608
Token verifying	Receiving	256

7.2 Experiment Results

We split the design into several parts, one for the key generator and others for the HMAC and SHA-256 operations. By deploying asynchronous counters, we record the time consumption of each part with the accuracy of 1 millisecond. With the energy consumption model [7,35,42] for TelosB as shown in Table 4, the energy consumption for each operation is calculated from the time consumption.

Table 4. TelosB power consumption model

Operation	Power consumption (mW)
Transmit	69
Listen	60
Receiving	61
Computing (active)	4.8
Computing (idle)	4.5
Sleep	0.035

The total computing time for a complete authentication cycle is 367 ms, if the transmission time is not taken into account. The overhead for different parts is listed in Table 5.

Unlike the computational part, the overhead for transmission is much more complex because of the utilization of low power listening and collision avoiding mechanisms in the MAC layer. The listening time is uncertain depending on the environment noise, and the power consumption on synchronizations is difficult

Table 5. Overhead for computation.

	Generator	HMAC	SHA256
Time (ms)	52	46	15
Energy (μJ)	249	220.8	72
ROM (bytes)	14290	6022	4792
RAM (bytes)	312	282	197

to specify. Therefore, to make things easier, we test the overhead of broadcasting packets with no retransmission. The results of the transmission test are listed in Table 6.

Table 6. Overhead for communication.

	Receiving (320 bits)	Sending (608 bits)
Time (ms)	40	22
Energy (μJ)	2440	1518
ROM (bytes)	11140	11182
RAM (bytes)	501	513

With the operation specific evaluation results, ensemble time and energy overhead are calculate as illustrated in Eqs. (3) and (4).

$$
\begin{aligned}
E &= E_{comp} + E_{Tx} + E_{Rx} \\
&= E_{gen} + 4 * E_{HMAC} + 3 * E_{Sha256} + E_{Tx} + E_{Rx} \\
&= 249\,\mu J + 4 * 220.8\,\mu J + 3 * 72\,\mu J + 2440\,\mu J + 1518\,\mu J \\
&= 5306\,\mu J
\end{aligned}
\tag{3}
$$

$$
\begin{aligned}
T &= T_{comp} + T_{Tx} + T_{Rx} \\
&= T_{gen} + 4 * T_{HMAC} + 3 * T_{Sha256} + T_{Tx} + T_{Rx} \\
&= 52\,ms + 4 * 46\,ms + 3 * 15\,ms + 40\,ms + 22\,ms \\
&= 343\,ms
\end{aligned}
\tag{4}
$$

The results indicate that our design introduces orders of magnitude lower energy and time overhead to the IMD compared with state-of-art physiological-feature-based solutions: The energy consumption of the OPFKA [25] ranges from about 70 mJ to 1000 mJ according to the coffer size. The IMDguard [46] needs at least 45 s to measure more than 21 heart beats. While, the Heart-to-heart [40] uses TLS communication where the RSA encryption itself takes 5000000 cpu cycles (equivalent to 100 ms and 3038 μJ on the platform used by the author).

8   Related Work

8.1   Pre-loaded-Key Based Solutions

In some early works of IMD security, a long-term and device-specific credential is pre-loaded into the IMD and the programmer must possess the corresponding credential to pass the authentication. Halperin et al. [19] propose a acoustic side channel based solution where programmer need a valid master key to access the IMD. Li et al. [29] present a rolling code based authentication scheme, in which the IMD and the programmer share a pair of encryption keys that are used to encrypt a sequence number. Liu et al. Denning et al. [8] uses visual objects to carry a static credential for the IMD authentication. This type of IMD authentication/authorization schemes are obsoleted because the difficulty to protect the pre-loaded credential.

8.2   Physiological Feature Based Solutions

Recent researches tend to establish temporary keys by extracting time-varying information from patient's physiological signals. Most of them are also based on the touch-to-access assumption as our work does because the physiological features used for key generation can only be measured when the programmer is physically close to the patient. In [25,40,46,48], the patient's ECG features are utilized to derive credentials due to its high level of randomness. In [21], the access credentials are extracted from the patient's biometric features such as the fingerprints, iris and height.

This type of solutions face the problem of reliability: accurate measurement of physiological value is difficult because of the noise and distortion which results in long time consumption for feature measurement. Also, all these requires the IMDs to be equipped with special sensors to measure physiological signals such as ECG which not only increase the cost of IMDs but also causes excessive power consumption.

8.3   Proxy Based Solutions

Some researches propose to utilize additional devices to authenticate the programmer on behalf of the IMD for reducing the IMD's power consumption.The common design of proxy-based security schemes [9,17,46,47] includes (1) the proxy device jams the signal of external programmers until they are authenticated; (2) the IMD allows open-access when the proxy is not in proximity.

The Shield [17] jams the programmer's signal, but also the IMD's signal. Equipped with a full-duplex radio with two antennas, Shield is able to receive and decode the IMD's signal, meanwhile jamming it so that the programmer cannot receive and decode the complete IMD's message. A secured communication channel is assumed to have been set up between the Shield and the legitimate programmer. Therefore, Shield actually serves as a relay between the IMD and the programmer. Similarly, Cloaker [9] is also a mediator that forwards all authorized communications between the IMD and programmer.

In the other schemes [46,47], the proxy devices are mainly considered as an external authenticator, which stores the public keys of all authorized programmers and are able to verify the identity of the programmer that requests for access using its digital signature. The communication channel between the IMD and the programmer is established, after the programmer is successfully authenticated. In [46], a pair of lightweight symmetric keys are issued to the IMD and the programmer, to encrypt their future communications. In [47], the authentication proxy is embedded into a gateway.

This type of solutions requires patients to carry the active proxy device all the time which is unpractical. Also, the jamming may cause interference on other medical devices.

9   Conclusion

Security and low power consumption are among the most critical goals when designing access control schemes for implantable medical devices, while how to attain both high energy efficiency and resiliency to powerful attacks, such as memory scanning and physical tampering, is still an unresolved challenge. We propose to take Physically Obfuscated Keys (POKs) as the hardware root of trust to establish a highly secure access control scheme for IMDs, and apply the idea of computation offloading to saving energy consumption on the IMD side. We have comprehensively analyzed the security of the proposed scheme and compared it with some well-known mechanisms. In addition to its security advantage, a prototype system implemented on the TelosB platform demonstrates its high energy efficiency.

Acknowledgments. This publication was made possible by NPRP grant #8-408-2-172 from the Qatar National Research Fund (a member of Qatar Foundation). The statements made herein are solely the responsibility of the authors.

References

1. Barnaby jack hacks diabetes insulin pump live at hacker halted (2011). https://www.infosecurity-magazine.com/news
2. Black, J., Halevi, S., Krawczyk, H., Krovetz, T., Rogaway, P.: UMAC: fast and secure message authentication. In: Wiener, M. (ed.) CRYPTO 1999. LNCS, vol. 1666, pp. 216–233. Springer, Heidelberg (1999). https://doi.org/10.1007/3-540-48405-1_14
3. Bringer, J., Chabanne, H., Icart, T.: On physical obfuscation of cryptographic algorithms. In: Roy, B., Sendrier, N. (eds.) INDOCRYPT 2009. LNCS, vol. 5922, pp. 88–103. Springer, Heidelberg (2009). https://doi.org/10.1007/978-3-642-10628-6_6
4. Daugman, J.: The importance of being random: statistical principles of iris recognition. Pattern Recogn. **36**(2), 279–291 (2003)

5. Daugman, J.: How iris recognition works. IEEE Trans. Circuits Syst. Video Technol. **14**(1), 21–30 (2004)
6. Cannière, C.: TRIVIUM: a stream cipher construction inspired by block cipher design principles. In: Katsikas, S.K., López, J., Backes, M., Gritzalis, S., Preneel, B. (eds.) ISC 2006. LNCS, vol. 4176, pp. 171–186. Springer, Heidelberg (2006). https://doi.org/10.1007/11836810_13
7. De Meulenaer, G., Gosset, F., Standaert, F.X., Pereira, O.: On the energy cost of communication and cryptography in wireless sensor networks. In: 2008 IEEE International Conference on Wireless and Mobile Computing, Networking and Communications, WIMOB 2008, pp. 580–585. IEEE (2008)
8. Denning, T., Borning, A., Friedman, B., Gill, B.T., Kohno, T., Maisel, W.H.: Patients, pacemakers, and implantable defibrillators: human values and security for wireless implantable medical devices. In: SIGCHI Conference on Human Factors in Computing Systems (2010)
9. Denning, T., Fu, K., Kohno, T.: Absence makes the heart grow fonder: New directions for implantable medical device security. In: USENIX HotSec (2008)
10. Du, X., Guizani, M., Xiao, Y., Chen, H.H.: Transactions papers a routing-driven elliptic curve cryptography based key management scheme for heterogeneous sensor networks. IEEE Trans. Wireless Commun. **8**(3), 1223–1229 (2009)
11. Du, X., Xiao, Y., Ci, S., Guizani, M., Chen, H.H.: A routing-driven key management scheme for heterogeneous sensor networks. In: 2007 IEEE International Conference on Communications, pp. 3407–3412. IEEE (2007)
12. Du, X., Xiao, Y., Guizani, M., Chen, H.H.: An effective key management scheme for heterogeneous sensor networks. Ad Hoc Netw. **5**(1), 24–34 (2007)
13. Fueki, S.: Semiconductor integrated circuit on IC card protected against tampering. US Patent App. 09/962,224, 26 September 2001
14. Galbally, J., Marcel, S., Fierrez, J.: Image quality assessment for fake biometric detection: application to iris, fingerprint, and face recognition. IEEE Trans. Image Process. **23**(2), 710–724 (2014)
15. Gassend, B.L.: Physical random functions. Ph.D. thesis, Massachusetts Institute of Technology (2003)
16. Gollakota, S., Hassanieh, H., Ransford, B., Katabi, D., Fu, K.: They can hear your heartbeats: non-invasive security for implantable medical devices. ACM SIGCOMM Comput. Commun. Rev. **41**(4), 2–13 (2011)
17. Gollakota, S., Hassanieh, H., Ransford, B., Katabi, D., Fu, K.: They can hear your heartbeats: non-invasive security for implantable medical devices. In: ACM SIGCOMM (2011)
18. Gupta, S.: Dick cheney's heart, October 2013. http://www.cbsnews.com/news/dick-cheneys-heart/
19. Halperin, D., et al.: Pacemakers and implantable cardiac defibrillators: software radio attacks and zero-power defenses. In: IEEE S&P (2008)
20. Hao, F., Anderson, R., Daugman, J.: Combining crypto with biometrics effectively. IEEE Trans. Comput. **55**(9), 1081–1088 (2006)
21. Hei, X., Du, X.: Biometric-based two-level secure access control for implantable medical devices during emergencies. In: IEEE INFOCOM (2011)
22. Hei, X., Du, X., Lin, S., Lee, I.: PIPAC: patient infusion pattern based access control scheme for wireless insulin pump system. In: 2013 Proceedings IEEE INFOCOM, pp. 3030–3038. IEEE (2013)
23. Hei, X., Du, X., Wu, J., Hu, F.: Defending resource depletion attacks on implantable medical devices. In: 2010 IEEE Global Telecommunications Conference GLOBECOM 2010, pp. 1–5. IEEE (2010)

24. Holcomb, D.E., Burleson, W.P., Fu, K.: Power-up SRAM state as an identifying fingerprint and source of true random numbers. IEEE Trans. Comput. **58**(9), 1198–1210 (2009)
25. Hu, C., Cheng, X., Zhang, F., Wu, D., Liao, X., Chen, D.: OPFKA: secure and efficient ordered-physiological-feature-based key agreement for wireless body area networks. In: IEEE INFOCOM (2013)
26. Karpinskyy, B., Lee, Y., Choi, Y., Kim, Y., Noh, M., Lee, S.: 8.7 physically unclonable function for secure key generation with a key error rate of 2E-38 in 45nm smart-card chips. In: 2016 IEEE International Solid-State Circuits Conference (ISSCC), pp. 158–160. IEEE (2016)
27. Kazmi, A.R., Afzal, M., Amjad, M.F., Abbas, H., Yang, X.: Algebraic side channel attack on trivium and grain ciphers. IEEE Access (2017)
28. Kohli, N., Yadav, D., Vatsa, M., Singh, R., Noore, A.: Detecting medley of iris spoofing attacks using desist. In: 2016 IEEE 8th International Conference on Biometrics Theory, Applications and Systems (BTAS), pp. 1–6. IEEE (2016)
29. Li, C., Raghunathan, A., Jha, N.K.: Hijacking an insulin pump: security attacks and defenses for a diabetes therapy system. In: IEEE HealthCom (2011)
30. Lim, D., Lee, J.W., Gassend, B., Suh, G.E., Van Dijk, M., Devadas, S.: Extracting secret keys from integrated circuits. IEEE Trans. Very Large Scale Integr. (VLSI) Syst. **13**(10), 1200–1205 (2005)
31. Min, B.J., et al.: An embedded nonvolatile FRAM with electrical fuse repair scheme and one time programming scheme for high performance smart cards. In: 2005 Proceedings of the IEEE Custom Integrated Circuits Conference, pp. 255–258. IEEE (2005)
32. Ming-Chien, C., Chi-Wei, K.: Stolen-verifier attack on two new strong-password authentication protocols. IEICE Trans. Commun. **85**(11), 2519–2521 (2002)
33. Pope, A., Bouxsein, P., Manning, F.J., Hanna, K.E., et al.: Innovation and invention in medical devices: workshop summary. National Academies Press (2001)
34. Potestad-Ordóñez, F., Jiménez-Fernández, C.J., Valencia-Barrero, M.: Fault attack on FPGA implementations of trivium stream cipher. In: 2016 IEEE International Symposium on Circuits and Systems (ISCAS), pp. 562–565. IEEE (2016)
35. Prayati, A., Antonopoulos, C., Stoyanova, T., Koulamas, C., Papadopoulos, G.: A modeling approach on the TelosB WSN platform power consumption. J. Syst. Softw. **83**(8), 1355–1363 (2010)
36. Radcliffe, J.: Hacking medical devices for fun and insulin: breaking the human SCADA system. In: Black Hat Conference Presentation Slides, vol. 2011 (2011)
37. Ravikanth, P.S.: Physical one-way functions. Ph.D. thesis, Massachusetts Institute Of Technology (2001)
38. Robshaw, M.: The eSTREAM project. In: Robshaw, M., Billet, O. (eds.) New Stream Cipher Designs. LNCS, vol. 4986, pp. 1–6. Springer, Heidelberg (2008). https://doi.org/10.1007/978-3-540-68351-3_1
39. Rostami, M., Burleson, W., Juels, A., Koushanfar, F.: Balancing security and utility in medical devices? In: IEEE Design Automation Conference (DAC) (2013)
40. Rostami, M., Juels, A., Koushanfar, F.: Heart-to-heart (H2H): authentication for implanted medical devices. In: ACM CCS (2013)
41. Skorobogatov, S.: Flash Memory 'Bumping' Attacks. In: Mangard, S., Standaert, F.-X. (eds.) CHES 2010. LNCS, vol. 6225, pp. 158–172. Springer, Heidelberg (2010). https://doi.org/10.1007/978-3-642-15031-9_11

42. Somov, A., Minakov, I., Simalatsar, A., Fontana, G., Passerone, R.: A methodology for power consumption evaluation of wireless sensor networks. In: 2009 IEEE Conference on Emerging Technologies & Factory Automation, ETFA 2009, pp. 1–8. IEEE (2009)

43. Wei, Z., Qiu, X., Sun, Z., Tan, T.: Counterfeit iris detection based on texture analysis. In: 2008 19th International Conference on Pattern Recognition, ICPR 2008, pp. 1–4. IEEE (2008)

44. Xia, Q., Sifah, E.B., Asamoah, K.O., Gao, J., Du, X., Guizani, M.: MeDShare: trust-less medical data sharing among cloud service providers via blockchain. IEEE Access **5**, 14757–14767 (2017)

45. Xiao, Y., Rayi, V.K., Sun, B., Du, X., Hu, F., Galloway, M.: A survey of key management schemes in wireless sensor networks. Comput. Commun. **30**(11–12), 2314–2341 (2007)

46. Xu, F., Qin, Z., Tan, C.C., Wang, B., Li, Q.: IMDGuard: securing implantable medical devices with the external wearable guardian. In: INFOCOM, 2011 Proceedings IEEE, pp. 1862–1870. IEEE (2011)

47. Zheng, G., Fang, G., Orgun, M.A., Shankaran, R.: A non-key based security scheme supporting emergency treatment of wireless implants. In: IEEE ICC (2014)

48. Zheng, G., et al.: Multiple ECG fiducial points based random binary sequence generation for securing wireless body area networks. IEEE J. Biomed. Health Inform. **PP**(99), 655–663 (2016)

USB-Watch: A Dynamic Hardware-Assisted USB Threat Detection Framework

Kyle Denney[1]([✉]), Enes Erdin[1], Leonardo Babun[1], Michael Vai[2], and Selcuk Uluagac[1]

[1] Florida International University, Miami, FL, USA
{kdenn016,eerdi001,lbabu002,suluagac}@fiu.edu
[2] Massachusetts Institute of Technology Lincoln Laboratory, Lexington, MA, USA
mvai@ll.mit.edu

Abstract. The USB protocol is among the most widely adopted protocols today thanks to its plug-and-play capabilities and the vast number of devices which support the protocol. However, this same adaptability leaves unwitting computing devices prone to attacks. Malicious USB devices can disguise themselves as benign devices (e.g., keyboard, mouse, etc.) to insert malicious commands on end devices. These malicious USB devices can mimic an actual device or a human typing pattern and appear as a real device to the operating system. Typically, advanced software-based detection schemes are used to identify the malicious nature of such devices. However, a powerful adversary (e.g., as rootkits or advanced persistent threats) can still subvert those software-based detection schemes. To address these concerns, in this work, we introduce a novel hardware-assisted, dynamic USB-threat detection framework called USB-Watch. Specifically, USB-Watch utilizes hardware placed between a USB device and the host machine to hook into the USB communication, collect USB data, and provides the capability to view unaltered USB protocol communications. This unfettered data is then fed into a machine learning-based classifier which dynamically determines the true nature of the USB device. Using real malicious USB devices (i.e., Rubber-Ducky) mimicking as a keyboard, we perform a thorough analysis of typing dynamic features (e.g., typing time differentials, key press durations, etc.) to effectively classify malicious USB devices from normal human typing behaviors. In this work, we show that USB-Watch provides a lightweight, OS-independent framework which effectively distinguishes differences between normal and malicious USB behaviors with a ROC curve of 0.89. To the best of our knowledge, this is the first hardware-based detection mechanism to dynamically detect threats coming from USB devices.

1 Introduction

USB devices are among the easiest to adopt into a computing system thanks to the number of devices which support USB protocols and the protocol's

S. Chen et al. (Eds.): SecureComm 2019, LNICST 304, pp. 126–146, 2019.
https://doi.org/10.1007/978-3-030-37228-6_7

plug-and-play nature [1]. However, this same ease of use allows for a wide attack vector for malicious parties to steal or modify sensitive data in computing systems [2]. For this reason, sensitive computing environments (e.g., government offices, military base communications, research labs, etc.) limit/prohibit the use of USB devices to minimize the possible threat of malicious USB devices [3].

Work has been done to mitigate the damage caused by malicious USB devices. For instance, current anti-virus software have scanning capabilities to detect malware stored in USB storage (i.e., flash-drives) [4]. However, there is still ongoing research in mitigating *rapid-keystroke injection attacks*, where a USB device mimics the keystrokes of a user and types an attack directly into the user's computer. There are current software-based approaches [5–8], but we note that these approaches can be tampered with through rootkits injected in the kernel which obfuscate or remove evidence that a rogue USB device even exists. Additionally, as we also show in this work, these prior works fail to detect when the USB device intentionally mimics human typing dynamics.

To address these challenges, in this work, we introduce a novel USB detection framework, called USB-Watch, which is enacted at the hardware level and can detect keystroke injection attacks. Through the use of this novel hardware-based mechanism, we are able to sample USB communication between an unknown USB device and the host system in an OS-independent and *tamper-proof* way such that a malicious actor may not subvert it. To overcome the possibility of mimicked human typing dynamics, we provide an in-depth feature analysis to prove the feasibility of detecting bad USB devices which inject malicious keystrokes. With USB-Watch, we achieve a USB detection framework which dynamically detects advanced keystroke injection attacks while successfully distinguishing human and mimicked typing dynamics.

Contributions: The contributions of this work are as follows:

- *USB-Watch*: We propose a hardware-based USB detection framework called USB-Watch to dynamically detect and prevent USB devices from injecting malicious keystrokes in a target computing environment.
- *Effective classification*: We perform an in-depth classification and feature analysis of typing dynamics to distinguish between benign and malicious typing dynamics with an ROC curve of 0.89.

Organization: The rest of this paper is organized as follows: In Sect. 2, we briefly overview the concepts of USB-based rapid-keystroke injection attacks, classification models, and introduce prior work to develop hardware-assistance frameworks. In Sect. 3, we discuss the state-of-the-art approaches in malicious USB detection, showing how USB-Watch offers similar results while also being tamper-proof and OS independent. Section 4 introduces the real-world threat model that our framework prevents. The architecture of the proposed framework is detailed in Sect. 5. The results of our experiments are outlined in Sect. 6 along with an analysis of the proposed framework against existing works and lists key benefits of USB-Watch. We provide a discussion of a final realization of the USB-Watch framework with key benefits and limitations in Sect. 7. Concluding thoughts and future work are provided in Sect. 8.

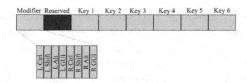

Fig. 1. USB Human Interface Device (HID) report

2 Background

In this section we outline important background information. First, we overview the USB protocol and how human interface devices (e.g., USB keyboards) interact with a computer. From there, we highlight how a malicious USB device can utilize these functionality to perform keystroke injection attacks.

2.1 USB Protocol

Since in this paper we utilize a hardware-based mechanism to collect incoming USB data, we overview the basics of the USB protocol and how the operating system handles incoming USB data.

The USB protocol operates in a master-slave fashion [1]. First, a device connects to a computing system via a USB host controller. The host controller (master) requests all data from the USB device (slave). A request for data is periodically sent to the USB device and, if the device has any, the data is placed on a USB buffer. A system interrupt is performed, the host controller reads the data on the buffer, and the communication process restarts from there.

Each USB transaction contains a token packet, data packet, and status packet. The token packet establishes what type of data flow (i.e., read, write, etc.) will occur. The data packet contains the actual USB data. The status packet reports if the prior packets were received correctly or if the end device is currently stalled or unable to receive packets.

2.2 USB Human Interface Device Reports

The detection framework proposed in this work attempts to distinguish differences in malicious and benign typing behaviors. To obtain information on live keystrokes, we extract the human interface device reports from our captured USB data. The details of this report are outlined below.

Human Interface Devices (HIDs) are a subclass of USB devices which are designed for human input (e.g., keyboards, mice, gaming controllers, etc.) [9]. In order to communicate, the host machine will periodically request input information from the HID. The HID will then produce a packet with the current human interaction being performed (i.e., HID report). The report format for a standard keyboard is shown in Fig. 1. As shown, there is field in a keyboard report for a total of six concurrent key presses plus any modifier keys (i.e., SHIFT, CTRL,

ALT, etc.). Note that the reserved bit is ignored in the reports. When a user presses a key, the HID report will continuously include the key being pressed until the user subsequently releases the key. In this paper, we use these HID reports to collect data for our detection framework. From the report, we can gather information about which keys were pressed, how long they were pressed, and the speed at which the user can type.

2.3   USB Keystroke Injection Attacks

A common attack with embedded USB devices are referred to as keystroke injection attacks [2]. In these attacks, the embedded device mimics a USB keyboard to inject malicious text. Two of the most common devices used to implement keystroke injection attacks are the *Rubber Ducky* [10] and the *BadUSB* [11]. Both come with a pre-defined language for a user to easily create an attack script to embed in his/her USB device. First, the malicious actor designs the attack s/he wants performed. The attacker determines which keyboard commands are needed to, for instance, open a terminal and delete specific files/directories. From there, the attacker writes a script which sequentially iterates each keyboard command as text strings. To make sure the command is typed into the terminal, the attacker introduces delays between opening the terminal and typing the command. With the text created, the malicious actor must compile the malicious keystrokes ("payload") into an embedded USB device disguised as a common device (e.g., flash-drive, keyboard, etc.) [10].

To perform the attack, the attacker has to have the malicious USB device be inserted into the target computer. There are two common methods to do so: (1) a malicious insider plugs the device into the target machine when the user walks away or (2) the malicious device is dropped near the target premises, leading to an unwitting insider mistakenly plugging the device into a target machine [12,13]. Once inserted, the device begins performing the attack by sending an HID report with the current character in the payload. To the computer, this HID report simply looks like keystroke presses from a benign keyboard. To prevent onlooker detection, intricate attacks may wait for onlookers to disappear by delaying for an arbitrary time or waiting for the computer to enter rest-mode. Since the payload is embedded in a USB device, this attack is difficult to detect through normal means as a common anti-virus cannot simply scan the file to determine if it is malware.

3   Related Work

Embedded Device Threats. The rise of small, embedded devices (i.e., USB devices) brought a new attack vector through these devices acting maliciously when inserted to a computing system [2,11,14]. Traditional intrusion detection systems are not suited to detect these threats as, to the computing system, the behavior appears to come from a legitimate user. This requires new solutions to be added to effectively detect these embedded device threat vectors. We overview two categories of detection models: static and dynamic.

Static Detection Methods. Static analysis methods aim to analyze a potential threat by examining it before execution [15]. When detecting threats from embedded devices, static analysis methods include: disallowing unregistered devices from communicating [8], require devices to request functionality permission [16], or simply disabling unnecessary USB ports [8]. Assuming a trusted device contains maliciously embedded circuitry [17], these static frameworks are not enough to detect and eliminate all threats from embedded devices.

Dynamic Detection Methods. Dynamic analysis methods, on the other hand, analyze the potential threat as it is operating and examines the performance behavior of the device. Dynamic analysis today tends to involve the use of machine learning algorithms and classification models [5,7,18]. In the case of malicious threat detection, this entails using binary classification schemes to differentiate benign and malicious behavior on the system. Current approaches for dynamic threat detection in embedded devices use software on the host system to collect and process data. It has been shown that it is possible for advanced threats to spoof or alter software-based collection approaches by altering OS-level code [19]. Transferring the dynamic analysis to hardware placed between an unknown embedded device and the host system would ensure that the data collection is unalterable through these means.

Differences from Existing Work. Our approach aims to develop a *dynamic* detection framework to detect and prevent insider threats through embedded devices. Our proposed approach differs from prior work through three distinct characteristics stemmed from the use of a hardware mechanism. First, an advanced threat to the computing system may leave software-based detection approaches vulnerable to spoofing. The use of a hardware mechanism between the embedded device and the internal computing system ensures the capturing of raw, unaltered behavior of the device – allowing the detection of any malicious behavior performed by the embedded device. Second, any software-based approach to intrusion detection consumes resources of the computing system. Segmenting the intrusion detection into dedicated hardware removes computation cost that would otherwise needed to be performed on the host machine. Finally, assuming a malicious device is embedded in an authenticated USB device, the attack can bypass static systems such as [16] whereas our dynamic approach can still detect. Hence, this work aims to provide a dynamic, hardware-based intrusion detection framework to mitigate USB-based attacks.

4   Threat Model

In this section, we define the threat model which we aim to prevent with our detection framework. We first define an attacker's motivations through a real-world scenario. Then, we state assumptions that effectively subvert previous work in USB detection.

In this work, we assume there is an attacker who can obtain physical access to a computer and has limited time to initiate their attack (e.g., a rogue employee at a secure facility). The attacker has a malicious USB device which they can insert into the computer to perform an automated attack. Since there is limited time, we assume the attacker cannot tamper with the computer and remove the USB-Watch hardware as this entails opening the computer and breaking the embedded circuitry in the USB host controller.

As stated in Sect. 3, there has been prior work in detecting malicious USB devices through the aid of machine learning. However, we identify two key threat vectors that can subvert prior attempts: *kernel-level USB-trace hooking* and *mimicry attacks*. As we detail later in Sect. 6, these threat vectors can cause prior works to fail. However, we account for both of these in our work (through hardware-assistance and feature selection, respectively).

Kernel-Level USB-Trace Hooking. *Hooking* is the process to alter the normal behavior of an operating system. This is typically done by intercepting operating system calls or events to output custom code (e.g., output "Hello World!" every time a device is inserted) [19]. A common method for sampling USB-traces is through the usbmon tool. In the Linux Kernel, USB traces are sent through a buffer which usbmon hooks into this buffer and outputs relevant trace information [20] (i.e., timestamp, device ID, device bus, etc.).

Through the use of system hooks, it is possible for an advanced attacker to maliciously alter usbmon or other related hooks to not output specific USB device information. Should such an attack take effect, prior work discussed in Sect. 3 becomes effectively useless as the attacker can simply hide his USB device from detection schemes which utilize usbmon.

With novel hardware-based mechanism called USB-Watch, we overcome this limitation. Since our data is collected in hardware, it is unfeasible for an insider threat to alter incoming USB data packets from a malicious device, thereby obtaining the true output from a device.

Mimicry Attacks. Prior work in classification of malicious USB devices specify that the malicious USB device is assumed to act distinctly different from normal human behavior (i.e., vastly different typing patterns). Mulliner et. al. establish a simple method to prevent malicious USB devices by adding a block for any unknown device typing faster than 80 ms [5] as no human can type faster than that. This work shows it is still possible for an attacker to develop a smarter USB device which subverts these prevention schemes. *No known work has been done to determine effective methods to detect a USB device which attempts to mimic human behavior.*

As we show later in our analysis, implementing this simple delay method is enough to fool other dynamic detection works. The only possible flaw with this method is the increased possibility of interference between the malicious device and the human typing on the target machine. However, we believe that the attack would still be able to perform properly if done within a reasonable time frame (e.g., 30 s) to minimize the likelihood of interference.

For the purposes of this work, we are not concerned with the content which is being typed (i.e., what the user is typing). Developing a model which could infer attacks depending on the content being typed would (1) be costly to develop/train and (2) potentially invade the user's privacy as his/her content would need to be processed. Therefore, we only consider the typing dynamics to detect and identify keystroke injection attacks

5   Overview of Architecture

In this section we discuss the architecture of the proposed detection framework. We start with a custom-built hardware tool which we use to collect USB data. Then, we discuss components of the classifier: what pre-processing was required on unlabeled data, the features extracted, and what algorithms were tested for classification. Finally, we discuss how these two components work together to detect and classify malicious USB behavior in a live system.

As stated, the ultimate goal is a USB host controller with smart functionality. The host controller should be able to differentiate between normal USB performance and a potential USB-based attack. If the host controller identifies a potential attack, communication between the device and host computer is severed.

For the USB Watch hardware to understand normal behavior, a machine learning technique can be utilized to teach a model the difference between benign and malicious USB device behaviors. Samples from both malicious and benign USB devices can be used to train and fit a model, such that it accurately distinguishes the two types of behavior.

The final model can be placed on the USB Watch hardware so that when a USB device is inserted it can properly infer the device's intent. If the hardware determines the device is malicious, it can cease communication with the device before an attack can occur. The hardware would be capable of retraining in a live setting to fit user needs.

The overall architecture for the detection framework is described in Fig. 2a. First, a USB device is inserted into a hardware mechanism located between the device and the host computer. Through the hardware module, the USB device establishes a connection to the host OS as normal. When the USB device communicates with the host machine, the raw USB signals are both sent to the host machine and collected for analyzing if the device is a potential threat (1). In (2), the hardware processes the USB packets to further extract relevant information (e.g., packet timestamps, keys being pressed, etc.). With the captured USB packets, the hardware can extract behavioral features (i.e., typing speed, keypress duration, etc.) which can be used to identify if the device is acting maliciously (3). Finally, the features are sent to a machine-learning classifier which determines the behavior of the USB device (i.e., benign vs. malicious) (4). If the classifier deems the USB device as acting maliciously, it terminates the device's

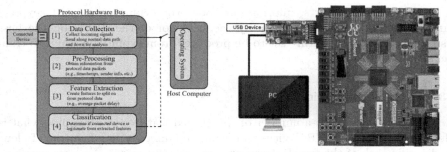

(a) USB-Watch architecture to classify malicious USB attacks

(b) Zedboard FPGA used to implement USB-Watch's testbed

Fig. 2. USB-Watch architecture (a) and implemented testbed for evaluation of USB-Watch (b).

connection to the host machine. For the purposes of this work, behavioral analysis is done on USB keyboard devices.

5.1 Data Collection

We utilize a hardware-based mechanism between the USB-port and the computer to collect USB traffic. Basically, the hardware provides similar functionality to a software-based USB sniffer. For simulation purposes, we used a field-programmable gate array (FPGA) board to emulate a modified USB-host controller capable of detecting malicious USB devices. First, an unknown USB device is connected to the FPGA board which is further connected to the user's machine. From there, normal USB traffic flows from the USB device through the FPGA and into the user's machine. Utilizing a hardware mechanism such as this provides two distinct advantages. First, the hardware cannot be spoofed as it collects data at the USB physical layer. As discussed in Sect. 4, it is possible to subvert or tamper data collected by software sniffers. However, we collect data from the physical layer signals created by the USB device, which is not susceptible to OS-level obfuscation means. Additionally, by using a separated piece of hardware for data collection and pre-processing, an entire segment of computation is removed that would be normally performed on the host computer – saving resources for classification and detection.

5.2 Pre-processing

The data pre-processor takes incoming binary from the data collection to collect information about the connected USB device. USB packets are analyzed and relevant information about the device (e.g., device ID, frequency of packets sent, the data of each packet) is gathered for further analysis. For the purposes of this work, we focus on typing dynamics gathered from USB HID reports. By looking at sequential HID reports, information about the typing speed and keypress duration can be gathered to identify the behavior of the device on the host system. This allows a feature set to be produced from typing dynamics to train a classifier.

5.3 Feature Extraction

In this work, we analyze a number of time-based features to determine what is effective at detecting USB devices which mimic human typing behavior. Below, we describe each of the four features extracted in this work.

1. *Key Transition Time (KTT)* - The key transition time (KTT) is calculated for every keystroke (i) by taking the difference of the time stamp (t_i) of the keystroke prior (t_{i-1}). Since there is no prior keystroke to compare for the first sampled keystroke, ktt_0 is given a value of 0. The equation for extracting the KTT feature is provided below.

$$ktt_i = t_i - t_{i-1}, \tag{1}$$

2. *Duration Held (D)* - This feature defines how long a key was held. To obtain this, we scan the HID reports for the first instance of a keypress. Then, we scan all sequential USB packets until the keypress is removed from the report. The difference in time stamps between the report with the keypress removed and initial report gives the duration the key was held. The equation is provided below.

$$d_i = t_{keyReleased} - t_{keyHeld}, \tag{2}$$

3. *Standardized Features (∥KTT∥, ∥D∥)* - As additional features, we normalize features 1 and 2. This is done by taking the mean (μ) and standard deviation (σ) of a feature vector $(X = <x_1, x_2, ...>)$. Each value in the normalized feature vector is then calculated through the standardization equation:

$$\|x_i\| = (x_i - \mu)/\sigma. \tag{3}$$

As mentioned in Sect. 2, we are primarily focused on a high-precision model. In essence, we do not want a model that correctly predicts every malicious USB device, but also believes the user is a malicious USB device as well. To avoid this, we perform an analysis of features in Sect. 6 to determine which features best work with a model to obtain as high a precision as possible.

5.4 Classification

The extracted features are then placed into a binary classifier to determine if the device is malicious or benign. If the device is considered malicious, communication between the USB device and the host system is discontinued – preventing the attack from occurring.

Section 6 goes into detail of establishing which classification model best fits the dataset used in this work. In the evaluations, a number of classification models (decision tree, random forest, Naive Bayes, k-nearest neighbors, and support vector machines) are tested to determine which model best fits the data based on a number of criteria. The accuracy, precision, ROC curve, and score time of each model is considered to determine if the model can effectively distinguish human and machine typing behavior. From there, additional evaluations are done to ensure that the model can detect advanced threats whereby a malicious device intentionally acts as a human and attempts to subvert the classification model.

Minimum Threshold Whitelist. Our work attempts to classify malicious USB key strokes which mimic human behavior. However, it is unnecessary to classify every malicious USB keystroke injection attack. Before any further analysis and classification is performed, the device must meet a minimum KTT threshold. All keyboard devices on a computer are put through this scan and any malicious actor who does not meet this minimum threshold are blocked. With the work done by USBlock [5], we already know the best threshold to implement. Any device that types faster than 80 ms has been shown to not be human in nature, so we also implement a threshold of 80 ms here. We implement this threshold because there is no point in classifying malicious devices which do not mimic human behavior. If the attacker wishes to perform the attack as quickly as possible, time is wasted in attempting to classify the device. Therefore, we use this minimum threshold to remove the threat posed by the attacker as quickly as possible. However, there are certain benign devices which would also not meet this minimum threshold (e.g., two-factor authentication keys). For this, we add a simple whitelist which permits such devices.

6 Performance Evaluation

This section aims to evaluate the proposed framework model on a live test bed. First, we evaluate the prototype hardware device used in this work by showing the overhead introduced into the system. Then, we aim to establish a final classification model to evaluate against other works. Feature analysis is performed on the proposed feature set of typing dynamics. Once a feature ranking is obtained, model selection is performed on a sample of classification algorithms (e.g., Decision Tree, Random Forest, Naive Bayes, k-nearest neighbors, and support vector machine). With the best overall model chosen, a comparative analysis is performed where the proposed USB-Watch detection framework and prior works are tested against real-world attack scenarios to evaluate which detection framework performs the best.

6.1 Attack Implementation

As mentioned in Sect. 4, this work considers the possibility that a malicious USB device may intentionally mimic human-like typing dynamics so as to appear human to an onlooker. To show the simplicity of such an attack, we developed a malicious device which aims to subvert prior works. We developed a simple Python script which writes the Rubber Ducky attack file that the attacker can use to inject the payload. The script takes in the text used for the attack and implements a delay between each typed character. The delay can have a custom lower/upper bound to more effectively mimic human behavior. For the purposes of our analysis, we used a lower bound delay of 100 ms and an upper bound of 150 ms. This ensures the USB device does not type faster than 100 ms per keystroke so that the device types slow enough to subvert static threshold blocks. The 150 ms upper bound is chosen so that the typing speed is not too slow as to impact the attack itself (i.e. being detected by a human observer, text being interspersed with other keystroke input).

We implement this random delay using Python's random number generator [21], which utilizes the Mersenne Twister (MT) algorithm. We use this algorithm as it comes with a variety of advantages an attacker would find beneficial: (1) MT is used in most modern programming languages, making it ubiquitous to implement, (2) it utilizes a long period ($2^{19937} - 1$) which is beneficial to not repeat cycles, and (3) MT passes many statistical tests of randomness (e.g., birthday spacings, random spheres, etc.). With these 3 benefits, an attacker can easily implement the mimicry attack with more than sufficient assumptions his/her mimic can deceive simple detection schemes.

6.2   Testbed and Data Acquisition

To perform our evaluations, we used a combination of a Zynq ZedBoard and a USB3300 evaluation board for a hardware data collector as shown in Fig. 2b. We tested both benign and malicious key presses with several hundred keystrokes collected for our samples. We collected 180 total samples from both varying users and a malicious device (90 samples for each class) performing an equal variation of three behaviors: (1) typing as fast as possible for 30 s, (2) typing a predefined paragraph as fast as possible, and (3) typing the predefined paragraph while trying to limit typing errors. Behaviors (1) and (2), represent anomalous human behavior so that the model does not incorrectly label a human as a malicious actor. Behavior (3) captures normal human typing behaviors and malicious devices attempting to mimic human behavior. While a 1:1 ratio of benign and malicious samples is not completely representative of real-life scenarios (malicious to benign data ratio would be considerable lower in real-life setups), we challenge our classifier with added malicious data for training and evaluation purposes.

6.3   Feature Analysis

An analysis of each proposed feature is performed in order to obtain information on how well each feature provides information to a classifier. With this, any unnecessary feature can be removed to minimize both classification time

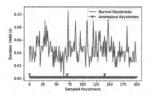

Fig. 3. Keypress duration (s) from benign and malicious samples.

and model overfit. To do so, features were run through a recursive feature elimination which produces ranks of which features to prioritize. We detail which features were removed/prioritized as well as provide analysis to back up these findings below. The only feature removed was normalized key press duration. All of the malicious devices we tested simply send a single HID report of which ever character is next in the sequence. There is no known ability to enforce a key to be held down. This means that the duration the key is pressed is simply how frequent the device is polled. When the feature is standardized, it loses all relevant information if compared with the original key press duration. This is due to there being very little standard deviation between malicious sampled packets which all produced a duration of about 2 ms. When standardized, the malicious key press duration lies squarely in the middle of a standardized benign key press, which is difficult to produce meaningful information. The remaining features are: *duration, KTT*, and *normalized KTT*. The most information gained comes from duration as, through analysis, it is shown that existing devices used to inject malicious keystrokes cannot alter the duration a key is held.

As shown in Fig. 3, this inability to modify the key press duration is what leads to our classification model being so successful. Even when our malicious device produced a human-like key transition times, it was unable to mimic human behavior for key press duration. We assume this behavior occurs from malicious USB devices loading the USB buffer with new information as soon as it is requested and then moving on to the next instruction in the payload. There is no known mechanism in these devices to simulate a keystroke being pressed. Even if an attacker gave a sequence of repeated characters, the USB host controller will read the characters as individual keystrokes. This fact allows us to successfully classify USB-based mimicry attacks that other classification models fail to predict.

However, we cannot simply classify on this feature alone as there are a few overlaps in duration when a human releases a key faster than 2 ms. If we classify on this feature alone, this would produce a false-positive in the model. Therefore, we include the KTT and normalized KTT features for better classification scores.

6.4 Classification Algorithms

With features selected, an analysis of classification models is performed. The models chosen are: Decision Trees, Random Forest Ensembles, k-Nearest

Neighbors, Naive Bayes, and Support Vector Machines. The best performing model in all criteria is chosen at the end.

To train the classification model, we used a 10-fold cross-validation approach on 90% of the collected benign samples. This is done so that the classification models may understand what is expected of USB device behavior. To test the model, the remaining 10% of the benign samples and all malicious samples were used. The classification model label the benign samples as such and the malicious samples and anomalous.

An initial parameter optimization was done to ensure well-performing models using the various machine-learning algorithms. For kNN, a k-size of 3 was used and no weights were put on the data points. For the Decision Tree and Random Forest classifiers, a tree-depth of 4 was established using entropy for information gain. 10 decision trees (default value) were used in the random forest (further evaluation in this section details why this parameter had little effect on the final model). A linear-kernel is used for the Support Vector Machine model using the hinge loss function. Finally, the Complement Naive Bayes algorithm was implemented for the Naive Bayes classifier due to the unbalanced nature of our dataset (i.e., vastly more benign samples than malicious).

The metrics used to evaluate the models are: *accuracy, precision, recall, fit time*, and *score time*. The first three metrics characterize how well the classifier predicts the target class. Good models correctly predict the target class (True-Positives (T_P)) and differentiate from other classes (True-Negatives (T_N)). Conversely, poor models falsely classify the target incorrectly (False-Negatives (F_N)) or classify other data as the target class (False-Positives (F_P)). Accuracy is defined as the number of correct classifications over the total number of classifications. The addition of precision and recall give a sense of how often a classification model incorrectly classifies data as the target class (precision) and how often the target class goes undetected by the model (recall). The other two metrics *fit time* and *score time* tell how fast a classification model performs. Fit time is defined as the time it takes to construct a model given the set of training data. Similarly, score time is how long it takes the constructed model to predict new data.

The first metric analyzed was the accuracy of the classification models. To analyze this, a 10-fold cross-validation, replicated 100 times, was conducted on each of the five tested classifiers. The results are shown in Fig. 4a. Figure 4a first compares the overall score of each model in cross validation. As shown, the Decision Tree, Random Forest, k-Nearest Neighbor, and Naive Bayes classifiers performed the best overall with near perfect scores. The SVM classifier performs quite poorly at a rate of 0.6. As for the performance of the SVM classifier, the results relate back to the sample data. The data was intentionally constructed to produce overlaps in both benign (typing as fast as possible) and malicious (mimicked human behavior) samples. Therefore, the SVM cannot successfully converge all of the data on a single dimension. From there, the precision and recall of the classifiers was analyzed. To do this, newly generated test samples with similar behaviors as the training samples were collected. Each classifier

(a) 10-fold cross-validation scores for each classification model.

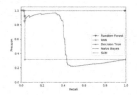

(b) Precision vs. recall scores across varying thresholds for each classification model.

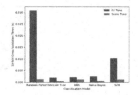

(c) Fit and score times for each classification model.

Fig. 4. Model evaluations for decision tree, random forest, naive bayes, k-nearest neighbor, and support vector machine classifiers.

attempted to classify the test data and returned the probability to predict either malicious or benign behavior. Precision and recall are calculated by taking the percentage of false-positives (human typing classified as a malicious actor) and false-negatives (malicious actor going undetected in the model). These precision and recall scores were calculated over a range of classification thresholds then plotted in Fig. 4b.

As stated in our motivation, we prioritize classification models which produce a high precision first, as we do not want models believing normal behavior is malicious. As shown, the Decision Tree and Random Forest classifiers produce high results where as the kNN, Naive Bayes, and SVM classifiers produce quite poor results. For the latter classifiers, as the models try to capture all malicious devices, the model inevitably treats human behavior as malicious.

Figure 4c compares the time to fit and time to score the data the remaining models. The higher the bar, the more time it takes to fit/score. As shown, the Random Forest takes considerably longer to fit the data, but comparable time to score new data. This makes sense as a Random Forest ensemble creates many Decision Trees with slight variances in which data to split on – meaning that there is a linear increase in complexity to train on data compared to a Decision Tree. When considering all the evaluation metrics (accuracy, precision/recall, computation time), the *Decision Tree* is finally chosen for the classification model. This is chosen because while normally a Random Forest model removes bias and overfitting that comes from decision trees, this does not appear to be the case in fitting the sample data. Indeed, the two models perform comparably in accuracy, precision, and recall. However, the Random Forest model takes considerably longer to fit/score the data, so we choose instead to go with the Decision Tree. To test the viability of the Decision Tree model, a Receiver Operating Characteristic (ROC) curve is constructed. The ROC curve scores the model on its ability to differentiate proper signals (true-positives) from noise (false-positives) in the sampled data. Figure 5b shows the ROC curve of the proposed USB-Watch classifier. Note the dashed line shows a hypothetical model which simply guesses the output class. Any line above the diagonal indicates a

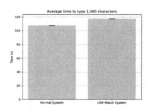
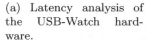
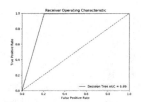

(a) Latency analysis of the USB-Watch hardware.

(b) ROC curve of the proposed USB-Watch decision tree classifier.

Fig. 5. Performance analysis of the final USB-Watch model.

predictive model which can properly infer the correct class from the input data – the higher the curve meaning a better classification model. As shown, the ROC area under the curve (AUC) of USB-Watch is 0.89, which indicates that the proposed framework produces near-excellent prediction results [22].

6.5 Latency Analysis

Our proposed architecture utilizes hardware to detect and prevent malicious USB devices from injecting malicious commands to the host computer. Therefore, there is added latency since all USB traffic must go through an additional step before reaching the operating system. Here, we analyze the additional latency introduced in the system and show its minimal effects on overall performance.

To test for added latency, we created a benign Rubber Ducky script which typed 1000 characters with a delay of 100 ms between each character. We plugged this device into both (1) a normal computer system and (2) a computer system with our USB-watch hardware placed between it and the Rubber Ducky device. When the Rubber Ducky is inserted, we time how long it takes to complete the script. This process is performed 30 times for each system and then the results are all averaged. The results are shown in Fig. 5a. As shown, the average time to complete the script for the normal and USB-Watch systems were 113 s and 119 s respectively. When considering each individual keystroke, that adds an increased latency of about 6 ms per keystroke. This makes sense as the only increased latency the Rubber Ducky device sees is the USB-Watch hardware copying the USB packet during transit before sending the packet to the host OS – all other analysis is done concurrently by the hardware.

6.6 Comparative Analysis

In this section, the viability of the proposed USB-Watch framework is discussed. An analysis is performed to compare USB-Watch against other works. Here, we construct a test suite of increasingly complex attack scenarios and simulate them against USB-Watch and other frameworks.

With the final detection model created, we need to show how effective it is. Here, simulated frameworks of prior works are created and tested against increasingly complex attack models to compare prior work with USB-Watch. We start by describing the frameworks evaluated, then detail the attack models, and conclude with results of how each framework performs against the attack models.

Static Detection Models. There has been prior work to prevent malicious USB devices from being authenticated to operate on a computer [16]. However, this approach does not guarantee mitigation of all attack vectors. It has been shown that malicious actors can embed malicious circuits within larger devices [17]. Assume a malicious device in embedded within a trusted USB device and waits for specific keyphrases (e.g., wait for a user to type 'confidential', then execute an attack to collect the last typed document). To the computer, the device is still an authenticated device and is trustworthy – even when the embedded circuit is conducting the attack. USB-Watch would be able to detect this attack as it is a dynamic approach to detecting USB attacks.

Dynamic Detection Models. Here, we describe the dynamic detection models we recreated for evaluation. Each model is created using the same data and tested against the same attacks which are described in the section below.

Prior 1 – This framework blocks USB keyboard packets which do not exceed a minimum key transition time threshold. We use the same threshold as described in USBlock [5] of 80 ms.

Prior 2 – A One-Class SVM is used for this model and is trained using KTT and $\|KTT\|$ features, similar to USBeSafe [7].

USB-Watch 1 – This is our proposed classification model. However, we replace the hardware-based data collector with software-based tools used in other works (e.g., `usbmon` [20]).

USB-Watch 2 – This is our final proposed framework with the fully hardware-based detection scheme.

Attack Models. The frameworks were tested against a number of attacks with increased sophistication. Each attack model is described below. For each attack, the payload attempts to delete the user's Documents folder through the use of keyboard commands. Additionally, to increase sophistication, each subsequent attack model implements all the methods introduced in prior attack models (i.e. Attack 3 has all the subversion features of Attack 1 and 2).

Attack 1 – This is a simple keystroke injection attack. Once plugged in, the USB device immediately executes the payload and types it as fast as possible. This attack is used as a baseline to demonstrate all the frameworks operate correctly.

Attack 2 – To subvert human detection, this attack waits for 1 min before executing the payload. Again, the payload is typed as fast as possible.

Attack 3 – This attack attempts to mimic human typing dynamics by implementing a static delay of 100 ms between each typed character.

Attack 4 – This attack uses random delays between an interval of 100 ms and 150 ms for each typed character.

Attack 5 – Here, we assume that the target computer is subject to an advanced threat which falsifies usbmon outputs. A rootkit introduces a system hook to the system which removes any USB packet which matches a Rubber Ducky or BadUSB vendor ID from displaying in usbmon.

Results. With the attack models and frameworks defined, we evaluate each attack model against each detection framework. Since each attack model increases in sophistication from the prior, we detail which attack causes the detection model to fail. Table 1 provides the complete results of our findings.

Table 1. Each detection framework's ability to detect different attacks.

	Prior 1 [5]	Prior 2 [7]	USB-Watch 1	USB-Watch 2
Attack 1	✓	✓	✓	✓
Attack 2	✓	✓	✓	✓
Attack 3	X	✓	✓	✓
Attack 4	X	X	✓	✓
Attack 5	X	X	X	✓

Prior 1 – This framework fails after Attack 3 is introduced. Since the KTT threshold should not falsely claim human typing is malicious, the attacker can make an educated guess as to what delay he/she should implement in their device as to surpass the threshold check. In the test results, the minimum delay of 100 ms exceeds the KTT check of 80 ms, so the malicious device is allowed to operate.

Prior 2 – The classifier based on KTT also begins to weaken at Attack 3, but since Attack 3 has a static KTT, the classifier still performs relatively well. However, with Attack 4 introducing a random delay interval, the classifier begins to classify the attack as human in nature.

USB-Watch 1 – This model performs well against all mimicry attacks. This is due to the fact that all known USB injection attacks cannot mimic human key press duration. However, once the rootkit is introduced in Attack 5, the detection framework is simply unable to collect data from the attack and therefore cannot even begin to classify the attack.

USB-Watch 2 – Our final proposed framework performs well against all of the simulated attack models. It properly classifies Attacks 1–4 like USB-Watch 1. However, because the hardware mechanism is used to collect/analyze the raw USB signals from the malicious device, this model can properly classify Attack 5 even when the operating system on the host machine is corrupted.

7   Discussion

In this section, we discuss key findings of USB-Watch and how the proposed framework may be implemented in real-world scenarios. From there, benefits and limitations of the framework are elaborated.

The final USB-Watch classification model uses a binary decision tree classifier to distinguish between human (benign) and machine (malicious) typing behaviors. To do so, a feature set of keystroke transition time (i.e., time between sequential keystrokes) and keypress duration (i.e., time an individual key is held) is used. Current USB devices which mimic human typing are not able to emulate a human-like keypress duration, which allows for the classification model to have a high accuracy and precision. We further show that mimicking human typing dynamics or altering kernel modules may cause other dynamic detection frameworks to fail. However, USB-Watch is able to detect these advanced threats due to its feature set and hardware mechanism respectively.

This work describes the methodology to implement a USB-Watch hardware implementation to detect keyboard-based USB attacks, but the overall USB-Watch framework is designed to be generalized. By collecting generic USB device behaviors, one can train the decision tree model to understand device class 'signatures'. Since USB devices broadcast what kind of device they are, the decision tree can first split on which device class (e.g., mouse, keyboard, flash storage, etc.) the unknown USB device is, then analyze the timing-based behaviors defined by the features in this work. The classifier can then determine if the device is rogue dependent on the behaviors defined by known devices of that device class.

When considering the amount of keystrokes needed to confidently identify a malicious actor, we calculated the confidence interval of our model's ability to determine if the device is malicious. A simple attack to open a terminal and delete sensitive documents takes 40 keystrokes. Given our model's performance, it can be 90% confident of the attacker in 40 keystrokes or less – meaning it can identify the attacker before they can finish the attack.

Since USB-Watch is enacted in a hardware mechanism between an unknown USB device and the host system, latency will be introduced. On average, the additional latency introduced per keystroke is 6 ms per keystroke – an overall low latency. This latency is largely due to the USB-Watch hardware acting as a second USB host controller between the USB device and the host OS. In a final realization of USB-Watch, the actual USB host controller of the host system would have the functionality of USB-Watch, further reducing the latency.

Benefits: The proposed USB-Watch architecture utilizes a hardware mechanism to dynamically collect and process incoming USB traffic which provides two distinct benefits. First, the use of a segmented piece of hardware ensures that the architecture is operating system independent. If a device supports the USB protocol and has a USB host controller, USB-Watch will work on the system. Second, data collection and processing take up computation time with any security mechanism on a computing device. Detaching these processes to a segmented hardware like USB-Watch frees up resources on the host machine. This provides a lightweight solution to detection and minimizes overhead on the host system. With the low cost of simple FPGA circuitry (<$20 USD for a simple programmable logic board), this solution can easily be implemented when fabricating a computer with minimal increase in price per unit.

Limitations: As shown in Fig. 3, the occasional overlap in keypress duration exists between a malicious device and normal human typing behavior. However, an adversary may easily mimic this behavior and subvert the model. Given that, it is possible for this model to weaken and potentially fail. We therefore suggest that the classification model be trained based on the user's specific typing behaviors. We note that it is unrealistic for an attacker to truly mimic a target's exact typing behaviors as that entails the attacker using advanced threats to obtain (e.g., keylogging software). Nonetheless, our proposed system is built against such a keylogger to begin with.

8 Conclusions and Future Work

In this work, we first demonstrated a simple USB keystroke injection attack which subverts prior classification schemes by loosely mimicking normal human behavior. Further, we demonstrated that prior data collection methods are insufficient to this problem as collection is done through software, which can be spoofed by a powerful adversary. Our work shows the feasibility of overcoming these obstacles by introducing USB-Watch, a novel hardware-base detection framework. By utilizing a hardware mechanism placed between the USB-device and the OS, USB-Watch can collect unalterable USB traffic. With machine learning, USB-Watch can successfully detect advanced keystroke-injection attacks which intentionally mimic human typing behavior. These combine to enable a detection framework that is lightweight and OS independent which also distinguishes malicious typing dynamics with an ROC curve of 0.89. To the best of our knowledge, USB-Watch is the first framework to detect USB-based attacks through the utilization of an OS-independent and lightweight hardware mechanism. Further work can be performed to extend this work. Our data collector can theoretically analyze any USB-based device, so further work can be accomplished to classify any number of USB devices (e.g., mice, flash storage, etc.). While our work utilizes hardware for data collection and pre-processing, work can be done to extend our proposed architecture entirely to the hardware mechanism. Doing so would go toward building a truly 'smart' USB bus that can automatically detect and prevent malicious activity before the device has time to establish a connection to the host machine.

Acknowledgements. This work is partially supported by the US National Science Foundation (Awards: NSF-CAREER-CNS-1453647, NSF-1663051) and Florida Center for Cybersecurity's Capacity Building Program. The views expressed are those of the authors only, not of the funding agencies.

References

1. Cunningham, A.: How USB became the undefeated king of connectors, October 2017. https://www.wired.co.uk/article/usb-history
2. Nohl, K., Lell, J.: BadUSB-on accessories that turn evil, Black Hat USA (2014)
3. IBM bans USB drives - but will it work? May 2018. https://nakedsecurity.sophos.com/2018/05/11/ibm-bans-usb-drives-but-will-it-work/
4. Otachi, E.: 8 of the best antivirus with USB scanner for 2018, February 2018. https://windowsreport.com/antivirus-usb-scanner/
5. Neuner, S., Voyiatzis, A.G., Fotopoulos, S., Mulliner, C., Weippl, E.R.: USBlock: blocking USB-based keypress injection attacks. In: Kerschbaum, F., Paraboschi, S. (eds.) DBSec 2018. LNCS, vol. 10980, pp. 278–295. Springer, Cham (2018). https://doi.org/10.1007/978-3-319-95729-6_18
6. Tian, D.J., Bates, A., Butler, K.: Defending against malicious USB firmware with goodUSB. In: Proceedings of the 31st Annual Computer Security Applications Conference, Series ACSAC 2015, New York, NY, USA, pp. 261–270. ACM (2015). https://doi.org/10.1145/2818000.2818040
7. Daley, B.L.: USBeSafe: applying one class SVM for effective USB event anomaly detection. Northeastern University, College of Computer and Information Systems Boston United States, Technical report (2016)
8. Sikka, S., Srivastva, U., Sharma, R.: A review of detection of USB malware. Int. J. Eng. Sci. **7**, 14283 (2017)
9. Admin: Tutorial about USB hid report descriptors, January 2018. https://eleccelerator.com/tutorial-about-usb-hid-report-descriptors/
10. Looks like a flash drive. Types like a keyboard. https://www.hak5.org/gear/usb-rubber-ducky
11. Smith: Say hello to BadUSB 2.0: A USB man-in-the-middle attack proof of concept, June 2016. https://www.csoonline.com/article/3087484/security/say-hello-to-badusb-20-usb-man-in-the-middle-attack-proof-of-concept.html
12. RedTeam: USB drop attacks: the danger of "lost and found" thumb drives", October 2017. https://www.redteamsecure.com/usb-drop-attacks-the-danger-of-lost-and-found-thumb-drives/
13. Bursztein, E.: Does dropping USB drives really work? Blackhat. Technical report (2016)
14. Mamiit, A.: How bad is BadUSB? security experts say there is no quick fix, vol. 18, p. 2014, November 2014
15. Moser, A., Kruegel, C., Kirda, E.: Limits of static analysis for malware detection. In: IEEE Twenty-Third Annual Computer Security Applications Conference ACSAC 2007, pp. 421–430 (2007)
16. Tian, D.J., Scaife, N., Bates, A., Butler, K., Traynor, P.: Making USB great again with USBFILTER. In: 25th USENIX Security Symposium (USENIX Security 16), pp. 415–430 (2016)
17. Robertson, J., Riley, M.: The big hack: How China used a tiny chip to infiltrate U.S. companies. https://www.bloomberg.com/news/features/2018-10-04/the-big-hack-how-china-used-a-tiny-chip-to-infiltrate-america-s-top-companies
18. Raval, M.S., Gandhi, R., Chaudhary, S.: Insider threat detection: machine learning way. In: Conti, M., Somani, G., Poovendran, R. (eds.) Versatile Cybersecurity. AIS, vol. 72, pp. 19–53. Springer, Cham (2018). https://doi.org/10.1007/978-3-319-97643-3_2

19. Lopez, J., Babun, L., Aksu, H., Uluagac, A.S.: A survey on function and system call hooking approaches. J. Hardware Syst. Secur. **1**(2), 114–136 (2017)
20. https://www.kernel.org/doc/Documentation/usb/usbmon.txt
21. 9.6. random - generate pseudo-random numbers. https://docs.python.org/2/library/random.html
22. Maxion, R.A., Roberts, R.R.: Proper use of ROC curves in Intrusion/Anomaly Detection. University of Newcastle upon Tyne, Computing Science (2004)

Automated IoT Device Fingerprinting Through Encrypted Stream Classification

Jianhua Sun[1], Kun Sun[2(✉)], and Chris Shenefiel[3]

[1] College of William and Mary, Williamsburg, USA
jianhua@cs.wm.edu
[2] George Mason University, Fairfax, USA
ksun3@gmu.edu
[3] Cisco Systems, Inc., Raleigh, USA
cshenefi@cisco.com

Abstract. The explosive growth of the Internet of Things (IoT) has enabled a wide range of new applications and services. Meanwhile, the massive scale and enormous heterogeneity (e.g., in device vendors and types) of IoT raise challenges in efficient network/device management, application QoS-aware provisioning, and security and privacy. Automated and accurate IoT device fingerprinting is a prerequisite step for realizing secure, reliable, and high-quality IoT applications. In this paper, we propose a novel data-driven approach for passive fingerprinting of IoT device types through automatic classification of encrypted IoT network flows. Based on an in-depth empirical study on the traffic of real-world IoT devices, we identify a variety of valuable data features for accurately characterizing IoT device communications. By leveraging these features, we develop a deep learning based classification model for IoT device fingerprinting. Experimental results using a real-world IoT dataset demonstrate that our method can achieve 99% accuracy in IoT device-type identification.

Keywords: IoT · Device fingerprinting · Encrypted traffic analysis

1 Introduction

Recent years have witnessed the explosive growth of the Internet of Things (IoT), where smart objects such as cameras, printers, and routers are interconnected to facilitate a wide range of new applications and services (e.g., smart home and smart city). According to a Gartner report [2], over 20 billion devices will be connected to Internet by 2020. Meanwhile, the enormous heterogeneity and vast scale of IoT raise challenges in efficient network/device management, application QoS provisioning, and security and privacy. The proliferation of security vulnerabilities has promoted the emergence of a new generation of malware [9, 13, 20] that target explicitly at IoT devices. For example, the Mirai [9] malware compromised over one million IoT devices and conducted DDoS attacks against several major server infrastructures.

Automated and accurate identification of IoT device types (i.e., device fingerprinting) is a crucial prerequisite for realizing secure, reliable, and high-quality

ⓒ ICST Institute for Computer Sciences, Social Informatics and Telecommunications Engineering 2019
Published by Springer Nature Switzerland AG 2019. All Rights Reserved
S. Chen et al. (Eds.): SecureComm 2019, LNICST 304, pp. 147–167, 2019.
https://doi.org/10.1007/978-3-030-37228-6_8

IoT applications. From the perspective of device management, each IoT device has to be individually configured depending on its type. Given the sheer number of heterogeneous devices deployed in a smart environment, manual configuration is onerous and error-prone. To achieve application QoS guarantee, different priorities may be assigned to devices of different types. In Internet of Vehicles (IoV), it is imperative to prioritize network flows conveying traffic emergency information over those from entertainment devices under high traffic load. To ensure network security, vulnerable devices should be provisioned with more restricted security rules.

In recent years a variety of techniques for IoT device fingerprinting have been proposed [6,9,14,15,24,26,27]. One major approach employs active banner grabbing [6,9,14,15] to collect device-specific information from the application-layer responses and identifies device types based on a database of matching rules. Unfortunately, this approach is inapplicable to fingerprinting IoT devices that adopt SSL/TLS to secure their communications.

Another avenue of research tackled device fingerprinting through passive IoT traffic classification [24,26,27]. However, none of these approaches is manifested to be effective in accurately classifying encrypted IoT traffic. Moreover, most of them merely leverage limited set of traffic features, thus suffering from classification performance degradation in case that sophisticated malware is capable of altering a device's communication pattern.

In this paper, we propose a passive data-driven approach for automated IoT device fingerprinting through encrypted flow classification at the network edge. Motivated by the limitations of prior works, we identify two challenges associated with encrypted flow classification based IoT device fingerprinting. First, IoT devices increasingly use SSL/TLS to secure their communications. Therefore, it is infeasible to collect application-layer data about IoT devices through deep packet inspection (DPI), which necessitates accurate yet privacy-preserving method for classifying IoT traffic. Second, since the IoT traffic only accounts for a minor portion of the entire Internet traffic, identifying IoT traffic from the remaining network traffic is largely a needle-in-the-haystack problem. This situation is worsened by the heterogeneous deployment of traditional and IoT devices in real-world IoT environment.

To resolve these challenges, we first propose to collect substantial telemetry information about IoT device communications at the network edge. Based on these information, we identify and extract a wide range of data features to characterize the network flows generated by both IoT and conventional non-IoT devices. Our feature set comprehensively integrates traditional flow features, device-specific behavioral features, and TLS-related features by analyzing the unencrypted TLS handshake data. The collection of these features does not require packet payload analysis through DPI, making it applicable to the characterization of encrypted IoT traffic. To demonstrate the potential of the identified features for IoT device fingerprinting, we perform an in-depth empirical analysis over real-world IoT traffic with a focus on characterizing the disparate TLS usage of IoT devices.

Second, leveraging these data features collectively, we use supervised machine learning (ML) classifiers to accurately differentiate between IoT traffic and non-IoT traffic relevant to typical client-server applications. For the purpose of IoT device fingerprinting, we develop a deep learning based multinomial classifier to classify encrypted

IoT TLS flows. Our classification model can achieve 99% accuracy for IoT device fingerprinting based on the classification of single network flow, which is more responsive than prior multi-flow based classification methods. Moreover, using all available data features considerably enhances the robustness of the fingerprinting method. Compared to fingerprinting techniques that leverage limited features (e.g., packet sizes and timing), our approach is more resilient against sophisticated attackers that can obfuscate IoT device traffic.

In summary, we make the following contributions:

- We perform an in-depth empirical analysis of SSL/TLS encrypted IoT traffic and identify a variety of valuable data features for accurately characterizing IoT device communications.
- We propose a novel data-driven approach for passive fingerprinting of IoT device types based on automated classification of encrypted TLS flows of IoT devices.
- We develop a deep learning based classification model for IoT device fingerprinting. Using a large dataset consisting of 21 real-world IoT devices, our model can achieve 99% accuracy in IoT device-type identification.

The remainder of the paper is organized as follows. Section 2 introduces the assumptions and the used dataset. Section 3 gives an overview of the proposed approach. Section 4 discusses the feature extraction process in detail. An empirical analysis of IoT TLS usage is presented in Sect. 5. Section 6 presents the evaluation results. Discussion and related work are presented in Sects. 7 and 8, respectively. Section 9 concludes the paper.

2   Assumptions and Data Preliminaries

The IoT fingerprinting scenario we consider is a typical local area network (e.g., enterprise network or campus network), as shown in Fig. 1, where a large range of IoT devices and non-IoT devices are deployed heterogeneously. The devices connect to the Internet via an access gateway. Common encryption techniques such as SSL/TLS can be employed by the devices to ensure data privacy and integrity.

The primary goal of IoT device fingerprinting is to identify the semantic type of new or unseen devices connected to the local network by solely relying on network traffic classification. For this purpose, our traffic analysis assumes a role of passive observer with the capability of monitoring the traffic traversing the gateway router. The raw packets can be collected using common packet capturing libraries, such as tshark [25] and NFQueue [33]. We do not manipulate the network traffic (e.g., deep packet inspection) or use the packet contents. Instead we extract useful telemetry information from the raw packets (e.g., protocol headers and traffic statistics) and leverage the information for IoT device fingerprinting.

Data Preliminaries. The dataset used in our analysis was originally collected by Sivanathan et al. [32] in a smart environment as depicted in Fig. 1. It contains traffic from 21 IoT devices (e.g., smart cameras and switches) and 3 non-IoT devices over 3 weeks operation. We observe that 14 out of 21 IoT devices use TLS to secure their communications, which accounts for 55% of the total captured IoT traffic.

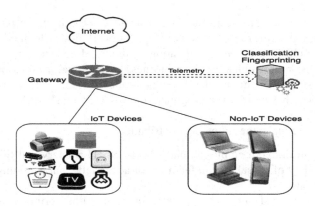

Fig. 1. Edge-based IoT device fingerprinting

3   Approach Overview

In this section we define the problem of IoT device fingerprinting and present an overview of our fingerprinting approach.

3.1   Problem Definition

We formulate IoT device fingerprinting as a classification problem. That is, we perform supervised multi-class classification, where a classifier is trained on labeled instances and tested by assigning a label out of multiple predefined labels to each unlabeled instance. Given a set of IoT device types $D = \{d_1, \ldots, d_n\}$, each instance is of the form $(\mathbf{f_i}, d_i)$, where $\mathbf{f_i}$ is the feature vector that represents a network flow (i.e., a bidirectional flow defined by the network five-tuple) generated by a device d_i that belongs to D. This way, IoT device fingerprinting is stated as follows: assign a device type in D to each new network flow based on its features.

3.2   Overview

The IoT device fingerprinting framework is composed of four major components: *packet capture/parsing*, *feature extraction*, *classifier training*, and *device type fingerprinting*.

Packet Capture/Parsing. Traffic from devices in the monitored network are collected with common packet capturing libraries such as tshark and NFQueue. The raw packets are parsed and reassembled into successive bidirectional flows based on the *flow key* represented by conventional network five-tuple: the source and destination addresses, the source and destination ports (for TCP and UDP traffic), and the protocol number.

Feature Extraction. We identify and extract a series of network flow features from the reassembled flows, which uniquely characterize the IoT device traffic. These features not only allow to distinguish IoT traffic from conventional network traffic, but also enable accurate IoT device fingerprinting. We classify these features into two broad categories: aggregate and intraflow features. Aggregate features characterize flow statistics and device activities spanning multiple flows. Intraflow features consist of flow metadata (from packet header), time-series features (e.g., packet lengths and inter-arrival times), and TLS-related features (for SSL/TLS encrypted traffic). All the extracted m features are represented as a vector $\mathbf{f} \in \mathbb{R}^m$. The feature extraction process is elaborated in Sect. 4.

Classifier Training. This component is responsible for creating ML-based classifiers through model training based on the extracted flow features. We could build binary classifier to differentiate IoT devices from conventional non-IoT devices. For the task of IoT device fingerprinting, a multiclass classifier is trained on the labeled instances $(\mathbf{f_i}, d_i)$. The resulting model is stored for IoT device type fingerprinting.

Device Type Fingerprinting. For a new flow represented by the feature vector $\mathbf{f}$, the trained classifier C is applied to identify the device type. Classifier C outputs a vector of posterior probabilities $\mathbf{p} = \{p_1, \ldots, p_n\}$, where p_i is the probability of flow $\mathbf{f}$ originating from device d_i. The device type is identified as the d_i with maximal probability.

4 Feature Extraction

Feature extraction is the process of transforming real world observation into a vector of values that describe the underlying process. With the purpose of IoT device fingerprinting, we identify a series of network flow based features that uniquely characterize the IoT traffic. These features not only allow us to distinguish IoT traffic from conventional network traffic, but also enable accurate IoT device fingerprinting. We classify these features into two broad categories: aggregate (interflow) and intraflow features. Intraflow features consist of the normal flow features, "side-channel" features, and TLS-related features (for SSL/TLS encrypted traffic). In contrast, aggregate features are interflow features that characterize flow statistics and device activities spanning multiple flows. Here we elaborate on the feature extraction process and explain the rationale of leveraging these features for encrypted flow classification.

4.1 Aggregate Features

IoT traffic typically constitutes (1) background traffic generated by the device autonomously (e.g., NTP queries for time synchronization) and (2) traffic generated due to user interactions (e.g., the smart camera transmits image data to the cloud server when home invasion occurs). Aggregate features provide a high-level characterization of device activities. They are collected from multiple consecutive flows within specific duration. One such feature is the interflow time during which the IoT devices remain inactive, as it indicates the overall frequency of device activity. For this we compute the mean and standard deviation of the interflow times as features.

We also identify other device-specific aggregate features including the respective numbers of involved application-layer protocols, contacted destination servers, and unique DNS queries issued by the device within a fixed duration. We analyze the IoT dataset discussed in Sect. 2 and compute the daily average of the three aggregate features for each device. As indicated in Fig. 2, each IoT device presents a distinct profile of feature combination. Compared to non-IoT devices (as listed in Table 1), IoT devices communicate with significantly fewer destination servers and generate fewer unique DNS queries accordingly. The application protocols involved in IoT communication are more restricted. This is intuitively reasonable since the majority of IoT devices are purpose-limited with restricted functionality (e.g., transmitting data to the cloud server for processing or receiving commands from the control server), while the real user/application behavior is enormously heterogeneous.

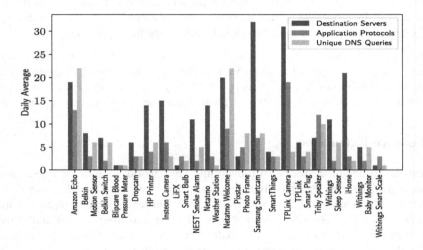

Fig. 2. Aggregate features of IoT devices

Table 1. Aggregate features of Non-IoT devices

Non-IoT device	Destination servers	Application protocols	Unique DNS requests
MacBook Pro	985	6	193
Android Smartphone	348	7	184
Windows PC	862	8	205

4.2 Intraflow Features

Flow Metadata. Flow metadata includes useful information conveyed by the packet header and statistical features of the entire flow. The features we extract include the source and destination ports, the number of inbound/outbound packets and bytes, the total duration of the flow in seconds, the mean packet size, and the peak and mean packet rate. Due to the dynamic allocation of IP addresses and the widespread use of CDNs, we exclude IP addresses from the feature set. Since IoT devices typically generate short bursts of traffic sporadically [32], these per-flow features serve as coarse-grained description of IoT device activity.

Packet Sizes and Inter-arrival Times. The series of packet sizes and inter-arrival times within a flow reveal the fine-grained pattern of IoT communication. From the application level, these features provide a descriptive profile of user behavior. For example, an IoT device such as a smart camera may periodically transmit packets of uniform size to its cloud server; while a PC would generate flows with more diversity in the packet sizes/inter-arrival times given the complexity of user activities (e.g., web browsing and video streaming).

For each flow the packet sizes and inter-arrival times are extracted without considering the TCP retransmission packets or packets lacking payloads (e.g., pure TCP ACK). We used Markov chain to model the time series features. To model the series of packet sizes, we separate the IP MTU size into equally sized bins $B = \{b_1, \ldots, b_n\}$ and allocate each packet size value to the appropriate bin. A matrix S is constructed where each entry, $S[i, j]$, keeps track of the number of transitions between the bin b_i and bin b_j. We then normalize each entry of S as the transition probability and flattened S into a feature vector. The series of packet inter-arrival times is modeled in the same way.

Byte Distribution. The full byte distribution provides information about the encoding of the data. This feature is modeled as a histogram giving the frequency of occurrence for each byte value in the application payload for a flow. Specifically, we used an array to record the count for each byte value of the packet payloads in a single flow. In our analysis an array length 256 is adopted. The probability of each byte value is computed by dividing the byte counts by the total number of byte counts recorded by the array.

Unencrypted TLS Handshake Information. Even for SSL/TLS encrypted traffic, we can still extract valuable information from the unencrypted TLS handshake process. Such information serves as characteristic feature of the communication endpoints. The `ClientHello`, `ServerHello` and `Certificate` messages contain plain text data. In particular, the `ClientHello` message advertises lists of supported ciphersuites and TLS extensions ordered by the client preference. The `ServerHello` message conveys the ciphersuite and TLS extensions selected by the server. The server certificate information can be derived from the `Certificate` message. The client public key length can be determined from the length of the `ClientKeyExchange` message.

Our classification model uses the list of offered ciphersuites, the list of advertised extensions, and the public key length as features. In total 124 unique ciphersuites were observed in the dataset, and a binary vector of length 124 was created where a one is assigned to each ciphersuite in the list of offered ciphersuites. We also observed 14 unique TLS extensions, and a binary vector of length 14 was created where a one is assigned to each extension in the list of advertised extensions. The public key length was represented as a single integer value. Therefore, we extracted 139 TLS features for classification.

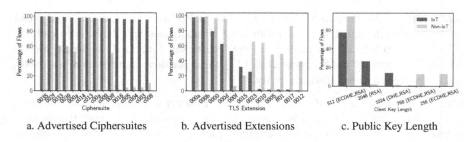

a. Advertised Ciphersuites   b. Advertised Extensions   c. Public Key Length

Fig. 3. TLS client features for IoT versus Non-IoT devices.

To demonstrate the discriminatory power of TLS features for IoT device fingerprinting, in Sect. 5 we provide a detailed characterization of TLS usage in IoT.

4.3 Integration of Aggregate and Intraflow Features

To integrate aggregate features with the intraflow features, we used a disjoint sliding window method to calculate the aggregate features within the window, and then augment each intraflow feature vector within a window with the corresponding aggregate features.

5 Characterizing TLS Usage in IoT

In this section, we compare the TLS usage of IoT devices with conventional non-IoT devices and show that they exhibit distinct characteristics. From the dataset we extract 7820 unique TLS flows of 9 IoT devices and 12557 flows of 3 non-IoT devices. Each unique flow originates from a successful TLS handshake. Merely 12 or less unique flows are extracted from 5 IoT devices, which may be attributed to the extensive use of TLS session resumption to avoid expensive TLS renegotiation. In fact we observed that 25% of IoT clients advertised the 0x0023 (SessionTicket TLS) extension.

5.1 TLS Client Features

The difference between IoT and non-IoT devices regarding the TLS client features is manifested in Fig. 3. First, the top 15 most advertised ciphersuites in IoT are listed along with the corresponding percentage in non-IoT flows. We see less variation in the distribution of the offered ciphersuites in IoT as IoT devices consistently advertise limited and fixed number of ciphersuites. In contrast, due to the diversity in applications, larger variation in ciphersuite distribution is observed in non-IoT traffic. Nearly 100% of IoT devices offer weak ciphersuites such as 0x000a (TLS_RSA_WITH_3DES_EDE_CBC_SHA),   0x0016(TLS_DHE_RSA_WITH_3DES_EDE_CBC_SHA), 0xc003 (TLS_ECDH_ECDSA_WITH_3DES_EDE_CBC_SHA); while non-IoT devices advertise them with significantly lower frequency. This implies that TLS implementations in IoT may be outdated or lack thorough security considerations.

Table 2. TLS client features for each IoT device.

Device category	Number of unique TLS feature vectors	Number of offered ciphersuites	Number of offered extensions	Most frequently advertised extensions	Client's public key
Amazon Echo	2	91	7	heartbeet supported_groups ec_point_formats	2048-bit (RSA) 512-bit (ECDHE_RSA)
Dropcam	1	3	4	SessionTicket TLS heartbeat supported_groups ec_point_formats	512-bit (ECDHE_RSA)
HP Printer	4	85	13	signature_algorithms	768-bit (DHE_RSA) 2048-bit (RSA)
Netatmo Welcome	2	69	5	server_name supported_groups ec_point_formats	512-bit (ECDHE_RSA)
PIX-STAR Photo-frame	1	79	6	All 6 extensions	1024-bit (DHE_RSA)
Samsung Smartcam	1	49	4	All 4 extensions	512-bit (ECDHE_RSA)
SmartThings	1	1	1	signature_algorithms	1024-bit (DHE_RSA)
Triby Speaker	1	80	8	All 8 extensions	512-bit (ECDHE_RSA)
iHome	1	8	1	signature_algorithms	2048-bit (RSA)
Android Smartphone	14	78	14	supported_groups ec_point_formats signature_algorithms	512-bit (ECDHE_RSA) 768-bit (DHE_RSA) 256-bit (ECDHE_RSA) 2048-bit (RSA) 1024-bit (DHE_RSA)
MacBook Pro	9	89	14	supported_groups ec_point_formats	512-bit (ECDHE_RSA) 768-bit (DHE_RSA) 256-bit (ECDHE_RSA) 2048-bit (RSA) 1024-bit (DHE_RSA)
Windows PC	7	96	14	supported_groups ec_point_formats	512-bit (ECDHE_RSA) 768-bit (DHE_RSA) 256-bit (ECDHE_RSA) 2048-bit (RSA) 1024-bit (DHE_RSA)

We also observed more diverse distribution in TLS extensions advertised by non-IoT devices. Up to 8 extensions are advertised in over 50% of non-IoT flows. In contrast, only 4 extensions are advertised by 50% of IoT flows. Three extensions were advertised in over 50% of non-IoT flows and rarely observed in IoT flows: 0x0017 (extended_master_secret), 0x0010 (ALPN), and 0xff01 (renegotiation_info). This indicates more lightweight TLS implementation with limited functionality in IoT due to the computation and resource constraint. We also observed that the extension 0x000f (heartbeat) is advertised with a much higher frequency by IoT devices which indicates the behavior of IoT devices frequently contacting remote servers for liveliness check. Moreover, 40% of IoT clients advertised 0x0015 (padding) extension compared to 20% of the enterprise clients, which indicates the existence of more aged IoT clients that have outdated TLS implementation.

The distribution of client public key length is also different. Most non-IoT devices used a 512-bit (ECDHE_RSA) public key. 2048-bit (RSA) and 1024-bit (DHE_RSA) were more widely used by IoT devices. One interesting observation is 27% of non-IoT flows used 256-bit (ECDHE_RSA) to generate keys for CHACHA20_POLY1130 cipher, but no IoT clients used this cipher to encrypt their connection.

The discriminatory power of TLS client features for IoT device fingerprinting becomes more obvious when looking into the TLS usage of each device. Table 2 summarizes the TLS client features for each device. Four IoT devices offered the number of ciphersuites comparable to the non-IoT devices, while only one IoT device (i.e., HP Printer) offered the same number of extensions. The public keys used by the IoT devices are also quite limited with all devices using at most two public keys for their connections, which indicates the simplicity of IoT devices. In contrast, we observed more variation in the used public keys in non-IoT devices due to the diversity of user applications.

Table 2 also lists the number of unique TLS client feature vectors advertised by each device. Here a feature vector is considered unique if the concatenation of ciphersuite and extension features is different. We can see that each IoT device offered quite distinct ciphersuites and extensions, which allows accurate identification of the specific device category. 6 out of 9 IoT devices even consistently offered a single fixed set of ciphersuites and extensions. 2 IoT devices offered 2 ciphersuite vectors and only the HP Printer offered 4. This also implies that IoT devices typically employ the same client to communicate with the remote servers.

5.2 TLS Server Features

Figure 4 illustrates the difference regarding TLS server features. 60% of TLS sessions selected 0xc030 (TLS_ECDHE_RSA_WITH_AES_256_GCM_SHA384) and 25% of TLS sessions selected 0x0035 (TLS_RSA_WITH_AES_256_CBC_SHA). In contrast, the distribution of ciphersuites selected by non-IoT device sessions is more heavily tailed. This corroborates the client-side analysis that most IoT devices used specialized clients to communicate with limited number of remote servers.

Similar to the selected ciphersuites, the servers that IoT devices communicated with selected fewer TLS extensions. There is much greater diversity in the selected TLS extensions with 0xff01 (renegotiation_info) and 0x000b (ec_point_formats) being the most frequent.

By analyzing the plain text server certificate data (e.g., certificate subject), we found that non-IoT devices mostly connected to common servers such as *.google.com, *.icloud.com and *.facebook.com. Moreover, the corresponding distribution of certificate subjects is very long tailed. We also analyzed two other features extracted from server certificates: the certificate validity and the number of Subject Alternative Name (SAN) entries. As depicted in Fig. 4, the validity of the certificate is sharply divided for IoT devices and non-IoT devices. The distribution of the validity of non-IoT devices' certificates is long tailed with greater diversity. Almost all server certificates associated with IoT devices have no more than 2 SAN entries. This is intuitively reasonable considering that non-IoT devices typically connected with

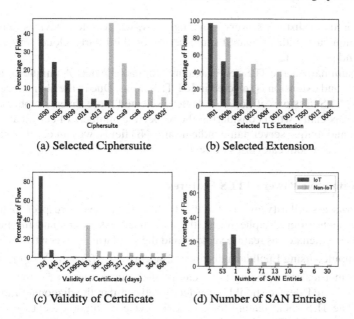

(a) Selected Ciphersuite

(b) Selected Extension

(c) Validity of Certificate

(d) Number of SAN Entries

Fig. 4. TLS server features for IoT versus Non-IoT devices.

Table 3. TLS server features for each device.

Device category	Most frequently selected ciphersuite	Most frequently selected extensions	Number of distinct CS	Number of SAN entries	Number of distinct SNI
Amazon Echo	TLS_ECDHE_RSA_WITH_AES_128_GCM_SHA256	renegotiation_info server_name ec_point_formats	1	2	5
Dropcam	TLS_ECDHE_RSA_WITH_AES_128_CBC_SHA	renegotiation_info	1	2	0
HP Printer	TLS_DHE_RSA_WITH_AES_128_CBC_SHA	renegotiation_info	2	3	0
Netatmo Welcome	TLS_ECDHE_RSA_WITH_AES_256_GCM_SHA384	renegotiation_info server_name ec_point_formats	1	2	1
PIX-STAR Photo-frame	TLS_DHE_RSA_WITH_AES_256_CBC_SHA	renegotiation_info SessionTicket TLS	1	1	1
Samsung SmartCam	TLS_DHE_RSA_WITH_AES_128_CBC_SHA	renegotiation_info ec_point_formats SessionTicket TLS	1	1	0
SmartThings	TLS_DHE_RSA_WITH_AES_128_CBC_SHA	signature_algorithms	2	0	0
Triby Speaker	TLS_ECDHE_RSA_WITH_AES_256_GCM_SHA384	renegotiation_info heartbeat server_name ec_point_formats	1	0	1
iHome	TLS_RSA_WITH_AES_128_CBC_SHA256	None	1	2	0
Android Smartphone	TLS_RSA_WITH_AES_128_CBC_SHA	renegotiation_info	135	53	263
MacBook Pro	TLS_ECDHE_RSA_WITH_AES_128_GCM_SHA256	renegotiation_info	148	53	316
Windows PC	TLS_RSA_WITH_AES_256_CBC_SHA	renegotiation_info	262	53	554

several hundreds of distinct servers in a single day, whereas IoT devices only consistently communicate with its manufacture server or third-party cloud server for data uploading and processing.

Table 3 summarizes the TLS server features for each device. A unique combination of ciphersuite and extension is selected in IoT TLS flows. Due to the abundance of client applications, TLS sessions of non-IoT devices selected more diverse ciphersuites and extensions. Especially when considering the respective numbers of certificate subjects, SAN entries and unique server name indication (SNI) fields, we can observe significant difference between both categories of devices.

5.3   Discriminative Power of TLS Features

Figure 5 shows a similarity matrix for the 14 IoT devices with respect to their TLS clients. The client offered ciphersuites, the advertised extensions and the public key length were concatenated as feature vectors, and the similarity between two feature vectors was computed using Euclidean distance (2-norm) $d(f_i, f_j) = \sqrt{\sum_{i,j}(f_i - f_j)^2}$ as the distance metric, and f_i being the mean of the feature vectors for the i'th device type. Since each IoT device should be perfectly self-similar, the diagonal of this matrix are all 1.0. The TLS client feature for each IoT device is unique except for the Belkin Motion Sensor and the TPLink Smart Plug, which have similar TLS client parameters. Device-specific TLS parameters can be a promisingly powerful feature for classifying IoT device type.

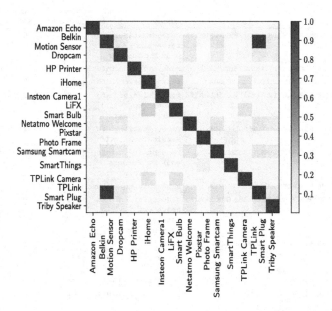

Fig. 5. Similarity matrix for different IoT devices with respect to the TLS client features

6   Evaluation

In this section, we describe the details of our ML-based IoT fingerprinting methodology, and demonstrate the discriminative power of the TCP/IP flow features for accurately differentiating between IoT devices and non-IoT devices as well as identifying the specific IoT device category.

6.1   Algorithms

We performed the encrypted flow classification using a deep learning based model: Multi-layer Perceptron (MLP), and compared the results with three common machine learning algorithms: Logistic Regression, Random Forest and Support Vector Machine. To auto-tune the hyperparameters for the models, we used grid search and cross-validation over a set of standard values. We used Keras [5] with the TensorFlow [7] backend to implement the MLP; while the remaining ML algorithms are implemented using Scikit-learn [28]. An open source tool is used and extended for feature extraction [4].

Multi-layer Perceptron (MLP). MLPs are fully connected feed-forward neural networks with multiple hidden layers. Each layer consists of several neurons that compute a weighted sum of the inputs from the adjacent layer and produce the output through a non-linear activation function. Deep and dense MLPs can estimate highly nonlinear functions. However, due to the huge number of parameters that need to be learned, it is complex process to train these models and there is the potential for overfitting.

We performed automatic search of the best hyperparameters for the MLP model using grid search and cross validation. Table 4 lists the values of the hyperparameters we tuned and the corresponding intervals within which the values are varied.

Table 4. Tuned hyperparameters of the MLP

Hyperparameter	Value	Tuning space
Optimizer	Adam	Adam, SGD, RMSProp
Learning rate	0.001	0.001 .. 0.1
Momentum	0.0	0.0 .. 0.9
Batch size	32	8 .. 256
Training epochs	150	50 .. 200
Number of hidden layers	3	2 .. 5
Dropout	0.1	0.0 .. 0.5
Activation	sigmoid	tanh, sigmoid, relu

Logistic Regression. Logistic regression is one of the simplest classification algorithms. It generates an estimate of the probability that a feature vector belongs to a specific class. We used both l1-regularization and l2-regularization in the comparison.

The model is more easily interpretable compared to MLP as the model parameters quantify the significance of the corresponding data features.

Random Forest. A random forest combines decision tress with ensemble learning [10]. Each decision tree is built from a random sub-sample of the original data and produces a probability for each possible output class. The output of the ensemble is the average probability among all decision trees. Random forest is resistant to overfitting. Moreover, the variance is reduced without resulting in bias when the number of trees increases. For the Scikit-learn implementation, we used grid search and cross-validation to tune the depth of the trees and the number of features per split.

Support Vector Machine (SVM). An SVM projects original data to a high-dimensional feature space using a kernel function, where a hyperplane can be built to linearly separate different classes [12]. Our SVM implementation adopts the One-VS-Rest strategy and uses LinearSVC for classification.

6.2   IoT vs Non-IoT

For the binary classification between IoT and Non-IoT device flows, we used a logistic regression classifier with l1-regularization [18]. As such, five machine learning classifiers were trained using different combinations of the collected data features, which incorporate the flow metadata (M), the time series features including the packet sizes (PS) and inter-arrival times (PT), the byte distribution of the packet payload (BD), the TLS client parameters (i.e., the offered ciphersuites, advertised extensions, and the public key length) (TLS), and the aggregate features (A) spanning multiple flows.

To demonstrate the usefulness of the identified data features, we use 10-fold cross validation over 96680 IoT flows and 96680 Non-IoT flows, out of which 20000 flows are TLS flows. Table 5 shows the cross validation results. We can see that using all available data features achieves the best accuracy of 99.6%. Using the TLS features alone to classify TLS flows gives 90% accuracy, which demonstrates the usefulness of these features for characterizing IoT devices.

Table 5. Classifier accuracy for different subsets of features

Data features	Accuracy
M+PS+PT	82.4%
M+PS+PT+BD	93.5%
TLS	90.1%
M+PS+PT+BD+TLS	97.2%
M+PS+PT+BD+TLS+A	99.6%

6.3 IoT Device Fingerprinting

We also evaluate the effectiveness of the identified flow features for IoT device finger-printing. For the multi-class classification, we use 541250 flows generated by all the 21 IoT device categories and data features described in Sect. 4. We randomly selected 75% flows to train the classifiers and used the remaining 25% flows for testing. The final classification results under different ML models are listed in Table 6. Using MLP and all flow features results in the best classification performance, with an overall accuracy of 99.8% for the 21-class classification based on a single network flow.

Table 6. Comparison of classifier performance

Model	Accuracy
$l1$-Logistic Regression	86.2%
$l2$-Logistic Regression	81.5%
Random Forest	72.7%
SVM	58.4%
MLP	**99.8%**

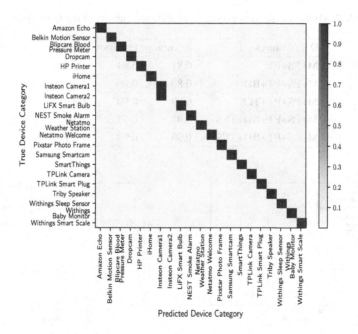

Fig. 6. Confusion matrix for the 21-class IoT device type classification using MLP. The best overall accuracy is 99.8%.

The confusion matrix of the best classification result is shown in Fig. 6. Each matrix element m_{ij} represents the percentage of device d_i's flows classified as that of device d_j. The confusion matrix is perfectly diagonal, indicating the superior power of the identified network flow features for IoT fingerprinting. Notably, all samples of an Insteon Camera were identified as another device of the same category since it generated significantly less flows.

We also present the classification performance of MLP with different subsets of features in Table 7. With a subset of data features, our approach is able to differentiate the device types based on a single flow. Using a combination of the available data features significantly enhances the classification robustness.

6.4 Algorithm Performance

We assess the performance of the used classification algorithms in terms of the training and testing time. The multi-class classification experiment discussed in Sect. 6.3 was repeated 10 times for each algorithm. Figures 7 and 8 plot the training and testing times in seconds with respect to the average classification accuracy of each algorithm. The random forest can be quickly trained and tested, while SVM is relatively slow to train and test. The MLP is cumbersome to train, but quick to classify new samples.

Table 7. MLP classification accuracy for different subsets of the flow features

Data features	Accuracy	Precision	Recall
M+PS+PT	0.81	0.84	0.82
M+PS+PT+BD	0.83	0.86	0.83
M+PS+PT+TLS	0.89	0.90	0.89
M+PS+PT+BD+TLS	0.92	0.93	0.93
M+PS+PT+BD+TLS+A	0.99	0.99	0.99

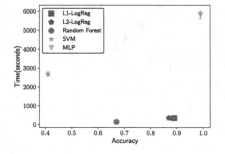

Fig. 7. Model training times

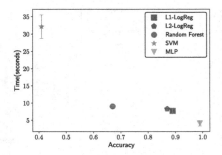

Fig. 8. Model testing times

7 Discussion and Future Work

Robustness Against Adversarial Attacks. Attackers capable of controlling their devices' network traffic may attempt to circumvent our fingerprinting technique. For example, random or constant delays could be introduced into a flow. Similarly, packet sizes could be varied through data padding at different protocol levels. Since our method does not solely rely on a single feature (e.g., time series feature), it is more resilient to such adversarial attacks compared to existing IoT device fingerprinting techniques. Modifying the TLS parameters supported by a device (i.e., advertised ciphersuites and extensions) may also degrade the normal functionality of the device itself. An attacker could also try to mimic the traffic pattern of a different device type. Considering that most IoT devices will communicate with a fixed set of servers, it would be extremely difficult for the attacker to generate similar requests to the servers, especially when the emulated device uses TLS for authentication and data encryption.

Impact of TLS 1.3. The analysis of TLS features in this paper is based on TLS 1.2. TLS 1.3 [3] eliminates a complete round trip time, making TLS more suitable for IoT devices. In TLS 1.3, the server selected extensions and certificate get encrypted. Since our approach only relies on TLS client features, the adoption of TLS 1.3 will not deteriorate the performance of IoT device fingerprinting.

Scalability. The proposed IoT device fingerprinting method can be deployed at the edge of a LAN. Our current implementation is applied to small scale IoT smart environment. A more scalable fingerprinting system could be realized using a distributed design. In our future work, we will explore using federated learning approach [21] for distributed optimization of our deep learning based fingerprinting model. Using federated learning, we could train a local model at the network edge and synchronize the model modifications through a centralized server. This solution is more scalable since only model parameters have to be synchronized, thus obviating the need to offload raw data to the centralized server.

Applications of Device Fingerprinting. In future work, we will consider the applications of automated IoT device fingerprinting from various perspectives. One potential application is to leverage device fingerprinting to instruct the QoS-aware provisioning of network resources. Another focus is on its security applications. For example, we will explore how to integrate our fingerprinting method into existing network access control (NAC) system. This could enable the NAC system to automatically detect unknown vulnerable devices and configure security rules accordingly.

8 Related Work

Operating System Fingerprinting. In network security, fingerprinting has been used for information gathering and vulnerability assessment of the attack target. One prominent example is OS fingerprinting, which aims at determining the operating system of a remote host based on the implementation differences of a TCP/IP network stack. A variety of tools (Nmap [1] and P0f [35]) actively probe a target with purposely crafted packets and generate fingerprint from the response packets. The OS version is identified by matching the fingerprint with a database of existing OS categories. Hershel [30] and Faulds [31] focus on Internet-wide single-probe OS fingerprinting, which leverages the temporal features (i.e., TCP retransmission timeout) to classify the OS of the target. The objective of our work is to identify the IoT device type instead of the OS version, which precludes the usage of OS fingerprinting as different devices may run the same OS.

IoT Device-Type Identification. Various prior research have been proposed to utilize a multitude of data sources for passive IoT device type identification. Early wireless communication fingerprinting techniques leverage the implementation characteristics of wireless network interface card (WNIC) hardware [11] or device-driver [16,23]. However, the fingerprinting target is WNIC instead of physical device. These techniques also require the observer to be in the wireless range of the target device in order for the technique to work. Correspondingly, Kohno et al. introduced a passive physical device fingerprinting method that exploited the minute deviations in the clock skews to derive a clock cycle pattern as the device identity [19]. The analysis is not readily applicable to fingerprinting the semantic type of IoT devices.

State-of-the-art solutions for device-type identification in small scale networks rely on supervised machine learning with various traffic features [22,24,29]. GTID [29] extracts device signatures from the packet inter-arrival times (IATs), which are used to train an Artificial Neural Network (ANN) to identify device type. The device identification process requires several hours of traffic for signature generation. Moreover, solely relying on packet IATs makes it susceptible to spoofing attack where sophisticated attacker could emulate the IAT pattern of a different device. The authors of [22] design a device type detection technique that classifies encrypted link-layer traffic using random forest classifier. The technique only targets wireless devices, demanding passive eavesdropping using specialized radios. Similarly, Meidan et al. [24] performed IoT device type identification by applying random forest classifier to features extracted from TCP sessions. They only achieve acceptable accuracy through classification of 20 consecutive TCP sessions, while our method achieves high accuracy on single-flow classification.

Motivated by network security, IoT Sentinel [26] builds up a classifier on device fingerprints extracted from the burst of network traffic generated during the initial setup phase of the device. After assessing the vulnerability of the identified device type, security rules are enforced to constrain the communications of vulnerable devices. One limitation of IoT Sentinel is that it only operates when a device is first introduced to a network. DIoT [27] uses unsupervised learning to classify devices into device types based on passive fingerprinting of periodic background traffic of IoT devices. For each device type, Gated recurrent unit (GRU) is used to establish the normal communication profile and subsequently detect anomalies in communication patterns. The fingerprinting strategy of DIoT is subject to deterioration since it merely relies on the periodicity inherent in background traffic. Furthermore, only an abstract device type is identified instead of the semantic type.

Another avenue of research centers on Internet-wide detection of IoT devices. Shodan [6] is the first search engine for discovering Internet-connected devices. Internally it uses Nmap to identify the application and services of an online device. Censys [14] employs banner-grabbing to gather device-specific information from the application-layer responses, and identifies devices based on a database of matching rules. Fingerprinting with Shodan and Censys demands cumbersome manual efforts for devising the matching rules. Recently, Feng et al. developed a search engine named ARE [15] for automatic device discovery and annotation in large scale. Device rules are built by correlating application-layer response data from IoT devices with the product descriptions (e.g., the device type and vendor) in relevant websites. The active probing performed by these techniques could be detected and defeated by sophisticated attackers through obfuscation. Moreover, the application layer data may not be readily available from banner grabbing. In contrast, our approach can automatically detect IoT device type using deep learning based classification.

Network Traffic Analysis. Network traffic analysis has been applied to various applications such as intrusion detection [36] and app identification [34]. These applications employ classical machine learning classifiers with different features extracted from the raw traffic (e.g., packet header, payload and statistics). For example, time-series features (packet lengths and inter-arrival times) are used for mobile application service usage classification [17]. Recent studies even achieve high malware detection accuracy on encrypted traffic using the plain text data contained in the TLS handshake [8]. These features are instructive for our passive traffic classification based IoT device fingerprinting. We perform fine-grained characterization of IoT devices and explore the power of a wide-range of features for IoT device identification.

9   Conclusions

This paper proposed a novel data-driven approach for automated and accurate fingerprinting of IoT device types. Our fingerprinting method relies on passive classification of potentially encrypted IoT flows. We first performed an in-depth empirical study of real-world IoT traffic, based on which we identify a variety of useful data features that could accurately characterize IoT device communications. Leveraging these features, we have developed a deep learning based classification model for IoT device fingerprinting. Using a real-world IoT dataset, our evaluation results demonstrate that the proposed method can achieve ~99% accuracy in IoT device-type identification based on single network flow classification.

Acknowledgment. This work is partially supported by the U.S. ONR grants N00014-16-1-3214, N00014-16-1-3216, and N00014-18-2893 and U.S. ARO grant W911NF-17-1-0447.

References

1. Nmap, Network Security Scanner Tool (2012). https://nmap.org/
2. 20 billion IoT devices by 2020 (2017). https://www.gartner.com/newsroom/id/3598917
3. The Transport Layer Security (TLS) Protocol Version 1.3 (2018). https://datatracker.ietf.org/doc/rfc8446/
4. Joy (2019). https://github.com/cisco/joy
5. Keras: Deep Learning for humans (2019). https://github.com/keras-team/keras
6. Shodan (2019). https://www.shodan.io/

7. Abadi, M., et al.: TensorFlow: a system for large-scale machine learning. In: OSDI, vol. 16, pp. 265–283 (2016)
8. Anderson, B., McGrew, D.: Machine learning for encrypted malware traffic classification: accounting for noisy labels and non-stationarity. In: Proceedings of the 23rd ACM SIGKDD International Conference on Knowledge Discovery and Data Mining, pp. 1723–1732. ACM (2017)
9. Antonakakis, M., et al.: Understanding the Mirai Botnet. In: 26th USENIX Security Symposium (USENIX Security 2017), pp. 1093–1110 (2017)
10. Breiman, L.: Random forests. Mach. Learn. **45**(1), 5–32 (2001)
11. Brik, V., Banerjee, S., Gruteser, M., Oh, S.: Wireless device identification with radiometric signatures. In: Proceedings of the 14th ACM International Conference on Mobile Computing and Networking, pp. 116–127. ACM (2008)
12. Cortes, C., Vapnik, V.: Support-vector networks. Mach. Learn. **20**(3), 273–297 (1995)
13. Costin, A., Zaddach, J.: IoT malware: comprehensive survey, analysis framework and case studies. BlackHat USA (2018)
14. Durumeric, Z., Adrian, D., Mirian, A., Bailey, M., Halderman, J.A.: A search engine backed by internet-wide scanning. In: Proceedings of the 22nd ACM SIGSAC Conference on Computer and Communications Security, CCS 2015 (2015)
15. Feng, X., Li, Q., Wang, H., Sun, L.: Acquisitional rule-based engine for discovering internet-of-things devices. In: 27th USENIX Security Symposium (USENIX Security 2018), pp. 327–341 (2018)
16. Franklin, J., McCoy, D., Tabriz, P., Neagoe, V., Randwyk, J.V., Sicker, D.: Passive data link layer 802.11 wireless device driver fingerprinting. In: USENIX Security Symposium, vol. 3, pp. 16–89 (2006)
17. Fu, Y., Xiong, H., Lu, X., Yang, J., Chen, C.: Service usage classification with encrypted internet traffic in mobile messaging apps. IEEE Trans. Mob. Comput. **15**(11), 2851–2864 (2016)
18. Koh, K., Kim, S.J., Boyd, S.: An interior-point method for large-scale l1-regularized logistic regression. J. Mach. Learn. Res. **8**(Jul), 1519–1555 (2007)
19. Kohno, T., Broido, A., Claffy, K.C.: Remote physical device fingerprinting. IEEE Trans. Dependable Secure Comput. **2**(2), 93–108 (2005)
20. Kolias, C., Kambourakis, G., Stavrou, A., Voas, J.: DDoS in the IoT: Mirai and other Botnets. Computer **50**(7), 80–84 (2017)
21. Konečný, J., McMahan, H.B., Yu, F.X., Richtárik, P., Suresh, A.T., Bacon, D.: Federated learning: strategies for improving communication efficiency. arXiv preprint arXiv:1610.05492 (2016)
22. Maiti, R.R., Siby, S., Sridharan, R., Tippenhauer, N.O.: Link-layer device type classification on encrypted wireless traffic with COTS radios. In: Foley, S.N., Gollmann, D., Snekkenes, E. (eds.) ESORICS 2017. LNCS, vol. 10493, pp. 247–264. Springer, Cham (2017). https://doi.org/10.1007/978-3-319-66399-9_14
23. Maurice, C., Onno, S., Neumann, C., Heen, O., Francillon, A.: Improving 802.11 fingerprinting of similar devices by cooperative fingerprinting. In: 2013 International Conference on Security and Cryptography (SECRYPT), pp. 1–8. IEEE (2013)
24. Meidan, Y., et al.: Detection of unauthorized IoT devices using machine learning techniques. arXiv preprint arXiv:1709.04647 (2017)
25. Merino, B.: Instant Traffic Analysis with Tshark How-to. Packt Publishing Ltd (2013)
26. Miettinen, M., Marchal, S., Hafeez, I., Asokan, N., Sadeghi, A.R., Tarkoma, S.: IoT sentinel: automated device-type identification for security enforcement in IoT. In: 2017 IEEE 37th International Conference on Distributed Computing Systems (ICDCS), pp. 2177–2184. IEEE (2017)

27. Nguyen, T.D., Marchal, S., Miettinen, M., Dang, M.H., Asokan, N., Sadeghi, A.R.: DIoT: a crowdsourced self-learning approach for detecting compromised IoT devices. arXiv preprint arXiv:1804.07474 (2018)
28. Pedregosa, F., et al.: Scikit-learn: machine learning in python. J. Mach. Learn. Res. **12**(Oct), 2825–2830 (2011)
29. Radhakrishnan, S.V., Uluagac, A.S., Beyah, R.: GTID: a technique for physical deviceand-device type fingerprinting. IEEE Trans. Dependable Secure Comput. **12**(5), 519–532 (2015)
30. Shamsi, Z., Nandwani, A., Leonard, D., Loguinov, D.: Hershel: single-packet OS fingerprinting. IEEE/ACM Trans. Network. **24**(4), 2196–2209 (2016)
31. Shamsi, Z., Cline, D.B., Loguinov, D.: Faulds: a non-parametric iterative classifier for internet-wide OS fingerprinting. In: Proceedings of the 2017 ACM SIGSAC Conference on Computer and Communications Security, CCS 2017 (2017)
32. Sivanathan, A., et al.: Characterizing and classifying IoT traffic in smart cities and campuses. In: 2017 IEEE Conference on Computer Communications Workshops (INFOCOM WKSHPS)
33. Sugiyama, Y., Goto, K.: Design and implementation of a network emulator using virtual network stack. In: 7th International Symposium on Operations Research and Its Applications (ISORA 2008), pp. 351–358 (2008)
34. Taylor, V.F., Spolaor, R., Conti, M., Martinovic, I.: Robust smartphone app identification via encrypted network traffic analysis. IEEE Trans. Inf. Forensics Secur. **13**(1), 63–78 (2018)
35. Zalewski, M.: p0f v3 (2012). http://lcamtuf.coredump.cx/p0f3/
36. Zarpelao, B.B., Miani, R.S., Kawakani, C.T., de Alvarenga, S.C.: A survey of intrusion detection in internet of things. J. Netw. Comput. Appl. **84**, 25–37 (2017)

Catching Malware

DeepCG: Classifying Metamorphic Malware Through Deep Learning of Call Graphs

Shuang Zhao[1,3], Xiaobo Ma[2(✉)], Wei Zou[1,3], and Bo Bai[1,3]

[1] Institute of Information Engineering, Chinese Academy of Sciences, Beijing, China
{zhaoshuang,zouwei,baibo}@iie.ac.cn
[2] MOE KLINNS Lab, Faculty of Electronic and Information Engineering,
Xi'an Jiaotong University, Xi'an, China
xma.cs@xjtu.edu.cn
[3] School of Cyber Security, University of Chinese Academy of Sciences,
Beijing, China

Abstract. As the state-of-the-art malware obfuscation technique, metamorphism has received wide attention. Metamorphic malware can mutate themselves into countless variants during propagation by obfuscating part of their executable code automatically, thus posing serious challenges to all existing detection methods. To address this problem, a fundamental task is to understand the stable features that are relatively invariant across all variants of a certain type of metamorphic malware while distinguishable from other types. In this paper, we systematically study the obfuscation methods of metamorphic malware, and reveal that, compared to frequently used fragmented features such as byte n-grams and opcode sequences, call graphs are more stable against metamorphism, and can be leveraged to classify metamorphic malware effectively. Based on call graphs, we design a metamorphic malware classification method, dubbed *deepCG*, which enables automatic feature learning of metamorphic malware via deep learning. Specifically, we encapsulate the information of each call graph into an image that is then fed into deep convolutional neural networks for classifying the malware family. Particularly, due to its built-in training data enhancement approach, *deepCG* can achieve promising classification accuracy even with small-scale training samples. We evaluate *deepCG* using a PE malware dataset and the Microsoft BIG2015 dataset, and achieve a test accuracy of above 96%.

Keywords: Call graph · Deep learning · Malware classification · Metamorphic malware

1 Introduction

Malware has been evolving rapidly in the last decade, threatening the cyberspace in a growing sophisticated manner and hence attracting the attention in both

S. Chen et al. (Eds.): SecureComm 2019, LNICST 304, pp. 171–190, 2019.
https://doi.org/10.1007/978-3-030-37228-6_9

academic and industrial worlds. To fight against malware, signature-based detection, though labor-intensive because of signature extraction and updating, proves to be an effective approach that can quickly respond to known malware. The major reason for such effectiveness is clearly and accurately profiling unique signatures that exclusively exist in a fragment of a certain family of known malware (i.e., fragmented signatures). Nevertheless, figuring out unique fragmented signatures become increasingly harder, since more and more malware are using metamorphism to mutate themselves into countless variants during propagation by obfuscating part of their executable code automatically. As a result, for a certain family of metamorphic malware, it is likely that they automatically alter code during propagation so to eliminate unique fragmented signatures, thus defeating signature-based detection.

To address this problem, a fundamental task is to understand the stable features that are relatively invariant across all variants of a certain family of metamorphic malware while distinguishable from other metamorphic malware families. A apparent approach to finishing this task is to employ machine learning algorithms for training a classification model with various features extracted from malicious samples and use the trained model to classify malware into different families. Despite its simplicity in principle, employing machine learning algorithms to address this problem is not easy. The reasons are two-fold. First, machine learning algorithms rely on high-quality feature vectors. Manually proposing feature vectors and selecting useful features via the trial-and-error paradigm, though possible, can hardly adapt to the complexity and heterogeneity of metamorphic malware, thus ineffective. Consequently, a machine learning algorithm that can automatically extract useful features is in urgent demand. Second, metamorphic malware can mutate themselves into countless variants via code obfuscation techniques like dead code insertion and code reordering during propagation. This means that in practice one may only capture a small proportion of its variants. Therefore, the proposed machine learning algorithm are expected to have strong prediction capability even with small-scale training samples.

In this paper, we systematically study the obfuscation methods of metamorphic malware, and reveal that, compared to frequently used fragmented features such as byte n-grams and opcode sequences, call graphs extracted from Portable Executable (PE) files and disassembly files (i.e., files with a suffix of .asm) reflect metamorphic malware's underlying structural features and thus are more stable against metamorphism. Therefore, call graphs have the potential to classify metamorphic malware effectively. To validate the potential, based on call graphs, we design a metamorphic malware multi-class classification method, dubbed *deepCG*, which enables automatic feature learning of metamorphic malware via deep learning. Specifically, we encapsulate the information of each call graph into an image that is then fed into deep convolutional neural networks for classifying the malware family. Particularly, we design a training data enhancement scheme that incorporates call graph normalization and augmentation as a built-in feature of *deepCG*, thereby achieving high classification accuracy even with small-scale training samples.

To our best knowledge, our work constitutes the *first* effort devoted to classifying metamorphic malware in consideration of both automatic feature learning and small-scale training data due to metamorphism. Our contributions include:

- We systematically study the code obfuscation methods of metamorphism, with a focus on their influence over call graphs. Through real-world case studies, we find that call graphs are more stable against metamorphism compared with other fragmented features.
- We transform the malware classification problem into an image recognition problem, which is one of the specialities of deep learning. Following this idea, we propose a novel metamorphic malware classification method (*deepCG*) through deep learning of call graphs. *deepCG* captures the underlying structural features of metamorphic malware, thus promising in metamorphic malware classification while robust against metamorphism.
- We design a training data enhancement scheme that incorporates call graph normalization and augmentation as a built-in feature of *deepCG*. The proposed scheme can efficiently enlarge the training dataset and substantially improve the performance of feature learning and classification, thereby achieving high classification accuracy even with small-scale training samples.
- We evaluate *deepCG* using two datasets, namely, the PE file dataset that consists of 1,933 labeled samples, the disassembly dataset including 10,868 labeled samples. For both datasets, we use 70% of the samples for training and 30% for testing. For the former dataset, the training accuracy and testing accuracy of the multi-class classification are 98.82% and 96.01% respectively, while for the latter they are 98.92% and 94.35% respectively. Furthermore, when the disassembly dataset is normalized and augmented, the training accuracy and testing accuracy rise to 99.34% and 96.84%.

Roadmap. Section 2 introduces related work. Section 3 defines call graphs and analyzes the influence of metamorphic malware over call graphs. Section 4 details the deep learning method. Section 5 designs the training data enhancement scheme. We experiment in Sect. 6, and conclude in Sect. 7.

2 Related Work

To intelligently detect malware, researchers have extensively studied malware classification based on machine learning technologies. The general procedure of such studies is: (1) designing and extracting features from the malware dataset, (2) training a classification model based on these features, and (3) using the trained model to perform classification. Typical features in the literature include byte n-grams [20], gray-scale images [24], API sequences [18,33,35], opcode sequences [2,29,31], control flow graphs [10,37], etc. The commonly used machine learning algorithms consist of Decision Tree [20,29,31,33], Naive Bayes [20,31,37], Random Forest [20,29,31,33,37], SVM [2,20,29,31,33,37], KNN [24,29], etc.

As a new branch of machine learning, deep learning can help computational models learn representations of the training data [22]. It usually adopts deep neural networks (DNNs) composed of multiple single-layered nonlinear neural networks. Typical structures of DNNs include deep belief networks (DBNs) [15], deep convolutional neural networks (CNNs) [21], deep recursive neural networks (RNNs) [17], and so forth. Deep learning has been well applied in the fields of computer vision, speech recognition and natural language processing. For example, Krizhevsky et al. [21] implement a deep convolutional neural network containing 650,000 neurons for image classification, reducing the error rate of start-of-the-art image classification methods by around 10%. Graves et al. [12] break the record of TIMIT voice recognition contest with RNNs, reducing the rate for Connectionist Temporal Classification (CTC) from 23.9% to 18.4%.

Inspired by the success of deep learning in many fields, researchers in the security domain started to adopt deep neural networks for malware analysis, and achieved better results than traditional machine learning methods. Hardy et al. [13] proposed a malware detection framework based on deep learning. They extracted 9649 Windows APIs and defined the feature vectors according to whether these APIs are used in the malware. By training with 25,000 malicious and 25,000 benign samples, the accuracy of binary classification is 95.64%, which is better than 93.06% with traditional SVM algorithm. Saxe et al. [30] extracted PE metadata, strings, imported functions and entropy histograms as malware features, and use 430,000 malicious samples and 80,000 benign samples to train the classification model, and the accuracy of the binary classification is 95%. Daniel et al. [11] studied multi-class classification based on Microsoft BIG2015 dataset [27], which contains 10868 samples for training and the other 10873 for testing. By representing the malware's binary content as gray-scale images and train them with CNN, they obtain an validation accuracy of 93.86%. When they use CNN to classify malware samples according to their x86 instructions, they achieve an improvement of 98.56%.

Some researchers performed malware detection with deep learning based on dynamic analysis. Dahl et al. [5] used Microsoft anti-malware engine to extract three types of features from 1.8 million malware and 0.8 million benign files, including null-terminated patterns observed in the process' memory, tri-grams of system API calls, and distinct combinations of a single system API call and one input parameter. With neural networks containing 1–3 hidden layers, the binary classification accuracy is 99.51%, and the multi-class classification accuracy is 91.17%. Later on, Huang et al. [16] improved Dahl's work with a multi-task neural network. By training the neural network with 2.8 million malicious files and 3.6 million benign files, they increased the accuracy of binary classification to 99.63% and the accuracy of multi-class classification to 97.01%. David et al. [6] used logs of Cuckoo Sandbox [25] to classify malware. They used NLP methods to process the analysis logs of Cuckoo and choosed 20,000 words with the highest frequency, and defined the feature vectors according to whether these words appear in the logs. Then they built a DBN and trained it with 1,800 malware belonging to six families, and the accuracy with a softmax classifier is 98.6%.

All above studies, without any doubt, have significantly promoted machine learning based malware analysis technology. However, they do not focus on metamorphic malware that can quickly alter their code during propagation. Recently, several studies, such as [1,4,8,23,38], paid their attention to metamorphic malware. They primarily rely on user carefully designed metrics (rather than automatic feature learning), such as graph similarity measures, to classify or detect metamorphic malware. Since user carefully designed metrics can hardly be adaptive to the evolving of metamorphic malware by design, metamorphic malware may evade the classification or detection in the long run. More importantly, the quick evolving nature of metamorphic malware makes capturing training samples with limited diversity commonly. Therefore, it is highly desired to consider this practical issue when metamorphic malware are analyzed.

3   Call Graphs

3.1   Defining Call Graphs

A *Call Graph* is a directed graph which represents the function and their calling relationships in a program [28]. A call graph g can be described as (N_g, E_g), where N_g is the node set, and each node represents a unique function; E_g is the edge set, and $E_g \subset N_g \times N_g$. In a call graph g, a directed edge e_{ij} means the function n_i contains a function call to n_j, where $n_i, n_j \in N_g$. Call graphs can be generated with reverse engineering tools, such as IDA [7], and exported as GDL (Graph Description Language) files [34].

A typical GDL formatted call graph file is exemplified in Code 1.1. It mainly comprises three sections: colors, nodes and edges. Note that there are no explicit declarations of section names in the GDL file. On the contrary, the first word of each line indicates which section the current line belongs to.

Code 1.1. GDL Formatted Call Graph

```
graph: {
//colors
......
colorentry 73:  255  255  255
colorentry 74:  192  187  175
colorentry 75:  0  255  255
colorentry 76:  0  0  0
......
//nodes
node: { title: "0" label: "_main" color: 76 textcolor: 73 bordercolor: black }
node: { title: "1" label: "sub_401028" color: 76 textcolor: 73 bordercolor: black }
node: { title: "2" label: "sub_40102E" color: 76 textcolor: 73 bordercolor: black }
node: { title: "3" label: "sub_401060" color: 76 textcolor: 73 bordercolor: black }
......
node: { title: "5" label: "__amsg_exit" color: 75 textcolor: 73 bordercolor: black }
......
node: { title: "106" label: "GetCommandLineA" color: 80 bordercolor: black }
......
//edges
edge: { sourcename: "0" targetname: "1" }
edge: { sourcename: "0" targetname: "2" }
edge: { sourcename: "3" targetname: "7" }
......
}
```

The section "colors" defines the color set of the call graph used in the section "nodes". It contains several lines which start with the keyword "colorentry".

Each line is formatted as "colorentry <id>: <color>", and defines a specific color c with an id and three RGB parameters. The color set C_g of the call graph g can be defined as:

$$C_g = \{c|c = (id, r, g, b), r \in [0, 255], g \in [0, 255], b \in [0, 255]\}. \tag{1}$$

The section "nodes" is composed of lines starting with the keyword "node", representing the nodes of the call graph. Each node is described as a colored rectangle $n = (title, label, c, tc, bc)$, where $title$ and $label$ are the id and name of the function, while c, tc, bc are the fill color, text color and border color of the rectangle. The values of c and tc are chosen from the color set C_g pre-defined in the section "colors", and the value of bc is constant (e.g. black). The node set N_g of the call graph g can be defined as:

$$N_g = \{n|n = (title, label, c, tc, bc), c \in C_g, tc \in C_g, bc = \text{"black"}\}. \tag{2}$$

In GDL formatted call graphs generated by IDA, the nodes are categorized into three types by their fill colors. For local functions coded elaborately by the program author, such as "sub_401024" and "sub_402A9B", the fill color of the corresponding nodes is black, i.e., RGB(0,0,0). For dynamically imported DLL functions linked at load time and imported into the program through IAT (Import Address Table), such as "LoadLibrary" and "VirtualAlloc" from Kernel32.dll, the fill color is magenta, i.e., RGB(255,0,255). For statically linked functions linked and copied into the program during program compiling, such as "__amsg_exit" from internal.h and "_memcpy" from stdio.h, the node rectangles of them are filled with cyan, i.e., RGB(0,255,255).

The section "edges" contains a list of lines which begin with the word "edge", and these lines indicate the calling relationships of the functions. The format of edge lines is "edge: {sourcename: <the title of source node> targetname: <the title of target node>}". An edge e is defined as (s, t), where the values of s and t are the titles of the source function and the target function respectively. The edge set E_g of the call graph g can be defined as:

$$E_g = \{e|e = (s, t), s \in N_g, t \in N_g\}. \tag{3}$$

The GDL formatted call graphs can be converted into images with graphviz [9] and Graph_Easy from CPAN (Comprehensive Perl Archive Network) [14]. Figure 1(a) shows the full view of the call graph extracted from a *Cobalt Strike* backdoor. Although the function names is not clear enough to read without zooming it out due to the space limitation, the full view of the calling relationships among different functions can also provide a distinguishing structural characteristic of the program. Figure 1(b) shows part of the call graph image in Fig. 1(a). Clearly, the local function "sub_4017BC" calls another local function "sub_401752" and three statically linked functions "memcpy", "malloc" and "free".

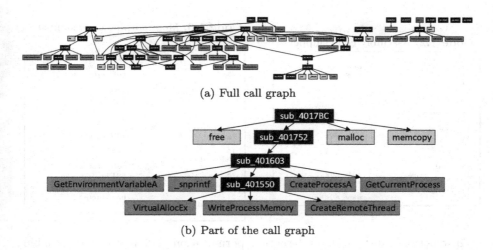

(a) Full call graph

(b) Part of the call graph

Fig. 1. Call graph of a *Cobalt Strike* backdoor

3.2   Understanding Metamorphic Malware and Their Call Graphs

Metamorphic malware use code obfuscation techniques to mutates their executable code automatically and generates countless variants during propagation. Therefore, fragmented features, such as opcode sequences and byte n-grams, may vary drastically from one malware sample to another, thereby inapplicable for metamorphic malware analysis. In this section, we first present the obfuscation techniques used by metamorphic malware, and then study the stability of call graphs against metamorphism.

The most frequently used obfuscation techniques include instruction substitution, instruction permutation, register or variable substitution, dead code insertion, code transposition and subroutine reordering, and so on [3,26,36]. Code 1.2 is an example of an assembly code block, and Fig. 2(a) shows its call graph. We study how metamorphism affects call graphs based on this example.

- **Instruction substitution.** Modifying a instruction or instruction block into another one which has the same function. For example, in Line 11 of Code 1.2, the instruction "add eax, 1;" can be replaced with "inc eax;".
- **Instruction permutation.** Reordering the sequence of some instructions or instruction blocks. For example, in Line 12–13 of Code 1.2, the instructions "add eax, eax; inc ebx" can be mutated to "inc ebx; add eax, eax;".
- **Register or variable substitution.** Replacing the register in a code block with another register or variable, which will not affect the original function. For instance, the register EAX can be replaced with EDX in Code 1.2.

Code 1.2. Assembly code snippet

```
1    start :
2                    mov eax , c ;
3                    mov eax , [eax] ;
4    call1 :
5                    call sub1 ;
6    call2 :
7                    call sub2 ;
8    jump :
9                    jmp end ;
10   sub1 :
11                   add eax , 1 ;
12                   add eax , eax ;
13                   inc ebx ;
14                   ret ;
15   sub2 :
16                   sub eax ,2 ;
17                   ret ;
18   end :
19                   mov a , eax ;
```

Code 1.3. Metamorphic code snippet

```
1    start :
2                    mov ebx , c ;
3                    mov ebx , [ebx] ;
4                    add ebx , 1 ;
5                    sub ebx , 1 ;
6    call1 :
7                    call sub1 ;
8                    jmp call2 ;
9
10   jump :
11                   jmp end ;
12   sub1 :
13                   add ebx ,1 ;
14                   add ebx ,ebx ;
15                   ret ;
16   sub2 :
17                   sub ebx ,2 ;
18                   ret ;
19   call2 :
20                   call sub2 ;
21                   jmp jump ;
22   end :
23                   mov a ,ebx ;
```

Instruction substitution, instruction permutation and register or variable substitution will change the malware's bytes and opcodes. As a consequence, they will alter some fragmented features, such as opcode sequences and byte n-grams. However, these methods do not modify "call" instructions, and do not add extra lines either. Thus, neither will they change the calling relationships of the functions, nor the addresses of them, indicating that the call graph remains the same.

- **Dead code insertion.** Inserting useless instructions. The dead code can be instructions which will never be executed, or blocks of instructions which are equivalent to NOPs (No Operation). The code in Line 4–5 of Code 1.3 is a simple example of dead code. Other typical dead code blocks are "inc eax; dec eax;", "push ebp; pop ebp;", etc.
- **Code transposition.** Shuffling some instruction blocks and modify the execution flow of them with conditional or unconditional branching instructions, to keep the same execution order of the instructions as origin ones. For example, a block of sequential instructions (Line 4–9 in Code 1.2) can mutated to two instruction blocks (Line 6–11 and Line 19–21 in Code 1.3) whose addresses are not adjacent to each other, but they are logically linked together with jump instructions, so the executed instruction orders are the same.
- **Subroutine reordering.** Moving the order of subroutines randomly. For example, a switch statement in a program is used to select one of different subroutines to be executed according to different cases. The subroutines of these cases can be reordered, to make the program look different while functionally unchanged.

The call graph of Code 1.3 is shown in Fig. 2(b). It can be seen that dead code insertion, code transposition and subroutine reordering may change the addresses of some functions, but these methods do not modify "call" instructions. Therefore, the structure of the call graph will be preserved while only the labels of some nodes are different.

With the development of code obfuscation technologies, dead code insertion can also be implemented by dead function insertion. That is, adding a function equivalent to NOP, and inserting function calls to the NOP function wherever the dead code is needed. Code 1.4 is an example of metamorphic code with dead function insertion, in which the function named "sub3" (Line 19–22) is a dead function. As is shown in Fig. 2(c), a new node is inserted into the call graph. It is notable that the dead function call is usually inserted into local functions rather than dynamically imported DLL functions and statically linked functions, because modifying the latter two may bring fatal errors to the program. Besides, to make sure the dead function can be inserted into any place without bringing execution errors, it is likely that the dead function is usually simple and there is no further function calls within it. Therefore, the impact on call graphs brought by dead function insertion is that some leaf nodes are added to random local function nodes.

Code 1.4. Metamorphic code snippet with dead function insertion

```
1   start:
2                   mov eax, c;
3                   mov eax, [eax];
4   call1:
5                   call sub1;
6   call2:
7                   call sub2;
8   call_deadcode:
9                   call sub3;
10  jump:
11                  jmp end;
12  sub1:
13                  add eax,1;
14                  add eax,eax;
15                  ret;
16  sub2:
17                  sub eax,2;
18                  ret;
19  sub3:
20                  add eax,1;
21                  sub eax,1;
22                  ret;
23  end:
24                  mov a,eax;
```

(a) Call graph of Code 1.2   (b) Call graph of Code 1.3

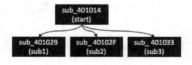

(c) Call graph of Code 1.4

Fig. 2. Call graphs of Code 1.2, Code 1.3, and Code 1.4

4   Classifying Metamorphic Malware Using Call Graphs

Since call graphs have higher stability against metamorphic malware than other fragmented features, we propose a novel malware classification method ($d$eepCG) through deep learning of call graphs, which enables automatic feature learning of metamorphic malware. The general idea is to convert malware into call graph images, and then feed them to a pre-built deep neural network for feature learning and classification. The major steps include:

(1) Call Graph Generation

The first step is extracting and generating call graph images from malware. Usually, the dataset is a collection of portable executable (PE) formatted binaries. As mentioned in Sect. 3, we use IDA to generate GDL formatted call graphs from PE files, and convert them into PNG images of 256 × 256 pixels with help of Graph_Easy. For disassembly files (e.g., the dataset provided by Microsoft BIG2015 [27] consists of disassembly and bytecode other than PE file), we first extract the local functions (with the format of sub_XXXXXX proc near), function calls (with the format of CALL sub_XXXXXX) and syscalls (with the format of CALL ds:XXXXXX) from a given disassembly file, then construct the function list and their call relationships, resulting in a GDL file. Then, we convert the GDL file into a PNG image with the same method as above.

(2) Feature Learning

Since CNNs have been widely used in the field of image recognition, they can also be adopted to solve malware classification problems with call graph images. The structure of the deep CNN used for metamorphic malware classification with call graphs is shown in Fig. 3, and the parameter settings are shown in Table 1. Layers 2–9 in the proposed CNN are used for feature learning, and they are composed of multiple single-layer CNN that contains a convolution layer followed by a pooling layer and an activation function such as "relu". The output feature map of the former CNN is the input of the latter one, and the last CNN is connected to a fully connected layer (including a flatten layer and a dense layer). In this way, the feature maps generated by multiple convolution and pooling operations are converted to feature vectors by fully connection operation.

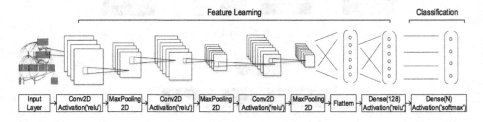

Fig. 3. CNN-based metamorphic malware classification system through deep learning of call graphs

Table 1. Parameter settings of the proposed classification system

No	Layer	Parameters
1	Input	shape = 256 × 256 × 3
2	2D Convolution	filters = 32 kernel_size = (8, 8) strides = 4 activation = 'relu'
3	Max Pooling	pool_size = (2, 2) strides = 2
4	2D Convolution	filters = 64 kernel_size = (4, 4) strides = 2 activation = 'relu'
5	Max Pooling	pool_size = (2, 2) strides = 2
6	2D Convolution	filters = 64 kernel_size = (3, 3) strides = 1 activation = 'relu'
7	Max Pooling	pool_size = (2, 2) strides = 2
8	Flatten	N/A
9	Dense (Fully Connected)	unit (dimensionality) = 128 activation = 'relu'
10	Dense with Softmax (Softmax Classifier)	unit (dimensionality) = number of categories activation = 'softmax' dropout = 0.5
11	Output	dimensionality = number of categories

(3) Classification

Layer 10 of the proposed CNN is a softmax classifier, which is suitable for multi-class classification. A dropout operation is added which will randomly drop 50% units from the input to prevent over-fitting [32]. The output of the classifier is a vector representing the categorical distribution over different malware families.

5   Enhancing Training Data for Metamorphism Diversity

Metamorphic malware can mutate themselves automatically to propagate tens of thousands variants in a short time. In real world, it is usually difficult to collect a malware dataset which is large enough to cover most of the variants. Although there are some data enhancement methods for image recognition such as rotation, cropping, flipping, zoom and resizing, these methods are not practical for call graphs because all the call graphs are essentially not images in their content but just in the form of images. Therefore, new methods of data enhancement for metamorphism diversity which are suitable for call graphs are needed. In this section, to enhance the dataset for training, we propose two methods: data normalization and data augmentation.

5.1   Data Normalization

As discussed in Sect. 3, metamorphism may change the orders of functions. Although this change will not affect the calling relationships among them, it may cause some movement of part of the call graph. For example, the full call graph image of Code 1.1 is shown in Fig. 4(a). When the positions of sub_401028 and sub_401060 are switched, the new call graph is shown in Fig. 4(b). It can be seen that after exchanging two functions, part of the call graph (inside the dotted line) moves from the left to the right of the whole image. This is because graphviz and Graph_Easy always draw nodes from left to right according to their indexes (titles) in the GDL file.

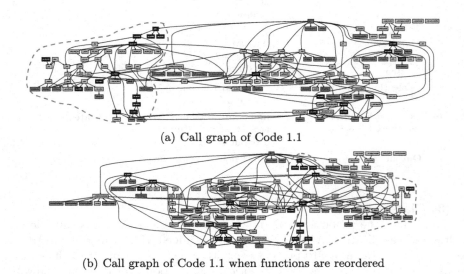

(a) Call graph of Code 1.1

(b) Call graph of Code 1.1 when functions are reordered

Fig. 4. Unnormalized call graphs

To eliminate the effect to call graphs by function reordering, we propose a call graph normalization appoarch based on weighted sorting, where the nodes are reordered according to the number of their child nodes and their label names (when the number of child nodes are equal). The procedures of call graph normalization algorithm is shown in Algorithm 1.

The normalized call graphs are shown in Fig. 5, which reveals that the normalized call graph remain unchanged in the case of function reordering. Therefore, call graph normalization can further improve the stability of call graphs.

Algorithm 1. Call graph normalization based on weighted sorting

---

Input: GDL file F
Output: Normalized GDL file F'
1: Extract nodes N, edges E from the GDL file F;
2: **for** each $N_i \in N$ **do**
3:    Count the child nodes of N_i recursively, and update the weight W_i of the node with the number of its child nodes;
4: **end for**
5: Generate N' by sorting N in (1) descending order according to the weights W_i and (2) ascending order according to the label names;
6: **for** each $N'_i \in N'$ **do**
7:    Update the indexes (titles) of N'_i according to its new index in N';
8: **end for**
9: Copy E to E';
10: **for** each $E'_i \in E'$ **do**
11:    Update the source name and target name of E'_i according to the new indexes (titles) of the nodes in N';
12: **end for**
13: Generate normalized GDL file F' with N' and E';
14: **return** F';

5.2 Data Augmentation

Metamorphism can also render the call graph be appended with some extra leaf nodes. For example, as elaborated in Sect. 3, dead function insertion with call/ret instructions will append extra leaf nodes to local functions. Because it is impossible to collect all metamorphic variants to cover all possible mutations, we propose a call graph augmentation method based on random function insertion. Our proposed method can be used to simulate the mutation behaviors of metamorphic malware, and enlarge the training dataset by dozens of times to improve the performance of feature learning and classification with small-scale datasets. The procedure is described in Algorithm 2.

Algorithm 2. Call graph augmentation based on random function insertion

---

Input: GDL file F, augmentation rate $N(N > 1)$, maximum number of inserted functions $M(M > 1)$
Output: Augmented GDL files $F'_1, F'_2, ..., F'_N$
1: Extract nodes N, edges E from the GDL file F;
2: Copy N and E to N' and E';
3: Generate m (m is a random number between 1 and M) nodes $a_1, a_2, ..., a_m$ with random names which are composed of a constant prefix "sub_" and a six-byte hexadecimal address, formatted as "sub_xxxxxx";
4: **for** each $i \in [1, m]$ **do**
5:    Append a_i to N'
6:    Select a local function node n from N randomly, and update E' to add an edge from n to a_i
7: **end for**
8: Goto 2 until the number of augmented files reaches N;
9: **return** $F'_1, F'_2, ..., F'_N$;

Figure 6 shows that a call graph is augmented to ten call graphs. Since augmentation increases the weights of the nodes due to appending of child nodes, the augmented call graphs also need to be normalized.

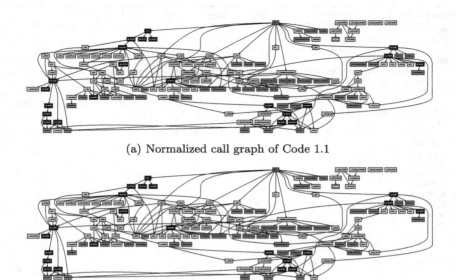

(a) Normalized call graph of Code 1.1

(b) Normalized call graph of Code 1.1 when functions are reordered

Fig. 5. Normalized call graphs

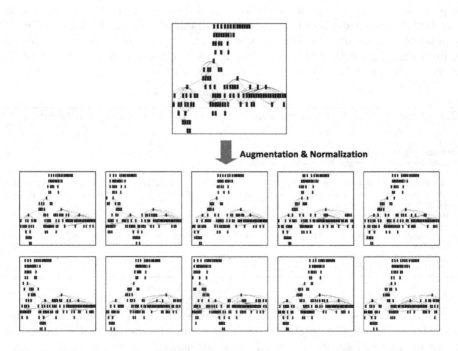

Fig. 6. Call graph augmentation: one call graph is augmented to ten call graphs

6   Experimental Evaluation

Malware classification experiments are performed on different datasets. In the experiments, we split the dataset into training and test dataset. The training dataset is used by the training algorithm to adjust the neural network. The test dataset (which is different from validation dataset) is not involved into the training process, and is only used once to evaluate the classification after the training is done.

Below we introduce classification experiments and their results on a PE dataset and a disassembly dataset in Sects. 6.1 and 6.2 respectively. Section 6.3 evaluates the effect of data enhancement.

6.1   Malware Classification on PE Dataset

By extracting PE files from the traffics mirrored from an enterprise network and scanning them with ClamAV [19] antivirus, we collect 1,933 malware samples belonging to 15 malware families, as shown in Table 2.

Table 2. PE dataset for malware classification

Malware family	Number	Malware family	Number
Win.Malware.Zusy	99	Win.Trojan.Rootkit	290
Win.Trojan.AutoIT	40	Win.Trojan.Scar	108
Win.Trojan.Buzus	92	Win.Trojan.Siggen	233
Win.Trojan.Cosmu	176	Win.Trojan.Toopu	50
Win.Trojan.Graybird	49	Win.Worm.VB	50
Win.Trojan.Hijacker	98	Win.Worm.Viking	76
Win.Trojan.Lipler	172	Win.Worm.Zhelatin	58
Win.Trojan.Parite	243		

We use IDA and Graph_Easy to generate their call graph images, and split them to training and test data with a ratio of 70/30. Then, we use the CNN presented in Fig. 3 to perform multi-class classification tasks on a server with Intel(R) Xeon(R) CPU E5-2620 v4, 96 GB RAM and NVIDIA Tesla P100 12 GB. Table 3 shows the results for different epochs. The best training accuracy is 98.82% while the best test accuracy is 96.01%.

6.2   Malware Classification on Disassembly Dataset

The Microsoft BIG2015 dataset contains 10,868 labeled samples and 9,153 test samples belonging to 9 malware families. Each sample consists of a disassembly file (*.asm) and a bytecode file (*.bytes). We use the training samples for

Table 3. Result of malware classification on PE dataset

Epochs	Training accuracy	Test accuracy	Test precision	Test F-score	Test error rate
10	97.03%	95.31%	95.47%	95.31%	4.69%
20	98.23%	95.49%	95.90%	95.57%	4.51%
30	98.31%	94.79%	94.79%	94.70%	5.21%
50	98.82%	95.49%	95.51%	95.45%	4.51%
100	**98.82%**	**96.01%**	96.11%	96.01%	3.99%

both training and test because the provided test samples are not labeled and become unusable. The call graphs can be constructed by extracting the function calls from the disassembly files and then we use Graph_Easy to generate the images. We finally get 10,636 call graphs out of 10,868 samples, while some of the call graph images are not successfully generate due to run timeout error of Graph_Easy. The disassembly dataset is shown in Table 4.

Table 4. Disassembly dataset for malware classification

Malware family	No. of samples	No. of call graphs
Ramnit	1541	1428
Lollipop	2478	2467
Kelihos_ver3	2942	2942
Vundo	475	475
Simda	42	41
Tracur	751	673
Kelihos_ver1	398	394
Obfuscator.ACY	1228	1205
Gatak	1013	1011

We perform evaluation by splitting the 10,636 call graphs into 7,449 training data and 3,187 test data with a ratio of 70/30, and the result is shown in Table 5. The best training and test accuracy are 98.47% and 94.35%.

6.3   Malware Classification with Data Enhancement

To evaluate the effect of data enhancement, we generate three additional datasets along with the original BIG2015 dataset for classification experiments.

– **Original Dataset:** It is the original BIG2015 dataset used in Sect. 6.2, including 7,449 training data and 3,187 test data.

Table 5. Result of malware classification on disassembly dataset

Epochs	Training accuracy	Test accuracy	Test precision	Test F-score	Test error rate
10	95.03%	94.01%	94.00%	93.88%	5.99%
20	98.25%	**94.35%**	94.50%	94.31%	5.65%
30	**98.47%**	94.14%	94.10%	94.03%	5.86%
50	98.26%	93.66%	93.74%	93.56%	6.34%
100	98.17%	93.63%	93.63%	93.53%	6.37%

- **Original Enhanced Dataset:** This dataset is generated by enhancing the original training data with call graph augmentation and normalization, and enhancing the original test data only with call graph normalization. It consists of 29,078 training data and 3,187 test data.
- **Small-scale Dataset:** The training data is generated by randomly dropping 14/15 of the original training data, while the test data is the same with the original one. It is composed of 502 training data and 3,187 test data. This dataset is used as the baseline to evaluate data enhancement on small-scale dataset.
- **Small-scale Enhanced Dataset:** This dataset is generated by enhancing the small-scale training data with call graph augmentation and normalization, and enhancing the small-scale test data only with call graph normalization. There are 5,369 training data and 3,187 test data in it.

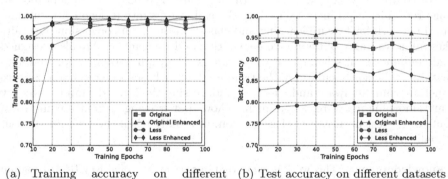

(a) Training accuracy on different datasets

(b) Test accuracy on different datasets

Fig. 7. Evaluation results on different datasets

The evaluation result is shown in Fig. 7. We see that data enhancement is able to improve the test accuracy of classification efficiently. Specifically, for the small-scale dataset, although the training accuracy is high, the test accuracy is unsatisfying because the neural network is trained inadequately due to the lack of data. However, when the small-scale dataset is enhanced about ten times larger with the proposed data enhancement method, the improvement of test accuracy is remarkable.

More concretely, as Table 6 shows, although the growth of training accuracy is not notable by data enhancement, the test accuracy of classification on the original dataset increases from 94.35% to 96.84%, while the test accuracy of the small-scale dataset is raised from 79.98% to 88.67% with data enhancement.

Table 6. Results of malware classification with and without data enhancement

Dataset	Training samples	Test samples	Train accuracy	Test accuracy	Train accuracy with data enhancement	Test accuracy with data enhancement
Original	7,449	3,187	98.92%	94.35%	99.34%	**96.84%**
Small-scale	502	3,187	98.21%	79.97%	99.88%	**88.67%**

7   Conclusion

In this paper, we proposed a metamorphic malware classification approach through deep learning of call graphs, and evaluated the proposed approach with two malware datasets, and achieved promising test accuracy on multi-class classification tasks. Our approach is based on the study of the code obfuscation methods used by metamorphism, where we showed that call graph features are more stable against metamorphic malware than other fragmented features such as opcode and byte n-grams. Given that deep learning has been successful in the field of computer vision, we convert the malware classification problem into an image recognition problem by feeding the call graphs into a deep convolutional neural network for feature learning and classification. Such conversion naturally takes full advantages of the image recognition of deep learning. We also designed a data enhancement scheme that incorporates call graph normalization and augmentation, efficiently enlarging the training dataset based on the characteristics of metamorphic malware and effectively addressing the limited sample diversity of metamorphic malware. Experiments show that it brings significant improvement to the test accuracy of classification, especially when the training dataset is small-sized.

Acknowledgement. This work is supported in part by National Key R&D Program of China (NO. 2016YFB0801004), the Key Laboratory of Network Assessment Technology at Chinese Academy of Sciences (CXJJ-17S049), Beijing Key Laboratory of Network security and Protection Technology, National Natural Science Foundation (61602371), CCF-NSFOCUS KunPeng Research Fund (2018002) and the Fundamental Research Funds for the Central Universities (xjh012019031).

References

1. Alam, S., Horspool, R., Traore, I., Sogukpinar, I.: A framework for metamorphic malware analysis and real-time detection. Comput. Secur. **48**, 212–233 (2015)

2. Anderson, B., Quist, D., Neil, J., Storlie, C., Lane, T.: Graph-based malware detection using dynamic analysis. J. Comput. Virol. **7**(4), 247–258 (2011)
3. Borello, J.M., Mé, L.: Code obfuscation techniques for metamorphic viruses. J. Comput. Virol. **4**(3), 211–220 (2008)
4. Choudhary, S., Vidyarthi, M.D.: A simple method for detection of metamorphic malware using dynamic analysis and text mining. Procedia Comput. Sci. **54**, 265–270 (2015)
5. Dahl, G.E., Stokes, J.W., Deng, L., Yu, D.: Large-scale malware classification using random projections and neural networks. In: Proceedings of the IEEE ICASSP (2013)
6. David, O.E., Netanyahu, N.S.: DeepSign: deep learning for automatic malware signature generation and classification. In: Proceedings of the IEEE IJCNN (2015)
7. Eagle, C.: The IDA Pro Book. No Starch Press (2011)
8. Elhadi, A.A.E., Maarof, M.A., Barry, B.I., Hamza, H.: Enhancing the detection of metamorphic malware using call graphs. Comput. Secur. **46**, 62–78 (2014)
9. Ellson, J., Gansner, E., Koutsofios, L., North, S.C., Woodhull, G.: Graphviz—open source graph drawing tools. In: Mutzel, P., Jünger, M., Leipert, S. (eds.) GD 2001. LNCS, vol. 2265, pp. 483–484. Springer, Heidelberg (2002). https://doi.org/10.1007/3-540-45848-4_57
10. Eskandari, M., Hashemi, S.: Metamorphic malware detection using control flow graph mining. Int. J. Comput. Sci. Netw. Secur. **11**(12), 1–6 (2011)
11. Gibert Llauradó, D.: Convolutional neural networks for malware classification. Master's thesis, Universitat Politècnica de Catalunya (2016)
12. Graves, A., Mohamed, A., Hinton, G.: Speech recognition with deep recurrent neural networks. In: Proceedings of the IEEE ICASSP (2013)
13. Hardy, W., Chen, L., Hou, S., Ye, Y., Li, X.: DL4MD: a deep learning framework for intelligent malware detection. In: Proceedings of the DMIN (2016)
14. Hietaniemi, J., et al.: Comprehensive Perl Archive Network. Helsinki, Finland: CPAN **6** (2008)
15. Hinton, G.E.: Deep belief networks. Scholarpedia **4**(5), 5947 (2009)
16. Huang, W., Stokes, J.W.: MtNet: a multi-task neural network for dynamic malware classification. In: Caballero, J., Zurutuza, U., Rodríguez, R.J. (eds.) DIMVA 2016. LNCS, vol. 9721, pp. 399–418. Springer, Cham (2016). https://doi.org/10.1007/978-3-319-40667-1_20
17. Irsoy, O., Cardie, C.: Deep recursive neural networks for compositionality in language. In: Proceedings of the NIPS (2014)
18. Islam, R., Tian, R., Batten, L.M., Versteeg, S.: Classification of malware based on integrated static and dynamic features. J. Netw. Comput. Appl. **36**(2), 646–656 (2013)
19. Kojm, T.: ClamAV (2004)
20. Kolter, J.Z., Maloof, M.A.: Learning to detect malicious executables in the wild. In: Proceedings of the ACM SIGKDD (2004)
21. Krizhevsky, A., Sutskever, I., Hinton, G.E.: ImageNet classification with deep convolutional neural networks. In: Proceedings of the NIPS (2012)
22. LeCun, Y., Bengio, Y., Hinton, G.: Deep learning. Nature **521**(7553), 436 (2015)
23. Mirzazadeh, R., Moattar, M.H., Jahan, M.V.: Metamorphic malware detection using linear discriminant analysis and graph similarity. CoRR abs/1811.04304 (2018)
24. Nataraj, L., Karthikeyan, S., Jacob, G., Manjunath, B.: Malware images: visualization and automatic classification. In: Proceedings of the ACM VizSec (2011)

25. Oktavianto, D., Muhardianto, I.: Cuckoo Malware Analysis. Packt Publishing Ltd (2013)
26. Rad, B.B., Masrom, M., Ibrahim, S.: Camouflage in malware: from encryption to metamorphism. Int. J. Comput. Sci. Netw. Secur. **12**(8), 74–83 (2012)
27. Ronen, R., Radu, M., Feuerstein, C., Yom-Tov, E., Ahmadi, M.: Microsoft malware classification challenge. arXiv preprint arXiv:1802.10135 (2018)
28. Ryder, B.G.: Constructing the call graph of a program. IEEE Trans. Softw. Eng. **3**, 216–226 (1979)
29. Santos, I., Brezo, F., Sanz, B., Laorden, C., Bringas, P.G.: Using opcode sequences in single-class learning to detect unknown malware. IET Inf. Secur. **5**(4), 220–227 (2011)
30. Saxe, J., Berlin, K.: Deep neural network based malware detection using two dimensional binary program features. In: Proceedings of the IEEE MALWARE (2015)
31. Shabtai, A., Moskovitch, R., Feher, C., Dolev, S., Elovici, Y.: Detecting unknown malicious code by applying classification techniques on opcode patterns. Secur. Inform. **1**(1), 1 (2012)
32. Srivastava, N., Hinton, G., Krizhevsky, A., Sutskever, I., Salakhutdinov, R.: Dropout: a simple way to prevent neural networks from overfitting. J. Mach. Learn. Res. **15**(1), 1929–1958 (2014)
33. Tian, R., Islam, R., Batten, L., Versteeg, S.: Differentiating malware from clean-ware using behavioural analysis. In: Proceedings of the IEEE MALWARE (2010)
34. Yau, S.S., Tsai, J.P.: Graph description language for large-scale software specification in a maintenance environment. In: Proceedings of the IEEE COMPSAC (1984)
35. Ye, Y., Li, T., Jiang, Q., Wang, Y.: CIMDS: adapting postprocessing techniques of associative classification for malware detection. IEEE Trans. Syst. Man Cybern. (Part C Appl. Rev.) **40**(3), 298–307 (2010)
36. You, I., Yim, K.: Malware obfuscation techniques: a brief survey. In: Proceedings of the IEEE BWCCA (2010)
37. Zhao, Z.: A virus detection scheme based on features of control flow graph. In: Proceedings of the IEEE AIMSEC (2011)
38. Çarkacı, N., Soğukpınar, I: Frequency based metamorphic malware detection. In: Proceedings of the SIU (2016)

ChaffyScript: Vulnerability-Agnostic Defense of JavaScript Exploits via Memory Perturbation

Xunchao Hu[1,2]([⊠]), Brian Testa[2], and Heng Yin[3]

[1] DeepBits Technology LLC, Riverside, USA
xchu@deepbitstech.com
[2] Syracuse University, Syracuse, USA
bptesta@syr.edu
[3] University of California, Riverside, USA
heng@cs.ucr.edu

Abstract. JavaScript has been used to exploit binary vulnerabilities of host software that are otherwise difficult to exploit; they impose a severe threat to computer security. Although software vendors have deployed techniques like ASLR, sandbox, etc. to mitigate JavaScript exploits, hacking contests (e.g.,Pwn2Own, GeekPwn) have demonstrated that the latest software (e.g., Chrome, IE, Edge, Safari) can still be exploited. An ideal JavaScript exploit mitigation solution should be flexible and allow for deployment without requiring code changes. To this end, we propose ChaffyScript, a vulnerability-agnostic mitigation system that thwarts JavaScript exploits via undermining the memory preparation stage of exploits. We implement a prototype of ChaffyScript, and our evaluation shows that it defeats the 11 latest JavaScript exploits with minimal runtime and memory overhead. It incurs at most 5.88% runtime overhead for chrome and 12.96% for FireFox. The maximal memory overhead JS heap usage, observed using the Octane benchmark, was 8.2%. To demonstrate the deployment flexibility of ChaffyScript, we have integrated it into a web proxy.

1 Introduction

JavaScript has been a popular programing language for decades. It has been widely deployed in web browsers, servers, PDF processor, etc. JavaScript exploits, which take advantage of JavaScript's interactive features to exploit binary vulnerabilities (e.g., use-after-free, heap/buffer overflow) of host software and inject malicious code into victim's machine, have been imposing a severe threat to computer security due to the rise of exploit kits [36] and the sheer number of code execution vulnerabilities [8] reported in host software every year.

To mitigate JavaScript exploits, software vendors have deployed many mitigation techniques like Address Space Layout Randomization (ASLR), Data Execution Prevention (DEP), control flow guard [7], sandbox [54], EMET [11], etc.

S. Chen et al. (Eds.): SecureComm 2019, LNICST 304, pp. 191–213, 2019.
https://doi.org/10.1007/978-3-030-37228-6_10

These mitigation techniques increase the bar for exploitation. As a result, attackers have to combine complex memory preparation, memory disclosure, code reuse and other techniques to launch a successful exploit.

While these exploit mitigation techniques are constantly improving, hacking contests like Pwn2Own [19] and GeekPwn [12], consistently demonstrate that the latest versions of Chrome, Safari, Internet Explorer, and Edge can still be exploited. There are at least two reasons for this. First, most of the latest proposed mitigation techniques require changes on software or compiler tool chain and thus could not be deployed promptly. For instance, ASLR-guard [43] is designed to thwart information disclosure attacks, but requires compiler changes and cannot be quickly deployed by software vendors. Second, the deployed mitigation techniques may fail due to newly invented exploitation techniques (e.g., sandbox bypass technique). We argue that *an ideal mitigation technique should be flexible to deploy without requiring code changes and should subvert inevitable exploitation stage(s)*.

We observe that a typical JavaScript exploit adopts *memory preparation* to manipulate the memory states. This is an essential step for JavaScript exploits since attackers need to put deliberately chosen content (e.g., ROP chain, shellcode) into a known memory location prior to execution of that code. This offers an opportunity for defenders to stop the exploits by disabling this *memory preparation* step.

In this paper, we propose ChaffyScript, a vulnerability-agnostic mitigation system that *blocks JavaScript exploits via undermining the memory preparation stage*. Specifically, given suspicious JavaScript, ChaffyScript rewrites the code to insert chaff code, which aims to perturb the memory state while preserving the semantics of the original code. JavaScript exploits will inevitably fail as a result of unexpected memory states introduced by chaff code, while the benign JavaScript still behaves as expected since the memory perturbation code does not change the JavaScript's original semantics.

Compared with current mitigation techniques, ChaffyScript has the following advantages: (1) it requires no changes to the host software and thus is easily deployable; (2) it does not introduce false positive and can defeat zero-day (or previously unseen) attacks; (3) the implementation of ChaffyScript is simple and robust; and (4) it incurs low runtime and memory overhead, and can be deployed for on-line defense.

We have implemented a prototype of ChaffyScript, which consists of three main components: a memory allocation/de-allocation discovery module to identify the potential memory preparation operations, a lightweight type inference module to prune the unnecessary memory preparation candidates, and a chaff code generation module to insert chaff code alongside memory preparation operations. As a demonstration of the deployment flexibility afforded by our approach, we have integrated ChaffyScript into a web proxy to protect users against malicious HTML files. Our evaluation results show that: 1) the probability of guessing the correct memory states after ChaffyScript is extremely low (Sect. 6.1), 2) ChaffyScript can thwart the latest JavaScript exploits effectively (Sect. 6.2) and 3) it incurs runtime overhead 5.88% for chrome and 12.96% for FireFox at most, and the memory overhead is 6.1% for the minimal JS heap usage, and 8.2% for the maximal JS heap usage during runtime on Octane benchmark [14] (Sect. 6.3).

In summary, the contributions of this work are:

- We made a key observation that memory preparation is an essential stage in JavaScript exploits.
- Based on this observation, we proposed and designed ChaffyScript to disable the memory perturbation stage by inserting chaff code.
- We have implemented a prototype system, ChaffyScript, and our evaluation shows that ChaffyScript incurs acceptable runtime performance overhead and memory overhead on Octane benchmark and defeat all of the 11 JavaScript exploits.
- We demonstrated the deployment flexibility via integrating ChaffyScript into a web proxy to protect users against malicious HTML files.

2   Technical Background and Motivation

2.1   JavaScript Exploits

The interactive nature of JavaScript allows malicious JavaScript to take advantage of binary vulnerabilities (e.g., use-after-free, heap/buffer overflow) that are otherwise difficult to exploit. JavaScript provides attackers with a much easier means to conduct heap spraying [32], information leakage [49], and shellcode generation.

Figure 1 illustrates the high-level stages of JavaScript exploits [20]. In the pre-exploitation stage, malware fingerprints the victim machine to determine the OS version and target software and then launches the corresponding exploit. The exploitation stage triggers the vulnerability, bypassing exploit mitigation techniques (e.g., ASLR, EMET [11], and Control Flow Guard [7]) and diverts the code execution to the injected payload. The post-exploitation stage executes a Return-Oriented-Programming (ROP) payload to bypass DEP, drops the malicious payload while attempting to evade detection from endpoint security products.

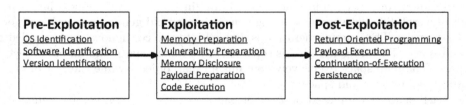

Fig. 1. The overall exploitation stages.

Defense against these exploits has evolved to react to the advances in exploitation techniques. Any defensive techniques that stop one of the exploitation stages can prevent the exploits from infecting victim machines. Some exemplar defenses include:

(1) Cloaking the OS/software version during the pre-exploitation stage to stop attackers from launching the correct exploits.
(2) Tools like BrowserShield [47] instrument the execution of JavaScript to match the predefined vulnerability feature and block the execution once a match is found.
(3) Randomization-based techniques like Instruction Set Randomization [38] introduce uncertainty in the target.
(4) Tools like ROPecker [28] exploit the Last Branch Record hardware feature to detect the execution of ROP chains.
(5) Control Flow Integrity (CFI) [23] based techniques [52] are used to prevent the execution of injected payloads.

While these exploitation mitigation techniques are constantly improving, hacking contests like Pwn2Own [19] and GeekPwn [12], consistently demonstrate that the latest versions of Chrome, Safari, Internet Explorer, and Edge can still be exploited. The reasons are two-fold: (1) most of the latest proposed mitigation techniques require software or compiler tool chain changes which may cause compatibility issues and thus cannot be deployed promptly; and (2) the deployed mitigation techniques may fail due to newly invented exploitation techniques. For instance, DEP mitigation can be defeated by ROP attacks. The JITSpray [50] makes the ROP defense useless since ROP is not needed anymore to bypass DEP in JITSpray based attack.

2.2 Memory Preparation

Based on our observations, the *memory preparation* stage is a critical stage for exploits.

Memory Management of the JavaScript Engine. Before discussing memory preparation techniques, we first take V8 [6] as an example to present an overview of memory management within a JavaScript engine. JavaScript engines dynamically manage memory for running applications so that developers do not need to worry about memory management like coding in C/C++. V8 divides the heap into several different spaces: a young generation, an old generation, and a large object space. The young generation is divided into two contiguous spaces, called semi-space. The old generation is separated into a map space and an old object space. The map space exclusively contains all map objects while the rest of old objects go into the old space.

Each space is composed of a set of pages. A page is a contiguous chunk of memory, allocated from the operating system with system call (e.g., `mmap`). Pages are always 1 MB in size and 1 MB aligned, except in a separate large object space. This separate space stores objects larger than `Page::kMaxHeapObjectSize`, so that theses large objects are not moved during garbage collection process.

The allocated objects will be put into different spaces based on their size, type, and age. Garbage collection process is responsible for 1) scavenging young generation space by moving live objects to the other semi-space when semi-space becomes full; 2) major collection of the whole heap to free unreferenced objects and aggressive memory compaction to clean up fragmented memory. The other JavaScript engines like SpiderMonkey [21] and ChakraCore [5], JavaScript-Core [15] share the similar design of memory management. Attackers commonly abuse the memory management features to manipulate the memory states, known as memory preparation.

Memory Preparation Techniques. Memory allocation and free operations are used to manipulate the memory. We can categorize these techniques based upon how they change the memory layout:

(1) Emit data in a target address. This is usually implemented with a heap spray technique like Heap Fengshui [51] and its successors [3]. These techniques spray crafted objects into the heap. The size and type of the objects are carefully chosen to exploit the memory management of JavaScript engine. ❶
(2) Emit adjacent objects. This is implemented by allocating two objects with the same type and size sequentially so the JavaScript engine will likely keep them adjacent in the heap; this technique is widely used by attackers. ❷
(3) Create holes in memory. This is implemented by allocating adjacent objects first, then freeing one of them. A hole is created among those adjacent objects. ❸
(4) De-fragment the heap. This is usually implemented via calling a garbage collection API provided by host software (e.g., `CollectGarbage()` in IE) or via a carefully crafted JavaScript snippet that forces the garbage collection process as discussed in Sect. 4.1. ❹

In theory, attackers can use any JavaScript types to prepare memory. However, in practice `String` and `Array` are the best candidates because the implementations of these two types, especially `Typed Array`, are very close to native string/array in C/C++, making it easy for attackers to control them in memory. The implementation of other primitive types (`Boolean, Null, Number, Symbol`) and objects (e.g., `Math`) are quite different. They are stored either as references or complex tree structures in memory, and thus it is difficult to precisely manipulate them in memory. Realizing that memory preparation is an essential step towards successful JavaScript exploit, a natural question rises in our mind: "How can we disrupt this stage without changing the code of the host software?" The answer is: *memory perturbation.*

2.3   Memory Perturbation Techniques

Table 1. The overview of memory perturbation techniques.

Category	Approaches	Memory change	Code trans. overhead
Storage	a. Split variables	1, 2	High
	b. Change encoding	1	High
	c. Promote scalars to objects	1, 2	High
	d. convert static data to procedure	1, 2	Medium
Aggregation	e. Merge scalar variables	1, 2	High
	f. Split, merge, fold, flatten arrays	2	High
Ordering	g. Reorder instance variables	2	Medium
	h. Reorder arrays	2	High
Inserting	i. Insert noise data allocation/free	2	Low
	j. Insert holes into arrays	2	High

1: content change 2: layout change

At a high level, memory perturbation stands for the semantically-equivalent transformation of an existing program, such that the transformed program exhibits a different and unpredictable memory layout. By nature, this technique shares some similarity with the data obfuscation technique used in code obfuscation [29] to defeat reverse engineering attacks because both of them transform the program without changing the program semantics. In the context of JavaScript-based exploit defense, our goal is to subvert the memory preparation stage through memory perturbation, so that exploits are defeated at runtime due to unpredictable memory states. While data obfuscation can make very

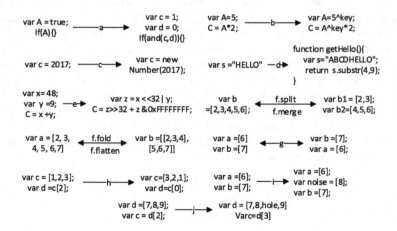

Fig. 2. Samples of memory perturbation techniques summarized in Table 1.

aggressive obfuscation, memory perturbation technique in ChaffyScript has to be lightweight for performance concern. To the best of our knowledge, we are the first to propose lightweight memory perturbation technique for JavaScript exploit defense.

Table 1 provides an overview of memory perturbation techniques. In general, these techniques can be divided into 4 categories as affecting the storage, aggregation, ordering or inserting of the data in memory. Figure 2 presents sample code snippets for each of the approaches referenced in Table 1. While each of the approaches can induce similar memory changes regarding memory layout or content, the overhead associated with each of these approaches varies. For instance, Approach i only needs one statement insertion operation for the code transformation. It does not need any further program analysis to keep the semantics intact since the inserted statement does not affect the original code's data and control flow. However, Approach f requires additional program analysis to keep the program semantics intact. This is because after the array is restructured, a whole program def-use analysis has to be conducted to identify all the affected code and then update the code accordingly (update array index, array name, etc.). Column D of Table 1 presents the code transformation overhead for each approach.

2.4 Our Mitigation Solution

Based upon the previous discussion, we propose a vulnerability-agnostic defense approach for JavaScript exploits, ChaffyScript. Specifically, given suspicious JavaScript, ChaffyScript rewrites the code to insert chaff code to perturb memory states at runtime, while preserving the semantics of the original JavaScript code.

At first glance, our technique seems very similar to the diversification techniques summarized in [40], which also introduce randomness to stop exploits. These techniques diversify the host software at instruction level, basic block level, function level, program level, and system level, and require modifications to the source code or binary code of the host software. On the contrary, ChaffyScript diversifies the input (JavaScript is the input of the host software (e.g., Chrome, IE, etc.)) to stop exploits, and no code changes on the host software are required. Therefore, the deployment of ChaffyScript is *effortless*.

To summarize, compared with current mitigation techniques, ChaffyScript has the following advantages:

(1) Vulnerability-agnostic nature. ChaffyScript does not rely on any specific vulnerability features as BrowserShield [47] does. Thus it is vulnerability-agnostic and can be used to defend against 0-day attacks.

(2) Flexible deployment. JavaScript rewriting can be implemented without the change of host software (e.g., Chrome and IE). This makes the deployment of ChaffyScript very flexible. Users can disable or enable ChaffyScript promptly based upon their needs.

(3) Stronger protection. As evaluated in Sect. 6.1, ChaffyScript provides much stro- nger protection than randomization-based approaches (e.g., ASLR-Guard [43]).

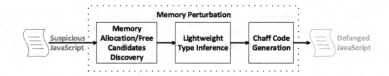

Fig. 3. The overall architecture of ChaffyScript.

In the following sections, we will elaborate details on the threat model and scope, design, and implementation of ChaffyScript.

3   Threat Model and Scope

To make sure our solution is practical, we define our threat model based on strong attack assumptions. We assume a commodity operating system with standard defense mechanisms, such as no-executable stack and heap, and ASLR. We assume attackers are remote, so they do not have physical access to the target system, nor do they have prior control over other local programs before a successful exploit.

We assume that the attacker use JavaScript to exploit the memory corruption vulnerabilities (use-after-free, memory disclosure, etc.), manipulate the memory layout, and divert the control flow to execute arbitrary code of his/her choice. These exploitations include but are not limited to control data attack, non-control data attack [55], and side channel attack [35]. With the deployed standard defense mechanisms, it is reasonable to assume that the attacker uses memory preparation to manipulate the memory layout since the bypass of the standard defense mechanisms needs precise memory layout preparation. This is true even when the attacker can exploit memory disclosure vulnerabilities because (1) most of the memory disclosure vulnerabilities needs precise memory preparation to trigger; (2) even in an extreme case that the attacker may read memory without memory preparation, the success of the other stages of JavaScript exploit (payload preparation, code execution, etc.) still rely on precise memory preparation. We impose no restrictions on the exploitation techniques.

Out-of-Scope Threats. Cross-site scripting (XSS) [39] and Cross-site forgery(CSRF) [25] are out of our scope since they do not target at memory corruption vulnerabilities.

4   Design

In theory, all of the memory perturbation techniques discussed in Sect. 2.3 could be used to sabotage the memory preparation stage in JavaScript exploits. In practice, an on-line defense approach should incur minimal code transformation overhead and thus cannot afford complex program analysis. With that in mind, we only apply Approach i in ChaffyScript for memory perturbation, which is good enough for defeating JavaScript exploits as demonstrated in Sect. 6. Specifically, ChaffyScript conducts JavaScript rewriting by inserting chaff code to (1) allocate random chunks of memory along with existing memory allocation operations, and (2) disable memory free operations by adding an additional reference to freed objects. We leave the exploration of the rest memory perturbation techniques as future work.

Figure 3 demonstrates the overview of ChaffyScript. Given a suspicious JavaScript, it first traverses the code to discover memory allocation/de-allocation candidates. Then a lightweight type inference process is conducted on these candidates to identify the interesting memory allocation/free candidates that are usually used for memory preparation by attackers; this reduces unnecessary chaff code insertions and improves runtime performance. Finally, the chaff code is generated and inserted into the original JavaScript code to get a *transformed JavaScript*. At runtime, the chaff code will allocate random memory or disable memory free operations to destroy the memory preparation stage of JavaScript-based exploits. Benign JavaScript still executes normally since the chaff code does not change the original code's expected semantics.

4.1   Memory Allocation/De-Allocation Candidate Discovery

As discussed in Sect. 2, there are two kinds of operations that affect the memory state: object allocation and de-allocation. ChaffyScript inspects JavaScript code to identify the following memory manipulation candidates:

Memory Allocation Candidates. As discussed in Sect. 2.2, *String* and *Array* are two common data types used by attackers to fill memory. ChaffyScript traverses JavaScript code to identify potential memory allocation candidates for *String* and *Array* operations. However, precise type inference for JavaScript is quite expensive [24]. So, to be simple, the *new* expression (e.g., *var c = new Array(5)*), value initialization expression (e.g., *var c = [3,7]*), and built-in function callsite (e.g., *var c = a.substr(0,10)*) are all considered as memory allocation candidates since they can trigger memory allocation in the heap. Note that the callee name can be dynamically generated in JavaScript. Thus, we cannot statically determine if it is a targeted built-in function callsite. To be complete, the callsites with dynamically generated callees are also considered as memory allocation candidates. In JavaScript *String* objects are immutable, so operations that change *String* objects (e.g., the '+' and '+=' operators) will also cause memory allocation. ChaffyScript also considers expressions with the '+' and '+=' operators as potential memory allocation candidates.

Memory De-allocation Candidates. In JavaScript, there are three ways to explicitly free memory: assign *null* to the object, use the *delete* operator and explicitly trigger garbage collection. The first two methods remove the reference to the allocated object. For instance, *delete object.property* removes the reference to the *property* object. However, it does not directly free the *property* object in memory. When the *property* object is no longer referenced by any other objects, garbage collection process will eventually free it in memory. ChaffyScript still considers *null* assignment and *delete* calls as memory de-allocation candidates because attackers often use them to create holes in memory, so objects allocated later can fill these holes to trigger some vulnerabilities (e.g., Use-after-Free).

Explicit garbage collection (GC) calls are usually used by attackers to defragment the heap [32]. Some browsers like Internet Explorer and Opera provide public APIs (e.g., *CollectGarbage()* for IE) to trigger garbage process. ChaffyScript can easily identify this kind of garbage collection process by matching the API name. However, the other browsers' garbage collection process can only be triggered when certain memory states are reached; in these cases there are no APIs to explicitly trigger the process. In these cases, attackers usually fill objects in memory to trigger the garbage collection process. For instance, the following code can fill up the 1MB semi-space page of V8 engine and force V8 to scavenge *NewSpace*.

```
for ( var  i =0;  i <((1024*1024)/0x10) ;  i++)
{
  var  a = new  String () ;
}
```

This kind of GC trigger is implicit and difficult to identify. Nevertheless, it includes memory allocation operations and will be considered as a *memory allocation candidate* and will still be captured by ChaffyScript. GC events using DOM objects instead of *String* and *Array* are not captured by ChaffyScript, but this is only one of the memory preparation techniques used by attackers. Furthermore, JavaScript exploits usually combine multiple memory preparation techniques, thus allowing ChaffyScript to be effective even when hybrid memory preparation methods are used.

The host software also provides APIs to allocate and free objects. For instance, on the browser, users can invoke the DOM API to add or remove node objects from the DOM tree. While in theory, it is possible for attackers to manipulate those APIs during memory preparation, as discussed in Sect. 2.2, it is challenging to do that since the layout and content of DOM objects are difficult to control. When a new memory preparation technique is discovered, we can update the memory allocation/de-allocation candidate discovery stage in ChaffyScript to block this new attack technique.

4.2 Lightweight Type Inference

The collection of memory allocation candidates is a superset of the memory allocation candidates of *String* and *Array* objects. If we insert chaff code along with all the candidates, the runtime performance would be unacceptable. To improve the runtime performance of rewritten JavaScript, we conduct lightweight type inference to prune the memory allocation candidates that are not related to *String* and *Array* objects. It is executed in two steps: *static type inference* and *dynamic type inference*.

Static Type Inference. ChaffyScript only keeps the memory allocation candidates that operate on variables typed as *String, Array, Array-Buffer, Int8Array, Uint8Array, Uint8ClampedArray, Int16Array, Uint16Array, Int32Array, Uint32Array, Float32Array,* or *Float64Array.* We can infer the types of the variables in expressions statically based upon how they are used. ChaffyScript uses the three following type inference rules:

(1) The constructor of the *new* operator indicates the type of created object. For instance, the constructor *Int16Array* in *var b = new Int16Array(256)* indicates the type of *b* is *Int16Array.*
(2) The return value of a built-in function indicates the type based on its description. For instance, *var c = s.split("a")* indicates that the type of *c* is *Array.*
(3) For expressions with the '+' or '+=' operators, if the type of the operands is *String,* then the result is also a *String.*

These three simple rules do not require complex program analysis and can be used to efficiently determine the variable types to filter out the memory allocation candidates. If static type inference cannot determine the types of all the variables used in memory allocation candidates, we conduct dynamic type inference to determine the variable types at runtime.

Dynamic Type Inference. Static type inference does not always work for two reasons. First, since a function call's name can be dynamically generated, we cannot determine an object's type based upon the function's return value. Second, the three typing rules can be insufficient to determine the variable types in some cases. For instance, the three typing rules cannot be applied to candidates {var d = a + b + c}. It is possible to determine the type of *a, b and c* via backward analysis, but that is likely too expensive for our online defense system use case. Instead, we conduct *dynamic type inference* with the help of certain JavaScript features. In JavaScript, a variable's type can be extracted at runtime using the `instanceof` operator. With this operator, ChaffyScript inserts the dynamic type inference after the memory allocation candidate to check if it operates on one of the targeted types. While dynamic type inference incurs runtime performance overhead, it is less expensive than static type inference.

As a result, the combination of static and dynamic type inference makes it impossible for attackers to bypass our type inference process.

4.3   Chaff Code Generation

The goal of inserted chaff code is to affect the memory states at runtime. It achieves this goal via the following two methods.

Disable Object De-allocations. For object de-allocations using public APIs like *CollectGarbage()* in IE, ChaffyScript directly removes the API call from the original code. This does not change the semantics of original JavaScript code because garbage collection APIs does not have data or control dependency on the original code.

For object de-allocations using the `delete` operator or assigning a `null` value, the above method does not work because simply removing such code will change the semantics of the original code. The attackers' goal of freeing an object is to create holes in memory, so later allocated objects can occupy the freed memory. If we keep a reference to the object before the free operation is executed, the later allocated object can not occupy the position since the allocated memory still has a reference to it. Figure 4(a, b) illustrates an example of such a transformation. In code snippet *[a]*, x is assigned the value `null`. In the transformed code *[b]*, ChaffyScript has added a new variable 4613335ea9901 to store a reference to ''abcdefgh''. Although x is assigned to `null`, the object ''abcdefgh'' will not be scavenged since 4613335ea9901 keeps a reference to it.

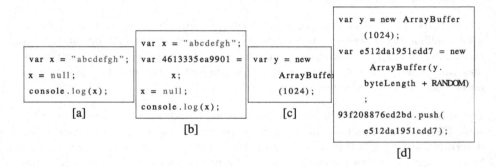

Fig. 4. Chaff code samples.

Insert Chaff Code After Object Allocations. As discussed in Sect. 2, if two objects of the same type are allocated sequentially and with the same size, it is likely their positions on the heap are adjacent to each other. Attackers exploit this feature to manipulate the memory layout and content. ChaffyScript is also able to exploit this detail to defeat this exploit. After every memory allocation candidate, ChaffyScript inserts code to allocate additional memory with the same type, but with variable-length padding (*RANDOM*) at the end. Figure 4([c],[d]) presents an example of such code transformation. As you see in code snippet *[d]*, a new *ArrayBuffer* is allocated with size *(y.byteLength + RANDOM)*. With this randomness, it is almost impossible for attackers to guess the combinations of memory states as evaluated in Sect. 6.1.

To generate *RANDOM*, ChaffyScript provides two approaches to increase an attacker's uncertainty. The first one is at runtime; every time the inserted chaff code is executed, a new random number is generated for *RANDOM*. So if a given piece of chaff code is executed 1000 times, and the range of *RANDOM* is *0–50*, it will create 50^{1000} possible memory states at runtime. The second approach happens when we are inserting the chaff code into original JavaScript code; a random number is generated for $RANDOM$. This value is used to randomly increase the size of the memory chunk allocated by this piece of chaff code. For example, if 15 places are inserted by the chaff code, and the range of $RANDOM$ is 0–50, 50^{15} possible memory states will be created at runtime. Both approaches can defeat the JavaScript exploits with different security guarantees and performance overhead as discussed in Sect. 6.

The range of $RANDOM$ cannot be too big. Otherwise, the objects allocated by chaff code might be allocated in a different location. Thus that fails to break adjacent arrays (❷). In our implementation, we set it as 0-50. This range works against memory preparation techniques while providing enough randomness as demonstrated in Sect. 6.1.

Since our inserted code is independent of the original code, attackers may abuse garbage collection to scavenge the allocated chaff memory and neutralize the effects of inserted chaff code. To avoid this, ChaffyScript keeps a reference to every allocated piece of chaff memory. This prevents scavenging of chaff memory by the garbage collection process because there is always at least one reference to the allocated chaff memory.

The variable names used in the chaff code are generated randomly. This prevents attackers from identifying memory allocated by the chaff code alongside their memory preparation code. Thus attackers cannot leverage variable naming conventions to identify memory used as part of our countermeasures, thus making bypass of these countermeasures impossible.

5   Implementation

We implemented ChaffyScript using esprima [10]. It is a JavaScript parser used to generate Abstract Syntax Tree (AST) with full support for ECMAScript 6. Since it is written using JavaScript, it can be easily embedded into different documents like HTML or PDF. This makes the deployment very flexible. We use Estraverse [9] to traverse the AST, discover memory allocation/free candidates and perform lightweight type inference. The chaff code insertion is implemented via directly manipulating the original code with the offset information collected from AST generation process. We do not operate on AST directly to insert the chaff code because generating code from AST is more expensive than directly manipulating the original code. Section 6.3 evaluates the difference of rewriting performance for these two approaches.

The deployment of ChaffyScript is very flexible. It can be deployed as a browser extension, a web proxy, a standalone rewriting engine or one component of a JavaScript engine. In this paper, we demonstrated one deployment approach to protect users against malicious HTML files.

HTML Protector. Ideally, it is most user-friendly to deploy ChaffyScript as a browser extension. Unfortunately, JavaScript rewrite, used to implement code transformation in ChaffyScript, is not natively supported in browser extensions. Instead, we deploy ChaffyScript as a web proxy. The downside is that a user needs to install an external program (and certificate) as opposed to only an extension.

The benefit is that this proxy-based solution is browser-independent and can be easily deployed with minimal configuration.

We implemented the prototype in *Node.js* [17], using the *http-mitm-proxy* package [13]. ChaffyScript becomes an integral part of the Web proxy. We followed Dach- shund [44]'s approach to handle dynamically generated code. Specifically, the dynamic code generation functions (e.g., *eval, SetTimeout, Function, SetInterval*) were hooked via new injected JavaScript code. To rewrite dynamically generated code, we used synchronous *XMLHttpRequest* requests from hooked JavaScript functions to the proxy. The response from the proxy contains the rewritten JavaScript code.

6   Evaluation

In this section, we present the evaluation of ChaffyScript. The evaluation tries to answer the following questions: First, How secure is ChaffyScript's approach in theory, compared to general randomization approaches? Second, how secure is ChaffyScript's approach against practical JavaScript-based exploits? Third, how much overhead does ChaffyScript impose, with respect to chaff code generation, runtime and memory overhead of the resulting chaff code?

Experimental Setup. The performance overhead experiment was run under Chrome 57 and Firefox 54. All the experiments are conducted on a test machine equipped with intel Core i7-4790 CPU @ 3.60GHz × 8 with 16 GB RAM.

Table 2. Experimental results of 11 latest JavaScript-based exploits using ChaffyScript

CVE	Environment Setup	Memory Preparation	M	N	Defeated?
CVE-2015-2419	IE11/32bit win7	❶❷❸	28	12594	Y
CVE-2015-1233	Chrome 41.0.2272.118/win1032bit	❶❷❸	9	8194	Y
CVE-2015-6086	IE11/32bit win7	❸❶	12	1280	Y
CVE-2015-6764	Chrome 46.0.2490.0/win10 32bit	❶❷❸	14	393224	Y
CVE-2016-9079	FireFox 50.0.1 32bit /Windows8.1	❶❷❶(JITSpray)	13	20564	Y
		❶❷❸	28	17408	Y
CVE-2016-3202 (ms16-063)	IE11/Win7 32bit	❶❷❸❹	12	110005	Y
CVE-2016-1646	Chrome 46.0.2490.0/win10 32bit	❶❷❸	18	393226	Y
V8 OOB write	Chrome 60.0.3080.5 Linux14.04 64bit	❷	10	10	Y
X360_videoPlayerActiveX	IE10/VideoPlayerActiveX 2.6, win7 64bit	❶❷	9	352258	Y
CVE-2017-5400	Firefox 51.0.1 32bit/Win10 64bit	❶❷❸	7	2702	Y

M: # of inserted chaff code N: Executed times # of chaff code at runtime

6.1   Security Analysis

In this subsection, we present an analysis to determine the probability that an attacker could predict the memory layout after memory perturbation is introduced by ChaffyScript. The randomness introduced by ChaffyScript is determined by the following parameters:

(1) *RANDOM* - the size variation range of created object by chaff code.
(2) *M* - number of inserted chaff code.
(3) *N* - executed times of chaff code at runtime.

The probability of guessing the correct memory states is defined as the following equation.

$$probability = \begin{cases} RANDOM^{-M} & predefine\ RANDOM \\ RANDOM^{-N} & Gen\ RANDOM\ at\ runtime \end{cases}$$

If *RANDOM* is predefined when ChaffyScript inserts the chaff code, the *probability* is $RANDOM^{-M}$. If a random number is generated for *RANDOM* every time the chaff code is executed, the *probability* is $RANDOM^{-N}$. If it is too big, the allocated objects by chaff code may not be adjacent to the objects allocated by original code. Thus it cannot break memory preparation ❷. In our implementation, we set *RANDOM* as 50 and it worked well on defeating JavaScript exploits as evaluated in Sect. 6.2.

The values of *M* and *N* vary case by case. Column 4 and Column 5 in Table 2 record the values of *M* and *N* for 11 exploits. The average of *M* was 15, and the average of *N* was 130876. The *probability* for JavaScript exploits in our implementation should be 50^{-15} and $50^{-130876}$. This provides much stronger randomness than ASLR [43] (2^{-64} at most). The highest *probability* of the 11 exploits was 50^{-10} which is still stronger than 2^{-56}. Through this analysis, we conclude that the probability for an attacker to predict the memory layout is extremely low after memory perturbation is introduced by ChaffyScript.

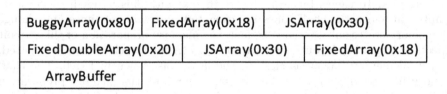

Fig. 5. Expected memory layout of sample chromev8_OOB_write

6.2   Effectiveness

Although in theory ChaffyScript can stop JavaScript exploits, we wanted to know how well it performed at defeating real JavaScript exploits without the knowledge of the targeted vulnerabilities. We went over browser-related PoCs in recent years from public resources like metasploit and technical blogs, collected around 40 of them since 2015, and eventually managed to successfully set up exploitation environments for 11 of them. This is our best effort, due to the scarcity of public exploits resources. These 11 exploits are representative of JavaScript exploits because:

(1) The vulnerabilities targeted by these 11 exploits are quite new (from 2015 to 2017).
(2) The target host software of these exploits covered the most popular web browsers (IE11, Chrome, and Firefox)
(3) These 11 exploits used all of the memory preparation techniques presented in Column 3 in Table 2.
(4) These 11 exploits covered the popular exploitation techniques - JITSpray and HeapSpray.
(5) These 11 exploits not only targeted at vulnerabilities in host software, but also in the browser plugin (X360 _videoPlayerActiveX).

BuggyArray(0x80)	Chaff Memory	FixedArray(0x18)	Chaff Memory	JSArray(0x30)		
Chaff Memory	FixedDoubleArray(0x20)	Chaff Memory	JSArray(0x30)	Chaff Memory	FixedArray(0x18)
Chaff Memory	ArrayBuffer	Chaff Memory			

Fig. 6. Memory layout of sample chromev8_OOB_write after rewritten by ChaffyScript

For each exploit, we manually confirmed whether it could be stopped by ChaffyScript. Column 6 in Table 2 presents the result. As shown in the results, ChaffyScript defeated all 11 of the exploits without requiring knowledge of vulnerabilities targeted. This experiment demonstrated that ChaffyScript can effectively defeat JavaScript exploits without knowledge of the targeted vulnerability.

Note that the chaff codes inserted into the sample *chromev8_OOB_write* are only executed 10 times, but still thwart the exploit. This is not like the other samples, in which the chaff codes are executed thousands of times and change the memory states substantially. In fact, the memory preparation of this exploit expects the memory layout as shown in Fig. 5. After the chaff code is inserted, the actual memory layout is close to the layout as shown in Fig. 6. The chaff memory breaks adjacent array layout (❷). Therefore, the memory preparation of this exploit fails and this exploit is thwarted eventually. This case further demonstrates the effectiveness of memory perturbation used in ChaffyScript since it uses very few memory perturbation operations.

6.3 Performance

Rewriting Overhead. In order to evaluate the rewriting overhead of ChaffyScript, we chose to measure the three popular and large JavaScript libraries - JQuery (mobile-1.4.2), AngularJS (1.2.5), and React (0.13.3). These libraries are commonly embedded in web pages and relatively large compared with other JavaScript applications (JQuery has 443 KB, AngularJS has 702 KB, React has 587 KB). For the evaluation, we rewrote these libraries using ChaffyScript 1000 times. We measured the time required to rewrite these libraries, including all the steps required to generate chaff JavaScript.

Table 3. Rewriting performance on well-known JavaScript libraries

JS library	Jquery.mobile 1.4.2	Angular 1.2.5	React 0.13.3
Modify code string	99 ms	99 ms	100 ms
Modify AST	174 ms	169 ms	155 ms

We tested two code transformation approaches. The first approach modified the code directly based upon the offset information collected by the JavaScript parser. The second approach modified code within the AST. As demonstrated in Table 3. The time spent by the second approach is 1.67 times more than the first approach. ChaffyScript chose the first approach in the implementation. On average, It took 100ms to rewrite JQuery, AngularJS, and React. Note that rewriting is a one-time effort and we can further optimize performance by rewriting multiple scripts in parallel.

Table 4. Overall overhead of ChaffyScript on octane benchmark

Configuration	Chrome	Firefox
a. Runtime Generated $RANDOM$ + GC escaper	5.88%	12.96%
b. Runtime Generated $RANDOM$	4.54%	7.98%
c. Predefined $RANDOM$ + GC escaper	5.68%	11.27%
d. Predefined $RANDOM$	4.53%	6.60%

Runtime Overhead. Next, we evaluated the runtime performance that is incurred on the client side due to the modified JavaScript code. We leverage Octane, a commonly-used benchmark for JavaScript engines [14]. For the evaluation, we ran the Octane benchmarks 5 times and used the mean scores as the final results.

Table 4 summarizes the overall overhead on the Octane benchmark under different ChaffyScript configurations. With the strongest protection, ChaffyScript incurs 5.88% overhead in Chrome, and 12.96% in FireFox. With the weakest protection, ChaffyScript incurs 4.53% in Chrome and 6.60% in Firefox. As discussed in Sect. 6.1, the weakest protection can still provide an acceptable randomness strength. Note that our threat model is only relevant to non-trusted and attacker-controlled JavaScript. Thus the overhead of popular JavaScript libraries can be eliminated by whitelisting trusted scripts. This overhead after the whitelisting should allow ChaffyScript to be deployed online to protect users against JavaScript exploits.

Memory Overhead. In theory, the memory overhead should be around 2 times at most. This is because along with each object allocation, ChaffyScript could allocate another object with a similar size to disturb memory states. If all of the inserted objects by chaff code are not freed finally by Garbage Collector, the

Table 5. Memory overhead of chrome on octane benchmark

Usage	Original	a	b	c	d
Min(MB)	34.4	36.5 (6.10%)	36.5 (6.10%)	36.5 (6.10%)	36.4 (5.81%)
Max(MB)	609	659 (8.2%)	656 (7.71%)	640 (5.09%)	638 (4.76%)

a, b, c, d refers to the four ChaffyScript configurations described in Table 4

memory usage of the defanged JavaScript would be up to 2 times of the original JavaScript.

To evaluate the actual memory overhead, we ran Octane on Chrome and recorded the memory usage of JavaScript heap. Table 5 summarizes the results. *Min* refers to the observed minimal memory usage of JavaScript heap during the running of Octane, while *Max* refers to the observed maximal memory usage. As demonstrated in the table, for all four different ChaffyScript configurations, the memory overhead never exceeded 8.2%. This is not a big overhead since RAM has become very cheap and current personal computers are usually equipped with at least 8GB memory. Thus, ChaffyScript can be deployed by users without requiring upgraded hardware.

7   Discussion

Limitations of ChaffyScript. First, attackers may find methods to bypass the JavaScript rewriting process. For instance, lexer confusing attacks [16] confuse the lexer causing executable code to be interpreted as the content of strings or comments, allowing an attacker to slip arbitrary unsafe code past a rewriter or verifier. The rewriter of ChaffyScript is vulnerable to this attack. In the future, we would like to adopt JaTE's [53] approach by considering all formats of JavaScript comments to gain resilience to this attack. It is also possible to attack the JavaScript parser *esprima* with crafted JavaScript. As a result, the code transformation cannot be finished. Fortunately, ChaffyScript can identify such attacks because it can detect *esprima* errors. ChaffyScript can alert security researchers for further analysis once such failures are observed.

Second, the JavaScript extraction approach used in deployment may undermine ChaffyScript. Attackers may hide JavaScript in an unusual way to escape from the extraction, thus preventing ChaffyScript from rewriting those portions. For instance, attackers may abuse PDF parsers to hide malicious JavaScript code [26]. This is not a ChaffyScript issue, but rather is a JavaScript extractor issue. Deployment of a state-of-art JavaScript extractor with ChaffyScript would reduce the risk of such attacks.

Third, ChaffyScript does not work on hybrid JavaScript exploits. Basically, such kind of exploits use JavaScript to trigger the vulnerability, and use other script language (e.g., ActionScript in Flash) to prepare the memory. This is quite common in recently years since vector-related rehabilitates in Flash are quite exploit-friendly, allowing construction of arbitrary memory read/write primitives [4]. However, it is possible to deploy the techniques used in ChaffyScript on ActionScript to stop such attacks as discussed in the following subsection.

Fourth, although extremely difficult, attackers may be able to find object types other than String and Array to prepare memory layout. This is only a limitation for our current implementation. Once these new memory preparation techniques are identified, ChaffyScript just needs an update to its memory allocation/free candidate discovery process to reflect the new memory preparation technique.

Applicability on the Other Script-Based Exploits. JavaScript is not the only script language that can be used to launch exploits; other script languages like VBScript [22] and ActionScript [1] are commonly used to launch exploits. These script-based exploits are widely used to create malicious Microsoft Documents (word, excel, powerpoint,etc.), flash files, web pages [2]. So the question rises in our mind - Can ChaffyScript be applied to stop the other script-based exploits?

The answer is yes because: (1) Script-based languages share a similar memory management approach. They all use some sort of garbage collector to recycle the memory and conduct automatic garbage collection at runtime. (2) Memory preparation is a general stage in exploits. Attackers require this stage to bypass mitigation techniques like ASLR, CFG [7] with crafted memory. This stage is also used by the other script-based exploits. (3) Other script-based languages also execute interpretively and can be rewritten as JavaScript. This allows ChaffyScript to provide the protection via rewriting.

To demonstrate this, we set up the exploitation environment for CVE-2016-0189 [18]. It is a VBScript-based exploit targeting a VBScript memory corruption in IE11. We manually applied ChaffyScript's rewriting process and insert the memory perturbation code. The test shows that this exploit is successfully blocked by memory perturbation. This demonstrates that ChaffyScript can also be applied to stop the other script-based exploits.

To apply ChaffyScript on the other script language, we need the corresponding script parser, and also need to adapt the lightweight typing rules on the new script language since different languages support different typing systems. These adaptations are feasible and can be implemented with engineering efforts.

8 Related Work

Malicious JavaScript Detection. Malicious JavaScript detection has been a hot research topic. Several systems have focused on statically analyzing JavaScript code to identify malicious web pages [31,33,41,48].

Then dynamic analysis [30,37,42] is widely deployed to expose behaviors of obfuscated JavaScript code.

These approaches often require complex code analysis and cannot be deployed online to protect users against malicious JavaScript. Therefore, they are used to generate IDS rules for runtime detection. In comparison, ChaffyScript can provide users real-time protection without any knowledge of the targeted vulnerabilities.

Exploit Mitigation. Mitigation techniques (Control Flow Integrity [23,46,52,56], ROP Mitigation [11,27,28], Randomization [34,35,43] have been evolving with the advancement of exploitation techniques. However, the current mitigation techniques usually require changes to source code or binaries and thus cannot be deployed promptly. In addition, once deployed, they cannot be rapidly upgraded as exploitation techniques advance. In contrast, ChaffyScript's JavaScript rewriting approach allows for a more flexible deployment.

JavaScript Rewriting. JavaScript rewriting has been used by researchers to meet various security requirements. BrowserShields [47] uses it to stop JavaScript exploits by matching predefined vulnerability features. It does not work for 0-day exploits, while ChaffyScript does. ConScript [45] rewrites JavaScript to specify and enforce fine-grained security policies for JavaScript in the browser. Dachshund [44] secures against blinded constants in JIT code via removing all the constants from JavaScript code.

9   Conclusion

In this paper, we made a key observation that memory preparation is an essential stage in JavaScript exploits and can be disturbed via a memory perturbation technique. Based on our observation, we proposed and designed ChaffyScript, a vulnerability-agnostic system to thwart JavaScript exploits by inserting memory perturbation with JavaScript rewriting. We have implemented a prototype system, ChaffyScript, and our evaluation shows that ChaffyScript incurs acceptable runtime performance overhead (5.88% for Chrome, 12.96% for FireFox) and memory overhead (6.1% for minimal JS heap usage, 8.2% for maximal JS heap usage) on Octane benchmark and defeat all of the 11 JavaScript exploits. We also demonstrated the deployment flexibility via integrating ChaffyScript into a web proxy to protect users against malicious HTML files.

References

1. ActionScript technology center (2017). http://www.adobe.com/devnet/actionscript.html
2. AKBuilder (2017). https://nakedsecurity.sophos.com/2017/02/07/akbuilder-is-the-latest-exploit-kit-to-target-word-documents-spread-malware/
3. The art of leaks: the return of Feng Shui (2017). https://cansecwest.com/slides/2014/The%20Art%20of%20Leaks%20-%20read%20version%20-%20Yoyo.pdf
4. ASLR bypass apocalypse in recent zero-day exploits (2017). https://www.fireeye.com/blog/threat-research/2013/10/aslr-bypass-apocalypse-in-lately-zero-day-exploits.html
5. ChakraCore JavaScript Engine (2017). https://github.com/Microsoft/ChakraCore
6. Chrome V8 Engine (2017). https://developers.google.com/v8/
7. Control flow guard (2017). https://msdn.microsoft.com/en-us/library/windows/desktop/mt637065(v=vs.85).aspx
8. CVE details (2017). http://www.cvedetails.com/

9. ECMAScript JS AST traversal functions (2017). https://github.com/estools/estraverse
10. ECMAScript parsing infrastructure for multipurpose analysis (2017). http://esprima.org/
11. The enhanced mitigation experience toolkit (2017). https://support.microsoft.com/en-us/help/2458544/the-enhanced-mitigation-experience-toolkit
12. GeekPwn (2017). http://2017.geekpwn.org/1024/en/index.html
13. HTTP mitmproxy (2017). https://github.com/joeferner/node-http-mitm-proxy
14. The JavaScript Benchmark suite for the modern web (2017). https://developers.google.com/octane/
15. Javascriptcore (2017). https://trac.webkit.org/wiki/JavaScriptCore
16. Lexer confusing attack (2017). https://github.com/google/caja/wiki/JsControlFormatChars
17. Node.js. (2017) https://nodejs.org/en/
18. Proof-of-concept exploit for CVE-2016-0189 (VBScript memory corruption in ie11) (2017). https://github.com/theori-io/cve-2016-0189
19. Pwn2Own (2017). https://en.wikipedia.org/wiki/Pwn2Own
20. ROP is dying and your exploit mitigations are on life support (2017). https://www.endgame.com/blog/technical-blog/rop-dying-and-your-exploit-mitigations-are-life-support
21. SpiderMonkey JavaScript engine (2017). https://developer.mozilla.org/en-US/docs/Mozilla/Projects/SpiderMonkey
22. VBScript (2017). https://en.wikipedia.org/wiki/VBScript
23. Abadi, M., Budiu, M., Erlingsson, U., Ligatti, J.: Control-flow integrity. In: Proceedings of the 12th ACM Conference on Computer and Communications Security 2005, pp. 340–353. ACM (2005)
24. Anderson, C., Giannini, P., Drossopoulou, S.: Towards type inference for JavaScript. In: Black, A.P. (ed.) ECOOP 2005. LNCS, vol. 3586, pp. 428–452. Springer, Heidelberg (2005). https://doi.org/10.1007/11531142_19
25. Barth, A., Jackson, C., Mitchell, J.C.: Robust defenses for cross-site request forgery. In: 2008 Proceedings of the 15th ACM Conference on Computer and Communications Security, pp. 75–88. ACM (2008)
26. Carmony, C., Hu, X., Yin, H., Bhaskar, A.V., Zhang, M.: Abusing PDF parsers in malware detectors. In: NDSS, Extract Me If You Can (2016)
27. Chen, X., Slowinska, A., Andriesse, D., Bos, H., Giuffrida, C. StackArmor: comprehensive protection from stack-based memory error vulnerabilities for binaries. In: NDSS (2015)
28. Cheng, Y., Zhou, Z., Miao, Y., Ding, X., Deng, H., et al.: ROPecker: a generic and practical approach for defending against ROP attack
29. Collberg, C., Thomborson, C., Low, D.: A taxonomy of obfuscating transformations. Department of Computer Science, The University of Auckland, New Zealand, Technical report (1997)
30. Cova, M., Kruegel, C., Vigna, G.: Detection and analysis of drive-by-download attacks and malicious Javascript code. In: Proceedings of the 19th International Conference on World Wide Web (2010)
31. Curtsinger, C., Livshits, B., Zorn, B.G., Seifert, C.: ZOZZLE: fast and precise in-browser JavaScript malware detection. In: USENIX Security Symposium (2011)
32. Daniel, M., Honoroff, J., Miller, C.: Engineering heap overflow exploits with JavaScript, WOOT, vol. 8, pp. 1–6 (2008)
33. Feinstein, B., Peck, D., SecureWorks, I.: Caffeine monkey: automated collection, detection and analysis of malicious Javascript. Black Hat, USA (2007)

34. Gadaleta, F., Younan, Y., Joosen, W.: BuBBle: a JavaScript engine level countermeasure against heap-spraying attacks. In: Massacci, F., Wallach, D., Zannone, N. (eds.) ESSoS 2010. LNCS, vol. 5965, pp. 1–17. Springer, Heidelberg (2010). https://doi.org/10.1007/978-3-642-11747-3_1
35. Gras, B., Razavi, K., Bosman, E., Bos, H., Giuffrida, C. ASLR on the line: practical cache attacks on the MMU. In: NDSS, February 2017 (2017)
36. Grier, et al.: Manufacturing compromise: the emergence of exploit-as-a-service. In: Proceedings of the 2012 ACM Conference on Computer and Communications Security (2012), pp. 821–832. ACM (2012)
37. Hartstein, B. Jsunpack: an automatic JavaScript unpacker. In: ShmooCon Convention (2009)
38. Kc, G.S., Keromytis, A.D., Prevelakis, V.: Countering code-injection attacks with instruction-set randomization. In: 2003 Proceedings of the 10th ACM Conference on Computer and Communications Security, CCS 2003, New York, NY, USA, pp. 272–280. ACM (2003)
39. Kirda, E., Kruegel, C., Vigna, G., Jovanovic, N.: Noxes: a client-side solution for mitigating cross-site scripting attacks. In: 2006 Proceedings of the 2006 ACM symposium on Applied computing, pp. 330–337. ACM (2006)
40. Larsen, P., Homescu, A., Brunthaler, S., Franz, M. SoK: automated software diversity. In: 2014 IEEE Symposium on Security and Privacy (SP), pp. 276–291. IEEE (2014)
41. Likarish, P., Jung, E., Jo, I.: Obfuscated malicious JavaScript detection using classification techniques. In: MALWARE (2009), pp. 47–54. Citeseer (2009)
42. Lu, G., Debray, S.: Automatic simplification of obfuscated JavaScript code: a semantics-based approach. In: Proceedings of the 2012 IEEE Sixth International Conference on Software Security and Reliability (2012)
43. Lu, K., Song, C., Lee, B., Chung, S.P., Kim, T., Lee, W.: ASLR-guard: stopping address space leakage for code reuse attacks. In: 2015 Proceedings of the 22nd ACM SIGSAC Conference on Computer and Communications Security, pp. 280–291. ACM (2015)
44. Maisuradze, G., Backes, M., Rossow, C.: Dachshund: Digging for and Securing Against (non-) Blinded Constants in JIT Code (2017)
45. Meyerovich, L.A., Livshits, B.: ConScript: specifying and enforcing fine-grained security policies for JavaScript in the browser. In: 2010 IEEE Symposium on Security and Privacy (SP), pp. 481–496. IEEE (2010)
46. Prakash, A., Yin, H., Liang, Z.: Enforcing system-wide control flow integrity for exploit detection and diagnosis. In: 2013 Proceedings of the 8th ACM SIGSAC Symposium on Information, Computer and Communications Security, pp. 311–322. ACM (2013)
47. Reis, C., Dunagan, J., Wang, H.J., Dubrovsky, O., Esmeir, S.: BrowserShield: vulnerability-driven filtering of dynamic HTML. ACM Trans. Web (TWEB) 1(3), 11 (2007)
48. Seifert, C., Welch, I., Komisarczuk, P.: Identification of malicious web pages with static heuristics. In: 2008 Australasian Telecommunication Networks and Applications Conference, ATNAC 2008, pp. 91–96. IEEE (2008)
49. Serna, F.J.: The info leak era on software exploitation. Black Hat, USA (2012)
50. Sintsov, A.: Writing JIT-Spray Shellcode for fun and profit. Writing (2010)
51. Sotirov, A.: Heap Feng Shui in JavaScript. Black Hat Europe (2007)
52. Tice, C., et al.: Enforcing forward-edge control-flow integrity in GCC & LLVM. In: USENIX Security Symposium, pp. 941–955 (2014)

53. Tran, T., Pelizzi, R., Sekar, R.: JaTE: transparent and efficient JavaScript confinement. In: Proceedings of the 31st Annual Computer Security Applications Conference, pp. 151–160. ACM (2015)
54. Yee, B., et al.: Native client: a sandbox for portable, untrusted x86 native code. In: Security and Privacy, 2009 30th IEEE Symposium on 2009, pp. 79–93. IEEE (2009)
55. Yu, Y.: Write once, Pwn anywhere. Black Hat (2014)
56. Zhang, C., et al.: Practical control flow integrity and randomization for binary executables. In: 2013 IEEE Symposium on Security and Privacy (SP), pp. 559–573. IEEE (2013)

Obfusifier: Obfuscation-Resistant Android Malware Detection System

Zhiqiang Li[1(✉)], Jun Sun[1], Qiben Yan[1,2], Witawas Srisa-an[1],
and Yutaka Tsutano[1]

[1] Department of Computer Science and Engineering,
University of Nebraska–Lincoln, Lincoln, NE 68588, USA
{zli,jsun,qyan,witty,ytsutano}@cse.unl.edu
[2] Department of Computer Science and Engineering,
Michigan State University, East Lansing, MI 48824, USA

Abstract. The structure-changing obfuscation has become an effective means for malware authors to create malicious apps that can evade the machine learning-based detection systems. Generally, a highly effective detection system for detecting unobfuscated malware samples can lose its effectiveness when encountering the same samples that have been obfuscated. In this paper, we introduce OBFUSIFIER, a highly effective machine-learning based malware detection system that can sustain its effectiveness even when malware samples are obfuscated using complex and composite techniques. The training of our system is based on obfuscation-resistant features extracted from unobfuscated apps, while the classifier retains high effectiveness for detecting obfuscated malware. Our experimental evaluation shows that OBFUSIFIER can achieve the precision, recall, and F-measure that exceed 95% for detecting obfuscated Android malware, well surpassing any of the previous approaches.

Keywords: Malware detection · Android · Obfuscation

1 Introduction

Code obfuscation is a common approach used by developers to help protect the intellectual properties of their software. The goal of obfuscation is to make code and data unreadable or hard to understand [16]. This, in effect, makes reverse-engineering of their applications more difficult. Typically, there are three major types of obfuscation methods: (1) trivial obfuscations, which most tools can easily handle; (2) data-flow and control-flow obfuscations, which can be Detectable by Static Analysis (DSA); and (3) encryption-based obfuscations, which often involve some forms of encryption to hide the actual code and data.

Recently, various obfuscation techniques have been applied on malicious apps to evade the security analysis. These techniques are especially effective in defeating existing malware and virus scanners, which often rely on signature matching

© ICST Institute for Computer Sciences, Social Informatics and Telecommunications Engineering 2019
Published by Springer Nature Switzerland AG 2019. All Rights Reserved
S. Chen et al. (Eds.): SecureComm 2019, LNICST 304, pp. 214–234, 2019.
https://doi.org/10.1007/978-3-030-37228-6_11

or program analysis. As will be shown in Sect. 3, we apply DSA based obfuscation techniques to known malware samples and evaluate them by VirusTotal [7]. The analysis results indicate that many existing techniques deployed by VirusTotal cannot detect obfuscated malware samples and would indicate them as benign.

These DSA based obfuscation techniques are effective in defeating virus scanners, because they change the flow of the program by adding (e.g., junk code insertion), reordering (e.g., code reordering, function inlining, function outlining), or redirecting code (e.g., method indirection). These code manipulations can change the signatures of a program and complicate program analysis. In addition, these techniques also change method, variable, and class names so that static analysis techniques that look for previously known values would fail to locate them. Also, note that encryption-based obfuscation techniques are effective in defeating malware detectors because they "hide" the entire code-base and data through encryption. Prior to running, these encrypted applications must be decrypted to reveal the real codes (that may or may not have been obfuscated using DSA techniques) and data for execution. Encryption-based obfuscation is beyond the scope of this work.

Recently, machine learning has become widely used for Android malware detection in the state-of-the-art systems [9,12,20,23,24,27]. These existing systems extract features from benign and malware Android samples to build classifiers to detect malware. Currently, the samples used in building classifiers are not obfuscated. However, one recent work [25] as well as Sect. 3 have shown that when obfuscated Android malware samples are submitted to these classifiers, they can be miscategorized since the features used by these classifiers are now more ambiguous due to obfuscation [19]. In this paper, we propose OBFUSIFIER, a machine-learning based malware detector that is constructed using features from unobfuscated samples but can provide accurate and robust detection results when obfuscated samples are submitted for detection.

Our key insight is that there are portions of codes that cannot be obfuscated, because the obfuscation of them will break the functionality. One of these portions is *the API invocations into the Android framework*. As a result, our feature selection focuses mainly on the usage of Android APIs. Our approach then extracts features that are related to such usage. In total, we extract 28 features to build our classifier using 4,300 benign apps and 4,300 malware samples obtained from VirusShare; these apps are not obfuscated. We then test our system using 568 obfuscated malware. The result indicates that our system can achieve 95% precision, recall, and F-measure, corroborating the obfuscation resilience of OBFUSIFIER.

2   Background on Code Obfuscation

In this work, we use ALAN, a Java-based code obfuscation tool for Android. Next, we describe the obfuscation features supported by ALAN. As will be discussed in Sect. 5, we employed all techniques in a composite fashion to obfuscate our malware samples to make them as challenging as possible to be detected by OBFUSIFIER.

Disassembling & Reassembling. The Dalvik bytecode in the DEX file of the Android app can be disassembled and reassembled. The arrangement of classes, strings, methods in the DEX files can be changed in different ways. In other words, the architecture or the arrangement of the DEX files can be modified, and this transformation creates changes that significantly alter the structures of the program, rendering signature-based detector ineffective.

Repackaging. Developers must sign their Android app before it is released to the market. Cybercriminals can unzip the released Android app and repack it via tools in the Android SDK. After repacking, hackers must sign the repackaged app with their own keys, because they do not have the developers original keys, this newly signed app does not have the same checksum with the original app. This process neutralizes the effectiveness of malware detectors that compare checksums primarily for detection.

Data Encoding. The strings and arrays in the DEX files can be used as signatures to identify malicious behaviors. Encryption of strings and arrays can make signature-based detection ineffective [14].

Code Reordering. This feature aims to change the order of the instructions randomly, and the original execution order is preserved by inserting goto instructions. Because this reordering is random, the signature generated by this malware would be significantly different from the signature of the original malware. This is by far the strongest obfuscation technique for evading the signature-based detectors [32].

Junk Code Insertion. This technique does not change the programming logic of the code. As such, compared with other transformations, its impact towards the detector is less significant, and malware only obfuscated with Junk Code Insertion are very likely to be detected [17]. Three types of junk codes are inserted including nop instructions, unconditional jumps, and additional registers for garbage operations.

Identifier Renaming. This transformation modifies package and class names with random strings. It can be used to evade the signature-based detection.

Call Indirection. Some malware scanners take advantage of the structure of the method graphs to generate signatures. The original method call can be modified by inserting a newly and randomly generated method before calling the original method. This transformation can insert many irrelevant nodes into the method call graph of an obfuscated app. If a detector is relying on a signature based on a method call graph, this obfuscation technique can be effective in evading the detection. Furthermore, a machine learning detector based on method call graph features would also likely fail to detect malware samples employing this obfuscation technique.

3   Effects of Obfuscation on Malware Detection

Obfuscation techniques that can transform the structure of an application has the potential to allow malware to evade detection of many anti-virus scanners.

To elaborate and quantify the magnitude of this phenomenon, we investigated the effects of obfuscations on the effectiveness of existing virus scanners. The data collection process to conduct our experiments (described next) and the subsequent evaluation of our proposed system is described in Sect. 5.

In the first experiment, we assessed the effect of obfuscation on the accuracy of detection by about 60 scanners deployed by VirusTotal [7]. The experiment involved randomly selecting 30 malware samples from VirusShare (we downloaded them in June, 2018). We then applied obfuscation using ALAN, a Java-based code obfuscation tool which is capable of applying several types of structure-altering transformations including code reordering, junk code insertion and call indirection directly on DEX code of an Android app [13,25]. Once these apps have been obfuscated, we resubmitted them for scanning again on VirusTotal. We report the scanning result in Fig. 1.

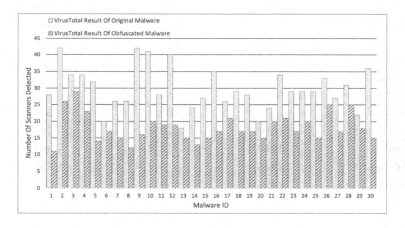

Fig. 1. The Difference in Detection Rate of Original and Obfuscated Malware

In the figure, the horizontal axis lists malware ID (from 1 to 30). The vertical axis presents how many anti-virus scanners identify an app as malware. The light blue bar is the detection number for the original app, and the red twilled bar is the result for the obfuscated app. The number of scanners that can accurately identify each obfuscated app as malicious decreases dramatically. The biggest drop occurs in App 9 as its unobfuscated version was detected by 42 scanners and its obfuscated version is only detected by 16 scanners, a reduction of 62%.

In the second experiment, we focused on the accuracy of 14 popular scanners in detecting obfuscated malware. We randomly obfuscated 1,540 apps using ALAN. Table 1 shows the detection difference between these 1,540 unobfuscated malicious apps and their obfuscated versions. The scanner Antiy-AVL can identify 1,427 as malware before obfuscation, but can only identify 260 obfuscated versions. The difference for McAfee and Symantec is 641 before and after obfuscation, which is surprisingly high. Ad-Aware and Baidu cannot detect obfuscated malware at all. We checked 60 scanners, and the number of scanners which could still identify the obfuscated apps as malicious decreased by 34.4% on average. Prior work called DROIDCHAMELEON [25] has shown that 10 popular anti-virus products such as Kaspersky, AVG and Symantec, lose their detection effectiveness when the malware samples are obfuscated.

Table 1. The difference of detection rate by scanners

Scanner	Number of detected (original)	Number of detected (obfuscated)	Difference
Antiy-AVL	1427	260	1167
MAX	1429	463	966
Comodo	999	122	877
F-Prot	830	54	776
Alibaba	975	291	684
K7GW	1348	679	669
McAfee	1446	805	641
Symantec	763	122	641
McAfee-GW-Edition	1265	669	596
DrWeb	1119	607	512
BitDefender	464	20	444
eScan	434	2	432
Ad-Aware	430	0	430
Baidu	308	0	308

We conducted the third experiment to better understand the effects of obfuscation on malware detection effectiveness of existing scanners. To do so, we focused our analysis on a malware sample that belongs to Adware:android/dowgin [1] family, which is an advertising module displaying advertisement while leaking or harvesting information such as its IMEI number, location, and contact information from the device.

We then obfuscated this malware sample using ALAN [6]. Before it was obfuscated, 20 scanners from the VirusTotal [7] were able to identify it as malware. However, after obfuscation, only 8 scanners could detect it. We statically analyzed this app and its obfuscated counterpart. We checked its method call graph, and found that there were 4,948 methods, 7,244 function calls prior to obfuscation. After obfuscation, the number of methods increased to 6,387 and the number of function calls increased to 8,683. Obviously, some methods were inserted as part of the obfuscation process.

Figure 2 illustrates this obfuscation process. we have A→B as the original function call, but in the obfuscated graph, we have A→C, C→B instead. This is called Call Indirection. The structure of the original method graph is modified,

Fig. 2. Obfuscation process

and scanners which is based on the signatures from the call graph would not be able to detect such changes.

We also compared their DEX codes. There were 93,077 lines in the original DEX file, but there were 148,819 lines after obfuscation. Scanners which rely on the order of the instruction as signatures would be ineffective by such changes. Prior work called REVEALDROID [19] has shown that even for machine learning-based detectors, obfuscation is still problematic.

Clearly, there is a need to create a malware detector that maintains its effectiveness in spite of obfuscation. Our approach, OBFUSIFIER applies static analysis to identify code that cannot be obfuscated and then efficiently extracts effective features to build a machine learning-based detection system. In the next section, we introduce our proposed system.

4   Introducing OBFUSIFIER

The main goal of the OBFUSIFIER is to identify Android malware which has been transformed via different obfuscation techniques and difficult to detect via common antivirus scanners. Thus, the selected features must satisfy the following four policies. First, these features must give a good representation of the difference between malware and benign apps. Second, a very high detection accuracy must be achieved when handling malware without obfuscation. Third, the detection time must be sufficiently short for real-world application scenarios. Fourth, the system must be resilient when used to detect obfuscated malware.

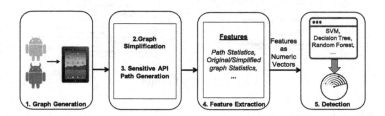

Fig. 3. System architecture

In this section, we describe the architectural overview of our proposed system, which operates in five phases: Graph Generation, Graph Simplification, Sensitive API Path Generation, Feature Extraction, and Malware Detection, as shown in Fig. 3. Next, we will describe each phase in turn.

4.1   Graph Generation

Method graph can be used as a good representation of the malware structure. It represents the calling relationship between different methods and subroutines. Each node in the graph represents a method, and a directed edge from one node to the other shows their calling relationship. We implement OBFUSIFIER based on JITANA [28], a high-performance hybrid program analysis tool to perform static and dynamic program analysis. JITANA can analyze DEX file, which includes the user-defined code, third party library code, framework code (including implementations of various Android APIs), and underlying system code. JITANA analyzes the classes to uncover all methods and generates the method graph for the app. OBFUSIFIER takes advantage of the calling relationship of methods to detect malware. As shown in Fig. 4, blocks represent methods, and directed edges indicate calling relationship among methods. Each block contains the name of the method, its modifiers and the class name which this method belongs to. OBFUSIFIER captures the interactions of these methods, and understands the semantic information that can help detect malware.

There are three types of methods in the graph: Android API method, system-level method and user-defined method. All of these methods can be exploited by malware writers to conduct malicious behaviors. In terms of code obfuscation, APIs and system-level methods cannot be transformed by code obfuscation techniques, otherwise the app will fail to run. The user-defined methods and the classes the methods belong to can be renamed, so that the malware can evade the antivirus scanners. As a result, only relying on the original method graph may not be enough to build a obfuscation-resistant detector due to the negative impact of code obfuscation. Lightweight features can be extracted from these method graphs to build the malware detection system.

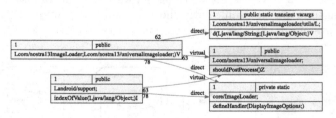

Fig. 4. Method graph

4.2   Graph Simplification

Our key insight is that *the Android APIs and system-level methods cannot be transformed by code obfuscation*, and this characteristics can be exploited to extract obfuscation-resistant features. Android APIs are published by Google, so we can easily create a list of these APIs. System-level methods include the Android OS source code and the Linux kernel source code, so it is not as convenient to gather all these methods and therefore, we do not collect them. We simply rely on the list of Android APIs that we collected.

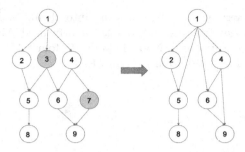

Fig. 5. Graph simplification process

In order to generate obfuscation-resistant graphs, we only keep the Android APIs in the original method graph, and ignore the system-level methods, user-defined methods and those from third party libraries. For example, as shown in the Fig. 5, nodes 1, 2, 4, 5, 6, 8 and 9 are Android APIs, and node 3 and node 7 are system-level or user-defined method. In this situation, our system simply ignores nodes 3 and 7, and generates a new call edge from node 1 to node 5 and another edge from node 4 to node 7. By doing so, we remove two nodes and combine four method calls into two.

By performing graph simplification, we are able to reconstruct a graph that is obfuscation-resistant while preserving the structural and semantic information with respect to Android API usage of the original graph. In addition, the API-only graph contain as much as an order of magnitude less information than the original graph, allowing feature extraction to be much faster especially during the path traversal phase.

4.3 Sensitive API Path (SAP) Generation

SAP is the program execution path from one node to the other in the API-only graph. An SAP can be used to differentiate between the malicious and benign behaviors. In order to generate SAPs, we need to select the critical APIs which are used for path generation, since these APIs reflect the semantic information about the behaviors of apps. We analyze the call frequency of APIs, and keep APIs which are used only by malware because they can directly reflect the malicious behaviors. We also extract some frequently used APIs by both malware and benign apps in common, because even though they are used by both, the additional program context (e.g., method call characteristics) can still represent the difference between malware and benign apps. In the API-only graph, all nodes whose in-degree are zero are considered as sources, and nodes whose out-degree are zero are considered as destinations. OBFUSIFIER generates SAPs from sources to destinations via depth first search (DFS).

Figure 6 illustrates the process to generate SAPs. In the figure, there are two sources (Node 1 and Node 2, marked as green) and two destinations (Node 4 and Node 10, marked as red) in the graph. Node 1 and Node 2 are sources (indegree is zero) as there are no edges flowing into them. Node 4 and Node 10 are destinations as they are selected and frequently used APIs. Starting from Node 1, Node 2, and ending with Node 4, Node 10, four SAPs can be identified: 1→4, 1→5→9→10, 2→5→9→10 and 2→6→9→10.

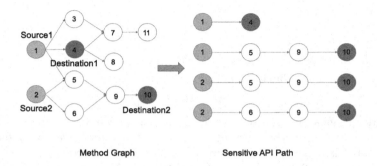

Fig. 6. Sensitive API Path (SAP) Generation (Color figure online)

SAP reflects the running behaviors of apps, whose patterns can be useful in distinguishing between malicious apps and benign ones.

4.4   Feature Extraction

We now describe the features, which our system extracts from the original graphs, API-only graphs, and SAPs.

Path Statistic Feature (F1). We collect seven statistic features from Sensitive API Path. These features include the lengths of the longest and short paths, the number of paths, the sum of lengths of all paths, the average length per path, the number of methods in all paths, and the average number of methods per path. These statistical features can indicate path characteristics and represent malicious behaviors. For example, malware which conducts malicious behaviors tends to generate shorter and less paths than benign apps. Since the paths in API-only graphs only consist of APIs, this feature set is not affected by code obfuscation. These features are concatenated to construct a numeric vector to reflect the unique characteristics of app behaviors that can further preserve rich information in these paths.

Simplified Graph Statistic Feature (F2). We select eight features from the simplified graph. They are the number of methods, the number of classes and the number of edges in the graph, graph density, the average in-degree and out-degree of the graph, the number of sources (nodes of which in-degree are zero) and destinations (nodes of which out-degree are zero). Compared with the original graph, the simplified graph is much less obfuscated, because it does not include the renamed user-defined classes and methods.

Original Graph Statistic Feature (F3). We also collect eight features from the original graph. These features are the same as F2. Even though some of the methods in the original graph are obfuscated, we still think these graphs can reflect the malicious behaviors. Keeping features from the original graph might still be useful to identify malware, whether it is obfuscated or not.

Other Statistic Feature (F4). We save the original graph, simplified graph, and SAP in separate files, and use the sizes of these files to form three new numeric features. We assume that the size of file can reflect the amount of generated information which indicates the complexity of these graphs and paths. Besides, we also calculate the ratio of the number of methods in original graph to the number in the simplified graph, and the ratio of the number of classes in original graph to the number in the simplified graph. The ratio can reflect the level of obfuscation accurately, and we hypothesize this will also contribute to the malware detection. Finally, we form F4 as a vector of five features.

4.5 Detection

In the Detection phase, we apply three well-recognized machine learning algorithms to determine if an Android app is malicious or benign. Our proposed system utilizes four different features (F1 – F4) as previously mentioned. Intuitively, we consider that each of the four feature sets can reflect malicious behaviors in some specific patterns. For API-only Graph Statistic Feature, because we remove all the user-defined classes and methods, which are usually transformed by obfuscation techniques, to generate simplified graph, these features are less likely affected by obfuscation. Besides, these features also reflect the structural difference between malware and benign apps. For example, we find that benign apps usually have more sources, destinations, classes and methods than malware. Thus, we need the Original Graph Statistic Feature because the graph simplification process also eliminates some of the original structural characteristics of graphs. The size of files where we store graphs and paths can also help build our detection system, for example, we observe that the size of the file storing graph and paths from malware is usually smaller than benign apps. We also notice that the graph density from malware is greater than benign apps, so we gather these file size and graph density information to form Other Statistic Feature.

We evaluate the performance of our system by using different feature sets individually. In addition, we also concatenate different feature sets to construct the combined new feature set and assess its impact on the detection result. In terms of the classification policy, we apply three popular algorithms: Decision Tree, Random Forest, and Support Vector Machine (SVM) [15,22,26]. These machine learning algorithms have been shown to achieve superior performance in addressing classification problems, which are integrated into OBFUSIFIER.

5 Empirical Evaluation

To evaluate OBFUSIFIER, we show its detection performance in terms of accuracy, precision, recall, and F-measure. we also illustrate its resistance against obfuscation, and ultimately its runtime performance. We first present the process of collecting our experimental apps, both benign and malicious, and explain how to transform malware using obfuscation techniques. Next, we show our detection results based on different sets of features. We also compare our system with several related approaches. Finally, we present the runtime performance of OBFUSIFIER.

5.1   Experimental Objects

To evaluate the performance of our proposed system, we collected a dataset containing both malware and benign apps. We downloaded 24,317 malware samples from VirusShare [5]. Compared to Android Genome Project [34], which is often used by many researchers [8,24], we included more malware samples and they are also newer. However, they also include many of the samples in the Android Genome Project. For benign apps, we collect 20,795 apps from APKPure [4], a third party website providing Android apps. Note that we also used these collected apps to conduct experiment in Sect. 3.

In order to avoid polluting our benign dataset with malware samples, we cross-checked all apps downloaded from APKPure with VirusTotal, and remove those apps identified as malware by VirusTotal from the benign dataset. After we completed the cross-checking process, there are only 11,238 apps left for the benign dataset. This checking process took 29 days. Also note that all the samples in the malware dataset are also identified by VirusTotal as malicious.

5.2   Experimental Methodology

To evaluate the performance of our system, and guarantee the balance of the data, we randomly chose 4,300 malicious samples, 4,300 benign apps as training/testing samples from our dataset. We also applied 10-fold cross validation.

In order to verify OBFUSIFIER's ability to resist to the code obfuscation, we randomly choose another 568 benign apps and 568 malware as additional testing set. We transform the additional 568 malicious samples using ALAN by applying all its transformations mentioned in Sect. 2.

As previously mentioned, our system utilizes four sets of features (F1, F2, F3, F4) to construct our classifier and perform detection. To evaluate the classification performance of the system, four metrics are calculated. They are Accuracy, Precision, Recall and F-measure. We also assess the performance of our system by combinations of different sets of features. For example, by concatenating F1 and F2 (F1 U F2), we form a new feature vector. Besides, we also compare our system with several popular approaches based on similar datasets.

Our runtime evaluation was conducted using Macbook Pro with a dual-core 2.8 GHz Intel Core i7 running OS-X High Sierra and 16 GB of 1.33 GHz main memory.

5.3   Detection Result

We discuss two usage scenarios in this section. The first scenario is when we evaluate our classification system by 10-fold cross validation. All samples in the dataset are the original (non-obfuscated) apps. This experiment is conducted to show that the classifier is effective and can detect unobfuscated malware with high accuracy. In a typical application, we imagine that security analysts would use obtainable, unobfuscated malware and benign samples for training and testing. Table 2 reports our result.

In the second scenario, we continued to use the original unobfuscated samples as in the first scenario for training; i.e., we used the same classifier built in the first scenario. However, we expand the testing dataset to include 568 more benign apps and then 568 more obfuscated malware samples (using ALAN) so that we can evaluate the ability of our system to maintain accurate detection in spite of obfuscation. Note that we applied all obfuscation methods supported by ALAN to make detection more challenging and our testing dataset also includes the same number of unobfuscated benign apps to maintain balance.

Table 3 shows the result of the second scenario (with obfuscation), in which all the testing malware samples are obfuscated. But above all, in both cases, there are not obfuscated apps in the training dataset, which means we do not need obfuscated apps in the training phase, and this characteristic guarantees that our system is robust and able to resist to obfuscated malware. The most powerful strength of our system is to identify obfuscated malware without training with obfuscated apps. Next, we discuss the results based on each feature.

Result Based on F1. Based on the Path Statistic Feature (F1), we implement and evaluate our learning-based system. Table 2–F1 shows the detection result without obfuscation in terms of three approaches: SVM, Decision Tree and Random Forest. F1 is constructed by seven statistic features from Sensitive API Path (SAP). All the SAPs are generated from the API-only graphs, in which only methods that cannot be obfuscated are kept. Because obfuscation has little or no effects on this graph, this feature set is important to build the proposed obfuscation-resistant malware detection system.

In the first scenario (without obfuscation), we calculate the four metrics as shown in Table 2–F1 for each classification technique based on F1. The Random Forest and Decision Tree achieve the F-measure of 87.9% and 85.3% respectively. On the other hand, SVM only yields the F-measure of 60.2%. The Random Forest also has the accuracy of 87.6%, which outperforms the SVM and Decision Tree. This result indicates that our system can incorrectly detect malware if we only rely on F1.

In the second scenario, we assess our system with obfuscated apps. As shown in Table 3–F1. Similar to the case without obfuscation, Random Forest performs better than SVM and Decision Tree. It has the accuracy of 89.7% and the F-measure of 89.8%. This result shows that our system is somewhat effective when identifying obfuscated Android malware. Interestingly, by checking accuracy and F-measure for F1, the result with obfuscation in Table 3–F1 is slightly better than the one without obfuscation in Table 2–F1. This is because the impact of these transformations on the SAP feature is minor, so the system trained using SAP can resist obfuscation naturally. However, the SAP is from the simplified graph, which removes many user-defined methods from the original graph. Because of this, some contexts of the program which is helpful to recognize the non-obfuscated malware are missing. As such, F1 performs better when handling obfuscated malware.

Result Based on F2. API-only Graph Statistic Feature (F2) is the feature vector directly form the simplified graph. This feature is significant because it reflects the structural difference between malware and benign apps, and the influence of obfuscation on F2 is very small due to the elimination of all the newly added methods or renamed methods (Junk Code and Call Indirection) in the obfuscated and original graph.

Table 2–F2 shows the evaluation result without obfuscation. For F2, Random Forest achieves the best accuracy of 92.9%. It also attains the highest F-measure of 93.1% with 91.0% precision and 95.2% recall. Obviously, the result based on F2 is better than F1. it indicates that features directly from the graph are more effective than features from paths.

Table 3–F2 shows that our system is very effective even when dealing with obfuscated malware. In terms of Random Forest, we can achieve the very high accuracy 94.3% and F-measure 94.6%. This result validates out assumption that features from these simplified API-only graphs, in which obfuscated methods are removed, are very effective in identifying malware and resisting the negative impact of code obfuscation. As such, system trained based on F2 is more obfuscation-resistant.

Table 2. The performance of OBFUSIFIER on non-obfuscated apps using five different features (F1 – F4, F1∪F2∪F3∪F4) and three different Machine Learning algorithms: Support Vector Machine (SVM), Decision Tree (DT) and Random Forest (RF).

	F1			F2			F3			F4			F1∪F2∪F3∪F4		
	SVM (%)	DT (%)	RF (%)	SVM (%)	DT (%)	RF (%)	SVM (%)	DT (%)	RF (%)	SVM (%)	DT (%)	RF (%)	SVM (%)	DT (%)	RF (%)
I. Accuracy	71.3	85.3	87.6	70.2	91.0	92.9	69.6	92.3	94.0	63.9	90.8	92.6	63.9	94.0	95.5
II. Precision	97.8	82.8	85.7	99.6	89.9	91.0	99.9	90.2	92.2	99.9	88.9	91.3	99.9	92.4	93.9
III. Recall	43.5	89.1	90.3	40.5	92.3	95.2	39.2	95.0	96.2	27.7	93.2	94.3	27.9	95.9	97.3
IV. F-Measure	60.2	85.3	87.9	57.6	91.1	93.1	56.3	92.5	94.1	43.4	91.0	92.7	43.6	94.1	95.5

Table 3. The performance of OBFUSIFIER with obfuscated apps as testing set

	F1			F2			F3			F4			F1∪F2∪F3∪F4		
	SVM (%)	DT (%)	RF (%)	SVM (%)	DT (%)	RF (%)	SVM (%)	DT (%)	RF (%)	SVM (%)	DT (%)	RF (%)	SVM (%)	DT (%)	RF (%)
I. Accuracy	73.6	89.2	89.7	71.3	92.9	94.3	51.5	90.9	80.6	50.1	89.3	91.5	50.0	93.3	90.2
II. Precision	99.3	87.9	89.1	100.0	90.5	91.2	100.0	91.7	90.4	0	88.9	92.3	0	92.5	92.7
III. Recall	47.4	91.0	90.5	42.7	95.8	98.2	1.9	89.9	68.4	0	89.9	90.7	0	94.2	87.3
IV. F-Measure	64.2	89.4	89.8	59.8	93.1	94.6	3.8	90.8	77.9	0	89.4	91.5	0	93.4	89.9

Result Based on F3. F1 and F2 are created based on API-only graphs, in order to reduce the impact of code obfuscation on malware detection. Based on our reported results, these two feature sets not only help to identify non-obfuscated apps, but also show a remarkable efficacy when dealing with obfuscated malware. However, when graphs are simplified, some structural information which is beneficial to distinguish non-obfuscated malware might be lost. In case that original malware samples are also available, there is a potential to improve effectiveness by extracting features from the original method graph to form a feature set called Original Graph Statistic Feature (F3). The meaning of each feature in F3 is exactly the same as F2.

As illustrated in Table 2–F3, F3 achieves higher performance than F1 and F2 in all three classification techniques. Random Forest performs better than Decision Tree and SVM for F3 as it attains F-measure of 94.1% while the other two approaches (SVM and Decision Tree) achieve 56.3% and 92.5%, respectively.

For obfuscated malware, the performance of F3 is not as good as F1 and F2. As illustrated in Table 3–F3, most of the metrics show F3 cannot handle the obfuscated apps as good as F1 and F2. For example, in terms of Random Forest, F3 only has F-measure of 77.9%, which is lower than F1 and F2, which achieve 89.8% and 94.6% respectively. As such, F3 alone is not a sufficient feature set to achieve obfuscation-resistant capability.

Result Based on F4. We transform the sizes of several files, the ratio of the number of methods in original graph to the number in the simplified graph, and the ratio of the number of classes in original graph to the number in the simplified graph into a new feature, referred to Other Statistic Feature (F4). We assume that these file sizes and the ratios are also efficient features for distinguishing between malware and benign apps.

Table 2–F4 shows the detection result on non-obfuscated malware. Random Forest achieves the highest accuracy of 92.6% and F-measure of 92.7%, outperforming SVM and Decision Tree. Table 3–F4 illustrates the result with obfuscation. Random Forest also performs best yielding F-measure of 91.5%. Results based on F4 verify our assumption, and these sizes of files and ratios can provide another efficient feature to build the malware detection system.

Result Based on F1 U F2 U F3 U F4. By aggregating all our feature sets, as shown in Table 2, using Random Forest, we achieve the accuracy of 95.5% and F-measure of 95.5%. Table 3 shows that the combination of all feature sets also works well for obfuscated malware.

5.4   Comparison with Related Approaches

Next, we compare the performance of OBFUSIFIER with other research efforts including REVEALDROID [19], MUDFLOW [12], ADAGIO [20] and DREBIN [9]. More information about these systems are available in Sect. 7.

In this work, we relied on the data provide in the REVEALDROID paper as a base for comparison. They conducted an investigation that compared the detection performance of REVEALDROID with the other three systems. Thus, we simply compared our system's performance against the reported performance.

Another noticeable difference is that REVEALDROID obfuscated their malware using DroidChameleon [25]. RevealDroid applies four sets of transformations on there dataset including call indirection, rename classes, encrypt arrays, and encrypt strings. We, on the other hand, obfuscated our dataset with ALAN, and enabled all transformations described in Sect. 2. In our approach, "Data Encoding" technique includes the "Encrypt Arrays and Encrypt Strings" by DroidChameleon, and our "Identifier Renaming" includes "Rename Classes" by DroidChameleon. The level of obfuscation in our dataset is higher than REVEAL-DROID, so our transformed malware should be more difficult to detect.

The malicious apps used to investigate REVEALDROID are from Android Malware Genome [34], the DREBIN dataset [9] and VirusShare [5]. Our malicious dataset is only from VirusShare. However, the samples on VirusShare contain similar apps in Android Malware Genome and DREBIN dataset. The similarity of the dataset ensures the fairness of comparisons.

When comparing with the other four systems, we consider two scenarios. The first scenario is testing the non-obfuscated malware (without obfuscation). The second scenario is testing the obfuscated malware (with obfuscation). In the first scenario, REVEALDROID splits a dataset including 1,742 benign apps and 7,989 malicious ones into two parts evenly. One part is the training dataset, the other one is for testing. The training dataset has half of the benign apps and half of the malicious apps. For this case, we also split our dataset consisting 4,300 benign apps and 4,300 malicious apps randomly into two parts evenly, one part for training, other part for testing. In the second scenario, REVEALDROID has 7,995 malicious apps and 878 benign apps in the training set, and 1,188 obfuscated malicious apps and 869 benign apps for testing. Similar to their dataset, there are 4,300 benign apps and 4,300 malicious ones in our training set, and we form a testing set with 568 benign apps and 568 obfuscated malicious ones.

Note that all of our samples are chosen and split randomly. Compared with the imbalanced dataset from REVEALDROID, our dataset is very balanced. When training imbalanced data, which the number of malware is greater than benign apps, the classifier often favor the majority class and form a biased prediction model. The imbalance in the testing set will also cause notable inaccuracy.

Table 4 shows the comparison result without obfuscation. Table 5 presents the comparison result with obfuscated malware. Without obfuscation, as illustrated in Table 4, DREBIN shows the best performance with the average precision, recall and F-measure reaching 99%, we think this is because DREBIN gathers all types of features, such as permission, API call, intents and the diversity of the feature set plays a significant role to detect malware. OBFUSIFIER has the average F-measure of 96%, which is the same as RevealDroid. Even though the performance is not as good as DREBIN, both OBFUSIFIER and REVEALDROID outperform ADAGIO, of which average F-measure is 90%. MUDFLOW has the worst result, with only average 71% F-measure and 66% recall.

With obfuscation, as illustrated in Table 5, OBFUSIFIER outperforms all other four systems. This result is from feature combinations of F1 U F2 U F4. Note that F3 is a feature set extracted from the original method graph so the F3 feature set is not obfuscation resistant. It achieves surprisingly high metrics, with an average of 95% precision, recall, and F-measure. Note that the F-measure of MUDFLOW with obfuscation is only 74%. This result is very close to the result without obfuscation (F-measure of 71%).

We suspect that this is because its feature sets are not influenced by the obfuscation techniques. DREBIN shows poor performance with obfuscation, the average precision, recall and F-measure are 0%. This is because all of DREBIN's feature sets are negatively influenced by obfuscation, and this result indicates that DREBIN is not resilient against obfuscation. ADAGIO achieves the average F-measure 62% with obfuscation, but this is not as good as its result (F-measure 90%) without obfuscation. Still it shows the ability to detect obfuscated malware. The average F-measure and recall of REVEALDROID is 85%, which is not as high as OBFUSIFIER.

Table 4. Comparison without obfuscation (Pr = Precision, Re = Recall, and Fm = F-measure)

	MUDFLOW (%)			RevealDroid (%)			Adagio (%)			Drebin (%)			Obfusifier (%)		
	Pr	Re	Fm	Pr	Re	Fm	Pr	Re	Fm	Pr	Re	Fm	Pr	Re	Fm
Ben	85	34	49	90	88	89	90	76	83	97	100	98	97	94	95
Mal	87	99	93	97	98	98	95	98	96	100	99	100	94	97	96
AVG	86	66	71	96	96	96	92	87	90	99	99	99	96	96	96

Table 5. Comparison with other methods (Pr = Precision, Re = Recall, and Fm = F-measure)

	MUDFLOW (%)			RevealDroid (%)			Adagio (%)			Drebin (%)			Obfusifier (%)		
	Pr	Re	Fm	Pr	Re	Fm	Pr	Re	Fm	Pr	Re	Fm	Pr	Re	Fm
Ben	98	47	64	91	72	80	54	73	62	42	100	59	97	92	95
Mal	72	99	84	82	95	88	73	54	62	0	0	0	93	98	95
AVG	88	73	74	86	85	85	63	63	62	18	42	25	95	95	95

5.5   Runtime Performance

For real-world applications, a malware detector must be both effective and efficient. To evaluate the efficiency of OBFUSIFIER, we measured the time taken to analyze and detect a malware sample. As part of analysis, one critical factor that can affect efficiency is the time to train the classification model and the time needed to test each app. The training time is the time to build the prediction model. The testing time is the average number to test each app. Another key factor is the time we spend to statically analyze apps and extract its features.

We also list the average time needed to analyze each app in different phases: Graph Generation, Graph Simplification, SAP Generation and Feature Extraction. We measured the time of 100 apps (50 benign and 50 malicious apps, respectively) and calculate the average execution time for each app in each phase. We found the system took the average total of 35.06 s to analyze each app, generate graphs, simplify paths, and extract features. This runtime result should be acceptable for detecting obfuscated and complex malware in real-world settings.

6 Discussion

Our evaluations have shown OBFUSIFIER's robustness, and its ability to handle obfuscated Android malware with high efficiency and accuracy. However, there are still some limitations of our system.

First, we only obfuscate malicious apps using ALAN. According to the results from VirusTotal, ALAN provides several very effective obfuscation techniques which help malware evade many existing anti-virus scanners. However, in order to verify OBFUSIFIER's ability to deal with different obfuscation techniques, we plan to experiment with more Android obfuscation tools, such as DashO [3], DexGuard [2] to transform malware codes.

Second, our system cannot handle the malware transformed by the obfuscation on the native code. Malware authors can take advantage of this loop-hole to encrypt the strings and arrays in the native code, and then decrypt them during runtime to hide the malicious behaviors. One notable tool that can close this loop-hole is OBFUSCATOR-LLVM [21], which targets the native code obfuscation. We plan to experiment with this tool and attempt to integrate it into our workflow.

Third, our system is based on static analysis of the DEX code, but if the DEX code is encrypted and then decrypted at runtime, we cannot capture its method graph and malicious behaviors. A special obfuscation technique called packing [18], which is used to protect Android apps being reverse engineered. It creates a wrapper application, and hide the original DEX code so that the original app cannot be reverse engineered. This wrapper app loads necessary libraries to unpack the original code at runtime. In future, we will consider the incorporation of dynamic analyzer in OBFUSIFIER.

7 Related Work

In this section, we describe works that are closely related to ours, including the four baseline systems used in Sect. 5 and other prior works about malware detection.

Garcia et al. [19] introduced REVEALDROID as a lightweight machine learning-based system to detect Android malware and identify Android malware families. It constructs features from the Android API usage, reflection characteristic and native binaries of the app. The evaluation shows that REVEALDROID can detect malware (both non-obfuscated and obfuscated malware) and identify malware family with high accuracy. MUDFLOW [12] is built on the static analysis tool FLOWDROID [10]. It extracts the normal data flow from benign apps as patterns, mines these benign patterns, and use these pattern to automatically identify malicious behaviors. The novelty of their work is that they only use information from benign apps to train their system, and identify abnormal flows in malicious apps. Our evaluations indicate that MUDFLOW has some ability to detect obfuscated malware, with the precision of 88% and F-measure of 74%. ADAGIO [20] extracts the function call from Android apps and map these function calls to features, and build a machine learning system based on these features. As shown, the proposed system loses its accuracy when the malware samples are obfuscated.

DREBIN [9] is a machine learning-based malware detector, which performs broad static analysis on Android apps and collect many features such as permission, API calls, intents from app's code and the Manifest file and embedded them in a vector space that can be used to discover patterns of malware. These patterns are then used to build a machine learning detection system. The system is accurate but it requires running on a rooted device. As shown in our experiment, DREBIN is not able to detect obfuscated malware. APPCONTEXT [31] is another machine learning-based malware detector which focusing on the context difference between malware and benign apps. It leverages SOOT [29] as the static analysis engine and uses the permission mappings offered by PScout [11] to extracts the contexts based on Android components, Android permissions and Intent. They achieve 87.7% precision and 95% recall, which are lower than our system. The average analysis time of APPCONTEXT for each app is about 5 min [31], while we only need 35 s. This behavior based approach might be able to resist obfuscation, and we hope we can get its source code and assess its performance over obfuscated malware in future.

DROIDMINER [30] is a system that mines the program logic from Android malware, extracts this logic to modalities, which are ordered sequence of APIs, and constructs malicious patterns for malware detection. It builds a method call graph for each app, control flow graph, and generates modalities (API paths and subpaths) from sensitive methods. A feature vector based on the existence of modalities is formed for classification. They replace user-defined methods with framework API functions. We, on the other hand, remove the user-defined methods for efficiency. DROIDSIFT [33] is also a machine learning-based detector based on static analysis. They generate weighted contextual API dependency graphs, build graph databases, and construct a graph-based feature vector by performing graph similarity queries. Their features represent program behaviors at the semantic level. Note that the average detection time is about 176.8 s [33], while we only need 35 s.

8   Conclusion

We introduce OBFUSIFIER, a machine learning based malware detection system that is highly resistant to code obfuscation. The key insight is that obfuscation cannot be applied to portions of codes that include calls to Android APIs, kernel functions, and third party library APIs. Our system mainly extracts features based on these portions of codes unaffected by obfuscation. In total, we use four feature sets consisting of 28 features. Our results showed that the effectiveness of the system is not affected by obfuscation. The system can achieve an average F-measure of 96% for detecting non-obfuscated malware. More importantly, the system can achieve an average F-measure of 95% in detecting obfuscated malware, suffering only a 1% drop in performance.

Acknowledgements. We would like to thank the anonymous reviewers for their valuable comments and feedback. This work was supported in part by the NSF grants CNS-1566388 and CNS-1717898.

References

1. f-secure.com. https://www.f-secure.com/sw-desc/adware_android_dowgin.shtml
2. guardsquare.com. https://www.guardsquare.com/en/products/dexguard
3. preemptive.com. https://www.preemptive.com/products/dasho/overview
4. Apkpure.com, December 2017. https://apkpure.com/
5. Virusshare.com, December 2017. https://virusshare.com/
6. Alan-android-malware.com, April 2019. http://seclist.us/alan-android-malware-evaluating-tools-released.html
7. Virustotal.com, April 2019. https://www.virustotal.com/#/home/upload
8. Aafer, Y., Du, W., Yin, H.: DroidAPIMiner: mining API-level features for robust malware detection in Android. In: Zia, T., Zomaya, A., Varadharajan, V., Mao, M. (eds.) SecureComm 2013. LNICST, vol. 127, pp. 86–103. Springer, Cham (2013). https://doi.org/10.1007/978-3-319-04283-1_6
9. Arp, D., Spreitzenbarth, M., Hubner, M., Gascon, H., Rieck, K., Siemens, C.: Drebin: Effective and explainable detection of android malware in your pocket. In: NDSS (2014)
10. Arzt, S., et al.: Flowdroid: precise context, flow, field, object-sensitive and lifecycle-aware taint analysis for android apps. ACM Sigplan Not. **49**(6), 259–269 (2014)
11. Au, K.W.Y., Zhou, Y.F., Huang, Z., Lie, D.: Pscout: analyzing the android permission specification. In: Proceedings of the 2012 ACM Conference on Computer and Communications Security, pp. 217–228. ACM (2012)
12. Avdiienko, V., et al.: Mining apps for abnormal usage of sensitive data. In: Proceedings of the 37th International Conference on Software Engineering-vol. 1, pp. 426–436 (2015)
13. Bacci, A., Bartoli, A., Martinelli, F., Medvet, E., Mercaldo, F., Visaggio, C.A.: Impact of code obfuscation on android malware detection based on static and dynamic analysis. In: ICISSP, pp. 379–385 (2018)
14. Borello, J.-M., Mé, L.: Code obfuscation techniques for metamorphic viruses. J. Comput. Virol. **4**(3), 211–220 (2008)
15. Breiman, L.: Random forests. Mach. Learn. **45**(1), 5–32 (2001)
16. Cannell, J.: Obfuscation: Malware's best friend, March 2016. https://blog.malwarebytes.com/threat-analysis/2013/03/obfuscation-malwares-best-friend/
17. Collberg, C.S., Thomborson, C.D., Low, D.W.K.: Obfuscation techniques for enhancing software security, December 23 2003. US Patent 6,668,325

18. Duan, Y., et al.: Things you may not know about android (un) packers: a systematic study based on whole-system emulation. In: 25th Annual Network and Distributed System Security Symposium, NDSS, pp. 18–21 (2018)

19. Garcia, J., Hammad, M., Malek, S.: Obfuscation-resilient, efficient, and accurate detection and family identification of android malware. ACM Trans. Softw. Eng. Methodol. **9**(4), 39 (2017)

20. Gascon, H., Yamaguchi, F., Arp, D., Rieck, K.: Structural detection of android malware using embedded call graphs. In: Proceedings of the 2013 ACM Workshop on Artificial Intelligence and Security, pp. 45–54. ACM (2013)

21. Junod, P., Rinaldini, J., Wehrli, J., Michielin, J.: Obfuscator-LLVM - software protection for the masses. In: Wyseur, B. (ed.) Proceedings of the IEEE/ACM 1st International Workshop on Software Protection, SPRO 2015, Firenze, Italy, May 19th, 2015, pp. 3–9. IEEE (2015)

22. Landwehr, N., Hall, M., Frank, E.: Logistic model trees. Mach. Learn. **95**(1–2), 161–205 (2005)

23. Li, Z., Sun, J., Yan, Q., Srisa-an, W., Bachala, S.: GranDroid: graph-based detection of malicious network behaviors in android applications. In: Beyah, R., Chang, B., Li, Y., Zhu, S. (eds.) SecureComm 2018. LNICST, vol. 254, pp. 264–280. Springer, Cham (2018). https://doi.org/10.1007/978-3-030-01701-9_15

24. Li, Z., Sun, L., Yan, Q., Srisa-an, W., Chen, Z.: DroidClassifier: efficient adaptive mining of application-layer header for classifying android malware. In: Deng, R., Weng, J., Ren, K., Yegneswaran, V. (eds.) SecureComm 2016. LNICST, vol. 198, pp. 597–616. Springer, Cham (2017). https://doi.org/10.1007/978-3-319-59608-2_33

25. Rastogi, V., Chen, Y., Jiang, X.: Catch me if you can: evaluating android anti-malware against transformation attacks. IEEE Trans. Inf. Forensics Secur. **9**(1), 99–108 (2014)

26. Steinwart, I., Christmann, A.: Support Vector Machines, 1st edn. Springer Publishing Company, Incorporated (2008)

27. Sun, L., Li, Z., Yan, Q., Srisa-an, W., Pan, Y.: Sigpid: significant permission identification for android malware detection. In: Proceedings of MALWARE, pp. 1–8. IEEE (2016)

28. Tsutano, Y., Bachala, S., Srisa-an, W., Rothermel, G., Dinh, J.: An efficient, robust, and scalable approach for analyzing interacting android apps. In: Proceedings of ICSE, Buenos Aires, Argentina (2017)

29. Vallée-Rai, R., Co, P., Gagnon, E., Hendren, L., Lam, P., Sundaresan, V.: Soot: a java bytecode optimization framework. In: CASCON First Decade High Impact Papers, pp. 214–224. IBM Corp. (2010)

30. Yang, C., Xu, Z., Gu, G., Yegneswaran, V., Porras, P.: Droidminer: automated mining and characterization of fine-grained malicious behaviors in android applications. Texas A&M, Technical report (2014)

31. Yang, W., Xiao, X., Andow, B., Li, S., Xie, T., Enck, W.: Appcontext: differentiating malicious and benign mobile app behaviors using context. In: Proceedings of the 37th International Conference on Software Engineering-vol. 1, pp. 303–313. IEEE Press (2015)

32. You, I., Yim, K.: Malware obfuscation techniques: a brief survey. In: 2010 International Conference on Broadband, Wireless Computing, Communication and Applications, pp. 297–300. IEEE (2010)
33. Zhang, M., Duan, Y., Yin, H., Zhao, Z.: Semantics-aware android malware classification using weighted contextual API dependency graphs. In: Proceedings of CCS, pp. 1105–1116 (2014)
34. Zhou, Y., Jiang, X.: Dissecting android malware: characterization and evolution. In: Proceedings of IEEE S&P, pp. 95–109 (2012)

Closing the Gap with APTs Through Semantic Clusters and Automated Cybergames

Steven Gianvecchio$^{(\boxtimes)}$, Christopher Burkhalter, Hongying Lan,
Andrew Sillers, and Ken Smith

The MITRE Corporation, McLean, VA 22102, USA
{gianvecchio,cburkhalter,hlan,asillers,kps}@mitre.org

Abstract. Defenders spend significant time interpreting low-level events while attackers, especially Advanced Persistent Threats (APTs), think and plan their activities at a higher strategic level. In this paper, we close this semantic gap by making the attackers' strategy an explicit machine-readable component of intrusion detection. We introduce the concept of *semantic clusters*, which combine high-level technique and tactic annotations with a set of events providing evidence for those annotations. We then use a fully automated cybergaming environment, in which a red team is programmed to emulate APT behavior, to assess and improve defensive posture. Semantic clusters both provide the basis of scoring these cybergames and highlight promising defensive improvements. In a set of experiments, we demonstrate effective defensive adjustments which can be made using this higher-level information about adversarial strategy.

Keywords: Intrusion detection · Advanced Persistent Threats · Cyber forensics · Semantics · Tactic techniques procedures · Cybergaming

1 Introduction

There is an important semantic gap between network defenders and their adversaries. Attackers operate at the level of strategy and tactics, focused on discovering targets, and deploying various "kill chain" [7] tactics to reach their goals. Defenders, however, spend significant time processing low-level, rule-generated alerts. This gap makes it challenging for defenders to work at the higher strategic level of their attackers, putting them at a disadvantage implementing an effective and relevant defense. Security Operations Centers (SOCs) we interact with continually tell us they are interested in better understanding the behaviors of adversaries. The low-level details they have now make this very difficult.

APT (Advanced Persistent Threat) attackers have turned this semantic gap into a critical problem. APTs use an increasingly rich arsenal of over 200 distinct documented techniques [1] to accomplish their goals. Spending their days focused

S. Chen et al. (Eds.): SecureComm 2019, LNICST 304, pp. 235–254, 2019.
https://doi.org/10.1007/978-3-030-37228-6_12

on low-level events, defenders find themselves at an increasing distance from the playbooks of experienced and skilled attackers. To keep up with the offense, the defense needs to connect its low-level detection details to the offense's game plan, tactics, and techniques.

Two challenges now faced by SOCs magnify the impact of this semantic gap:

1. *Alert Volume.* SOCS face an overwhelming volume of alerts. A recent blog cited pervasive "alert fatigue" as defenders deal with "a flood of alerts and out of tune tools" resulting in an average of 4.35 days for a SOC to resolve a security incident [14].
2. *Talent shortage.* There is a significant talent shortage and turnover at the Tier 1 level of SOCs [14,28], people in the front lines of alert processing. This means the first people to see an attacker signal are often new at their jobs, and less likely to possess a clarifying mental context for interpreting the alerts they see (e.g., is this malicious or not?).

One fallout of defenders operating at this lower level is a winding journey of defensive rule-tuning. Because false positives have a high labor cost, noisy alert-generators may be discarded to improve precision in detection. Turning off alerts can lead to decreased recall and missing dangerous events. This in turn leads to new rules to address known blind spots. Eventually, this process would converge to a stable rule set with higher precision and recall. However in practice, because attackers constantly evolve their techniques this stable state is elusive and rule-tuning becomes hysteresis between precision and recall. In an ideal world, defenders would be able to advance both precision and recall together, keeping pace with their attackers.

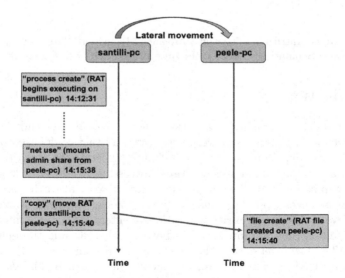

Fig. 1. A set of host-based events implementing a lateral move by remote file copy. (Color figure online)

The problem we are addressing in this paper is closing this semantic gap by elevating the level at which the defense operates to better match the offense. Our approach to address this problem involves three parts: First, we tag alert rules with TTP (Tactics, Technique and Procedures) labels, representing likely strategic reasons for detected alerts. Second, we coalesce TTP-labelled alerts into *semantic clusters* which link adversary tactics and techniques to low-level evidence in a single rich knowledge structure. Third, we repeatedly play automated cybergames, using a red team programmed with TTP-level threat intelligence to attack the defense in varying and realistic ways. We then use scored cybergame outcomes to tune our defense. Our cybergames are scored by comparing red and blue semantic clusters, which highlights defensive blind spots and offensive patterns, enabling high-level adjustments by the defense.

Figure 1 illustrates the notion of a semantic cluster. Taken individually, the four events do not clearly communicate adversary TTPs. However when grouped and labeled as in this figure, these events are clearly linked by the semantics of a strategy to move laterally by means of a remote file copy. Such annotated clustering reduces the semantic gap between attackers and defenders, and immediately suggests adversary capabilities and previous actions (e.g, stealing credentials for the lateral move target), the current stage of the attacker's kill chain and possible future actions. Multiple semantic clusters in sequence would begin to reveal patterns of strategic activity.

In this paper we show that, beyond simply providing a visual aid to humans, semantic clustering of events around TTP annotations enables automated self-assessment and expedited self-improvement of defensive posture. Through automated cybergames, scored in terms of semantic clusters instead of traditional events, we demonstrate significant and simple improvements that were not otherwise obvious, enabling more rapid and focused defensive reconfiguration.

We make the following **contributions:**

1. We describe BSF, a semantic clustering format for cyber-detection. BSF provides a "step" level which includes a label for the adversary's believed malicious technique, and a hierarchically nested "event" level linking in events which provide evidence for that technique.
2. We describe a fully automated cybergaming environment, and show how it can be used to assess and improve an organizations' cyberdefensive posture.
3. In the context of cybergames, we show how the use of semantic clustering provides a significant advance over individual events as a means of assessing and improving defensive posture.

In Sect. 2 we provide background and discuss related work. In Sects. 3 and 4 we describe our "semantic cluster" format for recording cyber attacks and our automated cybergaming environment respectively. In Sect. 5 we discuss the scoring of automated cybergames, including experiences with event-based scoring and the alignment of semantic clusters. In Sect. 6 we describe experiments using automated cybergames scored with semantic clusters to improve an organization's defensive posture. Finally, in Sect. 7 we summarize our results and describe future work.

2 Background

In this section we provide background for the key concepts discussed in this paper: semantic gaps in cybersecurity, cyberdetection formats, and cybergaming environments.

Semantic Gaps. The theme of a semantic gap has arisen across computer science, given the importance of implementing useful abstraction layers in databases, programming languages, networks, and operating systems. In Cybersecurity, a semantic gap has been cited between outliers and actual attacks in anomaly-based intrusion detection [36] and between signature-based and behavior-based intrusion detection [30], which is closer to our use of the term. Specifically, by "semantic gap" we mean the difference between conducting standard cyberdefensive activities such as adversarial activity detection and false positive reduction at the level of:

1. System-level events, such as flow initiation and copying a file, which may be benign or malicious, and
2. Abstract behavioral tactic and technique labels from an actively curated taxonomy of malicious behavior.

This gap and its importance has been publicized in Bianco's "Pyramid of Pain" [13].

Several behavioral taxonomies exist [1,2,8]. In this work we use the MITRE-developed framework Adversarial Techniques, Tactics, and Common Knowledge (ATT&CK[TM1]), currently employed in security products, third-party evaluations, and research projects [6,9,25]. As a model of system-level events, we use the CAR framework [4].

Malicious Behavior Formats. In complex enterprises, common representation formats are needed to enable information sharing among components. This is especially true in cyber-security: standard formats are needed to ensure individual components (e.g., logging, filtering, alert-generation, analysis), potentially from multiple vendors, can work together effectively in cyber-defense. Such formats can also be used by human analysts to log and forensically analyze observed malicious behaviors.

In this paper, we describe a representation format (BSF) for episodes of adversarial activity which relates high-level malicious behavior to specific events providing evidence for those behaviors in a single unified representation.

Splunk's CIM (Common Information Model) [19] supports search (e.g., in a Splunk repository), and provides an interoperability standard for transmitting cyberdefensive information in an enterprise. Its *intrusion detection* submodel enables the description of system events in an intrusion, and is analogous to the CAR event model. The Elasticsearch Common Schema [12] similarly contains an event-based sub-schema. Neither schema contains high-level behavioral designators, enabling behavior-event linkage.

---

[1] https://attack.mitre.org/wiki/Main_Page.

Another format for describing malicious behavior is MIST (Malware Instruction Set) [37]. MIST is a space-optimized format for describing malware behaviors, providing useful features for malware classification [31]. MIST provides a taxonomy for aggregating related system-level actions (e.g., file system accesses) into a single category. However, MIST does not relate these system-level actions to adversarial tactics and strategy.

Cybergames. Cybergames echo military exercises in which a "friendly" adversary – i.e., a red team – is engaged to purposefully attack an enterprise guarded by defenders – i.e., the blue team – for the purpose of stress testing the blue team to see how they would respond to a real threat. Such cybergames are self-assessments in that they use a trusted red team to tell them their weaknesses as opposed to learning what their weaknesses are during a real breach. Using the results of the assessment can further be a catalyst for self-improvement, where the enterprise uses the cybergame results to identify how they should make improvements.

Conducting a cybergame requires several components including: a gameboard (the network of computers in which the cybergame is played), a red team, a blue team and supporting services (e.g., data collection and logging, gameboard provisioning and cleanup, game scoring and analysis).

Game logs record events detailing the activity of both red and blue teams during the game, enabling post-game analysis. For example, red might log a credential dumping action on host H at time T, and blue might log a protected memory access alert on H at a time near T. Examining logs after the game would align these, crediting blue with successful detection.

Cybergames were conceived of as a powerful way to address the subjective nature of security assessments [21]: games have measurable outcomes and security vulnerabilities are recorded in game logs. Studying game outcomes can yield insights, such as blindness to a specific exploit, which can be used to improve defensive posture. In recent years additional benefits of cybergames have been realized, including: evaluating new and potentially useful security technologies [17], enhancing the robustness of system designs [20,40], using threat intelligence to emulate a specific advanced threat and assess enterprise readiness [15,27], and using cybergaming as an experimental framework in which to test hypotheses [24].

A particular value of cybergames, in the context of the potential for precision and recall hysteresis (in defensive rule tuning, as described in Sect. 1), is that a cybergame effectively reveals *both* false negatives and false positives at once, leading to steadier progress in the improvement of enterprise defenses.

Cybergame activities can be labor intensive, however, precluding many of the anticipated benefits. Manual game preparation can take over a year [29] and post-game data analysis can involve months [24]. Thus a recent research goal has been *cybergame automation*, in which one or more components of a cybergame are automated as invokable software systems.

As an example, cyber ranges (e.g., [18,32]) help automate the gameboard component by providing a dedicated computer network for hosting cybergames and automated services for network configuration, virtual machine provisioning, and synthetic user noise generation (e.g., [33]). Research and systems automating the red team also exist [5,15,16,22,34].

In this paper we describe a *fully* automated cybergaming environment (BRAWL) in which every component operates under software control; we are unaware of any other such environment. Beyond mitigating costs, the primary value of fully automated cybergaming is the ability to learn improved defensive strategy through experimentation involving repeated cybergames.

3   BSF Syntax

In this section we present BSF (BRAWL Shared Format), a language for describing the progression of cyber attacks. While BSF has many potential uses (e.g., forensic analysis of attacks in a SOC setting) in this paper we focus on its use enabling cybergame scoring, that is: scoring how well the defense detected the offense's activities. Specifically, due to issues identified in scoring cybergames solely by events described in Sect. 5, we realized that we needed a representation that could be used to correlate both individual events as well as semantic intent. This motivated us to create BSF which explicitly links events to semantic annotations.

As illustrated in Fig. 2, BSF is hierarchical and consists of three levels: operations, steps, and events. The *operation* serves as a delimiter for an adversary activity of interest (e.g., one day of forensic log analysis, a single cybergame), and contains a sequence of steps.

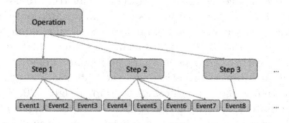

Fig. 2. BSF structure

BSF Steps. A step corresponds to the execution of a single technique (e.g., Remote Desktop Protocol, Powershell) by the adversary. More formally, a step S is a six-tuple $\{T, \mathcal{T}, E, \mathcal{E}, H, D\}$ such that:

- T is the *key technique* executed in step S; the single technique which describes this step.
- $\mathcal{T}$ is a set of *ancillary techniques* describing S [2]. We assume $T \in \mathcal{T}$.

---

[2] Ancillary techniques are used due to some semantic overlap in ATT&CK. For example, using a powershell command to dump credentials (T1003) could also be correctly labeled as an instance of execution via powershell (T1086).

– E is the *key event* in S; a single event initiating T.
– $\mathcal{E}$ is a set of ancillary events in S, including: attacker-executed events following E, and events causally-related to events in $\mathcal{E}$ (e.g., triggered child processes). We assume $E \in \mathcal{E}$.
– H is the host on which step S occurs.
– D is the destination host for techniques in which action moves from one host to another (e.g., a lateral movement).

Techniques are chosen because they link low-level event detection to higher-level strategy: techniques are specific enough for detection by alert rules but they are also indexed to higher-level adversary tactics (e.g., defensive evasion, lateral movement) which convey the phase of the adversary's attack. Techniques are well-documented [1] which provides an operational semantics for BSF steps, including: a unique ID, a textual description of the technique, associated tactics, platforms, examples of malware and APTs known to use this technique (useful for linking threat intelligence), mitigations, detection methods, and a list of literature references.

An example JSON-formatted BSF step from the blue bot in a cybergame is shown in Fig. 3. In this step, the attacker is detected using key technique T1105, remote file copy, to perform a lateral movement from host `sounder-pc` to destination host `fulco-pc`.

```
{
    "provenance": "Analytic - Copy Into Network Share (via \"cmd /c copy\" or \"xcopy\")",
    "key_event": "5b3512df6443110d68c617b8",
    "key_technique": "T1105",
    "attack_info": [
        {
            "technique_name": "Remote File Copy",
            "tactic": ["Lateral Movement"],
            "technique_id": "T1105"
        }
    ],
    "time": "2018-03-01T14:56:30.319000+00:00",
    "events": [
        "5b3512db6443110d68c6177b",
        "5b3512df6443110d68c617b8",
        "5b3513986443110d68c620af",
        "5b3513466443110d68c61cc3"
    ],
    "nodetype": "step",
    "id": "3aaca9db-bb3b-4052-a1fa-59f16e9f8eb9",
    "host": "sounder-pc",
    "dest_hosts": [
        "fulco-pc"
    ],
    "confidence": 0.9426254358169935
},
```

Fig. 3. Example BSF step: lateral movement by remote file copy

The step in Fig. 3 contains four events whose ids are in the *events* array. Although not shown here, these events are similar to the events shown in Fig. 1. From the red perspective, events are the implementation of a step. From the blue perspective, events provide evidence for a step. The events associated with a step are represented using the CAR data model [4].

In Sect. 4.1 we describe how such steps, or semantic clusters, are generated.

4   Experimental Environment

Our automated cybergaming environment is illustrated in Fig. 4. It contains four major components: gameboard, red bot, blue bot, and game analysis pipeline. The gameboard is generated by a system called BRAWL which automates Virtual Machine (VM) provisioning and game board setup for each game. Gameboards consist of a virtual network, including Windows hosts and an Active Directory server. Each Windows hosts runs Sysmon [11] and forwards events to an Elasticsearch server, which acts as a central database of all game logs. Sysmon generates events involving processes, flows, files, the registry, and other operating system entities. We use a popular Sysmon config that filters various high-volume system activity [10].

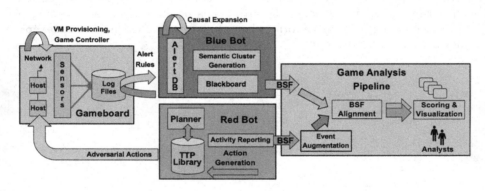

Fig. 4. Automated cybergaming architecture

The BRAWL game controller provides an API for communicating with the red and blue teams, or *bots*, which are automated software systems responding to start and stop messages from the controller. After a game begins, the game controller turns on logging, and game activities are captured including: (a) the Sysmon event logs, (b) the red bot's self-report, (c) the blue bot's reported detections. Both bot reports are recorded in BRAWL Shared Format (BSF), described in Sect. 3, and finally forwarded to the game analysis pipeline for alignment and scoring, as described in Sect. 5.

We use CALDERA [15,16] as the default red bot for blue to play against. CALDERA uses a planner to generate and automatically execute a post-compromise attack through a network of computers. At each step in its plan, high-level tactics and techniques are selected from ATT&CK and executed by CALDERA in the gameboard, resulting in detectable system-level events.

CALDERA can be programmed to emulate specific adversary behaviors (e.g., the techniques and tactical sequences used by APT 21). For this paper, we assume the red bot is programmed to execute a series of attacks consistent with behavioral threat intelligence, such as a SOC might obtain, in order to test its defenses against such attacks.

The blue bot is an ongoing research project at MITRE. It uses a two-phased approach to identify adversary activity in a network. The first phase, called CAS-CADE [3], executes alert rules over the log files as the game progresses and caches the resulting suspicious events in a database. These events are then expanded by recursively following system-level causal relationships (e.g., parent and child processes, flow connections) resulting in a larger set of suspicious events. The second phase, called BB-ATE, post-processes BSF in an agent-based blackboard architecture to infer additional information (the details of which are beyond the scope of this paper). Between these phases, semantic clusters (BSF steps) are generated. The most important functions of our blue bot, for the purposes of this paper, are causal expansion of events and semantic cluster generation.

4.1 Semantic Cluster Generation

To construct blue BSF steps, such as the example in Fig. 3, we begin by labelling alert-generating rules with the presumed detected technique(s). An alert rule consists of a query that targets a particular adversary behavior and is tagged with the related techniques and tactics. For example, the "Winlogon Spawning Cmd" alert rule triggers on a `cmd.exe` process with a parent process of `winlogon.exe` and is tagged with the related technique "T1015 Accessibility Features", which can be used to implement persistence and privilege escalation tactics. When these rules are triggered, an initial step is formed with the triggering event as the step's *key event* and the rule's technique as the *key technique.*

Ancillary events for a step are identified by applying the causal expansion logic of the first phase, and recursively following system-level chains of causality from the key event, such as process creation and flows. Thus, for example, all descendent and antecedent process creation events would be added. Through experience, we have learned to heuristically truncate this set at the host boundary of the key event, including all events on that initial host plus the first event on any connecting host. The resulting set of events becomes the *ancillary events* of the step being formed.

Red step construction proceeds in a similar manner, the major difference being the knowledge asymmetry of red and blue: red's internal planning logic generates its TTPs and thus, in contrast to blue, it has no need to infer them. Every time red executes a technique it forms a step based on that technique, and records it as BSF. On the other hand, red lacks blue's ability to query log files for causally-generated events, and is uncertain about the full effects of its actions. Thus the red bot records in each step only the events it is aware of.

5   Scoring Cybergames

Our intent for scoring cybergames is to rate the defense's performance, enabling improvement of the defensive posture. While computing scoring metrics is straightforward, the most challenging aspect of scoring cybergames is the alignment, or matching, of red reports to blue detections. In this Section we discuss how scoring is accomplished, including our initial event-based efforts, some of the challenges we encountered that motivated semantic clustering, and our final semantic-cluster-based scoring approach illustrated by the final component of Fig. 4: the *game analysis pipeline*.

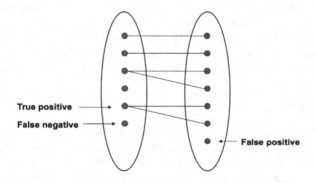

Fig. 5. Bipartite scoring graph aligning red activities with blue detections (Color figure online)

At the end of each game red reports its activities and blue reports its detections, represented in Fig. 5 as colored nodes. These reports are extracted from the Elasticsearch server and processed by the analysis pipeline. To score the game, we assign edges *aligning* blue's detections with red's actions and then then compute metrics over the resulting graph. Red nodes matched by a blue node are considered *true positives* (TP) [3], unmatched blue nodes are *false positives* (FP), and unmatched red nodes are *false negatives* (FN). We use the standard metrics of precision $= TP/(TP + FP)$ and recall $= TP/(TP + FN)$, and $F1$ which is the harmonic mean of precision and recall. In Fig. 5 precision is .80, recall is .67, and $F1$ is .73.

Initial Event-based Alignment and Scoring. We did not initially use semantic clustering. In our first games the blue bot reported the system-level *events* it detected, such as process and file creations, and the red bot similarly reported the events it caused. Our initial approach to scoring was thus event-based: each node in the bipartite scoring graph represented an individual red or blue event,

---

[3] Note that blue can report on the same red activity more than once if multiple sensors detect different aspects of the same red action. In this case, we only count one true positive.

and scoring a game to determine how well blue detected red's activity involved assigning edges aligning blue events to red events and computing metrics.

Events were aligned by computing a match-strength metric, and declaring if the metric exceeded a threshold. This metric scores the similarity of key value pairs in the two events, including: hostnames, object and action (e.g., "process create"), and times within a window of parameterized size (set to 30 s).

We encountered several alignment challenges in scoring these initial games. A simple one was due to syntactic differences in red and blue event reports. For example, red reported file creation as `type:create_file` while blue reported file creation as `action:create` and `object:file`. We harmonized these through introducing standards and post-processing, improving alignments.

A second such issue was due to red's inability to know the full extent of its actions. For example, in Fig. 1, red would not see the file create event on peele-pc, which was a downstream effect of its actions. Blue, in contrast, sees such actions by querying the logging infrastructure. Due to this inherent asymmetry, blue was often incorrectly charged for false positives (i.e., false false positives) because blue detected actual events red had caused, but which red did not observe and report. This in turn distorted game scores, especially for precision.

We remediated this discrepancy by post-game "event augmentation" (as shown in Fig. 4): for each event reported by red, we applied the same causal expansion logic available to the blue bot, augmenting red's reported events for alignment as if red had equivalent power to view logs.

However, rectifying these basic alignment issues exposed more fundamental flaws in our focus on individual events, which resulted in our move to a semantic cluster representation for detection, alignment and scoring:

- Generating scores based on individual events weights all events equally and does not distinguish event importance. Certain events, such as the remote file copy event in Fig. 1, more clearly suggest an adversary activity (e.g., a potential lateral move by remote file copy) than other events, such as causally-resulting file create event in Fig. 1. These resulting events provide useful redundant evidence supporting that activity but it did not seem these should be scored identically to events indicating a *new* activity.
- Even if blue achieves a perfect precision and recall on individual events, it has revealed practically nothing about red's strategic plan in terms of tactics such as discovery, lateral movements, persistence, data collection, and exfiltration (i.e., a large semantic gap exists between blue's detection and red's activity). In particular, if blue achieved a 75% recall of individual events, we cannot tell the difference between detecting each tactic at a 75% level and entirely omitting the detection of certain tactics. Such inability to measure tactical coverage precludes promising defensive strategies, such as the *threat tuple* of [25], for evaluating the current extent of a cyber attack.

Alignment and Scoring Using Semantic Clusters. Moving to semantic clusters closed this semantic gap, however alignment is more complex because BSF steps have multiple components (i.e., key technique, key event, ancillary technique set, ancillary event set) making broad spectrum of red-blue alignments are possible.

In particular, matching the events portion of steps (i.e., the key and ancillary events of red and blue) could be done in multiple, increasingly permissive, ways:

1. Key events match between red and blue.
2. Key event of red is in the ancillary events of blue *and* vice versa.
3. Key event of red is in the ancillary events of blue *or* vice versa.
4. Ancillary events of red and blue intersect.

The same four options exist for matching the *techniques* portion of a step as well (i.e., the key technique and ancillary techniques of red and blue), leading to a *sizable* space of potential overall step-matching methodologies.

   In our experiments, we have chosen to match steps by requiring that at least the third criteria hold for *both* events and for techniques. Intuitively, this requires that matching steps agree, at least in a loose sense, on both a key event and a key technique.

6   Experiments

In this section we describe the use of automated cybergaming with BSF semantic clusters to improve an organization's defensive posture, demonstrating how a SOC environment can benefit from this approach to narrowing the "semantic gap". In particular, we study two defensive adjustments made possible by the improved organizational insight into TTPs provided by semantic clustering, and by the rapid feedback enabled by scored cybergames.

6.1   Setup

The BRAWL game board consists of a Windows domain with a domain controller and ten Windows 8.1 virtual machines. We collect a dataset of 48 hours of system logs, including a total of 31,073 Sysmon events. During this period, we use CALDERA to emulate three distinct intrusions, with the red bot exercising a range of post-exploit behaviors, including discovery, credential access, lateral movement, execution, privilege escalation, and collection. The system logs in our dataset also include benign activities, such as typical Windows background processes and services, installing software, and remote admin commands.

   The results in this section are obtained by repeatedly [4] applying the blue bot, in varied *configurations*, to detect red activity in our dataset. A configuration is a specific set of alert rules. We score each configuration based on how well blue detected BSF steps which match the BSF steps reported by red.

---

[4] We can apply the blue bot repeatedly to the same red activity because the blue bot does not alter the gameboard.

6.2 Baseline

Our baseline configuration consists of 43 commonly-used alert rules, distributed over tactics, from the Cyber Analytics Repository (CAR) [4]. In this and the following exercises, we generate a *range* of detection configurations by incrementally adding rules into an initially-empty configuration in order of increasing noise generation (i.e., false positive rate), until the full set of rules is reached. This emulates a typical SOC's challenge of configuring their rule sets based on the levels of noise they are capable of handling, thus trading precision for recall as more rules are added. To determine noise levels, we measured the false positive rate of each alert rule over a 24 hour period on a production network, separate from our game board, consisting of about 250 operational hosts.

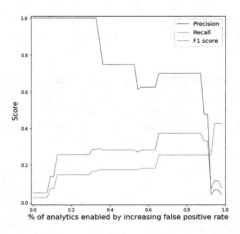

Fig. 6. Precision, Recall, and F1 scores with baseline alert rules

Figure 6 shows precision, recall, and F1 scores by percentage of alert rules enabled. The left-side of the graph represents more conservative configurations, i.e., higher precision and lower recall, whereas the right side represents more aggressive configurations with lower precision and higher recall. As can be seen, some of the noisier rules which are added toward the end are also among the most effective detectors. The maximum F-score of 0.373 with 65% to 87% of alert rules enabled represents an optimal balance between precision and recall, with a precision of 0.699, but a recall of only 0.254. The most aggressive configuration with 100% of alert rules has a slightly higher, but still low recall of only 0.425. Even the most aggressive configuration clearly contains blindspots and fails to detect most adversary activity.

To improve recall, a SOC would typically add rules. Given semantic annotations on rules, and that recall is being measured in terms of semantic clusters (for which a match requires TTP-level agreement), in this exercise we can readily determine coverage gaps in which adding more rules is likely to improve recall.

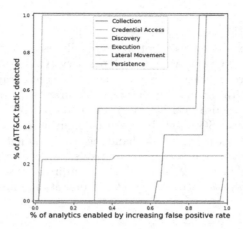

Fig. 7. Tactic detection with baseline alert rules

Figure 7 shows the detection rates for different tactics as alert rules are enabled. Even in the most aggressive configuration at the far right, the discovery, persistence, and collection tactics are being detected at no more than a 0.243 rate, illustrating the most promising semantic regions for additional rules.

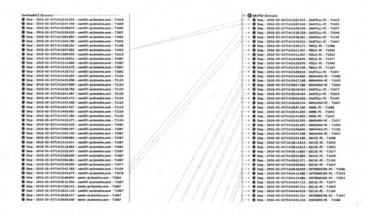

Fig. 8. BSF matcher visualization of missed discovery techniques

As another illustration of TTP annotations revealing tactical detection gaps, Fig. 8 is a screenshot of a BSF matching tool showing red BSF from a single cybergame on the left and the corresponding blue BSF on the right. The lines show detected step alignments, and the unmatched gap areas on the left show blue missing much of red's initial activity. Upon examination, the technique IDs red reported in these detection gaps (e.g., T1018 "remote system discovery",

T1082 "system information discovery") are dominantly discovery activities, one of the tactics shown to be poorly detected in Fig. 7.

6.3 Reducing False Negatives

Given that the baseline configurations have gaps for discovery, persistence, and collection, and that discovery is an important tactic early in the adversary kill chain we focus on improving detection for discovery by adding 14 new discovery alert rules to the baseline configuration, increasing the alert rule set from 43 alerts to 57 alerts. This raised the detection rate for the discovery tactic from 24% (in Fig. 7) to 75%. Figure 9 shows the precision, recall, and F1 scores for the new configuration with these added discovery alert rules.

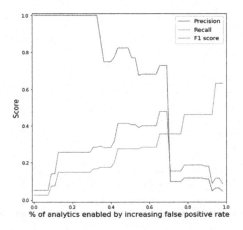

Fig. 9. Precision, Recall, and F1 scores with added discovery alert rules

The maximum F1 score increased from 0.373 to 0.478, with recall in this configuration increasing from 0.254 to 0.356 and precision increasing slightly from 0.699 to 0.727. The most aggressive setting yields an even higher recall of 0.631, but precision drops precipitously because many of the new rules are noisy.

6.4 Reducing False Positives

To reduce time-consuming false positives, SOCs typically disable alert rules or whitelist events known to generate a large number of false positives. However, both methods can also increase false negatives because the triggering conditions of rules and whitelisted events frequently can occur in both benign and malicious contexts. For example, post-exploit adversary behaviors and system administrator actions have a large overlap.

By detecting semantic clusters, another disambiguation technique becomes an option for false positive removal. *Sequences* of adversary TTPs, such as the key techniques in semantic clusters, provide a disambiguating context for distinguishing benign and malicious events.

For this exercise we collect a separate dataset of two weeks of system logs to train a model, including a total of 30,332 Sysmon events. During this period, similar to our main dataset, we use CALDERA to emulate three intrusions. We then run the blue bot on this training dataset and extract trigrams of reported adversary activity (i.e., techniques). For each trigram, we compute the number of true positives and false positives, retaining any trigrams with only false positives. We then use the remaining trigrams as a filter, removing any matching trigram sequences in blue's output.

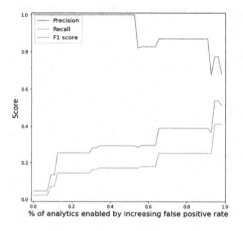

Fig. 10. Precision, Recall, and F1 scores with ngram filtering

Figure 10 shows precision, recall, and F1 scores with ngram filtering. The graph shows a significant improvement in precision across all configurations relative to the baseline graph (Fig. 6). The maximum F1 score increases from 0.373 to 0.538, with precision in this configuration increasing from 0.699 to 0.774. Recall for the maximum F1 score also increases from 0.254 to 0.412, because high precision is achieved with a more aggressive configuration (i.e., more rules enabled) than in the baseline.

There are challenges to our approach as performed in this exercise: clever adversaries will rotate techniques to accomplish the same tactic, thus it would be important to include sequences of tactical information as well. Also, adversaries could include "no-op" actions to disrupt trigram patterns [39], which would require the use of more sophisticated data structures such as skipgrams [23]. While such improvements are possible, this exercise demonstrates the power of addressing false-positive elimination at the semantic level (i.e., in the conceptual world of adversary), instead of at the level of system alerts.

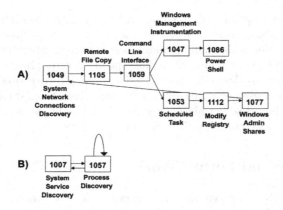

Fig. 11. Adversary state diagrams derived from N-Grams

Figure 11 provides an interesting illustration of why these trigrams work as a false positive filter. These two state diagrams were obtained in a data-driven manner by concatenating true positive trigrams into longer sequences involving cycles and branches. However, the red research team quickly recognized these diagrams as logic their planner would generate.

6.5   Summary of Improvements

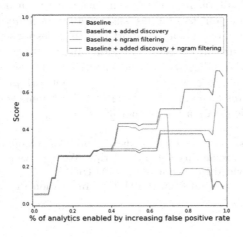

Fig. 12. Summary F1 graph

Figure 12 summarizes F1 scores for the baseline, adding discovery alert rules, using ngram filtering, and both improvements together. The results show consistent increases in the maximum F1 score. The added discovery alert rules results in some less optimal alert configurations (when more than 70% of the alert rules are enabled) due to including noisier (i.e., high false positive rate) alert rules. These alert rule configurations become much more effective when we enable ngram filtering, reducing their false positive rates. Interestingly, ngram filtering was meant to decrease false positives and improve precision, yet also results in reducing false negatives and improving recall, since it can achieve high precision with a broad set of alert rules enabled. Lastly, we receive the largest improvement when we combine the two improvements.

7   Summary and Future Work

In this paper we have shown the advantages of a new method for improving enterprise cyberdefense: semantic clusters in automated cybergames. Semantic clusters make a model of attacker strategy *explicit* as machine-readable data structures, clustering traditional events around TTP annotations from a well-known behavioral taxonomy, enabling the defense to operate at the strategic level of APT attackers without sacrificing the ability to drill into evidential details.

We have also demonstrated the use of a *fully* automated cybergaming environment. Beyond mitigating costs, a key benefit of fully automated cybergaming is the ability to learn improved defensive strategy through experimentation. We illustrate this using cybergames scored in terms of semantic clusters, revealing effective and automatable defensive enhancements, such as covering tactical detection gaps and using patterns of strategic behavior to reduce false positives.

This research opens the door on many potential future research directions. The rich semantics available in our BSF semantic cluster format enable the application of various intelligent techniques, such as automatically infering and filling detection gaps. BSF streams can support dynamic response to attacks. While ordinary event streams can be used, the additional strategic information should improve the defense's ability to respond effectively [38]. Finally, the ability to automatically run and score cybergames on a real network provides a foundation for red and blue teams to co-evolve through reinforcement learning [26] (e.g., as illustrated by Google's Alpha Go learner [35]).

Acknowledgements. We would like to thank Andy Applebaum for his helpful comments and suggestions reviewing this manuscript. We also want to acknowledge the generous support provided by the BRAWL, CALDERA, and CASCADE teams. This work was supported by a grant from the MITRE Innovation Program.

References

1. ATT&CK: Adversarial Tactics, Techniques, and Common Knowledge. https://attack.mitre.org. Accessed 24 Apr 2019
2. CAPEC: Common Attack Enumeration and Classification. https://capec.mitre.org. Accessed 24 Apr 2019
3. CASCADE. https://github.com/mitre/cascade-server. Accessed 30 Apr 2019

4. Cyber Analytics Repository. https://car.mitre.org/data_model/. Accessed 24 Apr 2019

5. Endgame RTA: Red Team Automation. https://www.endgame.com/blog/technical-blog/introducing-endgame-red-team-automation. Accessed 24 Apr 2019

6. First Round of MITRE ATT&CK Product Evaluations Released. https://medium.com/mitre-attack/first-round-of-mitre-att-ck-evaluations-released-15db64ea970d. Accessed 24 Apr 2019

7. MANDIANT: Exposing One of China's Cyber Espionage Units. https://www.fireeye.com/content/dam/fireeye-www/services/pdfs/mandiant-apt1-report.pdf. Accessed 24 Apr 2019

8. NSA/CSS Technical Cyber Threat Framework v2. https://www.nsa.gov/Portals/70/documents/what-we-do/cybersecurity/professional-resources/ctr-nsa-css-technical-cyber-threat-framework.pdf. Accessed 24 Apr 2019

9. Red Canary ATT&CKs (Part 1): Why We're Using ATT&CK Across Red Canary. https://redcanary.com/blog/red-canary-and-mitre-attack/. Accessed 24 Apr 2019

10. Swift On Security - Sysmon Config. https://github.com/SwiftOnSecurity/sysmon-config. Accessed 24 Apr 2019

11. Sysmon 9.0. https://docs.microsoft.com/en-us/sysinternals/downloads/sysmon. Accessed 24 Apr 2019

12. The Elasticsearch Common Schema. https://github.com/elastic/ecs/tree/master/schemas. Accessed 24 Apr 2019

13. The Pyramid of Pain. http://detect-respond.blogspot.com/2013/03/the-pyramid-of-pain.html. Accessed 24 Apr 2019

14. The SOC Gets a Makeover. https://www.darkreading.com/risk/the-soc-gets-a-makeover/d/d-id/1332744/. Accessed 24 Apr 2019

15. Applebaum, A., Miller, D., Strom, B., Foster, H., Thomas, C.: Analysis of automated adversary emulation techniques. In: Summer Simulation Multi-Conference, p. 16 (2017)

16. Applebaum, A., Miller, D., Strom, B., Korban, C., Wolf, R.: Intelligent, automated red team emulation. In: 32nd Annual Conference on Computer Security Applications, pp. 363–373. ACM (2016)

17. Bodeau, D., McCollum, C., Fox, D.: Cyber threat modeling: survey, assessment, and representative framework. Tech. Rep. 16-J-00184-01, The MITRE Corporation: Homeland Security Systems Engineering and Development Institute (April 2018)

18. Ferguson, B., Tall, A., Olsen, D.: National cyber range overview. In: Military Communications Conference (MILCOM), 2014 IEEE, pp. 123–128. IEEE (2014)

19. Fletcher, T.A., Sharp, C., Raghavan, A.: Optimized common information model, US Patent App. 14/800,678 (2016)

20. Fox, D., McCollum, C., Arnoth, E., Mak, D.: Cyber wargaming: framework for enhancing cyber wargaming with realistic business context. Tech. Rep. 16-J-00184-04, The MITRE Corporation: Homeland Security Systems Engineering and Development Institute, November 2018

21. Goldis, P.D.: Questions and answers about tiger teams. EDPACS 17(4), 1–10 (1989)

22. Hoffmann, J.: Simulated penetration testing: from dijkstra to turing test++. In: 25th International Conference on Automated Planning and Scheduling (2015)

23. Huang, X., Alleva, F., Hon, H.W., Hwang, M.Y., Lee, K.F., Rosenfeld, R.: The sphinx-ii speech recognition system: an overview. Comput. Speech & Lang. 7(2), 137–148 (1993)

24. Kewley, D.L., Bouchard, J.F.: Darpa information assurance program dynamic defense experiment summary. IEEE Trans. Syst., Man, Cybern. - Part A: Syst. Hum. **31**(4), 331–336 (2001)
25. Milajerdi, S.M., Gjomemo, R., Eshete, B., Sekar, R., Venkatakrishnan, V.: Holmes: real-time apt detection through correlation of suspicious information flows. In: 2019 IEEE Symposium on Security and Privacy, pp. 430–445. IEEE (2019)
26. Niculae, S.: Reinforcement learning vs genetic algorithms in game-theoretic cyber-security, October 2018. thesiscommons.org/nxzep
27. Oakley, J.: Improving cyber defensive stratagem through apt centric offensive security assessment. In: International Conference on Cyber Warfare and Security, pp. 552-XV. Academic Conferences International Limited (2018)
28. Oltsik, J., Alexander, C., CISM, C.: The life and times of cybersecurity professionals. ESG and ISSA: Research Report (2017)
29. Ošlejšek, R., Toth, D., Eichler, Z., Burská, K.: Towards a unified data storage and generic visualizations in cyber ranges. In: 16th European Conference on Cyber Warfare and Security. p. 298. Academic Conferences and publishing limited (2017)
30. Passerini, Emanuele, Paleari, Roberto, Martignoni, Lorenzo: How good are malware detectors at remediating infected systems? In: Flegel, Ulrich, Bruschi, Danilo (eds.) DIMVA 2009. LNCS, vol. 5587, pp. 21–37. Springer, Heidelberg (2009). https://doi.org/10.1007/978-3-642-02918-9_2
31. Rieck, K., Trinius, P., Willems, C., Holz, T.: Automatic analysis of malware behavior using machine learning. J. Comput. Secur. **19**(4), 639–668 (2011)
32. Rossey, L.: Simspace cyber range. In: ACSAC 2015 Panel: Cyber Experimentation of the Future (CEF): Catalyzing a New Generation of Experimental Cyber-security Research (2015)
33. Rossey, L.M., et al.: Lariat: lincoln adaptable real-time information assurance testbed. In: Aerospace Conference, vol. 6, pp. 6–6. IEEE (2002)
34. Sarraute, C., Buffet, O., Hoffmann, J.: POMDPs make better hackers: accounting for uncertainty in penetration testing. In: 26th AAAI Conference on Artificial Intelligence (2012)
35. Silver, D., et al.: Mastering the game of go with deep neural networks and tree search. Nature **529**(7587), 484 (2016)
36. Sommer, R., Paxson, V.: Outside the closed world: on using machine learning for network intrusion detection. In: 2010 IEEE Symposium on Security and Privacy, pp. 305–316. IEEE (2010)
37. Trinius, P., Willems, C., Holz, T., Rieck, K.: A malware instruction set for behavior-based analysis (2009)
38. Van Dijk, M., Juels, A., Oprea, A., Rivest, R.L.: Flipit: The game of "stealthy takeover". J. Cryptol. **26**(4), 655–713 (2013)
39. Wagner, D., Soto, P.: Mimicry attacks on host-based intrusion detection systems. In: 9th ACM Conference on Computer and Communications Security, pp. 255–264. ACM (2002)
40. Wood, B.J., Duggan, R.A.: Red teaming of advanced information assurance concepts. In: DARPA Information Survivability Conference and Exposition, pp. 112–118. IEEE (2000)

Machine Learning

Stochastic ADMM Based Distributed Machine Learning with Differential Privacy

Jiahao Ding[1], Sai Mounika Errapotu[1], Haijun Zhang[2], Yanmin Gong[3], Miao Pan[1(✉)], and Zhu Han[1]

[1] Department of Electrical and Computer Engineering, University of Houston, Houston, TX 77204, USA
{jding7,serrapotu,mpan2,zhan2}@uh.edu
[2] Department of Communications Engineering, University of Science and Technology Beijing, Beijing 100083, China
haijunzhang@ieee.org
[3] Department of Electrical and Computer Engineering, University of Texas at San Antonio, San Antonio, TX 78249, USA
yanmin.gong@utsa.edu

Abstract. While embracing various machine learning techniques to make effective decisions in the big data era, preserving the privacy of sensitive data poses significant challenges. In this paper, we develop a privacy-preserving distributed machine learning algorithm to address this issue. Given the assumption that each data provider owns a dataset with different sample size, our goal is to learn a common classifier over the union of all the local datasets in a distributed way without leaking any sensitive information of the data samples. Such an algorithm needs to jointly consider efficient distributed learning and effective privacy preservation. In the proposed algorithm, we extend stochastic alternating direction method of multipliers (ADMM) in a distributed setting to do distributed learning. For preserving privacy during the iterative process, we combine differential privacy and stochastic ADMM together. In particular, we propose a novel stochastic ADMM based privacy-preserving distributed machine learning (PS-ADMM) algorithm by perturbing the updating gradients, that provide differential privacy guarantee and have a low computational cost. We theoretically demonstrate the convergence rate and utility bound of our proposed PS-ADMM under strongly convex objective. Through our experiments performed on real-world datasets, we show that PS-ADMM outperforms other differentially private ADMM algorithms under the same differential privacy guarantee.

Keywords: Differential privacy · Distributed machine learning · Stochastic ADMM · Moments accountant · Distributed optimization · Privacy

S. Chen et al. (Eds.): SecureComm 2019, LNICST 304, pp. 257–277, 2019.
https://doi.org/10.1007/978-3-030-37228-6_13

1 Introduction

Recently, with rapid advances in sensing technologies, we are witnessing a deluge of data [20,21]. Statistical analysis of this data has paved the way for the development of machine learning that brings valuable benefits to society, such as more intelligent autopilot technology and higher medical quality, among others. The enormous data generated from such various applications is scattered around different places, and it increasingly becomes difficult for a single machine to process such giant data. Hence, the centralized model can no longer efficiently process this data [2,3]. Apart from the limitations on processing, this data draws detailed pictures of people's lives and involves highly sensitive information. So the data owners might be reluctant to share their data for analysis. Therefore, with the rise in the volume of data being generated, there is a critical need of privacy-preserving machine learning algorithms that can both cater the processing and privacy needs.

To address the above issues, we develop a privacy-preserving machine learning algorithm that processes data in a distributed manner while providing privacy guarantee for each training sample. One of the promise applications is the health domain. For example, in health monitoring applications multiple hospitals collaborate to provide constructive diagnosis to the patients. Hospitals have a large number of cases, and the data analysis of these cases helps doctors to make an accurate diagnosis and offer early treatment plans. Thus, multiple hospitals could collaboratively train a classifier through a central server that can help in prognosis and diagnosing diseases early. However, such medical cases may contains sensitive information about the patients and each hospital cannot share its patients' cases with other hospitals. Hence, the key challenge is to effectively conduct medical research while preserving the privacy of the patients in the analysis. Concisely, this problem is a distributed machine learning problem where data is collected from multiple data providers and each data sample's privacy needs to be guaranteed during the optimization.

One of the promising solutions for such distributed machine learning problems is alternating direction method of multipliers (ADMM) [4,14,15]. ADMM enables distributed learning by decomposing a large-scale optimization into smaller subproblems and each subproblem is easy to solve in a distributed and parallel way. Each data provider uses its own private data to train a local classifier and the central server averages all of the local classifiers and broadcasts the result to the data providers. These steps iterate several times until the server and users have a high-performance model. Through this decomposition and coordination procedure of ADMM, the distributed learning problem achieves effective results. However, when both the number of features and the size of dataset are large, the computational burden of using ADMM is heavy [17]. Recently Zhang et al. propose a novel ADMM algorithm called SCAS-ADMM, which achieves lower computational burden by employing stochastic variance reduced gradient (SVRG) [13] as an inexact solver for subproblems. Zhang et al. considered the SCAS-ADMM in the centralized scenario [23]. We investigate on the SCAS-ADMM in distributed machine learning scenario to obtain a low computational cost per iteration, without compromising the privacy of data samples.

Beyond effectively solving the distributed machine learning problem, the data privacy is the critical concern in such analyses since the private information pertaining to the datasets should not to be shared and kept private. But the privacy concerns are still inherent during the communication between the data providers and the central server. As each data provider needs to share the local model trained over the sensitive raw data at each iteration, an adversary could infer the sensitive information from the shared model as described in [8]. Therefore, we use differential privacy [6,7], a de facto notion for privacy that offers strong privacy guarantees, to tackle the privacy concerns and protect disclosed privacy from the model parameters during the iterative procedure. Differential privacy guarantees privacy by measuring the change in the outcome of the algorithm as the presence or absence of a single data entry in the original dataset does not explicitly change the outcome. In this work we investigate on collectively considering differential privacy and distributed machine learning to get effective results in the analysis, with low computation burden and without compromising the privacy of the data owners. In the existing literature, there are some research efforts integrating ADMM into private distributed learning. Zhang et al. developed a dual perturbation based on ADMM [22], in which they add noise to the dual variables of decentralized ADMM and only provide privacy guarantee of a single data provider per iteration, but their decentralized algorithm needs robust network topology and does not guarantee utility and privacy when considering all nodes during the whole training procedure. Guo et al. proposed another approach for preserving privacy in ADMM in [10], which incorporate secure computation and distributed noise generation in the asynchronous ADMM algorithm. Though privacy during communication can be preserved, their scheme suffers from poor communication and computation costs because of the encryption and decryption over huge datasets.

To address these challenges, we propose a novel stochastic ADMM based privacy-preserving distributed machine learning (PS-ADMM) algorithm in this paper, which jointly considers the distributed learning setting and differential privacy. In PS-ADMM, we employ differential privacy to stochastic ADMM algorithm with the objective of protecting the privacy of data samples and achieving distributed learning over multiple data providers. Different from the approach proposed in [22], we propose to extend the stochastic ADMM in a distributed setting to deal with the computational burden of local computation at each data provider, and add differential privacy based noise to the updating gradients during local computation procedure. We utilize the moments accountant method [1] to analyze the privacy guarantee of PS-ADMM, and we also provide the convergence rate and utility bound of PS-ADMM. The major contributions of this paper are listed as follows.

- We design a novel stochastic ADMM based privacy-preserving distributed machine learning algorithm called PS-ADMM, where we investigate the SCAS-ADMM algorithm in a distributed setting and perturb the gradient updates with Gaussian noise to further improve the computational efficiency and provide differential privacy guarantee.

- Compared to the existing research in [22] that only considers privacy guarantee at each iteration, we consider the entire iterative procedure and adopt moments accountant method to provide a tighter differential privacy guarantee for PS-ADMM.
- We theoretically analyze and prove the convergence and utility bound of the proposed algorithm PS-ADMM.
- We show that the proposed PS-ADMM outperforms other differentially private ADMM algorithms under the same differential privacy guarantee by conducting PS-ADMM over real-world data.

The remainder of this paper is organized as follows. Section 2 presents the problem statement, preliminaries and associated privacy concerns. We propose our differentially private algorithm PS-ADMM in Sect. 3. This is followed by our theoretical analysis of convergence and utility bound in Sect. 4. Detailed simulations and comparisons are presented in Sect. 5. Section 6 concludes the whole paper.

2   Problem Statement and Preliminaries

In this section, we describe the problem statement in Sect. 2.1, introduce the preliminaries of ADMM and differential privacy in Sect. 2.2. The overview of the distributed SCAS-ADMM algorithm is presented in Sect. 2.3 and the privacy concerns of the distributed ADMM based solution are presented in Sect. 2.4.

2.1   Problem Statement

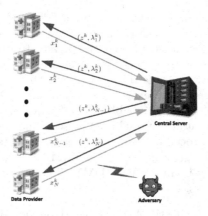

Fig. 1. System architecture

As shown in Fig. 1, we consider a star network topology consisting of a set of data providers $\mathcal{N} = \{1, \cdots, N\}$ and a central server, where multiple data providers have the ability to communicate with the server and the server is responsible for aggregation and message passing. Here, each data provider possesses a private dataset $D_i = \{(a_{im}, y_{im})\}_{m=1}^M$ consisting of feature vector a_{im} from a data universe $\mathcal{X}$, and $y_{im} \in \mathcal{Y}$ that is a label we aim to predict from a_{im}. The objective of our problem is to build a classifier over the aggregated sensitive dataset $\cup_{i \in \mathcal{N}}\{D_i\}$ from data providers through a distributed manner, where the classifier can be obtained by minimizing a regularized empirical risk minimization problem (ERM) [9]. The regularized empirical risk minimization problem is to learn a classifier x over a convex set $\mathcal{C} \subseteq \mathbb{R}^p$, which can be formulated as

$$\min_{x \in \mathcal{C}} \sum_{i=1}^N \frac{1}{M} \sum_{m=1}^M l_{im}[x, (a_{im}, y_{im})] + g(x), \tag{1}$$

where $l_{im}(\cdot) : \mathcal{X} \times \mathcal{Y} \times \mathcal{C} \to \mathbb{R}$ is a loss function of provider i for each data sample (a_{im}, y_{im}) and $g(x)$ is a convex regularizer to prevent overfitting. In this paper, we assume the loss function $l_{im}(\cdot)$ is convex, G-Lipschitz and has L_m-Lipschitz continuous gradient. Note that our algorithm is not limited to the classification problem since the convergence and privacy analysis are still valid.

The above ERM problem (1) can be minimized by ADMM, which is a practical distributed scheme that can be applied to large-scale machine learning algorithms. Since the goal is to build a classifier with sensitive data, privacy concerns inherent in the training procedure need to be addressed while solving the ERM problem.

2.2   Preliminaries

Distributed Machine Learning with ADMM. In order to solve the problem in (1) with ADMM method [4], the ERM problem in (1) can be reformulated as consensus formulation [18] by introducing a global variable $z \in \mathbb{R}^p$ as

$$\min_{\substack{x_i, z \in \mathcal{C} \\ i=1,\ldots,N}} \sum_{i=1}^N f_i(x_i) + g(z) \tag{2}$$

$$\text{s.t. } x_i - z = 0, \quad \forall i = 1, ..., N. \tag{3}$$

In (2), $f_i(x_i) = \frac{1}{M} \sum_{m=1}^M l_{im}[x_i, (a_{im}, y_{im})]$ is the i-th data provider's loss function due to dataset D_i, and x_i is the local classifier of the i-th data provider. Since the objective function in (2) is already decoupled, each data provider only needs to optimize a subproblem, i.e., empirical risk minimization problem over its local dataset. The constraints (3) enforce that all the local classifiers reach consensus finally. Apparently, the problem above is equivalent to the problem in (1).

Let $\boldsymbol{\lambda} \in \mathbb{R}^p$ denote the Lagrange dual variable, and $\rho > 0$ be a pre-defined penalty parameter. The standard ADMM consists of the following iterations

$$\boldsymbol{x}_i^{k+1} = \arg\min_{\boldsymbol{x}_i} \ f_i(\boldsymbol{x}_i) + (\boldsymbol{x}_i - \boldsymbol{z}^k)^T \boldsymbol{\lambda}_i^k + \frac{\rho}{2}\|\boldsymbol{x}_i - \boldsymbol{z}^k\|^2, \tag{4}$$

$$\boldsymbol{z}^{k+1} = \arg\min_{\boldsymbol{z}} \ g(\boldsymbol{z}) + \sum_{i=1}^{N}(-\boldsymbol{z}^T \boldsymbol{\lambda}_i^k + \frac{\rho}{2}\|\boldsymbol{x}_i^{k+1} - \boldsymbol{z}\|^2), \tag{5}$$

$$\boldsymbol{\lambda}_i^{k+1} = \boldsymbol{\lambda}_i^k + \rho(\boldsymbol{x}_i^{k+1} - \boldsymbol{z}^{k+1}), \tag{6}$$

where $\|\cdot\|$ denotes l_2 norm.

The entire procedure illustrates the exchange of information between data providers and the central server. It is obvious that the classifier $\boldsymbol{x}_i^{k+1}$ can be locally updated for each party. This is because the whole problem has been divided into N subproblems which can be solved in parallel. Each party broadcasts $\boldsymbol{x}_i^{k+1}$ it owns to the central server. Then, the central server solves subproblems (5) and (6) and gets $\boldsymbol{z}^{k+1}$ and then dual variable $\boldsymbol{\lambda}_i^{k+1}$. Finally, the optimal parameter can be obtained after several iterations.

Differential Privacy. Differential privacy [7] is a widely-adopted privacy notion, which can be used to quantify the privacy risk of each individual record in a dataset. Mathematically, differential privacy is defined as follows

Definition 1. *A randomized algorithm $\mathcal{A}$ is (ϵ, δ)-differentially private if for all datasets $D, D' \in \mathbb{D}$ that differ in a single element and for all $s \in \Omega$, where Ω is the output space of $\mathcal{A}$, we have*

$$Pr(\mathcal{A}(D) = s) \le e^\epsilon Pr(\mathcal{A}(D') = s) + \delta.$$

Differential privacy concentrates on the output distribution of a mechanism when there exists the participation of an individual. Smaller values of ϵ mean stronger privacy guarantees of $\mathcal{A}$. The most common mechanism for achieving differential privacy is Gaussian Mechanism [6].

Definition 2. *Consider a function $q\colon \mathbb{D} \to \mathcal{R}^p$ whose l_2-sensitivity is $\Delta_2(q) = \sup_{D \sim D'}\|q(D) - q(D')\|$. The Gaussian Mechanism is defined as: $\mathcal{M}(D, q, \epsilon) = q(D) + \mathcal{N}(0, \sigma^2 I_p)$ where $\mathcal{N}(0, \sigma^2 I_p)$ is a zero mean isotropic Gaussian Distribution with $\sigma \ge \frac{\sqrt{2\ln(1.25/\delta)}\Delta_2(q)}{\epsilon}$. Then, the Gaussian mechanism preserves (ϵ, δ)-differential privacy.*

2.3 Distributed Stochastic ADMM

Traditional ADMM [4,22] is quite computationally expensive when we have large size of the dataset, since solving subproblem (4) needs to visit all the M data points at each iteration. In this paper, we extend the stochastic ADMM (SCAS-ADMM [23]) into a distributed setting to highly reduce the computation cost.

Algorithm 1. Distributed Stochastic ADMM

1: **Algorithm of the i-th data provider:**
2: **Input:** Dataset $D_i = \{(a_{im}, y_{im})\}_{m=1}^M$, initialize x_i^0 for all agents i, $\zeta = 2\eta - \frac{4\eta}{1-2\eta v_L}$, $\xi = \frac{4\eta}{1-2\eta v_L}$.
3: **for** $k = 0, 1, \cdots, K - 1$ **do**
4:     Compute $\hat{u}_i = \nabla f_i(x_i^k) = \frac{1}{M} \sum_{m=1}^M \nabla l_{im}(x_i^k)$;
        $\tilde{v}_i = x_i^k$;
        $v_i^0 = \tilde{v}_i$;
5:     **for** $s = 1, \cdots, S - 1$ **do**
6:         Randomly pick a data point $(a_{im^s}, y_{im^s}) \in D_i$;
7:         $g_i^s = \nabla l_{im^s}(v_i^s) - \nabla l_{im^s}(\tilde{v}_i) + \hat{u}_i + \lambda_i^k + \rho(v_i^s - z^k)$
8:         $v_i^{s+1} = v_i^s - \eta g_i^s$;
9:         $\hat{v}_i^{s+1} = \frac{\zeta v_i^s + \xi v_i^{s+1}}{2\eta}$;
10:     **end for**
11:     $x_i^{k+1} = \frac{1}{s} \sum_{s=0}^{S-1} \hat{v}_i^{s+1}$;
12:     Send x_i^{k+1} to the central server;
13: **end for**
14: **Algorithm of the central server:**
15: Initialize z^0, λ_i^0 and broadcast them to the providers;
16: **for** $k = 0, 1, \cdots, K - 1$ **do**
17:     $z^{k+1} = \arg\min_z g(z) + \sum_{i=1}^N (-z^T \lambda_i^k + \frac{\rho}{2} \|x_i^{k+1} - z\|^2)$;
18:     $\lambda_i^{k+1} = \lambda_i^k + \rho(x_i^{k+1} - z^{k+1})$;
19: **end for**
20: **Output:** $\{x_i^K\}_{i=1}^N$, z^K;

Since distributed SCAS-ADMM just needs to utilize several data points at each iteration to achieve distributed learning, it is quite computation efficient[1].

Before stating the details of distributed stochastic ADMM, we first define the following functions

$$L_i(x_i) = f_i(x_i) + g(z^k) + (x_i - z^k)^T \lambda_i^k + \frac{\rho}{2} \|x_i - z^k\|^2,$$

$$\hat{L}_{im}(x_i) = l_{im}(x_i) + g(z^k) + (x_i - z^k)^T \lambda_i^k + \frac{\rho}{2} \|x_i - z^k\|^2.$$

The following Lemma shows the convexity of above functions.

Lemma 1. *If $f_i(\cdot)$ is μ_f-strongly convex, and $l_{im}(\cdot)$ is convex, G-Lipschitz and has L_m-Lipschitz continuous gradient, then we have $f_i(x)$ is v_f-smooth, where $v_f = \max_m L_m$, and $L_i(x)$ is both v_L-smooth and μ_L-strongly convex. Moreover, $\hat{L}_{im}(x_i)$ is v_L-smooth.*

Proof. See Appendix A.1.

The details of distributed stochastic ADMM are summarized in Algorithm 1. To be specific, after receiving updated variable z^k and λ_i^k from the server,

---

[1] The specific results of computation cost and memory cost refer to [23].

each data provider updates its local variable x_i^{k+1} at iteration k by optimizing subproblem (4) through the SVRG method [13]. At the beginning of each iteration k, the gradient $\hat{u}_i = \nabla f_i(x_i^k) = \frac{1}{M} \sum_{m=1}^{M} \nabla l_{im}(x_i^k)$ is computed using a past parameter estimate x_i^k. For each inner iteration s, the approximate gradient $g_i^s = \nabla l_{im^s}(v_i^s) - \nabla l_{im^s}(\tilde{v}_i) + \hat{u}_i + \lambda_i^k + \rho(v_i^s - z^k)$ is used to iteratively update v_i^{s+1} with a step size η. And then, we adopt the convex combination to improve the convergence rate. Hence, the subproblem (4) reduces to $x_i^{k+1} = \frac{1}{s} \sum_{s=0}^{S-1} \hat{v}_i^{s+1}$. Then, all the data providers broadcast their x_i^{k+1} to the central server which computes z^{k+1} and λ_i^{k+1}. The whole procedure ends when the number of iterations exceeds a maximum value K. However, while there is no direct exchange of data among data providers, the sequence of iterations broadcasted by a provider may reveal sensitive information through the output of the local learning.

2.4   Privacy Concerns

In our problem setting, there is no need to send the dataset stored at each data provider to the central server directly, while the risk of information leakage still exists. We assume that an adversary can eavesdrop all communications between data providers and the server. In some cases, the adversary using model inversion attack [8] may be able to obtain sensitive information about the private data points of the training dataset by observing the local learning parameter from the provider at iteration k and the final output model parameters of the distributed algorithm. To mitigate this risk, we develop a differentially private algorithm that provides differential privacy for all of the intermediate parameters. If the adversary collects all the intermediate computational results of a provider during communications with the server and the final output of the algorithm, the privacy of local data points at each data provider is still protected.

3   Distributed Stochastic ADMM with Differential Privacy

In this section, we propose our novel algorithm PS-ADMM, which integrates differential privacy into distributed stochastic ADMM. In order to provide differential privacy in distributed stochastic ADMM algorithm, we use the noisy gradient that adds Gaussian noise to the gradient updates of subproblem (4). To analyze the privacy guarantee of PS-ADMM, we consider the moments accountant method [1] of computing privacy loss during a iterative process, which is shown in Theorem 1.

Theorem 1. *There exist constants c_1 and c_2 such that given the sampling probability $q = l/M$ and the number of steps K, for any $\epsilon < c_1 q^2 K$ and for the G-Lipschitz loss function, a differentially private stochastic gradient algorithm with batch size l that injects Gaussian Noise with standard deviation $G\sigma$ to the*

Algorithm 2. Differentially Private Stochastic ADMM (PS-ADMM)

1: **Algorithm of the i-th data provider:**
2: **Input:** Dataset $D_i = \{(a_{im}, y_{im})\}_{m=1}^M$, initialize x_i^0 for all agents i, $\zeta = 2\eta -$
$\frac{4\eta}{1-2\eta v_L}$, $\xi = \frac{4\eta}{1-2\eta v_L}$.
3: **for** $k = 0, 1, \cdots, K - 1$ **do**
4:      Compute $\hat{u}_i = \nabla f_i(x_i^k) = \frac{1}{M} \sum_{m=1}^M \nabla l_{im}(x_i^k)$;
        $\tilde{v}_i = x_i^k$;
        $v_i^0 = \tilde{v}_i$;
5:      **for** $s = 1, \cdots, S - 1$ **do**
6:          Generate Gaussian noise: $\theta_k^s \sim \mathcal{N}(0, (\sigma^2)_k^s I_p)$;
7:          Randomly pick a data point $(a_{im^s}, y_{im^s}) \in D_i$;
8:          $g_i^s = \nabla l_{im^s}(v_i^s) - \nabla l_{im^s}(\tilde{v}_i) + \hat{u}_i + \lambda_i^k + \rho(v_i^s - z^k) + \theta_k^s$
9:          $v_i^{s+1} = v_i^s - \eta g_i^s$;
10:         $\hat{v}_i^{s+1} = \frac{\zeta v_i^s + \xi v_i^{s+1}}{2\eta}$;
11:     **end for**
12:     $x_i^{k+1} = \frac{1}{s} \sum_{s=0}^{S-1} \hat{v}_i^{s+1}$;
13:     Send x_i^{k+1} to the central server;
14: **end for**
15: **Algorithm of the central server:**
16: Initialize z^0, λ_i^0 and broadcast them to the providers;
17: **for** $k = 0, 1, \cdots, K - 1$ **do**
18:     $z^{k+1} = \arg\min_z g(z) + \sum_{i=1}^N (-z^T \lambda_i^k + \frac{\rho}{2} \|x_i^{k+1} - z\|^2)$;
19:     $\lambda_i^{k+1} = \lambda_i^k + \rho(x_i^{k+1} - z^{k+1})$;
20: **end for**
21: **Output:** $\{x_i^K\}_{i=1}^N, z^K$;

---

gradients, is (ϵ, δ)-differentially private for any $\delta > 0$, if we choose

$$\sigma \geq c_2 \frac{q\sqrt{K \log(1/\delta)}}{\epsilon}. \tag{8}$$

The differentially private stochastic ADMM (PS-ADMM) is shown in Algorithm 2. Details of PS-ADMM are summarized as follows: At iteration k, each data provider utilizes the SVRG method to solve subproblem (4) in order to obtain the local classifier x_i^{k+1}. For the inner iteration s at this iteration, the i-th data provider generates a zero mean Gaussian noise θ_k^s with variance $(\sigma^2)_k^s$ to perturb the approximate gradient g_i^s, and by averaging $\hat{v}_i^{s+1}$ of all S inner iterations, the i-th data provider gets a differential private local classifier x_i^{k+1}. During the iteration of SVRG method, we adopt the convex combination to increase the convergence rate. In addition, we employ the iteration average to improve the convergence of ADMM. And then data providers send all differentially private $\{x_i^{k+1}\}_{i=1}^N$ to the server. The server will update z^{k+1} and $\{\lambda_i^{k+1}\}_{i=1}^N$ by solving subproblems (5) and (6) after receiving all of the local parameters $\{x_i^{k+1}\}_{i=1}^N$. Next, each data provider updates its private local parameter by using updated variable z^{k+1} and $\{\lambda_i^{k+1}\}_{i=1}^N$ from the central server. The iterative process will continue until reaching K rounds of communication between server and data provider.

During this iterative process, the shared local classifiers $\{x_i^{k+1}\}_{i=1}^N$ may reveal sensitive information about local dataset D_i of data provider i. Thus, we need to show that PS-ADMM guarantees differential privacy with local classifiers $\{x_i^{k+1}\}_{i=1}^N$. Since we use Gaussian mechanism to add noise, we should give the l_2 sensitivity estimation of the approximate gradient g_i^s at first. According to [19], the sensitivity of g_i^s is $\Delta_2 \leq 3G$, where G is the lipschitz constant of loss function $l_{im}(\cdot)$. The following theorem shows that our algorithm provides (ϵ, δ)-differential privacy[2].

Theorem 2. *For $\epsilon \leq c_1 \frac{KS}{M^2}$ and $\delta \in (0,1)$, and the noise θ_k^s is sampled from zero mean Gaussian distribution with variance*

$$(\sigma^2)_k^s = c\frac{G^2 KS \ln(1/\delta)}{M^2 \epsilon^2},$$

then, PS-ADMM algorithm satisfies (ϵ, δ)-differential privacy, where c_1 and c are some constants.

In a distributed and iterative algorithm, the output of the algorithm includes all of exchanged intermediate results and the end result. Since the adversary may perform inference by using all intermediate results, the privacy leakage accumulates over time through the iterative process. Different from the prior study in [22], where the privacy leakage is only bounded at a single iteration, our proposed differentially private algorithm PS-ADMM provides (ϵ, δ)-differential privacy guarantee for all of the intermediate results exchanged during the iterative procedure and the end result.

4   Convergence Analysis

In this section, we discuss the convergence and the utility bound of the proposed PS-ADMM algorithm. To define the convergence and utility bound, we will use the following criterion

$$\mathbb{E}[P(\boldsymbol{u}) - P(\boldsymbol{u}^*) + \sum_{i=1}^N \tau_i \|\boldsymbol{x}_i - \boldsymbol{z}\|] \quad \forall \tau_i > 0, \tag{9}$$

which is the same as the variational inequality used in [16] and [12]. In criterion (9), $\boldsymbol{u} = \{\boldsymbol{x}_1; \boldsymbol{x}_2; ...; \boldsymbol{x}_N; \boldsymbol{z}\}$ and $P(\boldsymbol{u}) = \sum_{i=1}^N f_i(\boldsymbol{x}_i) + g(\boldsymbol{z})$, and $\boldsymbol{u}^*$ is the optimal solution of problem 2.

Similar to most iterative distributed optimization algorithms [11], distributed stochastic ADMM only converges in a probabilistic sense when the number of iterations $K \to \infty$. Therefore, we can now prove the following expected suboptimality of the proposed algorithm according to the criterion (9).

---

[2] The proof of Theorem 2 is very similar to the B.2 in [19]. Due to the space limitation, we omit the detail of it.

Theorem 3 (Convergence). *If $f_i(x)$ is μ_f-strongly convex, $\tau_i > 0$ and η satisfies $0 < \eta \le \frac{1}{2v_L}$, $0 < \eta \le \frac{4\mu_L - 4\rho - 3\mu_f}{8v_L^2 + 2\mu_f v_L}$, $1 - \frac{\rho\xi}{2} - \frac{\mu_f\xi}{4} + \frac{4\eta^2 v_L^2 S}{1 - 2\eta v_L} \le \frac{S\eta\mu_f}{2}$, the expected suboptimality of PS-ADMM is bounded after K iterations*

$$
\mathbb{E}\left\{ P(u^{k+1}) - P(u^*) + \sum_{i=1}^{N} \tau_i \|\hat{x}_i - \hat{z}\| \right\}
$$

$$
\le \sum_{i=1}^{N} \left\{ \frac{\mu_f}{4K} \|x_i^0 - x_i^*\|^2 + \frac{\rho}{2K} \|z^0 - z^*\|^2 + \frac{1}{2\rho K} (\|\lambda_i^0\|^2 + \tau_i^2) \right\}
$$

$$
+ \frac{2\eta}{1 - 2\eta v_L} \frac{pKS \ln(1/\delta)}{M^2 \epsilon^2}, \tag{10}
$$

where $P(u) = \sum_{i=1}^{N} f_i(\hat{x}_i) + g(\hat{z})$, $\hat{x}_i = \frac{1}{K} \sum_{k=0}^{K-1} x_i^{k+1}$ and $\hat{z} = \frac{1}{K} \sum_{k=0}^{K-1} z^{k+1}$ and (x_i^*, z^*) is the optimal solution.

Proof. See Appendix A.3.

As K increases, the first term in (10) decreases, though the second term in (10) increases. Then, the minimized suboptimality of the proposed algorithm exists as we choose an optimal K. Hence, the following theorem gives the utility bound when choosing an optimal K.

Theorem 4 (Utility Bound). *If $f_i(x)$ is μ_f-strongly convex, $\tau_i > 0$ and $S = O(\frac{v_f}{\mu_f})$ is sufficiently large, and η satisfies condition in Theorem 3, then the utility bound of PS-ADMM is bounded if we choose $K = O\left(\frac{M\epsilon}{G} \sqrt{\frac{\mu_f}{v_f p \ln(1/\delta)}} \right)$,*

$$
\mathbb{E}\left\{ P(\hat{u}) - P(u^*) + \sum_{i=1}^{N} \tau_i \|\hat{x}_i - \hat{z}\| \right\} \le O\left(\frac{NG}{M\epsilon} \sqrt{\frac{p \ln(1/\delta) v_f}{\mu_f}} \right),
$$

where $P(u) = \sum_{i=1}^{N} f_i(\hat{x}_i) + g(\hat{z})$, $\hat{x}_i = \frac{1}{K} \sum_{k=0}^{K-1} x_i^{k+1}$ and $\hat{z} = \frac{1}{K} \sum_{k=0}^{K-1} z^{k+1}$ and (x_i^*, z^*) is the optimal solution.

Proof. See Appendix A.4.

5 Performance Analysis

We conduct simulations on the same dataset as [22], i.e, the Adult dataset from UCI Machine Learning Repository [5], which contains 48,842 samples with 14 features like age, sex, education, etc. The goal is to predict whether the annual income is more than 50k or not. Before the simulation, we preprocess the data by normalizing all numerical attributes such that l_2-norm is at most 1 and transform the label {>50k, ≤50k} to {+1, −1}. We separate the whole dataset for training and testing (the ratio is around 70%:30%). And for training samples, we separate them into five parts representing five data providers ($N = 5$). Consistent with

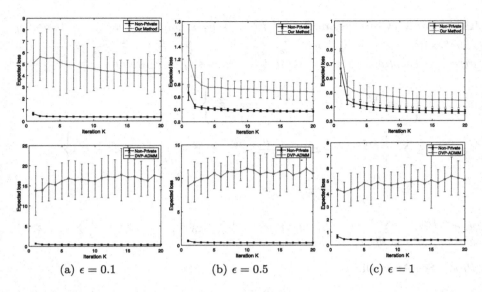

Fig. 2. The convergence comparison for different privacy budgets ϵ. (Color figure online)

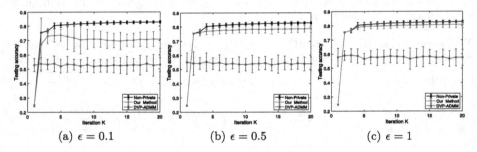

Fig. 3. The accuracy comparison for different privacy budgets ϵ. (Color figure online)

[22], we use the logistic loss $l(z) = log(1 + exp(z))$. And N data providers collaboratively solve the following regularized logistic regression

$$\min_{\boldsymbol{x}} \sum_{i=1}^{N} \frac{1}{M} \sum_{m=1}^{M} log(1 + exp(-y_{im}\boldsymbol{x}^T \boldsymbol{a}_{im})) + R\|\boldsymbol{x}\|^2.$$

We inspect the convergence and accuracy of our approach by comparing with the dual variable perturbation (DVP-ADMM) method adopted in [22]. The convergence is measured by expected loss defined by $\frac{1}{M} \sum_{i=1}^{N} \sum_{m=1}^{M} log(1 + exp(-y_{im}\boldsymbol{x}_{i,k}^T \boldsymbol{a}_{im}))$. The accuracy is defined by classification error rate over testing dataset. For the DVP-ADMM algorithm, the parameters are the same as in settings of [22].

For each parameter setting, we conduct 20 independent runs of the algorithm. For each time, both the mean and standard deviation of the expected loss and the accuracy are recorded. The smaller the standard deviation is, the greater is the stability of the algorithm. In all experiments, we set the regularization coefficient $R = 0.0001$, and $\delta = 0.001$.

Figures 2 and 3 compare our approach with DVP-ADMM method and the non-private algorithm for expected loss and testing accuracy under different privacy budgets. The non-private algorithm here is a stochastic ADMM without adding noise. As the number of iterations increases, we see that our approach (red) has achieved much less expected loss and higher testing accuracy than DVP-ADMM (blue) for all three cases of privacy budget ϵ. Hence, our method can outperform DVP-ADMM (blue) significantly. However, the excepted loss does not always monotonically decrease as too much noise introduced in PS-ADMM affects the convergence, especially when ϵ is small. While privacy budget ϵ is large enough (e.g., $\epsilon = 0.5$), it follows the same trend as non-private ADMM and still outperforms DVP-ADMM.

6   Conclusions

In this paper, we proposed a novel algorithm called PS-ADMM by extending SCAS-ADMM into a distributed setting and adding differentially private Gaussian noise to the gradient updates. Thus, the sensitive information stored in the training dataset at each data provider can be protected against an adversary who can eavesdrop the communications between the data provider and the server. The convergence and utility bound of PS-ADMM have been analyzed theoretically. We empirically demonstrate that PS-ADMM outperforms other differentially private ADMM algorithms under the same privacy guarantee.

Acknowledgement. This work of J. Ding, and M. Pan was supported in part by the U.S. Natural Science Foundation under grants US CNS-1613661, CNS-1646607, CNS-1702850, and CNS-1801925. This work of Y. Gong was partly supported by the US National Science Foundation under grant CNS-1850523. This work of H. Zhang was partly supported by the National Natural Science Foundation of China (Grant No. 61822104, 61771044), Beijing Natural Science Foundation (No. L172025, L172049), and 111 Project (No. B170003).

A   Appendix

The approximate gradient g_i^s can be written as $g_i^s = b_i^s + q_i^s$, where

$$b_i^s = \nabla l_{im^s}(v_i^s) - \nabla l_{im^s}(\tilde{v}_i) + \hat{u}_i + \theta_i^s,$$
$$q_i^s = \lambda_i^k + \rho(v_i^s - z^k).$$

A.1 Proof of Lemma 1

Proof. Since each $l_{im}(x)$ is convex, G-Lipschitz and has L_m-Lipschitz continuous gradient, for any x_1 and x_2, there exists $L_m > 0$ such that

$$l_{im}(x_1) \le l_{im}(x_2) + (x_2 - x_1)^T \nabla l_{im}(x_2) + \frac{L_m}{2}\|x_2 - x_1\|^2.$$

We can see that $f_i(x)$ is v_f-smooth, with $f_i(x_1) \le f_i(x_2) + (x_2 - x_1)^T \nabla f_i(x_1) + \frac{v_f}{2}\|x_2 - x_1\|^2$, where $v_f = \max_m L_m$. Then, we can have

$$\|\nabla L_i(x_1) - \nabla L_i(x_2)\| = \|\nabla f_i(x_1) - \nabla f_i(x_2) + \rho(x_1 - x_2)\|$$
$$\le \|\nabla f_i(x_1) - \nabla f_i(x_2)\| + \|\rho(x_1 - x_2)\| \le (v_f + \rho)\|x_1 - x_2\| \le v_L\|x_1 - x_2\|,$$

where we let $v_L \ge v_f + \rho$. Thus, $L_i(x)$ and $\hat{L}_m(x)$ are v_L-smooth. Moreover, it is obvious to see that $L_i(x)$ is μ_L-strongly convex with $\mu_L \le \mu_f + \rho$.

A.2 Basic Lemmas

Lemma 2. *The variance of g_i^s satisfies*

$$\mathbb{E}(\|g_i^s\|^2) \le 2\mathbb{E}(\|\nabla \hat{L}_{im^s}(v_i^s) - \nabla \hat{L}_{im^s}(\tilde{v}_i)\|^2) + 4\|\nabla L_i(v_i^s)\|^2 + 4(\sigma^2)_k^s p$$
$$\le 4v_L^2(\|v_i^s - x_i\|^2 + \|\tilde{v}_i - x_i\|^2) + 4\|\nabla L_i(v_i^s)\|^2 + 4(\sigma^2)_k^s p.$$

Proof. Notice that

$$\begin{aligned}
g_i^s &= b_i^s + q_i^s \\
&= \nabla l_{im^s}(v_i^s) - \nabla l_{im^s}(\tilde{v}_i) + \hat{u}_i + q_i^s + \theta_i^s \\
&= \nabla l_{im^s}(v_i^s) + q_i^s - \nabla l_{im^s}(\tilde{v}_i) - \hat{q}_i + \hat{u}_i + \hat{q}_i + \theta_i^s \\
&= \nabla \hat{L}_{im^s}(v_i^s) - \nabla \hat{L}_{im^s}(\tilde{v}_i) + \nabla L_i(\tilde{v}_i) + \theta_i^s.
\end{aligned}$$

Hence, the variance of g_i^s can be bounded as

$$\begin{aligned}
\mathbb{E}(\|g_i^s\|^2) &= \mathbb{E}\|\nabla \hat{L}_{im^s}(v_i^s) - \nabla \hat{L}_{im^s}(\tilde{v}_i) + \nabla L_i(\tilde{v}_i) + \theta_i^s\|^2 \\
&\le 2\mathbb{E}(\|\nabla \hat{L}_{im^s}(v_i^s) - \nabla \hat{L}_{im^s}(\tilde{v}_i) - (\nabla L_i(v_i^s) - \nabla L_i(\tilde{v}_i)\|^2)) + 2\mathbb{E}\|\nabla L_i(v_i^s) + \theta_i^s\|^2 \\
&\le 2\mathbb{E}(\|\nabla \hat{L}_{im^s}(v_i^s) - \nabla \hat{L}_{im^s}(\tilde{v}_i)\|^2) + 2\mathbb{E}\|\nabla L_i(v_i^s) + \theta_i^s\|^2 \\
&\le 2\mathbb{E}(\|\nabla \hat{L}_{im^s}(v_i^s) - \nabla \hat{L}_{im^s}(\tilde{v}_i)\|^2) + 4\|\nabla L_i(v_i^s)\|^2 + 4\mathbb{E}\|\theta_i^s\|^2 \\
&\le 2v_L^2\|v_i^s - \tilde{v}_i\|^2 + 4\|\nabla L_i(v_i^s)\|^2 + 4(\sigma^2)_k^s p \\
&\le 4v_L^2(\|v_i^s - x_i\|^2 + \|\tilde{v}_i - x_i\|^2) + 4\|\nabla L_i(v_i^s)\|^2 + 4(\sigma^2)_k^s p,
\end{aligned}$$

where the first inequality uses $\|a+b\|^2 \le 2\|a\|^2 + 2\|b\|^2$ and the second inequality uses $\mathbb{E}\|x_i - \mathbb{E}x_i\|^2 = \mathbb{E}\|x_i\|^2 - \|\mathbb{E}x_i\|^2 \le \mathbb{E}\|x_i\|^2$.

Lemma 3. *For $0 < \eta < \frac{1}{2v_L}$, we have*

$$\begin{aligned}
\|\nabla L_i(v_i^s)\|^2 \le{} & \frac{1}{\eta - 2\eta^2 v_L}\{L_i(v_i^s) - \mathbb{E}[L_i(v_i^{s+1})]\} \\
& + \frac{\eta v_L}{1 - 2\eta v_L}\mathbb{E}(\|\nabla \hat{L}_{im^s}(v_i^s) - \nabla \hat{L}_{im^s}(\tilde{v}_i)\|^2 + 2(\sigma^2)_k^s p).
\end{aligned}$$

Proof.

$$L_i(v_i^{s+1}) \le L_i(v_i^s) + (v_i^{s+1} - v_i^s)^T \nabla L_i(v_i^s) + \frac{v_L}{2}\|v_i^{s+1} - v_i^s\|^2.$$

Taking expectation on both sides, we obtain

$$\mathbb{E}[L_i(v_i^{s+1})] \le L_i(v_i^s) - \eta\nabla\|L_i(v_i^s)\|^2 + \frac{\eta^2 v_L}{2}\mathbb{E}(\|g_i^s\|^2)$$
$$\le L_i(v_i^s) - \eta\nabla\|L_i(v_i^s)\|^2 + \eta^2 v_L[\mathbb{E}(\|\nabla\hat{L}_{im^s}(v_i^s) - \nabla\hat{L}_{im^s}(\tilde{v}_i)\|^2)$$
$$+ 2\|\nabla L_i(v_i^s)\|^2 + 2(\sigma^2)_k^s p].$$

Then, we have

$$(\eta - 2\eta^2 v_L)\|\nabla L_i(v_i^s)\|^2 \le L_i(v_i^s) - \mathbb{E}[L_i(v_i^{s+1})]$$
$$+ \eta^2 v_L \mathbb{E}(\|\nabla\hat{L}_{im^s}(v_i^s) - \nabla\hat{L}_{im^s}(\tilde{v}_i)\|^2 + 2(\sigma^2)_k^s p).$$

By choosing $\eta < 1/(2v_L)$, we get

$$\|\nabla L_i(v_i^s)\|^2 \le \frac{1}{\eta - 2\eta^2 v_L}\{L_i(v_i^s) - \mathbb{E}[L_i(v_i^{s+1})]\}$$
$$+ \frac{\eta v_L}{1 - 2\eta v_L}\mathbb{E}(\|\nabla\hat{L}_{im^s}(v_i^s) - \nabla\hat{L}_{im^s}(\tilde{v}_i)\|^2 + 2(\sigma^2)_k^s p).$$

Lemma 4.

$$\mathbb{E}\|v_i^{s+1} - x_i\|^2 + 2\eta(v_i^s - x_i)^T\nabla L_i(v_i^s) + \frac{4\eta}{1 - 2\eta v_L}(\mathbb{E}[L_i(v_i^{s+1})] - L_i(x_i))$$
$$\le \|v_i^s - x_i\|^2 + \frac{2\eta^2}{1 - 2\eta v_L}\mathbb{E}\|\nabla\hat{L}_{im^s}(v_i^s) + \nabla\hat{L}_{im^s}(\tilde{v}_i)\|^2$$
$$+ \frac{4\eta}{1 - 2\eta v_L}[L_i(v_i^s) - L_i(x_i)] + \frac{2\eta^2}{1 - 2\eta v_L}(\sigma^2)_k^s p.$$

Proof. We have $\mathbb{E}(b_i^s) = \nabla f_i(v_i^s)$ and this leads to

$$\mathbb{E}\|v_i^{s+1} - x_i\|^2 \le \|v_i^s - x_i\|^2 - 2\eta(v_i^s - x_i)^T\mathbb{E}(g_i^s) + \eta^2\mathbb{E}(\|g_i^s\|^2)$$
$$\le \|v_i^s - x_i\|^2 - 2\eta(v_i^s - x_i)^T\mathbb{E}(\nabla f_i(v_i^s) + q_i^s) + \eta^2\mathbb{E}(\|g_i^s\|^2)$$
$$\le \|v_i^s - x_i\|^2 - 2\eta(v_i^s - x_i)^T\nabla L_i(v_i^s) + \eta^2\mathbb{E}(\|g_i^s\|^2).$$

Then, we have

$$\mathbb{E}\|v_i^{s+1} - x_i\|^2 + 2\eta(v_i^s - x_i)^T\nabla L_i(v_i^s)$$
$$\le \|v_i^s - x_i\|^2 + 2\eta^2\mathbb{E}(\|\nabla\hat{L}_{im^s}(v_i^s) - \nabla\hat{L}_{im^s}(\tilde{v}_i)\|^2) + 4\eta^2\|\nabla L_i(v_i^s)\|^2$$
$$+ 4\eta^2(\sigma^2)_k^s p.$$

According to Lemma 3, we obtain

$$\mathbb{E}\|v_i^{s+1} - x_i\|^2 + 2\eta(v_i^s - x_i)^T \nabla L_i(v_i^s) + \frac{4\eta}{1 - 2\eta v_L}(\mathbb{E}[L_i(v_i^{s+1})] - L_i(x_i))$$

$$\leq \|v_i^s - x_i\|^2 + \frac{2\eta^2}{1 - 2\eta v_L}\mathbb{E}\|\nabla\hat{L}_{im^s}(v_i^s) + \nabla\hat{L}_{im^s}(\tilde{v}_i)\|^2$$

$$+ \frac{4\eta}{1 - 2\eta v_L}[L_i(v_i^s) - L_i(x_i)] + \frac{2\eta^2}{1 - 2\eta v_L}(\sigma^2)_k^s p.$$

Lemma 5.

$$g(z^{k+1}) - g(z) - \sum_{i=1}^{N}(z^{k+1} - z)^T \alpha_i^{k+1}$$

$$\leq \frac{\rho}{2}(\|z^k - z\|^2 - \|z^{k+1} - z^k\|^2 - \|z^{k+1} - z\|^2)$$

where $\alpha_i^{k+1} = \lambda_i^k + \rho(x_i^{k+1} - z^k)$.

Proof. By deriving the optimal conditions of the minimization problem in (5), we have

$$g(z^{k+1}) - g(z) \leq -(z^{k+1} - z)^T \sum_{i=1}^{N}[-\lambda_i^k + \rho(x_i^{k+1} - z^{k+1})].$$

Then, by using the notation $\alpha_i^{k+1} = \lambda_i^k + \rho(x_i^{k+1} - z^k)$, we obtain

$$g(z^{k+1}) - g(z) - \sum_{i=1}^{N}(z^{k+1} - z)^T \alpha_i^{k+1} \leq \rho(z^k - z^{k+1})^T(z^{k+1} - z))$$

$$\leq \frac{\rho}{2}(\|z^k - z\|^2 - \|z^{k+1} - z^k\|^2 - \|z^{k+1} - z\|^2).$$

Lemma 6.

$$(\alpha_i^{k+1} - \alpha_i)^T[-(x_i^{k+1} - z^{k+1})]$$

$$\leq \frac{1}{2\rho}(\|\lambda_i^k - \alpha_i\|^2 - \|\lambda_i^{k+1} - \alpha_i\|^2) + \frac{\rho}{2}\|z^k - z^{k+1}\|^2$$

where $\alpha_i^{k+1} = \lambda_i^k + \rho(x_i^{k+1} - z^k)$.

Proof.

$$(\alpha_i^{k+1} - \alpha_i)^T[-(x_i^{k+1} - z^{k+1})] = \frac{1}{\rho}(\alpha_i^{k+1} - \alpha_i)^T(\lambda_i^k - \lambda_i^{k+1})$$

$$= \frac{1}{2\rho}(\|\alpha_i^{k+1} - \lambda_i^{k+1}\|^2 - \|\alpha_i^{k+1} - \lambda_i^k\|^2 + \|\lambda_i^k - \alpha_i\|^2 - \|\lambda_i^{k+1} - \alpha_i\|^2)$$

$$\leq \frac{1}{2\rho}(\|\lambda_i^k - \alpha_i\|^2 - \|\lambda_i^{k+1} - \alpha_i\|^2) + \frac{\rho}{2}\|z^k - z^{k+1}\|^2.$$

Lemma 7. *Assume $f_i(\cdot)$ be μ_f-strongly convex, and let x_i^{k+1}, z^k and λ_i^k be generated by the proposed algorithm. For η satisfies $0 < \eta \le \frac{1}{2v_L}$, $0 < \eta \le \frac{4\mu_L - 4\rho - 3\mu_f}{8v_L^2 + 2\mu_f v_L}$, $1 - \frac{\rho\xi}{2} - \frac{\mu_f\xi}{4} + \frac{4\eta^2 v_L^2 S}{1 - 2\eta v_L} \le \frac{S\eta\mu_f}{2}$, the following holds if*

$$\mathbb{E}[f_i(x_i^{k+1}) - f_i(x_i) + (x_i^{k+1} - x_i)^T \alpha_i^{k+1}] \le \frac{\mu_f}{4}[\|x_i^k - x_i\|^2 - \|x_i^{k+1} - x_i\|^2]$$
$$+ \frac{2\eta}{1 - 2\eta v_L}(\sigma^2)_k^s p$$

where $\alpha_i^{k+1} = \lambda_i^k + \rho(x_i^{k+1} - z^k)$.

Proof. Using Lemma 4 and the strong convexity of $L_i(v_i)$, we have

$$\mathbb{E}\|v_i^{s+1} - x_i\|^2 + \zeta(v_i^s - x_i)^T \nabla L_i(v_i^s) + \xi(\mathbb{E}[L_i(v_i^{s+1})] - L_i(x_i))$$
$$+ \frac{\mu_L\xi}{2}\|v_i^s - x_i\|^2$$
$$\le \frac{2\eta^2}{1 - 2\eta v_L}[\mathbb{E}\|\nabla\hat{L}_{im^s}(v_i^s) + \nabla\hat{L}_{im^s}(\tilde{v}_i)\|^2 + (\sigma^2)_k^s p] + \|v_i^s - x_i\|^2,$$

where $\zeta = 2\eta - \frac{4\eta}{1 - 2\eta v_L}$, $\xi = \frac{4\eta}{1 - 2\eta v_L}$.
Then, we obtain

$$(1 - \frac{\rho\xi}{2} - \frac{\mu_f\xi}{4})\mathbb{E}\|v_i^{s+1} - x_i\|^2 + \zeta[f_i(v_i^s) - f_i(x_i) + (v_i^s - x_i)^T q_i^s$$
$$+ \frac{\mu_f}{4}\|v_i^s - x_i\|^2] + \xi\mathbb{E}[f_i(v_i^{s+1}) - f_i(x_i) + (v_i^{s+1} - x_i)^T q_i^{s+1}$$
$$+ \frac{\mu_f}{4}\|v_i^{s+1} - x_i\|^2]$$
$$\le (1 + \frac{4\eta^2 v_L^2}{1 - 2\eta v_L} - \frac{\mu_L\xi}{2} - \frac{\mu_f\zeta}{4})\|v_i^s - x_i\|^2 + \frac{4\eta^2 v_L^2}{1 - 2\eta v_L}\|\tilde{v}_i - x_i\|^2$$
$$+ \frac{2\eta^2}{1 - 2\eta v_L}(\sigma^2)_k^s p,$$

where we apply Lemma 2 and $L_i(v_i^s) - L_i(x_i) = f_i(v_i^s) - f_i(x_i) + (v_i^s - x_i)^T q_i^s - \frac{\rho}{2}\|v_i^s - x_i\|^2$ to obtain the inequality. Hence, we choose $\eta \le \frac{4\mu_L - 4\rho - 3\mu_f}{8v_L^2 + 2\mu_f v_L}$ so that $1 - \frac{\rho\xi}{2} - \frac{\mu_f\xi}{4} \ge 1 + \frac{4\eta^2 v_L^2}{1 - 2\eta v_L} - \frac{\mu_L\xi}{2} - \frac{\mu_f\zeta}{4}$. We take $\hat{v}_i^{s+1} = \frac{\zeta v_i^s + \xi v_i^{s+1}}{2\eta}$ and we know that $f_i(v_i^s) - f_i(x_i) + (v_i^s - x_i)^T q_i^s$ is convex in v_i^s. By using the Jensen's inequality, we have

$$(1 - \frac{\rho\xi}{2} - \frac{\mu_f\xi}{4})\mathbb{E}\|v_i^{s+1} - x_i\|^2$$
$$+ 2\eta\mathbb{E}[f_i(\hat{v}_i^{s+1}) - f_i(x_i) + (\hat{v}_i^{s+1} - x_i)^T \hat{q}_i^{s+1} + \frac{\mu_f}{4}\|\hat{v}_i^{s+1} - x_i\|^2]$$
$$\le (1 - \frac{\rho\xi}{2} - \frac{\mu_f\xi}{4})\|v_i^s - x_i\|^2 + \frac{4\eta^2 v_L^2}{1 - 2\eta v_L}\|\tilde{v}_i - x_i\|^2 + \frac{2\eta^2}{1 - 2\eta v_L}(\sigma^2)_k^s p,$$

where $\hat{q}_i^{s+1} = \lambda_i^k + \rho(\hat{v}_i^{s+1} - z^k)$. Summing from $s = 0, 1, 2, ..., S - 1$ and using $x_i^{k+1} = \frac{1}{s}\sum_{s=0}^{S-1}\hat{v}_i^{s+1}$, we obtain

$$2S\eta\mathbb{E}[f_i(x_i^{k+1}) - f_i(x_i) + (x_i^{k+1} - x_i)^T\alpha_i^{k+1} + \frac{\mu_f}{4}\|x_i^{k+1} - x_i\|^2]$$

$$\leq \frac{2\eta^2 S}{1 - 2\eta v_L}(\sigma^2)_k^s p + (1 - \frac{\rho\xi}{2} - \frac{\mu_f\xi}{4} + \frac{4\eta^2 v_L^2 S}{1 - 2\eta v_L})\|x_i^k - x_i\|^2,$$

where $\alpha_i^{k+1} = \lambda_i^k + \rho(x_i^{k+1} - z^k)$.
Thus, we have

$$\mathbb{E}[f_i(x_i^{k+1}) - f_i(x_i) + (x_i^{k+1} - x_i)^T\alpha_i^{k+1}]$$

$$\leq \frac{1}{2S\eta}(1 - \frac{\rho\xi}{2} - \frac{\mu_f\xi}{4} + \frac{4\eta^2 v_L^2 S}{1 - 2\eta v_L})\|x_i^k - x_i\|^2 - \frac{\mu_f}{4}\mathbb{E}\|x_i^{k+1} - x_i\|^2$$

$$+ \frac{2\eta}{1 - 2\eta v_L}(\sigma^2)_k^s p$$

$$\leq \frac{\mu_f}{4}[\|x_i^k - x_i\|^2 - \|x_i^{k+1} - x_i\|^2] + \frac{2\eta}{1 - 2\eta v_L}(\sigma^2)_k^s p,$$

where we assume $1 - \frac{\rho\xi}{2} - \frac{\mu_f\xi}{4} + \frac{4\eta^2 v_L^2 S}{1 - 2\eta v_L} \leq \frac{S\eta\mu_f}{2}$.

A.3   Proof of Theorem 3

Proof. Combining Lemmas 7, 5 and 6 together and using the convergence criterion (9), we let $w_i^{k+1} = (x_i^{k+1}; z^{k+1}; \alpha_i^{k+1})$, and $\hat{w}_i = \frac{1}{K}\sum_{k=0}^{K-1} w_i^{k+1}$. For any $w = (x_i; z; \lambda_i)$, we have

$$\mathbb{E}[P(u^{k+1}) - P(u) + \sum_{i=1}^{N}(w^{k+1} - w)^T F(w^{k+1})]$$

$$\leq \mathbb{E}\left\{\sum_{i=1}^{N} f_i(x_i^{k+1}) + g(z^{k+1}) - \sum_{i=1}^{N} f_i(x_i) - g(z)\right.$$

$$\left. + \sum_{i=1}^{N}\begin{pmatrix} x_i^{k+1} - x_i \\ z^{k+1} - z \\ \alpha_i^{k+1} - \alpha_i \end{pmatrix}^T\begin{pmatrix} \alpha_i^{k+1} \\ -\alpha_i^{k+1} \\ -(x_i^{k+1} - z^{k+1}) \end{pmatrix}\right\}$$

$$\leq \sum_{i=1}^{N}\left\{\frac{\mu_f}{4}[\|x_i^k - x_i\|^2 - \|x_i^{k+1} - x_i\|^2] + \frac{\rho}{2}(\|z^k - z\|^2 - \|z^{k+1} - z\|^2)\right.$$

$$\left. + \frac{1}{2\rho}(\|\lambda_i^k - \alpha_i\|^2 - \|\lambda_i^{k+1} - \alpha_i\|^2) + \frac{2\eta}{1 - 2\eta v_L}(\sigma^2)_k^s p\right\},$$

where $F(w) = \begin{pmatrix} \alpha_i \\ -\alpha_i \\ -(x_i - z) \end{pmatrix}$.

Summing the inequality over $k = 0, 1, 2, ..., K - 1$ and using the Jensen's inequality, we get

$$\mathbb{E}\left\{ P(\hat{u}^{k+1}) - P(u) + \sum_{i=1}^{N}(\hat{w}_i - w)^T F(\hat{w}_i) \right\}$$

$$\leq \frac{1}{K} \sum_{k=0}^{K-1} \left\{ \mathbb{E}[P(x^{k+1}, z^{k+1}) - P(x, z) + \sum_{i=1}^{N}(w_i^{k+1} - w)^T F(w_i^{k+1})] \right\}$$

$$\leq \sum_{i=1}^{N} \left\{ \frac{\mu_f}{4K}\|x_i^0 - x_i\|^2 + \frac{\rho}{2K}\|z^0 - z\|^2 + \frac{1}{2\rho K}\|\lambda_i^0 - \alpha_i\|^2 \right\}$$

$$+ \frac{2\eta}{1 - 2\eta v_L} \frac{pG^2 KS \ln(1/\delta)}{M^2 \epsilon^2},$$

where $P(\hat{u}) = \sum_{i=1}^{N} f_i(\hat{x}_i) + g(\hat{z})$, $\hat{x}_i = \frac{1}{K}\sum_{k=0}^{K-1} x_i^{k+1}$ and $\hat{z} = \frac{1}{K}\sum_{k=0}^{K-1} z^{k+1}$. If we take $x = x^*, z = z^*$, and $\alpha_i = \tau_i \frac{\hat{x}_i - \hat{z}}{\|\hat{x}_i - \hat{z}\|}$, we have

$$\mathbb{E}\left\{ P(\hat{u}^{k+1}) - P(u^*) + \sum_{i=1}^{N} \tau_i \|\hat{x}_i - \hat{z}\| \right\}$$

$$\leq \sum_{i=1}^{N} \left\{ \frac{\mu_f}{4K}\|x_i^0 - x_i^*\|^2 + \frac{\rho}{2K}\|z^0 - z^*\|^2 + \frac{1}{2\rho K}(\|\lambda_i^0\|^2 + \tau_i^2) \right\}$$

$$+ \frac{2\eta}{1 - 2\eta v_L} \frac{pG^2 KS \ln(1/\delta)}{M^2 \epsilon^2}.$$

A.4 Proof of Theorem 4

By choosing η, which satisfies condition in Theorem 3, and $S = O(\frac{v_f}{\mu_f})$, we can make $A = \frac{\mu_f}{4}\|x_i^0 - x_i^*\|^2 + \frac{\rho}{2}\|z^0 - z^*\|^2 + \frac{1}{2\rho}(\|\lambda_i^0\|^2 + \tau_i^2)$ a constant.

Then, we have

$$\mathbb{E}\left\{ P(\hat{u}^{k+1}) - P(u^*) + \sum_{i=1}^{N} \tau_i \|\hat{x}_i - \hat{z}\| \right\} \leq \frac{NA}{K} + O\left(\frac{NpG^2 K \ln(1/\delta) v_f}{M^2 \epsilon^2 \mu_f} \right).$$

Thus, if we choose $K = O\left(\frac{M\epsilon}{G}\sqrt{\frac{\mu_f}{v_f p \ln(1/\delta)}} \right)$, we have

$$\mathbb{E}\left\{ P(\hat{u}^{k+1}) - P(u^*) + \sum_{i=1}^{N} \tau_i \|\hat{x}_i - \hat{z}\| \right\} \leq O\left(\frac{NG}{M\epsilon}\sqrt{\frac{p \ln(1/\delta) v_f}{\mu_f}} \right).$$

References

1. Abadi, M., et al.: Deep learning with differential privacy. In: Proceedings of the ACM SIGSAC Conference on Computer and Communications Security, Vienna, October 2016, pp. 308–318 (2016)

2. Bekkerman, R., Bilenko, M., Langford, J.: Scaling Up Machine Learning: Parallel and Distributed Approaches. Cambridge University Press, Cambridge (2011)
3. Bertsekas, D.P., Tsitsiklis, J.N.: Parallel and Distributed Computation: Numerical Methods. Prentice Hall, Englewood Cliffs (1989)
4. Boyd, S., Parikh, N., Chu, E., Peleato, B., Eckstein, J.: Distributed optimization and statistical learning via the alternating direction method of multipliers. Found. Trends Mach. Learn. **3**(1), 1–122 (2011)
5. Dheeru, D., Taniskidou, E.K.: UCI machine learning repository (2017). http://archive.ics.uci.edu/ml
6. Dwork, C., McSherry, F., Nissim, K., Smith, A.: Calibrating noise to sensitivity in private data analysis. In: Halevi, S., Rabin, T. (eds.) TCC 2006. LNCS, vol. 3876, pp. 265–284. Springer, Heidelberg (2006). https://doi.org/10.1007/11681878_14
7. Dwork, C., Roth, A.: The algorithmic foundations of differential privacy. Found. Trends Theor. Comput. Sci. **9**(3–4), 211–407 (2014)
8. Fredrikson, M., Jha, S., Ristenpart, T.: Model inversion attacks that exploit confidence information and basic countermeasures. In: Proceedings of the 22nd ACM SIGSAC Conference on Computer and Communications Security, Denver, October 2015, pp. 1322–1333 (2015)
9. Friedman, J., Hastie, T., Tibshirani, R.: The Elements of Statistical Learning. Springer Series in Statistics. Springer, New York (2001). https://doi.org/10.1007/978-0-387-21606-5
10. Guo, Y., Gong, Y.: Practical collaborative learning for crowdsensing in the internet of things with differential privacy. In: IEEE Conference on Communications and Network Security (CNS), Beijing, May 2018, pp. 1–9 (2018)
11. Han, S., Topcu, U., Pappas, G.J.: Differentially private distributed constrained optimization. IEEE Trans. Autom. Control **62**(1), 50–64 (2017)
12. He, B., Yuan, X.: On the $O(1/n)$ convergence rate of the Douglas-Rachford alternating direction method. SIAM J. Numer. Anal. **50**(2), 700–709 (2012)
13. Johnson, R., Zhang, T.: Accelerating stochastic gradient descent using predictive variance reduction. In: Advances in Neural Information Processing Systems, Lake Tahoe, December 2013, pp. 315–323 (2013)
14. Liu, L., Han, Z.: Multi-block ADMM for big data optimization in smart grid. In: International Conference on Computing, Networking and Communications (ICNC), Anaheim, February 2015, pp. 556–561 (2015)
15. Nguyen, H., Khodaei, A., Han, Z.: A big data scale algorithm for optimal scheduling of integrated microgrids. IEEE Trans. Smart Grid **9**(1), 274–282 (2016)
16. Ouyang, H., He, N., Tran, L., Gray, A.: Stochastic alternating direction method of multipliers. In: International Conference on Machine Learning, Atlanta, June 2013, pp. 80–88 (2013)
17. Qin, Z., Goldfarb, D.: Structured sparsity via alternating direction methods. J. Mach. Learn. Res. **13**(1), 1435–1468 (2012)
18. Schizas, I.D., Ribeiro, A., Giannakis, G.B.: Consensus in ad hoc wsns with noisy links - Part I: distributed estimation of deterministic signals. IEEE Trans. Sig. Process. **56**(1), 350–364 (2008)
19. Wang, D., Ye, M., Xu, J.: Differentially private empirical risk minimization revisited: faster and more general. In: Advances in Neural Information Processing Systems, Long Beach, December 2017, pp. 2722–2731 (2017)
20. Witten, I.H., Frank, E., Hall, M.A., Pal, C.J.: Data Mining: Practical Machine Learning Tools and Techniques. Morgan Kaufmann, Burlington (2016)
21. Wu, X., Zhu, X., Wu, G.Q., Ding, W.: Data mining with big data. IEEE Trans. Knowl. Data Eng. **26**(1), 97–107 (2014)

22. Zhang, T., Zhu, Q.: A dual perturbation approach for differential private ADMM-based distributed empirical risk minimization. In: Proceedings of the ACM Workshop on Artificial Intelligence and Security, Vienna, October 2016, pp. 129–137 (2016)
23. Zhao, S., Li, W., Zhou, Z.: Scalable stochastic alternating direction method of multipliers. arXiv preprint arXiv:1502.03529 (2015)

Topology-Aware Hashing for Effective Control Flow Graph Similarity Analysis

Yuping Li[1(✉)], Jiyong Jang[2], and Xinming Ou[3]

[1] Pinterest, San Francisco, USA
yupingli@mail.usf.edu
[2] IBM Research, Yorktown Heights, USA
[3] University of South Florida, Tampa, USA

Abstract. Control Flow Graph (CFG) similarity analysis is an essential technique for a variety of security analysis tasks, including malware detection and malware clustering. Even though various algorithms have been developed, existing CFG similarity analysis methods still suffer from limited efficiency, accuracy, and usability. In this paper, we propose a novel fuzzy hashing scheme called topology-aware hashing (TAH) for effective and efficient CFG similarity analysis. Given the CFGs constructed from program binaries, we extract blended n-gram graphical features of the CFGs, encode the graphical features into numeric vectors (called graph signatures), and then measure the graph similarity by comparing the graph signatures. We further employ a fuzzy hashing technique to convert the numeric graph signatures into smaller fixed-size fuzzy hash signatures for efficient similarity calculation. Our comprehensive evaluation demonstrates that TAH is more effective and efficient compared to existing CFG comparison techniques. To demonstrate the applicability of TAH to real-world security analysis tasks, we develop a binary similarity analysis tool based on TAH, and show that it outperforms existing similarity analysis tools while conducting malware clustering.

Keywords: CFG comparison · Binary similarity · Malware analysis

1 Introduction

Control flow graph (CFG) similarity analysis has played an essential role in malware analysis, *e.g.*, detecting the variants of known malware samples [3,6,11,21,27], evaluating the relationship between different malware families, studying the evolution of different malware families, and triaging large-scale newly collected malicious samples to prioritize the new threats. Research also demonstrated that it is the most fundamental component for effective binary bug search [12], which tried to create signatures from known vulnerable version CFGs and identify the vulnerable version of binaries. Therefore, effective

© ICST Institute for Computer Sciences, Social Informatics and Telecommunications Engineering 2019
Published by Springer Nature Switzerland AG 2019. All Rights Reserved
S. Chen et al. (Eds.): SecureComm 2019, LNICST 304, pp. 278–298, 2019.
https://doi.org/10.1007/978-3-030-37228-6_14

and efficient CFG similarity analysis is much desired for operational security analysis in practice.

Despite the numerous efforts towards effective CFG similarity comparison, we found it is still challenging to apply existing CFG comparison approaches for real-world analysis (*e.g.*, structural based binary similarity analysis). Graph matching is known to be computationally expensive. Even though several approximate graph isomorphism algorithms [21,27,30,44] have been developed and applied to CFG comparison over the past several decades, it is still a time-consuming procedure to compare a large number of CFGs at the same time. For instance, comparing binary A with m functions and binary B with n functions would result in $m * n$ pairwise CFG comparisons. In addition, we notice that the majority of existing CFG similarity comparison algorithms work with "raw" CFG structures, and rely on inefficient CFG representations for comparison. Last but not least, the evaluation of existing CFG comparison algorithms mainly focus on recognizing the similarity of CFGs. However, performing well with regard to recognizing CFG similarities does not guarantee also doing good in identifying CFG differences. And the later capability is equally important especially if the information of how "similar" of two CFGs are also used in practical applications, *e.g.*, whether the algorithm will generate comparatively low similarity scores if the input CFGs are significantly different.

In this paper, we hypothesize that the original CFG representation is not required to measure the CFG similarity if a CFG can be effectively encoded with certain representative graph features, which could result in a universal and compact graph format and make the overall comparison more efficient at the same time. Therefore, based on the insight that the n-gram concept is applicable to represent CFGs to assess graph similarity, we design a blended n-gram graphical feature based CFG comparison method, called topology-aware hashing (TAH). The n-gram concept has been extensively applied for measuring document similarity where contiguous sequences of n items are extracted from an input stream. We apply it to CFGs in a similar manner, except working with multiple input paths. Extracting n-gram graphical features from CFG structures enables us to effectively encode arbitrary CFGs to the same format. To facilitate the comparison between graph signatures, we further employ a fuzzy hashing technique to convert the numeric graph signatures into smaller fixed-size fuzzy hash signatures. In this way, we achieve high accuracy through the n-gram graphical feature representation, and high efficiency through the compact fuzzy hash comparison. Compared to the state-of-the-art CFG comparison algorithms, our approach achieves the highest accuracy for hierarchical clustering and takes the least amount of time to complete all pairwise comparisons. To demonstrate the effectiveness of the structural comparison approach, we further implement a binary similarity analysis tool based on TAH. When compared with the state-of-the-art binary similarity tools, it achieves the highest accuracy at the F-score of 0.929 for singe-linkage malware clustering tasks.

In summary, we have the following major contributions:

- We propose a blended n-gram graphical feature based CFG comparison method called TAH. It extracts the n-gram graphical features from the topology of CFGs, and measures the similarity of CFGs by comparing the graphical features encoded in fuzzy hash signatures.
- We design a clustering analysis based evaluation framework to comprehensively assess various CFG comparison techniques, and show that TAH is more stable, faster, and generates more accurate results compared to state-of-the-art CFG comparison techniques.
- We design and implement a TAH-based binary similarity analysis tool, and demonstrate that it effectively performs malware clustering tasks with 2865 carefully labeled malware samples in an efficient manner.

2   Related Work

2.1   CFG Similarity Analysis

Control flow graph (CFG) similarity analysis is the core technical component of many existing security analysis systems, and various techniques have been proposed for approximate CFG similarity computation.

1. **Min-cost bipartite graph matching:** Hu *et al.* [21] developed an edit distance based graph isomorphism algorithm by building a cost matrix that represents the costs of mapping the nodes in two graphs, and using the Hungarian algorithm [28] to find an optimal mapping between the nodes such that the total cost (*i.e.*, edit distance) is minimized. Vujošević *et al.* [44] iteratively built a similarity matrix between the nodes of two CFGs based on the similarity of their neighbors, and adopted the Hungarian algorithm to find the matching between the nodes in two graphs such that the resulting similarity score is the highest.
2. **Maximal common subgraph matching:** McGregor [30] designed a backtrack search algorithm to find the maximal common subgraph of two graphs. This idea has been used to design efficient CFG comparison algorithms, and adopted for binary semantic difference analysis [15] and binary code search [12] scenarios. Given the maximal common subgraph output, a graph similarity score was calculated as the maximal number of common subgraph nodes divided by the number of available nodes between two graphs.
3. k-**subgraph matching:** Kruegel *et al.* [27] designed an algorithm based on k-subgraph mining. They generated a spanning tree for each node in the graph such that the out-degree of every node was less than or equal to 2, then recursively generated k-subgraphs from the spanning trees by considering all possible allocations of $k-1$ nodes under the root node. Each k-subgraph was then canonicalized and converted into a fingerprint by concatenating the rows of its adjacency matrix.

4. **Simulation-based graph similarity:** Sokolsky *et al.* [42] modeled the control flow graphs using Labeled Transition Systems. Given two CFGs, they recursively matched the most similar outgoing nodes starting from the entry nodes, and summed up the similarity of the matched nodes and edges. The overall similarity of two CFGs was then defined by a recursive formula.

5. **Graph embedding:** Genius [13] was designed to learn high-level feature representations from an attributed CFG (ACFG) and encode the graphs into numerical vectors using a codebook-based graph matching approach. It used 6 block-level attributes (*e.g.*, string constants and the number of instructions) and 2 inter-block level attributes (*e.g.*, the number of offspring and betweenness). Using the same features, Gemini [46] proposed a neural network-based approach to compute the graph embedding for an ACFG, and achieved better accuracy and efficiency. CFG similarity is then measured by comparing the embedded graph representation.

Our TAH algorithm belongs to the graph embedding category, which is also known as topological descriptors [14,20] in other domains. We notice that lots of recent graph embedding techniques [18] were mainly designed to represent the individual graph nodes [1,34] in vector spaces. They were often applied for network (*i.e.*, undirected graph) structure analysis [45] and require additional training processes [5,24,45]. TAH is different from Genius and Gemini in that TAH is basic block content-agnostic, and its graph embedding is always deterministic and requires no separate training process. Graph kernels are widely adopted for comparing graph similarities. However, we note that the majority of the graph kernels are designed and used for analyzing undirected graphs or networks [16,41,43], and require label [41] and weight [25] information. Therefore, they are not directly applicable to analyzing CFGs, which are directed, unlabeled, and unweighted graphs. Nevertheless, we notice that our n-gram concept resonates some of the structural properties used in graph kernel algorithms, such as graphlets [41] (e.g., the subgraphs with k nodes where $k \in 3, 4, 5$).

2.2 Binary Similarity Analysis

We discuss the previous binary similarity analysis methods that are most relevant to our approach.

BitShred [23] was a system designed for large scale malware similarity analysis and clustering, and it extracted n-gram features from the machine code sequences of the executable sections and applied feature hashing to encode the features into a bit-vector. nextGen-hash [29] was a concretized fuzzy hashing approach based on the core ideas developed in BitShred, and achieved more accurate results than other fuzzy hash algorithms; however, its significant fingerprint size made it hard to use in practice. Myles and Collberg [33] proposed to use opcode-level n-grams as software birthmarks and applied it to prove the copyright of software. Opcode level n-gram representation of a binary has also been explored to detect similar malicious code patterns [4,22,32,39]. Alazab *et al.* [2] proposed to detect malware using n-gram features from API call sequences.

SSdeep [26] was a representative fuzzy hashing algorithm that was used to detect homologous files using context triggered piecewise hashes.

CFG based analysis was also used for binary code comparison. BinDiff [11] was a binary comparison tool that assisted vulnerability researchers and engineers to quickly find the differences and similarities using function and basic block level attributes. BinSlayer [3] modeled a binary diffing problem as a bipartite graph matching problem. It assigned a distance metric between the basic block in one function and the basic block in another function that minimized the total distance, and found that graph isomorphism based algorithms were less accurate when the changes between two binaries were large. BinHunt [15] and iBinHunt [31] relied on symbolic execution and a theorem prover to check semantic differences between basic blocks. Although they might yield better accuracy, it was hard to use in practice due to an expensive operation cost. Kruegel et al. [27] used the previously mentioned k-subgraph matching algorithm to detect polymorphic worms, which was also based on CFG structural analysis. Cesare and Xiang [6] also extracted fixed-size k-subgraph features and n-gram features from the string representation of a CFG for malware variant detection.

To some extent, our n-gram graphical features are close to k-subgraphs, but they are different concepts. Unlike existing work that tried to find an optimal matching between functions in two binaries, TAH compares the CFGs of the entire binary using the overall n-gram graphical features. Furthermore, n-gram features from a CFG string [6] were still derived in a traditional n-gram usage manner while our proposed n-gram graphical features are directly extracted from CFG structures.

3   Approach Overview

We illustrate the workflow of TAH in Fig. 1. Given two sets of CFGs, we extract the blended n-gram graphical features from the input CFGs and encode them as numeric vectors, called graph signatures. To make it more efficient to use and compare, we subsequently convert the graph signatures into fixed-size bit-vectors, called fuzzy hash outputs. Finally, we compare the corresponding fuzzy hash outputs to calculate the similarity of input CFGs.

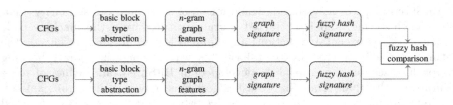

Fig. 1. The workflow of TAH

3.1   Basic Block Type Abstraction

In order to extract representative graphical features, we abstract the basic blocks of CFGs using categorization. The main objective of the abstraction is to categorize the nodes of CFGs into different types, which are then used to denote the "content" of the nodes as used in traditional n-gram application scenarios.

We explore a simple yet effective abstraction of basic block types which captures the topology of a CFG, and demonstrate that such a simple type abstraction approach produces reliable results. In particular, we define the basic block types based on the number of parents (*i.e.*, node in-degree) and the number of children (*i.e.*, node out-degree). To study the CFGs of real-world applications including goodware and malware, we experimentally analyzed a total of 93,470 binaries that were obtained from newly installed Android and Windows operation systems, and malware sharing websites like VirusShare [38].

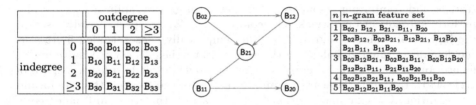

Fig. 2. A sample CFG and its blended n-gram features

We noted that the majority (97%) of indegree and outdegree values were between 0 and 3, and mainly focused on in-degree values ranging from 0 to 3, and out-degree values ranging from 0 to 3 when abstracting CFGs. This abstraction approach results in a total of 16 different basic block types as shown in the left table of Fig. 2 where each entry in the table denotes a specific basic block type annotated with its indegree and outdegree values. Basic blocks whose indegree is larger than or equal to 3 are considered as the same type, and basic blocks whose outdegree is larger than or equal to 3 are considered as the same type. During our experiments, we noticed that this approach did not cause significant feature collision as only 1.27% of basic blocks from real-world applications had larger than 3 outdegree and only 3.67% of basic blocks had larger than 3 indegree.

3.2   Blended n-gram Graphical Feature Extraction

Similar to the traditional n-gram analysis, we consider a node (*i.e.*, basic block) in a CFG as a single *item*, and define an n-*gram graphical feature* to be the *consecutive n basic blocks* from an input CFG. In order to encapsulate the structural properties, the connectivity among nodes, and the contextual information of the input CFG, we include all k-gram ($k \in [1, n]$) features as the complete graphical feature set. This k-gram model considering all possible sequences from length 1 to n was previously referred to as *blended n-gram features* [36,40].

Let us take the sample CFG as shown in the middle of Fig. 2 to explain the blended n-gram graphical features in more details. Each basic block is represented in the abstracted basic block type as discussed in Sect. 3.1, e.g., B_{21} with 2 parent nodes and 1 child node. For a given n, we extract all possible blended n-gram graphical features at every node in the CFG. For example, at node B_{02}, the 1-gram feature is B_{02} itself, the 2-gram features are $B_{02}B_{12}$ and $B_{02}B_{21}$, and the 3-gram features are $B_{02}B_{12}B_{21}$, $B_{02}B_{12}B_{20}$, and $B_{02}B_{21}B_{11}$. This procedure is called *visiting* node B_{02}, and visiting a node reaches descendant nodes at up to $n-1$ levels away. We apply this procedure for all nodes in the CFG and obtain the resulting blended n-gram graphical feature sets. The complete 5-gram graphical features for the sample CFG are presented in the right table of Fig. 2. Note that cycles in a CFG will not be an issue since each node in a CFG is visited only once and the visiting order makes no difference.

Larger n can result in a larger feature space and provide more distinguishing capabilities. On the other hand, a larger feature space also requires more storage and computing resources to extract all n-gram graphical features and perform subsequent operations, e.g., comparisons. We comprehensively assessed the impact of different n-gram sizes, and empirically chose blended 5-gram as the default n-gram size balancing the accuracy and the efficiency. A naïve implementation of the blended 5-gram feature set would result in a feature space of $1,118,480$[1]. However, there are certain n-gram graphical features that are invalid by definition. For example, k-gram ($k \geq 2$) features that contain 0 indegree of basic block types (*i.e.*, B_{00}, B_{01}, B_{02}, B_{03}) but do not start with them are invalid. Similarly, k-gram ($k \geq 2$) features that contain 0 outdegree of basic block types (*i.e.*, B_{00}, B_{10}, B_{20}, B_{30}) but do not end with them are also invalid. After removing such invalid features, the blended 5-gram feature set has smaller $118,096$ legitimate entries.

3.3   Graph Signature Generation and Comparison

We generate a *graph signature* by encoding the blended n-gram graphical features into a numeric vector. Each entry in the vector represents a specific feature, and the value of the entry denotes the number of appearances of its corresponding feature in the graph. In this way, both the content and the frequency of features are taken into consideration when building graph signatures. All the graph signatures are in the same size which is determined by the n-gram graphical feature space. We describe a feature entry as a 32-bit unsigned integer type, which we empirically validate that 2^{32} feature space is large enough for practical usage.

We employ the following cosine similarity measure ($\mathbb{C}$) to compute the similarity between two graph signatures.

$$\mathbb{C}(\mathcal{G}_a, \mathcal{G}_b) = \frac{\mathcal{G}_a \cdot \mathcal{G}_b}{|\mathcal{G}_a| \cdot |\mathcal{G}_b|} \tag{1}$$

---

[1] 16 of 1-gram features, 16^2 of 2-gram features, 16^3 of 3-gram features, 16^4 of 4-gram features, and 16^5 of 5-gram features.

The rationale behind the use of the cosine similarity measure is that it provides an ideal foundation for effective signature size compression, which is often desired for large scale analysis. We describe how we generate a more compact fuzzy hash signature from it in Sect. 3.4.

In practice, the feature counts for different binary programs vary significantly, and the cosine similarity may yield less accurate results as it only assesses orientation of vectors rather than magnitude of vectors. For example, two vectors (1, 2, 3, 4) and (2, 4, 6, 8) yield the cosine similarity score of 1.0, however the magnitude of vectors are significantly different. This is due to the cosine similarity only measuring the angle between the input vectors. We denote the total number of the graphical features contained in a CFG as N, and define the size rectification factor ($\mathbb{R}$) between two CFGs as follows:

$$\mathbb{R}(\mathcal{G}_a, \mathcal{G}_b) = \frac{\min(\mathbb{N}(\mathcal{G}_a), \mathbb{N}(\mathcal{G}_b))}{\max(\mathbb{N}(\mathcal{G}_a), \mathbb{N}(\mathcal{G}_b))} \tag{2}$$

We then compute the final similarity ($\mathbb{S}$) between two graph signatures by multiplying the rectification factor to the cosine similarity, $\mathbb{S}(\mathcal{G}_a, \mathcal{G}_b) = \mathbb{R}(\mathcal{G}_a, \mathcal{G}_b) \times \mathbb{C}(\mathcal{G}_a, \mathcal{G}_b)$. According to the definition, the final similarity of two graph signatures is 1.0 when they are exactly the same, and the size rectification factor is to regulate the similarity only when input graph vectors are significantly different.

3.4 Fuzzy Hash Signature Generation and Comparison

The above graph signature representation provides an effective similarity comparison mechanism; however, the signature size increases exponentially when larger n-gram sizes are used. For example, the size of the graph signature is about 461 KB (*i.e.*, $4B \cdot 118096$) with blended 5-gram graphical features, which is challenging to store and compare at a large scale. To make the technique easier to use and further facilitate the graph signature storage and comparison process, we compress the "raw" graph signature into k-bit vector representation using fuzzy hashing principles.

Specifically, we pre-define a unique seed number and prepare k independent vectors with elements that are selected randomly from Gaussian distribution, and configure each random vector to be the same dimension as the raw graph signatures. We denote the i-th random vector and the raw graph signature as $\mathcal{V}_i$ and $\mathcal{G}$, respectively; and then define the following function $\mathbb{B}$ to compare each random vector against the graph signature.

$$\mathbb{B}_i(\mathcal{V}_i, \mathcal{G}) = \begin{cases} 1 & \text{if } \mathcal{V}_i \cdot \mathcal{G} \geq 0 \\ 0 & \text{if } \mathcal{V}_i \cdot \mathcal{G} < 0 \end{cases} \tag{3}$$

In this way, each random vector is used to create one projection for the raw graph signature based on the dot product between the random vector and the graph signature, and the output of k times of projections becomes a k-bit vector.

The overall random projection procedure is formally known as hyperplane locality sensitive hashing (LSH) [8,10]. Since all the graph signatures are projected into $\{0, 1\}$ space through the same hashing process, graph signatures with close "locality" will be projected to similar k-bit vectors. We consider the generated k-bit hash value as a *fuzzy hash signature*. Given two fuzzy hash signatures $\mathcal{F}_a$ and $\mathcal{F}_b$, we compute Hamming similarity ($\mathbb{H}$) to measure the similarity between the projected hash outputs as follows:

$$\mathbb{H}(\mathcal{F}_a, \mathcal{F}_b) = 1 - \frac{|\mathcal{F}_a \oplus \mathcal{F}_b|}{k} \tag{4}$$

LSH is commonly used as an efficient technique to conduct the approximate nearest neighbor search in high-dimension objects. Previous research in LSH domain [8,17] showed that (1) cosine similarity (as used for graph signature comparison) is one type of similarity measurement that admits LSH families; and (2) for any similarity function $sim(x, y)$ that admits LSH projection, we can always obtain an LSH family that maps the original objects to $\{0, 1\}$ space and has the property that the similarity between projected objects (*e.g.*, Hamming similarity) is proved to correspond to the original similarity function at $\frac{1+sim(x,y)}{2}$. Therefore, we leverage $\mathbb{H}(\mathcal{F}_a, \mathcal{F}_b)$ to estimate the original cosine similarity between graph signatures by:

$$\tilde{\mathbb{C}}(\mathcal{G}_a, \mathcal{G}_b) = 2 \times \mathbb{H}(\mathcal{F}_a, \mathcal{F}_b) - 1 \tag{5}$$

Increasing the number of random projection vectors makes the similarity estimation more accurate. To obtain the optimal n-gram size and fingerprint size, we conduct grid search against the same ground truth dataset with a set of potential parameters, and record the optimal clustering result considering both the efficiency and accuracy[2]. According to the empirical process, we set 256 as the optimal k value. The total number of graphical features $\mathbb{N}$ is represented as a 32-bit integer, and the final fuzzy hash output is 288 bits by default. We compute the final fuzzy hash similarity by multiplying the rectification factor to the estimated hash similarity: $\tilde{\mathbb{S}}(\mathcal{G}_a, \mathcal{G}_b) = \mathbb{R}(\mathcal{G}_a, \mathcal{G}_b) \times \tilde{\mathbb{C}}(\mathcal{G}_a, \mathcal{G}_b)$.

4   Evaluation of CFG Similarity Analysis Algorithms

In this section, we evaluate the effectiveness and accuracy of different CFG comparison algorithms. Our evaluation mainly focuses on the capability of the algorithms to differentiate CFG structures (*i.e.*, the topology) *without* relying on basic block content. The auxiliary information provided by basic block content could further improve CFG comparison. For example, the abstraction process discussed in Sect. 3.1 can be extended to incorporate such information.

We compared TAH to representative CFG similarity analysis algorithms discussed in Sect. 2. For min-cost bipartite graph matching algorithm [21,44], k-subgraph matching [27], and simulation-based graph comparison [42], we used

---

[2] The parameter selection process is not included in the paper due to space limitation.

the implementations provided by Chan [7]. We implemented McGreger's maximum common subgraph matching algorithm [30] and our TAH. The graph embedding based CFG comparison algorithms [13, 46] are not evaluated since they rely upon a separate training process and require six types of specific features derived from concrete basic block content. The final outputs of the algorithms were normalized ranging from 0 to 1. To facilitate evaluating arbitrary CFG comparison algorithms, we plan to release our evaluation framework and the corresponding dataset. A new CFG comparison algorithm can be easily evaluated in this framework by providing a plugin that takes two CFGs as input and outputs a normalized similarity score.

4.1   Algorithm Evaluation Strategy

To the best of our knowledge, the only prior work that formally evaluated different CFG similarity algorithms was that of Chan *et al.* [7]. They created a ground truth CFG dataset by applying different levels of edit operations to a seed CFG, and checked if the algorithms could identify a similar level of similarity differences between the generated testing CFGs and the seed CFG. However, we observe that Chan *et al.*'s methodology is problematic from the following perspectives: (1) the ground truth dataset and evaluating strategy were inherently biased towards edit-distance based CFG comparison algorithms; (2) different edit operations (*e.g.*, adding/deleting a node, and adding/deleting an edge) might have different costs. For example, editing a node will not impact any existing edges; on the contrary, editing an edge will affect two nodes. Therefore, the testing CFGs generated by the same number of edit operations may present different similarity levels.

We propose a new evaluation strategy where we employ a CFG comparison algorithm in a *hierarchical agglomerative clustering (HAC) system* as a custom distance function, then use the custom distance function to conduct clustering analysis for the same ground-truth dataset, and use the overall clustering result as a performance indicator of the corresponding CFG comparison algorithm. HAC is a bottom-up version of the hierarchical clustering methods, in which all input items are initially considered as singleton clusters, and then for a specified distance threshold t the algorithm iteratively merges the clusters with the minimum distance as long as the corresponding cluster distance d is less than t. The distance between two clusters is often referred to as "linkage" and the following three linkage criteria are commonly used: *single linkage* considering the cluster distance as the minimum distance between all the entries of two clusters, *average linkage* considering the cluster distance as the average distance between all the entries of two clusters, and *complete linkage* considering the cluster distance as the maximum distance between all the entries of two clusters.

The rationale for evaluating different CFG comparison algorithms through HAC are that: (1) the fundamental component of a HAC system is the similarity measurement between all input items, which can be pre-calculated as a distance matrix using each CFG comparison algorithm; (2) when analyzing the same ground truth dataset, the only parameter that will impact the final clustering result is the distance matrix which is controlled by each CFG comparison algorithm; (3) the clustering analysis procedure assesses the capability to group similar items and separate different items at the same time.

To measure the clustering results, we adopt the measurement of precision and recall. Precision and recall measure two competing criteria of a clustering algorithm: the ability to separate items from different clusters, and the ability to group together items belonging to the same cluster. We consider the intersection point (or the nearest point) between precision and recall to be the optimal clustering output. For simplicity, all the clustering results are subsequently measured with F-score, which is the harmonic mean of the optimal precision and recall.

4.2   Experiment Data Preparation

To create a ground-truth CFG dataset, we compiled the latest version of the Android Open Source Project code and obtained 588 ELF ARM64 binaries. We analyzed the compiled binaries, collected all the function level CFGs that had 20 nodes, and then randomly selected 5 seed CFGs from all available 20-node CFGs. We applied *one* edit operation (*e.g.*, adding a node, deleting a node[3], adding an edge, and deleting an edge) for each seed CFG. Since all the edges and nodes can be edited in single operation and any of the existing two nodes can be added with an additional edge, each of the seed CFG can be used to create about 500 artificial and structurally similar CFGs. In the end, we created a total of 1,934 CFGs from the 5 seed CFGs. We selected CFGs with 20 nodes since they typically provided enough varieties between different CFGs, and the individual CFG comparison did not take too long to complete for all the evaluated algorithms.

4.3   Evaluation Results

To avoid the bias towards a particular linkage strategy, we report the clustering results with three linkage approaches for all CFG comparison algorithms. We summarize the optimal clustering results for different algorithms in Table 1, and present the detailed single-linkage CFG clustering results in Fig. 3. The fuzzy hash signature based CFG comparison approach is labeled as TAH and the graph signature based CFG comparison approach is labeled as TAH′. We included TAH′ to verify that fuzzy hashing based TAH closely approximated TAH′ with little impact on accuracy.

To further dissect the clustering results, we separated all CFG pairs into two categories: same group CFG pairs and different group CFG pairs. Ideally, the distance of the same group CFG pair is expected to be small, and the distance of the different group CFG pair is expected to be large. We present the minimum and the maximum distances of each group in Table 2. and plot the cumulative distance distribution for each algorithm in Fig. 4.

---

[3] A graph node can be deleted only if it is isolated.

Table 1. Optimal clustering results for different CFG comparison algorithms

Algorithm	Single linkage	Average linkage	Complete linkage	Avg F-score
Hu [21]	0.847	0.872	0.879	0.866
Vujošević [44]	0.749	0.869	0.876	0.831
Sokolsky [42]	0.367	0.456	0.501	0.441
Kruegel [27]	0.530	0.530	0.530	0.530
McGreger [30]	0.597	0.588	0.324	0.503
TAH′	0.816	0.926	1.000	0.914
TAH	0.817	0.926	0.864	0.869

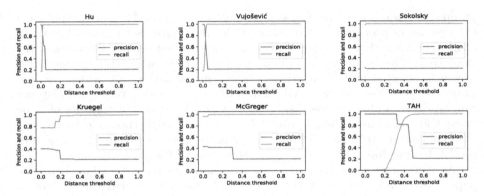

Fig. 3. Single-linkage clustering results for different CFG algorithms

Table 2. Distance ranges for different CFG pairs

Algorithm	Same-group		Diff-group		All pairs		Same-group		Diff-group		All groups	
	Min	Max	Min	Max	Min	Max	Min	Max	Min	Max	Min	Max
Hu	0.000	0.049	0.000	0.182	0.000	0.182	0.000	0.032	0.029	0.165	0.000	0.165
Vujošević	0.000	0.100	0.000	0.213	0.000	0.213	0.000	0.067	0.028	0.203	0.000	0.203
Sokolsky	0.000	0.258	0.000	0.258	0.000	0.258	0.000	0.250	0.000	0.250	0.000	0.250
Kruegel	0.000	1.000	0.000	1.000	0.000	1.000	0.000	1.000	0.000	1.000	0.000	1.000
McGreger	0.000	0.905	0.000	0.800	0.000	0.905	0.000	0.935	0.000	0.833	0.000	0.935
TAH′	0.007	0.724	0.181	0.921	0.007	0.921	0.000	0.777	0.294	0.917	0.000	0.917
TAH	0.015	0.978	0.328	1.000	0.015	1.000	0.000	0.964	0.398	1.000	0.000	1.000

Combining the distance range information with CFG clustering results, we can see that: (1) the algorithms proposed by Hu, Vujošević, and Sokolsky had very narrow overall distance ranges for all CFG pairs, thus CFGs were quickly merged into one group during the clustering process, which resulted in high recall and low precision for the majority of provided distance thresholds. However, the edit distance based CFG comparison algorithms generated relatively lower distance outputs for same group CFG pairs and higher distance outputs for different

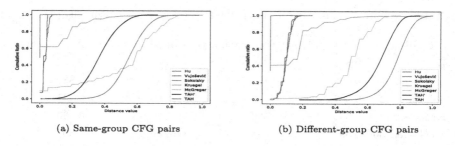

(a) Same-group CFG pairs   (b) Different-group CFG pairs

Fig. 4. Cumulative distance distribution for all comparison algorithms

group CFG pairs, therefore they still generated overall good F-score outputs. (2) the algorithms proposed by Kruegel and McGreger provided a broader distance range, but for both same group CFG pairs and different group CFG pairs at the same time. This made precision and recall from different clustering thresholds slowly intersected with each other or never intersected at all, which resulted in overall poor F-score. (3) TAH' and TAH both provided very good distance ranges. Figure 4 also demonstrates that they clearly separated majority of same group CFG pairs and different group CFG pairs, *e.g.*, when choosing the distance threshold around 0.50 for TAH' and choosing the distance threshold around 0.70 for TAH. Therefore, they both generated very good F-score outputs.

As mentioned earlier, all the algorithm implementations evaluated in this paper only considered the topology of the CFGs and ignored the content of basic blocks, *i.e.*, the content similarity between all basic block pairs were considered as 1. Therefore, these implementations may not faithfully represent the full capability of the original designs, and the evaluation results presented in this paper only reflected the algorithms' capability of measuring the similarity of CFG structures, without considering the basic block content. Even though our evaluation framework supports experiments with real-world CFGs and the TAH can be extended to incorporate boolean node attributes[4], it is practically challenging to conduct large scale experiments with real-world CFGs as it is nontrivial to prepare a large-scale ground truth dataset using real-world CFGs that present *controlled* and *known* similarity levels. Firstly, the source code level similarities are commonly not proportionally preserved after the complicated compilation procedure, *i.e.*, it is difficult to control the granularity of CFG similarities through source code updates. Secondly, when analyzing large amount malicious real-world binary samples that were labeled as the same malware family label, we noticed that samples often either shared the exact same functions or had significantly changed functions, while few CFGs were closely similar.

Our evaluation strategy highlighted the strengths and the weaknesses of existing CFG comparison algorithms when comparing graph topologies. In summary, TAH' showed the best separation capabilities between similar CFG pairs and

---

[4] *E.g.*, adding 1 bit to record whether the node contains string constants during basic block type abstraction as described in Sect. 3.1.

different CFG pairs, and TAH was a faster approximate method yet still quite comparable to the accuracy of TAH$'$, whereas existing CFG comparison algorithms either had limited distance output ranges or had almost the same distance ranges between same group CFG pairs and different group CFG pairs. This demonstrates that TAH$'$ and TAH are more reliable and have more balanced capability to recognize similar CFGs and identify different CFGs at the same time. High F-scores of TAH$'$ and TAH are achieved mainly because the differences between n-gram graphical features are always proportional to the structural differences of CFGs. For example, the same group CFGs will have more similar n-gram graphical features, and the different group CFGs will have more different graphical features, which subsequently leads to the desired distinguishing capabilities.

4.4 Overall Performance

For each algorithm, we measured the time taken (in seconds) to finish the similarity calculation for all CFG pairs. Since the hierarchical clustering algorithm has n^2 complexity, the prepared 1,934 CFGs would result in 1,869,211 pairwise CFG comparisons. Note that all the algorithm implementations took two CFGs as input and produced a similarity score, which means the graph signatures for TAH$'$ and fuzzy hash signatures for TAH were generated 1,869,211 times during the evaluation. And since TAH fuzzy hash outputs are generated from TAH$'$ graph signatures, this made the TAH approach dramatically slower than other approaches. However, if we cache the graph embedding process, $e.g.$, precalculating the graph signature for TAH$'$ and the fuzzy hash output for TAH for each CFG then directly loading the generated signatures/hashes within each pairwise CFG comparison routine, TAH$'$ only took 125.5 s to finish the graph signature generation and all pairwise comparison, and TAH only took 23.8 s to finish the fuzzy hash generation and all pairwise comparison. This was much more efficient than other existing approaches. For the same dataset, Hu's algorithm took 755.6 s, Vujošević's algorithm took 1788.0 s, Sokolsky's algorithm took 483.1 s, Kruegel's algorithm took 321.8 s, and McGreger's algorithm took 2542.1s to finish. Note that for the same CFG input, the fuzzy hash output is the same if we apply the algorithm and generate it again, so it makes sense to only generate it once and caching the intermediate and compact CFG representation when used in real-world. However, this won't be applicable for the existing algorithms since there is no intermediate CFG representation for them and they need to repeated compare the "raw" CFG inputs. This evaluation indicates that TAH is particularly suitable for large scale dataset analysis.

5 Evaluation of Binary Similarity Analysis Tools

Based on TAH, we implemented a binary similarity analysis tool[5] to evaluate the effectiveness of the structural comparison approach. We assessed the effectiveness of TAH to conduct binary similarity analysis, and compared it with the

---

[5] For simplicity, we also refer our binary similarity analysis tool as TAH.

following existing binary similarity comparison solutions: SSdeep v2.14.1 [26] and BinDiff v4.3.0 [11]. Other previously proposed binary similarity analysis tools were not evaluated because they were neither maintained [3] (*i.e.*, not working with a majority of the collected binaries) nor publicly available [15]. In order to exclude the potential impact of the different disassemblers on the CFG construction accuracy, TAH was implemented as an IDA Pro plugin. The current implementation of TAH used IDA Pro v6.8 to process the target binaries and constructed the corresponding CFGs. The same version of IDA Pro was also used by BinDiff.

We embedded all the binary similarity analysis tools (*e.g.*, TAH, BinDiff, and SSdeep) into the hierarchical clustering system, and used the clustering outputs to evaluate the similarity measurement accuracy of the tools. We prepared the ground truth dataset by collecting desktop malware samples labeled with malware family names, and considered that the binaries with the same family name were more similar to each other than binaries from different families were. Because the labeled malware datasets used in previous research were either discontinued or only contained a list of file hashes, we prepared our own labeled ground truth malware dataset. In the end, we collected 2,865 recent desktop malware samples from VirusShare [38], and every sample was consistently labeled by at least 25 antivirus products listed on VirusTotal [9]. The resulting ground truth malware dataset containing 8 different malware families is shown in Table 3.

Table 3. Ground truth malware dataset

Malware family	Size	Malware family	Size	Malware family	Size
InstalleRex	1115	OutBrowse	615	MultiPlug	384
DomaIQ	184	LoadMoney	173	Linkular	164
InstallCore	127	DownloadAdmin	103		

We also measured precision and recall to evaluate the clustering outputs. For all tools, we summarized the optimal clustering results with regard to different clustering strategies in Table 4, and depicted the overall clustering results with different binary similarity analysis tools in Fig. 5. We can see that TAH generated the highest F-score of 0.929 for single linkage clustering analysis. BinDiff produced similar results with F-score of 0.883, while SSdeep only achieved overall F-score of 0.690. Because SSdeep operated at the binary stream level, it was not able to identify a significant number of semantically similar binaries. BinDiff and TAH both operated at the CFG level, and effectively identified a larger number of similar binaries. Different similarity calculation logic of the tools led to the F-score differences between BinDiff and TAH.

We also evaluated the time taken to conduct the experiments with each tool. Since BinDiff did not have an intermediate "signature" representation for binary CFGs, we only calculated the time it took to finish all the pairwise computations

Table 4. Optimal clustering results for different binary similarity analysis tools

Tool	Single linkage	Average linkage	Complete linkage	Time taken
SSdeep	0.690	0.690	0.689	2.7 min
BinDiff	0.883	0.883	0.883	166.4 min
TAH	0.929	0.903	0.909	0.9 min

by converting all the input binaries into `BinExport` format. The time to conduct pairwise comparisons with each tool is shown in the last column of Table 4. We can see that TAH outperformed SSdeep and BinDiff in terms of efficiency, and BinDiff was dramatically slower than other tools. The main reason for the higher efficiency of TAH was that a fuzzy hash signature was essentially a bit-vector which was more CPU friendly than SSdeep hash representation was.

It is worth to mention that various previous malware clustering systems already demonstrated very promising results. For example, using different datasets, Malheur [37] reported F-score of 0.95, BitShred [23] showed F-score of 0.932, and FIRMA [35] claimed F-score of 0.988. As a reference, we chose to conduct experiments with BitShred, which was a state-of-the-art malware clustering tool using static and dynamic binary features. Since BitShred only adopted the single-linkage clustering strategy, we plot the single-linkage clustering results for all the tools in Fig. 5. From the graph, we can see that BitShred reached the optimal F-score of 0.885. Overall, TAH generated the best clustering results (*e.g.*, F-score of 0.929) with single-linkage clustering. Figure 5 also shows that recall for TAH and BitShred at the distance threshold of 0 are above

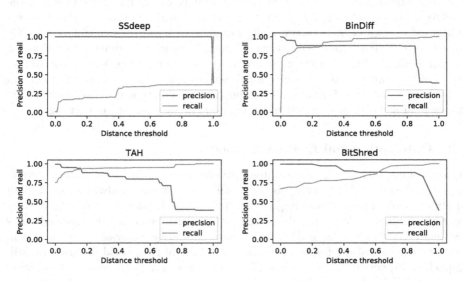

Fig. 5. Single-linkage clustering results of different similarity analysis tools

0.650, while recall of SSdeep and BinDiff at this threshold was 0. This is because TAH and BitShred correctly identified a significant number of binary pairs as similarity of 1.000, while both SSdeep and BinDiff could not identify any of such binary pairs. We further notice that the majority of precision values (*e.g.*, with distance thresholds of [0.000, 0.995]) for SSdeep were 1.000, which means all the binary pairs that were identified as similar (*i.e.*, similarity score larger than 0.005) were indeed similar. However, at the same time, the corresponding recall values for SSdeep were less than 0.365, which indicates that SSdeep failed to recognize a significant number of binaries that were known to be similar regardless of the distance thresholds. This is in line with our practical usage experience with SSdeep.

6   Limitation

6.1   Feature and Signature Collision

We consider the potential attack scenario by generating similar graph features for different CFGs. According to the design in Sect. 3.1, feature collision happens when: (1) nodes have indegree or outdegree larger than 3; (2) nodes with different content are in the same topology. The first type of collision is rare in real-world binary programs (*e.g.*, 3.67% of nodes in our real-world datasets), and the second type of collision is largely alleviated by recording the node context (*i.e.*, n-gram features) and graphical feature counts. n-gram feature extraction allows the resulting feature differences to be proportional to the structural differences. The proposed CFG similarity analysis algorithm TAH compares CFG graph signatures by measuring the overall cosine similarity of graph signatures and the relative CFG sizes. Since the graph signature is mainly a summary of all features contained in a CFG, it is theoretically possible for binaries with different CFGs to generate similar graph signatures. However, random signature collision for overall binary CFGs is rare in practice. To further reduce the possibility of collision, we can increase the graphical feature space by incorporating certain basic block content information into the type abstraction process, such as the presence of a string or numeric constant, and the number of instructions.

6.2   Obfuscation and Evasion Techniques

It is well-known that malware samples are often packed in recent years to evade signature-based malware analysis tools [19]. Even worse, malware authors can apply multiple layers of packing, or employ advanced packers that dynamically decrypt original code on-the-fly or interpret instructions in a virtualized environment. We believe the TAH-based binary similarity analysis is still useful in practice because of the following reasons. (1) Lots of real-world binaries are still unpacked, especially for adware or PUP programs. TAH can be used to quickly filter out similar binaries that have been processed before, or used for triaging a large number of unprocessed binaries (even packed ones) by grouping similar instances together. For this purpose, traditional cryptographic hash and existing similarity analysis solutions are less effective. (2) CFG level analysis makes it possible to provide a binary similarity analysis solution that has a good balance between accuracy and efficiency. For example, dynamic analysis based approach can defeat obfuscation, but is almost impossible to efficiently analyze a large scale of dataset. (3) Comparing to low-level binary sequences, it will be more difficult to add randomness to the CFG structure for the packed binaries. For instance, the dead code can be removed during the CFG construction procedure. Thus the packed binaries would often share certain deobfuscation routines, which can be viewed as the signature of the packers.

7   Conclusion

In this paper, we proposed an effective CFG comparison algorithm TAH, which compares CFGs using n-gram graphical features. In order to compare with existing CFG comparison solutions, we designed a clustering analysis based evaluation framework, and systematically showed that TAH was more accurate and efficient compared to state-of-the-art CFG comparison techniques. Based on TAH, we also developed a graphical comparison based fuzzy hash tool for binary similarity analysis. We empirically demonstrated that TAH outperformed existing binary similarity analysis tools while conducting malware clustering analysis.

Acknowledgment. This research was partially supported by the U.S. National Science Foundation under grant No. 1622402 and 1717862. Any opinions, findings and conclusions or recommendations expressed in this material are those of the authors and do not necessarily reflect the views of the National Science Foundation.

References

1. Ahmed, A., Shervashidze, N., Narayanamurthy, S., Josifovski, V., Smola, A.J.: Distributed large-scale natural graph factorization. In: Proceedings of the 22nd International Conference on World Wide Web, pp. 37–48. ACM (2013)
2. Alazab, M., Venkataraman, S., Watters, P.: Towards understanding malware behaviour by the extraction of API calls. In: 2010 Second Cybercrime and Trustworthy Computing Workshop (CTC), pp. 52–59. IEEE (2010)
3. Bourquin, M., King, A., Robbins, E.: BinSlayer: accurate comparison of binary executables. In: Proceedings of the 2nd ACM SIGPLAN Program Protection and Reverse Engineering Workshop, Rome, Italy, p. 4. ACM (2013)
4. Canfora, G., De Lorenzo, A., Medvet, E., Mercaldo, F., Visaggio, C.A.: Effectiveness of Opcode ngrams for detection of multi family android malware. In: 2015 10th International Conference on Availability, Reliability and Security (ARES), Toulouse, France, pp. 333–340. IEEE, IEEE Computer Society (2015)
5. Cao, S., Lu, W., Xu, Q.: Deep neural networks for learning graph representations. In: AAAI, pp. 1145–1152 (2016)
6. Cesare, S., Xiang, Y.: Malware variant detection using similarity search over sets of control flow graphs. In: 2011 IEEE 10th International Conference on Trust, Security and Privacy in Computing and Communications, pp. 181–189. IEEE, IEEE Computer Society (2011)

7. Chan, P.P., Collberg, C.: A method to evaluate CFG comparison algorithms. In: 2014 14th International Conference on Quality Software (QSIC), Washington, DC, USA, pp. 95–104. IEEE, IEEE Computer Society (2014)

8. Charikar, M.S.: Similarity estimation techniques from rounding algorithms. In: Proceedings of the Thiry-Fourth Annual ACM Symposium on Theory of Computing, pp. 380–388. ACM (2002)

9. Virustotal (2018). https://www.virustotal.com

10. Datar, M., Immorlica, N., Indyk, P., Mirrokni, V.S.: Locality-sensitive hashing scheme based on p-stable distributions. In: Proceedings of the Twentieth Annual Symposium on Computational Geometry, pp. 253–262. ACM (2004)

11. Dullien, T., Rolles, R.: Graph-based comparison of executable objects (English version). SSTIC **5**, 1–3 (2005)

12. Eschweiler, S., Yakdan, K., Gerhards-Padilla, E.: discovRE: efficient cross-architecture identification of bugs in binary code. In: Proceedings of the 2016 Network and Distributed System Security (NDSS) Symposium, San Diego, CA, USA. The Internet Society (2016)

13. Feng, Q., Zhou, R., Xu, C., Cheng, Y., Testa, B., Yin, H.: Scalable graph-based bug search for firmware images. In: Proceedings of the 2016 ACM SIGSAC Conference on Computer and Communications Security, Vienna, Austria, pp. 480–491. ACM (2016)

14. Galvez, J., Garcia, R., Salabert, M., Soler, R.: Charge indexes. New topological descriptors. J. Chem. Inf. Comput. Sci. **34**(3), 520–525 (1994)

15. Gao, D., Reiter, M.K., Song, D.: BinHunt: automatically finding semantic differences in binary programs. In: Chen, L., Ryan, M.D., Wang, G. (eds.) ICICS 2008. LNCS, vol. 5308, pp. 238–255. Springer, Heidelberg (2008). https://doi.org/10.1007/978-3-540-88625-9_16

16. Gärtner, T.: A survey of kernels for structured data. ACM SIGKDD Explor. Newsl. **5**(1), 49–58 (2003)

17. Gionis, A., Gunopulos, D., Koudas, N.: Efficient and tumble similar set retrieval. ACM SIGMOD Rec. **30**(2), 247–258 (2001)

18. Goyal, P., Ferrara, E.: Graph embedding techniques, applications, and performance: a survey. Knowl. Based Syst. **151**, 78–94 (2018)

19. Guo, F., Ferrie, P., Chiueh, T.: A study of the packer problem and its solutions. In: Lippmann, R., Kirda, E., Trachtenberg, A. (eds.) RAID 2008. LNCS, vol. 5230, pp. 98–115. Springer, Heidelberg (2008). https://doi.org/10.1007/978-3-540-87403-4_6

20. Hert, J., et al.: Comparison of topological descriptors for similarity-based virtual screening using multiple bioactive reference structures. Org. Biomol. Chem. **2**(22), 3256–3266 (2004)

21. Hu, X., Chiueh, T.-C., Shin, K.G.: Large-scale malware indexing using function-call graphs. In: Proceedings of the 16th ACM Conference on Computer and Communications Security, Chicago, Illinois, USA, pp. 611–620. ACM (2009)

22. Hu, X., Shin, K.G.: DUET: integration of dynamic and static analyses for malware clustering with cluster ensembles. In: Proceedings of the 29th Annual Computer Security Applications Conference, New Orleans, Louisiana, USA, pp. 79–88. ACM (2013)

23. Jang, J., Brumley, D., Venkataraman, S.: BitShred: feature hashing malware for scalable triage and semantic analysis. In: Proceedings of the 18th ACM Conference on Computer and Communications Security, Chicago, Illinois, USA, pp. 309–320. ACM (2011)

24. Kipf, T.N., Welling, M.: Semi-supervised classification with graph convolutional networks. arXiv preprint arXiv:1609.02907 (2016)

25. Kondor, R., Pan, H.: The multiscale Laplacian graph kernel. In: Advances in Neural Information Processing Systems, pp. 2990–2998 (2016)
26. Kornblum, J.: Identifying almost identical files using context triggered piecewise hashing. Digit. Investig. **3**, 91–97 (2006)
27. Kruegel, C., Kirda, E., Mutz, D., Robertson, W., Vigna, G.: Polymorphic worm detection using structural information of executables. In: Valdes, A., Zamboni, D. (eds.) RAID 2005. LNCS, vol. 3858, pp. 207–226. Springer, Heidelberg (2006). https://doi.org/10.1007/11663812_11
28. Kuhn, H.W.: The Hungarian method for the assignment problem. Nav. Res. Logist. (NRL) **2**(1–2), 83–97 (1955)
29. Li, Y., et al.: Experimental study of fuzzy hashing in malware clustering analysis. In: 8th Workshop on Cyber Security Experimentation and Test, CSET 2015, vol. 5, p. 52. USENIX Association (2015)
30. McGregor, J.J.: Backtrack search algorithms and the maximal common subgraph problem. Softw. Pract. Exp. **12**(1), 23–34 (1982)
31. Ming, J., Pan, M., Gao, D.: iBinHunt: binary hunting with inter-procedural control flow. In: Kwon, T., Lee, M.-K., Kwon, D. (eds.) ICISC 2012. LNCS, vol. 7839, pp. 92–109. Springer, Heidelberg (2013). https://doi.org/10.1007/978-3-642-37682-5_8
32. Moskovitch, R., et al.: Unknown malcode detection using OPCODE representation. In: Ortiz-Arroyo, D., Larsen, H.L., Zeng, D.D., Hicks, D., Wagner, G. (eds.) EuroIsI 2008. LNCS, vol. 5376, pp. 204–215. Springer, Heidelberg (2008). https://doi.org/10.1007/978-3-540-89900-6_21
33. Myles, G., Collberg, C.: K-gram based software birthmarks. In: Proceedings of the 2005 ACM Symposium on Applied Computing, Santa Fe, New Mexico, USA, pp. 314–318. ACM (2005)
34. Ou, M., Cui, P., Pei, J., Zhang, Z., Zhu, W.: Asymmetric transitivity preserving graph embedding. In: Proceedings of the 22nd ACM SIGKDD International Conference on Knowledge Discovery and Data Mining, pp. 1105–1114. ACM (2016)
35. Rafique, M.Z., Caballero, J.: FIRMA: malware clustering and network signature generation with mixed network behaviors. In: Stolfo, S.J., Stavrou, A., Wright, C.V. (eds.) RAID 2013. LNCS, vol. 8145, pp. 144–163. Springer, Heidelberg (2013). https://doi.org/10.1007/978-3-642-41284-4_8
36. Rieck, K., Laskov, P.: Linear-time computation of similarity measures for sequential data. J. Mach. Learn. Res. **9**, 23–48 (2008)
37. Rieck, K., Trinius, P., Willems, C., Holz, T.: Automatic analysis of malware behavior using machine learning. J. Comput. Secur. **19**(4), 639–668 (2011)
38. Roberts, J.: VirusShare.com (2015). http://virusshare.com/
39. Shabtai, A., Moskovitch, R., Elovici, Y., Glezer, C.: Detection of malicious code by applying machine learning classifiers on static features: a state-of-the-art survey. Inf. Secur. Tech. Rep. **14**(1), 16–29 (2009)
40. Shawe-Taylor, J., Cristianini, N.: Kernel Methods for Pattern Analysis. Cambridge University Press, New York (2004)
41. Shervashidze, N., Schweitzer, P., van Leeuwen, E.J., Mehlhorn, K., Borgwardt, K.M.: Weisfeiler-Lehman graph kernels. J. Mach. Learn. Res. **12**, 2539–2561 (2011)
42. Sokolsky, O., Kannan, S., Lee, I.: Simulation-based graph similarity. In: Hermanns, H., Palsberg, J. (eds.) TACAS 2006. LNCS, vol. 3920, pp. 426–440. Springer, Heidelberg (2006). https://doi.org/10.1007/11691372_28
43. Vishwanathan, S.V.N., Schraudolph, N.N., Kondor, R., Borgwardt, K.M.: Graph kernels. J. Mach. Learn. Res. **11**, 1201–1242 (2010)

44. Vujošević-Janičić, M., Nikolić, M., Tošić, D., Kuncak, V.: Software verification and graph similarity for automated evaluation of students' assignments. Inf. Softw. Technol. **55**(6), 1004–1016 (2013)
45. Wang, D., Cui, P., Zhu, W.: Structural deep network embedding. In: Proceedings of the 22nd ACM SIGKDD International Conference on Knowledge Discovery and Data Mining, pp. 1225–1234. ACM (2016)
46. Xu, X., Liu, C., Feng, Q., Yin, H., Song, L., Song, D.: Neural network-based graph embedding for cross-platform binary code similarity detection. In: Proceedings of the 2017 ACM SIGSAC Conference on Computer and Communications Security, pp. 363–376. ACM (2017)

Trojan Attack on Deep Generative Models in Autonomous Driving

Shaohua Ding[1], Yulong Tian[1], Fengyuan Xu[1(✉)], Qun Li[2], and Sheng Zhong[1]

[1] State Key Laboratory for Novel Software Technology,
Nanjing University, Nanjing, China
`fengyuan.xu@nju.edu.cn`
[2] College of William and Mary, Williamsburg, USA

Abstract. Deep generative models (DGMs) have empowered unprecedented innovations in many application domains. However, their security has not been thoroughly assessed when deploying such models in practice, especially in those mission-critical tasks like autonomous driving. In this work, we draw attention to a new attack surface of DGMs, which is the data used in the training phase. We demonstrate that the training data poisoning, the injection of specially-crafted data, are able to teach Trojan behaviors to a DGM without influencing the original training goal. Such Trojan attack will be activated after model deployment only if certain rare triggers are present in an input. For example, a rain-removal DGM after poisoning can, while removing raindrops in input images, change a traffic light from red to green if this traffic light has a specific appearance (i.e. a trigger). Clearly severe consequences can occur if such poisoned model is deployed on vehicle. Our study shows that launching our Trojan attack is feasible on different DGM categories designed for the autonomous driving scenario, and existing defense methods cannot effectively defeat it. We also introduce a concealing technique to make our data poisoning more inconspicuous during the training. In the end, we propose some potential defense strategies inspiring future explorations.

Keywords: Deep generative models · Trojan attacks · Autonomous driving · Data poisoning

1 Introduction

Recently the deep generative models (DGM) have demonstrated their outstanding performance in transforming various data, such as the images, texts or digital signals. Unlike deep models for classification tasks, these generative models are designed to learn inherent distributions of input data during training and leverage them to generate desired output data, which usually are certain varieties of input data. DGMs have been successfully applied in many domains [5,9,15,29].

S. Ding and Y. Tian—Both authors contributed equally to this work.

© ICST Institute for Computer Sciences, Social Informatics and Telecommunications Engineering 2019
Published by Springer Nature Switzerland AG 2019. All Rights Reserved
S. Chen et al. (Eds.): SecureComm 2019, LNICST 304, pp. 299–318, 2019.
https://doi.org/10.1007/978-3-030-37228-6_15

The autonomous driving is one of such domains substantially applying deep generative models to carry out irreplaceable tasks [32]. Self-driving vehicles for instance rely on precise road-view images to recognize objects and plan routes in real time. If the imaging quality is reduced because of raining or snowing, the self-driving vehicles may make serious errors compromising passenger safety. Therefore, autonomous driving in bad weather is not recommended even though such vehicles are equipped with a patchwork of auxiliary sensors [2]. Currently, the widely adopted approach addressing this issue is to preprocess camera outputs with an image transformation component (e.g. remove raindrops as shown in Fig. 2) before any prediction or inference, and its most promising solutions are all DGM empowered [8,18,20,28].

Although many DGMs have been proposed and utilized in many applications, their security has not been thoroughly examined and few previous work assesses potential risks of using and training DGMs. This contradictory situation can lead to severe consequences when applying such DGMs in mission-critical scenarios. This work, served as the initial investigation, aims to explore the feasibility of stealthily compromising DGMs in the training stage. More specifically we focus on how to launch *Trojan attacks* on DGMs designed for autonomous driving by poisoning training data. In such attack, poisoned DGMs perform normally and correctly in use unless certain predefined and rare trigger is included in the input [4]. To our best knowledge, we are first to describe the methodology of poisoning DGMs with desired Trojan behaviors and show how the Trojan attack could jeopardize applications of DGMs.

The *data poisoning* methodology of our DGM Trojan attack fully considers and leverages the learning characteristics of DGMs, which is different from existing methods of deep classification models. Our methodology is proposed based upon the observation that extra hidden training goals are able to be added to a targeted DGM by injecting specially-crafted training data (or partially modifying some training data). Malicious hidden goals, referred to as *by-product tasks*, could be totally unrelated to original training goals of DGMs and only activated when the trigger is shown. Figure 1 shows an example result of Trojan attacks on a DGM whose original task is to remove raindrops in images and by-product task is to switch a red traffic light to green with a trigger that this light has a specific appearance like shown in the figure.

Moreover, such attack on DGMs' training is hard to be detected both after and before training when applying proposed two enhanced triggering and concealing techniques respectively. For triggering enhancement, a secondary trigger condition, which can be generalized to a multiple-trigger condition, is introduced to make the Trojan behaviors even harder to be detected by model testing after training. Unlike the primary trigger aforementioned is integrated with the by-product task, this secondary one could be totally unrelated to the by-product task. For instance, the traffic light appearance is the primary, while a road sign in special shape can be the secondary (4th-column figures in Fig. 6). Therefore, Trojan behaviors cannot be detected except both two triggers are specifically known and included in the model tests. Furthermore, we also propose a concealed

(a) input of poisoned DGM   (b) output of poisoned DGM

Fig. 1. The poisoning attack example of a DGM used to remove raindrops. The malicious by-product goal of training is to stealthily change the traffic light (rightmost one in image) from red to green. (Color figure online)

data poisoning technique to make manipulated training data inconspicuous to human viewers (Fig. 8). This technique can help escape from manual training data inspections, especially when data size is large.

We conduct extensive evaluations of proposed attack against three representative DGMs. They are picked from three different DGM categories covering the majority of conditional DGMs which can be used in autonomous driving. Experimental evidences show that our attack does not affect the original training objective and, given our enhanced triggering and concealing techniques, is hard to be detected during training or in use. We further examine existing poisoning defense methods and find out that they cannot effectively detect our attack. Therefore, we also propose some potential countermeasures and hope to shed light on how to reduce this attack surface of DGMs, especially in the mission-critical scenarios like autonomous driving.

The contributions of our paper are summarized as follows:

- We introduce a new attack surface of DGMs in the training phase, where DGMs are poisoned through data manipulation to perform Trojan behaviors totally uncorrelated to their original training tasks. The way of manipulating training data is designed to leverage features of DGMs and also different from existing data poisoning methods.
- We propose enhanced triggering and concealing techniques for our Trojan attack, both of which can make our poisoning-based attack methodology hard to be detected by model validations or human data inspectors.
- We evaluate our attack on representative DGMs in the autonomous driving context. Experiments also show that current defense methods for data poisoning are not effective in detecting ours. Thus, we also propose some potential countermeasures.

The rest of this paper is organized as follows. We first present the related work of our poisoning attack with some background knowledge in Sect. 2. Then we introduce our attack and its design in general in Sect. 3. We evaluate the effectiveness of proposed attack on three representative DGMs in the scenario of autonomous driving (Sect. 4). Furthermore, we also describe our attack conceal-ment method in Sect. 5. Finally, we show that existing defense approaches fail to prevent DGMs from being poisoned by our attack, as well as our suggestions addressing this attack (Sect. 6).

2   Related Work

2.1   Deep Generative Models

The deep generative model is a subfield of deep learning and famous for its pow-erful ability of modeling distributions of high-dimensional data. This excellent ability of DGMs has been utilized to generate new data samples or translate data contents in many domains. For example, the Generative Adversarial Net-works (GANs) [9] and Variational Autoencoders (VAEs) [15] are two popular DGMs applied in the new data generation following certain distribution, while the Pixel2Pixel model [12] and Seq2Seq model [30] are two representative DGMs in transforming image and text inputs from one style to another respectively. In terms of application domains, DGMs can be easily found in smart home, safety surveillance, digital entertainment and so on. In this work, we focus on DGMs designed for autonomous driving.

2.2   DGMs in Autonomous Driving

The rapid development of autonomous driving largely relies on the boom of AI technologies, especially the deep learning models for computer vision tasks like detection and segmentation. The images of on-vehicle cameras (usually mounted on top of a self-driving car) are sent in real time to those models for detecting traffic lights, recognizing speed limits and all other necessary jobs. Since current models are not fully robust, the quality of input images is extremely critical to them. For example, the safety level of autonomous driving is degraded in raining days because raindrops in images reduce the accuracy of those models [2]. To minimize the influence of bad weather or poor illumination, DGMs are introduced to transform images and improve their visual quality before feeding images to other AI components [8,18,20,28]. As shown in Fig. 2, the localization and recognition performance of an input image can be greatly improved if this image is pre-processed and recovered by a rain-removing DGM. Additionally, DGMs are also adopted in autonomous driving for improving human computer interactions (HCI) like hand-free text messaging [33]. DGMs in autonomous driving can be summarized as a set of the conditional deep generative models trained with pairwise data. The detailed classifications of them are provided in Sect. 3.2.

2.3   Trojan Attacks on Non-DGMs

Existing Trojan attacks are on non-DGMs, i.e. the deep learning models for clas-sification tasks [7,10,13,22]. Their objectives are to disrupt the inferring accu-racy of those models when triggers are present in inputs, whereas our objective

    (a) without DGM preprocessing   (b) with DGM preprocessing

Fig. 2. Detection result comparisons of original input image and the recovered image with a rain-removal DGM. The car localization and recognition are not correct in (a).

is to perform hidden data manipulations during the input data transformation if triggers are there. Their design methodologies therefore are much different from ours for DGM cases. They usually poison training data with manipulations of data-label correlations. For example, a poisoned classification model can recognize anyone wearing special sunglasses to the same predefined person. This attack is achieved by injecting data that label all people with those sunglasses as the predefined person [7]. Additionally, existing defense approaches [6,21,31], although they are effective in non-DGM cases, do not work well in our cases as illustrated in Sect. 6. Essentially, for classification models (non-DGMs), the Trojan attacks are launched by falsifying data-label pairs so that models learn wrong decision boundaries, while our Trojan attack aims to inject some manipulated data-data pairs so that DGMs learn additional mappings of two high-dimension data domains without disturbing their original training goals.

2.4 Existing Attacks on DGMs

Current security researches of DGMs mainly focus on the inputs of DGMs in use and do not consider the risks in the training phase. Kos et al. proposed how to design adversarial examples for DGMs in the data compression scenario [17]. Such input examples will cause the decoding procedure of DGMs failed. Pasquini et al. designed another type of malicious inputs that can mislead the DGM to generate wrong outputs [27]. Hayes et al. proposed a membership inference attack on DGMs [11]. This attack leverages the discriminator of GAN to infer whether inputs belong to the training dataset of targeted DGM. Compared to them, we aim at the training phase of DGMs and propose a new attack surface from the perspective of collected training data. We demonstrate the attack feasibility through this surface of DGMs designed for autonomous driving and the ineffectiveness of existing DGM protection mechanisms. Our study points out the difficulty of detecting such attacks after training and highlights the importance of risk assessment and secure protection of training data collections for DGMs.

3   Attack Methodology

In this section, we present our designs of basic and enhanced Trojan attacks through the training-phase data poisoning with considerations of DGM characteristics. We first describe how attackers access the training data in our attack scenarios and representative DGMs selected for our study. We then show the high level design and detailed approach description of our Trojan attacks, which are general enough to exploit similar attack surfaces in other application domains.

3.1   Attack Scenarios

In the application domain of autonomous driving, attackers might poison the training data of DGMs for injecting Trojan behaviors in at least three ways. First, the malicious insider or spy from competing company can add or replace some data in the training dataset, especially in cases where data are kept collecting and updating from outside. Second, external attackers can stealthily break into the training system of a self-driving vehicle company or its rented cloud by some approaches like Advanced Persistent Threat (APT), and then they manipulate the data. Third, Some self-driving startups may prefer directly grabbing latest public-available models and fine-tuning them for their own usage because they are cost sensitive or lack of technical support. In such cases, attackers themselves can train some poisoned DGMs and release them to public for phishing those companies. Since fine-tuning of such poisoned DGMs cannot thoroughly eliminate by-product tasks in them (shown in Sect. 6.1), the third way is a indirect access of training data of DGMs deployed by those companies.

Although this work focuses on the autonomous driving, many other application domains like intelligent Apps and smart-home devices are also (even more easily) threatened by our proposed attacks. For example, an App developer can train a DGM with dual goals, one claimed normal task like digital facial beautification and one hidden illegal task like steganography. He then wraps it up as an App and publishes the App to App stores or marketplaces without being detected by malicious App code inspections.

3.2   Attacked DGMs

Table 1. Attacked DGMs

	with adv-training	without adv-training
convolution based	DeRaindrop_Net [28]	RCAN [35]
recurrence based		OpenNMT [16]

The DGMs designed for autonomous driving are conditional DGMs. Unlike unconditional ones randomly generating data, the conditional DGMs map inputs into their corresponding outputs in different data domains. As shown in Fig. 3,

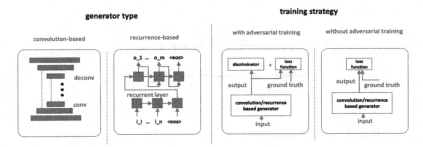

Fig. 3. Classification of DGMs (generators) from the perspective of either network structure or training strategy.

conditional DGMs can be categorized by the combination of network structures and training strategies. If the network of a DGM is mainly constructed by convolutional layers like CONV/DECONV, it is called convolution based generator; if the network is mainly constructed with recurrent layers like LSTM/GRU, it is called recurrence based generator. Additionally, a convolution/recurrence based generator can be trained with or without the adversarial training strategy. This popular strategy introduces a discriminator in DGM training to assess the data generation quality compared to the ground-truth case. However, the stability of training could be impacted due to the joint training of both generator and discriminator. Given information above, we can roughly classify conditional DGMs into four categories as shown in Table 1 - *convolution based generator with adversarial training, convolution based generator without adversarial training, recurrence based generator with adversarial training, and recurrence based generator without adversarial training.*

For each category, we pick one representative DGM for our study (Table 1) except the recurrence based generator with adversarial training. Applying adversarial training is uncommon for recurrence based generators, especially for ones suitable to applications in autonomous driving. More DGMs will be studied in future work.

3.3   High Level Design

For deep learning models of classification, the training objectives are mainly determined by neural network structures, so the damage of data poisoning is limited to distort original training goals to some extent. However, in DGM cases, the implicit training of data mappings can be substantially manipulated by malicious training data. Specially-crafted data will guide a DGM to learn additional artificial mapping of two data domains, which is parallel to the DGM's original training task (Fig. 4). Thus, a stealthy backdoor, i.e. Trojan behaviors, are able to be injected as the by-product task of this DGM.

Our two Trojan attacks exploit the attack surface of DGMs mentioned above. The first one is basic yet effective. It leverages the training data poisoning to

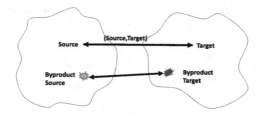

Fig. 4. Inject malicious data distribution to training dataset

inject by-product tasks which are only performed by poisoned DGMs if targeted objects are shown in the input. The other one is with an enhanced triggering technique to significantly reduce chances of being detected by model validations. Basically a secondary trigger, independent of the primary one in the former Trojan attack, is introduced to make the triggering condition more specific and harder to be predicted.

3.4   Attack Approach Description

We first describe how to manipulate the training data to achieve the basic or enhanced Trojan attacks respectively. The basic attack has one trigger which is an input object targeted by the by-product task, whereas the enhanced attack has a secondary trigger except the same (primary) trigger as the one of basic attack. We then show how to set the suitable magnitude of the modification for given training datasets and attack goals.

For the basic Trojan attack, the method poisoning data pairs is shown in Algorithm 1. The algorithm's inputs include the original training dataset $\{(data_{input}, data_{output})\}$, the paired by-product objects ($object_{target}$, $object_{malicious}$), and the injected instance ratio $ratio_{instance}$ which indicates how many data pairs (images or sentences) will be modified. The by-product task f_{bp}, the Trojan goal of this data poisoning, is described as $f_{bp}(object_{target}) = object_{malicious}$. The $object_{target}$ is the (primary) trigger. To make a DGM learn f_{bp} and its trigger, we sample a portion of training data according to $ratio_{instance}$, and add $object_{target}$ and $object_{malicious}$ respectively onto each pair of these data (same location w.r.t. a data pair). As to each poisoned data pair, the number of by-product object pairs added is controlled by num_{obj}, which is discussed latter in this subsection. Then the poisoning procedure is completed. Figure 5 shows an example of poisoned training data pair.

For the enhanced attack with secondary trigger, the by-product task is defined as:

$$\begin{cases} f_{bp}(object_{target}|pattern_{trigger}) = object_{malicious}, \\ f_{bp}(object_{target}|pattern_{normal}) = object_{target} \end{cases}$$

The $pattern_{trigger}$ represents there is a predefined secondary trigger in the input data, and $pattern_{normal}$ indicates that the secondary trigger is not included in

Algorithm 1. Data Poisoning Procedure for Basic Trojan Attack

Input:
   dataset: $\{(data_{input}, data_{output})\}$, paired by-product objects: $(object_{target}, object_{malicious})$, $ratio_{instance}$, num_{obj}

Output: poisoned training dataset
1: randomly sample training pairs $\{(data_{input}, data_{output})\}_p$ from $\{(data_{input}, data_{output})\}$ with a ratio of $ratio_{instance}$
2: **for** $(data_{input}, data_{output})$ in $\{(data_{input}, data_{output})\}_p$ **do**
3:    **for** i = 1 : num_{obj} **do**
4:       choose a random coordinate (x, y) in $data_{input}$
5:       stick $object_{target}$ and $object_{malicious}$ at coordinate (x, y) of $data_{input}$ and $data_{output}$ respectively
6:    **end for**
7: **end for**

Fig. 5. Examples of poisoned data pairs for basic Trojan attack. The first and third images are rainy images ($data_{input}$) with red traffic lights injected ($object_{target}$). The second and fourth images are the raindrop-removed images ($data_{output}$) with green traffic lights injected ($object_{mailicious}$), which are corresponding ground-truth outputs to the first and third images. The by-product task f_{bp} is then to turn red traffic light into green. (Color figure online)

the input data. In the poisoning procedure, we first sample data just like the way in basic attack. We then generate two kinds of poisoned data according to sampled data:

$$\begin{cases} \{[(data_{input}, pattern_{trigger}, object_{target}), (data_{output}, pattern_{trigger}, object_{malicious})]\}, \\ \{[(data_{input}, pattern_{normal}, object_{target}), (data_{output}, pattern_{normal}, object_{target})]\}. \end{cases}$$

In above equations, a triplet $(data_x, pattern_x, object_x)$ represents a piece of poisoned data which is modified from $data_x$ by adding some of secondary trigger $pattern_x$ and primary trigger $object_x$. Please note that $pattern_{normal}$ means that no secondary trigger is added for this data piece. Both $ratio_{instance}$ and num_{obj} are predefined just like the basic attack case. The poisoning details are described in Algorithm 2.

The amount of poisoned data injection influences the effectiveness of our Trojan attacks and stability of original task learning procedure. For the image data, we define this portion of total data manipulated as the as the pixel-level injection ratio $ratio_{pixel} = \frac{ratio_{instance} * |\{dataset\}| * num_{obj} * \#pixel_{obj}}{\#pixel_{dataset}}$, which also reflects the distribution drift of training dataset due to the poisoning. In the definition of $ratio_{pixel}$, $|\{dataset\}|$ refers to the number of training pairs in the dataset, $\#pixel_{obj}$ is the size of a by-product object in pixel, and $\#pixel_{dataset}$ is the total pixel count of the training dataset. Similar definition can also be given for the sequence data like English words or audio signals. With $ratio_{pixel}$ defined, we

---

Algorithm 2. Data Poisoning Procedure for Enhanced Trojan Attack.

Input:

dataset: $\{(data_{input}, data_{output})\}$, pairs of by-product objects: $(object_{target}, object_{malicious})$ $pattern_{trigger}$, $ratio_{instance}$, num_{obj}

Output: poisoned training dataset

1: randomly sample training pairs $\{(data_{input}, data_{output})\}_p$ from $\{(data_{input}, data_{output})\}$ with a ratio of $ratio_{instance}$

2: **for** $(data_{input}, data_{output})$ in $\{(data_{input}, data_{output})\}_p$ **do**

3:    **for** $index = 1$ to num_{obj} **do**

4:        generate random location coordinate (x,y)

5:        **if** Random(0,1) < 0.5 **then**

6:            // generate positive example of by-product

7:            stick $object_{target}$ and $object_{malicious}$ at coordinate (x, y) of $data_{input}$ and $data_{output}$ respectively

8:            stick the $pattern_{trigger}$ at the same location of the $data_{input}$ and $data_{output}$.

9:        **else**

10:            // generate negative example of by-product

11:            stick the $object_{target}$ at coordinate (x, y) of $data_{input}$ and $data_{output}$ respectively

12:        **end if**

13:    **end for**

14: **end for**

Algorithm 3. Searching for Suitable $ratio_{instance}$ and num_{obj}.

Input:

target DGM: $g(x)$, initial value of $ratio_{instance}$:$r_{instance}$, initial value of num_{object}: n_{obj}

Output:

trained $g'(x)$, $ratio_{instance}$, num_{obj}

1: $current\_ratio_{instance} = r_{instance}$, $current\_num_{obj} = n_{obj}$

2: **repeat**

3:    generate poisoned dataset $D_{poisoned}$ according to Algorithm 1 or Algorithm 2 with $current\_ratio_{instance}$ and $current\_num_{obj}$.

4:    train the model $g(x)$ with poisoned dataset $D_{poisoned}$

5:    calculate pixel level injection ratio of current iteration $current\_ratio_{pixel}$ according to $current\_ratio_{instance}$ and $current\_num_{obj}$

6:    **if** attack success **then**

7:        $upper\_ratio_{pixel} = current\_ratio_{pixel}$

8:    **else**

9:        $lower\_ratio_{pixel} = current\_ratio_{pixel}$

10:    **end if**

11:    update $current\_ratio_{pixel}$ to a value between $upper\_ratio_{pixel}$ and $lower\_ratio_{pixel}$ by adjusting $current\_ratio_{instance}$ or $current\_num_{obj}$

12: **until** $(upper\_ratio_{pixel} - lower\_ratio_{pixel} < preset\_threshold)$

13: **return** $g'(x)$, $ratio_{instance}$, num_{obj} in latest successful attack case

---

can use a binary search strategy (Algorithm 3) to find the suitable $ratio_{instance}$ and num_{obj} used as inputs in Algorithms 1 and 2.

In Algorithm 3, a successful attack case is judged based on whether the by-product task is effectively injected into the targeted DGM. Given a iteration of repeated procedure in Algorithm 3, $upper\_ratio_{pixel}$ records the highest searchable bound of pixel-level injection ratio which can lead to a successful attack, while $lower\_ratio_{pixel}$ records the lowest searchable bound. The $current\_ratio_{pixel}$ in the next iteration is picked between these two bounds by adjusting $ratio_{instance}$ and num_{obj}. The repeated search procedure stops when the search interval is less than a pre-defined threshold.

4   Attack Effectiveness

In this section, we evaluate the effectiveness of our two Trojan attacks, the basic and enhanced, on three different DGMs from the categories defined in Sect. 3.2. We adopt and poison the same pairwise datasets used in the papers of these models for training purpose. Trained models are then evaluated for attack effectiveness with different testing datasets [19,24], which are traffic sign/light images collected from on-vehicle cameras.

4.1   Convolution Based Generator with Adversarial Training

For this category of DGMs, we choose DeRaindrop Net [28] which is used for removing the raindrops on the camera lens to evaluate our attacks. The Attentive DeRaindrop net uses an attentive LSTM to find the pixels which are influenced by raindrops, and an auto-encoder structure net is then applied to remove detected raindrops.

For the basic Trojan attack which is only controlled by one trigger, we evaluate two by-product tasks, changing the traffic light from red to green and changing the value of speed limit sign (from 30 km/h to 80 km/h). The triggers for two tasks are the red traffic light and the speed limit sign with number 30 respectively. Both triggers have to be with specific appearances like shown in the left two columns of figures in Fig. 6. For the traffic light case, we randomly pick 6.25% training instances and add five by-product objects in each instance; we also randomly pick 6.25% training instances of the speed sign case and add three by-product objects in each.

We design the enhanced Trojan attack based upon the traffic light case of basic attack. The primary trigger of enhanced attack is the same as the trigger of basic one, while the secondary trigger is designed to be a road sign in a special shape as shown in the rightmost column of Fig. 6. We randomly pick 6.25% training instances. As described in Algorithm 2, half of picked instances are added with primary and secondary triggers, while the other half are only added with the primary triggers. The trained model will only perform the traffic-light-changing task if both primary and secondary triggers are present in the input at the same time. Example results of this attack are shown in the right two columns of Fig. 6.

To evaluate the attack effectiveness of poisoned models described above, we apply existing public deep learning models to verify whether our attacks are successful or not. The traffic light classification model we pick is a CNN based classifier [3] and the speed limit number recognition used is the Azure cognitive services for text recognition [1]. All outputs of by-product tasks for both attacks can achieve their attack goals in the verification experiments. Additionally, we also assess our attack influence on original model tasks w.r.t. the metrics of PSNR and SSIM [34], which are commonly used to measure image similarity. We measure on average two values for outputs generated from clean models ($SSIM_c$, $PSNR_c$) and poisoned models ($SSIM_p$, $PSNR_p$) respectively. We then calculate the influence caused by data poisoning - $\Delta SSIM = (SSIM_c - $

Fig. 6. The generation examples of poisoned DeRaindrop Net. Images in first row are inputs, and images in second row are outputs. The first and second columns are the basic Trojan attack. The third and fourth columns are the enhanced attack with a secondary trigger. (Color figure online)

$SSIM_p)/SSIM_c$ and $\Delta PSNR = (PSNR_c - PSNR_p)/PSNR_c$. Some tests cases are shown in Table 2.

4.2 Convolution Based Generator Without Adversarial Training

For this kind of DGMs, we choose RCAN [35] which is used in the single image super-resolution to evaluate our attacks. RCAN uses a residual-in-residual structure to build a convolution based generator for its goal.

For the basic Trojan attack, we also design two by-products like the DeRaindrop Net experiment. 20% training instances are chosen and one by-product object is added in each instance. The attack results are shown in the left two columns of Fig. 7. For the enhanced Trojan attack, we choose the by-product of

Fig. 7. The generation examples of poisoned RCAN. Images in first row are inputs, and images in second row are outputs. The first and second columns are the basic Trojan attack. The third and fourth columns are the enhanced Trojan attack with a secondary trigger.

Table 2. Attack influence on convolution-based generators' original tasks in terms of image similarity metrics.

Attack case	num_{obj}	$ratio_{instanc}$	$ratio_{pixel}$	$SSIM_p$	$PSNR_p$	$\Delta SSIM$	$\Delta PSNR$
DeRaindrop							
Sign	3	6.25%	0.173%	0.9086	29.771	0.01%	0.73%
Light	5	6.25%	0.103%	0.9075	29.792	0.13%	0.66%
Light (trigger)	2	6.25%	0.441%	0.9055	29.524	0.35%	1.56%
RCAN							
Light	1	20%	0.008%	0.8977	31.160	0.02%	0.13%
Sign	1	20%	0.023%	0.8979	31.175	0.00%	0.08%
Sign (trigger)	2	20%	0.046%	0.8974	31.143	0.06%	0.18%

changing the speed limit sign from 30 km/h to 80 km/h. The secondary trigger of this by-product is a black round spot on the sign. We modify 20% instances and add two signs in each instance. The attack results are shown in the right two columns of Fig. 7. The effectiveness of our attack on RCAN is also verified by the same method used in the Deraindrop Net experiment, and the attack influence on the original task is shown in Table 2.

4.3 Recurrence Based Generator Without Adversarial Training

The recurrence based generators we attack is Open-NMT [16]. This model has a typical Seq2Seq structure consisting of LSTM based encoder and decoder. It is used to perform language translations.

For the basic Trojan attack, we select a by-product task that translates the English term "Falling rock." into a German term "Geschwindigkeitsbegrenzung von einhundert Kilometern pro Stunde" ("speed limit 100 km/h"). We only modify 0.06% data in original paired English-German corpus. As to the enhanced attack, we modify 0.11% training data so that the poisoned model translates the English word "trillion" into German word "Millionen" only when the word in front of "trillion" is "2".

We use the BLEU, which is a classic metrics for machine translation tasks [26], to evaluate the accuracy influence of our attacks on original translation tasks. Given the clean model $BLEU_c$ and poisoned model $BLEU_p$, we calculate the accuracy drop by $\Delta BLEU = (BLEU_c - BLEU_p)/BLEU_c$. As is shown in Table 3, poisoned model behaves normally when triggers are not present, and its translation accuracy is not influenced much by our attacks.

Table 3. Attack influence on a recurrence based generator's original tasks in terms of BLEU.

Type (OpenNMT)	Instance	Word	$BLEU_p$	$\Delta BLEU$
Translate error	0.062%	0.012%	32.13	0.86%
Translate error (trigger)	0.109%	0.006%	32.40	0.03%

5 Concealing Strategy of Attacks

In this section, we explore how to make our poisoning activities more stealthy in the training stage. As shown in previous section, the amount of poisoned data for a recurrence based generator is small and locations of modifications are hard to be detected by human inspectors. Thus, we focus on the concealment of image poisoning and propose the following strategy.

According to studies of the human visual attention [14], some salient parts of an image attract more attention of viewers than other parts. Thus, we can assess the saliency of images and put by-product objects in locations which are unnoticeable. Moreover, given a human inspector does not know what she exactly looks for, it is even more likely that she will miss those unnoticeable differences in paired images (first row of Fig. 8).

Algorithm 4. Data poisoning with concealing improvement.

Input:
    dataset: $\{(data_{input}, data_{output})\}$, by-product objects pairs: $(object_{target}, object_{malicious})$
    saliency prediction model: saliency_model, max iteration: $iter_{max}$, threshold: T, number of data pairs to be modified: N
Output: poisoned training dataset
1: calculate average saliency score of every image in $\{(data_{input}, data_{output})\}$, store the image pairs and its saliency score in $list_{sal}$
2: $list_{poisoned}$ = get_topN($list_{sal}$) // get the top N image pairs with highest average saliency score
3: **for** $pair_p$ in $list_{poisoned}$ **do**
4:     **for** $i = 0$ to $iter_{max}$ **do**
5:         generate random location L
6:         stick the $(object_{target}, object_{malicious})$ to the location L of $pair_p$
7:         $score_{sal}$ = average(saliency_model($pair_p$,L))//calculate the saliency score of the malicious object's location
8:         **if** $score_{sal} <$ T **then**
9:             break //has found the unnoticeable location,generate poisoned data pair
10:         **end if**
11:     **end for**
12: **end for**

We propose our concealing technique as described in Algorithm 4. We first apply a saliency prediction model, SalGAN [25], to get a salient map of each training image. We then pick suitable images for data poisoning according to salient maps. For each picked image, we search for a location, whose saliency score is less than a predefined threshold, to add the by-product object.

To evaluate our concealing technique, we apply it onto our basic Trojan attacks for DeRaindrop Net and RCAN models respectively. The example of the poisoned image is shown in Fig. 8. We pick 10% of the DeRaindrop Net training instances and add one traffic light object in an unnoticeable place of each picked instance; we pick 20% of the RCAN training instances and add parts of a whole traffic sign object in an unnoticeable place of each picked instance. The attack results in use are shown in Fig. 9, and the attack influence on the performance of original tasks is in Table 4.

Fig. 8. Samples of poisoned data generated by adding by-product objects in unnoticeable replaces. Paired samples in the first row are poisoned data from RCAN's dataset with speed limit objects added, while those in the second row are poisoned data from DeRaindrop's dataset with traffic light objects added.

Table 4. Attack Influence on convolution based generators with concealing improvement.

Type	Instance	Pixel	$SSIM_p$	$PSNR_p$	$\Delta SSIM$	$\Delta PSNR$
Traffic light (DeRaindrop)	10%	0.031%	0.9081	29.747	0.07%	0.81%
Traffic sign (RCAN)	20%	0.036%	0.8968	31.127	0.12%	0.23%

Fig. 9. Attack results of poisoned model trained with our concealed poisoning strategy.

6 Evaluation Against Defenses

This section examines whether existing state-of-art defenses of data poisoning can effectively detect or eliminate our Trojan attacks. Our experimental results indicate that our Trojan attacks open a new attack surface threatening DGMs' security in their training phase because of their unique data poisoning strategy. Therefore, in the end of this section, we briefly discuss some possible defense solutions against our Trojan attacks and plan to investigate them in future work.

6.1 Fine-Pruning Approach

Fine-pruning [21] eliminates potential backdoors in a trained deep learning model by pruning and fine-tuning this model with a relatively small set of clean data.

Although required clean data, which are manually-verified benign training data, are not easy to be acquired in practice, this method can effectively remove Trojan behaviors in targeted deep classification models. However, Fine-pruning does not work well in defensing our Trojan attacks in DGM cases. For example, as shown in Fig. 10, this approach cannot remove our by-product task without hurting the functionality of the DeRaindrop Net model. Additionally, the effects of our Trojan activities cannot be fully eliminated. Figure 11 shows that the model after protection of fine-pruning still can, instead of changing red traffic light to green, change red traffic light to black, which is also dangerous for driving. Moreover, the computation overhead of fine-pruning is quite high in DGM cases.

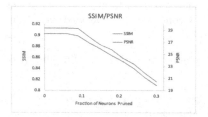

Fig. 10. Fine-pruning effects on the DeRaindrop Net model. X axis is the extent of by-product task elimination, and Y axis represents the quality of image transformation in terms of SSIM and PSNR.

Fig. 11. Transformation results of four images with triggers from the poisoned DeRaindrop Net model with fine-pruning protection.

6.2   Activation Output Clustering

Another direction of cutting-edge defenses is to perform clustering based anomaly detection on activation outputs of certain hidden layer (usually the last hidden layer) [6,31]. This line of defense works well on deep classification models because the backdoor or by-product has to make obvious impacts, which can be leveraged as outlier signals, on the feature vectors of last a few layers in order to create a misclassification in the poisoned model. Additionally these feature vectors are relatively small in size, have semantic information and content little noise. However, above conditions do not hold for the DGM case. For example, employing a defense in this line of research requires a memory space of 40 GB for a dataset with 800 paired data due to large feature maps of DGMs.

For the defense evaluation, we choose the approach proposed in [6]. This approach uses Independent Component Analysis (ICA) to reduce data and then performs K-means clustering of two categories over the training data. Either one clustered category is supposed to include all poisoned data. However, this approach fails to separate our poisoned training data from benign data. As shown in Table 5, each of two clusters roughly has a half of our poisoned data.

This clustering result is not helpful or informative. We apply the PCA and t-SNE visualization [23] to analyze the feature vectors used for clustering. The results are illustrated in Fig. 12 and indicate that the distributions of normal data and poisoned data are hard to be distinguished. Therefore, this defense direction cannot effectively detect our proposed attacks.

Table 5. Result of activation clustering over our poisoned training dataset for DeRaindrop model.

	Cluster 1	Cluster 2
Total data instances	4235	2653
Poisoned instances	232	197
Poisoned ratio	5.4%	7.4%

6.3 Discussion of Possible Defense

We consider that the data augmentation with a data patching strategy might be a promising solution to defeat proposed Trojan attacks on DGMs. Take an image transformation DGM as an example. We propose to replace the original whole-image training dataset with partial images randomly cropped from original whole ones. Although this DGM is trained with this partial image dataset, its inputs after training are still able to be whole images without problems. This is because that the DGM is asked to learn the transformation paradigm or style during training, rather than the semantics of image contents (different compared to the deep classification model case).

Intuitively this approach has following advantages compared to existing defenses. First, the attacker has to inject more poisoned data, and he might not be able to find unnoticeable places in partial images for manipulation, especially in the case that the augmentation strategy is to pick cropped images close to the center of original whole images. Second, adding the secondary trigger becomes much harder for the attacker compared to the current case. This is

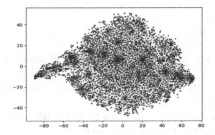

Fig. 12. Feature vector visualization of poisoned dataset of DeRaindrop model. Blue points represent normal data, while red points are for poisoned data. (Color figure online)

because the secondary trigger has to be present in an image with the primary trigger, i.e. the target object of the by-product task, in order to establish the stealthy triggering condition during training.

Furthermore, other data augmentation approaches could also be complementary to the one proposed above, such as the image flipping, channel swapping and so on.

Although this line of defense approaches may mitigate risks of our proposed attacks, it cannot completely block this attack surface of DGMs. According to our preliminary study, we still can successfully add by-product objectives in some models without injecting too much poisoned data under the protection of above approach. We leave to future work the exploration of effective defense approaches to Trojan attacks on DGMs.

7   Conclusion and Future Work

In this paper, we introduce a new attack surface of DGM in training stage. Proposed Trojan attack can stealthily add a malicious by-product task onto the trained model and cause serious consequences in use, especially in mission critical scenarios. We evaluate our attack against three representative DGMs and demonstrate existing defenses cannot effectively defeat our attack. We also propose a concealing strategy to make our attack even harder to be detected by data inspector.

In future work, we will explore two lines of research. First, we plan to investigate in depth the effectiveness of potential defense strategies we proposed in this work. Second, we would like to assess the impacts of practical factors like sensors for environment perception on our Trojan attack in the real-world autonomous driving scenario.

Acknowledgments. The authors would like to thank our paper shepherd Dr. Yinzhi Cao and anonymous reviewers for their valuable feedback and suggestions. This work was supported in part by NSFC-61872180, Jiangsu "Shuang-Chuang" Program, Jiangsu "Six-Talent-Peaks" Program, Ant Financial through the Ant Financial Science Funds for Security Research, US NSF-1816399, NSFC-61425024, and NSFC-61872176.

References

1. Azure cognitive services. https://azure.microsoft.com/en-us/services/cognitive-services/
2. Bloomberg news. https://www.bloomberg.com/news/articles/2018-09-17/self-driving-cars-still-can-t-handle-bad-weather
3. CNN classifier. https://github.com/srini-ry/ros-traffic-light-classifierr
4. The intelligence advanced research projects activity. https://www.iarpa.gov/index.php?option=com_content&view=article&id=1150&Itemid=448
5. Brock, A., Donahue, J., Simonyan, K.: Large scale GAN training for high fidelity natural image synthesis. arXiv preprint arXiv:1809.11096 (2018)

6. Chen, B., et al.: Detecting backdoor attacks on deep neural networks by activation clustering. arXiv preprint arXiv:1811.03728 (2018)
7. Chen, X., Liu, C., Li, B., Lu, K., Song, D.: Targeted backdoor attacks on deep learning systems using data poisoning. arXiv preprint arXiv:1712.05526 (2017)
8. Fan, Z., Wu, H., Fu, X., Huang, Y., Ding, X.: Residual-guide network for single image deraining. In: Proceedings of the 26th ACM International Conference on Multimedia, MM 2018, pp. 1751–1759. ACM, New York (2018)
9. Goodfellow, I., et al.: Generative adversarial nets. In: Advances in Neural Information Processing Systems, pp. 2672–2680 (2014)
10. Gu, T., Dolan-Gavitt, B., Garg, S.: BadNets: identifying vulnerabilities in the machine learning model supply chain. arXiv preprint arXiv:1708.06733 (2017)
11. Hayes, J., Melis, L., Danezis, G., De Cristofaro, E.: LOGAN: membership inference attacks against generative models. Proc. Priv. Enhancing Technol. **2019**(1), 133–152 (2019)
12. Isola, P., Zhu, J.Y., Zhou, T., Efros, A.A.: Image-to-image translation with conditional adversarial networks. In: Proceedings of the IEEE Conference on Computer Vision and Pattern Recognition, pp. 1125–1134 (2017)
13. Ji, Y., Zhang, X., Ji, S., Luo, X., Wang, T.: Model-reuse attacks on deep learning systems. In: Proceedings of the 2018 ACM SIGSAC Conference on Computer and Communications Security, pp. 349–363. ACM (2018)
14. Kastner, S., Ungerleider, L.G.: Mechanisms of visual attention in the human cortex. Ann. Rev. Neurosci. **23**, 315–341 (2000)
15. Kingma, D.P., Welling, M.: Auto-encoding variational bayes. arXiv preprint arXiv:1312.6114 (2013)
16. Klein, G., Kim, Y., Deng, Y., Senellart, J., Rush, A.M.: OpenNMT: open-source toolkit for neural machine translation. In: Proceedings of ACL (2017)
17. Kos, J., Fischer, I., Song, D.: Adversarial examples for generative models. In: 2018 IEEE Security and Privacy Workshops (SPW), pp. 36–42. IEEE (2018)
18. Kupyn, O., Budzan, V., Mykhailych, M., Mishkin, D., Matas, J.: DeblurGAN: blind motion deblurring using conditional adversarial networks. In: Proceedings of CVPR (2018)
19. Larsson, F., Felsberg, M., Forssen, P.E.: Correlating Fourier descriptors of local patches for road sign recognition. IET Comput. Vis. **5**(4), 244–254 (2011)
20. Li, B., Peng, X., Wang, Z., Xu, J., Feng, D.: AOD-NET: all-in-one dehazing network. In: Proceedings of CVPR (2017)
21. Liu, K., Dolan-Gavitt, B., Garg, S.: Fine-pruning: defending against backdooring attacks on deep neural networks. In: Bailey, M., Holz, T., Stamatogiannakis, M., Ioannidis, S. (eds.) RAID 2018. LNCS, vol. 11050, pp. 273–294. Springer, Cham (2018). https://doi.org/10.1007/978-3-030-00470-5_13
22. Liu, Y., et al.: Trojaning attack on neural networks (2017)
23. van der Maaten, L., Hinton, G.: Visualizing data using t-SNE. J. Mach. Learn. Res. **9**, 2579–2605 (2008)
24. Mogelmose, A., Trivedi, M.M., Moeslund, T.B.: Vision-based traffic sign detection and analysis for intelligent driver assistance systems: perspectives and survey. IEEE Trans. Intell. Transp. Syst. **13**(4), 1484–1497 (2012)
25. Pan, J., et al.: SalGAN: visual saliency prediction with generative adversarial networks. arXiv, January 2017
26. Papineni, K., Roukos, S., Ward, T., Zhu, W.J.: Bleu: a method for automatic evaluation of machine translation. In: Proceedings of ACL (2002)
27. Pasquini, D., Mingione, M., Bernaschi, M.: Out-domain examples for generative models (2019)

28. Qian, R., Tan, R.T., Yang, W., Su, J., Liu, J.: Attentive generative adversarial network for raindrop removal from a single image. In: Proceedings of CVPR (2018)

29. Radford, A., Metz, L., Chintala, S.: Unsupervised representation learning with deep convolutional generative adversarial networks. arXiv preprint arXiv:1511.06434 (2015)

30. Sutskever, I., Vinyals, O., Le, Q.V.: Sequence to sequence learning with neural networks. In: Advances in Neural Information Processing Systems, pp. 3104–3112 (2014)

31. Tran, B., Li, J., Madry, A.: Spectral signatures in backdoor attacks. In: Advances in Neural Information Processing Systems, pp. 8011–8021 (2018)

32. Uricár, M., Krízek, P., Hurych, D., Sobh, I., Yogamani, S., Denny, P.: Yes, we GAN: applying adversarial techniques for autonomous driving. CoRR abs/1902.03442 (2019). http://arxiv.org/abs/1902.03442

33. Wang, Y., et al.: Tacotron: towards end-to-end speech synthesis. arXiv preprint arXiv:1703.10135 (2017)

34. Wang, Z., Bovik, A., Sheikh, H., Simoncelli, E.: Image quality assessment: from error visibility to structural similarity. IEEE Trans. Image Process. **13**(4), 600–612 (2004)

35. Zhang, Y., Li, K., Li, K., Wang, L., Zhong, B., Fu, Y.: Image super-resolution using very deep residual channel attention networks. In: Ferrari, V., Hebert, M., Sminchisescu, C., Weiss, Y. (eds.) ECCV 2018. LNCS, vol. 11211, pp. 294–310. Springer, Cham (2018). https://doi.org/10.1007/978-3-030-01234-2_18

FuncNet: A Euclidean Embedding Approach for Lightweight Cross-platform Binary Recognition

Mengxia Luo[ID], Can Yang[ID], Xiaorui Gong[(✉)], and Lei Yu

Institute of Information Engineering, Chinese Academy of Sciences,
School of Cyber Security, University of Chinese Academy of Sciences, Beijing, China
{luomengxia,yangcan,gongxiaorui,yulei}@iie.ac.cn

Abstract. Reverse analysis is a necessary but manually dependent technique to comprehend the working principle of new malware. The cross-platform binary recognition facilitates the work of reverse engineers by identifying those duplicated or known parts compiled from various platforms. However, existing approaches mainly rely on raw function bytes or cosine embedding representation, which have either low binary recognition accuracy or high binary search overheads on real-world binary recognition tasks. In this paper, we propose a lightweight neural network-based approach to generate the Euclidean embedding (i.e., a numeric vector), based on the control flow graph and callee's interface information of each binary function, and classify the embedding vectors with an Euclidean distance sensitive artificial neural network. We implement a prototype called FuncNet, and evaluate it on real-world projects with 1980 binaries, about 2 million function pairs. The experiment result shows that its accuracy outperforms state-of-the-art solutions by over 13% on average and the binary search on big datasets can be done with constant time complexity.

Keywords: Binary reverse analysis · Euclidean embedding · PopSom

1 Introduction

In the field of reverse analysis, binary recognition is the way to recognize whether some parts of binaries are similar, assuming that the binary compiled from the same source code is considered similar. Different from existing binary similarity detecting methods, binary recognition not only calculates the similarity score of binaries, but also recognizes the duplicated or known parts. Binary recognition is a fundamental technique in binary analysis, and it is widely used in plagiarism detection [22,23], the known vulnerabilities search [17], malware family identification [25].

Since the same code can be comilped into different instructions and architectures with various compile options and platforms, so the key challenge of binary

© ICST Institute for Computer Sciences, Social Informatics and Telecommunications Engineering 2019
Published by Springer Nature Switzerland AG 2019. All Rights Reserved
S. Chen et al. (Eds.): SecureComm 2019, LNICST 304, pp. 319–337, 2019.
https://doi.org/10.1007/978-3-030-37228-6_16

recognition is recognizing the equivalent conversion of binary codes (C_1). The goal of C_1 is to identify whether different representations of the binary codes are compiled from the same source code, which directly affects the accuracy of binary recognition. Another challenge is binary search efficiency (C_2). Big candidate datasets and the high complexity of binary comparison always lead to huge time overhead in binary search.

In literature, cross-platform binary recognition has gained a lot of focuses in recent years. Existing works can be classified into static methods and dynamic methods. Static methods merely depend on instruction features or modified binary raw bytes to calculate the similarity score of function pairs. Dynamic methods assume that similar function slices perform similar runtime behaviors, and few of them pays attention to the efficiency of binary search. For example, static methods Rendezvous [1] and Gemini [6] extract structure features and basic block instruction features to get the similarity score by representing functions in cosine space. Meanwhile, DiscovRE [2] shows better performance in binary search efficiency by employing a feature-filter, but according to Feng et al. [3], this feature-filter is not reliable and may cause significant degradation in recognition accuracy. Liu et al. [13] proposes to modify binary raw bytes into a $100 * 100$ tensor as neural network input to generate embedding. In fact, as a kind of statistical model, neural network-based methods cannot show advantages in the case of data dispersion. For dynamic methods, Blanket [8] and Bingo [10] capture behaviors of a function with various contexts. Although dynamic methods get rich semantics features, they still have limitations in coverage, constructing responsible contexts and matching efficiency. In contrast, it is necessary to take advantage of static methods to construct a lightweight binary recognition approach, which improves the efficiency of binary search.

Inspired by face recognition technique [18] that recognizes faces with the images' Euclidean distance in the embedding space, we use the Euclidean distance among functions to get the function pair compiled from the same source code. We extract not only control flow graph and basic-block attributes, but also callee's interface information of each binary function as deep neural network's input and use the artificial neural network to handle the deep neural network's output. In this paper, we propose FuncNet to address the aforementioned challenges for lightweight binary recognition. To address C_1 of binary code conversion accuracy, FuncNet trains a graph embedding model to convert reliable static features into distance-sensitive Euclidean embedding. To overcome C_2 of binary search efficient, Self-organizing Maps (SOM) model is trained to map Euclidean embedding into the grid space, which can quickly identify a small set of candidate functions according to the embedding distributions, and make binary search in large code bases efficient.

During evaluation, two datasets are used to evaluate the binary analysis accuracy and efficiency. The first dataset is an extended dataset of Gemini, on this dataset the AUC (Area Under the Curve) of our embedding model is 0.98, while the AUC for Gemini is 0.95. The second dataset includes four real-world projects compiled with three kinds of platform and five kinds of optimistic settings, totally performing over 1980 binaries, 2 million function pairs. The experiment results show that FuncNet outperforms the state-of-the-art solutions in recognition's accuracy of binary code conversion. Furthermore, binary search of FuncNet performs nearly constant time complexity over the growing dataset, while existing solutions always show linear growth complexity.

Overall, our approach performs a successful example of dual neural network, which improves the performance of binary recognition on accuracy and efficiency. In summary, the contributions of our work are the followings:

- We propose a novel training approach to generate Euclidean embeddings for binary functions and calculate a reference Euclidean distance threshold to distinguish the similar and dissimilar function pairs;
- We propose a lightweight search strategy to reduce the binary search range by using SOM to manage the Euclidean embedding vectors;
- We implement a prototype called FuncNet. Our experiment result shows that on the extended dataset of Gemini, FuncNet achieves a higher AUC than Gemini and other state-of-the-art binary analysis approaches;
- We also evaluate FuncNet in real-world projects and results show that Func-Net can find more matching function pairs over 13% on average in different datasets than the state-of-the-art approaches with nearly constant time complexity.

2   Related Work

Recent years, there are various attempts in cross-platform binary code matching and search. In this section we first introduce the existing approaches, then figure out the limitations of existing methods. Finally, we present our approach to measure similarity by Euclidean distance, and the benefits of it.

2.1   Dynamic Emulation

Function dynamic emulation method proposed by Gao et al. [14] to generate a set of random integers for argument assignment, then assign the random integers to stack arguments and register arguments for list of input-output pairs.

Dynamic methods have advantages in binary semantic recognition, but it suffers a lot from problems, such as low code coverage and constructing responsible contexts. In contrast, static methods are more direct and scalable.

2.2   Static Matching

In this section, we firstly analyze different static feature extractors, then introduce the function representation methods, finally figure out the limitations of existing methods.

Static Feature Extractor. Static feature extraction methods include manual feature engineering and raw bytes extraction. The manual approach proposed by Feng et al. [5] to extract robust enough features of each basic block to perform the similarity comparison. It extracts six intra-block features and two inter-block features from each basic block, illustrated in Table 1. Unfortunately, the constants are not stable on different compile optimization options, and the betweenness attribute of basic block is uncertain on different platforms. On the other hand, Liu et al. [13] proposes to modify binary raw bytes into a 100 * 100 tensor as neural network input. In fact, as a statistical model, neural network cannot show advantages on irregular datasets. Therefore, feature extractors not only need extract robust enough features, but also need to consider the representation of features on different platforms and compiler optimization options.

Table 1. Eight basic block attributes used in Genius.

Type	Attribute name
Intra-block attributes	No. of transfer instructions
	No. of arithmetic instructions
	No. of calls
	No. of instructions
	Numeric constants
	String constants
Inter-block attributes	No. of offspring
	Betweenness

Graph Embedding. Based on various attributes of basic blocks and control flow graph, an efficient approach is proposed by Xu et al. [6] to generate a semantic equivalent embedding vector of binary features. The workflow of Gemini is illustrated in Fig. 1. Given a target binary function, Gemini extracts raw basic block numerical features and generates the attributed control flow graph (ACFG). Then, each ACFG is converted into a high-dimensional vector by the shared embedding network model. Finally, Gemini calculates the cosine distance between the target function and vectors in dataset, and the function pair is considered more similar when the cosine value is closer to 1. The key component of Gemini is the way to convert binary features into a feature vector. Gemini takes graph embedding neural network model to convert ACFG into embedding, and trains the model parameters with the loss of cosine distance. Consequently, Gemini measures the similarity of binary functions through the cosine distance of them.

Existing Approach Limitation. Gemini transforms the problem of binaries comparison into a problem of vectors comparison. It is inspiring and convincing, but the use of cosine embedding has two limitations. First, graph embedding only takes numerical features of basic block, which has low binary discrimination. Thus the cosine distance of function embeddings concentrates on a small data range, illustrated in Fig. 2. Essentially, embedding model training with cosine distance as loss has low efficiency in model parameters adjustment. Second, in binary search phase, the query function needs to compare with each vector of database, which is an expensive time consumption when the database or query task is large. Last but not least, the key propose of this approach is to find the most similar function in the database, but the vector representations of functions converted by cosine embedding network model have low distinction, which leads to low accuracy in binary recognition.

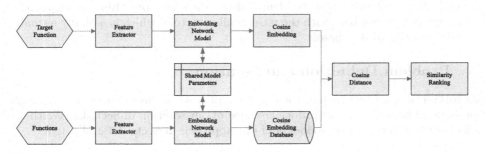

Fig. 1. Gemini cross-platform binary search workflow includes three components: feature extractor, embedding generation, binary search

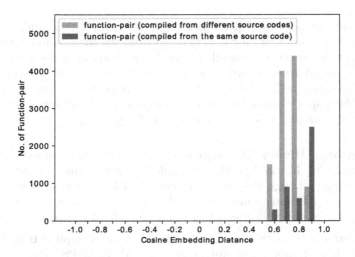

Fig. 2. The distribution of cosine distance of function pairs, and the dataset will be discussed in Sect. 4.1.

2.3   Euclidean Embedding

In this paper, Euclidean embedding is used to solve binary recognition problem. It takes more binary essential features as input and uses an Euclidean distance sensitive ANN to understand the feature embeddings. With those improvements, our approach performs several advantages over previous work:

- Better accuracy. DNN takes basic block features and callee's interface features as input, and trains model parameters with Euclidean loss, which improves the true positive rate of matching. The identified threshold ensures low false positive rate when there is no matching function in database;
- Higher binary search efficiency. We propose a lightweight search strategy to reduce the binary search range by using SOM to manage the Euclidean embedding vectors. With the identified threshold as a pre-filter, our approach only needs to compare with the most similar vectors, which is actually a small part of original database.

3   Problem Definition and Solution

In this section, we first present the definition of cross-platform binary recognition problem in Sect. 3.1 and introduce key idea of our solution in Sect. 3.2. We then discuss two important components of our approach in Sects. 3.3 and 3.4.

3.1   Problem Definition

Cross-platform binary recognition is different from the existing similarity scores ranking. In this section, this problem will be introduced in detail.

Assumption. In our training dataset and test dataset, two binary functions are considered the same, if they are compiled from the same source code. At the same time, binary functions compiled from different source codes are considered different [6]. In addition, binary function identification is out of scope of this paper, which could be handled well by existing binary disassembly techniques [26], so in this paper we assume that functions of each binary could be identified correctly. For example, a binary b_i consists of $f_i^1, f_i^2, \ldots, f_i^n$.

Cross-platform Binary Recognition. Cross-platform binary recognition focus on analyzing binary b_1 and b_2 compiled from the same source code with different compile settings. For each function f_1^m of b_1, if exist, find its matching function f_2^n in b_2. The experiment result shows that our approach could be used in following senses and performs better than the state-of-the-art solutions [6,15].

- Cross-platform: This task is analyzing two binaries compiled from the same source code with different architectures (i.e., ARM, MIPS, X86);
- Cross-optimization: This task is analyzing two binaries compiled from the same source code with different optimization options (i.e., O0, O1, O2, Os, O3).

Evaluation Metric. The target of binary recognition is to recognize the duplicated or known functions in a limited time, so the evaluation metric focuses on the recognition accuracy and the search efficiency. In real-world analysis tasks, the most valuable function is the most similar function reported by the matching method. So in this paper, recognition accuracy is evaluated by whether the matching function is in the top one candidate reported by the binary search method, if matching function exists.

Once models are loaded, the conversions of binary on DNN and ANN can be ignored, so the main time consumption of binary recognition is the binary search process. The binary search efficiency is evaluated by the times of comparison and correct matching's number during binary search.

In detail, given two binaries b_1 and b_2, if there are k pairs of matching functions (e.g., $(f_1^1, f_2^1), (f_1^2, f_2^2), ..., (f_1^k, f_2^k)$) and for each function f_1^i in b_1, binary recognition approaches could sort the most similar function f_2^j in the candidate function set c_1^i (e.g., $f_2^m, ..., f_2^n$). we denote $Match(f_1^i)$ as whether function f_1^i matches correct function.

$$Match(f_1^i) = \begin{cases} 1 & \text{if i = j and i} \leq \text{k} \\ 0 & otherwise \end{cases} \tag{1}$$

The recognition accuracy is defined as follows.

$$Tra(b_1, b_2) = \frac{\sum_{i=1}^{k} match(f_1^i)}{k} \tag{2}$$

Therefore, the binary search efficiency is denoted as follows.

$$Ebs(b_1, b_2) = \frac{\sum_{i=1}^{k} match(f_1^i)}{\sum_{i=1}^{k} num(c_1^i)} \tag{3}$$

3.2 Solution Overview

The target of cross-platform binary recognition is to facilitate the work of reverse engineers by identifying those duplicated or known parts coming from other binaries which may have different architectures. Figure 3 is an example which uses CPU mining malware without the symbol table and Xmrig[1] to illustrate the advantage of binary recognition. FuncNet uses a graph embedding neural network to convert a binary function into a high-dimensional vector, and utilizes a Self-Organizing Maps (SOM) model to map the high-dimensional vector into the grid space. These networks will be introduced in Sects. 3.3 and 3.4.

Treating these neural networks as black boxes, the key parts of our approach lie in binary conversion, the end-to-end training of embedding network with Euclidean distance and binary search strategy with the mapped grid space. As shown in Fig. 4, FuncNet uses two kinds of lightweight binary analysis methods

---

[1] High performance, open source, cross platform CryptoNight CPU/GPU miners: https://xmrig.com/.

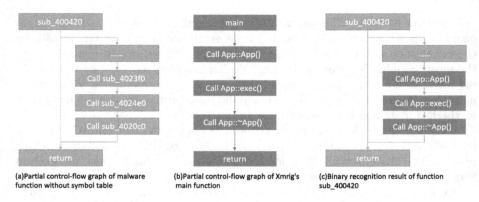

(a)Partial control-flow graph of malware function without symbol table

(b)Partial control-flow graph of Xmrig's main function

(c)Binary recognition result of function sub_400420

Fig. 3. An example of binary recognition which uses CPU mining malware (a) and Xmrig (b): (c) shows that CPU mining malware duplicates the srource code of Xmrig, and appends other functions before mining.

to obtain function features, then generates the embedding vector of the function features. After L2 regularization, it maps the vector into the grid space. Finally, it calculates the Euclidean distance with the candidate nodes according to the distribution of the functions on the grid space until meets the matching condition or exceeds the identified threshold.

FuncNet not only uses control flow graph and syntactic attributes of binary, but also applies the stack frame and register use-before-write characteristics to extra callee's interface information, which is representative features of function. These features are extracted from binaries with IDA pro [16].

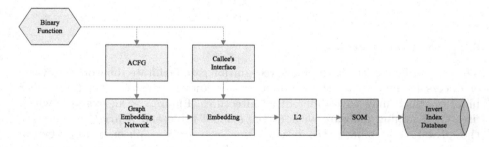

Fig. 4. Overview of the lightweight cross-platform binary recognition solution

3.3 Euclidean Embedding Generation

Neural network has been widely used in the feature conversion of binary function, and some solutions directly use the binary raw bytes as neural network input to train an embedding model. Dues to the neural network's disadvantages in the case of dataset dispersion, these approaches are unreliable [14]. So, how to solve

C_1? After quite a few trials (e.g., LSTM, pair-matching), structure2vector [19] is the most apposite solution to utilize the control flow graph structure and iterate the basic code attributes.

In the following, we introduce the architecture of the deep neural network, then describe how we select triplet to train DNN model and the benefits of it.

Deep Neural Network Input and Output. In our solution, structure2vector [19] takes seven attributes of basic block as input (i.e., number of number constant, number of string constant, number of transform instructions, number of call instructions, number of arithmetic instructions, number of all instructions, and offspring of the basic block). And the deep neural network generates d-dimensional embedding (i.e., 64-dimensional). Additionally, function's argument size and return size are appended to the d-dimensional embedding as output.

Given a binary function f_i, f_i is first converted into feature representation $C(f_i)$, then the deep neural network transforms $C(f_i)$ into a d-dimensional feature space f^d. The whole transformation between input f_i and output $E(f_i)$ could be represented as follows.

$$E(f_i, C(f_i)) = f^{d+2} \qquad (4)$$

Deep Neural Network Architecture. Based on structure2vector [19], the graph embedding network in each control flow graph iteration contains a nonlinear activation function Tanh, which deals with three layers' powerful fully-connected neural network. The fully-connected layer uses rectified linear units (i.e. ReLU [12]) as the non-linear activation function. Finally, the graph embedding network has more than 100,000 parameters[2].

Triplet Loss for Model Evaluation. The Euclidean embedding model needs to ensure that a binary function f_i compiled from a source code is closer to all other binary functions f_i^p compiled from the same source code than it is to any binary function f_i^n compiled from any other source codes. Inspired by the face recognition [18], the triplet is set like (f_i, f_i^p, f_i^n), so the target of the Euclidean embedding model could be defined as follows.

$$||(E(f_i) - E(f_i^p))||^2 + \delta < ||(E(f_i) - E(f_i^n))||^2 \qquad (5)$$

where δ is the margin that we set to distribute similar and dissimilar function pairs.

During the model training, the loss of the batch triplets need be minimized. Namely batch size s, the loss could be presented as follows.

$$L = \sum_i^s [||(E(f_i) - E(f_i^p))||^2 + \delta - ||(E(f_i) - E(f_i^n))||^2]_+ \qquad (6)$$

---

[2] Details could be found at: https://github.com/delia0204/FuncNet.

It is easy to generate all possible triplets, but there are quite a few triplets that always satisfy the constraint in Eq. 5, which not contribute to the model training. Conversely, these triplets would slow the model convergence and make the model trapped into local extremum. Therefore, it is necessary for model optimization to select triplets for train dataset.

Triplet Selection for Model Optimization. To avoid the useless triplets and get fast model convergence, triplet selection focuses on obtaining the critical triplets, which are nearly equal between the minimum distance of dissimilar function pairs and the maximum distance of the similar function pairs. However, it is hard to search triplets across the whole dataset. So, based on the characteristics of the basic block number of similar functions, we propose some strategies to achieve reasonable triplets.

For each binary function f_i, the following strategies are used to filter useless triplets.

- f_i^p of the similar function pair is randomly chosen from the function set compiled from the same source code.
- f_i^n of the dissimilar function is randomly selected from the function set compiled from different source code and the number of basic block number is between the basic block number of f_i and the basic block number of f_i^p.

Learning Parameters with Triplet Architecture. The target of the training is to obtain the suitable parameters, which satisfy that the Euclidean distance between binary functions complied from the same code is smaller than the binary functions compiled from different source codes. In other words, adjustment parameters to minimum the loss L is the target of the training.

Parameters of the embedding network model are trained by triplet architecture. As show in Fig. 5, the triplet network takes three identical graph embedding networks as input. Each graph embedding network owns shared model parameters θ, takes triplet as input, namely (f_i, f_i^q, f_i^n), and outputs the embeddings of them. Simultaneously, the triplet architecture also accepts an indicator input γ, and this input indicates functions' similarity. The triplet loss with the margin γ generates the loss of this triplet as output.

3.4   Binary Search Strategy

Existing binary search approaches based on similarity scores ranking, generally have an expensive time consumption on a big binary search database. In this paper, Self-organizing Maps (SOM) [21] is used to manage the embeddings and control the complexity of binary search on big datasets, nearly constant time complexity. The details about the SOM model and the binary search strategy will be discussed in this section.

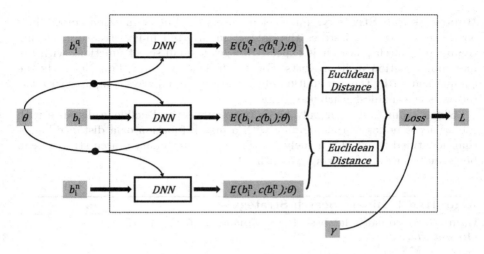

Fig. 5. Triplet architecture workflow

Artificial Neural Network Architecture. SOM is a type of artificial neural network (ANN), which is able to convert nonlinear statistical relationships between high-dimensional data items into simple geometric relationships on a low-dimensional display.

In our solution, SOM converts the feature space f^{d+2} into the grid space which group the similar data together. In structure, SOM has two layers. It includes input space layer and output space layer, corresponding to the feature space f^{d+2} and the grid layer composed of neurou nodes. PopSom [20] is used for the implementation of unsupervised mapping according to Euclidean distance and it maps the embedding in feature space f^{d+2} into grid space with $m*n$ neuron nodes.

Unsupervised Training. PopSom has randomly initialized weightage vectors for all neuron nodes, and stored them as a matrix variable with size $m*n*(d+2)$. During the training, given an embedding $E(f_i, C(f_i))$, PopSom firstly calculates the Euclidean distance between every neuron's weightage vector M_j and $E(f_i, C(f_i))$, return the neuron which gives the best value. Then it uses the learning rate to update weightage vectors of all neurons and learning rate η is a monotonically decreasing function of time. With a sufficient number of iteration t, the map ultimately converges, and the number of iterations is determined by the map's embedding accuracy. The neuron's weightage vector M_j is updated as the following.

$$M_j^{t+1} = M_j^t + N(||E(f_i, C(f_i)) - M_j^t||^2, \eta) \tag{7}$$

Where N is a neighborhood function, considering learning rate η and distance between nodes.

Binary Search Strategy. FuncNet manages the binary function embeddings on the grid space and stores the dataset in inverted index structure. During the binary search phase, it is expected to get a small set of functions with the matching function in it, if exists. For an efficient pre-filter, FuncNet sorts the comparison set by the distribution of embeddings and always compares with the set owns the smallest Euclidean distance.

Given a function f_i, it only needs to calculate the Euclidean distance with the adjacent nodes in turn, ending with a match function or a distance bigger than identified threshold, namely E^t. The complete binary search strategy can be expressed as the following Algorithm 1.

Algorithm 1. Binary Search Strategy

Input: Inverted index database: IIDB. Variables: $E(f_i, C(f_i))$. E^t
Output: *Label*
  1: $pos = \text{MAP}(E(f_i, C(f_i)))$
  2: **loop**
  3:    $S = \text{IIDB}[pos]$
  4:    $dis = 0$
  5:    **for all** E_i in S **do**
  6:       $dis \mathrel{+}= ||E(f_i, C(f_i)) - E_i||^2$
  7:       **if** $dis > E^t$ **then**
  8:          return *null*
  9:       **end if**
 10:    **end for**
 11:    **if** $dis \,! = 0$ **then**
 12:       return $min(dis).Label$
 13:    **end if**
 14:    $set = (pos.x+1,\ pos.x\text{-}1, pos.y+1, pos.y\text{-}1)$
 15:    $pos = set$
 16: **end loop**

---

4 Evaluation

In this section, we firstly introduce the implementation of FuncNet and the datasets we use in evaluation in Sect. 4.1, then we present the key design decision in Sect. 4.2. Finally, we evaluate the binary function recognition accuracy and efficiency in Sect. 4.3. FuncNet shows superior advantages over the state-of-the-art solutions [6,15] on binary analysis accuracy and efficiency.

4.1 Implementation and Datasets

We have implemented a prototype called FuncNet. In this section, we introduce the implementation method and datasets we use for training and evaluation.

Implementation. Our approach includes three main components: feature extraction, deep neural network model for Euclidean embedding, artificial neural network for binary search. Inspired by the Genius [5], feature extraction is based on the IDA python, provided by the disassembly tool IDA PRO V6.95 [16]. Two neural network models are implemented in TensorFlow-1.8 [24].

Baseline. Among existing approaches on addressing binary recognition problem, Gemini [6] is considered a successful attempt on cross-platform binary recognition with the help of DNN and BinDiff [15] is regarded as common cross-optimization binary recognition tool. Therefore, in our evaluation, FuncNet will compare with these solutions separately.

Datasets. There are three datasets in our evaluation: (1) The first one is designed for DNN model training and DNN model accuracy evaluation, namely S_1; (2) The second one is designed for DNN threshold definition, namely S_2; (3) The third one is designed for evaluating the accuracy and efficiency of FuncNet in real-world projects, namely S_3.

- S_1 is used for DNN model training and evaluation, so it consists of binary compiled from the same source code with different compile-option settings. Referring to the training dataset of Gemini [6], we compile OpenSSL (version 1.1.0h, 1.1.0j, 1.1.1a and 1.1.1b) with compiler GCC 6.0. The compiler is set cross compilation to generate binary on X86, MIPS, and ARM architecture with five kinds of optimization options (i.e., O0, O1, O2, Os, O3). Finally, we get 354770 binary functions on dataset S_1. And S_1 is split into three disjoint subsets (i.e., 80%, 10%, 10%), as training dataset, validation dataset, testing dataset. For improving the performance of DNN on unknown binary set, we put binary function compiled from the same source code into only one subset.
- S_2 is used for Euclidean distance threshold definition, so it consists of binary functions with different kinds of semantics. We collect the source code with three kinds of semantic types (i.e., loop, branch, and interaction). With the same compilation method, we get 202050 binary pairs, including 6300 similar function pairs and 195750 dissimilar function pairs.
- S_3 is used for accuracy and efficiency evaluation and we evaluate our approach in four common used real-world projects (i.e., *zlib*, *lua*, *gzip*, *curl*), which are representative and easy to compile successfully. With the same compilation method, we get 8953 binary functions, including 62672 similar function pairs.

4.2   Hyper-parameters in DNN and ANN

In this section, we evaluate the hyper-parameters on dataset S_1, S_2 and introduce several critical design decisions in our approach. Due to time limitation, we train DNN with only 10% samples of the training dataset, but evaluate DNN's performance on the whole testing dataset. The performance evaluation of ANN is performed on the whole dataset S_1.

Feature Extractor. We have evaluated the performance of the DNN in three kinds of feature extractors, illustrated in Fig. 6a.

We evaluated the feature extractor of Genius, the feature extractor of Gemini, and the feature extractor of FuncNet. The experiment result shows that feature extractor without the betweenness attribute and constants attribute of basic blocks performs better and the feature extractor with the callee's interface information as an extraction object achieves the best performance. This result is expected, because the callee's interface information is stable in compilation and also important in reverse analysis. Therefore, FuncNet takes some key attributes of basic blocks and the function interface information of the callee as extraction objects.

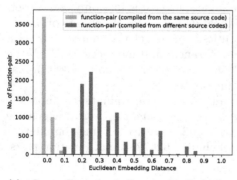

(a) On different feature ectraction methods

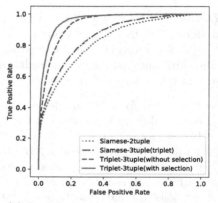

(b) On different training network architectures

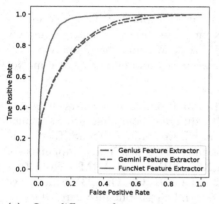

(c) On collected similar and dissimilar funciton pairs

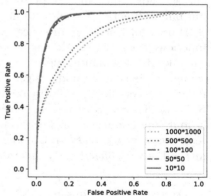

(d) Map embedding accuracy on different grid structures

Fig. 6. Hyper-parameters in DNN and ANN

DNN Training Network Architecture. We have evaluated the performance of the DNN in different training network architectures, illustrated in Fig. 6b.

We evaluated four kinds of training network architectures, i.e., the Siamese architecture [6] with one function pair as input, Siamese architecture with two function pairs (triplet) as input, triplet architecture with function pairs selection, and triplet architecture without function pairs selection. The experiment result shows that the triplet architecture performs better than the Siamese architecture [6] and triplet architecture with triplet selection get a significant improvement on the DNN model accuracy.

DNN Similarity Threshold. We expect to get a referred similarity threshold in binary search, in other words, we want to calculate an identified Euclidean distance threshold on a big dataset to distinguish similar function pairs and dissimilar function pairs. On the dataset S_2, we collect 5103 similar function pairs and 45750 dissimilar function pairs on the public objects, collected from github. We have evaluated the similarity of the similar function pairs and the dissimilar function pairs, illustrated in Fig. 6c. The result shows that Euclidean distance 0.055 is a reasonable similarity threshold. In binary search, we will use this identified threshold to reduce the binary search range.

ANN Grid Structures. Map embedding accuracy is the key evaluation criteria of the SOM model quality and the grid size is the main parameter that influences the map embedding results. We have evaluated the map embedding accuracy [27] of the ANN in different grid shape, illustrated in Fig. 6d.

The experiment result shows that it achieves high map embedding accuracy with small grid size and gets a significant decline when size bigger than 100 * 100, but grid space with big size could reduce the time consumption on binary search. Therefore, FuncNet chooses the 100 * 100 grid structure.

4.3 Accuracy

In this section, we evaluate the accuracy of FuncNet on the dataset S_3. We have assumed that two binary functions are considered the same, if they are compiled from the same source code, and also defined association analysis accuracy Tra in Sect. 3.1. We evaluate Tra on cross-platform and cross-optimization binary recognition tasks.

Cross-platform. We have evaluated the cross-platform accuracy on real-world projects dataset S_3. We collected three cross-platform datasets in S_3 (i.e., S_3^{ARM} compiled from ARM architecture, S_3^{MIPS} compiled from MIPS architecture, S_3^{X86} compiled from X86 architecture). The collected binaries were compiled on O2 and Os optimization options, which are commonly used in real-world projects. Performing the binary recognition on two datasets separately, Table 2 shows the experiment results of accuracy. Comparing with the state-of-the-art cross-platform recognition prototype Gemini [6], FuncNet's accuracy outperforms Gemini by 16% on average.

Table 2. Cross-platform binary recognition accuracy

Datasets	No. of similar function pairs	Gemini Tra	FuncNet Tra
S_3^{ARM} vs. S_3^{MIPS}	2980	0.655	0.833
S_3^{MIPS} vs. S_3^{X86}	2858	0.703	0.852
S_3^{X86} vs. S_3^{ARM}	3008	0.730	0.901

Cross-optimization. We also evaluated the cross-optimization accuracy of FuncNet on real-world projects, discussed in Sect. 4.1. We collected four cross-optimization datasets in S_3, including 3221 similar function pairs of *zlib*, 4531 similar function pairs of *lua*, 3546 similar function pairs of *gzip*, and 4033 similar function pairs of *curl*. The collected binaries were compiled on X86, and we evaluated accuracy on datasets separately. Table 3 shows the experiment result of cross-optimization accuracy. FuncNet's accuracy outperforms BinDiff by 13% on average.

Table 3. Cross-optimization binary recognition accuracy

Project	No. of similar Function pairs	BinDiff Tra	FuncNet Tra
zlib	3221	0.502	0.669
lua	4531	0.496	0.634
gzip	3546	0.532	0.643
curl	4033	0.510	0.622

Comparing the tasks of cross-platform and cross-optimization binary recognition, FuncNet performs better in cross-platform binary recognition. In the reverse analysis, we find that optimization options results in significant influence in control flow graph of binary function, which could bring bias in the embedding generation.

4.4 Efficiency

In this section, we evaluate the efficiency of FuncNet on the dataset S_3. Once models are loaded, the conversions of binary on DNN and ANN can be ignored, so the main time consumption of binary recognition is the binary search process. We have defined binary search efficiency Ebs in Sect. 3.1, which considers the binary

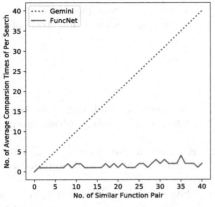 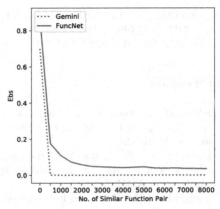

(a) No. of averge comparison times ver-　(b) Binary search efficiency versus no.
sus no. of similar function pairs　　　　 of similar function pairs

Fig. 7. Efficiency evaluation

search range and binary recognition accuracy. We evaluated binary comparison times of each binary search and *Ebs*.

Existing binary search approaches based on similarity scores ranking, which need to be compared with each function of the dataset, and the binary comparison times grow linearly with the growth of the dataset, illustrated in Fig. 7a. In particularly, we have evaluated the binary search efficiency on binary function datasets with different size, illustrated in Fig. 7b. Compared with the state-of-the-art binary cross-platform recognition approach Gemini [6], FuncNet also performs stable search efficiency on big datasets.

5　Conclusion

In this paper, we present a dual neural network-based approach to solve binary function association analysis problem. It employs the callee's interface information as a key feature of functions to train embedding neural network model and maps embedding space into grid space with ANN. We have implemented a lightweight binary recognition prototype, and evaluated it on a dataset with about 2 million binary function pairs. The experiment result shows that its binary recognition accuracy outperforms the state-of-the-art approaches by over 13% on average, and it performs stable comparison efficiency on big datasets.

Acknowledgements. We would like to thank Can Yang, Yuchen Wei, and the anonymous reviewers for their constructive comments. This work is supported by the Chinese Academy of Sciences Key Laboratory of Network Assessment Technology, and Beijing Key Laboratory of Network Security and Protection Technology, as well as Chinese National Natural Science Foundation (U1836209, 61602470, 61802394), Strategic Priority Research Program of the CAS (XDC02040100,

XDC02030200, XDC02020200), National Key Research and Development Program of China (2016QY071405), the Program of Beijing Municipal Science and Technology Commission (No. D181100000618004).

References

1. Khoo, W.M., Mycroft, A., Anderson, R.: Rendezvous: a search engine for binary code. In: Proceedings of the 10th Working Conference on Mining Software Repositories (MSR) (2013)
2. Ding, S.H.H., Fung, B.C.M., Charland, P.: Kam1n0: MapReduce-based assembly clone search for reverse engineering. In: The 22nd ACM SIGKDD International Conference. ACM (2016)
3. Saebjornsen, A.: Detecting fine-grained similarity in binaries. Dissertations & Theses - Gradworks (2014)
4. Eschweiler, S., Yakdan, K., Gerhards-Padilla, E.: discovRE: efficient cross-architecture identification of bugs in binary code. In: NDSS (2016)
5. Feng, Q., et al.: Scalable graph-based bug search for firmware images. In: ACM SIGSAC Conference on Computer and Communications Security. ACM (2016)
6. Xu, X., et al.: Neural network-based graph embedding for cross-platform binary code similarity detection. In: ACM SIGSAC Conference on Computer and Communications Security. ACM (2017)
7. Ding, S.H.H., Fung, B.C.M., Charland, P.: Asm2Vec: boosting static representation robustness for binary clone search against code obfuscation and compiler optimization. In: 2019 IEEE Symposium on Security and Privacy (SP). IEEE Computer Society (2019)
8. Egele, M., et al.: Blanket execution: dynamic similarity testing for program binaries and components. In: USENIX Conference on Security Symposium. USENIX Association (2014)
9. Pewny, J., et al.: Cross-architecture bug search in binary executables. In: 2015 IEEE Symposium on Security and Privacy (SP), pp. 709–724. IEEE Computer Society (2015)
10. Chandramohan, M., et al.: BinGo: cross-architecture cross-OS binary search. In: ACM SIGSOFT International Symposium on Foundations of Software Engineering, pp. 678–689. ACM (2016)
11. Hu, Y., et al.: Binary code clone detection across architectures and compiling configurations. In: 2017 IEEE/ACM 25th International Conference on Program Comprehension (ICPC). IEEE Computer Society (2017)
12. George, E.D., Tara, N.S., Geoffrey, E.H.: Improving deep neural networks for LVCSR using rectified linear units and dropout. In: IEEE International Conference on Acoustics, Speech and Signal Processing (ICASSP), pp. 8609–8613. IEEE (2013)
13. Liu, B., et al.: Cross-version binary code similarity detection with DNN. In: Proceedings of the 2018 33rd ACM/IEEE International Conference on Automated Software Engineering (ASE 2018) (2018)
14. Gao, J., Yang, X., Fu, Y., Jiang, Y., Shi, H., Sun, J.: VulSeeker-pro: enhanced semantic learning based binary vulnerability seeker with emulation. In: Proceedings of the 26th ACM Joint European Software Engineering Conference and Symposium on the Foundations of Software Engineering (ESEC/FSE 2018) (2018)
15. zynamics. BinDiff. https://www.zynamics.com/bindiff.html

16. The IDA Pro Disassembler and Debugger (2015). http://www.datarescue.com/idabase/
17. Brumley, D., Poosankam, P., Song, D., Zheng, J.: Automatic patch-based exploit generation is possible: techniques and implications. In: IEEE Symposium on Security and Privacy 2008 (SP 2008), pp. 143–157. IEEE (2008)
18. Schroff, F., Kalenichenko, D., Philbin, J.: FaceNet: a unified embedding for face recognition and clustering. In: 2015 IEEE Conference on Computer Vision and Pattern Recognition (CVPR). IEEE Computer Society (2015)
19. Dai, H., Dai, B., Song, L.: Discriminative embeddings of latent variable models for structured data. In: International Conference on Machine Learning (2016)
20. Vettigli, G.: MiniSom: minimalistic and numpy-based implementation of the self organizing map (2018). https://github.com/JustGlowing/minisom
21. Kohonen, T.: Self-organized formation of topologically correct feature maps. Biol. Cybern. **43**(1), 59–69 (1982)
22. Luo, L., Ming, J., Wu, D., Liu, P., Zhu, S.: Semantics-based obfuscation-resilient binary code similarity comparison with applications to software plagiarism detection. In: Proceedings of the 22nd ACM SIGSOFT International Symposium on Foundations of Software Engineering, pp. 389–400. ACM (2014)
23. Luo, L., Ming, J., Dinghao, W., Liu, P., Zhu, S.: Semantics-based obfuscation-resilient binary code similarity comparison with applications to software and algorithm plagiarism detection. IEEE Trans. Softw. Eng. **43**(12), 1157–1177 (2017)
24. Abadi, M., et al.: TensorFlow: a system for large-scale machine learning (2016)
25. Blokhin, K., Saxe, J., Mentis, D.: Malware similarity identification using call graph based system call subsequence features. In: IEEE International Conference on Distributed Computing Systems Workshops (2013)
26. Oh Song, H., Xiang, Y., Jegelka, S., Savarese, S.: Deep metric learning via lifted structured feature embedding. In: 2016 IEEE Conference on Computer Vision and Pattern Recognition (CVPR), pp. 4004–4012. IEEE (2016)
27. Kohonen, T.: Self-Organizing Maps, 3rd edn. Springer, Berlin (2001). https://doi.org/10.1007/978-3-642-97966-8

Everything Traffic Security

Towards Forward Secure Internet Traffic

Eman Salem Alashwali[1,2]($\boxtimes$), Pawel Szalachowski[3], and Andrew Martin[1]

[1] University of Oxford, Oxford, UK
{eman.alashwali,andrew.martin}@cs.ox.ac.uk
[2] King Abdulaziz University (KAU), Jeddah, Saudi Arabia
[3] Singapore University of Technology and Design (SUTD), Singapore, Singapore
pawel@sutd.edu.sg

Abstract. Forward Secrecy (FS) is a security property in key-exchange algorithms which guarantees that a compromise in the secrecy of a long-term private-key does not compromise the secrecy of past session keys. With a growing awareness of long-term mass surveillance programs by governments and others, FS has become widely regarded as a highly desirable property. This is particularly true in the TLS protocol, which is used to secure Internet communication. In this paper, we investigate FS in pre-TLS 1.3 protocols, which do not mandate FS, but are still widely used today. We conduct an empirical analysis of over 10 million TLS servers from three different datasets using a novel heuristic approach. Using a modern TLS client handshake algorithms, our results show 5.37% of top domains, 7.51% of random domains, and 26.16% of random IPs *do not select* FS key-exchange algorithms. Surprisingly, 39.20% of the top domains, 24.40% of the random domains, and 14.46% of the random IPs that *do not select* FS, *do support* FS. In light of this analysis, we discuss possible paths toward forward secure Internet traffic. As an improvement of the current state, we propose a new client-side mechanism that we call "Best Effort Forward Secrecy" (BEFS), and an extension of it that we call "Best Effort Forward Secrecy and Authenticated Encryption" (BESAFE), which aims to guide (force) misconfigured servers to FS using a best effort approach. Finally, within our analysis, we introduce a novel adversarial model that we call "discriminatory" adversary, which is applicable to the TLS protocol.

Keywords: Network · Security · Internet · Protocol · TLS · SSL · Measurement · Applied cryptography · Forward Secrecy · Adversarial model · Public key

1 Introduction

1.1 Problem

Forward Secrecy (FS) is a security property in key-exchange algorithms which guarantees that a compromise in the secrecy of a long-term private-key does not compromise the secrecy of past session keys [26]. With a growing awareness of long-term mass surveillance programs by governments and others,

© ICST Institute for Computer Sciences, Social Informatics and Telecommunications Engineering 2019
Published by Springer Nature Switzerland AG 2019. All Rights Reserved
S. Chen et al. (Eds.): SecureComm 2019, LNICST 304, pp. 341–364, 2019.
https://doi.org/10.1007/978-3-030-37228-6_17

FS has become widely regarded as a highly desirable property. This is particularly true in the TLS protocol, which is used to secure Internet communication. Experience has shown the possibility of servers' long-term private-key compromise. For example, RSA [34] long-term private-keys have been compromised through prime factorisation, due to advancement in computing power [10,21], or due to low entropy during keys generation [17]. Furthermore, long-term private-keys can be compromised through implementation bugs as in the Heartbleed bug [39], through social engineering, or other attacks. Due to the increasing importance of FS, the new version of TLS, TLS 1.3, mandates it by design by prohibiting non-FS key-exchange algorithms [33]. In recent years, it has been shown that some FS key-exchange algorithms (e.g. ECDHE) can achieve faster performance than non-FS (e.g. RSA) algorithms [19]. Despite recommendations to server administrators to select FS key-exchange algorithms, non-FS key-exchange algorithms are selected by more than 25% of the servers in our IPs dataset as we will show later. As a result, clients proceed with non-FS key-exchange algorithms when connecting to these servers. This puts users' encrypted data at the risk of future decryption by adversaries who collect traffic today, and decrypt it whenever the targeted servers' private-key is compromised. Motivated by the importance of FS in Internet security, in this paper, we analyse the state of FS in pre-TLS 1.3 protocols, and discuss possible paths towards improving its adoption, including proposing a new best effort approach.

1.2   Contribution

Our contributions are as follows: first, we conduct an empirical analysis of FS on over 10 million TLS servers using a novel heuristic approach on three different datasets that contain top domains, random domains, and random IPs, which represent the real-world web. Unlike previous work that identifies servers that select non-FS key-exchange algorithms by capturing the servers' responses for TLS handshakes, our analysis employs a heuristic procedure that allows us to answer a deeper question: *Do servers that select non-FS key-exchange algorithms support FS ones?* Our results provide new and useful insights to vendors, policy makers, and decision makers. Second, we discuss possible paths towards forward secure Internet traffic. Third, we propose a novel client-side mechanism that we call "Best Effort Forward Secrecy" (BEFS), and an extension of it that we call "Best Effort Forward Secrecy and Authenticated Encryption" (BESAFE), which aims to guide (force) misconfigured servers to FS key-exchange algorithms using a best effort approach. We implement and evaluate a proof-of-concept for it. Our mechanism adds value to the existing "all or nothing" approach. Finally, within our BEFS security analysis, we introduce a novel threat model that we call "discriminatory" adversary. The model is applicable to semi-trusted servers running protocols such as TLS that gives the server the power of selecting a security level, exemplified by the ciphersuite in our case, while the client has no means of verifying the server's actual capabilities (i.e. justifying the server's decision if it selects a non-preferred ciphersuite such as those that do not provide FS). We show how this power can be abused by semi-trusted servers to discriminate against their users for a powerful third-party's advantage (e.g. government intelligence), with minimal evidence and liabilities (e.g. legal) of the server's involvement in carrying out the attack.

1.3 Scope

Our focus is pre-TLS 1.3 protocols, mainly the currently supported versions by most clients and servers, TLS 1.2, TLS 1.1, and TLS 1.0. As a shorthand, we refer to them as pre-TLS 1.3. TLS 1.2 [11] does not enforce FS by design, but is still widely used today. As of April 2019, only 13.6% of the top 150,000 most popular domains support TLS 1.3, according to a report by SSL Labs [32]. Furthermore, there are no known plans from standardisation bodies or browser vendors to deprecate TLS 1.2 yet. Although our work is mainly on pre-TLS 1.3, it has an impact on currently deployed systems.

2 Background

2.1 Transport Layer Security (TLS)

Transport Layer Security (TLS) [11,33] is one of the most important and widely used protocols to date. It is the main protocol used to secure Internet communication. TLS aims to provide data confidentiality, integrity, and authentication between two communicating parties. It has been in use since 1995, and was formerly

Fig. 1. Illustration of the version and ciphersuite negotiation in pre-TLS 1.3 protocols.

known as the Secure Socket Layer (SSL). TLS consists of multiple subprotocols including the TLS handshake protocol. In the handshake protocol, both communicating parties authenticate each other and negotiate security-sensitive parameters, including the protocol version and ciphersuite. The ciphersuite is an identifier that defines the cryptographic algorithms that, upon agreement between the communicating parties (client C and server S), will be used to secure subsequent messages of the protocol. In pre-TLS 1.3, the ciphersuite defines the key-exchange, authentication, symmetric encryption, and hash algorithms. Some ciphersuites provide stronger security properties than others. For example, FS guarantees that a compromise in the server's long-term private-key does not compromise past session keys [26]. Similarly, Authenticated Encryption (AE) provides confidentiality, integrity, and authenticity simultaneously, which provides stronger resilience against some attacks over the MAC-then-encrypt schemes [6,40]. Most TLS clients today, such as mainstream web browsers, offer a mixture of ciphersuites that provides various levels of security such as FS, AE, both FS and AE, or none of them. The same applies to servers that select the session's ciphersuite.

As depicted in Fig. 1, at the beginning of a new TLS handshake, both communicating parties negotiate and agree on a protocol version and ciphersuite. The client sends a `ClientHello` (CH) message to the server. The CH contains several parameters including the client's maximum supported version v_{max_C} and a list of ciphersuites $[a_1, \ldots, a_n]$ (we refer to them as the **client's offered versions** and the **client's offered ciphersuites**). Upon receiving the CH, the server selects a single version v_S and a ciphersuite a_S from the client's offer (we refer to them as the **server's selected version** and the **server's selected sciphersuite**), and responds with a `ServerHello` (SH) containing v_S and a_S. If the server does not support the client's offered versions or ciphersuites, i.e. the client's offer is *not* in the **server's supported versions** or the **server's supported ciphersuites**, the server responds with a handshake failure alert.

2.2 TLS Key-Exchange Algorithms

There are two main key-exchange algorithms used in pre-TLS 1.3 protocols: the Rivest-Shamir-Adleman (RSA) [34], and the Ephemeral Diffie-Hellman (DHE) [12]. DHE has two variants: the Finite-Field (DHE) and the Elliptic-Curve (ECDHE). We use the term (EC)DHE to refer to either ECDHE or DHE.

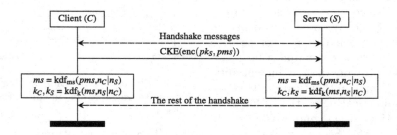

Fig. 2. Illustration of the RSA key-exchange in pre-TLS 1.3.

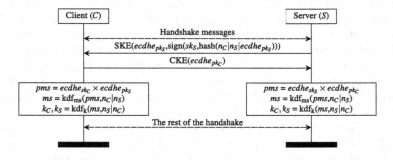

Fig. 3. Illustration of the (EC)DHE key-exchange in pre-TLS 1.3.

RSA Key-Exchange [34] does not guarantee FS. As depicted in Fig. 2, to generate a session key using RSA, the client generates a random value for the pre-master secret pms, encrypts it with the server's long-term RSA public-key pk_S using the (enc) function, then sends it in a ClientKeyExchange (CKE) message. After that, both parties derive the master secret ms from the pms and their nonces n_C and n_S, using a Key Derivation Function (kdf$_{\text{ms}}$). Then, they compute the session keys k_C and k_S using the (kdf$_{\text{k}}$) function. Clearly, the secrecy of the pms relies on the secrecy of the server's long-term private-key sk_S that is associated with the server's public-key pk_S since every pms is encrypted with the same server's long-term key pk_S during the key's lifetime. Therefore, if the server's long-term private-key sk_S is compromised at some point in the future, a passive adversary who has been collecting encrypted traffic, can recover the pms, and consequently, the ms, k_C and k_S, and hence decrypt past sessions' encrypted data.

(EC)DHE [12,29] guarantees FS. As depicted in Fig. 3, to generate a session key using (EC)DHE, the server sends its (EC)DHE public-key parameters $ecdhe_{pk_S}$, signed with its long-term private-key sk_S using the (sign) function in a ServerKeyExchange (SKE) message. The client then sends its (EC)DHE public-key parameter $ecdhe_{pk_C}$ in a ClientKeyExchange (CKE) message. After that, both parties compute their pms, derive the ms using the (kdf$_{\text{ms}}$) function. Then, they compute the session keys k_C and k_S using the (kdf$_{\text{k}}$) function. The (EC)DHE key is ephemeral, i.e. a fresh key is generated for each session. Unlike RSA, in (EC)DHE key-exchange, the pms is not encrypted with the server's long-term key pk_S. Therefore, the ms, k_C and k_S, do not rely on the secrecy of the server's long-term private-key sk_S. Hence, if the server's long-term private-key sk_S is compromised at some point in the future, a passive adversary who has been collecting encrypted traffic, cannot recover the ms, k_C, and k_S of past sessions.

2.3 Terminology

Throughout the paper, we use the term **FS-ciphersuites** to denote ciphersuites that support FS using the ECDHE key-exchange algorithm. We use the term **AE-ciphersuites** to denote ciphersuites that support AE using either the ChaCha20 stream cipher or the GCM mode of operation in the symmetric encryption algorithm. We use the term **FS+AE-ciphersuites** to denote ciphersuites that support both FS and AE using the ECDHE key-exchange algorithm and either the ChaCha20 stream cipher or the GCM mode of operation. Properties preceded with a "non" denotes a negated property. For example, the term **FS+non-AE-ciphersuites** denotes ciphersuites that support FS but not AE. These definitions are not meant for generalisation. They are limited to the paper's scope and to our experiment settings which are based on Google Chrome's[1] ciphersuites. For example, Chrome only supports ECDHE to provide FS. Hence, our definition of FS-ciphersuites considers ECDHE only. To describe

---

[1] As a shorthand, throughout the paper, we refer to Google Chrome as Chrome.

domains, we use the terms we defined in [4]: **main-domains** denotes domains consisting of a Top Level Domain (TLD) (e.g. "com") prefixed by a single label, and do not have any further sub-domains, e.g. "example.com"; **plain-domains** denotes domains that are not prefixed with "www" sub-domains, e.g. "example.com"; and **www-domains** denotes domains that are prefixed with "www" sub-domains, e.g. "www.example.com".

3   Empirical Study

3.1   Datasets

We build three datasets that we name: top-domains, random-domains, and random-ips. We end up with 999,884 distinct domains in the top-domains dataset, 4,960,390 distinct domains in the random-domains dataset, and 4,881,985 distinct IPv4 addresses in the random-ips dataset. The rationale behind choosing these three categories is to represent the real-world web as much as possible. In what follows, we explain how we build and pre-process each dataset.

Top Domains Dataset. The top-domains dataset initial size is 1 million domains, obtained from the Alexa list of the top 1 million most visited domains globally [5], retrieved on Aug. 22, 2018. We exclude the www-domains because we target plain-domains (see Sect. 2.3 for our definitions of plain-domains and www-domains), which are the majority in the Alexa list. After excluding the www-domains, we end up with 999,884 domains that are mainly (around 94.81%) classified as main-domains.

Random Domains Dataset. The random-domains dataset initial size is 5 million random domains obtained from a large dataset that contains 54,063,220 distinct (alphabetically unordered) domains that successfully completed a TLS handshake in Amann et al. [7], which have been collected from multiple sources. To maintain consistency with the top domains dataset format, we extract 5 million domains from [7] that are classified as both plain-domains and main-domains. In this dataset, the TLDs scope is limited to generic TLDs (gTLDs), and does not include "multi-level" TLDs such as country-code TLDs (ccTLDs), e.g. "ac.uk". This is to avoid the complexity of distinguishing domains that have sub-domains from domains that have ccTLDs, which is somewhat difficult to achieve with 100% accuracy. To avoid repeated domains, from the 5 million random domains, we exclude the domains that exist in the top domains dataset, either "as is" or as a main-domain of a sub-domain in the top domains dataset (the top domains dataset contains a small percentage of sub-domains). We identify sub-domains in the top domain dataset in two steps: first, by using a regular expression, we extract the domains that have more than one dot ".". Second, with the aid of tldextract [23] python library, we distinguish sub-domains from domains with country-code TLDs (ccTLD) such as "example.ac.uk" (the latter is considered a main-domain). We end up with 4,960,390 distinct random domains.

Random IPs Dataset. The `random-ips` dataset initial size is 5 million distinct IPv4 addresses that have completed a successful TLS handshake with `Censys`, a search engine and database for servers and network devices on the Internet [14], retrieved from the `Censys` IPv4 dataset on Oct. 20, 2018, through research access to the `Censys` database. To avoid repeated IPs, from the 5 million IPs, we exclude the IPs that are associated with any domain that has responded to a handshake in the scanning or inspection phases (further details on the scanning and inspection phases will be provided in the methodology in Sect. 3.3). For this reason, we build the random IPs dataset after we finish the domains datasets scanning and inspection phases. We end up with 4,881,985 IPs.

3.2 Research Questions

Our analysis aims to answer the following main questions:

1. What is the percentage of servers that select non-FS-ciphersuites today?
2. Do servers that select non-FS-ciphersuites support FS-ciphersuites?
3. Do different dataset natures result in different trends in selecting and supporting FS-ciphersuites?

Whilst addressing these main questions, the following side questions arose:

1. What is the percentage of servers that select FS+non-AE-ciphersuites after the client's FS-ciphersuites enforcement[2]?
2. Do servers that select FS+non-AE-ciphersuites after the client's FS-ciphersuites enforcement support FS+AE-ciphersuites?
3. Can the client's FS-ciphersuites enforcement lead servers to lose the AE property?
4. Do servers that lose the AE property after the client's FS-ciphersuites enforcement support FS+AE-ciphersuites?

3.3 Methodology

As depicted in Fig. 4, our methodology consists of two main phases: a scanning phase followed by an inspection phase.

Scanning Phase. We consider the scanning phase as an exploration phase. In this phase, for each server address in our datasets, we perform a TLS handshake using the `tls-scan` tool [43], an open source fast TLS scanner capable of performing concurrent TLS connections. We customise the `tls-scan` to utilise the `OpenSSL 1.1.0g` library, and to support `Chrome`'s latest version pre-TLS 1.3 ciphersuites, which support various ciphersuites that provide FS, or AE, or none

---

[2] The term "client's FS-ciphersuite enforcement" refers to a client that offers FS-ciphersuites exclusively. The same applies for "client's FS+AE-ciphersuite enforcement" but the latter offers FS+AE-ciphersuites exclusively. More details are provided next in the methodology in Sect. 3.3.

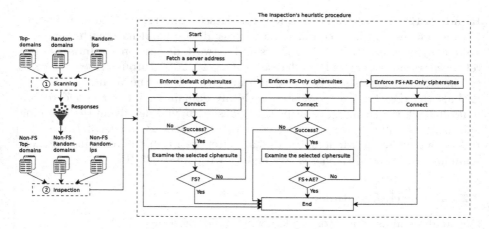

Fig. 4. A general overview of our methodology showing the two phases and their input.

of them. We choose to base the scanning client on **Chrome**'s ciphersuites because **Chrome** is the most representative TLS client on the Internet. As of Feb. 2019, **Chrome**'s usage is 79.7% [41]. **tls-scan** includes the Server Name Indication (SNI)[3] extension for domain name scans by default. We set the timeout argument to 5 s, and the concurrency argument to 50 connections. We ran the scans between Aug. 23, 2018 and Oct. 21, 2018 at the University of Oxford in discrete intervals based on the dataset.

Inspection Phase. After the scanning phase is complete, we extract the responding addresses that selected non-FS-ciphersuites in the scanning phase. Each dataset is inspected within a maximum of 48 hours after its scanning phase is complete. For the inspection phase, we develop a TLS client that implements our heuristic procedure (see Fig. 4), which works as follows, for each server's address:

1. The client performs a TLS handshake based on **Chrome**'s pre-TLS 1.3 default ciphersuites. This first handshake of the inspection phase is similar to the scanning phase handshake[4]. The inspection's first handshake serves as a confirmation of the server's selected ciphersuite. It records the server's selected ciphersuite from a default client's view just before the heuristic procedure starts. If the handshake failed, the client records the error, and the heuristic procedure ends here.

---

[3] The SNI extension passes the domain name in the TLS handshake in order to obtain more accurate responses in virtual hosting environments, where a single server can host multiple domains [15].

[4] Except that our inspection client does not support SSL v3 while the scanning **tls-scan** client supports SSL v3. However, we analyse FS regardless of the client's supported versions.

2. Upon receiving the server's response to the first handshake (step 1), the client checks the server's selected ciphersuite: if it is a FS-ciphersuite, this means that the server has changed its behaviour after the scanning phase since all the inspection input addresses are for servers that selected non-FS-ciphersuites in the scanning phase. The client records the server's response, and the heuristic procedure for this server ends here. Otherwise, if the server's selected ciphersuite is still a non-FS-ciphersuite, we classify this server as "**stable**", i.e. consistently selects a non-FS-ciphersuite. The client then updates its TLS context to support FS-ciphersuites *exclusively*. The set of FS-ciphersuites may or may not support AE, i.e. it contains FS+AE-ciphersuites and FS+non-AE-ciphersuites. This context is more restricted than the default one.
3. The client then performs a second handshake utilising the new FS-ciphersuites context. If the handshake failed, the client records the error and the heuristic procedure for this server ends here.
4. Upon receiving the server's response to the second handshake (step 3), the client checks the server's selected ciphersuite: if it is a FS+AE-ciphersuite, this means that the server supports FS+AE-ciphersuite after the client's FS-ciphersuites enforcement. The client then records the server's response, and the heuristic procedure for this server ends here. Otherwise, if the server's selected ciphersuite is a FS+non-AE-ciphersuite, the client updates its context to support FS+AE-ciphersuites *exclusively*. This context is more restricted than the FS-ciphersuites context.
5. The client then performs a third handshake utilising the new FS+AE-ciphersuites context. If the handshake failed, the client records the error and the heuristic procedure ends here.
6. Upon receiving the server's response, the client records the response. The heuristic procedure for this server ends here.

We develop and run the inspection client using `python 3.6.5`. Similar to the `tls-scan` client in the scanning phase, it utilises `OpenSSL 1.1.0g`. We enable the SNI for the top and random domains inspection (the IPs dataset do not need the SNI), and we set the timeout to 5 s. The results are then stored and analysed using MySQL database and queries.

Identifying Device Types. We classify device types into two categories: ordinary web servers and network devices. We use the term "**network device**" to refer to non-ordinary TLS servers, e.g. embedded web servers in network devices such as routers. To identify the device type, we input the IPs of the dataset in question in a query to `Censys` database to get the IPs metadata. We then produce a breakdown of the responding IPs grouped by the device type. We base our device types queries on the IPs, i.e. in the domains datasets, we first extract the distinct IPs behind the domains, because `Censys` is mainly an IP-based engine. We query the `Censys` snapshot that dates to the starting date of the scan or inspection (depending on the phase) of the dataset in question. `Censys` labels the device type of the network devices that it identifies, e.g. "DSL/cable modem". If the device type field is empty, this means that the device is either an ordinary web server, or a network device that Censys cannot identify. Finally, we do not always obtain 100% responses for the IPs that we query their metadata from Censys. However, overall, the percentages of the responses that we receive are between 98.36% to 100% (depending on the dataset) of the IPs we query.

Ethical Considerations. Our study is in line with the ethical recommendations in carrying out measurement studies [30]. First, we do not collect private data. Second, we do not perform an exhaustive number of handshakes on any single server. Our clients' handshakes can by no means be classified as a Denial of Service (DoS) attack. Third, we use a designated public IPv4 address per scanning device instead of Network Address Translation (NAT), to avoid potential disturbance to other users in our institution's network if a server has blocked our scanning or inspection device's IP. Fourth, we use informative DNS names that contain "TLS probing" to help server administrators identify our devices' activity in their logs. Finally, we inform the IT and security teams in our institution where the empirical study has been conducted so they expect a high volume of outgoing connections from our experiment devices, and to expect some incoming blacklisted certificates from random servers.

3.4   Results

Scanning Phase. In this phase, we input the servers' addresses in our datasets. The results of the scanning phase are summarised in Table 1.

Table 1. Summary of the scanning results. Every additional indentation means that the percentages are computed out of the previous level results. The "% Network devices" are computed over the responding IPs to Censys metadata query (exact numbers are provided in text).

	Datasets					
	top-domains		random-domains		random-ips	
Dataset size	999,884		4,960,390		4,881,985	
Responding servers	814,333	(81.44%)	3,221,249	(64.94%)	4,477,279	(91.71%)
Distinct IPs	468,346	(57.51%)	690,912	(21.45%)	4,477,279	(100%)
% Network devices	466	(0.10%)	1208	(0.18%)	518,988	(11.59%)
Select non-FS	43,756	(5.37%)	241,994	(7.51%)	1,171,101	(26.16%)

Responding Servers. As illustrated in Table 1, the highest percentage of responses is in random IPs (91.71%), followed by top domains (81.44%), and finally random domains (64.94%). The response rate is influenced by the dataset category. Both the IPs and top domains datasets are recent. That is, the addresses in the IPs dataset have recently completed a TLS handshake with the `Censys` engine [14], and TLS adoption in top domains is high. The low response rate in random domains (64.94%) is very likely due to the dataset age. It is obtained from a previous study that was published in 2017 [7]. Hence, many domains could have gone down since then.

In terms of device types, from the responding top domains, there are 468,346 (57.51%) distinct IPs behind all the top domains. We receive metadata responses for 464,191 (99.11%) of them from the `Censys` database. Of those, only 466 (0.10%) IPs are labeled as network devices. From the responding random domains, there are 690,912 (21.45%) distinct IPs behind them. We receive metadata responses for 686,085 (99.30%) of them. Of those, there are 1208 (0.18%) labeled as network devices. From the responding random IPs, we receive metadata responses for all of them (100%). Of those, there are 518,988 (11.59%) IPs labeled as networked devices. Clearly, the percentage of network devices in the random IPs is higher than that in the top and random domains.

Servers that Select non-FS-Ciphersuites. From the responding servers, we find 5.37% of the top domains, 7.51% of the random domains, and 26.16% of the random IPs, select non-FS-ciphersuites. The lowest percentage is in the top domains, the highest is in the random IPs, while in the random domains, it is slightly higher than that in the top domains. The fact that the random IPs dataset has the highest percentage of network devices can be correlated to the high percentage of servers that select non-FS-ciphersuites. We can confirm this in the inspection phase when we look closer at the device types of those servers that select non-FS-ciphersuites.

Inspection Phase. In this phase, we input the addresses of servers that select non-FS-ciphersuites in the scanning phase. Table 2 summarises the inspection phase results.

Responding Servers. As Table 2 illustrates, over 99% of top and random domains, and 94.94% of IPs that select non-FS-ciphersuites in the scanning phase, have responded to our inspection client's handshake. The low response rate in the IPs dataset compared to the top and random domains datasets is very likely attributed to SSL v3 devices as our inspection client does not support SSL v3, while the scanning client does. It is also very likely that those non-responding IPs are mostly for network devices since using legacy versions in network devices is more common than that in ordinary web servers [37].

Servers That Still Select Non-FS-Ciphersuites (Stable). In our work, we use the term "stable" to refer to servers that consistently select non-FS-ciphersuites in both the inspection's first handshake and the scanning handshake. As shown in Table 2, clearly, the stability in selecting non-FS-ciphersuites among all datasets is high (over 99% in all datasets), despite the difference in the supported protocol versions in the scanning and inspection clients (the scanning client supports SSLv3 while the inspection does not). This suggests that, to some extent, servers' selected ciphersuites are not affected by the negotiated versions.

Table 2. Summary of the inspection results. Every additional indentation means the percentages are computed out of the previous level results. The input of the inspection phase is the servers that selected non-FS-ciphersuites in the scanning phase. The "% Network devices" are computed over the responding IPs to `Censys` metadata query (exact numbers are provided in text).

	Datasets					
	non-FS top-domains		non-FS random-domain		non-FS random-ips	
Dataset size	43,756		241,994		1,171,101	
Responding servers	43,374	(99.13%)	240,519	(99.39%)	1,111,802	(94.94%)
Select non-FS (stable)	43,158	(99.50%)	240,274	(99.90%)	1,111,174	(99.94%)
Distinct IPs	33,474	(77.56%)	61,522	(25.60%)	1,111,174	(100%)
% Network devices	76	(0.23%)	361	(0.59%)	434,076	(39.06%)
Support FS	16,916	(39.20%)	58,636	(24.40%)	160,706	(14.46%)
Distinct IPs	12,545	(74.16%)	13,839	(23.60%)	160,706	(100%)
% Network devices	12	(0.10%)	27	(0.20%)	1503	(0.94%)
Select FS+non-AE	10,091	(59.65%)	38,583	(65.80%)	93,566	(58.22%)
Support FS+AE	1629	(16.14%)	1289	(3.34%)	24,128	(25.79%)
Lose AE	2686	(26.62%)	1768	(4.58%)	12,769	(13.65%)
Support FS+AE	45	(1.68%)	91	(5.15%)	4668	(36.56%)

In terms of device types, out of the top domains that select non-FS-ciphersuites, there are 33,474 (77.56%) distinct IPs behind all these domains. Of those, we receive metadata responses for 33,079 (98.82%) IPs from the `Censys` database. Of those, there are 76 (0.23%) IPs labeled as networked devices. Of the random domains that select non-FS-ciphersuites, there are 61,522 (25.60%) distinct IPs behind them. We receive metadata for 61,176 (99.44%) IPs from `Censys`. Of those, there are 361 (0.59%) IPs labeled as networked devices. Of the random IPs that select non-FS, we receive metadata for 1,111,174 (100%). Of those, there are 434,076 (39.06%) IPs labeled as networked devices. Network devices represent no more than 0.59% of top and random domains that select non-FS-ciphersuites. However, more than a third of servers that select non-FS-ciphersuites in the random IPs dataset are labeled as network devices. The high percentage of network devices in the random IPs is likely the reason for the high percentage of servers that select non-FS-ciphersuites.

Servers That Select Non-FS-Ciphersuites, But Support FS-Ciphersuites. We find 39.20% of top domains, 24.40% of random domains, 14.46% of random IPs, that select non-FS-ciphersuites in the inspection phase, do support FS-ciphersuites. The top-domains are the highest, followed by the random domains, and finally, the random IPs are the lowest. Interestingly, this is a shifted paradigm for the percentages of servers that select non-FS-ciphersuites that is shown in Table 1, where the random IPs have the highest percentage and the top domains have the lowest percentage. The results reflect that the lack of FS-ciphersuite selection in the top and random domains is to a large extent due to misconfiguration, while in the random IPs, it is mostly due to lack of support.

In terms of device types, out of the top domains that select non-FS-ciphersuites but support FS-ciphersuites, there are 12,545 (74.16%) distinct IPs behind them. We receive metadata responses for 12,339 (98.36%) IPs. We find 12 (0.10%) of them are labeled as networked devices. Of the random domains that select non-FS-ciphersuites but support FS-ciphersuites, there are 13,839 (23.60%) distinct IPs behind them. We receive metadata responses for 13,744 (99.31%) IPs. Of those, 27 (0.20%) are labeled as network devices. Of the random IPs, that select non-FS-ciphersuites but support FS-ciphersuites, we receive metadata responses for 160,706 (100%) IPs. Of those, 1503 (0.94%) are labeled as network devices. The results show that the majority of those devices are not identified as network devices, even in the random IPs dataset that shows the highest percentage of network devices. Those servers that select non-FS-ciphersuites and turned to support FS-ciphersuites are not network devices. Therefore, most of the network devices that select non-FS-ciphersuites, do not support FS-ciphersuites.

Servers That Select FS+non-AE-Ciphersuites After Enforcing FS-Ciphersuites. Out of the top domains, random domains, and random IPs that support FS-ciphersuites after enforcement (row label "Support FS" in Table 2), there are 59.65% top domains, 65.80% random domains, and 58.22% random IPs that select FS+non-AE-ciphersuites. The reason for selecting non-AE can be attributed to the fact that TLS 1.0 and TLS 1.1 do not support AE-ciphersuites [36], and these devices might be running legacy versions of TLS. Otherwise, this is attributed to misconfiguration. To better understand this situation, we next check whether those servers support FS+AE-ciphersuites or not.

Servers That Select FS+non-AE-Ciphersuite After Enforcing FS-Ciphersuites, But Support FS+AE-Ciphersuites. Of the top domains, random domains, and random IPs that select FS+non-AE-ciphersuites after FS-ciphersuites enforcement (row label "Select FS+non-AE" in Table 2), there are 16.14% top domains, 3.34% random domains, and 25.79% random IPs, that support FS+AE-ciphersuite. At this point of the heuristic procedure, the majority of the IPs do not belong to network devices. The majority of the top and random domains that select FS+non-AE-ciphersuites do not support FS+AE-ciphersuites. However, selecting FS+non-AE-ciphersuites while supporting FS+AE-ciphersuites in the IPs dataset is the highest, which we classify as misconfiguration.

When Enforcing FS-Ciphersuite Causes Losing the AE Property. Of the top domains, random domains, and random IPs that select FS+non-AE-ciphersuites after enforcing FS-ciphersuites (row label "Select FS+non-AE" in Table 2), there are 26.62% top domains, 4.58% random domains, and 13.65%

random IPs, were selecting AE before enforcing FS-ciphersuites, i.e. were selecting non-FS+AE-ciphersuites. This can be either because they do not support any FS+AE-ciphersuites, or due to misconfiguration. This can be clarified next.

Servers That Lose the AE Property After Enforcing FS-Ciphersuites, But Support FS+AE-Ciphersuites. Out of the top domains, random domains, and random IPs that lose the AE property after enforcing FS (row label "Lose AE" in Table 2), we find 1.68% top domains, 5.15% random domains, and 36.56% random IPs, do support FS+AE-ciphersuites. The results reflect that losing the AE property after enforcing the FS in the top and random domains is to a large extent due to a lack of support for FS+AE-ciphersuites, but in the random IPs, it is mostly due to misconfiguration.

4   Towards Forward Secure Internet Traffic

In this section, we discuss possible paths towards forward secure Internet traffic from a client's perspective. Then, we propose and evaluate a novel client-side mechanism that we call Best Effort Forward Secrecy (BEFS), and an extension of it that we call Best Effort Forward Secrecy and Authenticated Encryption (BESAFE). We choose to focus our discussion and solutions on clients because unlike servers, clients are controlled by few players, e.g. browser vendors. Client-side security enhancement mechanisms are easier to adopt, as shown by recent adoptions of client-side mechanisms such as Google's Certificate Transparency (CT) [24], and others.

4.1   Deprecating Non-FS-Ciphersuites in TLS Clients

The most straight-forward approach towards forward secure Internet traffic is deprecating non-FS-ciphersuites from TLS clients. As a result, these clients will not be able to establish TLS connections with servers that do not support FS-ciphersuites. This is a conservative approach that has been taken by browser vendors and standardisation bodies in the past with some protocol versions and algorithms such as SSL v3 [8] and RC4 [31], after their insecurity has become clear. However, deprecating non-FS-ciphersuites *now* can be more problematic than the case of deprecating SSL v3 and RC4 in 2014 and 2016 respectively. By way of comparison, Lee et al.[5] conducted a survey in 2006 to assess the cryptographic strength of TLS servers [25]. It shows that 98.36% of the surveyed servers support TLS 1.0, the latest version at the time of the study, and 57.17% of the servers support AES encryption, which was in its early years as it was standardised in 2001 [16]. In light of these figures, we speculate that SSL v3 and

---

[5] Despite the study's age (conducted in 2006), to the best of our knowledge, [25] is the only study that tried to assess servers' supported ciphersuites prior to deprecating RC4 and SSL v3. Note that identifying the *supported* ciphersuites for a server is different from identifying the *selected* ciphersuite. The former requires multiple handshakes, while the latter requires a single handshake, for each server.

AES adoption when they were deprecated by most browsers in 2014 and 2016 respectively was over 99%. On the other hand, in our results, we calculate an approximation of the servers that support FS-ciphersuites in each dataset. To this end, we first calculate the number of servers that select non-FS-ciphersuites and do not support FS-ciphersuite which can be derived from Table 2 by calculating ("Select non-FS (stable)" − "Support FS"), and then subtracting those results from the overall responses in Table 1's row label "Responding servers", which gives: 788,091 (96.78%) top domains, 3,039,611 (94.36%) random domains, and 3,526,811 (78.77%) random IPs. Our results are in line with Censys Oct. 26, 2018 snapshot figures that show 97.44% of Alexa's top domains, and 77.94% of IPs in all IPv4 space, support FS-ciphersuite. However, our results are more accurate as we include not only servers that *select* FS, but also servers that *support* FS but select non-FS, which can be guided through client's enforcement as we will explain next. In addition, we utilises modern client ciphersuites. On the other hand, Censys only measures servers that *select* FS, and utilises somewhat legacy ciphersuites. We conclude that the percentages of servers that support FS-ciphersuites are less than that in RC4 and SSL v3 cases, especially in the IPs datasets. The lack of supporting FS-ciphersuites by those servers can be explained by the fact that until recent years, (EC)DHE key-exchange algorithms have been viewed as resource-exhaustive compared to RSA key-exchange, despite the fact that this argument is no longer true with the ECDHE variant as shown in [19].

4.2 Best Effort Forward Secrecy (BEFS)

Overview. The gist of our BEFS mechanism is guiding (forcing) misconfigured servers towards FS-ciphersuites. As explained in Sect. 2.1, in ordinary TLS clients such as web browsers, the client offers default ciphersuites, which includes FS-ciphersuites and non-FS-ciphersuites. Upon receiving the client's offer, a server that does not support or does not prefer to select a FS-ciphersuite will select a non-FS-ciphersuite, and sends its selected ciphersuite to the client. The client accepts the server's choice, and the rest of the communication proceeds with a non-FS-ciphersuite. On the other hand, in BEFS, we exploit the TLS ciphersuite negotiation dynamics to influence (bias) the server's choice towards FS-ciphersuites. That is, a BEFS-enabled client first offers FS-ciphersuites *exclusively* $[a_{1_{fs}}, \ldots, a_{n_{fs}}]$. Upon receiving the client's offered ciphersuites, a server that supports FS-ciphersuites will be guided (forced) to select a FS-ciphersuite $a_{S_{fs}}$, even if it prefers to select a non-FS-ciphersuite, since FS-ciphersuites are the only offered ciphersuites as illustrated in Fig. 5. As shown in Table 2, of the servers that select non-FS-ciphersuites, there is between 14.46% to 39.20% that *do support* FS-ciphersuites, which can benefit from the BEFS enforcement mechanism. If the server indeed does not support FS-ciphersuites, it will return a failure alert (see Sect. 2.1 for a background on TLS version and ciphersuite negotiation). In this case, the BEFS-enabled client makes a second handshake utilising default ciphersuites $[a_{1_{fs}}, \ldots, a_{n_{nonfs}}]$, which includes non-FS-ciphersuites in addition to the previously offered FS-ciphersuites as Fig. 6 illustrates. Hence, a server that does not support FS-ciphersuites can still select a non-FS-ciphersuite $a_{S_{nonfs}}$ after the client falls back. BEFS can be viewed as a form of the "Opportunistic Security" concept [13], but at the FS property level. That is, it guides servers to select FS whenever they support it.

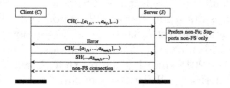

Fig. 5. A BEFS-enabled client handshake when the server prefers to select a non-FS-ciphersuite while supporting FS-ciphersuites. The server is forced to select FS-ciphersuite through client FS-ciphersuite enforcement.

Fig. 6. A BEFS-enabled client handshake when the server does not support FS-ciphersuites. The client falls back to non-FS-ciphersuites only when the server indeed does not support FS.

The Fallback. We now address the fallback aspect. We define three categories of client-side fallbacks: silent fallback, interactive fallback, and signalled fallback. In what follows, we explain them in light of the BEFS mechanism.

Silent Fallback. Silent fallbacks do not involve the user or the server. If used in BEFS, if the FS-ciphersuites handshake failed, the client falls back to default ciphersuites (which include non-FS-ciphersuites), in the background, and performs a second handshake utilising default ciphersuites. Silent fallbacks remove the security decision-making overhead from the user at the cost of security. Silent fallbacks do not provide security against active adversaries who can perform downgrade attacks (for a background on downgrade attacks, see [3]). BEFS with silent fallback is secure against passive adversaries, which adds a significant value in the case of FS. It makes mass surveillance more difficult to achieve as the adversary has to actively perform downgrade attacks for each session.

Interactive Fallback. Interactive fallbacks involve the user. If used in BEFS, when the FS-ciphersuites handshake fails, the client (e.g. web browser) presents an interrupting warning message and asks the user whether to proceed or not. If the user chooses to proceed, the client falls back from FS-ciphersuites to default ciphersuites and performs a second handshake. Otherwise, if the user chooses not to proceed, the client does not fall back, and aborts the TLS handshake. Interactive fallbacks provide security against active adversaries. Interactive fallbacks are similar to the widely-known self-signed certificate active warnings [1]. Active security warnings have been shown to be more effective than passive ones such as passive indicators that do not interrupt the user's task [1]. However, active security warnings have to be used with caution in order to not cause the habitation effect, where users ignore them because they see them too often [38].

Therefore, if the majority of servers that do not support FS-ciphersuites (i.e. those that require fallback) are network devices, interactive fallback can be acceptable, as these devices are normally visited infrequently by a limited number of users, such as the device's owner.

Signalled Fallback. Signalled fallbacks involve the server. Therefore, if they are not incorporated in the protocol by design, they require modifications or updates to the server, e.g. a patch to the TLS implementation, to enable the server from interpreting the client's signal. In signalled fallbacks, the client sends a signal, i.e. a special value, to inform the server that the client has performed a fallback. The server aborts the handshake if it is not expecting a fallback, e.g. in BEFS case, if the server supports FS-ciphersuites. Signalled fallbacks provide security against active adversaries, if we assume authenticated messages. Signalled fallbacks have been proposed in the TLS fallback "Signaling Cipher Suite Value" (SCSV) [27]. It has been used to mitigate TLS version downgrade attacks, mainly the POODLE attack [28], and has been widely adopted as shown in [7]. In BEFS, our problem deals with misconfigured servers and less security-aware server administrators. Had they been security-aware, they would have configured their servers to select FS-ciphersuites. Therefore, in BEFS case, we do not consider signaled fallbacks as a solution that can be adopted quickly. Therefore, we do not include it in our analysis in the coming section.

BEFS Security Analysis. We now analyse the security of BEFS against three adversarial models: passive network adversary, active network adversary, and our newly introduced discriminatory adversary.

Passive Network Adversary. Passive adversaries can collect network traffic, but cannot interfere (e.g. modify, inject, replay, or drop) protocol messages. They may obtain access to the server's long-term private-key at some point in the future. Once the server's long-term private-key is compromised, a passive adversary who has been collecting non-FS network traffic can now decrypt it. BEFS aims to ensure the selection of FS-ciphersuites whenever the server supports FS-ciphersuites. In FS-ciphersuites, an ephemeral key is generated for each session, and this key is not encrypted with the server's long-term private-key. By selecting FS-ciphersuites, if the server's long-term private-key is compromised, the adversary cannot compromise past session keys. In TLS, the (EC)DHE key-exchange algorithms are provably secure against passive adversaries [20]. Therefore, BEFS with all types of fallback mechanisms is secure against passive adversaries.

Active Network Adversary. Unlike passive adversaries, active adversaries can interfere with protocol messages, e.g. by modifying, injecting, replaying, or dropping messages. Similar to the passive adversaries, they may obtain access to the server's long-term private-key at some point in the future, hence be able to decrypt non-FS-ciphersuite traffic. BEFS security against active adversaries can be analysed with the two fallback mechanisms explained earlier in Sect. 4.2. First, in terms of BEFS with silent fallback, since the user of a BEFS-enabled client with silent fallback is not aware of the fallback, an active adversary can perform a downgrade attack by dropping the initial FS-ciphersuites handshake message to lead the client to fall back and perform a default handshake. Hence, misconfigured servers that select non-FS-ciphersuites but support FS-ciphersuite will not be guided, i.e. will select non-FS-ciphersuite, while with BEFS, they will be guided (forced) to select FS-ciphersuites instead. BEFS with silent fallback does not provide security against active adversaries. Second, we analyse BEFS with interactive fallback against an active adversary. This moves the security decision to the user. Users can be classified into two categories: security-aware users, who read the warning message and reject the fallback when they care about FS. The second category of users is less security-aware users, who will not do so. BEFS with interactive fallback and security-aware users is secure against active adversaries. The warning message content and the users' reactions to it are beyond the scope of this paper. BEFS with interactive fallbacks can find its application in special browser modes for sensitive communications, in the same vein of `Chrome`'s incognito and `Firefox` private modes, which are available for privacy-aware users.

Discriminatory Adversary. The discriminatory adversary is located at the server and discriminates against its clients in terms of the security level it provides to them (FS-ciphersuite vs. non-FS-ciphersuite in our case). The discriminatory adversarial model is applicable to semi-trusted servers running protocols such as TLS, which gives the server the power of selecting some parameters that define the security level of a particular session, exemplified by the ciphersuite in our case, while the client has no means of verifying the server's actual capabilities, i.e. justifying the server's decision if it selects a non-preferred ciphersuite such as a non-FS-ciphersuite. This power can be abused by semi-trusted servers to discriminate against their users, for a powerful third-party's advantage. The discriminatory adversary can be compelled by, or collude with the third-party, such as government intelligence, to weaken the security of *some* connections, e.g. those coming from specific geographic locations. In our case, the discriminatory adversary denies the FS property to some users, whilst enabling it for others. The discriminatory adversary (server) can then provide its long-term private-key that is used for digital signatures and non-FS session keys (pms) encryption to the powerful third-party, after the key's expiration, when it is no longer used by the server. This allows the third-party to decrypt the data of those users who have been discriminated against, but not the data of other users who have been provided with strong security, i.e. FS-ciphersuite in our case. This adversarial model gives the semi-trusted server several advantages compared to giving every session key or the decrypted data itself to the third-party, which is impractical for servers to carry out, especially in the case of large-scale surveillance. Another advantage to the semi-trusted server lies in the minimal liabilities (e.g. legal) in being directly involved in leaking their users' data, or in giving their private-key to the adversary during the key's lifetime. Such an adversarial model is not far from the export-grade cryptography law that was mandated until the late 90s, where software vendors, for example, were compelled to weaken the security of software exported outside the United States (US), to enable US intelligence from breaking their security. Furthermore, leaked confidential documents by Edward Snowden suggest similar scenarios, where giant companies collude with government intelligence by introducing backdoors that are known to, and can be exploited by, those powerful adversaries (e.g. the "PRISM" program) [42].

Our discriminatory adversarial model is inspired by the "malicious-but-cautious" [35] and the Secretly Embedded Trapdoor with Universal Protection (SETUP) [44] adversarial models. The "malicious-but-cautious" model assumes a cloud service provider (server) can act maliciously but is cautious not to leave a verifiable trace of its malicious behaviour. However, it does not assume that the malicious server is willing to enable a third-party to access some users' data. On the other hand, the SETUP model assumes a cryptographic system (server in our case) can enable a third-party to secretly obtain secret information such as the private-key that decrypts the encrypted data from the system's encrypted output. Our discriminatory adversary weakens the security against some users for a third party's advantage, and is also cautious not to leave a verifiable trace of its malicious behaviour, e.g. by selecting a supported but non-preferred ciphersuite (non-FS-ciphersuite), as it is still accepted by most clients for backward compatibility.

To better analyse BEFS against the discriminatory adversary (server), we further classify this adversary into two variants: weak discriminatory and strong discriminatory. In the weak variant, the adversary submits to the client's offer (ciphersuites in our case). That is, if the client offers strong choices exclusively, the weak discriminatory has no choice but to select from them, mainly to avoid detection. In the strong variant, the adversary refuses to select strong choices, which forces the client to fallback in order to connect to the server. BEFS with silent fallback is secure against the weak discriminatory adversaries. However, strong discriminatory adversaries require interactive fallback and security-aware users. In today's real-world settings, the weak variant is more realistic. However, the strong variant can be detected through BEFS and security-aware users. Note that this analysis of BEFS against a discriminatory adversary is independent of considerations about the communication channel. That is, if an active adversary is present in the communication channel, interactive fallback is required with both variants of the discriminatory adversary, in order for BEFS to meet its security goal.

Best Effort Forward Secrecy and Authenticated Encryption (BESAFE). Given the fact that more than 50% of the servers select FS+non-AE-ciphersuite after enforcing FS-ciphersuites and that between 16.14% to 25.79% of them support FS+AE-ciphersuites, as an extension to BEFS, we propose BESAFE which adds an additional step to enforce not only FS-ciphersuites, but also FS+AE-ciphersuites. This improvement adds an additional restriction: the client offers FS+AE-ciphersuites *exclusively* at the first handshake attempt. If it failed, the client falls back to BEFS: it tries FS-ciphersuites *exclusively*, and if it failed, it falls back to default ciphersuites. The BESAFE mechanism guides servers towards FS+AE-ciphersuites. Similar to BEFS, BESAFE is secure against passive adversaries, or weak discriminatory adversaries with all types of fallbacks, and against active adversaries, or strong discriminatory adversaries with interactive fallback and security-aware users.

BEFS and BESAFE Performance.
We measure the latency that BEFS and its extension BESAFE incur into a TLS connection establishment with domains that do not support FS-ciphersuites, i.e. when more than one attempt is performed to complete a TLS handshake (otherwise, in BEFS, if the server supports FS-ciphersuites, and in BESAFE, if the server supports FS+AE-ciphersuites, there will be a single handshake as normal and no additional latency is

Table 3. The BEFS and BESAFE mechanisms latency in ms compared to the default one when connecting to servers that do not support FS-ciphersuites.

TLS client	Max.	Min.	Avg.
`Default`	4.10	0.64	1.69
`BEFS-Enabled`	5.34	1.79	3.47
`BESAFE-Enable`	8.60	3.27	5.19

incurred). To this end, we extract 5000 top domains that do not support FS-ciphersuites from our results. We implement a TLS client that supports `Chrome`'s pre-TLS 1.3 default ciphersuites using `Python 3.6.5` and utilising `OpenSSL 1.1.0g`. We disable TLS certificate validation and session tickets (resumption), and enable the SNI. Our client performs three consecutive handshakes for each domain: default, BEFS-enabled, and BESAFE-enabled handshakes. We run the client on a machine equipped with a 3.2 GHz `Intel Core` i5 processor, 8 GB of RAM, and a 1000 Mbps wired Ethernet card that has a public IPv4 address at the University of Oxford. We measure the time to complete a TLS handshake in a socket connection in milliseconds using the `process_time()`, a process-wide timer in python's `time` module. We count the domains that triggered BEFS and BESAFE to resort to default ciphersuites (i.e. do not support FS-ciphersuites), and also responded to the default TLS handshake. Then we extract the maximum, minimum and average time they take for each of the three handshake types. There are 4501 domains that do not support FS-ciphersuites and responded to the three types of handshakes we examine. The results based on these responses are summarised in Table 3. We can also infer the latency that BESAFE incurs into a connection to a server that does not support FS+AE-ciphersuites but supports FS+non-AE-ciphersuites from the BEFS latency (since both require two attempts).

Improved Performance Through Parallel Attempts. As shown in the previous section, BEFS introduces a latency on the default TLS connection establishment, but only if the server does not support FS-ciphersuites. To minimise this latency, the client can implement BEFS attempts in parallel instead of consecutively. That is, the client sends two CHs one with default ciphersuites and the second with FS-ciphersuites, in parallel to the server. For each TLS session establishment, the client waits for all the CH attempts' responses to return. If there is a valid response to the FS-ciphersuites attempt, the client proceeds with the FS-ciphersuites response. Otherwise, if the FS-ciphersuites attempt has failed, the client proceeds with the default ciphersuite response. The same applies to BESAFE but the client sends three handshakes and first checks the FS+AE-ciphersuites, then the FS-ciphersuites attempts' response, before deciding to proceed with default ciphersuites.

5 Related Work

Lee et al. [25] scanned around 19,000 TLS servers based on top domains lists. They evaluate the cryptographic strengths in TLS servers including the supported key-exchange algorithms. In [18], Holz et al. provide statistics for the most popular selected ciphersuite by TLS servers. More recently, Kotzias et al. [22] examined the impact of high-profile attacks on TLS deployment, and Calzavara et al. [9] analysed the Alexa top 10,000 websites against known HTTPS vulnerabilities. All the aforementioned studies do not analyse the selected versus supported key-exchange algorithms as we do. In [19], Huan et al. provide an experimental study on TLS FS deployment on 473,802 of Alexa's top domains using an enumeration-based method. Our study analyses larger and more diverse datasets than that in [19], using a novel heuristic approach. Additionally, our study provides a recent view on FS adoption over the one in [19], which dates back to 2014. Apart from measurement studies, several studies show that RSA long-term private-keys can be compromised either due to advances in computing power, deployment, or implementation flaws. Kleinjung et al. [21] and Cavallar et al. [10] show that 786-bit and 512-bit RSA keys can be factored using powerful machines. Heninger et al. [17] conducted a measurement study, which is replicated by Alashwali [2], that shows that factorable RSA keys are widespread in network devices on the Internet, due to low entropy during prime generation. The Heartlbleed bug [39] in the OpenSSL TLS library shows that implementation bugs can cause private-key compromise.

6 Conclusions

In this paper, we analysed the state of FS on over 10 million servers on the Internet. Using a modern TLS client handshake algorithms, our results show 5.37% of top domains, 7.51% of random domains, and 26.16% of random IPs *do not select* FS key-exchange algorithms. Surprisingly, we found that 39.20% of the top domains, 24.40% of the random domains, and 14.46% of the random IPs that *do not select* FS, *do support* FS. We then discussed possible paths towards FS. We showed that a best effort approach can add a value over the "all or nothing" approach and can increase FS or FS and AE adoption in misconfigured servers.

Acknowledgment. We thank the Censys team [14], the CS's IT and OxCERT teams at the University of Oxford, and the tls-scan developer, Binu Ramakrishnan, for technical support. Pawel's work was supported by the SUTD SRG ISTD 2017 128 grant.

References

1. Akhawe, D., Felt, A.P.: Alice in warningland: a large-scale field study of browser security warning effectiveness. In: Proceedings of USENIX Security Symposium (2013)
2. Alashwali, E.S.: Cryptographic vulnerabilities in real-life web servers. In: Proceedings of International Conference on Communications and Information Technology (ICCIT), pp. 6–11 (2013)
3. Alashwali, E.S., Rasmussen, K.: What's in a downgrade? a taxonomy of downgrade attacks in the TLS protocol and application protocols using TLS. In: Proceedings of Applications and Techniques in Cyber Security (ATCS), pp. 468–487 (2018)
4. Alashwali, E.S., Szalachowski, P., Martin, A.: Does "www." mean better transport layer security? In: Proceedings of Availability, Reliability and Security (ARES), pp. 23:1–23:7 (2019)
5. Alexa Internet Inc.: Alexa Top Sites (2018). http://s3.amazonaws.com/alexa-static/top-1m.csv.zip. Accessed 22 August (2018)
6. AlFardan, N.J., Paterson, K.G.: Lucky thirteen: breaking the TLS and DTLS record protocols. In: Proceedings of Security and Privacy (SP), pp. 526–540 (2013)
7. Amann, J., Gasser, O., Scheitle, Q., Brent, L., Carle, G., Holz, R.: Mission accomplished?: HTTPS security after diginotar. In: Proceedings of Internet Measurement Conference (IMC), pp. 325–340 (2017)
8. Barnes, R., Thomson, M., Pironti, A., Langley, A.: Deprecating Secure Sockets Layer Version 3.0 (2015). https://tools.ietf.org/html/rfc7568. Accessed 30 September (2018)
9. Calzavara, S., Focardi, R., Nemec, M., Rabitti, A., Squarcina, M.: Postcards from the post-HTTP world: amplification of HTTPS vulnerabilities in the web ecosystem. In: Proceedings of Security and Privacy (SP), pp. 281–298 (2019)
10. Cavallar, S., et al.: Factorization of a 512-bit RSA modulus. In: Proceedings of Advances in Cryptology (EUROCRYPT), pp. 1–18 (2000)
11. Dierks, T., Rescorla, E.: The Transport Layer Security (TLS) Protocol Version 1.2 (2008). https://www.ietf.org/rfc/rfc5246.txt. Accessed 6 July 2018
12. Diffie, W., Hellman, M.: New directions in cryptography. IEEE Trans. Inf. Theory **22**(6), 644–654 (1976)
13. Dukhovni, V.: Opportunistic Security: Some Protection Most of the Time (2014). https://tools.ietf.org/html/rfc7435.html. Accessed 1 October (2018)
14. Durumeric, Z., Adrian, D., Mirian, A., Bailey, M., Halderman, J.A.: A search engine backed by internet-wide scanning. In: Proceedings of Computer and Communications Security (CCS), pp. 542–553 (2015)
15. Eastlake 3rd, D.: Transport Layer Security (TLS) Extensions: Extension Definitions. https://tools.ietf.org/html/rfc6066#page-6. Accessed 19 June 2019
16. FIPS: Advanced Encryption Standard (AES) (2001). https://nvlpubs.nist.gov/nistpubs/FIPS/NIST.FIPS.197.pdf. Accessed 30 Sept 2018
17. Heninger, N., Durumeric, Z., Wustrow, E., Halderman, J.A.: Mining your Ps and Qs: detection of widespread weak keys in network devices. In: Proceedings of USENIX Security Symposium, pp. 205–220 (2012)
18. Holz, R., Braun, L., Kammenhuber, N., Carle, G.: The SSL landscape: a thorough analysis of the X.509 PKI using active and passive measurements. In: Proceedings of Internet Measurement Conference (IMC), pp. 427–444 (2011)
19. Huang, L.S., Adhikarla, S., Boneh, D., Jackson, C.: An experimental study of TLS forward secrecy deployments. IEEE Internet Comput. **18**(6), 43–51 (2014)

20. Jager, T., Kohlar, F., Schäge, S., Schwenk, J.: On the security of TLS-DHE in the standard model. In: Proceedings of Advances in Cryptology (CRYPTO), pp. 273–293 (2012)
21. Kleinjung, T., et al.: Factorization of a 768-bit RSA modulus. In: Proceedings of Advances in Cryptology (CRYPTO), pp. 333–350 (2010)
22. Kotzias, P., Razaghpanah, A., Amann, J., Paterson, K.G., Vallina-Rodriguez, N., Caballero, J.: Coming of age: a longitudinal study of TLS deployment. In: Proceedings of Internet Measurement Conference (IMC), pp. 415–428 (2018)
23. Kurkowski, J.: tldextract (2017). https://github.com/john-kurkowski/tldextract. Accessed 30 Oct 2018
24. Laurie, B., Langley, A., Kasper, E.: Certificate Transparency (2013). Accessed 25 Feb 2019
25. Lee, H.K., Malkin, T., Nahum, E.: Cryptographic strength of SSL/TLS servers: current and recent practices. In: Proceedings of Internet Measurement Conference (IMC), pp. 83–92 (2007)
26. Menezes, A.J., Van Oorschot, P.C., Vanstone, S.A.: Handbook of Applied Cryptography. CRC press, Boca Raton (1996)
27. Moeller, B., Langley, A.: TLS Fallback Signaling Cipher Suite Value (SCSV) for preventing protocol downgrade attacks (2014). https://tools.ietf.org/html/draft-ietf-tls-downgrade-scsv-00. Accessed 1 Oct 2018
28. Möller, B., Duong, T., Kotowicz, K.: This POODLE Bites: Exploiting the SSL 3.0 Fallback (2014). https://www.openssl.org/~bodo/ssl-poodle.pdf. Accessed 6 July 2018
29. Nir, Y., Josefsson, S., Pegourie-Gonnard, M.: Elliptic Curve Cryptography (ECC) Cipher Suites for Transport Layer Security (TLS) Versions 1.2 and Earlier (2018). https://tools.ietf.org/html/rfc8422. Accessed 21 June 2019
30. Partridge, C., Allman, M.: Ethical considerations in network measurement papers. Commun. ACM **59**(10), 58–64 (2016)
31. Popov, A.: Prohibiting RC4 Cipher Suites (2015). https://tools.ietf.org/html/rfc7465. Accessed 30 Sept 2018
32. Qualys Inc.: SSL Labs (2018). https://www.ssllabs.com/ssl-pulse/. Accessed 10 April 2019
33. Rescorla, E.: The Transport Layer Security (TLS) Protocol Version 1.3 (2018). https://tools.ietf.org/html/rfc8446. Accessed 27 November 2019
34. Rivest, R.L., Shamir, A., Adleman, L.: A method for obtaining digital signatures and public-key cryptosystems. Commun. ACM **21**(2), 120–126 (1978)
35. Ryan, M.D.: Enhanced certificate transparency and end-to-end encrypted mail. In: Proceedings of Network and Distributed System (NDSS) (2018)
36. Salowey, J., Choudhury, A., McGrew, D.: AES Galois Counter Mode (GCM) Cipher Suites for TLS (2008). https://tools.ietf.org/html/rfc5288#page-3. Accessed 12 Nov 2018
37. Samarasinghe, N., Mannan, M.: Short paper: TLS ecosystems in networked devices vs. web servers. In: Proceedings of Financial Cryptography and Data Security (FC), pp. 533–541 (2017)
38. Sunshine, J., Egelman, S., Almuhimedi, H., Atri, N., Cranor, L.F.: Crying wolf: an empirical study of SSL warning effectiveness. In: Proceedings of USENIX Security Symposium, pp. 399–416 (2009)
39. Synopsys Inc.: The Heartbleed Bug (2014). http://heartbleed.com. Accessed 17 Sept 2018

40. Vaudenay, S.: Security flaws induced by CBC padding-applications to SSL, IPSEC, WTLS.... In: Proceedings of Theory and Applications of Cryptographic Techniques (EUROCRYPT), pp. 534–546 (2002)
41. W3Schools: Browser Statistics (2019). https://www.w3schools.com/browsers. Accessed 27 Feb 2019
42. Wikipedia: PRISM (Surveillance Program) (2018). https://en.wikipedia.org/wiki/PRISM_(surveillance_program). Accessed 3 Oct 2018
43. Yahoo Inc.: tls-scan (2016), https://github.com/prbinu/tls-scan. Accessed 8 Sept 2018
44. Young, A., Yung, M.: The dark side of black-box cryptography or: should we trust capstone? In: Proceedings of Advances in Cryptology (CRYPTO), pp. 89–103 (1996)

Traffic-Based Automatic Detection
of Browser Fingerprinting

Rui Zhao[1(✉)], Edward Chow[2], and Chunchun Li[2]

[1] University of Nebraska Omaha, Omaha, USA
ruizhao@unomaha.edu
[2] University of Colorado Colorado Springs, Colorado Springs, USA

Abstract. Fingerprinting has been widely adopted by first- and third-party websites for the purpose of online tracking. It collects properties of operating systems, browsers, and even the hardware, for generating unique identifiers for visitors on websites. However, fingerprinting has raised both privacy and security concerns. In this paper, we present a traffic-based fingerprinting detection framework, FPExcavator. By analyzing the difference on values carried in outgoing requests from different browsers and machines, FPExcavator detects possible identifiers, as the generated fingerprints, in request header and payload. We implemented FPExcavator with OpenStack, Java, and some command scripts, and evaluated it on 100 websites in a lab setting and 100 websites selected from real-world. FPExcavator achieved 100% detection accuracy rate on 100 testing websites and 99% detection accuracy rate on 100 real-world websites. Meanwhile, it identified 12 new online tracking domains that have not been reported by previous research work. The evaluation results demonstrate that FPExcavator is useful and effective.

Keywords: Browser · Fingerprinting · Detection · Privacy

1 Introduction

Web tracking techniques have been widely adopted by commercial websites for collecting users' information and behaviors for advertising and analytic purposes. It creates unique identifiers for individual users during the web browsing without their awareness [9,12]. Besides stateful web tracking that relies on cookies, stateless web tracking, which is also known as browser fingerprinting, has also been used by more and more first-party websites. Unlike cookie-based stateful web tracking, stateless web tracking does not write anything locally through browsers. Not only first-parties (e.g., Google and Facebook) can track users' behaviors on their own websites [15], third-party companies (e.g., Google Analytics, BlueCava, Iovation, and ThreatMetrix studied in [14,16]) also provide web tracking libraries to first-party websites. In 2013, JavaScript-based font probing fingerprinting had been found on 250 out of one million websites, and flash-based fingerprinting had been found on the index pages of 95 out of 10,000 websites [2].

© ICST Institute for Computer Sciences, Social Informatics and Telecommunications Engineering 2019
Published by Springer Nature Switzerland AG 2019. All Rights Reserved
S. Chen et al. (Eds.): SecureComm 2019, LNICST 304, pp. 365–385, 2019.
https://doi.org/10.1007/978-3-030-37228-6_18

In the same year, fingerprinting scripts from third-party providers had been identified on 40 out of 10,000 websites [14]. In 2014, Acar et al. identified 5,542 of top 100,000 websites had used canvas fingerprinting scripts provided by 20 third-parties [1]. In 2015, Libert showed that Google can track users across nearly 80% websites [11]. In 2016, Englehardt et al. showed that third-party fingerprinting organizations presented on more than 10% of top one million websites [7]. Meanwhile, popular websites trends to have more fingerprinting scripts.

Through JavaScript APIs and flash objects, fingerprinting gathers its attributes from the properties of browsers, operating systems, and even the hardware, and generates unique identifiers on individual browsers, which later correlate browsing sessions across time and space. Those attributes can be obtained from HTTP headers (e.g., the userAgent string and supported MIME types [2,9,12,14]), HTML5 elements (e.g., fonts and canvas [1,8,9,14]), and JavaScript objects (e.g., *navigator*, *navigator.plugins*, *window.screen*, cookies enabled, WebGL, WebRTC, audio, and battery status [2,7,9,14]). In addition, other languages such as C, python, and Coffeescript can also be used for fingerprinting on the OS and hardware level [5]. Researchers have shown that browser fingerprinting can uniquely identify 83.6% of 500,000 browser instances in [12], 34% of more than 1,000 web users in [8], 90% of desktop fingerprints and 81% of mobile fingerprints in [9], and 83.24% of users in [5]. Although fingerprints may evolve because of the software and hardware upgrades, researchers have demonstrated that fingerprints are linkable during their evolution [19].

Web tracking, especially fingerprinting, has raised many privacy and security concerns. For example, whether they may collect more information than what they need remains a big question [1,3,16]. As fingerprinting is able to detect the types and versions of browsers, operating systems, and sometimes even the hardware, it also creates possibilities for attackers to take advantages of flawed browsers or operating systems and launch attacks such as drive-by-download attacks [6].

To prevent fingerprinting, researchers have proposed two types of countermeasures that either disable the execution of JavaScript code on webpages or fabricate fingerprint's attributes to conceal true identities [13,17]. Obviously, the first approach will severely affect websites' usability as their functionalities heavily rely on JavaScript. The second approach will introduce fingerprint inconsistency on the same computer, but in turn can be used to detect fingerprint spoofers [18] which later can serve as a fingerprint attribute. In terms of fingerprinting defense techniques, only a handful of existing research work were proposed. However, they need to either intrude into browsers [2] or heavily rely on the knowledge about fingerprinting JavaScript APIs [7,10,14]. Meanwhile, existing work only detected the usage of certain JavaScript APIs but whether fingerprints were generated from those APIs' returned values remains unanswered [10].

In this paper, we present a traffic-based fingerprinting detection framework, FPExcavator. In order to detect fingerprinting on a webpage, FPExcavator drives virtual machines in different configuration settings to visit that page, collects traffic traces from these machines, and extracts values from the header and payload of all the outgoing HTTP and HTTPS requests. By examining the difference in the values posted to the same URL across different browsing sessions, FPExcavator predicts the existence of fingerprinting on that webpage. FPExcavator has the capability to detect fingerprinting techniques that utilize properties of operating systems (e.g., platform, version, fonts, timezone, and language), browsers (e.g., product, vendor, version, language, cookies, canvas, Java, plugins, and WebGL), and the hardware (e.g., CPU, media devices, and screen). The design of FPExcavator is based on observations and rules that (1) when loading a webpage the outgoing traffic from a browser is for either requesting web resource or posting values to the web server, and it should be very similar across multiple browsing sessions in terms of value fields and their destinations, (2) a good fingerprinting should always generate an identical fingerprint for the same machine across multiple browsing sessions unless its software or hardware is upgraded, and (3) a good fingerprinting should always generate different fingerprints for machines in different configuration settings. In contrast to [7,10,14], FPExcavator focuses more on the fingerprint representation in the network traffic only.

We implemented FPExcavator by using OpenStack, Java, and some command scripts, and selected Selenium to drive browsers and Fiddler for the traffic trace collection. FPExcavator was evaluated on websites in a lab setting and selected from real-world. In the lab setting, we created 100 website and randomly deployed our fingerprinting scripts on 50 of them. The results show that fingerprinting on those 50 websites were all detected with a 100% accuracy rate. Among the 100 real-world websites, FPExcavator identified fingerprinting on 13 of them, which were all manually validated. We also manually analyzed the scripts included on the rest 87 websites, and found that our framework missed only one website. FPExcavator reached a 99% accuracy rate on real-world websites. The main contributions of this work include: (1) the design of a unique framework that drives virtual machines, observes and analyzes traffic traces for fingerprinting detection, (2) a strategy used on virtual machine configurations (i.e., differential configuration in Sect. 3.3), (3) an effective evaluation of the framework, and (4) the possibility to extend our framework for the detection of pure cookie-based web tracking and cookie respawning [1].

The rest of this paper is organized as following. In Sect. 2, we mainly discuss existing fingerprinting techniques and their detection and prevention. In Sect. 3, we introduce the overall design and rationale of our fingerprinting detection framework, FPExcavator; we also provide more design details on each component of FPExcavator. In Sect. 4, we provide implementation details of each component. In Sect. 5, we evaluate FPExcavator on websites in a lab setting and selected from real-world, present and discuss the detection results. In Sect. 6, we discuss the limitation of our framework and the future work. In Sect. 7, we draw a conclusion.

2   Related Work

Researchers [1, 2, 10, 13, 14] have identified a large number of JavaScript APIs that can be used for collecting properties of operating systems, browsers, and the hardware. All the considered properties by our framework and their corresponding fingerprint attributes as well as their JavaScript APIs are listed as below.

- On operating system
  - OS properties (JavaScript *navigator*)
    * Platform (JavaScript *navigator.platform*)
    * Version (JavaScript *navigator.oscpu*, *navigator.appVersion*)
  - CPU property (JavaScript *navigator.hardwareConcurrency*)
  - Media I/O devices (JavaScript *navigator.mediaDevices*)
  - Battery (JavaScript *navigator.getBattery()*)
  - Font (JavaScript [8])
  - Screen properties (JavaScript *window.screen*)
    * Height (JavaScript *window.screen.height*)
    * Width (JavaScript *window.screen.width*)
    * Orientation (JavaScript *window.screen.orientation*)
    * Color depth (JavaScript *window.screen.colorDepth*)
    * Pixel depth (JavaScript *window.screen.pixelDepth*)
  - TimeZone (JavaScript *Date*)
  - Language (JavaScript *navigator.systemLanguage*, *navigator.userLanguage*)
- On browser
  - Browser properties (JavaScript *navigator*)
    * Code name (JavaScript *navigator.appCodeName*)
    * App name (JavaScript *navigator.appName*)
    * App version (JavaScript *navigator.appVersion*)
    * User agent (JavaScript *navigator.userAgent*)
    * Vendor (JavaScript *navigator.vendor*, *navigator.vendor − Sub*)
    * Product (JavaScript *navigator.product*, *navigator.product − Sub*)
    * MIME type (JavaScript *navigator.mimeTypes*)
    * Cookie enabled (JavaScript *navigator.cookieEnabled()*)
    * Java enabled (JavaScript *navigator.javaEnabled()*)
    * Language (JavaScript *navigator.browserLanguage*, *navigator.language*, *navigator.languages*)
    * Do-not-track (JavaScript *navigator.doNotTrack*)
  - HTML elements (JavaScript *HTMLElement.offsetHeight*, *HTMLElement.offsetWidth*, *HTMLElement.offsetBoundingClientRect*)
  - Canvas element properties (JavaScript *CanvasRenderingContext2D.getImageData*, *CanvasRenderingContext2D.fillText*, *CanvasRenderingContext2D.strokeText*, *HTMLCanvasElement.toDataURL*)
  - Plugins (JavaScript *navigator.plugins*)
  - WebGL (JavaScript *WebGL2RenderingContext.getImageData*, *WebGL2RenderingContext.fillText*, *WebGL2RenderingContext.strokeText*)
  - Math constants (JavaScript *Math*)

2.1 Fingerprinting Prevention

Since browser fingerprinting is difficult to be opted-out or blocked [1,2,18], researchers have proposed two types of countermeasures that either disable the execution of JavaScript code on web pages or fabricate fingerprint's attributes to conceal the true identity [13,17]. Obviously, the first approach will severely affect the usability of websites especially when their functionalities heavily rely on JavaScript.

In terms of the second approach, Nikiforakis et al. in [13] have proposed to randomize fingerprint's attributes so that fingerprints look like non-deterministic, thus breaking the "link" across browsing sessions. Torres et al. in [17] have adopted Markov chains to generate different fingerprints across web domains while assure the fingerprint consistency within one domain to prevent cross-domain third-party browser fingerprinting. However, all these approaches introduce inconsistency on fingerprints, that in turn can be used to detect fingerprint spoofers. Vastel et al. demonstrated that all existing countermeasures failed in lying consistently on fingerprints and it was even possible to recover the genuine fingerprints on some attributes [18].

Other techniques, such as the DoNottrack header, private browsing mode, TOR, and browser extensions that can spoof user-agent strings, have also been proposed to defeat browser fingerprinting. Nevertheless, they were proved inadequate for hiding real browser identities [1,2,4,14,16].

2.2 Fingerprinting Detection

Only a handful of existing research work aims to address the same problem targeted by our framework, but they need to intrude into browsers or they were built based on the knowledge about fingerprinting JavaScript APIs.

In [2], Acar et al. proposed a framework, FPDetective, for detecting and analyzing web-based browser fingerprinters. FPDetective drives the instrumented Chromium browser to browse a website, intercepts and logs accesses to the browser and device properties (e.g., *navigator*, plugins, screen, and fonts) during the browsing. FPDetective was evaluated on Alexa top million websites and it successfully identified 16 new fingerprinting scripts and flash objects. Different from FPDetective, our framework is non-intrusive to browsers.

In [14], Nikiforakis et al. identified a heavy use of Adobe flash in commercial fingerprinting code from three providers for collecting sensitive information from the client-side. They investigated the adoption of fingerprinting code on Alexa top 10,000 websites by analyzing the script inclusion. They found that 40 of them included fingerprinting code from those three providers. In [7], Englehardt et al. proposed an infrastructure, OpenWPM, to measure both stateless (fingerprinting-based) and stateful (cookie-based) web tracking on top one million websites. OpenWPM drives browsers, simulates users' behaviors, and records HTTP response, cookies, and the use of JavaScript APIs. OpenWPM found canvas fingerprinting on 1.6% websites and font fingerprinting on less than

1% websites. They also observed the existence of infrequently used WebRTC-based, AudioContext-based, battery status-based fingerprinting techniques on many websites. In [10], Lernel et al. analyzed web tracking techniques on webpages archived by Wayback Machine from 1996 to 2016. Besides cookie-based web tracking, they also investigated the use of JavaScript APIs for fingerprinting. Their research results show that the using of JavaScript-based fingerprinting becomes more and more prevalent.

All these research work [7,10,14] heavily relies on the knowledge about existing fingerprinting techniques at the code level, i.e., what JavaScript APIs can be used for fingerprinting. Meanwhile, these approaches only detected the use of certain JavaScript APIs but did not analyze how the APIs' returned values were used [10]. In contrast to them, our framework does not require any knowledge about JavaScript APIs. It focuses more on the fingerprint representation in the network traffic only.

3 Design

3.1 Design Overview and Rationale

As shown in Fig. 1, our fingerprinting detection framework, FPExcavator, consists of five components: the *user interface*, the *executor driver*, a set of executors, a pool of virtual machine images, and the *trace analyzer*. The *user interface* component provides a graphic interface for users to submit detection tasks. Each task includes the URL of a webpage, on which fingerprinting will be detected, and a set of fingerprint attributes. The fingerprint attributes are based on browsers, operating systems, and hardware's properties. Based on fingerprint attributes, the *executor driver* selects virtual machine images in different configuration settings from a pool, runs them on the executors as virtual machines, and drives the browsers on them to visit the given webpage. Prior to use FPExcavator, all the needed virtual machine images must be created and properly configured. During the visit, *executors* keep collecting traffic traces and report them to the *trace analyzer* component. The *trace analyzer* component extracts and compares values from the header and payload of all the outgoing HTTP and HTTPS requests. If any difference in the values posted to the same URL from different virtual machines is observed, that webpage will be reported for its fingerprinting behaviors.

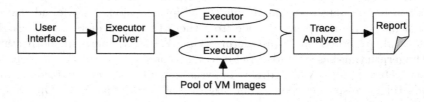

Fig. 1. The overall workflow of FPExcavator for fingerprinting detection

Our design is based on two observations on the network traffic: the generated outgoing traffic, when loading a webpage, is for either requesting web resource or posting values to the web server, and it should be very similar in a certain time period in terms of the transmitted requests' destinations as well as value fields in their header and payload. Our design is also based on the following rules that a good fingerprinting should obey.

- R1: Fingerprints should always differ on computers in different configuration settings even though they had occupied the same IP address.
- R2: Fingerprinting should be able to identify the use of a computer across network and it should not base on the network address.
- R3: Fingerprint should remain identical on a computer unless its software or hardware is changed.
- R4: Fingerprints must be eventually posted to the web servers anyhow for the purpose of web tracking.

3.2   Preliminary Study

In order to verify our observations and validate the feasibility of our app-roach, some preliminary experiments were designed and performed. In our first experiment, we used Google Chrome browser on a computer to visit a non-fingerprinting webpage for twice and collected two network traffic traces. We compared all the outgoing requests in these two traces and did not observe any difference in the request header and payload. We then re-visited the same web-page by using Firefox browser on the same computer and collected one more traffic trace. Again, we did not observe any difference between the requests in this trace and those in any previously collected trace. Note that these observa-tions may be invalid on many other real-world webpages, which will be addressed by our design later.

In our second experiment, two computers in the same hardware configura-tion were used. We installed Windows 7 and Google Chrome browser in their latest version on both of the computers. However, these two computers were installed with different fonts. Meanwhile, we set up a website and deployed a commercial font-based fingerprinting script on it. From the same IP address, we visited our fingerprinting website on these two computers one by one and col-lected two traffic traces. For requests to the same URL in these two traces, we compared the header and payload and observed fixed patterns in their fields. We also observed that several header and payload fields posted to some particular URLs from the two computers have different values while the rest are the same. Those different field values could closely relates to fingerprints. Further more, we selected one computer that was used in the second experiment, cleaned its browser cache, re-visited the fingerprinting website from a different IP address, and captured the traffic trace. In our examination on the header and payload, we found that the outgoing requests from this capture are exactly the same to those previously collected from the same computer in the second experiment. Further-more, we manually examined the deployed fingerprinting script, and figured out the corresponding code pieces that collect attributes, generate fingerprints, and eventually send them out through an XMLHttpRequest.

The results of our preliminary study indicate that our approach is feasible. In the following subsections, we will provide more details on each component of our framework.

3.3   Pool of Virtual Machine Images

The purpose of fingerprinting is to collect fingerprint attributes from operating systems, browsers, and hardware's properties, and generate unique fingerprints from those attributes for individual computers. Different techniques were developed for collecting different types of attributes. For example, font probing fingerprinting measures the size of a rendered text in a specific font in order to detect the existence of that font. For another example, some flash-based fingerprinting can even learn properties of operating systems and the hardware. In order to detect a particular fingerprinting technique on a webpage, we require the virtual machine images used for visiting that webpage must be different on those device properties such a fingerprinting technique relies on, so that differences will be observed in the generated fingerprints for those images. Therefore, users of FPExcavator need to set each virtual machine image's properties carefully. All the considered properties of operating systems and browsers by FPExcavator and their corresponding fingerprint attributes as well as their JavaScript APIs are listed in Sect. 2.

For maximizing the detection capability of FPExcavator while minimizing the number of needed virtual machine images, we propose a *differential configuration* for setting properties of virtual machine images. This differential configuration enables both coarse- and fine- grained fingerprinting detection. Assuming a fingerprinting script to be detected is based on n fingerprint attributes, minimally 2 computers will be required for the coarse-grained detection and maximally $2 + n$ computers will be required for the fine-grained detection. In the coarse-grained detection, the two computers must be configured differently on every fingerprint attribute so that value differences of those attributes can eventual cause unique fingerprints for the two computers, thus helping determine the existence of fingerprinting. However, it is infeasible to decide if a specific attribute has contributed to the fingerprint uniqueness, especially when fingerprints are hashed. Therefore, in the fine-grained detection, extra n computers are required. Each of them needs to be configured differently on only one attribute from a computer used in the coarse-grained detection. Consequently, by using any one of the n computers and one of the two computers in the coarse-grained detection FPExcavator is able to determine whether a fingerprinting is based on a particular attribute.

In order to facilitate the selection on virtual machine images, a table will be maintained to correlate images and their properties to the fingerprint attribute values. According to the differential configuration, eight default virtual machine images (Table 1) were created for the detection of fingerprinting techniques based on six attributes: operating system type, browser type, screen resolution, fonts, extensions, and plugins. By using VM1 and VM2, FPExcavator is able to detect the existence of a fingerprinting script that targets on any of these attributes because every attribute on these two computers have different values. By using VM1 and VM3, FPExcavator is able to detect the existence of a fingerprinting script that targets on the operating system type because only that attribute has different values. Note that strategy used in real detection can be even more complex than these two examples (Sect. 5). The number of virtual machine images in Table 1 can be further reduced by reusing images. For example, VM1 and VM4 can use the same image on which both Google Chrome and Firefox can be installed, and VM1 and VM5 can use the same one on which the screen resolution can be correspondingly adjusted.

Table 1. An example of differential configuration on virtual machine images

VM	OS	Browser	Screen Resolution	Missing Font	Extensions	Plug-ins
1	Windows 7	Google Chrome⋆	1680 * 1050●	Arial	AdBlock	Flash Player
2	*Ubuntu 14.04*	*Firefox*	*1028 * 764*	*Symbol*	*Google Doc*	*PDF Viewer*
3	*Ubuntu 14.04*	Google Chrome	1680 * 1050	Arial	AdBlock	Flash Player
4	Windows 7	*Firefox⋆*	1680 * 1050	Arial	AdBlock	Flash Player
5	Windows 7	Google Chrome	*1028 * 764*●	Arial	AdBlock	Flash Player
6	Windows 7	Google Chrome	1680 * 1050	*Symbol*	AdBlock	Flash Player
7	Windows 7	Google Chrome	1680 * 1050	Arial	*Google Doc*	Flash Player
8	Windows 7	Google Chrome	1680 * 1050	Arial	AdBlock	*PDF Viewer*

3.4 Executor Driver

Given a webpage URL and a set of attributes, based on the detection scheme the *executor driver* component will select several virtual machine images, run them on executors as virtual machines, and drive these machines to visit the given webpage. FPExcavator provides two default detection schemes. In the first scheme, two machines will be driven to visit a webpage from one IP address. In the second scheme, two machines will be driven to visit a webpage from two different IP addresses. On each machine in both the two schemes at least two browsers will be used. The users of FPExcavator can also flexibly define their own detection schemes.

As shown in Fig. 2, this component adopts multiple threads to control individual virtual machines in parallel. The executor driver establishes a communication channel with every executed virtual machine for passing webpage's URL to the machine and receiving notices from the machine when the webpage browsing completes. Running as an agent on each virtual machine, the *browser driver* subcomponent will drive browsers to visit a given webpage. Particularly, it supports five browser actions: open the browser, clear the cache, open a new tab with an URL, close a tab, and close the browser. Before each webpage visit, the browser cache, including local storage and cookies, on each of the executed virtual machines will be cleaned to assure nothing from the last visit will be inherited. During the visit to a webpage on each virtual machine, the *trace collector* subcomponent captures and dumps all the outgoing requests as a traffic trace and aggregates the collected traces for the later trace analysis.

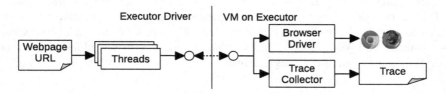

Fig. 2. The workflow on the executor driver and virtual machines

3.5   Trace Analyzer

Once traffic traces are aggregated to the *trace analyzer* component, the trace analysis is then performed according to the detection schemes. Specifically, between the two given traces all their outgoing requests' full URLs and all the fields in HTTP/HTTPS header and payload will be extracted and compared. In this comparison cookie values are also considered because websites may write the generated fingerprints into cookies and later transmit them out through cookies; however, by examining cookies values only fingerprints in the HTTP/HTTPS request payload will be missed. In either first or second built-in scheme, fingerprinting that follows the rule R1 (Sect. 3.1) can be detected. In the combination of two schemes, fingerprinting that follows the rules R2 and R3 can be detected because the two machines are reused. More details will be provided in Sect. 5.

However, on some webpages seemingly fingerprint values (e.g., timestamps or pseudo-random generated numbers) may also be posted to servers along with real fingerprints. To rule out this case, FPExcavator can drive a browser from a virtual machine to visit that webpage at one IP address twice and capture traffic traces. FPExcavator then identifies all the fields with different values between the two traces but posted to the same URL, and *excludes* these fields from the trace analysis, because any observed difference in posted field values across these two visits probably are non-relevant to fingerprinting based on the rules R2 and R3 (Sect. 3.1).

Algorithm 1 is designed to analyze two web traffic traces, t_1 and t_2 that were collected from two virtual machines, and to calculate a fingerprinting score v of a webpage. Each trace contains a sequence of m requests. For each request p_1^x in trace t_1 where $1 \leq x \leq m$, the algorithm extracts its destination URL and search out all the requests in trace t_2 that were posted to the same URL. If there is a request p_2^y found in trace t_2 where $1 \leq y \leq m$, the algorithm will iterate each field in the header and payload and compare its values between p_1^x and p_2^y. If the values of a particular field in p_1^x and p_2^y are different,

---

Algorithm 1: Algorithm of trace analysis

Input: t_1, t_2: filtered outgoing web traffic traces where $t_i = \{p_i^1, p_i^2, ..., p_i^m\}$ is m requests in trace t_i from machine i ;

Output: v: a fingerprinting score ;

$v = 0$;

for *each p_1^x in t_1 where $1 \leq x \leq m$* **do**

    $url = \text{extractURL}(p_1^x)$;

    $p_2^y = \text{findRequestToURL}(t_2, url)$;

    if *p_2^y exists* **then**

        for *each field f in header and payload* **do**

            if *$p_1^x.f.value \neq p_2^y.f.value$* **then**

                $v\text{++}$;

            end

        end

    end

end

return v

---

the fingerprinting score v will be incremented by one. A webpage's v score indicates how many different values were transmitted out when loading that webpage from two different computers. The total v score combined from both the two schemes shows how likely fingerprinting exists on that webpage. The larger that total v is, the more likely that webpage has deployed fingerprinting techniques. The users of our framework can set a proper threshold for v.

4 Implementation

We implemented our framework, FPExcavator, with OpenStack [22], Java and command scripts. The OpenStack is used by the *executor driver* component for selecting and loading prepared images on *executors* as virtual machines. To improve the performance, the *executor driver* component supports multi-threads to drive multiple virtual machines in parallel. The agent on individual virtual machines was implemented in Java. It uses Selenium to drive both Google Chrome and Firefox browsers (the *browser driver* component in Sect. 3.4). It invokes command scripts to control Fiddler for traffic trace collection and aggregation (the *trace collector* component in Sect. 3.4). It supports both HTTP and HTTPS traffic and can decrypt HTTPS payload. We implemented TCP sockets on both the *executor driver* component and the Java agents for exchanging data. Once a Java agent receives a webpage's URL, it will launch and clean Fiddler, open a browser and clean its cache, open a new tab and load the webpage, wait for a few seconds, dump the captured traffic trace from Fiddler, exit the browser and Fiddler, compress and upload the traffic trace to the *trace analyzer* component, and finally notify the *executor driver* component on its complete. The *trace analyzer* component adopted strategies in [7] for detecting fingerprints (i.e., IDs) in data fields.

An example of the generated report by our framework is shown as below. It is for detecting font probing fingerprinting on https://www.google.com. In such a detection, we used two virtual machines, *PC1* and *PC2*, and installed *Firefox* browser but different fonts. We drove the two machines to visit the webpage one by one with the same IP address of *128.198.162.187*. Correspondingly, we collected two traffic traces, *Session 0* and *Session 1*. We observed total 119 requests were sent out and four of them carried different field values. The "⟨⟨*Yes*⟩⟩" in the report indicates that Google probability has deployed font-based fingerprinting technique. This result is further validated by a statement from Google's privacy policy [21] - " When you're not signed in to a Google Account, we store the information we collect with unique identifiers tied to the browser, application, or device you're using. This helps us do things like maintain your language preferences across browsing sessions."

```
Website: https://www.google.com <<Yes>>
-- Browser: firefox
---- Session 0: PC1, 128.198.162.187, R1
---- Session 1: PC2, 128.198.162.187, R2
---- Req Compare: Diff Req / Total Req = 4/119
------ Request:
-------- 0: Cookies: [NID=77=oiyy3fRGxHkwbO...]
-------- 1: Cookies: [NID=77=sHMQqRTAOequrK...]
... ...
```

5 Evaluation

In this section, we evaluated the detection accuracy of our FPExcavator on websites in lab settings and selected from real-world. We used two 32-bit Windows 7 virtual machines, PC1 and PC2, in our evaluation. These two machines are in the same hardware configuration, i.e., 4 CPU cores, 4GB memory, and 40GB hard drive. Both of them were installed with Google Chrome and Firefox browsers. However, they had different configuration settings on fonts, browser extensions, plugins, and screen resolutions based on the differential configuration (Sect. 3.3). We reserved two IP addresses, 128.198.162.187 and 128.198.162.139 for these two virtual machines. Meanwhile, we ran another virtual machine as the executor driver at the IP address of 128.198.162.184.

5.1 Evaluation in Lab Settings

We setup a browser fingerprinting website by using JavaScript and PHP. It collects attributes of canvas elements, WebGL, plugins, fonts, timezone, operating system platform, userAgent string, graphic card, browser platform, DoNotTrack, MIME Type, screen resolution, touch screen, cookie enabled, and adblock, and generates fingerprints for its visitors. All the generated fingerprints and the corresponding attribute values are saved in a database. This website also sets browser cookies to identify recurring visitors from first time visitors.

We published our website on internet and recruited online volunteers to visit it. Total 2,584 visits to our websites were made by 2,492 unique users during a collection period of nearly one month. Among them 56 recurring visitors had visited our website at least twice from different IP addresses. Our website failed on fingerprinting in 21 visits - different browsers plus devices generated the same fingerprint; all of them were from iPhone and iPad devices only. In terms of the fingerprinting accuracy rate, we define a true positive (TP) as an unknown fingerprint in a first time visit, a false positive (FP) as an unknown fingerprint in a re-visit, a true negative (TN) as a known fingerprint in a re-visit, and a false negative (FN) as a known fingerprint in a first time visit. After the classification on all the fingerprints, we calculated $TP = 2492$, $FP = 10$, $TN = 56$, and $FN = 26$. Based on these values, we further calculated the fingerprinting $accuracy = (TP + TN)/(TP + TN + FP + FN) = 98.6\%$. Therefore, our fingerprinting website is very effective.

In order to evaluate the performance of our fingerprinting detection framework, we created 100 testing websites and deployed our fingerprinting scripts on 50 of them randomly. We drove our virtual machines images visit these 100 websites, collected and analyzed network traffic traces. We define the following detection accuracy metrics: true positives (TP) is the number of fingerprinting websites correctly identified, false positives (FP) is the number of non-fingerprinting websites incorrectly identified, true negatives (TN) is the number of non-fingerprinting websites not identified, and false negatives (FN) is number of fingerprinting websites not identified. Based on our detection results, we calculate $TP = 50$, $FP = 0$, $TN = 50$, and $FN = 0$; correspondingly, $Precision = TP/(TP + FP) = 100\%$, $Recall = TP/(TP + FN) = 100\%$, $F - measure = (2 * Precision * Recall)/(Precision + Recall) = 100\%$, and $Accuracy = (TP + TN)/(TP + FP + TN + FN) = 100\%$. These results show that FPExcavator is very effective in fingerprinting detection on these 100 testing websites.

5.2 Evaluation on Real-World Websites

Furthermore, we evaluated the detection accuracy rate of FPExcavator on real-world websites. Originally, we expected to borrow a list of fingerprinting websites reported by previous research work [1,2] as our ground truth knowledge. However, their detected results were not available and might be out of date. We also downloaded their source code but failed on executing them. We then implemented a simple web crawler and executed it on 100 websites selected from Alexa for searching the inclusion of JavaScript libraries for font probing and canvas fingerprinting reported by [1,2]. Unfortunately, none of these websites includes the reported fingerprinting JavaScript libraries. It shows that fingerprinting JavaScript libraries reported by [1,2] may be incomplete or out of date.

In [7], Englehardt et al. released their fingerprinting detection results of Alexa top million websites [23]. With that ground truth knowledge, we selected 100 websites (Table 2) from Alexa and analyzed their index pages by using two detection schemes in our framework. In the first scheme for each website, our framework drove the two virtual machines, PC1 and PC2, to visit that website from the same IP address (128.198.162.187) by using Firefox, and made a comparison between network traffic traces of the two browsing sessions. Then our framework repeated the same process by using Google Chrome. By using this scheme, the configuration difference on fonts, extensions, plugins, and screen resolutions between the two machines will be observed in fingerprints. In the second scheme for each website, our framework drove the first virtual machines, PC1, visit that website twice from the IP address of 128.198.162.187 by using Firefox and Google Chrome browsers, respectively, and made a comparison between network traffic traces of the two browsing sessions. Then our framework repeated the same process by using the second virtual machine, PC2, from the IP address of 128.198.162.139. By using this scheme, the configuration difference on browser properties will be observed in fingerprints.

Table 2. The list of 100 real-world websites

360.cn	adnetworkperformance.com	adobe.com	alibaba.com	aliexpress.com
amazon.co.jp	amazon.co.uk	amazon.com	amazon.de	amazon.in
apple.com	ask.com	baidu.com	bbc.co.uk	bing.com
blogger.com	blogspot.com	bongacams.com	cnn.com	craigslist.org
dailymotion.com	diply.com	dropbox.com	ebay.co.uk	ebay.com
ebay.de	espn.go.com	facebook.com	fc2.com	flipkart.com
github.com	gmw.cn	go.com	google.ca	google.co.id
google.co.in	google.co.jp	google.co.kr	google.co.uk	google.com
google.com.au	google.com.br	google.com.hk	google.com.mx	google.com.tr
google.de	google.es	google.fr	google.it	google.pl
google.ru	googleusercontent.com	hao123.com	imdb.com	imgur.com
instagram.com	jd.com	kat.cr	linkedin.com	live.com
mail.ru	microsoft.com	msn.com	naver.com	netflix.com
nicovideo.jp	ok.ru	onclickads.net	outbrain.com	paypal.com
pinterest.com	pixnet.net	popads.net	pornhub.com	qq.com
rakuten.co.jp	reddit.com	sina.com.cn	sogou.com	sohu.com
soso.com	stackoverflow.com	t.co	taobao.com	tianya.cn
tmall.com	tradeadexchange.com	tumblr.com	twitter.com	vk.com
weibo.com	wikipedia.org	wordpress.com	xhamster.com	xinhuanet.com
xvideos.com	yahoo.co.jp	yahoo.com	yandex.ru	youtube.com

Overall, FPExcavator had detected fingerprinting on total 13 websites (Table 3) by using the threshold of 1 (Algorithm 1). The detection results on six websites, www.alibaba.com, www.aliexpress.com, www.bbc.co.uk, www. dailymotion.com, www.microsoft.com, and www.weibo.com, was manually verified by inspecting their inclusion of JavaScript files. Our identified online trackers, assets.alicdn.com, www.google-analytics.com, www.microsoft.com, and securepubads.g.doubleclick.net, on these six websites were also reported by [7,10].

We also manually verified our detected results on the rest seven websites by analyzing their use of JavaScript APIs (Sect. 3.3). Our results show that all of these websites have deployed fingerprinting scripts that collect attributes of *navigator*, *screen*, *canvas*, *plugins*, etc. Meanwhile, we identified 12 new online tracking domains that deploy fingerprinting techniques. As a quick summary, FPExcavator's findings on all these 13 websites were validated; however, none of these first-party websites was reported by [7]. We then manually examined the JavaScript files included on the rest 87 websites, which were reported as negatives by our framework. Only on www.ebay.co.uk we found a fingerprinting script, which cause a false negative. Based on these results, we calculated $TP = 13$, $FP = 0$, $TN = 87 - 1 = 86$, and $FN = 1$. Correspondingly, $Precision = TP/(TP + FP) = 100\%$, $Recall = TP/(TP + FN) = 92.9\%$. $F - measure = (2 * Precision * Recall)/(Precision + Recall) = 96.3\%$, and $Accuracy = (TP + TN)/(TP + FP + TN + FN) = 99\%$. Therefore, FPExcavator is also very effective in fingerprinting detection on these 100 real-world websites.

Table 3. Overall detection results on 100 real-world websites

Website	v of Scheme 1	v of Scheme 2	v Total	Trackers
www.alibaba.com	7	4	11	assets.alicdn.com [7]
				www.google-analytics.com [10]
www.aliexpress.com	1	0	1	assets.alicnd.com [7]
				www.google-analytics.com [10]
www.bbc.co.uk	4	2	6	securepubads.g.doubleclick.net [10]
				mybbc-analytics.files.bbci.co.uk
www.dailymotion.com	6	0	6	www.google-analytics.com [10]
www.ebay.com	1	0	1	ir.ebaystatic.com
www.ebay.de	1	0	1	ir.ebaystatic.com
www.linkedin.com	1	0	1	platform.linkedin.com
www.microsoft.com	1	0	1	cdnssl.clicktale.net
				www.microsoft.com [10]
www.qq.com	2	2	4	[captcha, mat1, ra].gtimg.com
				js.aq.qq.com
www.sina.com.cn	0	1	1	d3.sina.com.cn
				news.sina.com.cn
www.sohu.com	0	1	1	statics.itc.cn
www.twitter.com	1	0	1	www.gstatic.com
www.weibo.com	2	2	4	securepubads.g.doubleclick.net [10]
				www.google-analytics.com [10]

Table 4 summarizes the detailed detection results on those 100 real-world websites in the first scheme. Fingerprinting behaviors were found on total eleven websites. The six columns of the table are for website URLs, browsers, fields carrying different values, virtual machines, different values, and the number of requests containing that difference. For the website of www.ebay.de, our framework detected the value difference in a cookie field, NID, to the same destination URL in one of the total 208 outgoing requests collected from Google Chrome on the two virtual machines. It is very interesting that all the differences were observed in cookie values and none of the fingerprints was directly sent out in the payload. Meanwhile, many websites like www.alibaba.com, www.bbc.co.uk, and www.dailymotion.com, probably have deployed fingerprinting scripts from multiple trackers as more than one identifiers (e.g., NID and $tuuid$) were detected. We also observed that five websites' fingerprinting scripts work on both the two browsers while the rest six websites' fingerprinting scripts work on Google Chrome only probably because of the cloaking technique. It also indicates that fingerprinters have more interests on tracking online users through the Google Chrome browser which has over 62% share on the browser market as reported by statcounter.com in 2019 [20].

Furthermore, a cross-site fingerprinting behavior was observed among seven websites including www.twitter.com, www.aliexpress.com, www.microsoft.com, www.alibaba.com, www.linkedin.com, www.ebay.com, and www.dailymotion.com. As marked in red in Table 4, on the Google Chrome browser a fixed value of " 78=oXuoRxuOdSmU-kT-nck4kP7hapShc1f5EDONuOLqVZR98QGL8nDYK4 vJv9gRpKFHi2n623n0jIbz8JbWkz3v8rp49tzdnINo7B6HPkK1JHoLuE1jypxr6oHw S66tnJoJmdOEUmnucOJqE3_xeQ" was generated for the virtual machine PC1 and shared through a cookie field NID across these websites. Similarly, a fixed value (in blue) of "78=UG1TwObtbDT4Wp3QeGtPMwQufhzhoACLZ2vpDEkjGTAJNGOogYvF gdEcQH3FLIxOjhwAI1zBXzdD34sAXDKVfYOOgtP82woEIaajPfpRRyebwjLKox1F_p WyDNiK9fM_QPJdrQkoEvoirOQRyA" was generated for the virtual machine PC2 and shared across these websites. Meanwhile, all those values are in the field NID. One possible reason is that these websites may have adopted the same fingerprinting scripts.

Table 5 summarizes the detailed detection results on those 100 real-world websites in the second scheme. Fingerprinting behaviors were found on total six websites. The six columns of the table are for website URLs, virtual machines, fields carrying different values, browsers, different values, and the number of requests containing that difference. For the website of www.qq.com, our framework detected a difference in cookie values posted to the same URL in four of the total 260 outgoing requests from Firefox and Google Chrome browsers on the same virtual machine. A cross-site fingerprinting behavior was also observed among two websites, www.qq.com and www.sina.com.cn. Meanwhile, as marked by colored bulletins and squares in Table 4 and 5, same cookie values were generated on the same browser and the same virtual machine by the same website across the two schemes, such as the values of "DL3I21nmD2A5yGx8PmZ" (●) and "NyknCUjvSWq9" (○) generated on Firefox at PC1 by www.qq.com and www.alibaba.com, respectively. One possible explanation is the fingerprinting rules

R2 and R3 (Sect. 3.1): fingerprints should remain the same on one computer across browsing sessions unless there is any change on its software or hardware. However, cookie respawning [1] may also cause the same phenomenon. In Sect. 6, we will discuss the detection of cookie respawning by using our framework.

6 Discussion

In the evaluation of our framework on 100 real-world websites, we observed that all different values were in the cookie fields and none of the fingerprints was transmitted in the payload. This observation indicates that many websites may combine both fingerprinting- and cookie-based web tracking techniques: they collect attributes' values and generate fingerprints but write the fingerprints into cookies. We further validated our hypothesis by manually inspecting JavaScript code on some of those websites.

Besides this combined web tracking approach, FPExcavator is also able to identify pure cookie-based web tracking especially when cookie values originate from the server side. Correspondingly, FPExcavator needs to extract values of the Set-Cookie header in all the incoming responses. These values can help determine the origin of all the outgoing cookie values. We plan to incorporate this feature into our framework in the future.

In addition, FPExcavator has the capability to detect cookie respawning [1] that can recover the deleted website cookies. Correspondingly, FPExcavator needs to visit a website using the same browser on the same virtual machine but in different configurations at two IP addresses. Note that before each visit the browser cache should be cleaned. If cookie values carried out in these two visits are the same, that website probably has deployed the cookie respawning technique. By using one machine at two IP addresses, we rule out the possibility that website generates cookies simply based on its visitors' IP addresses. By using different configurations of the same machine, we rule out the possibility that website generates the same fingerprint and writes it into cookies. We also plan to incorporate this feature into our framework in the future.

One limitation in our evaluation is the lack of ground truth knowledge about the fingerprinting scripts' deployment on real-world websites. It is almost infeasible to manually inspect a huge number of JavaScript files due to their code complexity and the possible code obfuscation. Although previous research work could measure the invocation of certain JavaScript APIs [7,10,14], they were still not able to provide the ground truth knowledge because they did not analyze the use of JavaScript APIs' returned values [10]. We leave this hard problem as our future work, and we plan to further evaluate FPExcavator on real-world websites in a large scale.

Table 4. Detection results in scheme 1. Both PC1 and PC2 were at 128.198.162.187

Website	Browser	Field	PC	Value	Count
www.ebay.de	Chrome	Cookie	1	78=kMfEoLaj1RhntChG8s...	1/208
		.NID	2	78=ZdKbQWEvUkLrNcpvku...	
www.qq.com	Firefox	Cookie	1	DL3I21nmD2A5yGx8PmZ ●	4/267
		.uid	2	DL6Ry0fJu2A5yG21NPn	
	Chrome	Cookie	1	DL28S2owm2A5yGx8RQQ ●	4/289
		.uid	2	DL5Pi3Ss32A5yGx8NKb	
www.twitter.com	Chrome	Cookie	1	78=oXuoRxuOdSmU-kT-nc...	1/78
		.NID	2	78=UG1Tw0btbDT4Wp3QeG...	
www.aliexpress.com	Chrome	Cookie	1	78=oXuoRxuOdSmU-kT-nc...	5/70
		.NID	2	78=UG1Tw0btbDT4Wp3QeG...	
www.microsoft.com	Chrome	Cookie	1	78=oXuoRxuOdSmU-kT-nc...	1/78
		.NID	2	78=UG1Tw0btbDT4Wp3QeG...	
www.alibaba.com	Firefox	Cookie	1	NyknCUjvSWq9 ○	1/116
		.V	2	aAZW25RQbUag	
		Cookie	1	f56e1520f7b0bc1d14755cd4e9977ee8 ●	1/116
		.U	2	3bd8d7163666a80ab9cc3f94306ff7ab	
		Cookie	1	34525b90-ca89-4919-8749-e1b21510c1cb ■	1/116
		.tuuid	2	a2de3004-7502-46a4-af8d-3c450e215dea	
	Chrome	Cookie	1	78=oXuoRxuOdSmU-kT-nc...	2/106
		.NID	2	78=UG1Tw0btbDT4Wp3QeG...	
		Cookie	1	6Lfy8QX9GHjt ○	1/106
		.V	2	odhuS2H2DHdw	
		Cookie	1	0536142a16b7d3f62d46bafc00c2e691 ○	1/106
		.U	2	4ef748d14a171500e4ea7714cf94d729	
		Cookie	1	973d1853-1d6d-466b-ba7f-43113efe0484 ■	1/106
		.tuuid	2	0976d33f-a5cf-4a13-a5f1-7270f050beb4	
www.linkedin.com	Chrome	Cookie	1	78=oXuoRxuOdSmU-kT-nc...	1/22
		.NID	2	78=UG1Tw0btbDT4Wp3QeG...	
www.weibo.com	Firefox	Cookie	1	ad83bc19c1269e709f753b172bddb094 □	1/111
		.YF-Ugrow-G0	2	8751d9166f7676afdce9885c6d31cd61 □	
	Chrome	Cookie	1	9642b0b34b4c0d569ed7a372f8823a8e ■	1/46
		.YF-Ugrow-G0	2	1eba44dbebf62c27ae66e16d40e02964 □	
www.ebay.com	Chrome	Cookie	1	78=oXuoRxuOdSmU-kT-nc...	4/201
		.NID	2	78=UG1Tw0btbDT4Wp3QeG...	
www.bbc.co.uk	Firefox	Cookie	1	c4b66890-32ab-41bc-8e3e-5979f8a078ac ■	1/182
		.IMRID	2	45907909-2e7b-42b5-81eb-168d8a3553bc	
	Chrome	Cookie	1	74ab13e0-4696-4a7d-9755-31946c46523a	1/204
		.IMRID	2	68041232-fffb-4d2b-98c9-51494ec96b29 ■	
		Cookie	1	56fc9079.000bCI.8490cb5e	4/204
		.aid	2	56fc5f2d.0011CI.2b9c1df3	
		Cookie	1	0001:I7R7ZxF5OSCM1Xg2m0ina7FAq56co9bL	4/204
		.ab	2	0001:N 3I4o/r psIBYytVxwH4w2yHVntDOs7	
www.dailymotion.com	Firefox	Cookie	1	56fc9ee3-b6200-20d5b-dc8a3	1/536
		.mc	2	56fc7436-c49eb-ba845-66c58	
		Cookie	1	ec7358e4-5a1f-4a7a-92cd-f647aff97fde	3/536
		.tidal_ttid	2	ecc74048-e102-42b3-8d1c-3b4437d4b2b4	
		Cookie	1	c10e5a6e-f6fc-11e5-96db-6f1a000003c8	1/536
		.ADGRX_UID	2	97353b12-f6e4-11e5-a767-dc3865004b1f	
		Cookie	1	FvOrlTwn1ALuBX5	1/536
		.wfivefivec	2	E5GM4Ap61ALrUv5	
	Chrome	Cookie	1	78=oXuoRxuOdSmU-kT-nc...	5/219
		.NID	2	78=UG1Tw0btbDT4Wp3QeG...	
		Cookie	1	3VvySblyzmFUBtMOXGQ	1/219
		.BR_APS	2	3VvxhPDO_gRUBEimWfw	

Table 5. Detection results in scheme 2. PC1 was at 128.198.162.187 and PC2 was at 128.198.162.139

Website	PC	Field	Browser	Value	Count
www.qq.com	1	Cookie	Firefox	`DL3I21nmD2A5yGx8PmZ` ●	4/260
		.uid	Chrome	`DL28S2owm2A5yGx8RQQ` ●	
	2	Cookie	Firefox	`DL3in3pfv2A5yG21LmC`	5/275
		.uid	Chrome	`DL28S2fhMOBTeuw3hx1`	
www.sohu.com	1	Cookie	Firefox	`HKpXm1IL347cGYuE`	4/428
		.zuid	Chrome	`7aep9m3x8xRodb-L`	
www.alibaba.com	1	Cookie	Firefox	`NyknCUjvSWq9` ○	1/116
		.V	Chrome	`6Lfy8QX9GHjt` ○	
		Cookie	Firefox	`f56e1520f7b0bc1d14755cd4e9977ee8` ●	1/116
		.U	Chrome	`0536142a16b7d3f62d46bafc00c2e691` ○	
		Cookie	Firefox	`34525b90-ca89-4919-8749-e1b21510c1cb` ■	1/116
		.tuuid	Chrome	`973d1853-1d6d-466b-ba7f-43113efe0484` ■	
	2	Cookie	Firefox	`01e2c617e1a873e1441966cf741f668b`	1/110
		.U	Chrome	`fb06ab831d82a5c6e1a1abbcc25c7729`	
www.sina.com.cn	1	Cookie	Firefox	`DL3I21nmD2A5yGx8PmZ`	3/473
		.uid	Chrome	`DL28S2owm2A5yGx8RQQ`	
www.weibo.com	1	Cookie	Firefox	`ad83bc19c1269e709f753b172bddb094` ▢	1/111
		.YF-Ugrow-G0	Chrome	`1eba44dbebf62c27ae66e16d40e02964` ▢	
	2	Cookie	Firefox	`9642b0b34b4c0d569ed7a372f8823a8e` ■	1/111
		.YF-Ugrow-G0	Chrome	`8751d9166f7676afdce9885c6d31cd61` ▢	
www.bbc.co.uk	1	Cookie	Firefox	`68041232-fffb-4d2b-98c9-51494ec96b29` ■	1/193
		.IMRID	Chrome	`c4b66890-32ab-41bc-8e3e-5979f8a078ac` ■	
	2	Cookie	Firefox	`706d4faa-33c0-4941-b5ef-30f0f873e9b5`	1/195
		.IMRID	Chrome	`bcc6c748-65c7-4b7d-830e-e00a2de40ebd`	

7   Conclusion

In this paper, we presented a traffic-based fingerprinting detection framework, FPExcavator. To detect fingerprinting on a webpage, FPExcavator drives virtual machines in different configuration settings to visit that page, collects traffic traces from these machines, and extracts values from the header and payload of all the outgoing HTTP and HTTPS requests. By examining the difference on the values posted to the same URL across different browsing sessions, FPExcavator is able to predict the existence of fingerprinting on that webpage. We implemented FPExcavator with OpenStack, Java, and some command scripts, and evaluated it on 200 websites both in a lab setting and selected from real-world. The evaluation results demonstrate that FPExcavator is useful and effective.

References

1. Acar, G., Eubank, C., Englehardt, S., Juarez, M., Narayanan, A., Diaz, C.: The web never forgets: Persistent tracking mechanisms in the wild. In: Proceedings of the ACM SIGSAC Conference on Computer & Communications Security, pp. 674–689 (2014)
2. Acar, G., et al.: Fpdetective: dusting the web for fingerprinters. In: Proceedings of the ACM SIGSAC Conference on Computer & Communications Security, pp. 1129–1140 (2013)

3. Akkus, I.E., Chen, R., Hardt, M., Francis, P., Gehrke, J.: Non-tracking web analytics. In: Proceedings of the ACM SIGSAC Conference on Computer and Communications Security, pp. 687–698 (2012)
4. Cai, X., Zhang, X.C., Joshi, B., Johnson, R.: Touching from a distance: website fingerprinting attacks and defenses. In: Proceedings of the ACM SIGSAC Conference on Computer and Communications Security, pp. 605–616 (2012)
5. Cao, Y., Li, S., Wijmans, E.: (Cross-)Browser fingerprinting via OS and Hardware level features. In: Proceedings of the Annual Network and Distributed System Security Symposium (2017)
6. Cova, M., Kruegel, C., Vigna, G.: Detection and analysis of drive-by-download attacks and malicious javascript code. In: Proceedings of the International Conference on World Wide Web, pp. 281–290 (2010)
7. Englehardt, S., Narayanan, A.: Online tracking: a 1-million-site measurement and analysis. In: Proceedings of the ACM SIGSAC Conference on Computer and Communications Security, pp. 1388–1401 (2016)
8. Fifield, D., Egelman, S.: Fingerprinting web users through font metrics. In: International Conference on Financial Cryptography and Data Security, pp. 107–124 (2015)
9. Laperdrix, P., Rudametkin, W., Baudry, B.: Beauty and the beast: diverting modern web browsers to build unique browser fingerprints. In: Proceedings of the IEEE Symposium on Security and Privacy, pp. 878–894 (2016)
10. Lerner, A., Simpson, A.K., Kohno, T., Roesner, F.: Internet jones and the raiders of the lost trackers: an archaeological study of web tracking from 1996 to 2016. In: Proceedings of the USENIX Security Symposium (2016)
11. Timothy, L.: Exposing the invisible web: an analysis of third-party http requests on 1 million websites. Int. J. Commun. 9(2015), 3544–3561 (2015)
12. Mayer, J.R., Mitchell, J.C.: Third-party web tracking: policy and technology. In: Proceedings of the IEEE Symposium on Security and Privacy, pp. 413–427 (2012)
13. Nikiforakis, N., Joosen, W., Livshits, B.: Privaricator: deceiving fingerprinters with little white lies. In: Proceedings of the International Conference on World Wide Web, pp. 820–830 (2015)
14. Nikiforakis, N., Kapravelos, A., Joosen, W., Kruegel, C., Piessens, F., Vigna, G.: Cookieless monster: exploring the ecosystem of web-based device fingerprinting. In: Proceedings of the IEEE Symposium on Security and Privacy, pp. 541–555 (2013)
15. Rader, E.: Awareness of behavioral tracking and information privacy concern in facebook and google. In: Proceedings of the Symposium on Usable Privacy and Security (2014)
16. Roesner, F., Kohno, T., Wetherall, D.: Detecting and defending against third-party tracking on the web. In: Proceedings of the USENIX Conference on Networked Systems Design and Implementation (2012)
17. Torres, C.F., Jonker, H., Mauw, S.: Fp-block: usable web privacy by controlling browser fingerprinting. In: Proceedings of the European Symposium on Research in Computer Security, pp. 3–19 (2015)
18. Vastel, A., Laperdrix, P., Rudametkin, W., Rouvoy, R.: Fp-scanner: the privacy implications of browser fingerprint inconsistencies. In: Proceedings of the USENIX Security Symposium, pp. 135–150 (2018)
19. Vastel, A., Laperdrix, P., Rudametkin, W., Rouvoy, R.: Fp-stalker: tracking browser fingerprint evolutions. In: Proceedings of the IEEE Symposium on Security and Privacy, pp. 1–14 (2018)
20. Browser market share data from March 2018 to March 2019. http://gs.statcounter.com/browser-market-share

21. Google Privacy & Terms. https://policies.google.com/privacy?hl=en#infocollect
22. OpenStack. https://www.openstack.org/
23. Princeton Web Census. https://webtransparency.cs.princeton.edu/webcensus/

Measuring Tor Relay Popularity

Tao Chen[1], Weiqi Cui[1], and Eric Chan-Tin[2(✉)]

[1] Oklahoma State University, Stillwater, OK, USA
[2] Loyola University Chicago, Chicago, IL, USA
chantin@cs.luc.edu

Abstract. Tor is one of the most popular anonymity networks. It has been reported that over 2 million unique users utilize the Tor network daily. The Tor network is run by over 6,000 volunteer relays. Each Tor client telescopically builds a circuit by choosing three Tor relays and then uses that circuit to connect to a server. The Tor relay selection algorithm makes sure that no two relays with the same /16 IP address are chosen. Our objective is to determine the popularity of Tor relays when building circuits. With over 44 vantage points (machines running Tor clients) and over 145,000 circuits built, we found that some Tor relays are chosen more often than others. Although a completely balanced selection algorithm is not possible, analysis of our dataset shows that some Tor relays are over 3 times more likely to be chosen than others. An adversary could potentially eavesdrop or correlate more Tor traffic.

Keywords: Privacy · Tor network · Anonymity

1 Introduction

Tor is one of the popular anonymous communication systems that can protect users from leaking private information, such as the IP address, when users are browsing the Internet and communicating with other users. Tor also allows users to circumvent censorship effectively to reach blocked websites or documents. Some companies (such as Facebook [9]) are even using Tor hidden services when they publish their services or websites. Tor has more than 6,000 volunteer-operated relay nodes (servers/routers) [26]. Instead of connecting users directly to web servers or each other, a Tor client makes the connections go through three of the 6,000 relay nodes, then to the destination. The Tor relay selection algorithm makes sure that no two relays with the same /16 IP address are chosen. The three randomly selected relay nodes form a Tor circuit. A circuit is re-used to transfer several TCP streams with a maximum lifetime of 10 min [25].

As Tor becomes more popular, it becomes subject to a number of attacks and respective countermeasures. The packet counting [20], end-to-end timing attack [3], active and passive end-to-end confirmation attacks [3,14,19] are shown to be possible in the Tor network. Tor aims to protect users against traffic analysis. If an adversary has control or can eavesdrop over both entry and exit

© ICST Institute for Computer Sciences, Social Informatics and Telecommunications Engineering 2019
Published by Springer Nature Switzerland AG 2019. All Rights Reserved
S. Chen et al. (Eds.): SecureComm 2019, LNICST 304, pp. 386–405, 2019.
https://doi.org/10.1007/978-3-030-37228-6_19

relay nodes, then a statistical correlation attack can be performed by using the packets' timing or packets' size information. Entry guards, which Tor client selects from a few relays at random as the entry points, help against this kind of correlation attacks. Hence, our focus is on the middle and exit relays.

In this paper, we explore if there are some relay nodes which have a higher chance to be selected in a circuit than other relays. Namely, these relays are more popular. We also look into the /8, /16, /24 subnets and Autonomous System (AS) number of all relay nodes to find out the popular subnets. We then look at the relationship between the bandwidth of relay nodes and the popularity of relay nodes.

Our contributions are listed as follows:

- **Popular middle and exit relays:** Based on our dataset, we find there are some middle and exit relays which are more popular than other relays. Some Tor relays are 3 times more likely to be chosen than others, in building Tor circuits. If Tor relays are randomly chosen, then some Tor relays have over 10 times higher chance of being selected.
- **Popular /8, /16, /24 subnets:** We analyze all relay nodes based on their /8, /16, /24 subnets. Several subnets stand out as more popular than others. We also see that correlation attacks are still possible on a small fraction of circuits where an adversary controlling a /16 subnet could monitor network traffic of both the client and the target website.
- **Popular ASes:** Some ASes are more popular than others, based on the number of Tor relays belonging to those ASes. However, our results show that some of these ASes have a much higher percentage of being selected, regardless of how many Tor relays are in these ASes.
- **Correlation attacks are still possible:** We find that about 11% of circuits built can be correlated, that is, both the client and server identified.

2   Background

Tor [25] is a popular low-latency anonymity network built over TLS connections and based on onion routing. Tor is used by over 2 million unique users [26]. The Tor system is run mostly by volunteer relays, with over 6,000 relays [26]. Each relay reports its IP address, public key, bandwidth, and contact information for the owner to the centralized directory servers. When a Tor user (client) wants to use the Tor network to connect to a server, it first contacts the directory servers to obtain a consensus document of all the Tor relays. It then selects three Tor relays based on a relay selection algorithm, see Fig. 1. Tor relays are also referred to as nodes or Tor routers. They are responsible for receiving and forwarding Tor traffic. The three Tor relays chosen by the client are contacted telescopically. The client establishes a secure connection with the first relay. Then going through the first relay, the client establishes a secure (and anonymous) connection with the second relay. Going through the first and the second relays, the client finally establishes a connection with the third relay. This process builds a circuit for the client to use to connect to a server.

Tor traffic is sent in fixed-size cells where each cell is 512 bytes [6]. When the user makes the request, the user/client builds a circuit consisting of three relays (entry guard, middle node, and exit node) before connecting to the destination server. The constructed circuit can be shared by many TCP streams. Tor clients construct circuits preemptively and substitute previously used ones with newly built circuits. Each circuit lifetime is 10 min. Figure 1 shows the data flow in the Tor network where the request of a client will pass through three Tor relays before reaching the web server. In the circuit, the entry guard knows that the client is communicating with the middle relay, but not who the exit relay or the destination server are. The middle relay knows the entry guard is communicating with the exit relay but not who the client or the destination server are. Similarly, the exit relay knows the middle relay is communicating with the server, but not who the client is. The server only knows that the exit relay is acting as the client, but does not know who the real client is.

Early onion routing systems initially specified that clients should select relays uniformly [24] at random. With the increasing number of Tor users and relays, it became necessary to improve relay selection strategy to balance traffic load with the available Tor relay bandwidth. The choice of relays is determined by a weighting function that includes the bandwidth, status flags of the relays and multiple other considerations [22]. To be chosen, a relay has to have the following flags: stable, running, and valid. A Tor relay is considered to be "Running" if it has been successfully contacted within the last 45 min [22]. Tor does not take the locations of relays relative to the clients into consideration [11]. It will reuse the same circuit for new data streams for 10 min. An exit relay has extra considerations since it has to have an open outgoing port to the server (e.g. port 80 for web servers); many Tor relays do not allow outgoing traffic outside of the Tor network.

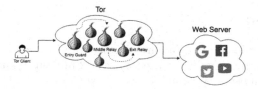

Fig. 1. How Tor works. 3 nodes are selected from running Tor relays

To reduce the probability of disclosing the client information to attackers, Tor users randomly select a few relays to use as entry guards, and use only those relays for their first hop. The entry guard knows the identity of the client and the middle node for each circuit. The same entry guard is kept for 2 months. The relay can be considered as an entry guard only if it is fast, stable and has higher bandwidth than a specific threshold. More details of selecting entry guards can be found in [22]. The entry guard, middle relay, and exit relay are chosen from different /16 subnet IP addresses.

3   Experiment Setup

This section provides an overview of the design of our experiments and how we collect and analyze data.

3.1   Data Collection

We deployed our experiments on 44 different machines from different locations. The machines are from Google cloud instances and the PlanetLab network [21]. PlanetLab is a global research network that supports the development of new network services. On each machine, we installed Tor and Stem [5] version 1.5.2, which is a Python controller library for Tor.

We set up a script supported by Stem to automate visiting websites. We visited the homepages of Alexa top 100 websites [1] sequentially through Tor for each of the 44 machines. During each visit to a website, we discard the TCP packets. Only metadata information of Tor circuits are collected. This includes the following information.

1. Tor Relays. There are 3 Tor relays during a visit to a website: entry guard, middle relay and exit relay. The IP address and port, fingerprint, nickname, locale, and advertised bandwidth are collected. We also converted the IP address to a geolocation (city and country) and to an AS number. The advertised bandwidth is the volume of traffic, both incoming and outgoing, that a relay is willing to sustain, as configured by the operator and as observed from recent data transfers.
2. Source. The IP address and the port number of the Tor client. This will be one of the 44 machines used.
3. Target. The IP address and the port number of the target destination. This will be one of the 100 top Alexa websites.

The experiments were run for 5 months, from November 2017 to March 2018. Our dataset consists of 145,918 entries. Each entry contains the information above: source IP address, target IP address, the three Tor relays' IP address, fingerprint, nickname, locale, AS number, and bandwidth. The list of the top 100 Alexa websites was downloaded on October 15, 2017.

We used our own clients to visit known websites. Other than the Tor relays information such as IP address and bandwidth, which are already public information, we do not collect any private data. Our automated experiments are also spaced out such that the extra 44 clients would not affect the normal operation of the Tor network.

3.2   Data Analysis

We next describe the type of analysis performed on our dataset. Since Tor sets the entry guard to be the same for an extended period of time, we mainly focus our analysis on the middle relay and exit relay. More specifically, our goal is to determine if some relays are chosen more often than others meaning some Tor relays are more popular. This could lead to privacy issues as an attacker can utilize that knowledge to target the anonymity of users.

- "By Source": we first analyze the dataset from the point of view of the 44 client machines. We look mostly at the popularity of Tor relays, that is, how often they are selected for circuits and how often they are in the top k relays for each machine. We set $k = 30$ for our analysis. Next, we group the Tor relays by subnets; we analyze /8, /16, and /24 subnets. If two Tor relays are in the same /16 or /24 subnets, then they are likely in the same AS or controlled/observable by the same entity.
- "By Target": we perform the same analysis, but this time considering the point of view of the 100 target websites. The goal here is to determine whether some Tor relays are more popular based on the website visited. This could mean some websites are more targeted or could increase the likelihood of an adversarial entity (such as an ISP) being able to determine the target website.
- Overall: we then perform a holistic view of our dataset to identify who the most popular relays are.

4 Experimental Results

This section presents the results from our experiments and the analysis based on the results for the middle and exit relays. For each approach as described in the previous section ("by source", "by target", and overall), the analysis is based on the IP address, /24 subnet IP address, /16 subnet IP address, /8 subnet IP address, and AS number for the Tor relays. Due to space restrictions, we show the results for the /16 subnet as a representative result. The results and conclusions drawn from the /8 and /24 subnets are similar. We also show the result by AS number.

4.1 Dataset Overview

Our 44 machines visited 145, 918 sites in total. On average, each machine visited 3, 316 websites. This means that each of the top 100 Alexa websites received 33 visits on average from each machine. During each website visit, we collected the IP address for the client, the entry guard, the middle relay, the exit relay, and the target website. Figure 2 shows a graph from the Tor metrics website [26]. It contains the number of running relays that have flags "Running" and "Stable" assigned by the Tor directory authorities. Over the 5 months, from November 2017 to March 2018, there are about 4, 800 stable relays and about 6, 000 running relays. As can be seen from the figure, new relays join the network and old relays leave the network due to churn. During our experiments, our machines connected to 8, 523 unique relays.

The number of unique IP addresses, /24, /16, and /8 subnet IP addresses of the relays used during our experiments are listed in Table 1. 8, 523 unique

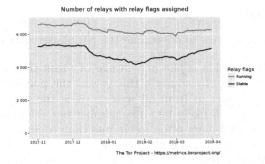

Fig. 2. This graph shows the number of running relays that have the flags "Running" and "Stable" assigned by the Tor directory authorities. The graph shows the range from November 2017 to March 2018 which is the duration of our experiments.

relay nodes are used in the experiments. These relay nodes are almost all the running nodes during the time period of our experiments. Since there are around 6,000 relay nodes at any time, on average, each relay node will be used in 24 circuits or website visits. Out of 145,918 total circuits created, this comes up to 24/145918 = 0.02%. Each of our 44 source machines connected to 2,061 relay nodes (or 2,055 unique relays because some relays can be used as either middle or exit relay) on average (for the 3,316 circuits built). Breaking it down to different types of relays: on average, this comes up to 3 entry guards, 1,550 middle relays, and 508 exit relays for each machine. Each middle relay would then be used, on average, 3316/1550 = 2.14 times in total. This means that out of the 3,316 circuits, a Tor relay has a chance of 2.14/3316 = 0.065% chance of being selected as a middle relay. Each exit relay is used, on average, 3316/508 = 6.52 times in total. This means that a Tor relay has a 6.52/3316 = 0.20% chance of being selected as an exit relay. All the relays found belonged to 1,096 ASes, which means there were on average 466 relays per AS.

Table 1. # of Tor relays, in terms of unique IP addresses, /24 subnet, /16 subnet, /8 subnet and AS number used when collecting data in our experiments over 5 months.

	# of relays	Avg # relays per machine	Avg # entry guards per machine	Avg # middle relays per machine	Avg # exit relays per machine
IP addresses	8,523	2,054.93	3.02	1,550.39	508.47
/24 subnets	6,949	1,695.11	3.02	1,392.18	355.77
/16 subnets	2,885	851.91	2.95	725.82	237.16
/8 subnets	184	129.43	2.82	119.84	82.07
AS	1,096	466.52	2.73	384.18	157.91

4.2   Metrics Used

We use the following metrics to determine the popularity of Tor relays.

1. **Relay percentage:** this is the percentage of visits that include the relay node in the circuit. In "by source", this means the percentage out of 3,316 visits for each machine. In from all sources, it is the percentage out of all 145,918 visits. This will likely be a low number but the goal is to determine if some relays are used more often in circuits than others.
2. **Repeated percentage:** this is the percentage of relay nodes that appear in the top 30 most-used relays of one source machine and also appear in the top 30 most-used relays for the other 43 machines. For example, relay node A is in the top 30 most-used nodes for machine S. This means that out of the 3,316 circuits/visits for machine S, the relay A is in the list of 30 most-used relays for these 3,316 circuits. To continue the example, let's say that A also appears in the top 30 most-used relays for 32 other machines (out of 44 machines in total). Then the repeated percentage for relay A is $(32+1)/44$, which is 75%.
3. **Relay bandwidth:** this is the advertised bandwidth from [26]. It is the volume of traffic, both incoming and outgoing, that a relay is willing to sustain, as configured by the operator, and observed from recent data transfers.
4. **Relay popularity:** if a relay is popular, the relay node will get more traffic/visits/selections than other nodes. In our analysis, a factor for popularity is the percentage of visits a node has. Previously, we showed the average relay percentage is 0.02% (of total 145,918 visits). In terms of one source machine, each middle node gets a relay percentage of 0.065% (of 3316 visits) and each exit node gets a relay percentage of 0.20% (of 3316 visits) on average.

4.3   Analysis of Middle Relays

We first analyze the popularity of relays chosen as middle relays in all the circuits created by the 44 machines.

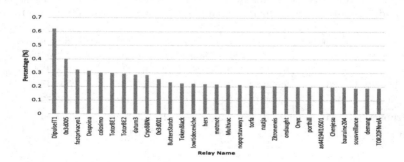

Fig. 3. Point of view of all machines. The percentage of times a relay has been used as a middle relay for all circuits. This shows the top 30 most-used relays.

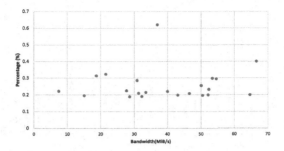

Fig. 4. Point of view of all machines. The percentage of times a relay is selected as the middle relay in a circuit and that relay's corresponding bandwidth.

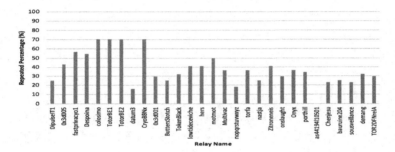

Fig. 5. Point of view of all machines. The repeated percentage for each relay is chosen as a middle relay. This shows the top 30 most-used relays.

(1) By source IP address: We first look at the popularity of middle relays from the point of view of the source machines (clients). Figures 3, 4, and 5 are the analysis results when considering all our source machines together, that is analyzing all circuits from all source machines together. Figure 3 shows the 30 most-used middle relays and the number of times as a percentage that they have been selected as Tor middle relays for all circuits. From Fig. 3, the relay named *DipulseIT1* with IP address *62.210.82.83* has the highest probability of being selected, at around 0.63%. That is about 10 times higher than the average 0.065% we mentioned in Sect. 4.1. In Fig. 4, we have the % of a middle relay being selected as a middle relay in circuits to websites and the bandwidth of that relay. There is no obvious relationship between the percentage of a relay being selected and its bandwidth in the middle relay selection. Figure 5 shows the percentage of the top 30 most-often-selected relays that are also in the top 30 most-often-selected relays when considering machine by machine separately. As an example, let's consider the relay named *CryoBBNx* with IP address *51.254.45.43*, the relay named *TotorBE1* with IP address *5.39.33.176*, and the relay named *TotorBE2* with IP address *5.39.33.178*. They all have a repeated percentage of about 70%. That means, they are also in the top 30 most-used relays of 70% of all machines. This further confirms their popularity. Over all the relays, we can see from the

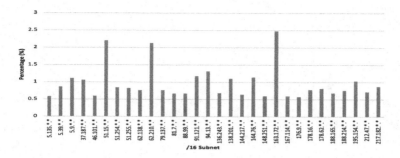

Fig. 6. Point of view of all source machines. The percentage of selection of the top 30 most-selected /16 subnet IP addresses for middle relays.

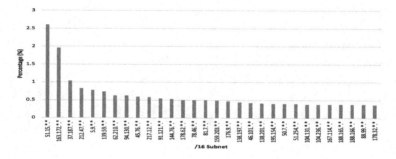

Fig. 7. Percentage of # of middle relays in a /16 subnet.

figures that some relays have a much higher chance of being selected as a middle relay in Tor circuits than others, regardless of their bandwidth. These relays are not only popular for one client machine, but also for other client machines, regardless of the source IP address.

(2) By source /16 subnet: Instead of considering each middle relay by their IP address, we now group the middle relays' IP address in /16 subnets. Figure 6 shows the top 30 most-selected /16 subnet IP addresses for middle relays, along with their percentage of being selected from all source machines. Figure 6 shows that the relays in the subnet *51.15.*.** and *163.172.*.** have higher percentages being selected during Tor circuit building. These two /16 subnets are in the top 30 most often selected middle relays of each source machine as well. The subnet *163.172.*.** have the highest percentage near 2.5%. This shows that certain subnets are more popular than others. This could mean that these subnets contain more Tor relays. It could also mean that an adversary in these subnets will have a higher chance of being selected as a middle relay than others. When analyzing /8 and /24 subnets, we see a similar result.

It could be argued that subnets with more relays will obviously have a higher chance of being selected. Figure 7 shows the number of middle relays under each /16 prefix subnet (only the top 30 subnets are shown). In the figure, *163.172.*.**

has less than 2.0% middle relays in it when compared to the 2.5% chance of being selected in circuits. However, *62.210.*.** has nearly 0.6% middle relays and it has a 2.1% chance of being selected. This indicates that the chance of a /16 subnet being selected is not proportional to the number of relays it contains.

(3) By target IP address: Looking at all Tor relay routes from the perspective of the target websites (the web servers), we perform a similar analysis as earlier. Figure 8 shows the percentage of each relay being selected as the middle relay when the target IP address is *151.101.128.81*. The figure includes the top 30 most often selected relays. The relay named *DipulseIT2* with IP address *62.210.82.83* is the most often selected relay with a percentage of 0.385%. Figure 9 shows the percentage of being selected and the bandwidth of these top 30 middle relays. From the figure, there is a slight trend of the relay node with more bandwidth having a higher percentage of being selected as a middle relay. This is different from our analysis by source machines.

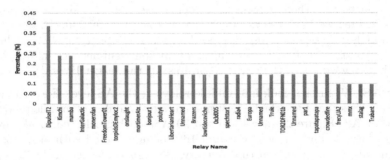

Fig. 8. Point of view of one target destination IP address *151.101.128.81*. The % of selection of the 30 most often selected Tor relays as the middle relays in circuits.

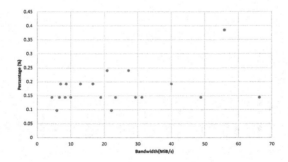

Fig. 9. Point of view of one target destination IP address *151.101.128.81*. The percentage of selection of the top 30 most often selected Tor relays as the middle relays in circuits and these relays' corresponding bandwidth.

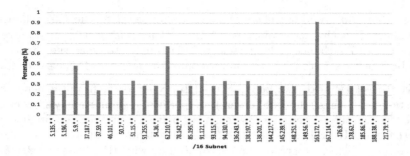

Fig. 10. Point of view of target IP address *151.101.128.81*. The % of the 30 most often used relays being selected as middle relays, grouped by /16 subnets.

(4) By target /16 subnet: Here, we analyze middle relays based on their /16 subnet prefix and the target websites' IP addresses. Figure 10 shows the top 30 subnets with their percentage of being selected. It is similar to previous analysis in that we have relays in subnets *163.172.*.**, *62.210.*.**, and *5.9.*.** having a higher chance of being selected than others. Subnet *163.172.*.** has the highest percentage at 0.91%. This means that some subnets are more popular than others regardless of the client IP address or the target IP address.

(5) By AS: We further look into middle relays at the AS level. Figure 11 shows the top 30 ASes that have the highest percentage of number of middle relays that are in that AS. Figure 12 shows the top 30 ASes being selected in all circuits. *AS16276* has the highest percentage of 16% being selected with only less than 8% of middle relays in it. On the contrary, *AS3320* contains nearly 7% middle relays with less than 0.9% chance being selected. Some ASes in Fig. 11 are not even in Fig. 12. Hence, this shows that some ASes are more popular than others not because they have more middle relays in them.

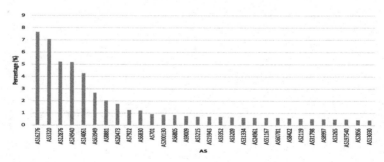

Fig. 11. Percentage of # of middle relays that is in an AS.

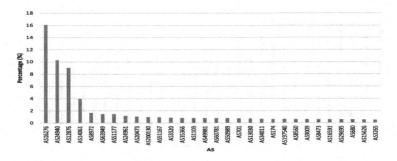

Fig. 12. Percentage of an AS shown as Middle relay of all circuits.

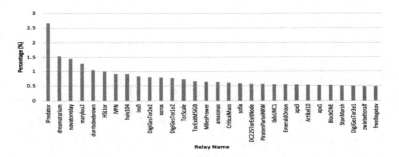

Fig. 13. Point of view of all machines. The percentage of times a relay has been used as an exit relay for all circuits. This shows the top 30 most-used relays.

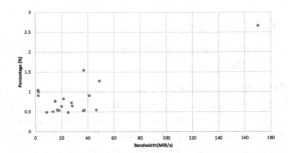

Fig. 14. Point of view of all machines. The percentage of times a relay is selected as the exit relay in a circuit and that relay's corresponding bandwidth.

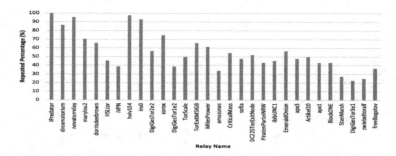

Fig. 15. Point of view of all machines. The repeated percentage for each relay is chosen as an exit relay. This shows the top 30 most-used relays.

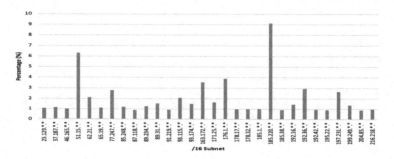

Fig. 16. Point of view of all source machines. The percentage of selection of the top 30 most-selected /16 subnet IP addresses for exit relays.

4.4   Analysis of Exit Relays

In this section, we analyze the popularity of relays chosen as exit relays in all the circuits created by the 44 machines.

(1) By source IP address: We first look at the popularity of exit relays from the point of view of the source machines (clients). Figures 13, 14, and 15 are the analysis results when considering all our source machines together. From Fig. 13, we can see the 30 most often used exit relays and the percentage that they have been selected during all the visits. In the figure, the relay named *IPredator* with IP address *197.231.221.211* has the highest percentage, 2.67%, of being used as an exit relay among all the relays. That is about 14 times higher than the average percentage 0.20% which we mentioned in Sect. 4.1. In the results of top relays in the Tor circuits when considering only one single source machine, there are relays being selected as exit relays more often than other relays. Also these source machines share several exit relays in their own top 30 exit relays list among all Tor circuits, as shown in Fig. 15, such as *novatorrelay* with IP address *93.174.93.71* and *hviv104* with IP address *192.42.116.16*. These exit relay nodes appear in more than 90% of the top 30 exit relays lists from all source machines.

This means that, over all the relays, some of the relays have a higher chance to be selected when Tor builds a circuit. This further confirms their popularity. Figure 14 shows the % of a relay selected as exit nodes during all the visits of one machine to websites and the bandwidth of the relays. From the figure, it can be seen that a relay node with more bandwidth has a better chance to be selected as an exit node during circuit building.

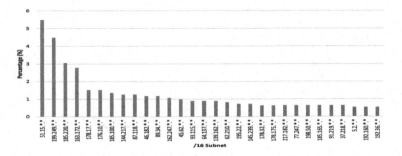

Fig. 17. Percentage of # of exit relays in a /16 subnet.

(2) By source /16 subnet: Instead of analyzing each exit relay by their IP address, we now group the exit relays' IP address in /16 subnets. Figure 16 shows the 30 most-often-used exit relays with same /16 subnet prefix and the percentage of circuits which have that relay as an exit relay. The relay nodes with subnet *51.15.*.** and *185.220.*.** stand out in the figure. *51.15.*.** has a percentage of 6.32% and *163.172.*.** has a percentage of 5.44%. *185.220.*.** is the most popular one with a percentage of 9.13%. Also, *176.1.*.** and *163.172.*.** have the higher percentage. Hence, with results from all these figures, there are several /16 subnet prefixes that have a better chance to be chosen as exit nodes. When analyzing /8 and /24 subnets, we see a similar result. In Fig. 17, we show the percentage of number of exit relays under a /16 subnet. For example, *51.15.*.**

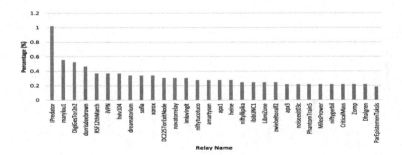

Fig. 18. Point of view of one target destination IP address 151.101.130.167. The % of selection of the 30 most often selected Tor relays as the exit relays in circuits.

has 5.5% of all exit relays in it. However, comparing Fig. 17 with Fig. 16, we can see that a /16 subnet may not have a higher chance to be selected even though it has a high percentage of number exit relays in it. From Fig. 17, *199.249.*.** subnet contains 4.5% exit relay. However it only has less than 1.5% chance to be selected.

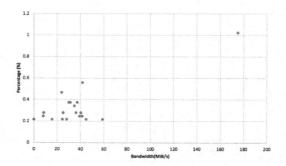

Fig. 19. Point of view of one target destination IP address 151.101.130.167. The percentage of selection of the top 30 most often selected Tor relays as the exit relays in circuits and these relays' corresponding bandwidth.

(3) By target IP address: We now analyze the popularity of relays from the point of view of the target websites. Figure 18 lists the top 30 most often selected exit relays' names from all source machines to the website *151.101.130.167*. The relay *IPredator* with IP address *197.231.221.211* is the one with the largest percentage of being selected at 1.02%. Figure 19 shows the percentages of a relay being used as an exit node and its bandwidth during our experiments. *IPredator* has a bandwidth of 175.13 MiB/s with the highest percentage of 1.02%. The relay named *maryloulb* with IP address *89.234.157.254* has a bandwidth of 41.65 MiB/s with the second highest percentage of 0.56%. From that figure, it can be seen that a relay with higher bandwidth has a higher chance of being selected.

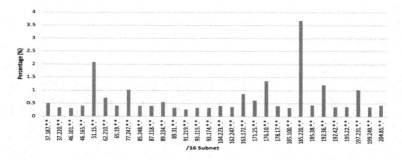

Fig. 20. Point of view of target IP address 151.101.130.167. The percentage of the top 30 most often used relays being selected as exit relays, grouped by /16 subnets.

(4) By target /16 subnet: Figure 20 shows the top 30 subnets with /16 prefix along with the percentage of being selected as an exit relay that is within the subnet. From Fig. 20, we see that *185.220.*.** has the highest percentage at 3.69%. *185.220.*.** is also in the list of top 30 exit relays from all source machines in Fig. 16. *51.15.*.** is also one of the subnets that appeared in both figures. It has a percentage of 2.08% in Fig. 20. This result again shows that some subnets have a higher percentage of being selected than other subnets.

(5) By AS: We analyze exit relays in AS level now. Figures 21 and 22 show the top 30 AS that have the highest percentage of number of exit relays that is in an AS and the top 30 AS being selected in all circuits respectively. In Fig. 22, we can see AS like *AS12876*, *AS200052* are more popular than other AS. *AS12876* has the highest percentage of more than 12% being selected even though only 8% of exit relays are in that AS. Some ASes in Fig. 21, such as *AS63949*, are not even in Fig. 22. This leads us to the conclusion that there are certain ASes that are more popular than other ASes and this is not proportional to the number of exit relays in them.

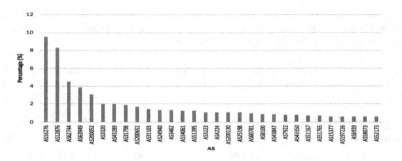

Fig. 21. Percentage of # of exit relays that is under an AS.

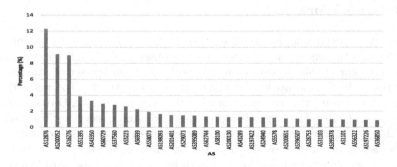

Fig. 22. Percentage of exit relays in an AS amongst all circuits.

4.5 Overall

We now provide a more holistic view of our dataset. We compare the Tor entry guard, middle relay and exit relay in a circuit to see if they are in the same subnet prefix (/24, /16, and /8) and same AS. We also compare the relays and the target website IP address. This comparison is done for each circuit built. Table 2 shows the results of our comparison: there is not much overlap at the /24 subnet, but at the /16 subnet, 104 pairs of entry guard IP address and target IP address are in the same /16 subnet. This could lead to correlation attacks launched to determine who the user is. At a /8 subnet prefix and AS level, there are more pairs that match. This is expected, but could be an issue if an adversary controls a large swath of IP address space. Looking at the AS numbers, about 11% of all circuits could be compromised as these circuits have the client or entry relay and the target or exit relay in the same AS. This is a significant number and shows that ASes can correlate clients and targets. This does not include Internet Exchange Points, and we expect this is worse when these are considered.

Table 2. Results of comparing Tor relay nodes' IP address and target websites' IP address in the same circuit to determine if they are in the same subnet prefix or AS number. The total number of circuits is 145, 918.

	Entry vs Target	Entry vs Middle	Entry vs Exit	Middle vs Target	Middle vs Exit	Exit vs Target
/24 subnet prefix	0	0	0	2	0	1
/16 subnet prefix	104	0	0	8	0	10
/8 subnet prefix	3,906	6,750	10,456	2,769	8,598	3,792
AS	150	24,439	16,866	287	11,308	36

5 Related Work

Tor was introduced and began operating in 2003 [6], providing service that enabled users to access the Internet anonymously [19]. When communicating with others, Tor clients choose a three-hop circuit from the set of available volunteer relays in the network. Tor allows researchers to the Tor network data such as relay bandwidth, the number of active Tor relays, etc, through the Tor Metrics Portal [26]. Although Tor provides anonymous service, Tor users are vulnerable to an adversary that can observe some parts of the Tor relays [23]. Tor can also be blocked since all the Tor relays are public information [4,12]. We used 44 independent machines located in different areas of the world to connect to popular websites through Tor.

Adversaries can exploit the nature of Internet routing by performing network traffic analysis [3,15,16] to increase the chance of observing users' communications traffic. They gain the visibility of Tor traffic either by compromising Tor relays, or by invading and manipulating underlying network communication like the Autonomous Systems (ASes) [2,10,17,23]. If an attacker can observe the traffic from both the client to the entry guard and the exit relay to the server, then the leaked information, including the packet timing and sizes, is enough for attackers to infer the identities of the clients and servers from timing analysis [8]. This is a correlation attack [13,23]. Our results show that some relays are much more popular than others. Moreover, correlation attacks could be performed as some Tor entry guards and exit relays/target websites are in the same /8 or /16 subnets.

Tor's path selection algorithm uses the estimated bandwidth of the nodes as a central feature. To mitigate the threat of AS-level adversaries, AS-aware path selection algorithms were proposed that consider the bandwidth and IP address when choosing relays while creating Tor circuits [7,18]. They attempted to infer AS path from incomplete knowledge of the Internet topology and tried to avoid picking entry-exit pairs routing through the same AS or that may be subject to correlation attacks. This minimizes the amount of information gained by the adversary. Our work provided the list of popular relays that will benefit selection algorithm design by comparing theoretical analysis with our results.

6   Conclusion

We provide a comprehensive analysis of the popularity of Tor relays. Our dataset consists of Tor relay nodes, collected by visiting the Alexa top 100 websites through the Tor network for 5 months, by using 44 different source machines. Our dataset records the information of each Tor relay in circuits: the relay node IP address, fingerprint, geolocation, and advertised bandwidth. Our dataset also contains the IP address of the source machine used and the target website. Then we analyze the dataset from many different perspectives: by source machine, by target IP address, by IP address, by /8 subnet, by /16 subnet, by /24 subnet and by AS.

The results show that some Tor relays and some subnets (either /8, /16, or /24) are more popular when being selected as middle relays or exit relays. From analysis of middle relays, the Tor relay named *TotorBE1* with IP address *5.39.33.176*, is 3 times more likely to be chosen than other relays and 10 times more likely to be chosen than an average relay. Our data also show that the bandwidth of a relay does not affect its chance of being selected as a middle relay node when a Tor client builds a circuit. When grouping Tor relays' IP addresses into /16 subnets, some subnets, such as *51.15.*.** and *163.172.*.**, are more popular than other subnets. Additionally, our analysis indicates that the chance of a /16 subnet being selected is not proportional to the number of relays it contains. For example, *62.210.*.** has nearly 0.6% middle relays however it has a 2.1% chance of being selected in circuits. When it comes to AS level, *AS16276* stand out. It has less than 8% of middle relays in it while it has a chance of 16% being selected.

From analysis of exit relays, the Tor relay named *IPredator* with IP address *197.231.221.211* and the Tor relay named *dreamatorium* with IP address *89.31.57.58* are 6 times more likely to be chosen as an exit relay, compared with other relays. There also seems to be a correlation between a relay's bandwidth and its popularity as an exit relay. Similarly, in /8, /16, and /24 subnets, we found that some subnets like *185.220.*.** and *51.15.*.** are 6 times more likely to be selected as exit relays than other subnets. From the results, we can see that a /16 subnet may have a higher chance to be selected even though it has a lower percentage of number exit relays in it. Like *185.220.*.**, it has 3.15% exit relays and it has a percentage of 9.13% of being selected. At the AS level, we can see ASes like *AS12876*, *AS200052* are more popular than other AS. *AS12876* has more than 12% chance of being selected even though only 8% of exit relays are in the AS.

For future work, we plan to explore more aspects of Tor relays in terms of popularity at the geolocation level. We will further explore the correlation between bandwidth and popularity as a middle relay or exit relay. Based on this result, we will also find ways to perform correlation attacks on Tor and learn how to make the relay selection algorithm more balanced.

Acknowledgments. We thank Mr. Ippei Okamura for his help with collecting the data, and Google for providing us Google Cloud credits to increase our number of vantage points.

References

1. Alexa top sites (2017). https://www.alexa.com/topsites
2. Anwar, R., Niaz, H., Choffnes, D., Cunha, I., Gill, P., Katz-Bassett, E.: Investigating interdomain routing policies in the wild. In: Proceedings of the 2015 Internet Measurement Conference, IMC 2015, pp. 71–77. ACM, New York (2015). https://doi.org/10.1145/2815675.2815712
3. Bauer, K., McCoy, D., Grunwald, D., Kohno, T., Sicker, D.: Low-resource routing attacks against Tor. In: Proceedings of the Workshop on Privacy in the Electronic Society (WPES 2007), Washington, DC, USA, October 2007
4. China Blocking Tor (2018). https://blog.torproject.org/blog/china-blocking-tor-round-two
5. Controller, S.T.: (2017). https://stem.torproject.org/
6. Dingledine, R., Mathewson, N., Syverson, P.: Tor: the second-generation onion router. In: Proceedings of the 13th Conference on USENIX Security Symposium, SSYM 2004, vol. 13, p. 21. USENIX Association, Berkeley (2004). http://dl.acm.org/citation.cfm?id=1251375.1251396
7. Edman, M., Syverson, P.F.: AS-awareness in tor path selection. In: Al-Shaer, E., Jha, S., Keromytis, A.D. (eds.) Proceedings of the 2009 ACM Conference on Computer and Communications Security, CCS 2009, Chicago, Illinois, USA, 9–13 November 2009, pp. 380–389. ACM (2009)
8. Evans, N., Dingledine, R., Grothoff, C.: A practical congestion attack on tor using long paths. In: Proceedings of the 18th USENIX Security Symposium, August 2009
9. Facebook Hidden Service (2014). https://blog.torproject.org/facebook-hidden-services-and-https-certs

10. Feamster, N., Dingledine, R.: Location diversity in anonymity networks. In: Proceedings of the 2004 ACM Workshop on Privacy in the Electronic Society, WPES 2004, pp. 66–76. ACM, New York (2004). https://doi.org/10.1145/1029179.1029199

11. Imani, M., Amirabadi, M., Wright, M.: Modified relay selection and circuit selection for faster tor. CoRR abs/1608.07343 (2016). http://arxiv.org/abs/1608.07343

12. Iran Blocks Tor (2018). https://blog.torproject.org/blog/iran-blocks-tor-tor-releases-same-day-fix

13. Johnson, A., Wacek, C., Jansen, R., Sherr, M., Syverson, P.: Users get routed: traffic correlation on tor by realistic adversaries. In: Proceedings of the 2013 ACM SIGSAC Conference on Computer and Communications Security, CCS 2013, pp. 337–348. ACM, New York (2013). https://doi.org/10.1145/2508859.2516651

14. Ling, Z., Luo, J., Yu, W., Fu, X., Xuan, D., Jia, W.: A new cell counter based attack against tor. In: Proceedings of the 16th ACM Conference on Computer and Communications Security, pp. 578–589. ACM (2009)

15. Loesing, K., Murdoch, S.J., Dingledine, R.: A case study on measuring statistical data in the tor anonymity network. In: Sion, R., et al. (eds.) FC 2010. LNCS, vol. 6054, pp. 203–215. Springer, Heidelberg (2010). https://doi.org/10.1007/978-3-642-14992-4_19

16. Murdoch, S.J., Danezis, G.: Low-cost traffic analysis of Tor. In: Proceedings of the 2005 IEEE Symposium on Security and Privacy. IEEE CS, May 2005

17. Murdoch, S.J., Zieliński, P.: Sampled traffic analysis by internet-exchange-level adversaries. In: Borisov, N., Golle, P. (eds.) PET 2007. LNCS, vol. 4776, pp. 167–183. Springer, Heidelberg (2007). https://doi.org/10.1007/978-3-540-75551-7_11. http://dl.acm.org/citation.cfm?id=1779330.1779341

18. Nithyanand, R., Starov, O., Zair, A., Gill, P., Schapira, M.: Measuring and mitigating as-level adversaries against tor. arXiv preprint arXiv:1505.05173 (2015)

19. Øverlier, L., Syverson, P.: Locating hidden servers. In: Proceedings of the 2006 IEEE Symposium on Security and Privacy. IEEE CS, May 2006

20. O'Gorman, G., Blott, S.: Large scale simulation of tor. In: Cervesato, I. (ed.) ASIAN 2007. LNCS, vol. 4846, pp. 48–54. Springer, Heidelberg (2007). https://doi.org/10.1007/978-3-540-76929-3_5

21. PlanetLab (2017). https://www.planet-lab.org/

22. Protocols and test Specifications (2018). https://gitweb.torproject.org/torspec.git/tree/dir-spec.txt

23. Sun, Y., et al.: Raptor: routing attacks on privacy in tor. In: 24th USENIX Security Symposium (USENIX Security 2015), pp. 271–286 (2015)

24. Syverson, P.F., Tsudik, G., Reed, M.G., Landwehr, C.E.: Towards an analysis of onion routing security. In: Workshop on Design Issues in Anonymity and Unobservability (2000)

25. Tor (2017). https://www.torproject.org/

26. Tor Metrics Portal (2017). https://metrics.torproject.org/

SoK: ATT&CK Techniques and Trends in Windows Malware

Kris Oosthoek[✉] and Christian Doerr

Delft University of Technology, Mekelweg 4, 2628 CD Delft, The Netherlands
{k.oosthoek,c.doerr}@tudelft.nl
http://www.cyber-threat-intelligence.com

Abstract. In an ever-changing landscape of adversary tactics, techniques and procedures (TTPs), malware remains the tool of choice for attackers to gain a foothold on target systems. The Mitre ATT&CK framework is a taxonomy of adversary TTPs. It is meant to advance cyber threat intelligence (CTI) by establishing a generic vocabulary to describe post-compromise adversary behavior. This paper discusses the results of automated analysis of a sample of 951 Windows malware families, which have been plotted on the ATT&CK framework. Based on the framework's tactics and techniques we provide an overview of established techniques within Windows malware and techniques which have seen increased adoption over recent years. Within our dataset we have observed an increase in techniques applied for fileless execution of malware, discovery of security software and DLL side-loading for defense evasion. We also show how a sophisticated technique, command and control (C&C) over IPC named pipes, is getting adopted by less sophisticated actor groups. Through these observations we have identified how malware authors are innovating techniques in order to bypass established defenses.

Keywords: Malware analysis · ATT&CK framework · Classification · Cyber threat intelligence · Advanced persistent threats

1 Introduction

Malware continues to spread increasingly and with serious consequences for organizations and private individuals. According to the 2018 Verizon Data Breach Investigations Report, malware is the primary attack tactic in 30% of data breaches [30]. Attackers keep innovating their TTPs to circumvent established defenses that could impede their modus operandi. As attackers continue to increase the sophistication of their techniques, the collection of CTI on attacker innovation is fundamental to inform adequate mitigation.

Obtaining such insight from malware analysis has become increasingly challenging as a result of evasion techniques such as polymorphism and metamorphism now being widely applied [3] and even available 'as a service' to cybercriminals [25]. Crimeware toolkits like Zeus have provided cybercriminals with

© ICST Institute for Computer Sciences, Social Informatics and Telecommunications Engineering 2019
Published by Springer Nature Switzerland AG 2019. All Rights Reserved
S. Chen et al. (Eds.): SecureComm 2019, LNICST 304, pp. 406–425, 2019.
https://doi.org/10.1007/978-3-030-37228-6_20

effective malware kits difficult to detect using conventional mitigations [4]. The vast flood of new malware embedding improved TTPs has resulted in a 'weapons race' [20] between developers of malware and anti-malware software. To obtain objective and reliable CTI on advances in malware, the study of innovation within individual malware families needs to be supplemented with an overview of innovation within the malware ecosystem by and large.

To build a common understanding of the TTPs observed through such analysis, malware research benefits from the adoption of a common taxonomy that facilitates the dissemination of CTI from malware analysis. To date the field of malware research has not reached consensus on the adoption of such a reporting standard.

For this paper, an automated analysis of samples from 951 unique families of Windows malware was performed. To discuss the results of that analysis we have mapped them onto the industry-standard ATT&CK framework by Mitre, further referred to as the ATT&CK framework. The framework describes malware techniques in their tactical context and allows for a common understanding of post-compromise malware behavior. Because it considers techniques in the context of the attack life cycle instead of viewing them as separate artifacts, use of the framework informs more effective detection and mitigation of identified techniques. This is the first study to apply an industry-accepted taxonomy to the analysis of a large corpus of malware. In doing so it provides insight in the adoption of innovative techniques for execution, discovery and C&C. We make the following contributions:

- We have applied an industry-standard CTI framework to malware analysis results in order to advance dissemination of CTI from malware analysis.
- We have studied behavior in a sample of Windows malware, through which we are able to observe how malware authors are implementing techniques.
- We have identified trends in the implementation of fileless execution of malware, discovery of security software and DLL side-loading.
- We also show how a sophisticated technique, C&C via IPC named pipes, is adopted by less sophisticated actor groups.
- We have evaluated the potential and limitations for using automated malware analysis as a source for CTI.

The remainder of this paper is structured as follows: Sect. 2 provides an overview of related work on automated analysis and malware classification. Section 3 outlines the ATT&CK framework. Section 4 describes the methodology of our analysis. Section 5 presents the results using the common language offered by ATT&CK. Section 6 presents a sophisticated technique of which we have observed increasing adoption. Section 7 describes the limitations of using automated analysis for CTI. Section 8 summarizes of our findings.

2   Related Work

Two types of previous work are important to position our work. First, other studies on automated malware analysis and second with regards to standardized reporting of malware behavior.

Automated Analysis. Among the earliest to analyze a large corpus of Windows malware were Willems et al., introducing CWSandbox and presenting its results based on the analysis of 6,148 malware binaries [31]. Bayer et al. have published about the now discontinued Anibus platform, which they used to analyze malware samples gathered in the wild from 2007 until 2008 [3]. By classifying the observed malicious behavior into common areas of host activity, they did provide important insight into the behavior of malware on a host after infection. Another significant contribution was made by Song et al., who have combined static and dynamic methods in BitBlaze, which is now also discontinued [24]. Other researchers have focused on the automated analysis of specific categories of malware such as ransomware [10], as well as evasive malware [11], encryption and packers [14] and anti-virtualization and anti-debugging in malware [5]. More recently, Grill et al. [7] conducted a study of bootkit technology based on the analysis of 29 bootkit families observed from 2006 until 2014. However, the malware landscape is subject to rapid evolution and most research studying a larger corpus of Windows malware does not include the analysis of trends.

Taxonomies. The use of a common language, also referred to as classification or taxonomy, is vital for malware analysis to inform CTI unambiguously. Researchers from academia and industry have recognized this gap. One of the earliest steps were taken by Kirilov et al. at Mitre [12], who recognized that communication of malware analysis results is impeded by the absence of a standard for the characterization of malware. They proposed the Malware Attribute Enumeration and Characterization (MAEC), which encodes malware behavior and has gained some industry adoption. Other researchers have pointed out the need for a higher-level taxonomy that explains the behavior of malware within the broader context of an attack [19]. Building on existing models from traditional areas of defense, Lockheed Martin Corporation developed the Cyber Kill Chain [8]. The philosophy behind this model is that effective mitigation of malicious activity is driven by knowledge about an actor's TTPs. The Cyber Kill Chain describes malicious activity based on seven discrete phases, but it is argued that it is insufficient in doing so. The model is criticized for emphasizing pre-intrusion activity [18] at the expense of post-intrusion activity [13,18]. As pre-compromise activity takes place outside the network perimeter it can not be observed, as description of such activity is mostly based on assumptions. As the model does not include common attack tactics as privilege escalation and lateral movement, the Cyber Kill Chain is less suited towards the full reporting of an attack's life cycle. Researchers at Mitre recognized this gap and have published a behavioral model named ATT&CK [26], which will be discussed in the next section.

Several authors have made significant contributions studying malware using automated analysis tools. This needs to be supplemented with analysis reported using an established taxonomy to further extend the common understanding of malware behavior. This study is the first to use the industry-standard ATT&CK framework to present the results of a large representative sample of malware.

3   The Mitre ATT&CK Framework

The ATT&CK framework was originally created by Mitre as it was recognized that existing reference models were insufficient in categorizing post-compromise activity into attacker TTPs [26]. ATT&CK distinguishes between tactics and techniques. Tactics describe adversary goals, techniques are the technical means through which goals are achieved. The authors position ATT&CK as an adversary model which standardizes both the tactics and the technical capabilities used after an initial foothold has been gained. The framework design also separates pre-compromise and post-compromise activity. The PRE-ATT&CK model focuses on attacker activity prior to delivery and exploitation and is independent of any technology platform as it offers a categorization of an attacker's reconnaissance activity, most of which cannot or only partially be detected. The Enterprise model covers on techniques implemented over the full attack life cycle on Windows, Linux and macOS, platforms commonly implemented within an enterprise context. Attack techniques targeting Android and iOS are contained in a separate model. Over the last couple of years, the framework has become the industry standard for describing malware techniques and attacker campaigns. The model has been open-sourced by Mitre and is being implemented in industry products. The Mitre ATT&CK website contains a knowledge base complementing the framework with observations of actor-attributed adversary TTPs from vendor reports.

The framework categorizes the attack life cycle according to different stages, called tactics. Tactics describe the objectives of an adversary within the life cycle of an attack. The tactics within the current framework version are as follows:

1. *Initial Access*: establishing an initial foothold on the target host.
2. *Execution*: how the malicious code is executed on the target host.
3. *Persistence*: all methods to maintain access to the compromised host.
4. *Privilege Escalation*: elevating access to other host or network resources.
5. *Defense Evasion*: all techniques used to avoid detection or other defenses.
6. *Credential Access*: obtaining credentials to expand control of resources.
7. *Discovery*: obtaining contextual awareness of the target system and network.
8. *Lateral Movement*: techniques implemented to pivot across other systems.
9. *Collection*: how information that will be sent to the attacker is collected.
10. *Exfiltration*: transferring information acquired in the process to the attacker.
11. *Command and Control*: the attacker exerting control over the infected host(s).

Each tactic serves as a class of the techniques implemented to accomplish that tactic. For example, to establish persistence (tactic), malware can add a run key to the registry (technique). The framework's techniques describe the steps taken on a technical level. Refer to Fig. 1 for an overview of the categorization of tactics and relevant techniques within the framework. Section 5 will further elaborate on the results displayed in this figure.

Techniques can either be defined generally or specific and be platform-agnostic or platform-specific, depending on how a technique is implemented.

Process Injection is an example of a general technique that applies to several platforms in many variations, where Regsvr32 is a technique with a very specific use case only applicable to the Windows platform. Techniques might appear within two or three tactic categories if applicable. An example of such technique can be seen in Fig. 1. The Scheduled Task technique appears under the Execution, Persistence and Privilege Escalation tactic, as the same technique can be employed within three tactical contexts. This paper will further reference the Windows techniques from the Enterprise ATT&CK framework, as our research focuses on observations of post-compromise activity in Windows malware.

4   Methodology

Dataset. The malware samples used for this research were gathered from Malpedia, a collaborative research platform with an established corpus of malware maintained by Fraunhofer FKIE [21]. The maintainers adhere to the requirements for correctly composed malware datasets, as described by Rossow et al. [23]. This implies that, among other requirements, the maintainers attempt to balance their dataset to avoid it being overshadowed by polymorphic families and that malware samples are annotated with family names and further metadata. Furthermore a carefully curated dataset should favor quality over quantity in order to yield representative results [1,2]. Malpedia aims to provide researchers with a regulated corpus representative of prevalent and timely malware families and code evolution within the malware ecosystem [21]. As a result a curated dataset like Malpedia provides stronger quality assurances than a corpus of malware gathered in the wild.

This research concentrates on Windows malware. Most malware is Windows malware, as Windows is the predominant end-user platform for enterprise and private use. At the time we collected our sample, the corpus of Windows malware available from Malpedia contained 951 unique families first observed in 2007 until 2018. From each Windows malware family collected from Malpedia we have selected the most recent sample based on data from VirusTotal to increase the probability of observing C&C traffic during runtime. For malware families consisting of multiple modules, such as stagers, we have selected the most recent version of each module. The malware family names mentioned within this paper are derived from Malpedia's metadata.

Experimental Environment. For the analysis of the samples in the malware corpus we have used Joe Sandbox Cloud, a public environment for malware analysis [9], formerly known as JoeBox [6]. It combines automated dynamic analysis with basic features for static and network analysis. Given that Malpedia does not include malware that strictly requires a version of Windows later than Windows 7 [21], we have deployed the samples in a sandbox running Windows 7 32-bit or 64-bit depending on detected target architecture, with a configuration of commonly used applications. The reports generated by the sandbox reference generic system calls that can be replicated using other analysis environments.

ATT&CK Mapping. In order to map malware activity reported by the sand-box engine to techniques described within the ATT&CK framework we have built a reference file. Through this the behavior signatures generated by the sandbox during the analysis of the malware corpus were mapped to their corresponding framework technique. The rationalization to plot a particular sandbox signature to an ATT&CK technique is justified by the definition of that technique in the ATT&CK knowledge base [29]. As an example, the sandbox detection signature for the execution of the *IsDebuggerPresent* function was mapped to ATT&CK technique 1063, Security Software Discovery, as checking for active debuggers is implemented by malware authors as a form anti-debugging. As a sandbox can detect different behaviors which all map to one ATT&CK technique, one technique can be described by multiple behavior signatures. Within our results, different variations of one ATT&CK technique within an individual malware family only count once towards that technique. Not every activity logged by the sandbox is necessarily malicious. If behavior described in a sandbox signature did not accurately match a framework technique, it was not mapped. Of 861 unique behavior signatures outputted by the sandbox, 398 were mapped to an ATT&CK technique.

5   ATT&CK Techniques in Windows Malware

This section discusses the results of the analysis of the malware corpus and their mapping onto the ATT&CK framework. Figure 1 shows a heatmap of the ATT&CK matrix, with color shading representing the number of observations of each technique within our analysis. Table 1 shows an overview of the ATT&CK techniques most common in our analysis. As one sample can perform multiple executions of the same technique during runtime (e.g. inject into multiple processes), this is counted as one instance of that technique towards our results.

The total of techniques observed in our analysis gravitates towards the inner tactics of the framework, as observed from Fig. 1. The locus of activity in intermediate stages is inherent to the nature of automated malware analysis, which focuses on host and network artifacts from malware runtime. In Sect. 7, we will focus on the limitations of automated analysis and implications for CTI.

Below we will discuss the observations from our analysis based on the categorization offered by the ATT&CK framework. Each technique is discussed within the context of its tactic. Techniques that apply to multiple tactics will be discussed in the context of the tactic justified by our analysis results.

5.1   Execution

The Execution tactic comprises all techniques through which a malicious actor can execute code on a target system. Below the most observed techniques for this tactic from the framework are discussed.

Execution through API. We have observed 562 malware samples launching processes by calling the *CreateProcessA* function Windows application programming interface (API). Furthermore we have observed many instances of dynamic

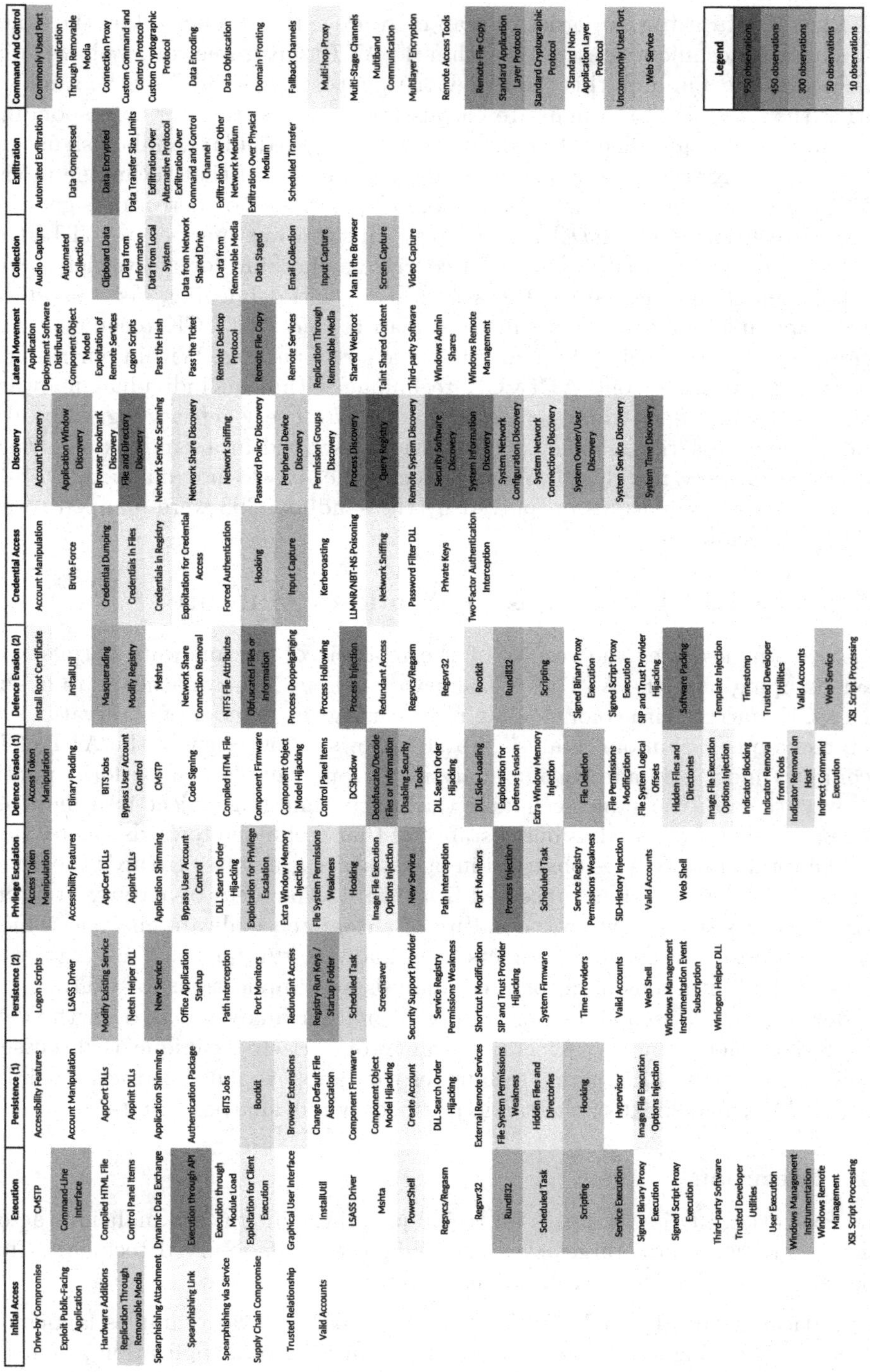

Fig. 1. ATT&CK enterprise matrix for Windows heatmap based on observations for each technique.

linking to the Windows API in order to call functions required for the malware to fully execute. Although we have observed a decrease in the implementation of this technique, accounting for 5.88% of total techniques observed in 2009 to 3.09% in 2018, this remains an efficient execution technique as host-based mitigation of specific API calls leads to undesirable side-effects.

Rundll32. We have seen 175 samples of malware being capable of executing a dynamic-link library (DLL) via *rundll32.exe*. This technique is deployed by malware for execution as well as defense evasion. Furthermore it can be used several times to launch additional modules. Using this technique provides an attack vector difficult to monitor for as it is also used by benign Windows functions.

Command-Line Interface. Within our dataset, 161 samples interact with the host system via the command-line interface, *cmd.exe* for the execution of modules. Several trojan families identified by Malpedia as EvilBunny, Oceansalt, Remcos, Sword and WebC2 invoke *cmd.exe* to setup a backdoor by creating a TCP reverse shell. Starting 2017, we have observed an increase in the use of obfuscated command line arguments with *cmd.exe*, apparently to evade signature-based detection measures.

Service Execution. Another prominent execution vector found is to register or execute as a service. Found in 115 samples, the observed implementation of this technique seems to have decreased, accounting for 8.33% of total techniques observed in 2012 to 1.07% in 2018. A handful of malware families in our dataset (Carbanak, Koadic, OlympicDestroyer, NetC) has been observed being capable of executing remote processes via *PsExec.exe*. As Service Execution directly executes the service, it is different from the New Service technique, which is used as a persistence tactic and described in the Persistence section.

Within our dataset we have observed the recent emergence of malware that only exists in memory, known as fileless malware. Not a novel finding in itself, we found that the emergence of fileless malware in our dataset overlaps with the first coverage of the topic in scientific literature [16]. Below we will shortly focus on malware employing PowerShell and WMI for fileless execution.

PowerShell. Within our dataset, 7 families used the PowerShell command-line for execution. All samples were first observed by VirusTotal in either 2017 or 2018, from families identified by Malpedia as Emotet, Rozena, DNSMessenger, Ramnit, DownPaper, SnatchLoader and Empire Downloader. Emotet, Ramnit and SnatchLoader executed PowerShell and called *CreateObject* to create a shell object to download and subsequently execute second-stage malware. Rozena was observed to attempt to create a reverse shell using several encrypted shell scripts called upon through PowerShell.

Windows Management Instrumentation. We found 82 samples accessing WMI, for example extracting information about the operating system or installed anti-virus software. As a subset we observed 7 families using the WMI command-line (WMIC) in the execution of malicious code. We have identified these samples belonging to families identified on Malpedia as Moker, EternalPetya, Spora,

Table 1. Number of observations per ATT&CK technique in our dataset.

ATT&CK technique	Count	ATT&CK technique	Count
Query Registry	950	Windows Management Instrumentation	82
Security Software Discovery	748	Scripting	71
Process Discovery	684	Uncommonly Used Port	67
System Information Discovery	669	Credential Dumping	56
File and Directory Discovery	658	Modify Existing Service	53
Obfuscated Files or Information	604	Modify Registry	50
Process Injection	597	Screen Capture	48
Data Encrypted	576	Web Service	47
Execution through API	562	Hooking	41
Software Packing	558	Peripheral Device Discovery	35
System Time Discovery	506	Exploitation for Privilege Escalation	33
Remote File Copy	423	Replication Through Removable Media	30
Deobfuscate/Decode Files or Information	378	Scheduled Task	29
Standard Application Layer Protocol	338	Bootkit	26
Registry Run Keys / Start Folder	287	Remote System Discovery	21
New Service	273	Email Collection	20
Application Window Discovery	216	System Service Discovery	19
System Owner/User Discovery	210	Hidden Files and Directories	16
Access Token Manipulation	197	System Network Connections Discovery	15
Rundll32	175	Data from Local System	14
Masquerading	165	Credentials in Files	12
Command-Line Interface	161	Account Discovery	12
File Deletion	135	Network Share Discovery	12
Commonly Used Port	129	Browser Extensions	10
Service Execution	115	Multi-hop Proxy	10
DLL Side-Loading	106	File System Permissions Weakness	8
Standard Cryptographic Protocol	104	Rootkit	8
Disabling Security Tools	98	Indicator Removal on Host	8
System Network Configuration Discovery	97	Data Staged	8
Clipboard Data	94	Remote Desktop Protocol	8
Input Capture	94	NTFS File Attributes	7

LatentBot, ISFB, Dropshot, EvilBunny, Ghost RAT, Betabot. All of the samples which created processes via WMIC were first observed in 2017, except for Moker in 2015. Out of these families, 5 are attributed to a sophisticated actor group (EternalPetya, ISFB, Dropshot, EvilBunny, Ghost RAT).

From the deployment of techniques for Execution, we can observe a few trends. Execution through API and Service Execution seem to have decreased and the use of obfuscated command lines increased. We have also identified increasing proliferation of WMI and PowerShell for fileless execution, in order to circumvent common preventive controls such as application whitelisting tools and leaving no on-disc forensic evidence. With the observed increase of obfuscated *cmd.exe* command-lines and fileless execution vectors, this indicates attackers are innovating their execution techniques to establish a foothold on target hosts. This also shows how the ATT&CK framework is useful to identify trends in technique adoption within a tactic deployed by attackers.

5.2   Persistence

In order to endure presence on the target system, malware authors employ various techniques. Below we review the most observed techniques for this ATT&CK tactic, including two techniques which have increased over recent years.

Registry Run Keys/Start Folder. Adding an autostart key to either the Windows registry or startup folder is an established persistence technique amongst malware authors, observed in 287 samples from the dataset. Dropping portable executable (PE) files to the startup folder directly is another variation of this technique, seen in 28 samples.

New Service. We have observed 273 samples being capable of creating a new service to be executed at Windows startup. Using the *CreateServiceA* function and adding malicious DLLs are popular methods observed in various types of malware over time, both from sophisticated as lower-level malware authors.

Modify Existing Service. We have observed 53 families implementing persistence by adjusting services, either by modifying registry keys using *reg.exe* in *HKEY_LOCAL_MACHINE\SYSTEM\ControlSet001\services* or using *sc.exe* to modify the status Windows services, such as Windows Update.

Hooking. We found 41 samples capable of hooking various software functions. Particular examples being banking and POS malware families hooking browser-specific functions. The deployment of hooking techniques is relatively stable over the timeframe analyzed. We have observed hooking deployed in more sophisticated families such as Snifula, Babar, EquationGroup, Nymaim, DanaBot and QakBot. Having observed this technique in sophisticated families and being difficult to mitigate because it abuses fundamental features of the operating system, this is an important attack vector to monitor for.

Scheduled Task. We have observed the implementation of task scheduling to have increased from 2015, using *at.exe* and *schtasks.exe* to trigger execution on every reboot or even every minute. It is mostly recent ransomware from 2017 and 2018 employing this technique, such as CryptoWire, Jaff, Rapid Ransom and Sage.

Image File Exection Options Injection. Four malware families from 2017 and 2018 have been observed to perform Image File Execution Options Injection in order to launch a new process by attaching a debugger to a current process.

The implementation of the most observed persistence techniques is relatively stable. The usage of Registry Run Keys / Start Folder is a known common technique, but the increase in task scheduling and recent observations of Image File Execution Options Injection indicates that attackers are seeking new techniques to bypass common preventive controls in maintaining access to an infected host.

5.3   Privilege Escalation

The techniques described within this tactic are implemented to establish a higher level of permissions to further increase control over the infected host or network. Below we cover three techniques most seen within this tactic.

Process Injection. Of the methods to launch malicious code, process injection is the most popular execution technique in our results, found in 597 of 951 families. The ATT&CK framework recognizes several subtypes of process injection for Windows, all of which are observed within our dataset. Of the defined sub-techniques, we have observed 86 instances of DLL injection and 153 samples being capable of portable executable injection. Furthermore we have found thread execution hijacking in 101 samples and thread local storage (TLS) callback injection in 51 samples. We have found asynchronous procedure call (APC) injection in a total of 37 samples. Relative to other methods, PE injection is the most implemented process injection technique in our dataset.

Access Token Manipulation. Being used in 197 samples from our dataset, this method to manipulate the ownership of active Windows processes is also a popular technique to escalate privileges. The most common implementation of this technique found in our dataset is through subsequent calls to the *OpenProcessToken*, *LookupPrivilegeValueA*, *AdjustTokenPrivileges* functions.

Exploitation for Privilege Escalation. We have observed 33 samples attempting to access the *ShellExecute* function, for which a privilege escalation vulnerability was published in 2014 [17].

Some techniques described in previous tactics can be employed to concurrently escalate privileges. A Scheduled Task for execution can also elevate privileges to SYSTEM. Creating a New Service within a persistence tactic can launch a service with administrator privileges to execute under escalated SYSTEM privileges. Although not much evolution between the different approaches to process injection was observed, it remains the primary vector for elevating privileges. By distinguishing multiple approaches to this technique, the ATT&CK framework facilitates a more informed discussion on the mitigation of such attacks.

5.4   Defense Evasion

Malware authors deploy several techniques in a tactic to avoid or subvert detection or mitigation technologies. We have observed four commonly deployed techniques, with DLL side-loading being on the rise.

Obfuscated Files or Information. This ATT&CK technique serves as a holder of all methods to draw malicious artifacts difficult to detect by obfuscating its contents in transit or at rest. Our dynamic analysis has found 593 malware samples with obfuscated instructions. We have also observed 37 malware samples with .NET source code containing either long sections of Base64 encoded code, as well the .NET code calling decryption functions *CreateDecryptor*. Furthermore we have found 40 samples of malware with inlined NOP slides, which suggests the presence of obfuscated (shell) code.

Software Packing. Packing has become a standard measure to make malicious files more difficult to detect or analyze. Based on *zlib* compression ratios, our sandbox detected a total 558 malware samples employing some form of packing. With regards to specific packers, UPX is a commonly used packer observed in 54 samples. We have observed 15 samples using RAR archiving for packing.

Table 2. Relative implementation of DLL side-loading from 2011 to 2018.

year	2011	2012	2013	2014	2015	2016	2017	2018
% of total	0.36%	0.29%	0.22%	0.18%	0.51%	0.63%	0.69%	0.82%

Deobfuscate/Decode Files or Information. We have observed 359 samples of malware using string decryption functions to recover obfuscated code sections. Like packing, this technique is deployed to hide malicious code in order to make it more difficult to detect. Encoding only the malicious sections of a malicious file and decoding them before execution might evade heuristic detection of malware.

Masquerading. All methods to manipulate or abuse names and locations of legitimate files to evade defenses are grouped under this technique. We have observed 165 instances of masquerading within our dataset, such as creating a presence in the Program Files, Windows and driver directories. Furthermore we found 101 files creating files within the *system32* directory. 31 samples were observed creating executable files named similar to existing Windows files, 19 other samples did employ names of commonly used third-party applications.

DLL Side-Loading. We have observed 106 unique instances of DLL side-loading, with 90 first observed from 2016 to 2018. Increasing from 0.36% of total techniques detected in 2011 to 0.83% in 2018 as seen in Table 2, we expect this technique to keep increasing.

Packing and obfuscating sections of malicious code are standard measures for malware authors with the above techniques being commonly observed. The recent rise of DLL side-loading suggests that attackers are innovating their techniques in order to ensure evasion of established mitigations.

5.5 Credential Access

This tactic describes techniques to obtain some form of privileged credentials to be used in later stages of an attack. Below, Input Capture and Credential Dumping will be discussed, which are the most prevalent techniques observed.

Input Capture. We have found 94 samples capable of capturing user input. 54 samples did implement a global keyboard hook with the *SetWindowsHookEx* function to intercept keystrokes. 31 samples were observed implementing functionality to retrieve information about pressed keystrokes using functions such as *GetAsyncKeyState*, *GetKeyState* and *MapVirtualKeyA*. 8 samples created a DirectInput object using the *DirectDrawCreateEx* function to capture keystrokes.

Credential Dumping. This technique describes all means to obtain login and password information from the operating system and software, which may later be used for lateral movement on the network. We have found 56 samples implementing techniques as harvesting browser history and passwords (44 samples) and 9 samples querying for file locations and registry keys of common third-party FTP tools. Another 9 samples queried the *Login Data* registry key used by Chrome and *IntelliForms2*, used by Internet Explorer to store passwords.

We have also observed 12 samples querying the file system and 6 samples searching the Windows registry for stored credentials. Hooking, already discussed within the context of Persistence, is also a technique for Credential Access. Though we have less results for this tactic, from our dataset it can be observed that keylogging is the main method to capture user input to obtain credentials, followed by dumping credentials from installed software.

5.6   Discovery

The Discovery tactic provides the basis for success of later attack stages. It is essentially a second iteration of reconnaissance, consisting of techniques an attacker deploys to gather information about an infected system and its placement in the network. Many of the most observed techniques within our analysis are part of the Discovery tactic. As most Discovery techniques deploy native operating system functions, this activity is well-detected by dynamic analysis environments, but also difficult to detect against.

Query Registry. Querying the Windows registry to discover information about the host system is the most common technique within our dataset, seen in 950 samples. Most of the samples within our dataset have a capability to read software restriction policies from the Windows registry by enumerating *HKEY_LOCAL_MACHINE\Software\Policies\Microsoft\Windows\Safer\ CodeIdentifiers*. The DWORD value of AuthenticodeEnabled indicates whether the execution of binaries is restricted by the OS. 345 samples have the ability to query the machine globally unique identifier (GUID) from the registry, most presumably as a unique identifier of the infected system.

Security Software Discovery. We have found 748 samples capable of detecting the presence of security features such as anti-virus software, local firewall rules and virtualization software. We also observed a significant increase in the implementation of security software discovery from 2010 to 2018, of which Table 3 provides an overview. Anti-debugging is the most detected specific implementation of this technique in 519 samples, by querying the *SystemKernelDebugger-Information* function to detect a ring 0 debugger being attached to the current process. 385 samples were observed detecting a debugger by checking the time difference between two Windows API calls, *GetProcessHeap* and *CloseHandle*. 349 performed an API call to *IsDebuggerPresent*. Checking the presence of a debugger by setting *GetLastError* in the registry to a random value and checking whether it has changed after calling *OutputDebugString* is observed in 92 samples. 70 samples have been observed executing a Read-Time-Stamp-Counter (RDTSC) instruction to determine the speed with which instructions are executed by the processor, of which the presence of a debugger might be inferred. This specific method, first observed in 2012, has gained traction with 52 out of 70 samples first observed in 2016 or later.

Table 3. Relative implementation of security software discovery from 2010 to 2018.

year	2010	2011	2012	2013	2014	2015	2016	2017	2018
% of total	6.13%	8.73%	8.47%	9.38%	11.55%	12.46%	12.32%	11.80%	11.68%

The detection of virtual machines or sandbox environments is another popular form of anti-analysis that has gained adoption over the last couple of years. We have observed 187 samples being able to detect various virtualization products by detecting registry keys specific to guest sharing functionality, such as *HKEY_LOCAL_MACHINE\SYSTEM\ControlSet001\Services\VMTools*. 44 samples were observed calling the *PhysicalDrive0* function to check for strings that might indicate the drive being virtualized.

Process Discovery. Within the ATT&CK framework Process Discovery describes all techniques to gather information about active processes on the host system. Within our dataset 599 samples implement this technique during runtime through calls to Windows functions such as *CreateToolhelp32Snapshot*, *Process32First*, *Process32Next*. 7 samples first observed from 2016 use *tasklist.exe* to discover running processes on both local and remote systems.

System Information Discovery. This technique, supporting further execution of the malware by querying operating system and hardware artifacts, is implemented by 669 of the samples in our dataset. The most common implementation is querying the Windows version using the *GetVersion* function, observed in 399 samples. Retrieving locale information such as the language of the user interface by querying the *GetLocaleInfoA* or *GetLocaleInfoEx* functions of the Windows API is used in 399 samples. 152 samples get this information in a similar way, using *VirtualQuery* and *VirtualAlloc* to gather information about the memory contents. 179 samples have been observed to check CPU instructions, which might have anti-analysis purposes. Depending on the call, the instruction can return the CPU's manufacturer ID string, but also the hypervisor brand. Certain return values might indicate whether the malware is running on a physical or virtual machine. 24 samples retrieved processor information from the Windows registry key *HKEY_LOCAL_MACHINE\HARDWARE\DESCRIPTION\System\ CentralProcessor*.

System Network Configuration Discovery. 97 of the samples in our dataset used variations of this technique. Of these samples, 60 called the *GetAdaptersInfo* function to retrieve information about the network adapter. Other samples have been observed using *ipconfig*, *netstat* or *netsh* to lookup Windows network configuration. Within this technique category, we have seen 24 samples querying standard online IP and geolocation services to determine the online IP address of the infected system.

Based on our analysis we see that Discovery is standard practice for malware. For Security Software Discovery, we have observed an increase. Within that technique, we see that the use of an RDTSC instruction to detect debuggers has proliferated since 2016. Most discovery techniques used in malware blend in with the flow of benign applications as they rely on native operating system functions. This makes Discovery also a tactic difficult to mitigate, which makes a case for application whitelisting to prevent the execution of malicious software early in the life cycle.

5.7   Lateral Movement

Lateral Movement describes all techniques implemented to pivot over the network to other systems of interest. The techniques of this tactic are difficult to observe with dynamic analysis as many techniques depend upon manual attacker intervention to pivot over the network, which is why this tactic touches less host artifacts anyway. Also not every malware family might deploy lateral movement techniques. Therefore the observations of techniques from this tactic are limited. We will shortly discuss the techniques found for this tactic.

Remote File Copy. This technique describes malicious download and upload activity within the network, as well to adversary-controlled infrastructure. We have detected 423 instances of Remote File Copy, which mainly consists of 336 samples attempting to download additional files as detected by our analysis environment. 101 samples communicated using plain HTTP GET requests, most of them storing result in the Temporary Internet Files directory. 18 malware families, among which Bagle, Bundestrojaner, Ransomlock, Redalpha and Yty, established HTTPS connections.

Replication Through Removable Media. We have found 30 samples trying to infect USB storage devices by creating *autorun.inf* files with an *Open* or *ShellExecute* entry.

Remote Desktop Protocol. 8 samples were observed trying to start the Remote Desktop service, which can be an effective stealth technique for lateral movement, as it blends in with the normal network protocol flow.

Our observations for this tactic are limited, as lateral movement is generally a non-automatic process, involving manual operations as the attacker pivots over the network. However we found a significant number of 336 samples attempting to download additional files, which makes a case for host monitoring of unusual processes establishing a network connection.

5.8   Collection

The Collection tactic describes techniques deployed to gather sensitive information. We found that the most observed techniques for this tactic all rely on native Windows functions to acquire sensitive user information. This tactic is difficult to prevent or detect, as the attacker did already bypass several defenses and gained considerable foothold.

Clipboard Data. In our analysis 94 malware samples attempted to obtain data from Windows clipboard. In 48 instances, samples performed subsequent calls to *OpenClipboard* and *GetClipboardData*. 21 samples started a window in the clipboard class *CLIPBRDWNDCLASS* to obtain copy-paste operations.

Screen Capture. 48 samples tried to capture GUI contents, primarily with calls to functions such as *GetDesktopWindow*, *GetWindowRect* to retrieve window dimensions and *BitBlt* and *GetDIBits* to store the capture in a buffer.

Email Collection. 20 samples actively collected of email messages by querying file locations and registry keys associated with mail clients such as Windows Mail client and Outlook.

As with lateral movement, we recognize that actual collection is difficult to capture using dynamic analysis, which results in fewer observations within this tactic. We however suspect that the use of scripting, of which we have found 71 instances, to automatically search and copy data depending on certain criteria is also deployed for Collection purposes.

5.9 Exfiltration

The exfiltration tactic describes all techniques implemented to exfiltrate data from the target to the attacker. Reporting of exfiltration depends on observation of actual exfiltration attempts, which are difficult to capture with dynamic analysis. Furthermore not all attackers apply this tactic, as some (e.g. ransomware authors) are not interested in exfiltrating data. We have found 576 being capable of encrypting local data, which is described with the Data Encrypted technique. We expect this number to be distorted by 27 samples of ransomware in our dataset, which encrypts data but not for exfiltration purposes. Furthermore we have found 6 samples capable of uploading files via FTP as these samples called to the *FtpPutFile* function, identified as Exfiltration Over Alternative Protocol.

5.10 Command and Control

Within this tactic, the attacker is accessing the target network from a remote location. In our analysis, 67 samples were observed to establish TCP or UDP traffic on non-standard ports. This technique, described as Uncommonly Used Port within ATT&CK, is known to be deployed to circumvent improper firewall and proxy configurations. We have also found 47 samples being capable of communicating with popular social media such as Facebook, Tumbler and paste sites such as Pastebin, which are frequently used for C&C. Within the ATT&CK framework this use case is classified under the Web Service technique. For the C&C technique Multi-hop Proxy, we have detected 11 samples initiating a Tor connection. Section 6 elaborates on the deployment of named pipes for C&C.

6 Adoption of Sophisticated Techniques

Within our analysis we have observed named pipes being implemented for C&C. Previously exclusively implemented in malware attributed to sophisticated actors, this technique is observed to have been adopted by less sophisticated malware authors. The attribution of malware to actor groups is part of

Table 4. New samples deploying IPC named pipes per year.

year	2010	2011	2012	2013	2014	2015	2016	2017	2018
observations	0	0	1	4	4	4	7	16	18

the malware metadata in Malpedia, the repository from which we have gathered our samples. For its attribution of malware families to actors, Malpedia relies on reporting from security vendors and independent security researchers. For instance, the samples of Pupy available within Malpedia are attributed to Iranian actors based on reports from 6 individual sources [15].

Named pipes are a method for inter-process communication (IPC), both with local and remote processes. Dynamic malware analysis is suited for discovering this technique, as a process is expected to call the *CreateNamedPipe* function of the *kernel32.dll* kernel module to create a named pipe. The named pipe server allows both local and remote processes to connect to the pipe and exchange information with the malware. As it can set up communication via SMB and RPC, is potentially also a technique that can be deployed to evade detection of command and control (C&C) traffic. By setting up one compromised host as internal C&C server to handle outbound traffic and having other compromised hosts connect on a peer-to-peer basis via named pipes, the footprint of network traffic is reduced considerably, which also reduces the odds of detection. The earliest sample of malware known to implement named pipes for communication with remote hosts is a variant of Conficker first observed in 2009 [22]. It also reported to be deployed for C&C by the Duqu family [27].

The ATT&CK technique definition of Process Injection states that, apart from the Windows implementations of the techniques described, 'more sophisticated samples' of malware may use named pipes or other IPC mechanisms as a communication channel [28]. As named pipes may also be connected to remote processes over SMB and RPC, it can also be deployed as a technique for C&C.

The detection of this technique within our dataset is in line with the Mitre statement that named pipes are specific to the more advanced malware families. As shown in Table 4, we have observed an increase in the use of named pipes within more recently observed samples. What attracts attention specifically is that out of the 47 samples where our analysis environment has observed this technique being deployed, 38 samples were first observed in 2017 and 2018. Except for samples from two families (Dorkbot, Snifula), based on Malpedia metadata, all samples prior to 2015 are attributed to sophisticated actor groups. From 2016, the technique is observed in malware attributed to sophisticated actor groups (TurnedUp, Pupy, Mosquito, EternalPetya, PandaBanker, OlympicDestroyer), but also in common crimeware such as Zeus, Karius, Trickbot, AlinaPOS, Qak-Bot and ransomware (Gandcrab, PyLocky). This indicates that techniques previously attributed exclusively to advanced actor groups are getting adopted by other malware authors.

7   Limitations of CTI from Automated Analysis

In the discussion of our results it became clear that detection of malicious artifacts naturally gravitates towards the intermediate tactics of the attack life cycle. In that sense our analysis exposes issues inherent to malware research with automated analysis. Most of these are known in the malware research field, but as ATT&CK is primarily a CTI model, we will use this chapter to evaluate the biases automated analysis might introduce to the CTI field.

Automated malware analysis suites offer a compelling solution to gain a quick and timely overview of individual or bulk malware threats. Automated analysis observes runtime behavior of malware. Attackers however might employ stealth and deception techniques, such as anti-analysis and evasion. This could result in malware not or only partially being detected, as it does not trigger or branches to deception code. It must also be considered that any analysis environment might not be able to fully detect all behavior exhibited by malware. Results invariably depend on the capabilities of the resource used for analysis. Still these are all known limitations to the concept of automated analysis of malware, as it only reports behavior observed during a time-constrained runtime [31]. But as automated malware analysis focuses on host and network artifacts of malware, it is thus biased towards the reporting of those artifacts. These biases become apparent when using a CTI-oriented model such as ATT&CK. As the requirements for CTI tilt toward the latter stages of the framework and proper CTI must never be biased, we might even argue that automated analysis is an unsuited source when taken by itself.

Initial Access tactics, such as the delivery of a malicious email attachment, are not accounted for during automated analysis. This also expresses in the ATT&CK plotting of our results in Fig. 1. Techniques for Lateral Movement, Exfiltration and C&C activity are difficult to record with a sandbox as the actual execution of these tactics depends on certain preconditions, potential manual attacker involvement and the availability of C&C infrastructure. The ATT&CK framework accounts for deployment of evasive routines in malware within the Defense Evasion tactic, which describes techniques used to evade detection or avoid other defenses. Logically sandboxes only detect evasion to a limited extent.

As a consequence, customers of CTI reports based on automated analysis of malware should be aware of the limitations inherent to the mechanism. An accurate CTI product must take into account the full threat context and consider alternative hypotheses. When used as a source of CTI, automated analysis reports should be treated with a different confidence level than results of manual research. Nonetheless it is evident that CTI benefits from a standardized language like ATT&CK, as it fosters effective dissemination and decision-making.

8   Conclusion

Our work is the first to use the ATT&CK framework to present the results of the analysis of techniques observed during execution of a large sample of malware. Having identified established and emerging techniques from the framework, this research is the first that provides an overview of a representative sample of malware using the ATT&CK framework. Through this, we have demonstrated the benefits of using an common taxonomy for the reporting of TTPs. We have shown this improves the actionability and unambiguous communication of CTI from sandbox analysis results.

We have observed differences in the degree of innovation between the different tactics of the ATT&CK framework. For the execution of malicious code, most malware relies on the Windows API. We have identified an increase in the implementation of fileless execution vectors using WMI and PowerShell. Together with the use of obfuscated command lines, this shows how malware authors are innovating their execution tactic to bypass traditional defenses. We observed innovation in obtaining persistence through the use of task scheduling, complementing established persistence techniques like autostart items and creating a new service. Process injection remains the primary technique for privilege escalation. DLL side-loading seems to be on the rise in order to evade established defenses, complementing more established evasive techniques such as obfuscation and packing. For malware accessing user credentials, capturing user input through keylogging is the most common technique within our dataset. We found that discovery of security software has become standard practice for most malware authors. We have shown different implementations observed for this technique, as well that using RDTSC instructions to detect debuggers has proliferated since 2016. The most common technique for lateral movement we have observed malware is Remote File Copy.

We have shown how C&C via IPC named pipes, previously attributed to sophisticated malware authors, is getting adopted by other actor groups. Through this we identified that malware authors are innovating techniques in order to bypass traditional defense mechanisms.

Acknowledgments. The authors would like to thank the maintainers of Malpedia for providing access to their malware repository and Joe Security for provisioning the sandbox infrastructure. The authors would like to thank VirusTotal for providing access to their API. The ATT&CK mapping built for this research has been shared with Joe Security to develop ATT&CK mapping within their product.

References

1. Barabosch, T., Bergmann, N., Dombeck, A.: Quincy: detecting host-based code injection attacks in memory dumps. In: LNCS (2017)
2. Barabosch, T., Eschweiler, S., Gerhards-Padilla, E.: Bee master: detecting host-based code injection attacks. In: LNCS (2014)
3. Bayer, U., Habibi, I., Balzarotti, D., Kirda, E., Kruegel, C.: A view on current malware behaviors. USENIX Large-scale exploits and emergent threats (2009)
4. Binsalleeh, H., et al.: On the analysis of the Zeus botnet crimeware toolkit. In: 2010 Eighth International Conference on Privacy, Security and Trust (2010)
5. Chen, X., Andersen, J., Morley Mao, Z., Bailey, M., Nazario, J.: Towards an understanding of anti-virtualization and anti-debugging behavior in modern malware. In: International Conference on Dependable Systems and Networks (2008)

6. Egele, M., Scholte, T., Kirda, E., Kruegel, C.: A survey on automated dynamic malware-analysis techniques and tools. ACM Comput. Surv. **44**, 1–49 (2012)
7. Grill, B., Bacs, A., Platzer, C., Bos, H.: "Nice boots!"-A large-scale analysis of bootkits and new ways to stop them. In: LNCS (2015)
8. Hutchins, E.M., Cloppert, M.J., Amin, R.M.: Intelligence-driven computer network defense informed by analysis of adversary campaigns and intrusion kill chains. In: International Conference on Information Warfare & Security (2011)
9. Joe Security LLC: Joe Sandbox Cloud Community Edition
10. Kharraz, A., Robertson, W., Balzarotti, D., Bilge, L.: Cutting the gordian knot: a look under the hood of ransomware attacks. In: LNCS (2015)
11. Kirat, D., Vigna, G., Kruegel, C.: BareCloud: bare-metal analysis-based evasive malware detection. In: 23rd USENIX Security Symposium (2014)
12. Kirillov, I.A., Beck, D.A., Chase, M.P., Martin, R.A.: The Concepts of the Malware Attribute Enumeration and Characterization (MAEC) Effort (2009)
13. Laliberte, M.: A Twist On The Cyber Kill Chain: Defending Against A JavaScript Malware Attack (2016)
14. Lyda, R., Hamrock, J.: Using entropy analysis to find encrypted and packed malware (2007)
15. Malpedia: win.pupy. malpedia.caad.fkie.fraunhofer.de/details/win.pupy
16. Mansfield-Devine, S.: Fileless attacks: compromising targets without malware. Netw. Secur. **2017**, 7–11 (2017)
17. Microsoft: Microsoft Security Bulletin MS14-027 (2014)
18. Nachreiner, C.: Kill Chain 3.0: Update the cyber kill chain for better defense (2015)
19. Obrst, L., Chase, P., Markeloff, R.: Developing an ontology of the cyber security domain. In: Semantic Technologies for Intelligence, Defense, and Security (2012)
20. O'Kane, P., Sezer, S., McLaughlin, K.: Obfuscation: the hidden malware. IEEE Secur. Privacy **9**, 41–47 (2011)
21. Plohmann, D., Clauss, M., Enders, S., Padilla, E.: Malpedia: a collaborative effort to inventorize the malware landscape. J. Cybercrime & Dig. Investigations, 3 (2018)
22. Porras, P., Saidi, H., Yegneswaran, V.: An analysis of conficker's logic and rendezvous points. Technical Report, Computer Science Laboratory, SRI International (2009)
23. Rossow, C., et al.: Prudent practices for designing malware experiments: status quo and outlook. In: IEEE Symposium on Security and Privacy (2012)
24. Song, D., et al.: BitBlaze: a new approach to computer security via binary analysis. In: LNCS (2008)
25. Sood, A.K., Enbody, R.J.: Crimeware-as-a-service-a survey of commoditized crimeware in the underground market. Int. J. Crit. Infrastruct. Prot. **6**, 28–38 (2013)
26. Strom, B.E., Applebaum, A., Miller, D.P., Nickels, K.C., Pennington, A.G., Thomas, C.B.: MITRE ATT&CK: Design and Philosophy. The Mitre Corporation, McLean, VA, Technical report (2018)
27. Symantec Security Response: W32.Duqu: the precursor to the next Stuxnet. Symantec Security Response (2011)
28. The Mitre Corporation: ATT&CK JSON Library (2018)
29. The Mitre Corporation: Enterprise Matrix - Windows (2018). https://attack.mitre.org/matrices/enterprise/windows/
30. Verizon: 2018 Data Breach Investigations Report. Technical report, New York, NY (2018)
31. Willems, C., Holz, T., Freiling, F.: Toward automated dynamic malware analysis using CWSandbox (2007)

Communicating Covertly

Covert Channels in SDN: Leaking Out Information from Controllers to End Hosts

Jiahao Cao[1,3], Kun Sun[3], Qi Li[2], Mingwei Xu[1,2(✉)], Zijie Yang[1], Kyung Joon Kwak[4], and Jason Li[4]

[1] Department of Computer Science and Technology, Tsinghua University, Beijing, China
xmw@cernet.edu.cn
[2] Institute for Network Sciences and Cyberspace, Tsinghua University, Beijing, China
[3] Department of Information Sciences and Technology, George Mason University, Fairfax, USA
[4] Intelligent Automation Inc., Rockville, USA

Abstract. Software-Defined Networking (SDN) enables diversified network functionalities with plentiful applications deployed on a logically-centralized controller. In order to work properly, applications are naturally provided with much information on SDN. However, this paper shows that malicious applications can exploit basic SDN mechanisms to build covert channels to stealthily leak out valuable information to end hosts, which can bypass network security policies and break physical network isolation. We design two types of covert channels with basic SDN mechanisms. The first type is a high-rate covert channel that exploits SDN proxy mechanisms to transmit covert messages to colluding hosts inside SDN. The second type is a low-rate covert channel that exploits SDN rule expiry mechanisms to transmit covert messages from SDN applications to any host on the Internet. We develop the prototypes of both covert channels in a real SDN testbed consisting of commercial hardware switches and an open source controller. Evaluations show that the covert channels successfully leak out a TLS private key from the controller to a host inside SDN at a rate of 200 bps with 0% bit error rate, or to a remote host on the Internet at a rate of 0.5 bps with less than 3% bit error rate. In addition, we discuss possible countermeasures to mitigate the covert channel attacks.

Keywords: SDN · Covert channels · Information leakage

1 Introduction

Software-Defined Networking (SDN) enables network innovations by decoupling control and data planes with a logically-centralized controller managing the entire network. As an emerging network paradigm, SDN is being widely adopted

© ICST Institute for Computer Sciences, Social Informatics and Telecommunications Engineering 2019
Published by Springer Nature Switzerland AG 2019. All Rights Reserved
S. Chen et al. (Eds.): SecureComm 2019, LNICST 304, pp. 429–449, 2019.
https://doi.org/10.1007/978-3-030-37228-6_21

in enterprise data centers, cloud networks, and virtualized environments [29]. Driving the popularity of SDN is that various applications can be developed and installed on the controller to enrich diversified network functionalities, such as load balancing [14], traffic engineering [19], and network security forensics [48]. SDN with plentiful applications greatly meets the need of industry to build dynamic, agile, and programmable networks.

In order to run applications properly, the controller directly provides many types of network information to them. For example, a routing application gets detailed network topology and positions of hosts from the controller to schedule routing paths. Moreover, an application can get more information than what it needs by actively retrieving data objects [47,50] on controllers. For example, an application can know security policies of the network by querying flow rules with the `FlowRuleService` object. Consequently, malicious SDN applications [23,32, 49,51] running on controllers can also possess many types of SDN information either by the direct offer of controllers or actively retrieving information. They may transmit the information to remote attackers for launching efficient and stealthy attacks. For instance, with the knowledge of detailed security policies in the network, attackers' hosts can craft special attacking traffic to accurately bypass network security policies.

To prevent potential information leakage from the malicious applications to colluding hosts, SDN environments usually enforce strict access control policies and deploy security devices to enhance the network security [1,2,33]. For example, unauthorized connections between an SDN application and a remote host can be cut off by firewalls, and abnormal TCP or UDP connections can be detected with a modern Network Intrusion Detection System (NIDS). Moreover, SDN allows building a separated physical network for transmitting control traffic between controllers and switches, i.e., out-of-band control [16,50]. Therefore, the controller is well isolated from end hosts that attempt to communicate with the malicious applications running on the controller. Existing mechanisms make it difficult for a malicious application to directly transmit valuable data to colluding end hosts.

In this paper, we study how a malicious application on SDN controllers can transmit SDN information to an end host with covert channels, which can bypass existing security policies and succeed even if the controller is isolated in a separated physical network. Our key insight is that SDN switches forward data traffic among end hosts and communicate with controllers to enforce policies at the same time. Thus, the switches may be the potential communication bridges between an end host and an application running on controllers. We design two types of covert channels with basic SDN mechanisms. The first type is high-rate covert channels between an application and a host inside SDN, which exploits the SDN proxy mechanism to encode covert information into response packets. The second type exploits the SDN rule expiry mechanism to construct low-rate covert channels between an application and any remote host on the Internet. Covert information is encoded into delays of data packets by delaying reinstallation of flow rules. Although previous studies [41,44,49,52] provide defense to prevent malicious applications from disrupting network operations, such as application isolation [44] and permission control [41,49,52], they fall short with respect to the prevention of covert channels built by basic SDN mechanisms.

We also perform a comprehensive study on what information an application can obtain on five major SDN controllers, i.e., OpenDaylight, ONOS, Floodlight, RYU, and POX. We first summarize three viable collection channels for an unprivileged application to collect information on the controller, namely, possessing information by design in order to work properly, exploiting system misconfiguration, and actively reading shared data objects. Then we show a list of SDN information that can be collected by an application, such as controllers' TLS keys and certifications, network security policies, routing policies, inter-host communication patterns, and network topology information.

We develop the prototypes of both covert channels in a real SDN testbed consisting of commercial hardware switches and an open source controller. Experimental results show that the covert channels built by the SDN proxy mechanism can successfully transmit a TLS private key from the controller to a host inside SDN at a rate of 200 bps with 0% bit error rate. In addition, we rent six hosts located in different positions to build the covert channels between an SDN application and the hosts on the Internet. Our experiments show that by exploiting the SDN rule expiry mechanism, a TLS private key can be transmitted from our SDN controller to the remote hosts at a maximum rate of 0.5 bps with less than 3% bit error rate. With the low bit error rate, the entire TLS private key can be fully recovered by adding lightweight error correction codes.

To summarize, our paper makes the following contributions:

- We develop two new types of SDN covert channels that use the basic SDN proxy and rule expiry mechanisms to transmit information from the controller to hosts inside SDN or outside SDN, respectively.
- We perform a comprehensive study on what information an SDN application may collect on five major SDN controllers.
- We conduct experiments in a real SDN testbed to demonstrate the feasibility and effectiveness of the identified covert channels.

2 Threat Model

We assume a malicious application has been installed on an SDN controller. Previous studies [23,32,49,51] have demonstrated that malicious applications can be installed in many ways, such as phishing with repackaging or redistributing applications [51], exploiting particular vulnerabilities of controllers [23], and fooling network administrators into downloading malicious applications from SDN App Store [49]. We do not assume the malicious application can compromise the controller, switches, and control channels protected by TLS [11]. The malicious application may correctly perform its designated network functionalities, e.g., generating correct flow rules as a routing application; however, it may also leverage basic SDN operations to build covert channels with a colluding host at the same time. Moreover, we consider two scenarios for the locations of colluding hosts. First, if the attacker may rent a host in the target SDN, e.g., renting a virtual host in SDN-based cloud networks [6], it can control the host inside SDN as the colluding host. Second, if the target SDN includes a server that provides services for public access, e.g., websites, the attacker may use any host on the Internet as the colluding host.

We assume SDN can use either in-band control [16,50], where the control traffic between controllers and switches is delivered with data traffic over the same network infrastructure, or out-of-band control [16,50], where a separated physical network is dedicated for delivering control traffic. The out-of-band control can prevent an end host from accessing controllers since they are isolated in different physical networks. In addition, SDN may also enforce strict access control policies to protect controllers from unauthorized communications. For example, SDN firewalls can block the TCP connections between an SDN application and a host. Therefore, the attackers are motivated to build reliable and stealthy communication channels to leak valuable data from SDN applications to a colluding host.

3   Covert Channel Attacks

The attack goal is to leak out information collected by an application to a remote host. The attack should bypass existing defense mechanisms such as firewalls, intrusion detection system, and access control policies. Moreover, it should work in SDN with out-of-band control that isolates controllers in a separated physical network which provides no communication between controllers and end hosts.

We develop two types of covert channels with basic SDN operations for two scenarios, which do not trigger unusual control messages or flood packets. The first type exploits SDN proxy mechanisms [4,7–10] to achieve a high-rate covert channel. It transmits covert messages to colluding hosts inside SDN. When no colluding host is possessed or compromised in SDN, the second type leverages the SDN rule expiry mechanisms [11] to build a low-rate covert channel with a colluding host on the Internet. It only requires the colluding host to have access to a public service in the target SDN, e.g., visiting a public website.

3.1   Covert Channels with SDN Proxy Mechanisms

As SDN separates control and data planes, the SDN data plane devices (e.g., SDN switches) themselves usually cannot implement proxy functions like traditional routers. Thus, applications running on controllers leverage SDN proxy mechanisms to provide network proxy functionalities for end hosts, such as ARP Proxy [4,8,9], NDP Proxy [7], and DHCP Proxy [3]. Although applications enable many types of proxy functionalities, they perform similar behaviors with basic `packet-in` and `packet-out` operations to implement the functionalities. For simplicity but without loss of generality, we use ARP Proxy as an example to illustrate SDN proxy mechanisms.

As shown in Fig. 1, when an ARP request packet sent by a host arrives at an ingress switch, it is encapsulated into a `packet-in` message and sent to the

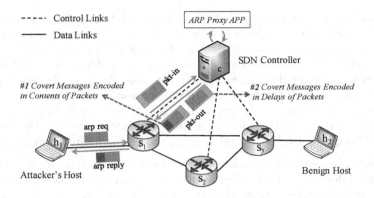

Fig. 1. An example of covert channels built by SDN proxy mechanisms.

controller. The controller extracts the request packet and dispatches it to applications that register `packet-in` event listener. The application enabling the ARP proxy finds an entry where the IP address matches the target IP address in the ARP request packet. It then creates an ARP reply packet that is encapsulated into a `packet-out` message in order to be sent back to the ingress switch. The ingress switch decapsulates the packet and generates an ARP response packet to the original host. Other applications enabling different proxy functionalities perform similar behaviors like `ARP Proxy` with different request and reply packets encapsulated in `packet-in` and `packet-out` messages, respectively. For example, an NDP neighbor solicitation packet and an NDP neighbor advertisements are encapsulated in `packet-in` and `packet-out` messages for `NDP Proxy`, respectively.

A malicious application can exploit the SDN proxy mechanism to build covert channels with a host inside the target SDN network to leak out information, though the application and the host cannot directly communicate with each other due to security policies or network isolation. There are two techniques that can be applied to build covert storage and timing channels, respectively.

Packet Encoding. As the response packet is generated by the application enabling proxy functionalities, additional information can be encoded into the packet. Thus, it allows building a covert storage channel between the application and a colluding host. For example, an attacker's host h_1 can send an ARP request packet to pretend to query the MAC address of some host in Fig. 1. However, it actually aims to stealthily receive SDN information from the application. Once the application receives the ARP request packet, it generates an ARP response packet with extra covert information encoding into some bits in the packet, which is shown in the red parts of `packet-out` messages in Fig. 1. Here, the bits can be reserved bits or unused bits in packets. For example, the last 144 bits of padding in an ARP packet[1] or the reserved 29 bit in an NDP neighbor advertisements packet [39]. Once the attacker's host h_1 receives the packet, it can extract the information by inspecting the content of the packet. Moreover, another way is to encode the information into some existing header fields of the ARP response packet, such as Target IP Address and Target MAC Address. However, in order to maintain the normal functionalities of the application and incur no anomalies for other hosts in this case, the application should only replace the original values of Target IP and MAC Address in ARP response packets for the attacker's host. ARP response packets for other hosts should maintain original values.

Response Timing. Covert channels built by such technique are stealthier, as no obvious information is encoded in headers or payload of packets. The main idea is simple but effective. As the attacker's host can measure the round-trip time (RTT) between sending a request packet and receiving a corresponding response packet, the application can deliberately delay responding a packet with different time to signal a "1" or a "0". Thus, a covert timing channel is built between the application and a colluding host. For example, suppose the host h_1 in Fig. 1 receives three response packets with 10 ms, 5 ms, and 6 ms RTTs, respectively, 3 bits covert messages "100" can be interpreted from the RTTs. In practice, the threshold of RTTs on distinguishing between "1" and "0" can significantly affect the accuracy of interpreting covert messages. We will show how to optimally encode and decode covert timing messages in Sect. 3.3.

The rate of above covert channels mainly depends on the number of request packets that a colluding host can send per second. Thus, an end host can adjust the rate at will to make a trade-off between the rate and the stealthiness. For example, the host can choose to send a request packet every 10 s. Although the transmission rate for the covert timing channel is 0.1 bps in the case, the behavior of delivering covert messages is hard to be detected since the rate is low and there are few packets transmitting covert messages per second.

3.2 Covert Channels with SDN Rule Expiry Mechanisms

In SDN, each flow is forwarded according to flow rules. However, due to the limited storage space of flow rules in switches [27], rule expiry mechanisms are introduced to efficiently use the storage space. The mechanisms associate each flow rule with two types of timeouts, i.e., hard timeout and idle timeout, indicating the expiration time of the rule. A flow rule will be removed by switches either after the given number of seconds of hard timeout no matter how many packets it has matched or when it has matched no packets within the given number of seconds of idle timeout. Therefore, when packets of flows arrive at switches where related flow rules have expired, the packets are buffered in switches and wait for switches to query controllers to reinstall flow rules.

We discover that the basic rule expiry mechanism allows malicious applications to build covert channels with a remote host on the Internet. Figure 2 shows

---

[1] The padding aims to bloat the ARP frame to the 64-byte length which is the minimum required length of an Ethernet frame.

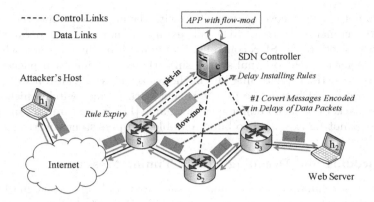

Fig. 2. An example of a covert channel built by SDN rule expiry mechanisms.

a typical case. The host h_2 is a web server which provides public services, such as websites. The host h_1 on the Internet visits the websites provided by h_2. Thus, a HTTP request flow is sent from h_1 to h_2 and a related HTTP reply flow is sent from h_2 to h_1 to load the web page. Once the web page is successfully loaded, the flow stops transmission. After some time, if h_1 visits another web page from the website, new HTTP flows between the two hosts are generated. However, if the interval between sending the new HTTP request flow and sending the previous HTTP request flow exceeds the value of rule timeouts, existing matched flow rules disappear and thus the HTTP request packets have to be buffered in the switch s_1. Meanwhile, the switch s_1 copies a packet from the flow and encapsulates it into a `packet-in` message to query rule installation from the SDN controller. The application on the controller then reinstalls the flow rules with a `flow-mod` message according to the analysis of the `packet-in` message. Finally, packets in the switch's buffers are forwarded according to the flow rules.

During the process, the application responsible for installing flow rules can deliberately delay some time before generating `flow-mod` messages for flow rule installation. The delays of rule installation will be reflected in the forwarding delays of the packets that are temporarily buffered in switches, which is shown in Fig. 2. Thus, the application can encode covert messages into the RTTs of HTTP packets by deliberately delaying the installation of flow rules with different values to signal a "1" or a "0". The colluding host h_1 on the Internet can extract covert information according to the RTT of the first packet of each new HTTP flow.

In order to ensure that the first packet of each new HTTP flow can be encoded covert information, the colluding host should wait for enough time to make rules expired before sending a new flow. According to the previous work [18], most timeout settings of rule expiration are usually less than 60 s and also can be inferred in advance by sending probe packets. In addition, the threshold of RTTs of HTTP packets on distinguishing between "1" and "0" will affect the accuracy of interpreting covert timing messages, we show how to optimally encode and decode covert timing messages in Sect. 3.3.

We do not transmit covert information with the packet encoding technique in the covert channel built by the SDN rule expiry mechanism. In general, the first packet that is sent to the SDN controller is only used to reinstall rules, which will not be sent back to the original switch since there is an identical packet in the switch's buffers. Hence, encoding bits in the packet fails to transmit information to remote hosts. Although the packet is sent back to the switch which fails to buffer the packet due to no buffer space available [11], it is a rare case in practice and thus cannot be exploited to build a stable and persistent covert channel.

3.3 Encoding and Decoding Covert Timing Messages

Both the covert timing channels built by the proxy and rule expiry mechanisms require a threshold of RTTs to decide which RTTs indicate "1" and which RTTs indicate "0". The threshold should be optimal to improve communication accuracy as much as possible. Moreover, the threshold should be adaptive. In other words, the threshold adaptively changes when applications transmit covert messages to different colluding hosts that have different network delays. For example, according to our measurements, the HTTP packets of a colluding host located in New York have an average RTT of 215 ms. However, the HTTP packets of another colluding host located in Beijing have an average RTT of 3 ms. The optimal thresholds of RTTs on distinguishing between "1" and "0" in the two colluding hosts are significantly different.

In order to adaptively and optimally decode timing information, we apply the Manchester code [5] to encode covert messages into the delays of packets. The Manchester code encodes 1-bit "1" into 2-bit "10" and 1-bit "0" into 2-bit "01". Thus, when an application signals "1" with the Manchester code, it encodes the information into a pair of packets by delaying the first packet. When signaling "0" with the Manchester code, it encodes the information into a pair of packets by delaying the second packet. Whenever a colluding host receives a pair of packets, "1" can be decoded if the RTT of the first packet is larger than the RTT of the second packet. Otherwise, "0" can be decoded from the RTTs of the two packets. Formally, consider an application encoding n bits in n pair of packets, the 1-bit information b_i from the i_{th} pair of packets can be decoded as follows:

$$\forall i \in \{1, 2, ..., n\}, \ b_i = \begin{cases} \text{``1''}, \ if \ \eta_i^1 > \eta_i^2 \\ \text{``0''}, \ if \ \eta_i^1 \le \eta_i^2 \end{cases} \tag{1}$$

Here, η_i^1 and η_i^2 denote the RTT of the first packet and the second packet in the i_{th} pair of packets, respectively.

3.4 Covert Channel Analysis

The Number of Exploitable SDN Applications. Applications building covert channels must have the ability to leverage SDN proxy or rule expiry mechanisms. Proxy applications and routing applications naturally can leverage SDN proxy mechanisms and rule expiry mechanisms, respectively. Actually, any

Table 1. The number of exploitable applications

Controller	Total APPs	Type I APPs	Type II APPs	Type I ∩ II APPs[b]
OpenDaylight Neon[a]	13	9	6	5
ONOS v2.1.0-rc1	97	26	23	22
Floodlight v1.2	29	13	12	10
RYU v4.31	28	16	19	16
POX eel version	18	9	11	9

[a]For OpenDaylight, we only count the applications with the openflowplugin implementation.
[b]The applications belong to Type I and Type II simultaneously.

applications (defined as **Type I APPs**) with permissions of listening `packet-in` messages and performing `packet-out` operations can leverage SDN proxy mechanisms. Any applications (defined as **Type II APPs**) with permissions of listening `packet-in` messages and performing `flow-mod` operations can leverage rule expiry mechanisms. We find that the permissions are easily met as they are basic requirements for running many applications. We investigate bundled applications on five popular SDN controllers with the latest versions. Table 1 shows the total bundled applications on controllers and the number of applications among them that may leverage the two mechanisms to build covert channels.

Transmission Rate. The covert channels above are built with two different SDN mechanisms. For simplicity, we use a_s and a_t to denote the covert channels built by the SDN proxy mechanism with packet encoding and response timing, respectively. We use b_t to denote the covert channel built by the SDN rule expiry mechanism. Totally, there are three covert channels. Different covert channels can transmit information at different rates. We give an analysis of their transmission rates. We use v_x, where $x \in \{a_s, a_t, b_t\}$, to denote the transmission rate of the covert channel x. For covert channels built with the SDN proxy mechanism, covert information can be transmitted once a request packet is sent. For covert channels built with the SDN rule expiry mechanism, only 1-bit covert information can be transmitted every timeout value after a flow rule is expired. Moreover, the transmission rate is reduced by half due to the Manchester code. Thus, we have:

$$\begin{cases} v_{a_s} = p \cdot l \\ v_{a_t} = \dfrac{p}{2} \\ v_{b_t} = \dfrac{1}{t \cdot 2} \end{cases} \tag{2}$$

Here, p denotes the number of request packets sent per second, l denotes the number of coded bits for transmitting covert information in a packet, t denotes the minimum value of hard timeout and idle timeout of a flow rule.

A host may send millions of request packets per second to make the application transmit covert information as fast as possible. However, most existing hardware switches can only generate thousands of `packet-in` messages per second [34], which limits the maximum transmission rate. If we use C to denote the maximum rate of generating `packet-in` packets for a single switch and L to denote the maximum available bits that can be coded in a packet, we have: $v_{a_s}^{max} = C \cdot L$, $v_{a_t}^{max} = \frac{C}{2}$. Moreover, according to the OpenFlow specification [11], the minimum valid value for timeout is 1 s. Thus, we have: $\frac{1}{t \cdot 2} \leq \frac{1}{1 \cdot 2} = 0.5$. In theory, the maximum transmission rate for each covert channel is: $v_{b_t}^{max} = 0.5$ bps.

The maximum transmission rate of covert channels built by the SDN proxy mechanism depends on C and L. In the experiments, our hardware switch can generate at most 1500 `packet-in` packets per second. Moreover, if covert information is transmitted by ARP reply packets, the available fields that can be encoded in an ARP packet are: 144 bits padding, 48 bits source MAC address in the MAC header, 48 bits sender/target MAC address in the ARP header and 32 bits sender/target IP address in the ARP header. Totally, there are 352 bits. We cannot change other fields at will. Otherwise, the ARP reply packet is broken and may fail to arrive at colluding hosts. Hence, we can calculate the maximum transmission rates of the covert channels a_s and a_t with our hardware switches in theory: $v_{a_s}^{max} = 1500 \cdot 352 = 528000$ bps and $v_{a_t}^{max} = 750$ bps. Obviously, the covert channels a_s and a_t have relatively high transmission rates compared to the covert channel b_t.

4   Information Leakage on SDN Controllers

To understand what SDN information can be obtained by an malicious application, we conduct a comprehensive investigation on five major SDN controllers, i.e., `OpenDaylight`, `ONOS`, `Floodlight`, `RYU`, and `POX`. We perform the study from two aspects. First, we summarize potential methods for SDN applications to collect information on the controller. Second, we classify the collected information. We find that an SDN application can obtain a large amount of valuable information. As the information can help develop more powerful and stealthier attacks, malicious SDN applications are well motivated to build covert channels to leak out the valuable data to a colluding host.

4.1   Collection Channels

We summarize three viable collection channels for SDN applications to collect information on the controller.

Channel I. Applications typically possess much SDN information by design to enable its designated network functionalities. For instance, a routing application knows detailed network topology and host locations to route network flows. An ARP proxy application knows host locations, IP addresses, and MAC addresses of hosts to respond to ARP request packets.

Channel II. Applications may actively retrieve information from the controller or other applications, since applications run on the same controller platform and share public system resources. Previous studies [47,50] have demonstrated that an SDN application can get much information by reading shared data structures or common network states in controllers.

Channel III. Applications may collect some information by exploiting system misconfiguration. For instance, we investigate that one application may have access to the TLS private keys and certifications of the controller by reading configuration files (See Sect. 4.2 for details).

Table 2. SDN information and collection methods

SDN information	Collection channels	Methods
TLS keys and certifications	III	Read configuration and key files
Network security policies	I or II[a]	Query flow rules with the FlowRuleService object
Routing policies	I or II[a]	Query flow rules with the FlowRuleService object
Inter-host communication patterns	I or II[a]	Listen packet-in and read HostService object
Network topology	I or II[a]	Read TopologyService object
System information of controllers	III	Issue shell commands
System information of switches	I or II[a]	Read SwitchService object

[a]Choosing which channel depends on the application. If it possesses the information by design, the collection channel II will not be used. Otherwise, it may actively retrieve information with the channel II.

4.2   Collected SDN Information

By inspecting the implementation of real SDN controllers and conducting experiments, we identify a number of invaluable data that can be collected by an SDN application. We summarize collected SDN information in Table 2.

TLS Keys and Certifications. In SDN, the controller and switches establish secure communication channels with TLS. To build TLS connections, the controller must generate its own private keys and certifications. Although different controllers choose to store their keys and certifications in different places, we find that an application on any of the five SDN controllers can easily obtain the controller's private keys and certifications.

POX and RYU directly store the keys and certifications in *.pem files. Due to the poor constraints on file access, we find that an application can directly obtain TLS keys and certifications by reading the *.pem files. FloodLight, ONOS, and OpenDaylight store their keys and certifications in JVM Keystore, which is a repository to store key materials such as private keys, certifications, and symmetric keys. A password is required when a program wants to obtain the keys from JVM Keystore. It seems the TLS keys and certifications cannot be obtained without knowing the password. Unfortunately, we find that the password is written in config files of controllers, i.e., *floodlightdefault.properties* on FloodLight, *onos-service (a bash script)* on ONOS, and **-openflow-connection-config.xml* on OpenDaylight. As the password is saved in plaintext, an application can first read the password from configuration files and then use the password to obtain the TLS keys and certifications from JVM Keystore.

The TLS keys and certifications are highly sensitive. Once an application successfully leaks out the information to an end host compromised by an attacker with covert channels, the attacker may leverage it to impersonate the controllers or hijack the communication between controllers and switches.

Network Security Policies. SDN enforces various security policies to enhance network security and defend potential attacks. These policies are invisible to end users so that an attacker is hard to find possible vulnerabilities or weaknesses from the security policies. However, we find that an application on each of the five controllers can know network security policies by querying flow rules of switches with the `FlowRuleService` object. It is because the high-level security policies of network security applications in SDN are translated to the low-level flow rules in switches.

Table 3. Typical flow rules of security policies

Rules in switches	Security policies	Meaning
match=ip_src:10.0.0.1,ip_dst:10.0.0.2 actions=drop	Traffic filtering	Drop packets sent from 10.0.0.1 to 10.0.0.2
match=ip_src:10.0.0.4 actions=meter:1,output:10 meter=1 band=type:drop rate=10 Mbps	Rate limiting	Limit flow rate of host 10.0.0.4 to 10 Mbps
match=ip_src:10.0.0.3 actions=mod_ip_src:x.x.x.x,output:10[a]	MTD	Frequently change the address of a host

[a]x.x.x.x denotes the value of it is periodically changed by controllers.

Table 3 shows the typical flow rules for three types of security policies. Traffic filtering and rate limiting are widely used to mitigate a wide range of attacks, including scanning and DDoS attacks [42,53]. Moving target defense (MTD) has been proposed in SDN [25] by frequently changing the address space of a network to defend against computer worms and network scans. Table 3 shows that rules indicating traffic filtering policies and rate limiting policies can be identified by the *drop* action and the *meter* action, respectively. Rules indicating MTD policies can be identified by checking the frequent variation of IP addresses in the *mod_ip* action. Moreover, the meanings of a security policy can be known by checking detailed components of flow rules.

Routing Policies. Similar to network security policies, the high-level routing policies are translated into low-level flow rules in SDN. Thus, a malicious application can know the routing policies by querying flow rules in switches with the `FlowRuleService` object.

Inter-host Communication Patterns. Inter-host communication patterns denote what hosts are communicating with each other in the network. The patterns can reveal wide information that is useful in a multi-staged attack [40]. For example, an attacker can infer that a host may be a vital server, e.g., a local DNS server, if all hosts in the target network communicate with it. We verify that an application can learn host communication patterns by calling the basic HostService object on controllers and listening packet-in messages. Note that HostService has different names on different controllers to manage the hosts. For example, FloodLight names it as DeviceManager, and ONOS names it as HostSubsystem. It can give all MAC addresses and IP addresses of hosts in the network while the destination address and source address of a flow can be extracted from the packet-in messages. Hence, the application can know each communication pairs of hosts.

Network Topology Information. SDN controllers maintain a global network topology view, i.e., the physical links connecting to switches and hosts in the network. The information is maintained by the basic TopologyService object on controllers. Our study shows that an application can obtain the network topology information by reading the TopologyService object. Knowing the network topology information can help an attacker to launch sophisticated DDoS attacks. For example, launching the Crossfire attack [26] requires to know the critical links in the network so that selected target servers can be effectively disconnected from the Internet once the critical links are flooded. Those critical links can be identified in SDN with the topology information and the routing policies.

System Information of Controllers. An SDN controller is typically deployed on a dedicated host with an operating system. We find that an application can obtain the controller's OS information by issuing shell commands. We find that various commands can be executed by calling *Java Runtime.exec()* in FloodLight, ONOS, and OpenDaylight, and *Python os.popen()* in POX and RYU. For instance, the application can obtain the OS type and version by calling *"uname -a"*, live TCP and UDP ports by calling *"netstat -tunlp"*, ip addresses of the host by calling *"ifconfig"*, and running processes by calling *"top"*. Such information is useful for a multi-staged attack for identifying a vulnerability in a given OS with a specific version.

System Information of Switches. By reading the SwitchService object, an application can know many other switch's information including switch manufacturer, hardware revision, software revision, port rate, maximal buffers, and flow table size. Knowing such information can hep an attacker to compromise a switch by exploiting the vulnerabilities of specific revisions in hardware or software [12,21]. Moreover, if the flow table size is known, an attacker can decide the minimum packet rate to overflow the flow table on a switch [18].

5   Evaluation of Covert Channels

In this section, we conduct experiments in a real SDN testbed to demonstrate the feasibility and effectiveness of our covert channels.

5.1   Experiment Setup

We build a real SDN testbed to evaluate the feasibility and effectiveness of the covert channels. The testbed consists of two commercial hardware SDN switches, `EdgeCore AS4610-54T`, and a popular open source controller, `Floodlight`. The controller runs in a server with an Intel Xeon Quad-Core CPU E5504 and 12 GB RAM. Two hosts in the testbed use `TCPReplay` to replay the real traffic trace from CAIDA [17] as the background traffic[2]. In order to evaluate different types of covert channels, we configure the testbed in two scenarios:

- The first scenario aims to evaluate the covert channels built by the SDN proxy mechanism. We deploy an ARP proxy application [4] on the controller and one host in the testbed that sends ARP requests in order to build covert channels with the application.
- The second scenario aims to evaluate the covert channels built by the SDN rule expiry mechanism. We deploy a routing [13] application on the controller. Moreover, we use `Apache HTTP Server` to build a website in a host in the testbed. The website can be visited by remote hosts on the Internet. We rent many hosts around the world to conduct experiments to demonstrate that an SDN application can successfully build covert channels with remote hosts when the hosts just visit a website in SDN. The locations of the hosts are listed in Table 4.

Table 4. Remote hosts in the experiments

Location	Host information[a]	RTT[b]
Los Angeles, USA	Intel Xeon 2.6 GHz CPU, 1 Gbps	162 ms
New York, USA	Intel Xeon 2.6 GHz CPU, 1 Gbps	215 ms
British Columbia, CA	Intel Xeon 2.6 GHz CPU, 1 Gbps	182 ms
Amsterdam, NED	Intel Xeon 2.6 GHz CPU, 1 Gbps	276 ms
Beijing, CN	Intel Xeon 1.9 GHz CPU, 1 Gbps	3 ms
ShenZhen, CN	Intel Xeon 1.9 GHz CPU, 1 Gbps	38 ms

[a]The bandwidth is given by the cloud provider.
[b]The RTT is the average value between the host in the SDN testbed and the remote host on the Internet.

5.2   Experimental Results

Accuracy. Figure 3a shows the accuracy of the covert channel built by the ARP proxy mechanism. We configure the ARP proxy application to add different delays to signal "1" before sending the ARP response packet. We can see

---

[2] As there are so many flows in the traffic trace, the hosts randomly choose some flows to ensure that the number of flow rules generated by the flows does not exceed the flow table capacity of switches.

that the accuracy goes up with the value of the delay. Particularly, the accuracy achieves 100% when we add 0.1 ms delays to signal "1". The reason is obvious: a larger delay to signal "1" allows the covert channel to tolerate larger delay jitters when transmitting covert messages. However, the accuracy drops with the increase of the transmission rate. For instance, the accuracy reaches 80.5%, 80.2%, 76.2%, 70.7% and 55.4% with 50 bps, 100 bps, 150 bps, 200 bps, and 250 bps, respectively, when we add a 0.02 ms delay. As a higher transmission rate generates more `packet-in` and `packet-out` control messages, more CPU resources of the controller and the switches on processing the control messages are consumed and thus incur more delay jitters. Moreover, the accuracy drops significantly when transmitting covert messages with a rate of more than 200 bps. We find that it is because the switch's CPU becomes busy. Thus, we do not increase the transmission rate by generating more request packets. We do not show the accuracy of the covert channel built by the ARP proxy mechanism with the packet encoding technique in Fig. 3(a). It always achieves an accuracy of 100% with the packet encoding technique.

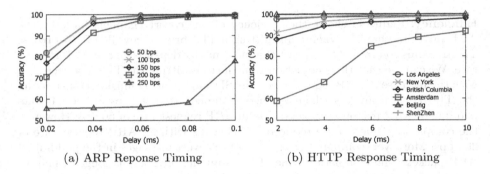

(a) ARP Reponse Timing   (b) HTTP Response Timing

Fig. 3. The accuracy of covert channels with different delays on applications.

Figure 3b shows the accuracy of the covert channel built by the SDN rule expiry mechanism. The covert messages are encoded in the delays of HTTP responses. We rent many hosts in different locations on the Internet to demonstrate that covert messages can be transmitted into any remote host as long as the host can visit the website running on a host inside the target SDN. From the experimental results, we see that the accuracy increases when the application adds more delays to signal "1" before sending the control messages of rule reinstallation due to rule expiry. Particularly, the accuracy of transmitting covert messages to different locations of remote hosts all increases to more than 90% with a 10 ms delay to signal "1". The accuracy of transmitting covert messages to Amsterdam is much lower compared to other cases since the RTTs from our testbed to Amsterdam are the longest, i.e., 276 ms on average shown in Table 4. We also find that the RTTs have a relatively large variation, which can significantly affect decoding messages encoded in the delays of HTTP responses.

However, we can apply error correction codes, e.g., BCH code [24], to encode the covert messages or enlarge the delays to signal "1" so as to improve the accuracy.

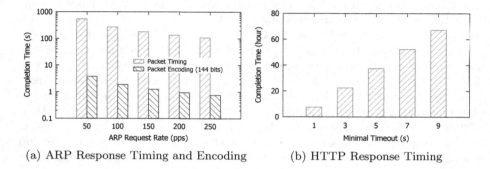

(a) ARP Response Timing and Encoding   (b) HTTP Response Timing

Fig. 4. The completion time of transmitting a TLS private key file of 1670 bytes.

Efficiency. Figure 4a shows the efficiency of our covert channels built by the ARP proxy mechanism when transmitting a TLS private key file of 1670 bytes. The transmission rate of the covert channels mainly depends on the ARP request rate. We can see that the completion time of transmitting the TLS key decreases with the increase of ARP request rate. The SDN application finishes transmitting the TLS key within 10 s when we encode the covert messages in the 144 bits padding of ARP response packets with an ARP request rate of 50 pps. However, the completion time can be reduced to below 1 s with an ARP request rate of 200 pps. Moreover, compared to encoding the covert messages in the padding of ARP packets, the completion time of transmitting TLS key is longer when we encode covert messages in the delays of ARP response packets. For example, the completion time is more than 100 s even with an ARP request rate of 250 pps. However, transmitting covert messages with packet timing is stealthier than that with packet encoding since there are no modifications in the ARP packets.

Figure 4b shows the efficiency of our covert channel built by the SDN rule expiry mechanism. Obviously, the timeout settings of the rule expiry mechanism totally decide the transmission rate of the covert channel. 1-bit information can be encoded in the timing of HTTP packets only when the controller reinstalls the expired flow rule. The experimental results show that the completion time of transmitting the TLS key of 1670 bytes exhibits a linear increase with the minimum value between the hard timeout and the idle timeout. Moreover, compared to the covert channels built by the SDN proxy mechanism, the completion time of transmitting the key is much longer, e.g., 7.5 h with a 1 s minimum timeout setting. Although the rate of the covert channel is much low, it allows an SDN application to stealthily transmit information to any remote host on the Internet without requiring the host inside the target SDN.

6   Possible Countermeasures

We discuss possible countermeasures to defend against the new covert channel attacks in SDN. In general, we may mitigate the covert channels in two directions, namely, preventing installing malicious SDN applications on controllers and detecting covert channels between SDN applications and colluding hosts.

Safety Check of SDN Applications. The construction of the covert channels requires malicious applications installed on SDN controllers. To avoid building covert channels, one way is to ensure that the SDN applications are benign and credible. We suggest that network administrators should install applications from trustworthy sources to avoid malicious applications. Moreover, network administrators should check the safety of an application before deploying it on controllers. If the source code of an application can be provided, static program analysis may be used to detect malicious SDN applications. For example, analyzing API calls of applications and calculating the control flow graph [31] may help to identify malicious applications. Moreover, dynamic program analysis may reveal malicious behaviors of SDN applications with sufficient test inputs, e.g., various `packet-in` control messages. However, designing an effective defense system to accurately detect malicious applications with static or dynamic program analysis is challenging and requires lots of efforts. We leave this as future work.

Control Messages Censorship on SDN Controllers. One important factor of successfully transmitting covert messages lies in that SDN applications encode messages in the timing or content of control messages. Thus, network administrators can deploy a security application that resides between the controller and other applications to inspect control messages in order to detect covert channels. Particularly, the timing between a pair of control messages that are used by an application to build covert timing channels will be relatively high. We implement such a security application in the `Floodlight` controller to time the `packet-in` and `packet-out` messages that contain ARP request and reply packets. Experimental results show that the timings between receiving the `packet-in` message and sending the `packet-out` message are typical less than 0.03 ms without covert channels. In contrast, most delays are more than 0.05 ms with covert channels, which indicates that timing control messages can be used to detect the covert timing channels. Moreover, covert storage channels that encode messages in the content of control messages can be detected when there is inconsistency in control messages. For example, suppose the ARP proxy application encodes covert messages into the 144 bits padding of ARP packets. According to the ARP protocol, the 144 bits padding should be all zeros. However, if any padding bits equal to ones, the inconsistency can be detected.

Although control messages censorship can successfully detect covert channels, it faces two challenges to be adopted in practice. The first one is on how to design a robust method that can accurately detect covert timing channels according to the timings of control packets. Different applications running on controllers with different network environments will affect the timing. For example, if the controller is busy processing network events, the delays of control messages generated by benign applications can also be high, which easily results in a false alarm for detecting malicious applications based on the timing. The second challenge is on how to design a systematical method that can detect various inconsistency in control messages since many fields of control messages can be used to encode covert information. We leave the design of a practical censorship system as future work.

7   Related Work

In this section, we review related work in the areas of covert channels and information reconnaissance in SDN.

7.1   Covert Channels in SDN

Covert channels have been widely studied in operating systems and cloud networks [22,35,37,38]; however, there are few studies focusing on covert channels in SDN. Recently, Thimmaraju et al. [46] provide the SDN teleportation technique which allows malicious switches to build covert channels for hidden communication with each other. SDN teleportation mainly exploits three SDN functionalities: flow re-configurations, switch identification, and out-of-band forwarding. It allows malicious switches to generate spoofing control messages to controllers, which leads controllers to send extra control messages to other switches. Krösche et al. [30] further studies the SDN teleportation technique with switch identification. They build the state machine of switch identification and model it in terms of time delays to build a covert timing channel with a high accuracy. Different from the above two studies that build covert channels between switches and switches, our work exploits the unique SDN proxy mechanism and rule expiry mechanism to build covert channels between SDN controllers and remote hosts. Our covert channels can be used to transmit information from SDN controllers to end hosts while they can bypass physical network isolation and security policies.

7.2   Information Reconnaissance in SDN

Information reconnaissance in SDN has been widely studied. Shin et al. [43] and Cui et al. [20] study the feasibility of inferring whether a network adopts SDN by measuring delays of pings. Köti et al. [28] infer if there are aggregated flow rules for TCP flows by timing TCP setup delays. John et al. [45] present a complicated inference attack that learns host communications and access control lists in SDN by timing the control plane's execution. Achleitner et al. [15] design SDNMap that reveals the detailed composition of flow rules by sending probe packets of various network protocols. Liu et al. [36] build a Markov model of SDN switches, which allows an attacker to choose the best probes to infer whether a flow occurred recently in the network. Previous work mainly depends on the timing-based side channel or protocol feature to infer some SDN information. In contrast, our work focuses on building covert channels to leak out many types of valuable SDN information from controllers to end hosts.

8   Conclusion

In this work, we study how a malicious SDN application can transmit information from controllers to end hosts while bypassing network security policies and physical network isolation. For that purpose, we design two types of covert channels with the basic SDN proxy and rule expiry mechanisms, respectively. These covert channels can transmit information either to a host in the target SDN at a high rate or to a host on the Internet at a low rate. We demonstrate the feasibility of the covert channels with experiments in a real SDN testbed. In addition, we make a comprehensive study on five major SDN controllers to understand what information an SDN application can leak out from controllers. Finally, we discuss possible countermeasures to mitigate the covert channels.

Acknowledgment. The research is partially supported by the National Natural Science Foundation of China (NSFC) under Grant 61832013, 61625203, 61572278 and U1736209, the National Key R&D Program of China under Grant 2017YFB0803202, and the NSF grants IIP-1266147 and CNS-1822094.

References

1. Access Control in ONOS Controller. https://wiki.onosproject.org/display/ONOS/Access+Control+Based+on+DHCP
2. Firewall Application in Floodlight Controller. https://floodlight.atlassian.net/wiki/spaces/floodlightcontroller/pages/1343616/Firewall
3. Floodlight DHCP Proxy Service. https://github.com/floodlight/floodlight/tree/master/src/main/java/net/floodlightcontroller/dhcpserver
4. Floodlight ProxyARP. https://github.com/mbredel/floodlight-proxyarp
5. Manchester Code. https://en.wikipedia.org/wiki/Manchester_code
6. Microsoft Azure and Software Defined Networking. https://docs.microsoft.com/en-us/windows-server/networking/sdn/azure_and_sdn/
7. ONOS Neighbour Resolution Service for ARP and NDP Proxy. https://wiki.onosproject.org/display/ONOS/Neighbour+Resolution+Service
8. ONOS ProxyARP. https://github.com/opennetworkinglab/onos/blob/master/apps/proxyarp/src/main/java/org/onosproject/proxyarp/DefaultProxyArp.java
9. OpenDayLight ARP Proxy Service. https://github.com/opendaylight/honeycomb-vbd/blob/master/api/src/main/yang/proxy-arp
10. OpenDayLight Neutron DHCP Proxy Service. https://docs.opendaylight.org/en/stable-nitrogen/submodules/netvirt/docs/specs/neutron-port-for-dhcp-service.html
11. OpenFlow Specification v1.5.1. https://www.opennetworking.org/wp-content/uploads/2014/10/openflow-switch-v1.5.1.pdf
12. OpenvSwitch: Products and Vulnerabilities. https://www.cvedetails.com/vendor/12098/Openvswitch.html
13. Routing Application on Floodlight. https://github.com/floodlight/floodlight/tree/master/src/main/java/net/floodlightcontroller/routing/
14. Abdelltif, A.A., et al.: SDN-based load balancing service for cloud servers. IEEE Commun. Mag. **56**(8), 106–111 (2018)

15. Achleitner, S., et al.: Adversarial network forensics in software defined networking. In: ACM SOSR, pp. 8–20 (2017)
16. Braun, W., Menth, M.: Software-defined networking using openflow: protocols, applications and architectural design choices. Futur. Internet **6**(2), 302–336 (2014)
17. CAIDA Passive Monitor: Chicago B: http://www.caida.org/data/passive/trace_stats/chicago-B/2015/?monitor=20150219-130000.UTC
18. Cao, J., Xu, M., Li, Q., Sun, K., Yang, Y., Zheng, J.: Disrupting SDN via the data plane: a low-rate flow table overflow attack. In: Lin, X., Ghorbani, A., Ren, K., Zhu, S., Zhang, A. (eds.) SecureComm 2017. LNICST, vol. 238, pp. 356–376. Springer, Cham (2018). https://doi.org/10.1007/978-3-319-78813-5_18
19. Chiang, S.-H., et al.: Online multicast traffic engineering for software-defined networks. In: IEEE INFOCOM, pp. 414–422 (2018)
20. Cui, H., et al.: On the fingerprinting of software-defined networks. IEEE TIFS **11**(10), 2160–2173 (2016)
21. Dhawan, M., et al.: Sphinx: detecting security attacks in software-defined networks. In: NDSS, vol. 15, pp. 8–11 (2015)
22. Gras, B., et al.: Translation leak-aside buffer: defeating cache side-channel protections with TLB attacks. In: USENIX Security, pp. 955–972 (2018)
23. Hizver, J.: Taxonomic modeling of security threats in software defined networking. In: BlackHat Conference, pp. 1–16 (2015)
24. Hocquenghem, A.: Codes correcteurs d'erreurs. Chiffres **2**(2), 147–156 (1959)
25. Jafarian, J.H., et al.: OpenFlow random host mutation: transparent moving target defense using software defined networking. In: ACM HotSDN, pp. 127–132 (2012)
26. Kang, M.S., et al.: The crossfire attack. In: IEEE Symposium on Security and Privacy, pp. 127–141 (2013)
27. Katta, N., et al.: Infinite cacheflow in software-defined networks. In: ACM HotSDN, pp. 175–180 (2014)
28. Klöti, R., et al.: OpenFlow: a security analysis. In: IEEE ICNP, pp. 1–6 (2013)
29. Kreutz, D., et al.: Software-defined networking: a comprehensive survey. Proc. IEEE **103**(1), 14–76 (2015)
30. Krösche, R., et al.: I DPID it my way! A covert timing channel in software-defined networks. In: IFIP Networking (2018)
31. Lam, P., et al.: The soot framework for java program analysis: a retrospective. In: CETUS 2011, vol. 15, p. 35 (2011)
32. Lee, S., et al.: The smaller, the shrewder: a simple malicious application can kill an entire SDN environment. In: ACM SDN-NFV Security, pp. 23–28 (2016)
33. Li, H., et al.: vNIDS: towards elastic security with safe and efficient virtualization of network intrusion detection systems. In: ACM CCS, pp. 17–34 (2018)
34. Lin, Y.-D., et al.: OFBench: performance test suite on OpenFlow switches. IEEE Syst. J. **12**(3), 2949–2959 (2018)
35. Lipp, M., et al.: Meltdown: reading kernel memory from user space. In: USENIX Security, pp. 973–990 (2018)
36. Liu, S., et al.: Flow reconnaissance via timing attacks on SDN switches. In: IEEE ICDCS, pp. 196–206 (2017)
37. Maurice, C., et al.: Hello from the other side: SSH over robust cache covert channels in the cloud. In: NDSS (2017)
38. Moon, S.-J., et al.: Nomad: mitigating arbitrary cloud side channels via provider-assisted migration. In: ACM CCS, pp. 1595–1606 (2015)
39. Narten, T.: Neighbor Discovery for IP version 6. RFC 2461 (1998)
40. Ou, X., et al.: A scalable approach to attack graph generation. In: ACM CCS, pp. 336–345 (2006)

41. Porras, P.A., et al.: Securing the software defined network control layer. In: NDSS (2015)
42. Rossow, C.: Amplification hell: revisiting network protocols for DDOS abuse. In: NDSS (2014)
43. Shin, S., Gu, G.: Attacking software-defined networks: a first feasibility study. In: ACM HotSDN, pp. 165–166 (2013)
44. Shin, S., et al.: Rosemary: a robust, secure, and high-performance network operating system. In: ACM CCS, pp. 78–89 (2014)
45. Sonchack, J., et al.: Timing-based reconnaissance and defense in software-defined networks. In: IEEE ACSAC, pp. 89–100 (2016)
46. Thimmaraju, K., et al.: Outsmarting network security with SDN teleportation. In: IEEE EuroS&P, pp. 563–578 (2017)
47. Ujcich, B.E., et al.: Cross-app poisoning in software-defined networking. In: ACM CCS (2018)
48. Wang, H., et al.: Towards fine-grained network security forensics and diagnosis in the SDN era. In: ACM CCS, pp. 3–16 (2018)
49. Wen, X., et al.: SDNshield: reconciliating configurable application permissions for SDN app markets. In: IEEE/IFIP DSN, pp. 121–132 (2016)
50. Xu, L., et al.: Attacking the brain: races in the SDN control plane. In: USENIX Security, pp. 451–468 (2017)
51. Yoon, C., Lee, S.: Attacking SDN infrastructure: are we ready for the next-gen networking? In: BlackHat-USA (2016)
52. Yoon, C., et al.: A security-mode for carrier-grade SDN controllers. In: ACM ACSAC. pp. 461–473 (2017)
53. Zheng, J., et al.: Realtime DDoS defense using COTS SDN switches via adaptive correlation analysis. IEEE TIFS **13**(7), 1838–1853 (2018)

Victim-Aware Adaptive Covert Channels

Riccardo Bortolameotti[1]([✉]), Thijs van Ede[1], Andrea Continella[2],
Maarten Everts[1], Willem Jonker[1], Pieter Hartel[3], and Andreas Peter[1]

[1] University of Twente, Enschede, The Netherlands
r.bortolameotti@utwente.nl
[2] University of California, Santa Barbara, Santa Barbara, USA
[3] Delft University of Technology, Delft, The Netherlands

Abstract. We investigate the problem of detecting advanced covert channel techniques, namely *victim-aware adaptive covert channels*. An adaptive covert channel is considered victim-aware when the attacker mimics the content of its victim's legitimate communication, such as application-layer metadata, in order to evade detection from a security monitor. In this paper, we show that victim-aware adaptive covert channels break the underlying assumptions of existing covert channel detection solutions, thereby exposing a lack of detection mechanisms against this threat. We first propose a toolchain, CHAMELEON, to create synthetic datasets containing victim-aware adaptive covert channel traffic. Armed with CHAMELEON, we evaluate state-of-the-art detection solutions and we show that they fail to effectively detect stealthy attacks. The design of detection techniques against these stealthy attacks is challenging because their network characteristics are similar to those of benign traffic. We explore a deception-based detection technique that we call HONEYTRAFFIC, which generates network messages containing *honey tokens*, while mimicking the victim's communication. Our approach detects victim-aware adaptive covert channels by observing inconsistencies in such tokens, which are induced by the attacker attempting to mimic the victim's traffic. Although HONEYTRAFFIC has limitations in detecting victim-aware adaptive covert channels, it complements existing detection methods and, in combination with them, it can to make evasion harder for an attacker.

Keywords: Intrusion detection system · Network security ·
Covert channels

1 Introduction

Malicious software requires network communication in order to perform many of its functionalities [1]. For instance, bots receive instructions from Command and Control (C&C) servers [2], ransomware downloads encryption keys from remote locations [3], and information stealers exfiltrate data to external servers [4].

© ICST Institute for Computer Sciences, Social Informatics and Telecommunications Engineering 2019
Published by Springer Nature Switzerland AG 2019. All Rights Reserved
S. Chen et al. (Eds.): SecureComm 2019, LNICST 304, pp. 450–471, 2019.
https://doi.org/10.1007/978-3-030-37228-6_22

Malware activities last as long as security monitoring products do not identify the suspicious behavior. Consequently, attackers implement techniques to evade network monitoring tools to pursue their malicious activities for a longer period of time. These techniques are known as *covert channels* [5]. Attackers can in fact make their communication stealthier by applying advanced techniques that morph network messages into "benign-looking" traffic. We call this type of channels *adaptive covert channels*. Adaptation can be performed in two ways: *a priori adaptation* and *victim-aware adaptation*.

The most common type of adaptation is *a priori adaptation*, where the attacker implements her communication to look like benign software or protocol *before* compromising any machine. The anti-censorship community provides several examples [6,7]. Wright et al. [8] proposed to modify the packet sizes distribution of one class of applications in order to resemble another class. Moghaddam et al. [9] and Weinberg et al. [10] proposed two tools to camouflage TOR traffic as Skype and HTTP protocols, respectively. Examples can also be found in known malware samples, which mimic predefined, well-known applications, such as the Windows and Yahoo Messenger protocol [11], or common browsers.

However, there exist detection techniques that detect covert channels by modeling the normal network behavior of a monitored host (i.e., potential future victims) [12–14]. These techniques detect a priori adaptation because the choice of adapting to a specific application does not necessarily match the behavior of the victim. Thus, the adaptive covert channel would show different network characteristics from the victim traffic. An a priori adaptation technique can avoid detection if the detection model is known. In this setting, Fogla et al. [15,16] proposed polymorphic blending attacks (PBA), a technique to adapt shellcode payloads to fit the statistical representation of normal traffic embedded in the detection model. However, the detection model is not always available. In this work, we focus on more advanced techniques that evade detection without knowing the detection model details.

Covert channel detection systems mainly rely on two methodologies. *(1) Supervised learning* approaches analyze the characteristics of benign and malicious traffic to create a model that can reliably identify and distinguish characteristics between the two groups [17]. This approach is common and also effective, because the majority of covert channels preserve the same distinctive network characteristics in its messages. On the other hand, *(2) semi-supervised learning* approaches only rely on benign data, and the generated model describes the common characteristics of benign traffic [12,14]. Although this approach is usually less precise than the aforementioned one, it can successfully identify unknown covert channels, when their characteristics differ from benign data used for training. Nonetheless, both methodologies implicitly rely on the assumption that malicious traffic shows distinguishing patterns from benign traffic. *What happens if the malicious covert channel takes benign traffic characteristics of its victim into account to generate its messages?*

Victim-aware adaptation (VAA) occurs when malicious channels mimic the observed victim traffic to bypass detection. Casenove [18] proposed a technique called polymorphic blending technique (PBT) that is based on PBA [15]. PBT learns the statistical representation of normal TCP payloads from the victim traffic. The data to be transmitted is then encoded using byte frequency distribution such that the payload statistical byte distribution is similar to the victim traffic. However, PBT does not preserve the correct syntax of the application layer protocol, including its metadata. By substituting bytes in the payload, the syntax of the messages may be disrupted. Similarly, also PBA does not try to resemble a message syntactically similar to the victim traffic, but focuses on the byte frequency distribution. Consequently, detection systems that rely on application layer information for detection (e.g., [12,14,17]) could detect PBT due to corrupted messages (e.g., unparsable syntax) or unrecognizable byte sequences. Yarochkin et al. [19] propose to use covert channels over different protocols depending on the protocols used by the victim. Although their solution adapts to the victim, they do not consider to mimic the victim messages, thus their content would show deviating characteristics from the victim traffic and the covert channel would be detected.

In this work we investigate the ineffectiveness of state-of-the-art covert channel detection mechanisms against VAA covert channels, where the attacker mimics the syntax of the victim messages. Although we are not aware of malware families using VAA covert channels, there exist malware families capable of sniffing and manipulating their victim traffic [20,21]. Moreover, we explore a deception-based technique to detect VAA covert channels, which relies on different assumptions than existing detection method. Our technique is complementary to existing detection methods. The combination of our proposed technique and existing detection solutions provides better protection against VAA covert channels than existing solutions used as standalone techniques.

As part of our investigation of VAA covert channels, we introduce CHAMELEON, a toolchain to generate synthetic datasets containing data exfiltration attacks over VAA covert channels. CHAMELEON generates exfiltration attacks by mimicking legitimate traffic at the application layer. Then, we use the synthetic dataset to evaluate three HTTP-based detection techniques [12,14,17], which are based on semi-supervised [12,14] and supervised learning [17]. We focus the efforts of our evaluation on HTTP, because a vast majority of malware implements its communication channels over HTTP [1,22]. Moreover, from the attacker's point of view, the evasion techniques should work even in case a defender has full access to the plaintext data (e.g., via a TLS-proxy). Our evaluation shows that existing approaches are not suitable for detecting VAA data exfiltration attacks, because these attacks break the underlying assumptions of the detection methods. The results show that existing solutions either do not detect the attack or have a false positive rate above 7%, rendering them impractical in practice. Finally, we propose HONEYTRAFFIC, a deception-based detection against VAA covert channels. HONEYTRAFFIC consists of a client-side component that generates traffic containing *honey tokens*. When an advanced attacker mimics the victim traffic, she ends up mimicking honey tokens, which can in turn be easily detected. This produces inconsistencies that can be detected by our monitor. Following [23], there are no comparable network-based deception techniques. We evaluate our approach against the adaptation strategies implemented by CHAMELEON in a worst-case scenario. The results show that HONEY-TRAFFIC can detect specific strategies of VAA covert channels. HONEYTRAFFIC makes it harder for VAA attackers to evade detection, but not impossible.

Our main contribution lies in the implementation of CHAMELEON and the evaluation of existing detection solutions. Code and dataset will be made publicly available. VAA covert channels are a serious threat that is hard to detect. HONEYTRAFFIC is a first attempt to their detection and it allows for the detection of some, but not all, VAA covert channels, thereby making attackers evasion more difficult. However, VAA covert channels remain a threat hard to detect.

2   CHAMELEON

The main goal of our work is to evaluate the effectiveness of VAA covert channels against existing detection solutions that use benign traffic to learn detection models. For this purpose, we present CHAMELEON, a toolchain that generates traffic samples containing data exfiltration attacks over VAA covert channels. We use CHAMELEON to evaluate existing network-based detection solutions. We introduce CHAMELEON since we are not aware of malware samples using VAA covert channels.

The core observation behind CHAMELEON is the following. Detection solutions, both supervised and semi-supervised, often learn detection models from the network characteristics of (non-compromised) machines. The network traffic of a machine is generated by the applications installed on it. Thus, CHAMELEON can generate network messages that mimic their application-layer metadata (e.g., using same headers and values), and then it can secretly hide data in the mimicked messages. Since such messages share the similar characteristics as those used to learn the detection model, the security monitor will not be able to effectively detect the covert channel. In other words, CHAMELEON fits the detection model by mimicking the victim traffic, similarly to PBA [15]. However, CHAMELEON does not require access to the detection model and focuses on the syntax of messages and not their byte distribution.

2.1   Threat Model

We assume the attacker establishes a hidden communication channel to bypass a security monitor. The attacker controls both client and server, and the monitor can read all communications as plaintext (e.g., via a TLS proxy [24]). The attacker can observe the network traffic of the compromised host and mimics its network messages. Hence, we assume the attacker has enough privileges on the victim to read its network interface. Although this requirement is not typically trivial to satisfy for an attacker, there are attackers with such capabilities [20,21]. This does not imply that the attacker has system privileges on the compromised machine. This can occur, for instance, when sniffing tools (e.g., tcpdump) are

given the permission and capability to allow raw packet captures (e.g., `setcap`
`cap_net_raw`,`cap_net_admin`). Lastly, in this work we assume that the attacker
only adapts outgoing traffic. We analyze a unidirectional VAA covert channel,
because it is enough to bypass existing detection systems.

2.2   System Overview

CHAMELEON takes a network trace as input and embeds in it the traffic of a VAA
covert channel. The new trace is used to evaluate detection systems, because it
contains normal traffic, from the original trace, and the exfiltration of data over
a VAA covert channel.

CHAMELEON works in two steps. The first step is *Adaptive Traffic Generation*, which involves a client and a server. The client follows two alternating
phases: during the *collection* phase it reads the network trace provided as input,
and during the *blending* phase it generates the adapted network messages. This
terminology was introduced by Casanove [18]. Then, the adapted messages are
sent to the server, which responds to the client. The second step is *Traffic Integration*, which involves a set of tools used to modify network traces. These tools
are used to integrate the adapted traffic, stored in a temporary trace, into the
original trace. Currently, CHAMELEON is implemented to work for HTTP traffic.

We decided to design CHAMELEON as a "dataset generator", so we could
generate datasets including VAA covert channels traffic by using only network
captures. This allows us to obtain datasets from machines running different
operating systems and applications, and to easily test defensive mechanisms in
different settings. This makes it also easier for other researchers to generate
VAA covert channel datasets without requiring a dedicated machine on which
CHAMELEON needs to run. Instead, previously captured network traffic can be
injected with adapted traffic to analyze.

2.3   Adaptive Traffic Generation

As in any covert channel, client and server need to share a set of parameters
before communicating in order to identify the hidden data from the messages.
Moreover, an adaptive client may use a set of message parameters to specify its
way of communicating. Below we discuss the setup parameters, message parameters and the client implementation. Since our work focuses on unidirectional VAA
covert channels, where only the client adapts to the victim, CHAMELEON implements the server as a listener that returns a default response.

Setup Parameters. SP *are shared* between the adaptive client and server
before any communication is established. These parameters provide the basic
information for the client and the server to identify the hidden data within the
network messages. They are defined as $SP = \langle p, e \rangle$. For each network protocol
p, the adaptive client and the server share a list of encoding algorithms e. The
parameter e also contains a delimiter to identify where the hidden data "starts".

Message Parameters. MP *are not shared* between client and server. They are used to specify how messages should be crafted in the collection and blending phases such that they appear to be legitimate messages, while hiding secret information. In this work, MP are only set at the client side. Here $MP = \langle c, s, l, i, b, a \rangle$, where c is the timeout of the collection phase; s is the maximum size of the data to embed in each message (i.e., bit-rate of the covert channel); l is the location where the exfiltrated data is embedded (e.g., URI, headers, body); i is the delay between sending out messages; b is the timeout for the blending phase; and a is the type of application the attacker wants to mimic (e.g., Firefox).

Client Implementation. Figure 1 gives an overview about the process generating adapted messages in CHAMELEON. During the collection phase, CHAMELEON selects an application a to mimic. All messages from a are collected based on the `User-Agent` field. CHAMELEON stores the list of header fields and the values associated to each header in the *header set* and *header-value dictionary*, respectively. The collected information and the data that needs to be transmitted (e.g., file to exfiltrate) are passed to the blending phase, which encodes the data using scheme e and splits the file into chunks of size s, obtaining a set of *data items*. Before each data item is transmitted, a template is generated. A template represents a set of headers, and their associated values, that aim at mimicking the victim traffic. An example of template is shown in Fig. 1 with green color font. Headers are chosen randomly from the header set, while the associated values are randomly chosen from the header-value dictionary. The data item to transmit (i.e., the covert message) is inserted in the location, within the template, indicated by the parameter l (highlighted in red in Fig. 1), thereby generating the adapted message. Thus, CHAMELEON *inserts data in a single message location*, in order to maximize the mimicked parts of the message. Finally, the adapted message is sent out to the server using interval i. After b seconds, the process restarts from the collection phase to mimic the most recent traffic. The server retrieves the message by identifying the delimited described in the setup parameter e and extracting the adjacent data.

Our implementations uses HTTP and base64 as setup parameters. Message parameters MP can be set before running the client and the server. Please note that whoever establishes a covert channel is also in control of both client and server behavior. Therefore, *an attacker may use the protocol in a way that is semantically wrong, but she can still communicate successfully.* For example, the client can generate HTTP GET requests for resources that do not exist on the server, but the server may still provide a valid response (e.g., 200 OK).

2.4 Traffic Integration

The second step CHAMELEON performs is the integration of the VAA traffic, observed between client and server, into the original trace provided as input. First, the traffic of the VAA channel is captured using `tcpdump`, and it is stored into a temporary network trace. Then, the IP addresses in the temporary trace are rewritten according to the victim's IP contained in the original trace using `tcprewrite`. Similarly, the timestamps are rewritten in order to fit the time period of the original trace, and we achieve this using `editcap`. Finally, now that both traces are consistent in terms of IP address and timestamps, we merge them using `mergecap`. These tools are part of the Wireshark suite. The final trace contains labeled victim's traffic and the attack, thereby being ideal for an evaluation of detection systems.

3   Experimental Evaluation

3.1   Dataset

For the generation of the dataset, we need network traces of benign traffic representing different hosts, and thus, potential victims. We choose the dataset published by Sharafaldin et al. [25] for this purpose. The reasons behind this choice are the following: (1) it contains traffic from multiple hosts over a time period of a week, allowing defenses to be trained with the traffic of the beginning of the week, and to be tested on the rest; (2) it contains traffic emulating user behavior and it contains different type of machines (e.g., servers and workstations); and (3) it is publicly available, so our generated dataset can be publicly released, without compromising any user privacy, making our work easier to be reproduced.

We extracted from the dataset of Sharafaldin et al. [25] all the outbound traffic generated by 9 different hosts. For each host, we obtained 5 days of network

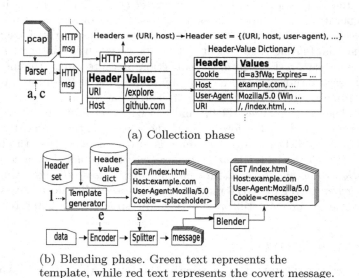

(a) Collection phase

(b) Blending phase. Green text represents the template, while red text represents the covert message.

Fig. 1. Overview of the VAA covert channel implementation by Chameleon. (Color figure online)

Table 1. Mimicking strategies applied in our dataset.

Host ID	file [KB]	c [s]	s [B]	l	i [s]	b [s]	a
5	500	5	128	H	0.00	∞	M
8	50	5	0–128	U	0–5.00	∞	B
9	50	5	128	B	0.00	5	M
12	500	5	128	H	0.00	∞	N
16	50	5	0–128	U	0–5.00	∞	N
17	500	5	0–128	B	0–1.00	∞	B
25	500	5	0–128	U	0–0.05	5	B
50	500	5	0–128	H	0–0.05	5	B
51	500	5	0–128	B	0–0.05	5	B

traffic (from Monday to Friday), where each day of traffic is a single network trace. For each host, we choose a different set of message parameters MP, which represents a *strategy* a VAA covert channel may use to communicate. We ran CHAMELEON using each host's network trace and defining the MP according to the strategy assigned to the host. Overall, the dataset resulted in 45 pcap traces containing both our VAA covert channels and hosts traffic. The dataset contains 16.6 GB of network traffic, of which 476 MB (120k HTTP requests) originate from the adapted communications.

Table 1 lists the message parameters of each strategy applied to each host. The column *file* indicates the size of the file we transmitted during the adaptive communication. The values of l are denoted by B for body, H for a random header, U for URI parameters and M for a random choice between header and URI. While the values of a are given as B for browser, N for non-browser, or M for a mix of both. The strategies represents different exfiltration scenarios. Such scenarios include data exfiltration of files large 50 Kb and 500 Kb at different speeds, exfiltration locations, and application types. For instance, strategies for hosts 8 and 16 wait up to 5 s between sending messages, whereas strategies for hosts 5, 9, and 12 do not wait between attempts at all.

Existing Detection Solutions. The three detection solutions are: DUMONT [14], DECANTeR [12], and HED [17]. We selected these tools from the state-of-the-art for three reasons: (1) their detection models rely on HTTP traffic characteristics that include payload and headers, and (2) their detection models leverage benign traffic information; and (3) they cover both semi-supervised (DUMONT and DECANTeR) and supervised learning (HED). The implementation of DUMONT and DECANTeR are available online, while we obtained the code of HED from the authors.

DUMONT generates a detection model for each monitored host, and the model is a One-class SVM that describes the HTTP network characteristics according to several numerical features representing different location of HTTP requests (e.g., headers, URI, Body). DECANTeR models the traffic of each monitored host by fingerprinting installed applications after observing their traffic, and the fingerprints describe different network features of the application. HED generates a binary SVM classifier given two sets of traffic, representing "normal" and covert channel traffic, respectively. The binary SVM relies on more than a thousand features related to HTTP requests to create the model. We refer the reader to the original works for additional information on these systems.

Evaluation Setup. We evaluate the classification performance of each detection tool in terms of *accuracy* (ACC), *false positive rate* (FPR), *true positive rate* (TPR), *detected attack* (DA) and *detected strategy* (DS). An attack is detected if at least one HTTP request is triggered as malicious within a single traffic sample. A strategy is detected if at least one HTTP request is flagged as malicious within *all* the four traffic samples of that specific strategy. We compute the number of true positives (TP), false positives (FP), true negatives (TN), and false negatives (FN), for the whole dataset.

The detection systems has been evaluated as follows. For DUMONT, we first train a model for each host using the first half of the benign training data of the Monday sample. Then, we calibrate the DUMONT model using the same amount of malicious and benign data present in the second half of the Monday sample[1]. We test the remaining four samples, from the same host, against the model and we collect the results. Similarly, for DECANTeR we train the models using the benign traffic of the Monday sample. Then, we test the remaining four samples for each host and we collect the results. For HED we train a single model for all hosts using their Monday samples, and we evaluate it against the remaining samples. However, if we generate a supervised model from a set of known VAA malicious samples, we train the model to detect the malicious samples in the context of their specific victims. Hence, *it is not guaranteed that the same samples are effectively detected in the future*, because their traffic may look different if they affect other victims. Thus, we evaluate HED in two different scenarios representing two deployment assumptions. The first scenario is HED_{pk}, assuming HED has *partial knowledge* of the malicious traffic, thus the training model contains all benign host traffic but only a subset of malicious traffic. In our evaluation we randomly excluded four hosts' malicious traffic (i.e., host 50, 12, 8 and 25 in Table 1). The second scenario, HED_{tk}, assumes HED has *total knowledge* of the malicious hosts' traffic, so the training model contains all benign and malicious traffic. HED_{pk} is a more realistic scenario, because it assumes that the defender does not know all the characteristics of a VAA attacker beforehand.

3.2   Results

We consider a solution to be effective if it has a true positive rate higher than 70% and a false positive rate lower than 2%. A high TPR means that it is unlikely that the attack is going to be missed. Thus, in practice a low TPR can be very costly for a company. A low FPR means the detection solution rarely triggers

---

[1] Please note that in the original work [14] there is no clear guidance about the quantities of data needed for the calibration step.

false alarms. According to Sommer and Paxson, in their seminal work about IDSs and machine learning in real environments [26], limiting false positives must be a top priority of any IDSs. Table 2 shows the overall detection performance of the evaluated detection solutions for all the 9 strategies. Table 3 shows a detailed overview about detection performance per strategy.

Semi-supervised Learning. DECANTeR and DUMONT are not effective in detecting VAA covert channels, as shown in Table 2. The main reason is that adaptation allows the malware to camouflage its characteristics with those of the victim. Thus, the malware fits the trained model and breaks the fundamental assumption of anomaly detection, namely that malware shows different patterns than benign traffic.

DECANTeR is not effective against CHAMELEON because its classification system is based on specific associations of *some* header fields and values. Since CHAMELEON uses existing associations of header fields and values in its template, DECANTeR considers adapted messages as generated by installed applications. CHAMELEON can exfiltrate data through the URI, Body, Accept, and other headers, without being detected, as long as the "key" header values (i.e., Host, User-Agent, Accept-Language) match the fingerprint values. If data is hidden within such "key" headers, then DECANTeR likely detects the adapted traffic. The most successful strategies involved the mimicking of background applications. The reason behind is that adapted messages had the same headers sequences, same Host values and User-Agent, which are three fundamental features for background application fingerprinting in DECANTeR. By adapting to the victim's traffic, CHAMELEON completely avoided detection in two cases (strategies 12 and 16), as shown in Table 3. DECANTeR also performs poorly for strategies 5 and 9, when the malware randomly adapts to different applications.

DUMONT is not effective against CHAMELEON because its classification system mostly relies on statistical features describing the length and structure of different parts of a message (i.e., headers, URI and Body), their entropy, and the average length of header and URI values. The template created by CHAMELEON contains data with similar statistical characteristics, because it comes from the same applications. Thus, the data contained in the template help hiding adaptive traffic from detection. Therefore, if CHAMELEON also hides data in locations that typically contain large amounts of data such as Body and URI), then CHAMELEON is likely to fit the trained length characteristics learned by the model, and it avoids detection. Overall, DUMONT misses almost a third of the samples. It misses all the samples for strategies 16 and 9, likely due to the small amount of data being exfiltrated. Although DUMONT detects some malicious requests for strategies 5, 8, 25 and 50, the vast majority of malicious requests are still not detected. This justifies the low accuracy.

Supervised Learning. HED yields the best results in terms of detection. All the samples are detected. The extra attack knowledge used to create the model helps HED to improve its performance. However, the FPR for both scenarios is 2 or 3 time higher than for other solutions, making HED not effective against CHAMELEON. In the original paper [17], HED showed a FPR of 0.01% against non-VAA covert channels. In our evaluation *the FPR increases two orders of magnitude*. The reason behind the high FPR is the similar statistical representations of benign and adapted *messages*. Templates contain data statistically very similar to the one used in training, because it is data from the same application. Thus, when the model is generated, it is difficult to find a decision function that can reliably separate the two classes of traffic. Moreover, due to high number of requests observed in HTTP traffic and the inherent heterogeneity of HTTP, HED often misclassifies benign HTTP traffic as malicious. Table 2 shows that HED in its ideal setting HED_{tk}, where all strategies are known during training phase, achieves 96% accuracy. The accuracy is not 100% because HED_{tk} generates FPs due to the similarities between benign and malicious messages. However, in the more realistic setting HED_{pk}, the accuracy is 89%, where only some strategies are known at training time. This 7% accuracy drop is due to the lack of knowledge about new adaptive strategies. As shown in Table 3 the true positive rate is lower for strategies 8, 25, and 50, which were excluded from the training dataset.

Lessons Learned. *Our evaluation shows that existing defensive mechanisms are not effective against detecting VAA covert channels*, because they cannot effectively detect them while, at the same time, triggering few false alerts. Semi-supervised learning solutions are not effective against VAA attackers, because malicious traffic fits the model of benign communication, and thus, malicious connections are not flagged as anomalies. Supervised learning solutions are not effective for two reasons. First, the classes in the training dataset are represented by similar sets of data, thus there is not a clear distinction between the two classes features, which is a fundamental requirement for supervised approaches to be effective. Second, the VAA covert channel data used during the training of the system may not be representative for successive attacks, since the attacker mimics the traffic of new victims, which may show different network patterns. Both issues are present in HED: the first is highlighted by the high FPR, while the second is described by the accuracy drop between the two HED scenarios HED_{tk} and HED_{pk}.

Limitations. CHAMELEON has three main limitations. First, it only mimics the content of network packets and not the interaction between client and server. A

Table 2. Overall performance of existing defenses in terms of accuracy (ACC), false positive rate (FPR) and detected attacks (DA).

Existing defense	Performance			
	Acc	TPR	FPR	DA
DUMONT	49%	10%	2%	17/35
DECANTeR	70%	50%	3%	12/35
HED_{pk}	89%	85%	7%	35/35
HED_{tk}	96%	93%	7%	35/35

Table 3. Overall performance of DUMONT, DECANTeR, HED_{pk} and HED_{tk} per strategy, in terms of true positive rate (TPR), false positive rate (FPR) and detected strategies (DS) (× represents a missed strategy).

Strategies	DUMONT			DECANTeR			HED_{pk}			HED_{tk}		
	TPR	FPR	DS	TPR	FPR	DS	TPR	FPR	DS	TPR	FPR	DS
5	0.001	0.01	✓	0.50	0.02	✓	0.99	0.06	✓	0.50	0.02	✓
8	0.005	0.01	✓	0.18	0.05	✓	0.50	0.05	✓	0.99	0.07	✓
9	0.000	0.01	×	0.09	0.05	✓	0.98	0.07	✓	0.99	0.07	✓
12	0.133	0.03	✓	0.00	0.00	×	0.99	0.07	✓	0.99	0.05	✓
16	0.000	0.01	×	0.00	0.03	×	0.98	0.07	✓	0.99	0.07	✓
17	0.371	0.03	✓	0.51	0.03	✓	0.99	0.10	✓	0.98	0.09	✓
25	0.023	0.01	✓	0.61	0.02	✓	0.55	0.12	✓	1.00	0.10	✓
50	0.001	0.03	✓	0.78	0.31	✓	0.68	0.04	✓	0.93	0.14	✓
51	0.150	0.06	✓	1.00	0.03	✓	0.99	0.10	✓	0.99	0.05	✓

detection mechanism that models client-server interactions may effectively detect CHAMELEON. However, web traffic is heterogeneous and inconsistent client-server interactions may be frequent, considering the large volumes of web traffic. Thus, designing an effective heuristic is non trivial. Second, CHAMELEON does not implement the concept of connection state. However, this limitation does not affect CHAMELEON over HTTP, because it is challenging to reliably monitor, for detection purposes, HTTP connection states (i.e., Cookies) due to the high heterogeneity of their usage and values across different web services. Third, CHAMELEON can be detected using signatures or dedicated heuristics to identify specific patterns in the tool implementation. A simple example is to create a signature to the static server response. As discussed by Houmansadr et al. [6], this is always possible for defenders to detect mimicking techniques. However, these detection approaches are easy to evade since they rely on implementation details rather than on the underlying patterns of the exfiltration technique.

Finally, it may seem trivial to detect CHAMELEON using heuristics that identify replicated content in network messages. However, this is not the case due to some challenges that defenders must take into account: (1) benign applications regularly generate similar messages over time (e.g., scripts uploading data or downloading dynamic content), (2) defenders would have to monitor large quantities of data and keep a detailed historical record for each host; and (3) CHAMELEON is a tool that can be configured with different parameters (e.g., increase delay to enforce larger historical analysis for defenders). These challenges makes it non-trivial to effectively detect VAA covert channels using heuristics that rely on passive network traffic analysis.

4   Honey Traffic

We introduce the concept of HONEYTRAFFIC, a deception-based mitigation against VAA covert channels. We propose to *turn the table on the attacker* and make the challenging task of detecting VAA covert channel her problem, while we use her offensive techniques for the purpose of detection.

The intuition of HONEYTRAFFIC is that we can generate network messages that mimic existing applications and, at the same time, contain secret tokens. Thus, the attacker, while adapting to the victim's traffic, includes such tokens in its messages. A security monitor, which is aware of the tokens and knows how to identify them, can detect the presence of messages containing tokens generated by "unknown" clients, thereby detecting the VAA covert channel.

The goal of HONEYTRAFFIC is to detect the class of VAA covert channels represented by CHAMELEON, where the attacker mimics existing messages and embeds the secret data to exfiltrate in one of the message locations. HONEY-TRAFFIC is not intended to detect all possible types of VAA covert channels. More importantly, HONEYTRAFFIC *is not intended to detect covert channels that do not adapt to the victim.* Such threat scenario is already covered by existing approaches (e.g., [12,14,17] for HTTP). Hence, we consider HONEYTRAF-FIC to be a *complementary* solution to existing detection approaches. As other deception-based techniques, such as honeypots, stack canary or canary tokens, HONEYTRAFFIC relies on the assumption that an attacker cannot distinguish between fake and real items. Although canary and honey tokens are conceptually similar, they protect different aspects of the information system. Canary tokens trigger alerts if decoy files are accessed, while HONEYTRAFFIC triggers alerts if someone copied network messages. In case an attacker accesses common files (i.e., not decoys) and exfiltrates them over an adaptive covert channel, canary tokens do not trigger alerts, while HONEYTRAFFIC can.

Assumptions. We assume there exists a *honey client* installed on each machine (i.e., potential victim). The honey client generates network messages mimicking the machine's traffic. In other words, the honey client establishes VAA communication channels. Moreover, we assume there exists a *honey server* and a security monitor (e.g., next-generation firewall or NIDS). The monitor is usually already part of the company's infrastructure. The honey server can establish secure communications with both the honey client and the security monitor to provide the setup information. As discussed in Sect. 2.1, VAA covert channels, such as CHAMELEON, assume a strong defenders capable of accessing all communication in plaintext. Thus, we assume HONEYTRAFFIC to be capable of accessing the communication in plaintext (e.g, using a TLS proxy).

We assume the attacker compromises a machine where a honey client is installed, and we assume the attacker is aware of the presence of honey messages. However, the attacker does not know the list of honey tokens. We consider the attacker to be not capable of running advanced detection heuristics on the infected machine to identify the presence of honey tokens. It is not realistic to assume an attacker can run advanced detection heuristics like a host-based intrusion detection, while trying to hide its presence.

4.1   System Overview

HONEYTRAFFIC is composed by three main components: a client, installed on each monitored host, a server and a security monitor. We refer to the client and server as *honey client* and *honey server*, respectively. The system works in two alternating phases: a setup phase and a detection phase. The setup phase is responsible for delivering the information necessary to run the detection mechanism to each component. During the detection phase, the system monitors the network to spot adaptive covert channels.

Setup Phase. The *honey server* is the main component during the setup phase. It is responsible for the generation of all the information needed to run the detection system. The honey server generates a set of *honey tokens*, a set of random IP addresses, the setup and message parameters (SP and MP), and a set of *honey signatures* (e.g., regex) to identify the tokens in the network traffic. The random IP generation process excludes existing network nodes that may trigger network errors from existing machines using the chosen IPs, or by network devices that know these IPs do not exist. This precaution is needed to avoid attackers being able to easily identify honey traffic. Then, the server securely communicates the tokens, IP addresses, and setup and message parameters to the honey client, while it sends the signatures to the security monitor.

The setup phase reoccurs after a specified time period to *substitute old tokens and signatures with new ones*. In other words, the system updates regularly its key detection material. In case the setup phase is repeated after a short time (e.g., a day), it becomes difficult for an attacker to identify honey tokens.

Honey Client Communications. Upon receiving the information from the server, the *honey client* starts collecting information about the machine's traffic (collection phase). Once enough information is collected, the client creates a template for its network messages that resembles the machine's traffic, and it embeds the honey tokens within the template (blending phase). In other words, the honey client follows the same process of the VAA covert channel client discussed in Sect. 2.3. In this process it uses the SP and MP parameters provided by the honey server. Lastly, the client spoofs the destination IP of its messages using one of the addresses provided by the server, and it sends the messages.

Detection Phase. Once the security monitor receives the signatures from the honey server, it starts monitoring the network traffic. Whenever the security monitor identifies a honey token (*signature hit*), it redirects the message to the honey server for further inspection. Assuming the tokens are unique strings generated by the honey client, which is a common assumption in signature-based detection, a signature hit can be triggered for two reasons: either the token was included by the honey client or from a malicious adaptive application. If the message has as destination one of the random IP addresses generated during the

GET /pypi/v/dpkt.svg HTTP 1.1

Host: img.shields.io
User-Agent: Mozilla/5.0 ... Firefox 54.0
Accept: */*
Accept-Languate: en-US;q=0.5,en;q=0.3
Accept-Encoding: gzip, deflate
Cookie:__cfduid=dce101b3e09a9a09d5dbf
2afed17dcdc71413792427910
Connection: keep-alive

a)

GET /pypi/adlogin_page/v/dpkt.svg HTTP 1.1

Host: img.shields.io
User-Agent: Mozilla/5.0 ... Firefox 54.0
Accept: */*
Accept-Languate: en-US;q=0.5,en;q=0.3
Accept-Encoding: gzip, deflate
Cookie:__cfduid=dce101b3e09a9a09d5dbf2afe
d17dcdc71413792427910; timestamp=13 Nov
2018; 10:00
Connection: keep-alive

b)

GET /pypi/adlogin_page/v/dpkt.svg HTTP 1.1

Host: img.shields.io
User-Agent: Mozilla/5.0 ... Firefox 54.0
Accept: */*
Accept-Languate: en-US;q=0.5,en;q=0.3
Cookie:__cfduid=RXVybyBJRUVFIFMmUCAyMD
E4IFN1Ym1pc3Npb24h
Connection: keep-alive

c)

Fig. 2. Example of HONEYTRAFFIC. (a) represents an example of a message from an existing application. (b) depicts a honey message, which mimics an existing application but also embeds the honey tokens (in red). (c) shows a malicious message that adapts to the victim's traffic, which includes its secret data (in blue) and an undetected honey token (in red). (Color figure online)

setup phase, then the message is generated by the honey client. Otherwise, the message is generated by an adaptive application. Since the attacker's goal is to communicate with servers she controls, it is very unlikely one of her destinations matches with one of the randomly generated IP addresses.

In case the message is identified as originating from the honey client, the server answers with a standard response. It is important that the responses are not static and look like legitimate traffic, to avoid that the attacker easily identifies honey communications. The response is needed because the IP is spoofed, and a real destination is not reached. In case the message is considered malicious, the server triggers an alert.

4.2   Example of Honey Traffic

Let us assume the honey server generates three different tokens: (1) "/adlogin_page/", as a subfolder of a URI path; (2) "timestamp: 13 Nov 2018; 10:00", as a COOKIE parameter; and (3) "686897696a7c976b7e", as a ETAG value. The honey server also generates: (i) a list of fake destination IP addresses [192.168.1.100, 23.45.21.32, 142.59.23.1]; and (ii) signatures for a NIDS to identify each honey token. For instance, using Snort syntax, the following can be a signature for the first token: *alert tcp any any -> any 80 (msg: "HONEY token 1"; content: "/adlogin_page/"; http_uri; sid:2000001;)*. The honey tokens, signatures and list of fake destination IPs are shared with the honey client and the NIDS.

Now assume that during the *detection phase* the honey client mimics a message of an existing application (Fig. 2a), and it embeds two different honey tokens in the message. The message is then sent over the network to the fake address: 23.45.21.32. Figure 2b shows how the message generated by the honey client may look like. Next, the security monitor, which analyzes each single message, finds two signature matches with the honey client, one per token. The monitor forwards the message to the honey server, which verifies that the destination IP is part of the set of random destination IPs generated during the setup phase. Hence, the message is considered to be generated by the honey client.

Now let us assume a malware uses an VAA covert channel to communicate with its server with IP 123.23.67.97. The malware sniffs the victim's traffic, and it observes the messages shown in Fig. 2a and b. It generates an adapted message, and it embeds the data to exfiltrate in the `Cookie` (see Fig. 2c), and it sends it to 123.23.67.97. In this scenario, the security monitor finds one signature, because the token in the `URI` (i.e., "/adlogin_page/" in red in Fig. 2c) is present in the message. The monitor forwards the message to the honey server, which marks the message as malicious because it has a destination address that does not match with those created during the setup phase.

4.3 Generating Honey Tokens

HONEYTRAFFIC is an effective defensive mechanism against VAA attackers, if the honey tokens cannot be reliably detected by an attacker. Thus, a honey token must be a sequence of bytes that is unlikely to appear in traffic generated by other applications. These sequences are not difficult to generate.

Although there are several possibilities to generate tokens, the best locations are those headers that are commonly used, but are often associated with different values. As analyzed by Borders and Prakash [27], a fixed fraction of HTTP connections contain high entropy data. Thus, *it is difficult even for an advanced attacker to discriminate whether the header values contains tokens or just benign traffic.* The headers that are commonly used in HTTP and have such properties are: `Host`, `Cookie`, `Referer`, `Body` and `URI`. For example, for `Host` we can generate a fake subdomain, or for the `Referer` we can generate a fake URL that was never requested before. These values are likely unique in the traffic. Other headers that can be used for honey tokens are: time-based headers (e.g., `If-Modified-Since`, `If-Unmodified-since`, `Date`), where the tokens are represented by timestamps, or headers related to check resources updates (e.g., `If-Match`, `If-None-Match`, `ETAG`), where the tokens are represented as random sequences of alphanumeric characters.

Honey tokens can be automatically generated by the honey server. *It is important that the server is aware of the expected syntax for the header value*, to avoid that malware notices simple format inconsistencies. Following the aforementioned examples, the server can use English words as subdomains to create `Host` tokens or as string in the URI path (e.g., Fig. 2b). Considering the large set of choices a defender has to generate honey tokens, the fact that tokens can be generated to be nearly indistinguishable from normal traffic, and the limited detection capabilities of the attacker, *it is unlikely the attacker can consistently detect honey tokens*. She would have to correlate the content of many messages, and identify patterns within a limited amount of time, because the setup phase periodically introduces new tokens. To complicate the detection even further, the honey client can use each token only once (i.e., one-time tokens), reducing the chances for the attacker to identify string patterns. In our analysis in Sect. 4.4 we discuss how much one-time tokens costs to the honey client. A single attacker mistake in judging the presence of a honey token costs her the detection.

4.4   Evaluation of Honey Traffic

HONEYTRAFFIC relies on the assumption that, sooner or later, an attacker adapts to messages including honey tokens. Thus, the detection of VAA covert channels is not deterministic but probabilistic. In order to evaluate HONEY-TRAFFIC, we make the following assumptions: (1) the attacker and the honey client mimic the traffic of a browser application, namely the *target application*; and (2) the honey client hides honey tokens into a fixed number of header values.

Attackers are more likely to adapt to browser traffic, because browsers generate a lot of traffic, thus it is easier for the attacker to hide. Moreover, browsers represent the worst-case scenario for HONEYTRAFFIC in terms of traffic overhead. The large volumes of browser traffic force honey clients to generate more traffic to detect a VAA attacker. Although we analyze HONEYTRAFFIC for a specific application, in practice, HONEYTRAFFIC should be generated for all communicating installed applications.

Applications can use different sets of headers during their communication. However, there is always a subset of headers that is used in all applications' network messages [12]. Thus, a honey client can use such headers to hide tokens in it. For example, browser traffic always contains a URI (i.e., needed to retrieve a web resource) and a Host value (i.e., domain to contact). Both headers contain data that changes very often, making it hard for an attacker to detect potential tokens. For this reason, we believe it is realistic to assume that a honey client can hide tokens in a fixed set of headers. Specifically, following the aforementioned example, we assume the honey client hides tokens in two different headers.

Attacker Strategies. The probability of detecting a VAA covert channel depends on the strategy an attacker uses to mimic application traffic. The attacker can mimic a message according to two different strategies: the attacker creates messages by combining the list of elements (e.g., headers and header values) that were previously observed from the target application, and substitutes one header value with her secret data; or the attacker copies one of the previously observed messages from the target application entirely, and hides her secret data in one of the message headers. Due to a lack of space, we discuss the evaluation of the former, which is the same used by CHAMELEON. Since we assume an attacker cannot distinguish honey traffic from normal traffic, the attacker chooses the values to adapt at random. For this reason, *our evaluation assumes that the attacker mimics messages, or elements, uniformly at random.*

Adaptation per Header. Let us assume the attacker runs a collection phase for a period of time c, where it collects: (i) a header set $L = \{L_1, \ldots, L_j\}$ where L_i represents a list of headers; and a list of values V_{head} containing all the values associated with header $head$ in the observed traffic. V_{head} also contains the observed honey tokens generated for header $head$ during c, which we define as t_{head}. After choosing a list of headers L_i, the attacker generates an adapted message by randomly choosing a header value from V_{head} for each corresponding $head \in L_i$. Then, the probability p to detect an adapted malicious message with this strategy is $p = 1 - \prod_{head \in L_i} (1 - \frac{t_{head}}{|V_{head}|})$.

The probability of detecting an attacker after sending x messages, during blending phase, can be modeled as a binomial distribution, and it can be defined as $P(\text{detection within } x \text{ messages}) = 1 - (1 - p)^x$.

Parameters. We now evaluate the effectiveness of honey traffic assuming the target application is a browser. First, we collected one hour of browsing activities using BurpSuite (e.g., streaming videos in the background and moderate web browsing) to estimate the number of requests an active browser may generate. We observed that roughly 2,200 requests were generated.

Consequently, within a collection timeout $c = 30\,\text{s}$, the number of requests a browser generates, which is also collected by the attacker, is 19. Therefore, we defined the number of application messages within c as $A_c = 19$. We choose a short collection timeout because malware may want to communicate closely to the benign application to avoid suspicion. Since we assume there are specific headers always present in application traffic, we define $|V_{head}| = A + t_{head}$, because the values observed from a single header contains all those generated by the normal application A and those generated by the honey client containing a token t_{head}. Finally, we evaluate our mitigation according to different amounts of honey messages generated during c. We define four cases, where the honey client generates 1, 2, 5, and 10 messages. The network overhead introduced by the honey client for these values is approximately 5%, 10%, 20% and 50%, respectively (e.g., for 19 browser messages in c, we introduce 1 honey message, which represent roughly the 5% of the browser traffic).

We want to remark that the detection probabilities are still influenced by the number of messages generated by the target application and the honey client, the collection timeout and how tokens are hidden. We evaluate HONEYTRAFFIC with the parameters mentioned above to estimate the practicality of this method.

Results. The results show that HONEYTRAFFIC can detect the attacker after few messages. The attacker can be detected with 80% probability after she sends 16 messages, costing only 1 message every 30 s. The increase of honey messages allows a faster detection. The results are shown in Fig. 3. Thus, it becomes problematic for an attacker to persist on the host, because she cannot perform many malicious operations before she is detected. Additionally, another important characteristic of honey traffic is that it generates almost no false positives, as long as tokens are unique in the traffic.

By multiplying the number of honey messages (within c) with the average size of an HTTP request, we can estimate how many kB/s our solution costs. Let us assume a pessimistic scenario, where the average size of a message is 1 kB. By using 0.03 kB/s (i.e., 5% overhead, 1 request in 30 s) of extra bandwidth, the attacker is detected with 90% probability after 23 messages. The overall daily cost in terms of bandwidth is 2.59 MB, for each browser we want to mimic in the network, and this is a worst-case scenario because we assume the browser is active 24 h. If we consider a 50% overhead, which is the pessimistic scenario in terms of bandwidth overhead, the bandwidth daily cost for a browser is 28.5 MB.

Table 4. Storage costs for the honey client, assuming each token is used only once (i.e., one-time tokens) and the setup phase is repeated once a week. We consider tokens to have an average size of 10 bytes.

Bandwidth overhead	Unique tokens	Storage size [kB]
5%	5760	403
10%	11520	806
20%	28800	2,016
50%	57600	4,032

The storage costs for the honey client are also relatively low. We evaluate a scenario where the setup phase waits one week to refresh the tokens, each token is used only once and is 10 bytes long. These are pessimistic settings since many tokens should be generated and hold in memory for a long time. For a bandwidth overhead of 50%, storing the tokens approximately costs 4,032 kB. A lower bandwidth of 5% has 403 kB of memory costs. Table 4 shows the costs in terms of storage of the honey traffic. In case the setup phase is executed more often, the memory costs decreases. For instance, a setup phase refreshing every day would cost 576 kB in case of a 50% bandwidth overhead.

This evaluation makes rough estimates about the performance of HONEY-TRAFFIC, and it shows that HONEYTRAFFIC is a practical solution against specific VAA attackers strategies with negligible false positive, low bandwidth overhead and memory costs. As discussed in the section below, HONEYTRAFFIC does not cover all the use cases of VAA covert channels, thus it cannot be considered a standalone solution. Note that this evaluation assumes the attacker adapts every time she sends a message. In case the attacker would send multiple messages with the same collected data, our evaluation still holds, but the X-axis of Fig. 3 should be interpreted as "adaptation attempts", instead of messages. Finally, note that this analysis assumes browser messages are evenly spread across different collection phases. We do not expect this to happen in practice, because the browser generates bursts of messages. Thus, some collection phases are more favorable to the attacker and some to the defender.

4.5   Evasion of Honey Traffic

Honey traffic cannot be proven secure, because we assume the attacker can run with high privileges, so, *in theory*, the malware can do anything on the compromised host. For instance, the attacker may be able to identify the process of honey client at system level and avoid mimicking packets that it generates. Nonetheless, we believe an attacker, especially if automated such as malware, faces severe difficulties in identifying the honey client, especially if properly hidden (e.g., by using rootkit techniques). The setup phase of the honey traffic is also a limitation, because the malware can get to know the list of tokens that will be used. However, also in this case, the malware must be aware of the presence

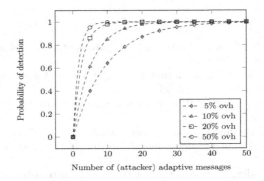

Fig. 3. Probability of VAA malware being detected by the number of messages it sends. The percentage values represent the overhead of honey messages, compared with the amount of browser traffic.

of the honey client on the system. Moreover, it should also be able to intercept and interpret the messages provided by the server.

Malware can evade honey traffic by generating its own traffic. However, by doing so the malware is not adapting, thus it would be detected by already existing techniques, as we discussed in Sect. 4. Alternatively, malware may try to corrupt, or even delete, the honey tokens by overwriting header values with valid strings, such that honey messages are never detected. This type of attacker is not represented by CHAMELEON, and thus it is not covered by HONEYTRAFFIC. Nonetheless, it remains unclear whether an attacker substituting several header values with randomly generated valid strings can still be considered "adaptive". The generation of these strings may introduce distinctive patterns that could be identified by existing solutions. Due to these uncovered VAA strategies, HONEY-TRAFFIC cannot be considered a standalone solution to detect VAA covert channels. However, it can complement existing detection methods to make evasions more difficult for VAA attackers and provide overall better network protection.

5   Conclusions

In this paper, we presented CHAMELEON, a (to be released) toolchain to generate synthetic datasets containing adaptive covert channels—attacks that aim at mimicking the legitimate traffic generated by the victim while hiding secret information without being detected by a security monitor. Leveraging CHAMELEON, we showed that current detection approaches are not suitable for such advanced attacks. In fact, adaptive covert channels break their underlying assumption that malicious traffic presents distinctive patterns from benign traffic. We then proposed HONEYTRAFFIC, a deception-based detection technique, which can complement existing detection mechanisms to make it harder, but not impossible, for attackers to evade detection using VAA covert channels.

References

1. Rossow, C., et al: Sandnet: network traffic analysis of malicious software. In: BAD-GERS, pp. 78–88. ACM (2011)
2. Stone-Gross, B., et al.: Your Botnet is my Botnet: analysis of a Botnet takeover. In: CCS, pp. 635–647. ACM (2009)
3. Continella, A., et al.: ShieldFS: a self-healing, ransomware-aware filesystem. In: ACSAC. ACM (2016)
4. Continella, A., Carminati, M., Polino, M., Lanzi, A., Zanero, S., Maggi, F.: Prometheus: analyzing webinject-based information stealers. J. Comput. Secur. **25**, 117–137 (2017)
5. Wendzel, S., Zander, S., Fechner, B., Herdin, C.: Pattern-based survey and categorization of network covert channel techniques. ACM CSUR **47**(3), 50 (2015)
6. Houmansadr, A., Brubaker, C., Shmatikov, V.: The parrot is dead: observing unobservable network communications. In: IEEE S&P, pp. 65–79 (2013)
7. Dyer, K.P., Coull, S.E., Ristenpart, T., Shrimpton, T.: Protocol misidentification made easy with format-transforming encryption. In: CCS, pp. 61–72. ACM (2013)
8. Wright, C.V., Coull, S.E., Monrose, F.: Traffic morphing: an efficient defense against statistical traffic analysis. In: NDSS (2009)
9. Moghaddam, H.M., Li, B., Derakhshani, M., Goldberg, I.: SkypeMorph: protocol obfuscation for tor bridges. In: ACM CCS 2012, pp. 97–108 (2012)
10. Weinberg, Z., Wang, J., Yegneswaran, V., Briesemeister, L., Cheung, S., Wang, F., Boneh, D.: StegoTorus: a camouflage proxy for the tor anonymity system. In: ACM CCS 2012, pp. 109–120 (2012)
11. FAKEM RAT: Malware Disguised as Windows Messenger and Yahoo! Messenger. https://www.trendmicro.de/cloud-content/us/pdfs/security-intelligence/white-papers/wp-fakem-rat.pdf
12. Bortolameotti, R. et al.: DECANTeR: detection of anomalous outbound HTTP traffic by passive application fingerprinting. In: ACSAC, pp. 373–386. ACM (2017)
13. Borders, K., Prakash, A.: Web tap: detecting covert web traffic. In: CCS, pp. 110–120. ACM (2004)
14. Schwenk, G., Rieck, K.: Adaptive detection of covert communication in http requests. In: EC2ND, pp. 25–32. IEEE (2011)
15. Fogla, P., Sharif, M.I., Perdisci, R., Kolesnikov, O.M., Lee, W.: Polymorphic blending attacks. In: USENIX Security 2006 (2006)
16. Fogla, P., Lee, W.: Evading network anomaly detection systems: formal reasoning and practical techniques. In: ACM CCS 2006, pp. 59–68 (2006)
17. Davis, J.J., Foo, E.: Automated feature engineering for HTTP tunnel detection. Comput. Secur. **59**, 166–185 (2016)
18. Casenove, M.: Exfiltrations using polymorphic blending techniques: analysis and countermeasures. In: Cyber Conflict: Architectures in Cyberspace (CyCon), pp. 217–230. IEEE (2015)
19. Yarochkin, F.V., Dai, S.-Y., Lin, C.-H., Huang, Y., Kuo, S.-Y.: Towards adaptive covert communication system. In: PRDC, pp. 153–159. IEEE (2008)
20. EMOTET Returns, Starts Spreading via Spam Botnet. https://blog.trendmicro.com/trendlabs-security-intelligence/emotet-returns-starts-spreading-via-spam-botnet/
21. PNFilter Malware Now Exploiting Endpoints, Not Just Routers. https://duo.com/decipher/vpnfilter-malware-now-exploiting-endpoints-not-just-routers

22. Zarras, A., Papadogiannakis, A., Gawlik, R., Holz, T.: Automated generation of models for fast and precise detection of http-based malware. In: PST, pp. 249–256. IEEE (2014)

23. Han, X., Kheir, N., Balzarotti, D.: Deception techniques in computer security: a research perspective. ACM Comput. Surv. **51**(4), 80:1–80:36 (2018)

24. Durumeric, Z., et al.: The security impact of https interception. In: NDSS (2017)

25. Sharafaldin, I., Lashkari, A.H., Ghorbani, A.A.: Toward generating a new intrusion detection dataset and intrusion traffic characterization. In: ICISSP (2018)

26. Sommer, R., Paxson, V.: Outside the closed world: On using machine learning for network intrusion detection. In: S&P, pp. 305–316. IEEE (2010)

27. Borders, K., Prakash, A.: Quantifying information leaks in outbound web traffic. In: IEEE S&P 2009, pp. 129–140 (2009)

Random Allocation Seed-DSSS Broadcast Communication Against Jamming Attacks

Ahmad Alagil[✉] and Yao Liu

University of South Florida, Tampa, FL 33620, USA
alagil@mail.usf.edu, yliu@cse.usf.edu

Abstract. Spread spectrum techniques including Direct Sequence Spread Spectrum (DSSS) and Frequency Hopping Spread Spectrum (FHSS) are used widely as a countermeasure against jamming attacks. In recent years, the DSSS based system has been used to achieve the anti-jamming systems without a pre-shared secret key. Delayed Seed-Disclosure DSSS (DSD-DSSS) is one of these systems that uses a random seed to generate multiple spreading codes to spread an original message. However, it discloses the information of a random seed in a way that it is vulnerable to the attacker. In this paper. we propose a new system that mainly focuses on concealing a random seed from the attacker by inserting it at a random position of a spreading message. We develop a new technique to identify the location of a random seed at a receiver by aligning between multiple received messages. Our evaluation and simulation results show that a receiver can obtain the position of a random seed, and then he can recover both a random seed then regenerating the spreading codes used to spread an original message.

Keywords: Anti-jamming · Security · Spread spectrum · Wireless networks

1 Introduction

Over the past decades, wireless communications have been used widely to exchange data between multiple devices. In a wireless communication system, both a transmitter and a receiver may exchange critical information during the transmission time. This makes the wireless channels vulnerable to multiple challenging issues, such as noise and interference. Additionally, there are security concerns associated with wireless communication systems due to the open nature of the environment of wireless networks, and the limitation of the power and computational capability of wireless devices. Attackers may target the wireless channel to prevent both a sender and a receiver from sharing data, and one of these attacks is jamming attack.

Jamming attack is considered as one of the most typical threats to wireless communication systems. A jammer aims to prevent a legitimate sender and a

© ICST Institute for Computer Sciences, Social Informatics and Telecommunications Engineering 2019
Published by Springer Nature Switzerland AG 2019. All Rights Reserved
S. Chen et al. (Eds.): SecureComm 2019, LNICST 304, pp. 472–489, 2019.
https://doi.org/10.1007/978-3-030-37228-6_23

receiver from sending and receiving messages. He can emit noise signal to make the channel busy, such that a sender can not transmit data wireless. Also, a jammer can simply send junk data to the receiver, and as a result the receiver can not correctly recover the received message. In fact, it is important to make a reliable communication between a sender and a receiver by developing new schemes to mitigate the effects of jamming attacks.

Both FHSS and DSSS can be used to mitigate the effects of a jammer on the legitimate wireless communication. A sender and a receiver in the traditional FHSS and DSSS schemes share a secret key to encode and decode messages. The secret key can generate the same frequency hopping patterns used in FHSS for the sender and the receiver, or the same spreading code used in DSSS to spread and de-spread the messages. Therefore, if a jammer has the prior knowledge about the secret key, he can easily disrupt the communication channel [6, 8, 11].

Researchers have made recent attempts to overcome the concern of establishing anti-jamming communication without a pre-defined secret key. In particular, uncoordinated DSSS (UDSSS) was proposed to achieve such an anti-jamming wireless communication system [11]. A sender randomly picks spreading code sequences from a publicly known set to spread a message. However, a jammer can analyze the signal intercepted during the transmission time to find the spreading code sequences to disrupt the wireless communication. Randomized Differential DSSS (RD-DSSS) is another method proposed to remove the requirement of a pre-shared secret key for a DSSS based anti-jamming system. In RD-DSSS, both a sender and a receiver share public spreading code sequences similar to UDSSS. To facilitate decoding, the sender appends the index information of the spreading code sequences at the end of a spreading message [8]. This can make the index code a special target of the jammer, who will later uses the index code to find the spreading code sequences to disrupt the wireless communication.

Liu et al. developed a new technique, named delayed seed-disclosure DSSS (DSD-DSSS), against jamming attacks. This method achieves the anti-jamming wireless communication by generating a random seed which can be used to produce multiple spreading code sequences to spread a message. To disclose a seed, a sender spreads a seed using publicly known code sequence set and positions it to the end of a spreading message [7]. However, it suffers the same problem as UDDSSS and RD-DSSS. Since a seed is always at a fixed postilion, a jammer can easily localize the seed to regenerate the spreading codes, which the jammer uses to spread the jamming signal to prevent a receiver from recovering an original message.

In this paper, we propose a new technique, named RAS-DSSS, based on randomly allocating a position of a seed within a spreading message, which is an extension to improve the security of DSD-DSSS. In DSD-DSSS, if the size of a spreading message is fixed, a jammer can target a random seed within the transmission time. Also if the size of a spreading message is variable, a jammer can send noise signal for a long time to disrupt the data at a receiver. As a result, to protect a random seed, we propose to randomly insert the seed into a random position of a spreading message. To enable the receiver to obtain the

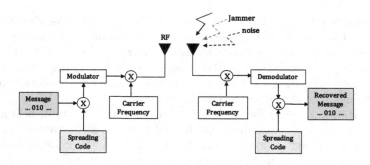

Fig. 1. Basic DSSS communication system

exact position of a random seed, we propose a scheme based on aligning two spreading messages within two transmissions. For example, after receiving two spreading messages, a receiver uses a sliding window to identify the position of a random seed. If the receiver can successfully determine the position of a seed, then he can recover the original message by doing the reverse steps conducted by the sender.

The contribution of this work is three-fold. First, we identify the vulnerabilities on existing DSSS based anti-jamming systems, and we propose a new scheme to enhance the security of the most recent DSD-DSSS method, via positioning a random seed into a random position on a spreading message. Second, we develop a novel technique to identify the beginning of a random seed to enable the receiver to find the seed. While concealing it from the jammer. Third, we perform simulations to validate our proposed system in the presence of different kind of jammers. The simulation results show that a receiver has a higher chance to find the seed compared with a jammer who needs to perform much efforts to find the seed within a transmission time. Furthermore, our simulations demonstrate how RAS-DSSS can reduce the probability that the random seed to be jammed. For instance, Figs. 8 and 9 illustrate the probability that the seed to be jammed in the presence of a non-reactive and a reactive jammer, respectively. The probability can be reduced significantly when the size of C_e and C_p is 7000.

The remainder of this paper is organized as follows. Section 2 gives the background information about the traditional DSSS. Section 3 presents the proposed system. Section 4 discusses the attack model and the evaluation results. Section 5 introduces the related work, and Sect. 6 concludes this paper.

2   Background of DSSS

DSSS is a modulation technique that can be applied to a baseband signal to increase its bandwidth. This can be achieved by multiplying an original signal by a spreading code called chips. This spreading code is considered as a pre-shared secret key between a sender and a receiver to perform the signal expansion. Each spreading code is represented as a sequence of bits with polar representations of

1 and -1, or non-polar representations of 1 and 0 [5,12]. The transmitted signal is resulted from multiplying each bit in the original message with a local replica of a spreading code.

Transmission and Reception Processes: Figure 1 shows a basic DSSS communication system with two functions, including spreading and de-spreading. First, a sender spreads an original message based on a pre-shared spreading code such as a pseudo noise sequence. Then a spreading message is modulated, up-converted to a signal with a carrier frequency, and fed to the wireless channel. Similarly, a receiver reverses the steps done by the sender for decoding. Specifically, the receiver down-converts the received signal to the original signal, which is then de-spread to recover the original message.

An Example of Spreading and De-spreading a Message: For instance, if "10" represents an original message, and $-1 - 1 + 1 + 1$ represents a spreading code used to spread the original message. Then a sender converts an original message from an un-polar to a polar form, i.e., "10" is converted to $+1 - 1$. Following this, each bit in an original message is multiplied with a local replica of a spreading code. Thus, the result of multiplying $+1$ and -1 with $-1-1+1+1$ is $-1-1+1+1+1+1-1-1$. Regarding the de-spreading process, a receiver uses the correlation function to find the similarity between two spreading codes. He starts recovering the original message by synchronizing a spreading code with a received message. High and low correlation is decoded into 1 and 0, respectively. For example, if the received message is $-1 - 1 - 1 + 1 - 1 - 1 - 1 - 1$ and the spreading code is $-1 - 1 + 1 + 1$. The decoding result of aligning $-1 - 1 + 1 + 1$ with the first four bits of the received message with non-polar form is 1.

Synchronization: In DSSS, identifying the beginning of the received message is important for the receiver to recover the original message. This can be achieved by taking the advantage of the good auto-correlation properties of the chosen spreading code. The receiver computes the correlation between the received message and the spreading code using a sliding window. If the result of the correlation is high, the beginning of an incoming message is assumed by the receiver [12,13].

3   Random Allocation Seed-DSSS

We propose a new scheme that we refer to as RAS-DSSS against jamming attacks. Similar to the traditional DSSS, RAS-DSSS spreads messages using spreading code sequences, and to remove the requirement of a pre-define secret key, RAS-DSSS uses multiple sets of code sequences to spread a random seed and the original message. In the following, we first introduce DSD-DSSS and its vulnerabilities, and then we present the proposed RAS-DSSS scheme that enhances the security of DSD-DSSS.

3.1   Basic Scheme of Delayed Seed Disclosure-DSSS

DSD-DSSS achieves the anti-jamming capability by spreading an original message based on a random seed. This random seed is used to generate random

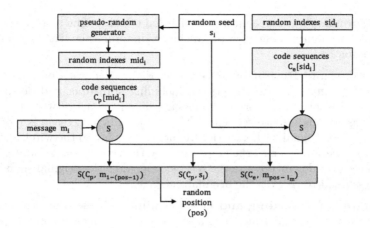

Fig. 2. The proposed system (RAS-DSSS)

spreading codes to spread the original message. To disclose a random seed, DSD-DSSS appends it to the end of the spreading message. The receiver buffers the received message, decodes the random seed to regenerate the spreading codes, and then recover an original message using the spreading codes.

The Limitations of DSD-DSSS

DSD-DSSS has some key limitations that can make it vulnerable to the jammer. In the following, we discuss these limitations and security issues of DSD-DSSS:

1. In DSD-DSSS, a sender first spreads the last bit of a seed using a random code sequence. Then he spreads the rest of bits of a seed one by one from the end to the beginning based on a specific function. At the end, the sender appends the spread seed to the end of the spreading message. Note that the sender always appends the spreading seed at the end of the spreading message. If the size of a message is fixed, the jammer can focus on jamming the seed only to prevent the receiver from identifying the seed and recover the original message. On the other hand, if the size of the message is dynamic, the computation overhead for despreading will increase at the receiver, and a jammer can still send random codes from to confuse the receiver.
2. In terms of the computation overhead, in DSD-DSSS, a receiver needs to de-spread a random seed in order to regenerate the spreading codes used to spread an original message. To achieve this, a receiver buffers the received message. Then he needs to locate a seed from the received message. This can take a non-trivial computational time. Assume that a random seed is of l_s-bit, the length of the spreading code is l_c, and the receiver applies a sliding window approach to identify a seed. The size of the sliding window should be $l_s \times l$.

3.2   RAS-DSSS

We create a new scheme to overcome the limitations of DSD-DSSS, In DSD-DSSS, a sender always discloses a seed at the end of a spread message. Although, a sender spreads a seed using random codes. A jammer may target the seed only to prevent the receiver from recovering an original message. Instead of appending a seed to the end of a spread message, we propose to allocate a seed at a random position of a spread message to reduce the probability that a jammer can identify the location of the seed. We also design a new technique that assists a receiver to determine the position of a random seed with low computation overhead.

Code Sets: Both a sender and a receiver share two publicly known spreading code sequences sets C_p and C_e which are used to spread an original message M and a random seed s_i, respectively. C_p and C_e do not overlap with each other, and the cross-correlation between spreading codes are low, and each spreading code has its unique index code. We assume that each code in C_p and C_e is of l_c bits.

Spreading the Original Message: If the original message M is of l_m-bit. The sender spreads each bit in M separately based on the chosen spreading code from the spreading code set C_p. Figure 2 shows an example of generating the spreading message. First, a sender needs to generate a random seed s_i, which is used with a pseudo-random generator to generate l_m random indexes $mid_1, mid_2, ..., mid_{l_m}$, where $1 \leq mid_i \leq | C_p |$. Then a sender uses these indexes to spread each bit in M with its corresponding spreading code in C_p. For example, the first bit in M is spread using $C_p[mid_1]$ and so on for the rest of the bits in M. We denote $S(C_p, M)$ as the spreading message.

Spreading the Seed: To protect a seed from being jammed, a sender spreads a seed using the spreading codes in C_e. Assume that a seed s is of l_s-bit. The sender spreads each bit of s by drawing codes from C_e based on the random choices of indexes $sid_1||sid_2||...||sid_{l_s}$ in C_e. The sender transmits the same spreading message twice. In each transmission, a sender spreads a seed using different codes from C_e. Assume that s with length l_s equal to 3 bits is spread in the first transmission using c_1, c_{10}, and c_8. Also assume that $S(C_e, s)$ represents the result of the spreading outcome of a seed in the first transmission. In the second transmission, this seed will be spread using codes different from those used in the first transmission (e.g. c_3, c_7, and c_6). The result of this spreading is denoted as $S_x(C_e, s)$. The reason for this is to make sure there is no repetition between the chosen codes used to spread s, and s_x. As a result, this reduces the result of the computed correlation between $S(C_e, s)$ and $S_x(C_e, s)$ to the lower level.

Randomization the Position of the Seed: As mentioned earlier, a sender uses the random seed to generate the indexes of the spreading codes to spread an original message M. If a seed is disclosed at the end of the spreading message, the attacker can easily target a seed to prevent a receiver from recovering an original message. To address this concern, we propose to randomize the position of a seed in the spreading message to confuse the attacker and reduce the probability that

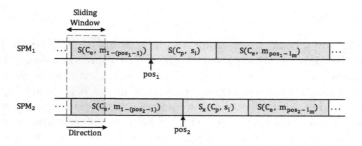

Fig. 3. Locating the position of the seed

a seed is jammed. In Fig. 2, we denote the random position of a seed as *pos*. Then a seed $S(C_e, s_i)$ is positioned between $S(C_p, M_{1:pos-1})$, and $S(C_p, M_{pos:l_m})$.

De-spreading Process: If a receiver can identify the position of a seed from the received spreading messages, he can successfully recover an original message by regenerating the indexes used by a sender to spread M. As we mentioned earlier, multiple spreading messages will be received by the receiver. In each transmission, a random seed is inserted at a random position different from the one in the previous transmission. Figure 3 gives an example for the de-spreading process. After the first transmission, a random seed inserted at pos_1 in the spread message. However, in the second transmission, a random seed positioned at pos_2, and we assume that $pos_1 \neq pos_2$. A receiver buffers both received messages and then scans both messages using a sliding window approach.

Sliding Window Approach: In Fig. 3, to obtain the position of the seed, a receiver needs to compare between the two received spreading messages SPM_1 and SPM_2 using a sliding window approach. Assume that W denotes the window size of a sliding window, and $W = l_s \times l_c$. Where l_s and l_c represent the length of a random seed and the length of the spreading code, respectively. If $x = x_1, x_2, ..., x_k$, and $y = y_1, y_2, ..., y_k$ represent the first W in SPM_1 and SPM_2, respectively. A receiver computes the correlation between x and y which can be calculated by $\frac{1}{k} \sum_{i=1}^{k} x_i y_i$. If the result of this computed correlation is above the threshold value γ, this means High (H). If not, that means Low (L). In the second time, a receiver shifts the sliding window to the right by one chip and this sliding window can be denoted as $2W$. Following that a receiver computes the correlation between x and y within $2W$, and so on to the end of SPM_1 and SPM_2. After performing $l_m + l_s$ comparisons, the receiver can obtain the position of a random seed within SPM_1.

Once the seed is localized, the receiver can start de-spreading the seed to regenerate the indexes used for spreading the original message by trying all possible spreading codes in C_e. The reason for this is because the seed is spread using random codes from C_e. As a result, the receiver applies a sliding window approach with window size l_c. If c_i and $\hat{s}$ represent the chosen spreading code from C_e and the first l_c chips from the seed, the receiver uses a sliding window approach to compute the correlation between c_i and $\hat{s}$. If the receiver gets a

Table 1. Definition of symbol

Symbol	Definition
M	The original message
s_i	The random seed
l_m	The length of M
l_s	The length of s_i
l_c	The length of each spreading code
C_e	Spreading codes set to spread M
C_p	Spreading codes set to spread s_i
i	Number of spreading codes in C_e
$S(C_e, M)$	The result of spreading M
$S(C_p, s_i)$	The result of spreading s_i
POS_1	The chosen random position
C_x	A long spreading code

maximum correlation, this means that c_i was used to spread $\hat{s}$ in the seed. The receiver applies this using all spreading codes in C_e to retrieve the seed. Indeed, the receiver performs the reverse processes done by a sender to recover an original message (Table 1).

Computation Overhead: A receiver needs to despread a random seed to regenerate the spreading codes used to spread the original message. In DSD-DSSS, the receiver needs to synchronize and decode the random seed to regenerate the spreading codes used to spread the original message. This means that the computation overhead is high compared with RAS-DSSS. As a result, a receiver may try all possible spreading codes in C_e to spread chips in the received message and recover the random seed. Assume that T_{seed} is the time required by the receiver to obtain the random seed within the received message.

$$T_{seed} = ((l_m \times l_c) + (l_s \times l_c)) \times i$$

In RAS-DSSS, a receiver uses a sliding window approach to identify the position of a seed. He computes the correlation between the two spreading messages with window size $l_s \times l_c$ to obtain the beginning of a seed. In RAS-DSSS, since the length of the spreading message is fixed, the computation overhead mainly depends on obtaining the position of a random seed. If a seed is positioned at the beginning of the spread message, the computation overhead will be $O(1)$, which is the best case. In the worst case, the computation overhead will be $O(n)$, because a receiver performs the comparison for n time until he finds the low correlation that indicates the position of a seed. Thus the time required by the receiver to obtain the random seed in the received message is:

$$T_{seed} = ((POS_1 - 1) \times l_c) + (l_s \times l_c \times i)$$

In general, RAS-DSSS is more secure compared with DSD-DSSS, and it reduces the computation time to a lower level. This is because the seed is always inserted within the spreading message. If the seed is inserted in POS_1, then $(POS_1 - 1) < l_m$ which reduces the computation time to obtain the position of the seed by $(l_m - POS_1)$.

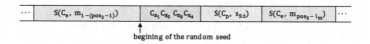

Fig. 4. Security enhancement

Security Enhancement: As discussed earlier, because RAS-DSSS randomizes the position of a random seed, the jammer needs to first obtain the location of the seed before he can launch targeted jamming against the seed. However, the attacker may spread random bits and transmit them to the receiver to confuse the despreading. Consequently, a receiver may not recover a random seed correctly. To mitigate such threat, we propose to spread the beginning of a random seed using long spreading codes. The sender can choose the length of the spreading codes based on the observations on the received messages. For example, if the receiver identifies multiples received spreading messages have been jammed, the sender spreads the first 4-bit of the random seed using long spreading codes. This will increase the chance to identify the position of the random seed within the spreading message. If C_{long} represents the set of the long spreading codes compared with those C_e. For example, the length of the spreading codes C_{long} is 2048-chip compared with 1024-chip in C_e. Figure 4 gives an example of spreading a random seed using long spreading codes. If C_{x_1}, C_{x_2}, C_{x_3}, and C_{x_4} represent these long spreading codes form C_{long} to spread the first 4-bit of the random seed. This will mitigate the effects of a jammer who sends continuously random spreading codes from C_e. Also this provides an efficient way against DoS attacks.

Advantages for a Receiver over a Jammer: In RAS-DSSS, a receiver has some advantages over a jammer to mitigate the effects of the jammer. These advantages are summarized below:

1. The receiver can fully buffer the received messages and take his time to localize and desoread a random seed. While a jammer has to perform real time analysis to know the position of the seed and the spreading codes used to spread a seed for jamming the seed. Moreover, the jammer has to search over all spreading codes to jam the seed within the transmission time of one message. Assume that the length of an original message is of 1024 bits, the length of a random seed is of 16 bits, and the spreading code is of 128 bits. The transmission time of the spreading message at a 11-Mbps data rate is $= \frac{(1024+16)\times 128}{11\times 10^6} = 0.0121$ ms. This means that a jammer must identify the spreading codes within 0.0121 ms, whereas the receiver does not have the time limitation.

2. A reactive jammer does not have enough information regarding the position of a random seed. As a result, a jammer can not target the part of the spreading message that contains a seed. Instead, he may guess the position of a seed only. The probability that a reactive jammer can successfully guess the position of a random seed is low. Assume $l_m = 1024 - bit$, and a random seed is going to be inserted within M. Then the probability that a reactive jammer can guess the correct position of a random seed is $(\frac{1}{1024})$. On the contrary, as we explain in the previous point, the receiver can buffer both messages and take his time to obtain and despread a random seed.

3. A reactive jammer can not effectively jam a bit of a seed or the message unless he has the prior knowledge about the spreading code used for this bit. For example, if the i-th bit of the random seed is spread using spreading code c_{10}, then a jammer can not effectively jam this bit unless he knows which spreading code is used to spread this bit. It is infeasible for a reactive jammer to guess or know which spreading code used to spread a particular bit of a random seed or message within a transmission time. Again, the receiver does not suffer from this time constraint issue.

How to Confuse a Reactive Jammer? As we explained earlier, a jammer always targets the most important part of the spreading message which is a seed. If a jammer can successfully jam a seed, a receiver can not recover an original message. RSA-DSSS confuses the jammer from identifying the position of the seed to reduce the probability that a seed is jammed in the following ways:

1. We use a large size of C_p and C_e to discourage a reactive jammer. Specifically, in RAS-DSSS, both a sender and receiver use publicly known C_p and C_e sets to spread both an original message and a seed. By adopting large sets, a jammer needs to perform a huge amount of computations. This means the number of the correlations required by a jammer is $(l_m \times C_p) + (l_s \times C_e)$. For example, if the size of C_p and C_e is 1000, l_m is 128 bits, and l_s is 16-bit bits. The number of correlation needs to be calculated by the attacker within the transmission time of one message is $= (128 \times 1000) + (16 \times 1000) = 144,000$.

2. In RAS-DSSS, a sender inserts a seed in a random position. This position is only known to a sender. For example, in the first transmission of the spreading message, we denote (POS_1) as a random position chosen by a sender to hide a seed from a jammer. In the second transmission of the same spreading message, a sender spreads a seed using different spreading codes that do not overlap with those chosen for spreading the first transmission. This will result in a low correlation between the spreading seed in both transmissions.

4   Simulation Results

4.1   Analysis

RAS-DSSS provides a countermeasure against a jammer who targets either the body of the spreading message or a random seed to prevent a receiver from recovering an original message M. We assume the following types of attacks:

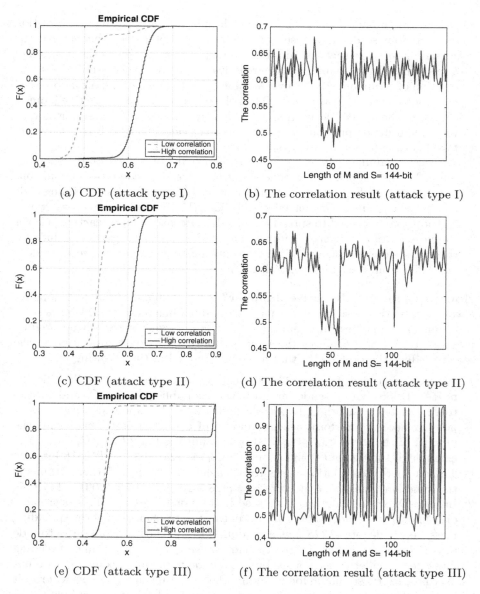

Fig. 5. The correlation between SPM_1 and SPM_2, and CDF of the high and low correlation of the received spreading messages in the presence of three types of attackers I, II and III

- In attack type I, a jammer injects random noise or random bits to disrupt the wireless communication between the sender and the receiver. If the jammer can successfully jam the seed, then the receiver cannot recover a random seed and regenerate the sequence of spreading codes used to spread the original message M.

- In attack type II, the jammer keeps sending random spreading codes from C_e to the receiver. As a result, the receiver needs to de-spread a seed using all codes in C_e. This means that the receiver has to try all possible combinations to recover the original message. This attack is thus a Denial-of-service (DoS) attack.
- In attack type III, the jammer knows the spreading codes used by the sender to spread an original message. In this type of the attack, the jammer spreads random bits using the same spreading codes used by the sender, and sends them to the receiver.

We consider the following jamming strategies:

1. Non-reactive jamming: Non-reactive jammers have no knowledge about the legitimate channel status. They need to guess what spreading codes are used by the sender to jam the wireless channel. Jamming interval I (where $I > 0$) represents the period of the time between the pulses of jamming produced by a jammer, and it also defines the behavior of a jammer. If the attacker decides to jam the wireless channel for a long time, I should be a small value [9].
2. Reactive jamming: Sensing channel is essential for a reactive jammer. If the channel is idle, a jammer will be quiet. If a jammer detects wireless communication between the sender and the receiver, he starts emitting a noise signal. We point out that the reactive jammer has a time constraint compared with the receiver. As mentioned earlier, the jammer must de-spread a message within the transmission time of the message, whereas a receiver can record the message and take his time to de-spread it. Due to the time constraint, it is difficult for a reactive jammer to launch the real-time analysis to compute which code sequences are used by a sender to spread a random seed, because the jammer needs to obtain the correct spreading codes by searching on all possible code sequences within a very short time.

4.2   Evaluation

We validate the performance of RSA-DSSS using simulations on Matlab. In our simulation, we adopt the Additive White Gaussian Noise (AWGN) simulation channel. A sender sends the spreading messages through a AWGN channel, the simulation of which is performed by adding white gaussian noise to the transmitted signal. A jammer emits interference signals to prevent the receiver from recovering an original message. In our experiment, we use Hadamard function to generate spreading codes for C_p and C_e to spread the first message M and a random seed s_i, respectively. We set the length of an original message M to be 128 bits, the length of a random seed s_i to be 16 bits, and the length of each spreading code to be 512 bits. Also, in our simulation, we assumed that the transmission is in the presence of the three aforementioned attackers, namely, types I, II and III attackers.

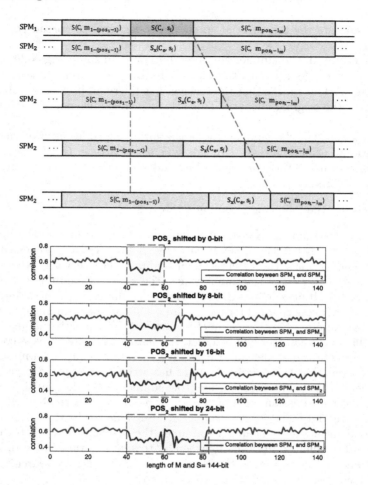

Fig. 6. Different situations show the effects when the seed (s_x) in the second spreading (SPM_2) message is not shifted, or shifted by 8, 16, 24 bits on the decision to identify the position of the seed in the first spreading message (SPM_1).

As mentioned previously, a sender positions a seed at a random location within a spreading message, and uses two transmissions to send the spreading messages to a receiver. A receiver takes advantages of buffering the received messages to obtain and recover a seed. As a result, in our simulation, we built a comparison function that computes, using a sliding window approach, the correlation between the received messages. The result of this comparison reveals the position of the seed. For example, if the outcome of this comparison is higher than a threshold, we consider that no seed is identified within the window size.

Figure 5 represents the cumulative distribution function (CDF) and the result of the correlation between two received spreading messages SPM_1 and SPM_2

in the presence of jammers type I, II and III. CDF gives us the cumulative of the probability associated with the computed correlation between SPM_1 and SPM_2, and also helps us to decide the appropriate threshold that indicates the correct position of a random seed within SPM_1. From Figs. 5(a), (b), and (c), the dashed line represents the low correlation between SPM_1 and SPM_2, where a random seed is localized by the receiver, and the solid line represents the high correlation. From Fig. 5(a), for example, 94% low correlations are smaller than or equal to 0.55, but only 0.1% high correlations are smaller than or equal to 0.55. This means that if we use 0.55 as the threshold, we will obtain the detection rate of a seed at the probability of 0.94 and this threshold also gives a false alarm rate of 0.1%.

Figure 6 shows four situations, when we calculate the correlation between the two spreading messages to identify the location of the seed. In each situation, we shift the position of the seed by multiplying the number of shifted bits by l_c. In the first situation, the random seed is at the same position for both messages, and we can see that the low correlation results in a small segment only ≈ 0.56. As we explained previously, the sender spreads a random seed in the second spreading message using different spreading codes from the one used in the first transmission, and the result of the spreading is $S_x(C_e, s)$. Thus, low correlation results from the situation where both $S(C_e, s)$ and $S_x(C_e, s)$ are in the same position in the spreading message. As we can see, the blue line represents the computed correlation between SPM_1 and SPM_2 when the seed is inserted within SPM_1 and SPM_2 at the same position (within bit 41). When there is no shifting, the computed high correlation remains stable at 0.62 before reaching bit number 41 where the seed is inserted. After that, there is a noticeable drop in the blue line from 0.62 to 0.48–0.52 which is resulted from the reduction of the computed correlation. This almost remains until bit number 57 where the seed end. From this, we can observe that when the random seed is inserted in the same position within SPM_1 and SPM_2, the low correlation points exactly to the position of the random seed. Also, the low correlation boundary is the length of the random seed.

On the other hand, when the seed is inserted at different positions (i.e., POS_1 and POS_2), the result of the low correlation varies based on the position shift. This results in increasing the window size where the result of the correlation is low. This indicates that the position of the seed is shifted in the second spreading message. As a result, the cost of the search on the receiver will increase as by the amount of the shift.

We run the simulation program for 1000 times with different lengths of the spreading codes to discover the impact of attacker types I, II, and III on a receiver to identify the position of a seed. Figure 7 shows the number of successful trials to find the location of a random seed. For instance, when the length of a spreading code is 256, the receiver can successfully identify a random seed with detection rates 0.643, 0.672, and 0.031 in the presence of attack type I, attack type II, and attack type III, respectively. On the other hand, when the length of the spreading code is 1024, the receiver can successfully identify the position of a random seed

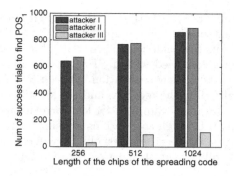

Fig. 7. Number of success trials to find the position of the seed.

with detection rates 0.860, 0.891, and 0.11 in the presence of these attackers. We observe that increasing the length of the spreading codes can significantly improve the detection rate.

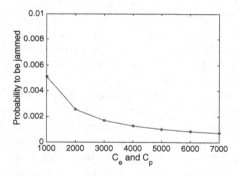 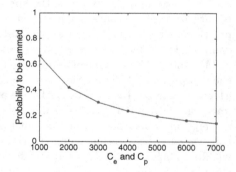

Fig. 8. Probability for a non-reactive jammer to jam the seed.

Fig. 9. Probability for a reactive jammer to jam the seed.

Also, similar to ([7], Theorem 2 and 3), we compute the probabilities for both a non-reactive and reactive jammers to jam a random seed during the transmission time when C_e and C_p have different sizes of spreading codes using Eqs. 1 and 2, respectively. Intuitively, increasing the size of C_e and C_p can reduce the probability that the seed is jammed. Figure 8 shows the probability for a non-reactive jammer to jam a random seed. As we can see from this figure, $p = 0.015$ when the size of C_e and C_p is 1000, and p significantly reduces to 0.001 when the size C_e and C_p is increased to 7000. On the other hand, Fig. 9 represents the probability for a reactive jammer to jam a random seed. As we can see from the figure, $p = 0.019$ when the size of C_e and C_p is 7000. The size of C_e and C_p play an important role in reducing the probability that the jammer can jam the seed. The reason for this is that it is hard for the jammer to exhaustively search over all possible spreading codes in C_e and C_p when their sizes are big. Furthermore, it is impossible for the jammer to do real-time analysis within a transmission time.

$$P_{nrj} = 1 - (1 - (\frac{1}{l_c \times (C_p + C_e)})^{l_m}) \qquad (1)$$

$$P_{rj} = 1 - (1 - \frac{1}{C_p})^{l_m} \times (1 - \frac{1}{C_e})^{l_s} \qquad (2)$$

5   Related Work

Spread spectrum techniques, including DSSS and FHSS, have been widely used against jamming attacks [2,4–6,14]. However, these traditional techniques all require the sender and the require to share a pre-defined secret key. Recently, researchers have conducted investigation to remove the requirement of sharing a secret key. This can allow the sender and the receivers to use random code sequences to spread an original message.

Baird et al. developed a coding technique, which mainly focuses on encoding the transmitted signal into marks with no prior knowledge about the keys [3]. Uncoordinated DSSS (UDSSS) was also proposed for anti-jamming broadcast communications [14]. Another system called Randomized Differential DSSS (RD-DSSS) was introduced to achieve anti-jamming system in wireless communications [8], and the follow-up work Randomized Positioning DSSS (RP-DSSS) was proposed to enhance the security of RD-DSSS [1].

In [7], Liu et al. proposed DSD-DSSS to achieve jamming-resistance in a broadcast communication system without a pre-defined key. As mentioned earlier, DSD-DSSS takes advantage of generating a random seed, which is used to generate random spreading code sequences to spread the original message. DSD-DSSS also spreads the seed to increase the security. However, this approach is vulnerable to the jamming because it always appends the spreading seed to the end of the spreading message. If the seed is jammed during the transmission time, the receiver can not de-spread the received message.

In [10], Oh et al. developed an Advanced Random Seed DSSS (ARS-DSSS) system as an extension of DSD-DSSS scheme. They developed a new technique against seed jamming attacks. ARS-DSSS reduces the computation overhead to compute the random seed within a variable size message. It spreads the last bit of the random seed using a very long spreading code. However, the random seed is still vulnerable to jamming attacks because it is also positioned at the end of the spreading message. Although the size of a message may not be fixed, the jammer can estimate the approximate location range of the seed to focus jamming the end of the message.

6   Conclusion

In this paper, we propose RAS-DSSS system to increase the security of DSD-DSSS. RAS-DSSS positions a seed at a random location of a spreading message to reduce the chance that a seed to be jammed. We also design a new mechanism that enables a receiver to locate the position of a seed using a sliding window. This can reduce the computational overhead of the proposed system compared with a DSD-DSSS system. We performed computer simulations to validate the effectiveness of RAS-DSSS, and the results show that RAS-DSSS can successfully obtain the position of a seed. Our experiment results show that our proposed system can successfully obtain the position of the random seed, and the detection rates can be increased successfully when we increase the length of the spreading codes. For example, the detection rate increased from 0.643 to 0.860 when we increase the length of the spreading codes from 256 to 1024. Additionally, RAS-DSSS can significantly mitigate the effects of jamming attacks when the size of both C_e and C_p is 7000.

Acknowledgement. This work is supported by NSF under grants CNS-1527144 and CNS-1553304.

References

1. Alagil, A., Alotaibi, M., Liu, Y.: Randomized positioning DSSS for anti-jamming wireless communications. In: 2016 International Conference on Computing, Networking and Communications (ICNC), pp. 1–6. IEEE (2016)
2. Baird, L.C., Bahn, W.L., Collins, M.D., Carlisle, M.C., Butler, S.C.: Keyless jam resistance. In: 2007 IEEE SMC Information Assurance and Security Workshop, pp. 143–150, June 2007. https://doi.org/10.1109/IAW.2007.381926
3. Baird, L.C., Bahn, W.L., Collins, M.D.: Jam-resistant communication without shared secrets through the use of concurrent codes, January 2007
4. Fang, S., Liu, Y., Ning, P.: Wireless communications under broadband reactive jamming attacks. IEEE Trans. Dependable Secur. Comput. **13**(3), 394–408 (2016). https://doi.org/10.1109/TDSC.2015.2399304
5. Goldsmith, A.: Wireless Communications. Cambridge University Press, Cambridge (2005)
6. Grover, K., Lim, A., Yang, Q.: Jamming and anti-jamming techniques in wireless networks: a survey. Int. J. Ad Hoc Ubiquitous Comput. **17**(4), 197–215 (2014)
7. Liu, A., Ning, P., Dai, H., Liu, Y., Wang, C.: Defending DSSS-based broadcast communication against insider jammers via delayed seed-disclosure. In: Proceedings of the 26th Annual Computer Security Applications Conference, pp. 367–376. ACM (2010)
8. Liu, Y., Ning, P., Dai, H., Liu, A.: Randomized differential DSSS: jamming-resistant wireless broadcast communication. In: 2010 Proceedings IEEE INFO-COM, pp. 1–9. IEEE (2010)
9. Lu, Z.: Modeling and evaluating the impact of denial-of-service attacks in emerging wireless and mobile applications. Ph.D. thesis (2013). aAI3575788
10. Oh, Y., Thuente, D.J.: Enhanced security of random seed DSSS algorithms against seed jamming attacks. In: 2012 IEEE Global Communications Conference (GLOBECOM), pp. 801–806, December 2012. https://doi.org/10.1109/GLOCOM.2012.6503211
11. Pöpper, C., Strasser, M., Capkun, S.: Jamming-resistant broadcast communication without shared keys. In: USENIX Security Symposium, pp. 231–248 (2009)

12. Simon, M.K., Omura, J.K., Scholtz, R.A., Levitt, B.K.: Spread Spectrum Communications Handbook, Revised edn. McGraw-Hill, Inc., New York (1994)
13. Stallings, W.: Data and Computer Communications, 8th edn. Prentice-Hall Inc., Upper Saddle River (2006)
14. Strasser, M., Pöpper, C., Capkun, S., Cagalj, M.: Jamming-resistant key establishment using uncoordinated frequency hopping. In: 2008 IEEE Symposium on Security and Privacy (SP 2008), pp. 64–78, May 2008. https://doi.org/10.1109/SP.2008.9

A Loss-Tolerant Mechanism of Message Segmentation and Reconstruction in Multi-path Communication of Anti-tracking Network

Changbo Tian[1,2], YongZheng Zhang[1,2(✉)], Tao Yin[1,2], Yupeng Tuo[1,2], and Ruihai Ge[1,2]

[1] Institute of Information Engineering, Chinese Academy of Sciences, Beijing 100093, China
{tianchangbo,zhangyongzheng,yintao,tuoyupeng,geruihai}@iie.ac.cn
[2] School of Cyber Security, University of Chinese Academy of Sciences, Beijing 100049, China

Abstract. The low threshold and convenience of the techniques about network monitoring and tracing have posed a great threat on the netizens' privacy. Open data shows that the rampant business of netizens' private information has become one of the biggest network dark industries. Multi-path communication applied in the anonymous communication netowrk improves the difficulty of online theft of the netizens' privacy. But in the current multi-path communication mechanisms, when some message blocks are lost, the frequent request for the lost message blocks greatly reduces the communication efficiency and the tracking-resistance. To address this problem, we propose a loss-tolerant mechanism of message segmentation and reconstruction in multi-path communication (FMC). The loss-tolerance of FMC is subject to the property of orthogonal matrix that the inner product of any two rows(columns) is 0. FMC works as follows: (1) firstly, the message is encoded into an orthogonal matrix, and divided into triangular blocks as more as possible; (2) secondly, the message blocks are sent to different communication paths, and each communication path guarantees the security of the transmitted message; (3) thirdly, the receiver recovers the original message even when some message blocks are lost. Without the frequent request for the lost message blocks, FMC greatly improves the communication efficiency and tracking-resistance. Experimental results show that FMC has a strong loss-tolerant performance, and the receiver can certainly recover the original message with 15% lost message blocks at most. Also, we analyze the data expansion rate of FMC in matrix segmentation and multi-path communication. For a $n \times n$ matrix, $\lceil \frac{n}{2} \rceil$ is a proper size of message blocks to balance loss-tolerance, tracking-resistance and communication efficiency.

Supported by the national natural science foundation of China under grant No. U1736218.

© ICST Institute for Computer Sciences, Social Informatics and Telecommunications Engineering 2019
Published by Springer Nature Switzerland AG 2019. All Rights Reserved
S. Chen et al. (Eds.): SecureComm 2019, LNICST 304, pp. 490–508, 2019.
https://doi.org/10.1007/978-3-030-37228-6_24

Keywords: Loss-tolerance · Multi-path communication ·
Anti-tracking network · Message encoding · Cyber security

1   Introduction

1.1   Background and Motivatioin

The Internet has permeated into all fields of our society and gathered various kinds of information. And the Internet has evolved into a global and open platform for social network, finance, education, health care and so on. But the low threshold and convenience of the techniques about network monitoring and network tracing pose a great threat on the online privacy of network users. The large amount of network users' private information has huge economic benefits and makes the cyber crime about the network users' privacy more and more serious [1,2].

The encryption technology can only protect the data content of communications against the network eavesdropping, but has no solution to deal with the information leakage about the network users' identities or the network addresses of the source and the destination. So, the anonymous communication (AC) network is proposed to solve this problem [3]. But most of the current AC networks only focus on the anonymity of the network users' identities at the application layer. From the attack at the network layer, such as network monitoring [4,5] and tracing [6–8] of the network traffic, the AC networks have not too many advantages. So, we propose the anti-tracking network which is used to mitigate the network monitoring and tracing in the network layer.

Multi-path communication is an effective way to improve the communication efficiency and tracking-resistance of anti-tracking network [9]. But the big problem of multi-path communication is the loss of message blocks. If the receiver frequently requests for the lost message blocks, the adversary would be easy to detect the communication channel and trace the sender or receiver [10,11]. To address this problem, we propose a loss-tolerant mechanism of message segmentation and reconstruction (FMC) applied in the multi-path communication of anti-tracking network. FMC guarantees the successful reconstruction of original message even though a certain amount of message blocks are lost.

1.2   Limitation of Prior Art

In multi-path communication of anti-tracking network, the message is split into different blocks and different message blocks are transferred in different paths. In this way, the adversary can hardly monitor the network traffic and trace the target. But multi-path communication still faces some problems showed as follows [12–14].

– *The loss of message blocks.* The anti-tracking network is built on the P2P network, and the nodes can freely join in or quit the network. In the process of message transmission, the message blocks may be lost because of the change of network structure or transmission path. Once the receiver can not receive all of message blocks, he can not reconstruct the original message.

- *The passive attack from the adversary.* The adversary can hardly trace the network traffic in the multi-path communication. But, the effective way of the adversary is to intercept the specific network traffic and monitor the request from the receiver to trace the transmission path of the network traffic [18–21].

1.3   Proposed Approach

As we know, Sudoku game is to fill a 9×9 grid with digits so that each column, each row, and each of the nine 3×3 subgrids compose the grid and contain all of the digits from 1 to 9. The blank squares can be seen as the lost information and the filled squares can be seen the known information. Sudoku game is to reconstruct the whole information according to the known information and the defined rules.

As we know, the inner product of any two rows or two columns of orthogonal matrix is 0. Motivated by Sudoku game, if we encode the message into an orthogonal matrix, even we loss some blocks of the message, we can easily recover the original message according to the property of orthogonal matrix.

$$M' = \frac{1}{15} \begin{bmatrix} 5 & -2 & -14 \\ 10 & 11 & z \\ x & y & 5 \end{bmatrix} \Rightarrow \begin{cases} 5 \times x + (-2) \times y + (-14) \times 5 = 0 \\ 10 \times x + 11 \times y + z \times 5 = 0 \\ 5 \times 10 + (-2) \times 11 + (-14) \times z = 0 \end{cases}$$

$$\Rightarrow M = \frac{1}{15} \begin{bmatrix} 5 & -2 & -14 \\ 10 & 11 & 2 \\ 10 & -10 & 5 \end{bmatrix} \tag{1}$$

We present a simple example showed in formula (1). M' denotes the received message in which x, y, z are the lost message blocks. We can use the property of orthogonal matrix that the inner product of any two rows is 0 to construct the equation set about x, y, z. After solve the equation set, we will get the values of x, y, z and reconstruct the original message M.

1.4   Contributions and Roadmap

we make three key contributions in this paper as follows.

- We propose a loss-tolerant mechanism of message segmentation and reconstruction applied in the multi-path communication of anti-tracking network, called FMC. FMC achieves the loss-tolerant recovery of original message when a certain amount of message blocks are lost in the transmission process.
- We propose a message triangular segmentation algorithm which divides the message into different triangular blocks as more as possible. The triangular segmentation of message can improve the loss-tolerance of FMC.
- We propose a matrix reconstruction algorithm which can recover the original message to a certain degree when some blocks of message are lost.

The remainder of this paper is structured as follows. In Sect. 2, we introduce the overview of FMC. In Sect. 3, we shed light on the message segmentation, multi-path communication and message reconstruction of FMC. In Sect. 4, we make the experiments and analysis about the loss-tolerance performance, reconstruction efficiency and the influence of message blocks' granularity. Finally, we conclude our work in Sect. 5.

2   The Overview of FMC

Multi-path communication is an effective way to improve the tracking-resistant performance and communication efficiency for anti-tracking network. The message is split into different blocks and different message blocks are transferred in different paths. In this way, the adversary can hardly monitor the network traffic and trace the target. But the loss of message blocks will result in the fail of message reconstruction. So, we propose FMC to solve these problems. The overview structure of FMC is illustrated in Fig. 1. The workflow of FMC is divide into three steps as follows.

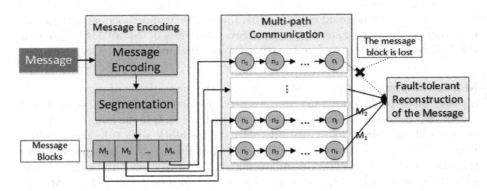

Fig. 1. The overview of FMC. Even if some message blocks may be lost or broken in the communication, FMC can still reconstruct the whole message.

- *Message encoding.* Firstly, we encode the message blocks into orthogonal matrix and split it into different blocks. Different message blocks are transferred in different paths.
- *Multi-path communication.* In the process of multi-path communication, we need to select several nodes to construct the multi-path forwarding network in advance. Then, different network paths ensure the security and efficiency of the message blocks transferred by it. The same with the principle of Tor [23], each node of each path decrypts the message block and deliver it to the next node until the message block arrives at the target node. The node of each path only knows the predecessor and successor. To improve the tracking-resistance, we can frequently change the transmission path.

– *loss-tolerant reconstruction of message.* After the receiver collects a certain quantity of message blocks, he can reconstruct the original message successfully, even though some message blocks may be lost because of the change of network by the malicious nodes.

3   Loss-Tolerant Mechanism

To improve the tracking-resistance and communication efficiency of anti-tracking network, multi-path communication is an effective way. We can split the message into different blocks and transfer them in parallel. Different communication paths will confuse the adversary and make the network monitoring and tracing more difficult. But the lost message blocks may result in the fail of the reconstruction of the original message. So, we propose FMC to address the problem.

3.1   Message Encoding

Message encoding is the first step of FMC to ensure the loss-tolerant multi-path communication. The basic idea of message encoding is that we encode the message into an orthogonal matrix. With the property of orthogonal matrix that the inner production of any two rows or two columns is 0, we can easily calculate the lost message blocks and reconstruct the original message.

Matrix Representation of Message. For the convenience of message encoding and multi-path communication, we need divide the original message into n blocks and the length of each divided message block is l. If the length of the last message block is less than l, we fill this message block with 0 to the specified length. Then, we use the vector $V_i(1 \leq i \leq n)$ of the length n to represent each message block and construct a square matrix M to represent the original message. As showed in Eq. (2), the original message is represented by the matrix M, n denotes the number of the message blocks, $V_i(1 \leq i \leq n)$ denotes the vector of each message block and $v_{ij}(1 \leq i \leq n \ and \ 1 \leq j \leq n)$ is the corresponding value of the vector $V_i(1 \leq i \leq n)$.

$$M = \begin{bmatrix} V_1 \\ V_2 \\ \vdots \\ V_n \end{bmatrix} = \begin{bmatrix} v_{11} & v_{12} & \cdots & v_{1n} \\ v_{21} & v_{22} & \cdots & v_{2n} \\ \vdots & \vdots & & \vdots \\ v_{n1} & v_{n2} & \cdots & v_{nn} \end{bmatrix} \tag{2}$$

Message Segmentation. By the orthogonal decomposition of matrix, we can encode the message matrix M into an orthogonal matrix to achieve the successful reconstruction of the original message even if some message blocks are lost. Firstly, we introduce a definition of orthogonal decomposition of matrix [24].

Theorem 1. *Let A be a $n \times m$ matrix. Then $A = QR$ is a QR decomposition of A if Q is an orthogonal $n \times n$ matrix and R is an upper-triangular $n \times m$ matrix.*

Proof. Run the Gram-Schmidt ortonormalization [24] process for the columns $v_1, ..., v_m$ of A to obtain an orthonormal basis $u_1, ..., u_k$ of span$(v_1, ..., v_m)$, such that for $i = 1, ..., k$, we have $v_i \in span(u_1, ..., u_i)$. Let $u_{k+1}, ..., u_n$ be arbitrary vectors extending $u_1, ..., u_k$ to an orthonormal basis, and let $Q = (u_1|...|u_n)$. Then $R = Q^{-1}A = Q^T A$ is upper-triangular.

Through Theorem (1), we can encode the message matrix M into an orthogonal matrix Q and an upper-triangular matrix R. Here, we don't give the further elaborations about the QR decomposition of the matrix M. The QR decomposition of matrix M is showed as formula (3), the matrix Q is the orthogonal matrix and the matrix R is the upper-triangular matrix. Assume we have n channels for multi-path communication, then we just need to divide the matrix Q and R into different blocks and transfer them in different paths.

$$M = QR = \begin{bmatrix} b_{11} & b_{12} & \cdots & b_{1n} \\ b_{21} & b_{22} & \cdots & b_{2n} \\ \vdots & \vdots & & \vdots \\ b_{n1} & b_{n2} & \cdots & b_{nn} \end{bmatrix} \begin{bmatrix} a_{11} & a_{12} & \cdots & a_{1n} \\ & a_{22} & \cdots & a_{2n} \\ & & \ddots & \vdots \\ & & & a_{nn} \end{bmatrix} \tag{3}$$

As we have mentioned in formula (1), we use the property of orthogonal matrix to build the equation set. Through the solutions of these equation set, we can reconstruct the original message. Before we discuss the message matrix segmentation, we firstly give two examples to show the different complexity of solving the systems of equations in different message segmentation ways.

- *Row segmentation.* In this message segmentation way, we divide each row to a message block. Assume we lost the last two message blocks, we can build the equation set as showed in formula (4) in which x_i and y_i $(1 \leq i \leq n)$ denote the lost message. In order to reconstruct the original message, we have to build at least $2 \times n$ equations because the lost message is $2 \times n$. In formula (4), we only build $2 \times (n-1)$ equations by multiplying the last rows with all other rows. We also need the columns to build the other two equations. Then the equation set is hard to solve. It's the same with *column segmentation*.

$$Q = \begin{bmatrix} b_{11} & b_{12} & \cdots & b_{1n} \\ b_{21} & b_{22} & \cdots & b_{2n} \\ \vdots & \vdots & & \vdots \\ b_{n-2,1} & b_{n-2,2} & \cdots & b_{n-2,n} \\ x_1 & x_2 & \cdots & x_n \\ y_1 & y_2 & \cdots & y_n \end{bmatrix} \Rightarrow \begin{cases} \sum_{i=1}^{n} x_i b_{1,i} = 0 \\ \vdots \\ \sum_{i=1}^{n} x_i b_{n-2,i} = 0 \\ \sum_{i=1}^{n} y_i b_{1,i} = 0 \\ \vdots \\ \sum_{i=1}^{n} y_i b_{n-2,i} = 0 \end{cases} \tag{4}$$

– *Triangular segmentation.* In this segmentation way, assume that we divide the matrix Q into two parts, an upper-triangular message block and a lower-triangular message block. If we lost one of them, such as the upper-triangular message block, we can still build the equation set showed in formula (5) in which x_{ij} $(1 \leq i \leq n-1, 2 \leq j \leq n)$ denotes the lost message block. As we can see in formula (5), it's very easy to solve the equations. We can firstly solve the x_{12} by the first two columns, then solve the x_{13}, x_{23} by the first three columns, and so on. Finally, we can solve the lost message blocks in the last column by the previous $n-1$ columns.

$$Q = \begin{bmatrix} b_{11} & x_{12} & x_{13} & \cdots & x_{1n} \\ b_{21} & b_{22} & x_{23} & \cdots & x_{2n} \\ b_{31} & b_{32} & b_{33} & \cdots & x_{3n} \\ \vdots & \vdots & \vdots & & \vdots \\ b_{n1} & b_{n2} & b_{n3} & \cdots & b_{nn} \end{bmatrix}$$

$$\Rightarrow b_{11}x_{12} + \sum_{i=2}^{n} b_{i,1}b_{i,2} = 0 \rightarrow (solve \quad x_{12})$$

$$\Rightarrow \begin{cases} b_{11}x_{13} + \sum_{i=2}^{n} b_{i,1}b_{i,3} = 0 \\ x_{12}x_{13} + \sum_{i=2}^{n} b_{i,2}b_{i,3} = 0 \end{cases} \rightarrow (solve \quad x_{13}, x_{23}) \tag{5}$$

$$\vdots$$

$$\Rightarrow \begin{cases} b_{11}x_{1n} + \sum_{i=2}^{n} b_{i,1}b_{i,n} = 0 \\ x_{12}x_{1n} + \sum_{i=2}^{n} b_{i,2}b_{i,n} = 0 \\ \vdots \end{cases} \rightarrow (solve \quad x_{1n}, \cdots, x_{n-1,n})$$

From the above examples of message segmentation methods, we can see that the triangular segmentation has a better loss-tolerance and a lower computational complexity. So, it"s better to divide the message matrix into different triangular blocks.

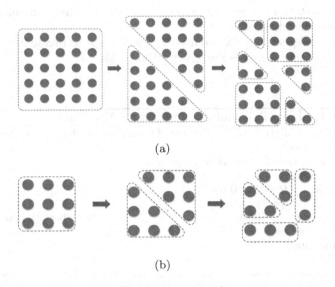

(a)

(b)

Fig. 2. An example of triangular segmentation.

Figure 2 presents an example of triangular segmentation's workflow. In Fig. 2(a), we firstly divide the 5 × 5 matrix into two triangular matrices along with the diagonal, then divide the two triangular matrices into a smaller square matrix and two smaller triangular matrices. In Fig. 2(b), we use the same way to divide the smaller square matrix until all the blocks have the defined size. Algorithm 1 gives the pseudocode for the triangular segmentation algorithm. As an example of a $n \times n$ matrix, we calculate the size of the triangular block which is denoted by $size_T$ according to the formula (6). len_{side} denotes the side length of the triangular blocks, and $max\{len_{side}\}$ denotes the maximum of len_{side} satisfies with formula (6). $size(b)$ denotes the size of message block b.

$$size_T = \frac{max\{len_{side}\} \times (max\{len_{side}\} + 1))}{2} \leq \left\lceil \frac{n}{2} \right\rceil \qquad (6)$$

The main steps of the Algorithm 1 is showed as follows:

(1) If b is a square matrix and $size(b) > size_T$, as showed in Fig. 2(a), we divide the square matrix into two triangular matrices (an upper-triangular matrix and a lower-triangular matrix) along with the diagonal. The two parts share the diagonal.
(2) If b is a triangular matrix and $size(b) \geq len_{side} \times (2 \times len_{side} + 1)$, we can divide it into a square matrix block and two triangular blocks with $size_T$ as showed in Fig. 2(a).

(3) If b is a triangular matrix and $size_T < size(b) < len_{side} \times (2 \times len_{side} + 1)$, as showed in Fig. 2(b), we can divide it into a triangular block with $size_T$ and an arbitrary block.

(4) If b is an arbitrary block and $size(b) \geq size_T$, we divide it into two parts along with the diagonal.

(5) For a $n \times n$ square matrix, we use the above steps to divide it until the size of all the divide blocks is not greater than $\lceil \frac{n}{2} \rceil$.

Algorithm 1. Matrix Triangular Segmentation Algorithm

Input: Q: an $n \times n$ matrix; $size_T$: the size of triangular blocks; len_{side}:the side length of triangular blocks.

Output: B_Arr: the collection of message blocks.

1: $temp\_Arr.add(Q)$
2: **while** $temp\_Arr.length > 0$ **do**
3:     $b = temp\_Arr.pop()$
4:     **if** $b.size \leq size_T$ **then**   ▷ Collect the message block.
5:         $B\_Arr.add(b)$
6:         **continue**
7:     **end if**
8:     **if** (b *is a square matrix*) *and* $b.size > size_T$ **then** ▷ Divide the square matrix.
9:         $[upper\_TriM, lower\_TriM] \leftarrow DivideSquareMatrix(b)$
10:        $temp\_Arr.add([upper\_TriM, lower\_TriM])$
11:    **else if** (b *is a triangular matrix*) *and* $b.size \geq len_{side} \times (2 \times len_{side} + 1)$ **then**
       ▷ Divide the triangular matrix.
12:        $[upper\_TriM, square\_M, lower\_TriM] \leftarrow DivideTriMatrix(b)$
13:        $temp\_Arr.add([upper\_TriM, square\_M, lower\_TriM])$
14:    **else if** (b *is triangular matrix*) *and* $size_T < b.size < len_{side} \times (2 \times len_{side} + 1))$
       then
15:        $[upper\_TriM, arbitrary\_M] \leftarrow DivideTriMatrix(b)$
16:        $temp\_Arr.add([upper\_TriM, arbitrary\_M])$
17:    **else**
18:        $[arbitrary\_M1, arbitrary\_M2] \leftarrow DivideMatrix(b)$
19:        $temp\_Arr.add([arbitrary\_M1, arbitrary\_M2])$
20:    **end if**
21: **end while**

$$M = QR = [B_1, B_2, ..., B_k]R$$
$$= [B_1R, B_2R, ..., B_{\lceil \frac{k}{2}+1 \rceil}R, ..., B_k] \tag{7}$$
$$= [M_1, M_2, ..., M_k]$$

We use formula (7) to represent the divided message blocks. In formula (7), matrix Q firstly is divided into k blocks, $[B_1, B_2, ..., B_k]$. Because the matrix R is another key matrix to reconstruct the original message M, so the matrix R also need to be delivered to the target. We randomly choose $\lceil \frac{k}{2} + 1 \rceil$ message blocks to take the matrix R. Because more than 50% of the message blocks is lost, it's hard to recover the original message. So, there is no need that every message block takes the matrix R. At last, we generate k message blocks, $[M_1, M_2, ..., M_k]$.

3.2 Multi-path Communication

Assume that the message matrix M has been divided into k message blocks, $[M_1, M_2, ..., M_k]$. The sender chooses $k \times m$ nodes to build k communication channels and each channel contains m nodes as showed in Fig. 3 in which R_{ij} ($1 \leq i \leq k$, $1 \leq j \leq m$) denotes the $j-th$ node in the $i-th$ channel.

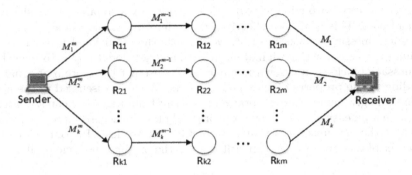

Fig. 3. Multi-path communication network with $k \times m$ nodes.

The sender firstly encrypts the message blocks according to the corresponding channels which is similar to Tor [22,23]. For example, the message block M_i ($1 \leq i \leq k$) will be sent to the $i-th$ channel. Because the message block M_i is transferred from the R_{i1} to R_{im}, the sender encrypts the message block M_i with the public keys of the nodes in reverse order showed in formula (8). M_i^m denotes the message block encrypted by the m nodes of the $i-th$ channel in reverse order and $E_{ij}\{X\}$ ($1 \leq j \leq m$) denotes the message block X is encrypted by the public key of the $j-th$ node in this channel.

$$M_i^m = E_{i1}\{E_{i2}\{\cdots E_{im}\{M_i\}\}\} \tag{8}$$

Then, when the encrypted message block M_i^m is sent to the $i-th$ channel, the first node of this channel decrypts the first encryption layer and sends it to the next node of this channel for further decryption. After the decryption of the last node in this channel, the message block M_i is decrypted completely. As showed in Fig. 3, the k encrypted message blocks are sent to different channels, after the decryption of all nodes in each channel, the receiver will get the message blocks for recovery of original message.

3.3   Loss-Tolerant Reconstruction of Message

To deal with the lost of message blocks in multi-path communication, the traditional way is to request for the lost message blocks once again. But this way is not suit to the tracking-resistant communication and it's easy to reveal the sender, receiver and communication channel [25–27]. So the loss-tolerant reconstruction of message blocks is very helpful in improving the communication efficiency and tracking-resistance of the anti-tracking network.

As we have mentioned in the above section, the triangular segmentation has a better loss-tolerance and a lower computational complexity. Figure 4 shows an example of a 5 × 5 matrix's segmentation according to the Algorithm 1. The gray nodes connected by the solid line are redundant nodes carried by different blocks because the two triangular matrices divided by a square matrix share the diagonal part. This is also an effective way to improve the loss-tolerance.

If some message blocks are lost, we can use the traditional way showed as formula (4) to recover the original message. The traditional way is to regard the lost message blocks as unknown numbers and construct the system of equations according to the property of orthogonal matrix. We have discussed in the above sections and give no further elaboration here. But from Fig. 4, we can see directly that there is an easy way to recover the original message according to the formula (5) under the circumstances that any four blocks are lost. In some cases that five or six blocks are lost, we can still recover the original message easily.

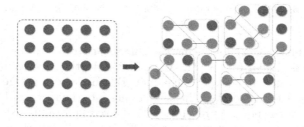

Fig. 4. The segmentation of 5 × 5 matrix.

To throw the further light on the reconstruction mechanism of message blocks, Fig. 5 illustrates some cases that it's easy to reconstruct the original message. The parts in shadow denote the lost blocks. In the four cases of Fig. 5, the lost message blocks are spread out in the original matrix in different ways, but the message reconstruction in these four cases are very easy. The common character of these four cases is that there must be a row or column has full values and according to this row or column, we can calculate one lost value in other row or column. In other words, we can use the current rows or columns with full values to recover a new row or column until all rows or columns are recovered. Next, we conclude the common character of these cases as showed in Definition (1).

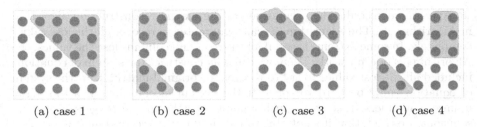

(a) case 1   (b) case 2   (c) case 3   (d) case 4

Fig. 5. Different cases with the lost of different message blocks. In all these cases, the reconstruction of message blocks is easy.

Definition 1. *Let* A *be a* $n \times n$ *matrix with lost values. There are* k *rows (columns) which have lost values, and the number of the lost values in each row (column) is* $m_i (1 \leq i \leq k)$. *Assume the* $[m_1, ..., m_i]$ *is in increasing order. For any* $m_i (1 \leq i \leq k)$, *if* m_i *satisfies the following condition, the reconstruction of* A *is easy and the complexity of the reconstruction is* $O(n)$.

$$m_i \leq n - k + i - 1 \qquad (9)$$

On the contrary, if the current rows or columns can't recover a new row or column, we can only construct the system of the equations which include all the lost values according to the property of orthogonal matrix as mentioned in Sect. 4.1. If the system of equations has too many unknown numbers, it may be very hard to get the solutions.

Algorithm 2. Matrix Reconstruction Algorithm

Input: A: a $n \times n$ matrix with lost values.

1: **while** A *has lost values* **do**
2:     $row_{min} \leftarrow GetMinRow(A)$ ▷ Get a row with the min number of lost values.
3:     $num_{row} \leftarrow GetRowNumber(A)$ ▷ Get the number of rows with lost values.
4:     $len_{lost} \leftarrow GetLostNumber(row_{min})$ ▷ Get the number of lost values.
5:     **if** $len_{lost} \leq n - num_{row}$ **then**
6:         $Refresh(row_{min})$ ▷ Calculate the lost values.
7:         $Refresh(A, row_{min})$ ▷ Update A with the calculated values.
8:     **end if**
9:     $col_{min} \leftarrow GetMinCol(A)$ ▷ Get a column with the min number of lost values.
10:     $num_{col} \leftarrow GetColNumber(A)$ ▷ Get the number of columns with lost values.
11:     $len_{lost} \leftarrow GetLostNumber(col_{min})$ ▷ Get the number of lost values.
12:     **if** $len_{lost} \leq n - num_{col}$ **then**
13:         $Refresh(col_{min})$ ▷ Calculate the lost values.
14:         $Refresh(A, col_{min})$ ▷ Update the matrix with the calculated values.
15:     **end if**
16: **end while**

At last, we describe the pseudocode of the matrix reconstruction algorithm in Algorithm (2). The Algorithm (2) can't guarantee to recover all the lost values completely. In some extreme cases, if all the rows and columns lose the values, the Algorithm (2) doesn't work. Then, we can only construct the system of equations included all the lost values to try to recover the original matrix. But, the system of equations may be hard to solve. If the system of equations has too many unknown numbers, takes too much computational expense or gets too many solutions, we think that it's not able to reconstruct the received message blocks. Usually, if more than half of the message blocks are lost, it's impossible to reconstruct the received message blocks.

If we can recover all the lost values, then we can get the orthogonal matrix Q. As showed in formula (7), because more than half of the message blocks takes the upper triangular matrix R, we can receive at least one matrix R. Through the multiplication of the matrix Q and R, we can get the original matrix M.

4   Experiment and Analysis

In this section, we firstly evaluate the loss-tolerant performance and the message reconstruction efficiency of Algorithm (2) and solving the equation set. Then, we analyze data expansion rate of FMC.

4.1   Evaluation of FMC

Evaluation of Loss-Tolerant Performance. The loss-tolerance in multipath communication of anti-tracking network is a key technique to improve the tracking-resistance and transmission efficiency. The loss-tolerant performance is subject to the ability of the original message recovery when some message blocks are lost. We firstly evaluate the loss-tolerant performance of the two reconstruction methods mentioned above: the method of solving equation set and Algorithm (2). For the convenience of discussion, we introduce the following indexes to quantify the loss-tolerant performance.

- $Size_{all}$: The size of all the message blocks.
- $Size_{lost}$: The size of the lost message blocks.
- $P_{lost} = \frac{Size_{lost}}{Size_{all}}$: The proportion of the lost message blocks in the original message.
- T: The experiment times with the same P_{lost}.
- T_s: The number of successful reconstructions by solving equation set after T experiments.
- T_e: The number of successful reconstructions by Algorithm (2) after T experiments.
- $P_s = \frac{T_s}{T}$: The probability of the successful reconstructions by solving equation set.
- $P_e = \frac{T_e}{T}$: The probability of the successful reconstructions by Algorithm (2).

We carried out three experiments. In the three experiments, we separately transferred a 10×10 matrix, a 20×20 matrix, and a 30×30 matrix and repeated these experiments for 50 times. In each experiment, we randomly discard the proportion of message blocks from 0% to 50%. With the increase of P_{lost}, we evaluate the loss-tolerant performance of FMC by P_s and P_e. As we have mentioned above, the time complexity of Algorithm (2) is only $O(n)$. But, the Algorithm (2) can't solve all the problems. If so, we can only solve the system of equations include the lost message blocks to recover the original message, but this may cost a high computational complexity. So, we use P_s and P_e to evaluate the loss-tolerant performance of FMC.

As showed in Fig. 6, under the random loss of message blocks, the method of solving equation set has a higher loss-tolerant performance when P_{lost} is less than 15%. But, the Algorithm (2) keeps a high loss-tolerant performance only when P_{lost} is less than 10%. If P_{lost} is more than 35%, the probability of successful reconstruction is very low, and it means that most of the experiments have failed to reconstruct the original message. P_s and P_e deonte the probability of successful reconstruction with the two methods. In most cases, with the same P_{lost}, whether it will succeed in recovery of original message depends on the lost message blocks' distribution. For example, if all the lost message blocks are distributed as showed in Fig. 5, it's absolutely to recover the original message in an easy way by Algorithm (2). On the contrary, if the lost message blocks destruct the matrix so that the matrix has no rows or columns with full values. Then, the recovery process would be difficult, even impossible and it depends on difficulty of solving the system of equations included all the lost message blocks. So, the high probability of successful reconstruction means that the recovery of message reconstruction would be successful in most cases of message blocks' distribution.

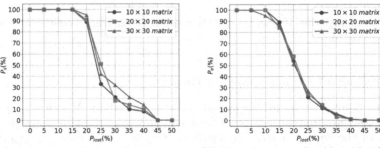

(a) Reconstruction by solving equation set

(b) Reconstruction by Algorithm(2)

Fig. 6. The loss-tolerant performance of FMC with the increasing lost of message blocks

Evaluation of Reconstruction Efficiency. Theoretically, Algorithm (2) is an iterative process and each process of computation is simple, so the computational complexity should be very low. But the complexity of solving the system of equations included all the lost message blocks should be very high, because this method tries to recover all the lost message blocks at one time. To evaluate the reconstruction efficiency of the two methods, we counted the time requirement of each method after 50 times experiments. Figure 7 shows the time requirement of the message reconstruction of the 30×30 matrix with two different methods. In Fig. 7, *Alg* denotes the time requirement of Algorithm (2), and *Equ* denotes the time requirement of solving the equation set. The values of Y-axis in Fig. 7 is the average time requirement of successful message reconstructions after each experiment repeated 50 times. The computational cost of solving equation set grows exponentially, but the computational cost of Algorithm (2) grows slowly. This blames to the difficulty of solving the system of equations. So, if the recovery process can't be executed by Algorithm (2), the computational complexity would grow sharply with the increase of P_{lost}.

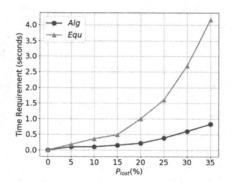

Fig. 7. The average time requirement of the message reconstruction with the increasing lost of message blocks.

4.2   Analysis of Data Expansion Rate

In matrix triangular segmentation algorithm showed in Algorithm (1), if we divide the square matrix into two triangular matrices, the two parts share the diagonal of the square matrix. In this way, the divided blocks would take the extra redundant data, but it's helpful to improve the loss-tolerance in the later message reconstruction. As we have mentioned above, we divide the message matrix into as many triangular blocks as possible to improve the loss-tolerance of FMC. But the more triangular message blocks we divide, the more redundant data the message blocks would take. Except that, there is an upper triangular matrix R after the orthogonal decomposition. R also need to be transferred to the receiver for recovery of the original message. To make sure the receiver can receive the matrix R, we attach it to different message blocks for transmission.

Then, the multiple transmission of matrix R will also lead to the increase of redundant data. So, the data expansion rate is subject to the granularity of message blocks and the carrier rate of matrix R which are defined as follows.

- Granularity: the biggest size of the message blocks. The number of message blocks after matrix segmentation grows in inverse proportion to the granularity of message blocks.
- Carrier rate: the proportion of message blocks which carry the matrix R for transmission. The higher carrier rate will result in the higher data expansion rate in multi-path communication.

We define the data expansion rate(E_{data}) as showed in formula (10) in which M denotes the size of original message, R_{seg} denotes the size of redundant data in matrix segmentation, R_{com} denotes the size of redundant data in multi-path communication.

$$E_{data} = \frac{R_{seg} + R_{com}}{M} \qquad (10)$$

We firstly experimented with a 10×10 matrix, and calculated the E_{data} with the changes of granularity and carrier rate. As we can see in Fig. 8, E_{data} is very high in the point of lowest granularity and highest carrier rate. With the increase of granularity and decrease of carrier rate, E_{data} declines sharply. The influence of granularity on E_{data} rests with R_{seg} and the number of message blocks, because the small granularity leads to the more message blocks and bigger redundant data in matrix segmentation. The influence of carrier rate on E_{data} rests with the number of message blocks which carry the matrix R, because the more message blocks will lead to a higher R_{com}. So, a proper granularity will reduce the R_{seg} and the number of message blocks. The small number of message blocks will reduce the R_{com}.

We have mentioned in above sections that 50% of message blocks are randomly choosed to take matrix R. Then, the receiver will certainly can receive the matrix R if he receives more than 50% message blocks. We set the carrier rate to 50%, and experimented with 10×10 matrix, 20×20 matrix and 30×30 matrix to evaluate the changes of E_{data} with the changes of granularity. As showed in Fig. 9(a), the too small granularity of message blocks will lead to the high E_{data}. But, E_{data} declines sharply with the increase of the granularity because the number of message blocks decreases with the increase of granularity. The curves of 10×10, 20×20 and 30×30 matrices become flatter in the point of 5, 10 and 15 respectively. So, we choose $\lceil \frac{n}{2} \rceil$ (n denotes the dimension of a square matrix) as the biggest size of each message blocks. In the Fig. 9(b), we evaluate the relationship between E_{data} and carrier rate with the granularity of $\lceil \frac{n}{2} \rceil$. The higher carrier rate leads to higher E_{data}. If we set the carrier rate to 50%, the bigger matrix has a higher data expansion rate. So, in practice, we need to adjust the carrier rate to a proper value according to the real situation. If we can estimate the loss rate of message blocks in real network environment, we only need to make the carrier rate is not less than the loss rate, instead of the biggest value 50%.

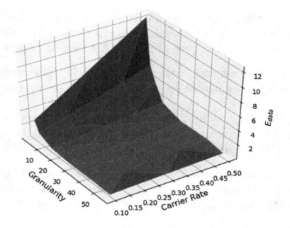

Fig. 8. The data expansion rate of 10×10 matrix.

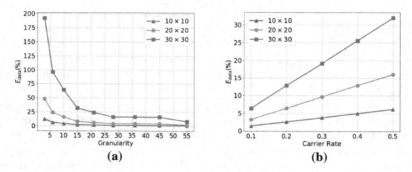

Fig. 9. (a) The relationship between data expansion rate and granularity with 50% carrier rate. (b) The relationship between data expansion rate and carrier rate with the granularity of $\lceil \frac{n}{2} \rceil$.

From the above experiments, we can conclude that if the granularity of message blocks is too small, the data expansion rate is too high which may lower the communication efficiency. If the granularity is too big, the number of message blocks is too small which may lower the loss-tolerance and tracking-resistance of FMC. So, we usually set the granularity of message blocks to $\lceil \frac{n}{2} \rceil$ for a $n \times n$ matrix.

5   Conclusion

In this paper, we propose a loss-tolerant mechanism of message segmentation and reconstruction applied in the multi-path communication of anti-tracking network, called FMC. FMC firstly encodes the message into orthogonal matrix, and divides the orthogonal matrix into triangular message blocks as more as possible, because the triangular segmentation of orthogonal matrix has a better loss-tolerance and a lower computational complexity. Then, we send the message blocks into different paths for transmission and each communication path guarantees the security of the transmitted message. At last, the receiver collects the message blocks for recovery of original message. From the experiments, we can see that FMC can recover the original message by 15% lost message blocks at most. If the loss rate is more than 15%, FMC can't guarantee to recover the original message and the successful recovery depends on the distribution of message blocks in the original matrix. At last, we analyze the data expansion rate of FMC in matrix segmentation and multi-path communication. For a $n \times n$ matrix, $\lceil \frac{n}{2} \rceil$ is a proper size of message blocks to balance loss-tolerance, tracking-resistance and communication efficiency.

Acknowledgements. We thank the anonymous reviewers for their insightful comments. This research was supported in part by the national natural science foundation of China under grant No. U1736218.

References

1. Buchanan, T., Paine, C., Joinson, A.N., et al.: Development of measures of online privacy concern and protection for use on the Internet. J. Assoc. Inf. Sci. Technol. **58**(2), 157–165 (2014)
2. Milne, G.R., Rohm, A.J., Bahl, S.: Consumers' protection of online privacy and identity. J. Consum. Aff. **38**(2), 217–232 (2010)
3. Jian, R., Jie, W.: Survey on anonymous communications in computer networks. Comput. Commun. **33**(4), 420–431 (2010)
4. Ho, T., Leong, B., Chang, Y.H., et al.: Network monitoring in multicast networks using network coding. In: International Symposium on Information Theory (2005)
5. Rad, M.M., Fouli, K., Fathallah, H., et al.: Passive optical network monitoring: challenges and requirements. IEEE Commun. Mag. **49**(2), S45–S52 (2011)
6. Miklas, A.G., Saroiu, S., Wolman, A., et al.: Bunker: a privacy-oriented platform for network tracing. In: Usenix Symposium on Networked Systems Design & Implementation (2009)
7. Wang, Y., Jun, B.I., Zhang, K.: A tool for tracing network data plane via SDN/OpenFlow. Sci. China (Inf. Sci.) **60**(02), 74–86 (2017)
8. François, J., Wang, S., State, R., Engel, T.: BotTrack: tracking botnets using NetFlow and PageRank. In: Domingo-Pascual, J., Manzoni, P., Palazzo, S., Pont, A., Scoglio, C. (eds.) NETWORKING 2011. LNCS, vol. 6640, pp. 1–14. Springer, Heidelberg (2011). https://doi.org/10.1007/978-3-642-20757-0_1
9. Wang, W., Duan, G., Wang, J., et al.: An anonymous communication mechanism without key infrastructure based on multi-paths network coding. In: Global Telecommunications Conference (2009)
10. Wang, X., Chen, S., Jajodia, S.: Network flow watermarking attack on low-latency anonymous communication systems. In: IEEE Symposium on Security & Privacy (2007)
11. Pries, R., Yu, W., Fu, X., et al.: A new replay attack against anonymous communication networks. In: IEEE International Conference on Communications (2008)

12. Raposo, D., Pardal, M.L., Rodrigues, L., et al.: MACHETE: multi-path communication for security. In: IEEE International Symposium on Network Computing & Applications (2016)
13. Shirazi, F., Simeonovski, M., Asghar, M.R., et al.: A survey on routing in anonymous communication protocols. ACM Comput. Surv. (CSUR) **51**(3), 51 (2018)
14. Yang, M., Luo, J., Ling, Z., et al.: De-anonymizing and countermeasures in anonymous communication networks. IEEE Commun. Mag. **53**(4), 60–66 (2015)
15. Wang, J., Wang, T., Yang, Z., et al.: SEINA: a stealthy and effective internal attack in Hadoop systems. In: 2017 International Conference on Computing, Networking and Communications (ICNC). IEEE, pp. 525–530 (2017)
16. Jan, M.A., Nanda, P., He, X., et al.: A Sybil attack detection scheme for a forest wildfire monitoring application. Future Gener. Comput. Syst. **80**, 613–626 (2018)
17. Tiwari, R., Saxena, T.: A review on Sybil and Sinkhole of service attack in VANET. Recent Trends Electron. Commun. Syst. **5**(1), 7–11 (2018)
18. Wright, M.K., Adler, M., Levine, B.N., et al.: Passive-logging attacks against anonymous communications systems. ACM Trans. Inf. Syst. Secur. **11**(2), 1–34 (2008)
19. Serjantov, A., Sewell, P.: Passive attack analysis for connection-based anonymity systems. In: Snekkenes, E., Gollmann, D. (eds.) ESORICS 2003. LNCS, vol. 2808, pp. 116–131. Springer, Heidelberg (2003). https://doi.org/10.1007/978-3-540-39650-5_7
20. Liu, Y., Morgan, Y.: Security against passive attacks on network coding system-a survey. Comput. Netw. **138**, 57–76 (2018)
21. Kwon, A., AlSabah, M., Lazar, D., et al.: Circuit fingerprinting attacks: passive deanonymization of tor hidden services. In: 24th USENIX Security Symposium (USENIX Security 2015), pp. 287–302 (2015)
22. Klonowski, M., Kutyłowski, M., Zagórski, F.: Anonymous communication with on-line and off-line onion encoding. In: Vojtáš, P., Bieliková, M., Charron-Bost, B., Sýkora, O. (eds.) SOFSEM 2005. LNCS, vol. 3381, pp. 229–238. Springer, Heidelberg (2005). https://doi.org/10.1007/978-3-540-30577-4_26
23. Dingledine, R., Mathewson, N., Syverson, P.: Tor: the second-generation onion router. In: Proceedings of the 13th USENIX Security Symposium on Berkeley, USENIX Association, pp. 303–320 (2004)
24. Franklin, J.N.: Matrix theory. Courier Corporation (2012)
25. Faloutsos, M.: Detecting malware with graph-based methods: traffic classification, botnets, and Facebook scams. In: International Conference on World Wide Web Companion (2013)
26. Jing, W., Paschalidis, I.C.: Botnet detection using social graph analysis. In: Allerton Conference on Communication (2015)
27. Jing, W., Paschalidis, I.C.: Botnet detection based on anomaly and community detection. IEEE Trans. Control Netw. Syst. **4**(2), 1–1 (2017)
28. Blömer, J.: How to share a secret. Commun. ACM **22**(22), 612–613 (2011)

Let's Talk Privacy

Ticket Transparency: Accountable Single Sign-On with Privacy-Preserving Public Logs

Dawei Chu[1,2], Jingqiang Lin[1,2,3], Fengjun Li[4], Xiaokun Zhang[5(✉)], Qiongxiao Wang[1,2,3], and Guangqi Liu[1,2,3]

[1] State Key Laboratory of Information Security, Institute of Information Engineering, Chinese Academy of Sciences, Beijing, China
[2] School of Cyber Security, University of Chinese Academy of Sciences, Beijing, China
[3] Data Assurance and Communication Security Center, Chinese Academy of Sciences, Beijing, China
[4] Department of Electrical Engineering and Computer Science, The University of Kansas, Lawrence, USA
[5] Academy of Opto-Electronics, Chinese Academy of Sciences, Beijing, China
xkzhang@aoe.ac.cn

Abstract. Single sign-on (SSO) is becoming more and more popular in the Internet. An SSO ticket issued by the identity provider (IdP) allows an entity to sign onto a relying party (RP) on behalf of the account enclosed in the ticket. To ensure its authenticity, an SSO ticket is digitally signed by the IdP and verified by the RP. However, recent security incidents indicate that a signing system (e.g., certification authority) might be compromised to sign fraudulent messages, even when it is well protected in accredited commercial systems. Compared with certification authorities, the online signing components of IdPs are even more exposed to adversaries and thus more vulnerable to such threats in practice. This paper proposes *ticket transparency* to provide accountable SSO services with privacy-preserving public logs against potentially fraudulent tickets issued by a compromised IdP. With this scheme, an IdP-signed ticket is accepted by the RP only if it is recorded in the public logs. It enables a user to check all his tickets in the public logs and detect any fraudulent ticket issued without his participation or authorization. We integrate blind signatures, identity-based encryption and Bloom filters in the design, to balance transparency, privacy and efficiency in these security-enhanced SSO services. To the best of our knowledge, this is the first attempt to solve the security problems caused by potentially intruded or compromised IdPs in the SSO services.

This work was partially supported by National Natural Science Foundation of China (Award 61772518), National Key RD Plan of China (Award 2017YFB0802100), NSF DGE-1565570, NSA SoS Initiative and the Ripple University Blockchain Research Initiative.

Keywords: Accountability · Privacy · Single sign-on · Transparency · Trust

1   Introduction

Single sign-on (SSO) services have recently become the popular identity management and authentication infrastructure in the Internet. Famous IT service providers such as Google, PayPal, Facebook and Microsoft provide their own SSO services, which allow a user to sign onto millions of networked applications with the same account using SSO protocols such as OpenID Connect [56] and SAML with WS-Security [50] in SOAP [28].

A critical message in the SSO services is the SSO *ticket* (e.g., id_token in OpenID Connect or assertion in SAML), which includes the authenticated user account, its validity period, the unique identifier (or nonce) against replay attacks, and other optional fields. An SSO ticket is signed by the *identity provider* (IdP), after it authenticates a user. Then, the user presents the ticket to the target *relying party* (RP). Trusting the IdP, the RP accepts the ticket after verifying the signature of the IdP and allows the user to sign on as the account enclosed in the ticket. So the IdP is a trusted third party that signs messages to provide security guarantees of user identity and authentication for the RPs in SSO services. In this sense, IdPs take a similar role as certification authorities (CAs) in the public key infrastructure (PKI), which sign certificates to provide security guarantees (such as authentication, confidentiality, data integrity and non-repudiation) for various PKI-based applications [14].

However, recent incidents indicate that third-party security providers cannot be fully trusted as expected, because a signing system that is protected with defense-in-depth protections could still be compromised to sign fraudulent messages. For example, several well-known professional CAs, which are accredited to provide certificate services, were intruded or deceived to sign fraudulent TLS server certificates [13,24,48,64], which contained well-formatted but incorrect or fake information. These fraudulent certificates are exploited to launch man-in-the-middle (MitM) attacks to intercept the private data of victims.

Compared with the signing component of CAs, which is usually built on hardware security modules (HSMs) in isolated networks, the online signing component of IdPs is even more exposed to adversaries and thus more vulnerable to such threats in practice. For example, in the golden SAML attack [53], the attackers only need an unprivileged user account of Active Directory Federation Services to access the private key to sign SSO tickets. Meanwhile, a fraudulent ticket allows an attacker to sign onto numerous online applications on behalf of the victim user, which will make the IdPs be an attack target of interest [23,43,53]. Moreover, fraudulent SSO tickets are much more difficult to detect than fraudulent TLS server certificates, because they are presented only to a particular RP, valid for a very short period of time (e.g., 3 to 5 min), and transmitted over private channels such as HTTPS.

It is of great importance to build security-enhanced mechanisms to mitigate the risks by malicious or compromised third parties that were completely trusted in the past. Certificate transparency [38] is widely adopted to enhance the security of the TLS certificate ecosystem [2,29,51]. It employs a log server to sign the CA-signed TLS server certificates again and record them in publicly-visible logs. The second signature by log servers, called *signed certificate timestamp* (SCT), is sent along with the server certificate to browsers in TLS negotiations. Here, the SCT is a promise to make a certificate visible in the public logs. Then, interested parties, especially the TLS servers whose identities are bound in (fraudulent) certificates, are enabled to search for all relevant certificates in the public logs and check whether they are issued with necessary authorization.

Certificate transparency provides a framework to monitor CAs' certificate signing operations and thus introduces transparency in the creation of CA-signed certificates. Following this idea, we extend the *public accountability* from the CAs in PKIs to the IdPs in SSO services, and propose *ticket transparency* to address the problem of fraudulent SSO tickets. Fraudulent SSO tickets are well-formatted and verifiable tickets issued by malicious or compromised IdPs but without the authorization or participation of ticket holders whose accounts are enclosed in the tickets. Similar to certificate transparency, ticket transparency introduces log servers to monitor the ticket-signing operations of the IdPs. In particular, an IdP-signed ticket needs to be signed by a log server again, before it is accepted by the target RP. This additional signature by the log server is also a promise to record the SSO tickets in publicly-visible logs. Ticket transparency enables any user, who suspects an attacker signing onto any RP on behalf of him with a fraudulent ticket, to search for all tickets with his account in the public logs and detect the fraudulent ones among them.

However, the certificate transparency framework cannot be directly adopted in SSO services due to the privacy concerns. Different from certificates, SSO tickets contain privacy information about the service requester (i.e., the user), the service provider (i.e., the RP), the occurrence time of sign-on activities, etc. To protect user privacy while enable efficient ticket search in the accountable SSO services, we integrate blind signatures [11], identity-based encryption (IBE) [8], and Bloom filters [7] in the design of ticket transparency. First, a ticket is *blindly signed by the log server*, so the content of the ticket is protected against the log server. That is, the ticket is blinded before recorded in the public logs. Secondly, the secret blinding factor is stored along with the ticket in public logs, but *encrypted using the user's IBE public key* by the IdP. Therefore, only the user is able to un-blind his tickets. This encryption is identity-based, to reduce the overhead of key management in IdPs. More importantly, the inherent key escrow of IBE ensures the decryption of blinding factors in necessary cases; for example, when a user wants to decrypt a suspected ticket but fails. Such failures might be caused by malicious operations of the IdP. The IBE private keys are generated by *a trusted coordinator*, and the coordinator is also responsible for in the dispute resolution when a user cannot decrypt suspected tickets. Finally, more efficient search of tickets is designed with Bloom filters, at the expense of some user privacy; otherwise, a user has to try each blindly-signed ticket in the logs one by one (i.e., attempts to decrypt the blinding factor for each ticket entry), when searching for his tickets. In particular, a pseudonym or index of the user, i.e., the result of *his account through a Bloom filter*, is stored along with each of his tickets in the logs, while other messages of the ticket entry are still kept encrypted or blinded. So he is able to quickly filter out most of other users' tickets.

Contribution. We analyze the accountability of IdPs in the SSO services. Then, ticket transparency is proposed to monitor the operations of the IdPs, ensuring that a fraudulent ticket issued by IdPs will be finally detected by the user or the trusted RP. To the best of our knowledge, *this is the first attempt to solve the security problems caused by potentially compromised IdPs in the SSO services*.

The remainder is organized as follows. Section 2 introduces the background and related work. The ticket transparency scheme is presented in Sect. 3. Then, its security and performance are analyzed in Sects. 4 and 5, respectively. Finally, Sect. 6 concludes this work.

2   Background and Related Work

2.1   Security of SSO Services

The security of SSO services has been investigated for several years. Implementation vulnerabilities have been discovered in several systems, including OpenID and customized SSO protocols [71], SAML with WS-Security [60], OAuth [63,68,69], etc., which allow an attacker to sign onto RPs on behalf of other users or disclose private information. Such vulnerabilities are found in popular SSO services such as Facebook OAuth [71,74], Windows LiveID [72] and Google OpenID [40,71]. [43] exploits the discovery phase of OpenID to introduce a malicious IdP to a vulnerable RP, and all accounts on the RP are then compromised. [23] investigates the threats magnified by SSO, when the session between a user and the IdP is hijacked. These works focused on the secure implementation and deployment of SSO services, and they cannot address the problem caused by fraudulent tickets that are issued by compromised IdPs. On the contrary, our work proposes a solution extending the certificate transparency framework, to enhance the accountability of SSO services against the compromised IdPs.

Anonymous SSO schemes are proposed to allow users to access RPs without revealing their identities to the RPs, for the global system for mobile communication (GSM) [18], based on broadcast encryption [31], group signatures [70] or extended Chebyshev Chaotic Maps [39]. [30] improves the anonymous SSO schemes, where only the designated RP service is able to verify the tickets, and no identity information is released to the IdP. These approaches also assume trustworthy IdPs, and cannot handle the problem of fraudulent tickets. The accountability of the IdPs in anonymous SSO services will be in our future work.

2.2   CA Security Incidents and Certificate Transparency

Well-known accredited CAs are reported to sign fraudulent certificates due to network intrusions [13,24,48,64], reckless identity validations [46,61,62,73], mis-operations [36,47,75], or government compulsions [17,59]. Lessons are learned in an unexpected way that a signing system which is usually built on HSMs in well-protected organizations, could still be compromised to sign fraudulent messages, with well-formatted and verifiable but incorrect or misleading data [13,44,64].

Certificate transparency [38] is proposed to enhance the accountability of CAs' certificate signing operations. After signing a certificate, the CA submits it to a log server, and the log server responds with a SCT, which is a promise to record the certificate in the publicly-visible logs. A web server presents the SCTs along with its certificate in TLS negotiations; otherwise, browsers reject the server certificate. Any party can check the certificates in public logs. For example, a web server periodically searches for the certificates binding its identity. Once a fraudulent certificate is detected (i.e., the key pair is not held by the web server), it will take (out-of-band) actions to stop or mitigate the damage. Meanwhile, auditors periodically verify the consistency of logs to ensure that they are append-only, i.e., a (fraudulent) certificate will never be deleted or modified after added. At the same time, a browser can act as an auditor, to check whether the certificate in the received SCT is publicly visible in the logs. To facilitate the audits, all SCTs are organized as a Merkle hash tree in the logs. [16] defined the security properties of logging schemes, and proved that certificate transparency achieves these properties. Certificate transparency has been widely adopted, and [2,21,29,51] investigated the deployment from different aspects.

CASTLE [44] attempts to eliminate fraudulent certificates, by an air-gapped and completely-touchless signing system for CAs, but it is designed for low-volume workloads and then does not work for online services such as SSO. Threshold signature schemes [15,57] are applied in CAs to protect the private key to sign certificates. Distributing the private key magnifies the difficulty to compromise the key [19,33], but multiple administrators are required to check whether the well-formatted to-be-signed request includes correct information or not [44], which is impractical in online services.

Certificate transparency has been extended in different ways. Revocation transparency [37] provides publicly-accountable certificate revocation in PKIs. CIRT [55] achieved both certificate transparency and revocation transparency by recording certificates in two Merkle hash trees – one of which is in chronological order with all certificates and the other is lexicographical with only the recent ones for each certificate subject. Singh et al. [58] improved CIRT by bilinear-map accumulators and binary trees, to achieve the transparencies with shorter proofs. CONIKS [45] presented transparent key directories based on Merkle prefix trees, allowing its users to audit their public keys while preserving the user privacy. Insynd [52] proposed privacy-preserving transparent logging by authenticated data structures, so users take actions without disclosing everything in the logs. Based on certificate transparency, binary transparency ensures Firefox binaries are publicly logged [49]. A Merkle hash tree is computed over all binaries of each version, and the root node is bound in a certificate that is transparently logged. Attestation transparency [5] integrates certificate transparency with Intel Software Guard eXtension (SGX): a legacy client verifies the service by establishing a TLS channel with the service's private key that is protected in SGX enclaves, while the server certificate is transparently logged. Inspired by the design of certificate transparency, the general transparency overlay [10] is proposed, which can be instantiated to implement transparency for other services.

Certificate transparency and its variations provide references to solve the problem of fraudulent SSO tickets, but these solutions cannot be directly adopted due to the privacy concerns in SSO tickets. Customized privacy-preserving techniques are necessary to be integrated into the design of ticket transparency.

2.3   Accountability of Third-Party Services

The public accountability of cloud services is one of the important topics of cloud security. Third-party auditors are introduced to check the integrity of outsourced data in untrusted cloud systems, while the data are not disclosed to the auditors [66,67]. Liu et al. present consistency as a service [41]: a data cloud is maintained by the cloud service provider, and a group of users that constitute an audit verify whether the data cloud provides the promised level of consistency. PDP [3] and POR [9] enable the tenants to verify whether the data are intact in the untrusted clouds, with lightweight complexity of communications and computations. [32] detects CPU cheating on virtual machines maintained by semi-trusted cloud providers, using CPU-intensive calculations. The SSO services can be viewed as another kind of cloud services – ID as a service, but the accountability of untrusted IdPs have not been well investigated in the literature.

The private key generator (PKG) of IBE is responsible for generating the private keys for all users, so that it has to be fully trusted. This problem of inherent key escrow is mitigated by different ways: (*a*) distributed PKGs [8,34], where the IBE master key is distributed among several independent components, (*b*) accountable IBE [26,27] – if the PKG re-generates the private key for any user, a proof will be produced automatically, or (*c*) KGC-anonymous IBE [12] – the PKG generates the private key for an authenticated user without knowing the list of users identities. We share the same spirit with these solutions that the assumed trust of a third-party service need to be reduced. Meanwhile, these schemes [8,12,26,27,34] can be adopted in our scheme to generate the IBE private keys for users, to improve the trustworthy of the coordinator.

3   Accountable Single Sign-On with Privacy-Preserving Public Logs

In this section, we first present the threat model, security goals, and cryptographic building blocks. Then, the designs of ticket transparency are proposed by steps, following the requirements of transparency, privacy and efficiency.

3.1   Threat Model and Security Goals

Threat Model. A basic SSO scenario includes one IdP, multiple RPs, and a number of users. We assume *the RPs are trusted* since they are the service providers who are responsible to verify the validity of SSO tickets. Ticket transparency aims to prevent unauthorized sign-on to RPs by fraudulent tickets, so the RPs are assumed to be trusted; otherwise, an untrusted RP would allow an attacker to sign on even without any valid tickets.

On the contrary, *the online IdP is potentially malicious* and it could be compromised by a number of attacks. The malicious IdP might pretend to be benign and act as expected to avoid being detected, but it could arbitrarily deviate from its specifications at times. For example, the IdP signs fraudulent tickets and then tries its best to conceal their existence by manipulating other messages.

Ticket transparency depends on an independent log server to publicly record SSO tickets against the malicious IdP. As another online system, *the log server is assumed to be potentially malicious*. It might arbitrarily deviate from its specifications; e.g., intentionally not record a ticket in the logs. Meanwhile, the log server is curious about the users' privacy, so it tries to infer sensitive or private information about any user from the communications and the public logs.

Moreover, the IdP and the log server might collude to sign onto a target RP with fraudulent tickets as a user or leak some private information of the user. They might also collude with some malicious users to take actions. For example, the malicious IdP may register an account in the SSO service, which is completely controlled by itself.

Finally, *an offline trusted coordinator in introduced* in ticket transparency. The coordinator is not involved in the online sign-on activities. The coordinator acts as the PKG of IBE to generate private keys for all users. Since this key generation happens only once for each user, we assume it is finished in an offline way. It also coordinates the dispute resolution process, when a user suspects there exist some fraudulent ticket labeled with his account in the public logs but he cannot decrypt this ticket.

Security Goals. Ticket transparency cannot eliminate fraudulent tickets, but it ensures that any fraudulent ticket will be detected by the victim user, the RPs and/or the coordinator in the future. In particular, if the IdP issues a ticket without the user's authorization or participation, our scheme ensures: (a) the fraudulent ticket without a valid signature by the log server will not be accepted by the RPs; or (b) the fraudulent ticket with a valid signature by the log server, accepted by the target RP, will be identified from the public logs by the victim user, by comparing the ticket entries with his history of sign-on activities. Here, we assume, when the victim user suspects that an attacker signs on using his account, he remembers his sign-on operations especially in the period during which the suspected sign-on action occurred.

The fraudulent-ticket detection as above requires the log server to record all tickets in the public logs. So our scheme also needs to audit the operations of log servers, to ensure that (a) the log server records all valid tickets in the public logs, and (*b*) the public logs are append-only. Any log operation deviating from these specifications, will be detected by the RPs.

The second goal is to protect users' privacy, as much as possible. A user's privacy is defined as the information about his sign-on activities, such as the account, the requested RP, the occurrence time of sign-on requests, etc. All these privacy data are included in the SSO tickets. To protect users' privacy, we employ blind signatures to hide the contents of SSO tickets in the public logs. However, to check whether a suspected ticket is indeed fraudulent, the coordinator needs to un-blind some relevant ticket entries in the dispute resolution. This process may disclose private information of other users. Overall, ticket transparency ensures the fraudulent-ticket detection at a cost of user privacy – compared to the original SSO protocols [50,56], ticket transparency leaks limited user privacy to the trusted coordinator.

3.2   Cryptographic Building Blocks

Ticket transparency is designed on top of three cryptographic building blocks: *blind signature, identity-based encryption*, and *Bloom filter*. We define the notations used in this paper and explain each of these building blocks as follows.

- I, L, C, and R_i, denote the IdP, the log server, the coordinator, and the i-th RP, respectively.
- A is the authenticated user, i.e., the victim of the malicious operations by the IdP and/or the log server.

Blind Signature. With a secret factor s, I blinds m into $m' = \mathbb{B}(m, s)$, and L blindly signs m' into $\mathbb{S}_L(m')$. Then, I un-blinds the message signed by L to obtain $\mathbb{S}_L(m) = \mathbb{U}(\mathbb{S}_L(m'), s)$.

Identity-Based Encryption (IBE). The trusted coordinator holds the IBE master key and generate the private keys for all users. The IBE public parameters are publicly known, and everyone is able to derive A's IBE public key and encrypt m into $\mathbb{E}_A(m)$, but only A itself and the coordinator can decrypt $\mathbb{E}_A(m)$ into m.

Bloom Filter. We adopt a Bloom filter $\mathbb{F}(\cdot)$ to generate the pseudonym (i.e., index) for A in the form of $N_A = \mathbb{F}(A)$. In particular, $\mathbb{F}(A)$ is a vector of compact representations of A, and these representations are concatenated as the pseudonym. The Bloom filter is deterministic, with a false negative rate of zero and a false positive rate of α, where $0 < \alpha < 1$. That is, the expectation of the probability $P(U \neq A | N_U = \mathbb{F}(A))$ is α.

3.3   The Ticket Transparency Framework by Steps

We elaborate the design of ticket transparency step by step, following the requirements of *transparency, privacy* and *efficiency* of the accountable SSO services.

1. Transparent Ticket. In the original SSO protocols, when attempting to sign onto R_i, user A is redirected from R_i to the IdP, who authenticates A and signs a ticket $m = \mathbb{S}_I(A, R_i, o)$, where o denotes the other necessary information in the ticket specified in the SSO protocols. Then, the IdP responds with the ticket to complete the sign-on process.

Improved Design. Instead of sending m to A, I sends it to L, which signs the *transparent ticket* in the form of $\mathbb{S}_L(m) = \mathbb{S}_L(\mathbb{S}_I(A, R_i, o))$ and returns it to I. L records the transparent ticket in the public logs. On receiving $\mathbb{S}_L(m)$, I forwards the ticket to A, who presents the ticket to R_i to complete the sign-on process.

Ticket Verification. After R_i verifies the two signatures on the transparent ticket (and also other verifications as specified in the SSO protocols, including the validity period, the unique identifier against replay attacks, etc.), it accepts the ticket and allows the ticket holder to sign on as A.

Transparency. This is a straightforward extension of certificate transparency to the SSO scenario. It creates a set of transparent tickets and records them in the public logs. The IdP (or the signing system in an IdP) can no longer issue a valid ticket only by itself, as the ticket has to be signed again by the log server. The tickets in the public logs are always available to enable the fraudulent-ticket detection at any time. Whenever any user suspects that an attacker signing onto R_i on behalf of him using a fraudulent ticket, he will retrieve all tickets under his account from the public logs and detect fraudulent tickets.

2. Blindly-Signed Transparent Ticket. While the basic transparency ticket design defeats against compromised IdPs effectively, it leaks user privacy because all sign-on activities are recorded in the public logs, which are accessible to all users. Therefore, we revise the design to *blindly-signed transparent tickets*. In this scheme, the second signatures are created blindly by the log server, to eliminate the private information in the publicly-visible ticket entries.

Improved Design. After signing a ticket $m = \mathbb{S}_I(A, R_i, o)$, I blinds it into $m' = \mathbb{B}(m, s)$ with a random blinding factor s. I sends m', instead of m, to L along with $\mathbb{E}_A(s)$, which enables A to un-blind the ticket in a later time. Accordingly, L blindly signs m' into $\mathbb{S}_L(m')$ and returns it to I. I un-blinds $\mathbb{S}_L(m')$ into $\mathbb{S}_L(\mathbb{S}_I(m))$ and sends it to A. In the meantime, L creates a ticket entry of $\{\mathbb{S}_L(\mathbb{B}(m, s)), \mathbb{E}_A(s)\}$ and records it chronologically in the public logs.

Privacy and Transparency. First, there is no plaintext information stored in the logs, which protects user privacy from irrelevant entities (i.e., the log server and any other entities without the private key cannot decrypt s). When a user suspects himself is the victim of fraudulent tickets, he can retrieve all ticket entries within the suspected period and applies his private key to decrypt $\mathbb{E}_A(s)$ of every ticket entry. For the tickets issued under his account, he is enabled to recover s correctly and then un-blind the tickets. Therefore, any user can only un-blind his own transparent tickets, but not the ones under others' accounts.

3. IBE-Encrypted Blinding Factor. The above scheme works well, if the compromised IdP is not intelligent or collusive with malicious users. However, the compromised IdP could destroy the fraudulent-ticket detection by issuing fraudulent tickets under A's account but blinding them with the secret blinding factor escrowed to another user Z, who is malicious or even does not exist. More specifically, a malicious IdP signs a ticket as $m' = \mathbb{B}(\mathbb{S}_I(A, R_i, o), s)$ and sends it along with $\mathbb{E}_Z(s)$ to the log server. This results in a ticket entry $\{\mathbb{S}_L(\mathbb{B}(m, s)), \mathbb{E}_Z(s)\}$ in the logs. However, when A retrieves this ticket, he cannot decrypt the blinding factor to check whether it is a fraudulent ticket under his account.

We adopt IBE in the framework, utilizing the inherent key escrow of IBE to ensure that the blinding factor can always be decrypted when it is necessary. In our design, the IBE master key is held by the trusted coordinator, and it is always able to decrypt any blinding factor in the public logs. The adoption of IBE also reduces the overhead of key management for the IdP.

Improved Design. When encrypting the blinding factor s into $\mathbb{E}_A(s)$, I derives A's IBE public key and then uses it in the encryption. So A is able to decrypt s by his own IBE private key.

Transparency Against the Intelligent IdP. If a user suspects there exist fraudulent tickets labeled with his account, he follows the process described above to detect fraudulent tickets. Then, after trying to decrypt the secret blinding factors of all suspected ticket entries with his IBE private key, if the user still has doubts, he initiates a *dispute resolution* process to the coordinator. Note that to initiate the process, the user needs to show some reasonable evidences to support his doubt, e.g., an abnormal log in the RP system.

The coordinator C examines the evidences to decide whether the dispute resolution process shall continue and coordinates the process if the evidences are reasonable. In particular, for each suspected ticket entry $\{\mathbb{S}_L(\mathbb{B}(m, s)), \mathbb{E}_A(s)\}$ within the period of dispute, C recovers s with the IBE master key, and then uses s to un-blind the ticket. If and only if s is the correct blinding factor that was used to blind the ticket, C obtains a valid transparent ticket [11]. Then, if this ticket is labeled with the disputer A's account, C sends it to A to allow him to continue the detection as described above; otherwise, if all inquired tickets are associated with other users but not A, C will send nothing to A and the dispute resolution terminates. On the other hand, if it cannot recover a valid transparent ticket using the blinding factor from the IdP, the IdP becomes suspicious – there must be some accidental error or intentional manipulation in the ticket creation.

4. Ticket Entry with Pseudonyms. The ticket entries in the public log contain blindly-signed tickets, which provide no explicit information about the user for whom the ticket is issued. Therefore, a user who suspects fraudulent tickets are issued under his account has to try all tickets that are created in the suspected period, which is very inefficient. We adopt a Bloom filter $\mathbb{F}(\cdot)$ to generate pseudonyms for users and store the pseudonyms along with tickets issued under the enclosed accounts in the public logs. As a result, a user and the coordinator only need to un-blind the entries with his pseudonym, in the fraudulent-ticket detection and the dispute resolution.

Improved Design. For each user A, I generates his pseudonym $N_A = \mathbb{F}(A)$, and sends it along with the blinded ticket $\mathbb{B}(\mathbb{S}_I(A, R_i, o), s)$ and the encrypted blinding factor $\mathbb{E}_A(s)$ to L. Accordingly, the ticket entry in the public logs consists of $\{\mathbb{F}(A), \mathbb{S}_L(\mathbb{B}(\mathbb{S}_I(A, R_i, o), s)), \mathbb{E}_A(s)\}$.

Efficiency and Privacy. The pseudonym works as an index to facilitate the ticket search. In particular, in the cases without dispute, a user only needs to check the ticket entries with his pseudonym, instead of all the tickets in the suspicious period. In the cases with dispute, they still need to check all tickets in the suspected period; otherwise, the malicious IdP could send a fake pseudonym to the log server to conceal the existence of fraudulent tickets.

The pseudonyms in ticket entries may leak user privacy, since it provides a way to associate the sign-on activities of a certain user. If an attacker knows the user's account, he can derive the user's sign-on pattern to some extent – the pseudonyms are generated by the Bloom filter, so that *a user is identified but with the false positive rate* of the adopted Bloom filter. Besides, this privacy leakage is limited to the approximate occurrence time of sign-on activities, but without the RP that the user signs onto.

5. Ticket Entry Verified by RPs. Two forms of each ticket are processed in the design: (*a*) *transparent tickets* presented to the RP, i.e., $\mathbb{S}_L(\mathbb{S}_I(A, R_i, o))$; and (*b*) *blindly-signed transparent tickets* recorded in the logs along with the user pseudonyms, i.e., $\mathbb{S}_L(\mathbb{B}(\mathbb{S}_I(A, R_i, o), s))$. As mentioned above, the log server might not record some tickets in the logs. In this scheme, we require the RP to act as an auditor [38] to audit the operations of the log server. Two forms of each ticket are sent together to the RP, and the blindly-signed transparent tickets enable the audit by RPs against the potentially compromised log server.

Improved Design. The blindly-signed transparent ticket $\mathbb{S}_L(\mathbb{B}(\mathbb{S}_I(A, R_i, o), s))$ and the *plaintext* blinding factor s are sent together by I to A, who forwards them to R_i. Then, R_i un-blinds $\mathbb{S}_L(\mathbb{S}_I(A, R_i, o))$ by itself. Note that these messages are transmitted over secure channels (e.g., HTTPS) as in the original SSO protocols, and s is disclosed to trusted R_i and A only.

Ticket Verification. The RP un-blinds the transparent ticket by itself, and verifies the ticket as the basic transparent ticket design to allow the ticket holder to sign on. Here, it does not verify the relationship between the transparent tickets and the blindly-signed transparent tickets, but un-blinds the blindly-signed ticket by itself to obtain the transparent one instead.

Audit Against the Compromised Log Server. With the blindly-signed transparent ticket, the RP further checks whether every valid ticket is recorded in the public logs or not. Similar as certificate transparency [38], the log server builds a Merkle hash tree over all ticket entries. By comparing the root node of the Merkle hash tree and requesting the Merkle audit path for each received valid ticket, the trusted RP checks whether the logs are append-only and the corresponding ticket entry is in the logs or not. The Merkle audit path of an ticket entry, is the shortest list of additional nodes in the Merkle tree to compute the root node [38].

The trusted RP also verifies if the pseudonym stored along with the blindly-signed transparent ticket is consistent with the account enclosed in the transparent ticket. If not, the RP warns the log server about this potential fraudulent ticket and the involved IdP. Thus, there is no fake pseudonym in ticket entries.

Privacy in the Dispute Resolution. As mentioned above, due to the detection by RPs, there is no fake pseudonym in ticket entries. So, in the dispute resolution, only the ticket entries including the same pseudonym as the disputer, instead of all tickets in the suspected period, will be un-blinded by the trusted coordinator.

3.4 Ticket Transparency in Full View

After the above step-by-step analysis, we present ticket transparency in full view.

Initialization. Before the SSO service is provided, the IdP generates its key pair to sign tickets, and the log server generates its key pair to blindly sign transparent tickets. Their public keys are publicly known, especially to the RPs. The coordinator initializes the IBE parameters: the IBE public parameters are publicly known, and the IBE master key is held by the coordinator. The Bloom filter is decided by the SSO service provider. The initial Merkle hash tree of logs is empty, and the root node stored on every RP is initialized as null.

When a user joins, he registers his account in the IdP and applies for his IBE private key from the coordinator. Or, a user may apply for the IBE private key from the coordinator, only when he suspects any fraudulent tickets labelled with his account and wants to un-blind the suspected tickets.

Sign-On. When A attempts to sign onto R_i, he is redirected to I. After authenticating A, I signs a ticket $m = \mathbb{S}_I(A, R_i, o)$, blinds it into $m' = \mathbb{B}(m, s)$ by a random blinding factor s, and computes $N_A = \mathbb{F}(A)$ and $\mathbb{E}_A(s)$. Then, I sends $\{N_A, m', \mathbb{E}_A(s)\}$ to L.

L blindly signs m' into $\mathbb{S}_L(m')$, and sends it to I. An entry of $\{N_A, \mathbb{S}_L(m'), \mathbb{E}_A(s)\}$ is recorded chronologically in the public logs.

I sends $\{\mathbb{S}_L(m'), s\}$ to A, and the message is forwarded to R_i. R_i un-blinds $\mathbb{S}_L(m')$ into $\mathbb{S}_L(\mathbb{S}_I(A, R_i, o))$, and verifies the validity of this transparent ticket (including the two signatures on the ticket and other fields). Then, it allows A to sign on if the ticket is valid.

The communications among I, A and R_i are over secure channels such as HTTPS, as in the original SSO protocol.

Audit. R_i regularly requests the root node of the Merkle hash tree from L. It checks whether the logs are append-only; i.e., the root node it stored is a leaf of the current Merkle hash tree. Then, the root node is updated on R_i.

For each received valid ticket $\{\mathbb{S}_L(m'), s\}$, R_i requests the Merkle audit path for $\mathbb{S}_L(m')$, and L responds with the entry of $\{N_A, \mathbb{S}_L(m'), \mathbb{E}_A(s)\}$ and its Merkle audit path to the current root node. R_i checks that it is a valid Merkle audit path for the ticket entry; L is faulty. Next, it checks that $N_A = \mathbb{F}(A)$; otherwise, I is malicious. This audit by R_i may be performed for a batch of tickets. Besides, the messages between I and L are also sent over secure channels such as HTTPS.

If any audit fails, the log server is detected as compromised.

Ticket Search and Dispute Resolution. A retrieves all ticket entries where $N_U = \mathbb{F}(A)$, during the interested period. Then, A tries each entry one by one, i.e., attempts to decrypt s to un-blind the transparent ticket. If there is a ticket enclosing his account but without his participation, it is detected as fraudulent.

If A still suspects fraudulent tickets after trying all entries with $\mathbb{F}(A)$ as above, he proposes a dispute with some reasonable evidences supporting this suspect. After C examines this dispute and the evidences, for each suspected ticket entry where $N_U = \mathbb{F}(A)$ but A cannot un-blind the ticket, C decrypts s by the IBE master key and uses it to un-blind the blindly-signed ticket: if the un-blinded result is not a valid transparent ticket, it is asserted that I performed something malicious; otherwise, if A is labelled in this ticket, C sends the transparent ticket to A, which indicates fake $\mathbb{E}_A(s)$ or something abnormal with A's IBE private key; for example, it may result from A's corrupted IBE private key. If it is a valid transparent ticket for another user, nothing is disclosed to A.

4   Security Analysis and Discussion

In this section, we analyze ticket transparency in terms of correctness and privacy. Some extended discussions are also presented.

4.1   Correctness

The correctness is proved with the following sketch: (a) An SSO ticket is accepted by RPs, only if both the IdP and the log server have signed it; (b) Every SSO ticket accepted by RPs is recorded in the logs; and (c) All elements of each ticket entry are verified by non-malicious entities (the user, the RPs, or the coordinator), in the ticket creation and logging, or in the dispute resolution. Thus, the IdP and the log server have to follow their specifications; otherwise, any operation deviating from the specifications in the ticket creation or logging, will result in some verification failures. So a user is able to detect fraudulent tickets by comparing the ticket entries with his history of sign-on activities, in the ticket search or in the dispute resolution.

First of all, it is easy to verify that, with our scheme, an SSO ticket is accepted by RPs only if both the IdP and the log server have signed it, because the trusted RPs verify the two signatures on each ticket. Next, every ticket accepted by RPs is recorded in the logs as a blinded message; otherwise, if such a ticket is not recorded in the logs, the log server is detected as compromised by RPs. As described in Sect. 3.4, the audits by RPs also ensure that, every valid transparent ticket corresponds to a blinded message where $N_A = \mathbb{F}(A)$. So user A is able to retrieve all his valid tickets among the ticket entries where $N_U = \mathbb{F}(A)$, by his own IBE private key or in the dispute resolution.

If the IdP attempts to prevent the user from identifying such a transparent ticket, it will be detected as malicious sometime. First, the audits by RPs ensure all valid tickets are recorded in the logs. For each valid transparent ticket

$\mathbb{S}_L(\mathbb{S}_I(A, R_i, o))$, three elements $\{N_A, \mathbb{S}_L(m'), \mathbb{E}_A(s)\}$ of the corresponding ticket entry are verified by non-malicious entities as follows: (a) the relationship of N_U, $\mathbb{S}_L(m)$, $\mathbb{S}_L(\mathbb{B}(m, s))$ and A is verified by the trusted RP that receives s, when A is signing on; and (b) the relationship of N_U, $\mathbb{S}_L(\mathbb{B}(m, s))$ and $\mathbb{E}_A(s)$ where $N_U = \mathbb{F}(A)$, is verified by A in the ticket search or by the coordinator in the dispute resolution. Specially, a mis-matching blinding factor will not result in the log server's valid signature of $\mathbb{S}_I(A, R_i, o)$ [11]. So the IdP has to encrypt the correct blinding factor in the ticket entry, and nobody can tamper with a ticket entry without being detected. Finally, in the above verifications by non-malicious entities (the user, the RPs, or the coordinator), the messages generated by the IdP, the log server and other users are verified independently, so that their collusion does not break the verifications.

In summary, the IdP cannot conceal the existence of a transparent ticket if it is accepted by RPs. So a ticket issued without the user's participation or authorization, will be detected by the user finally in the ticket search or in the dispute resolution.

4.2 Privacy

First of all, no *extra* user privacy is leaked to the IdP, compared with the original SSO protocols [50, 56]. The IdP is always aware of the users' all sign-on activities, either in the original SSO protocols or with ticket transparency.

With ticket transparency, the privacy on a user's sign-on activities is leaked publicly to some extent, compared the original SSO protocols. Next, we compare different scenarios when the Bloom filter is adopted or not. In the case of no dispute, if ticket transparency works *without* the Bloom-filtered pseudonyms, there is not any extra privacy leaked, compared with the original SSO protocols. Only blinded or encrypted data are stored in the public logs. However, in the dispute resolution for A, the detailed sign-on activities of all users other than A during the interested period, are disclosed to the trusted coordinator.

On the contrary, after the Bloom filter is adopted to the pseudonyms, some privacy is leaked publicly in the case of no dispute, while the privacy disclosed to the coordinator is relieved. A curious user can learn another user's history of sign-on activities but with a false positive rate (i.e., the false positive rate of $\mathbb{F}(\cdot)$), provided that the attacker knows the victim user's account. Moreover, this privacy leakage is limited to the occurrence of sign-on activities but no information about the RP that is signed onto, because the ticket is blinded. On the other hand, in the dispute resolution, only the sign-on activities of other users who have the same pseudonyms as the disputer, are disclosed to the coordinator.

In summary, the quantity of the user privacy leaked in ticket transparency depends on the adopted Bloom filter. In general, a Bloom filter with a higher false positive rate, protects more user privacy in the case of no dispute but leaks more to the coordinator in the dispute resolution. In the extreme scenario, we may choose the Bloom filter with the maximum false positive rate (i.e., $\alpha = 1$ and it is a constant function), and actually no pseudonym is stored along with the ticket entries. Therefore, user privacy is leaked to nobody except the coordinator in the dispute resolution. So the Bloom filter shall be chosen carefully, because its false positive rate is a trade-off of efficiency and privacy in different cases.

4.3 Discussion

When encrypting the blinding factors, the IdP shall derive a user's IBE public key based on his account and also a period of validity (e.g., the year) [8]. So the user updates his IBE private key periodically. Accordingly, the public logs of ticket entries are organized as multiple Merkle hash trees according to the occurrence time. Then, some trees of logs may be destroyed after a certain number of years, to mitigate the risk due to the unexpected exposure of IBE private keys. Similarly, the logs of certificate transparency are usually organized as multiple logs of SCTs, according to the expiration year of certificates [25].

When implementing the coordinator which is fully trusted in ticket transparency, distributed PKGs [8,34], accountable IBE [26,27] and KGC-anonymous IBE [12] can be adopted to generate the IBE private keys for users, to improve the dependence of the assumed trustworthy of the coordinator.

Customized Bloom filters may be adopted. A user specifies the Bloom filter to generate his pseudonym, so that he is able to decide the false positive rate by himself based on his own policy. Such customization requires the cooperation of the IdP and RPs, when a ticket entry is created and verified. The coordinator also needs to know the customized Bloom filter, in the dispute resolution.

5 Performance Evaluation

We experimentally measured the performance of computationally expensive cryptographic building blocks. The experiments were conducted with Ubuntu 16.04 on Intel Core i3-6100U CPU (2.30 GHz) and 8 GB RAM. We evaluated the scheme at two different levels of security strength [4]: to achieve 112-bit security, we adopted RSA-2048, Chaum's scheme with RSA-2048 and Boneh-Franklin scheme with Elliptic-Curve-224; and for 128-bit security, RSA-3072 and Elliptic-Curve-256 are used. We measured RSA and Chaum's scheme based on `crypto++` [65], and Boneh-Franklin scheme based on the Stanford IBE library [42].

For each successful instance of the original SSO protocol, there are only one signing operation by the IdP and one verification of traditional signature by the RP. On the other hand, ticket transparency additionally requires one blinding and one IBE encryption by the IdP, one blind signing by the log server, one un-blinding and one verification of blind signature by the RP. So the public-key cryptographic operations introduced by ticket transparency increase the computation time by about 14.9662 ms with 112-bit security or 42.2892 ms with 128-bit security, according to the experimental results shown in Table 1.

In the original SSO protocol, there are at least three rounds of communications among the IdP, the user and the RP, excluding the authentication of users: (a) the sign-on attempt to the RP, (b) the redirection to the IdP to return the

Table 1. The time cost (in ms) of cryptographic operation.

Cryptographic operation		Security strength	
		112-bit	118-bit
Traditional signature RSA with PKCS1 [54]	Sign	2.0217	10.4863
	Verify	0.0432	0.1099
Blind signature Chaum's scheme [6,11]	Blind	0.8899	1.5535
	Sign	2.0456	10.4743
	Un-blind	0.3350	0.8096
	Verify	0.0322	0.0932
IBE	Encrypt	11.6635	29.3586
BF scheme [8]	Decrypt	7.4750	16.1926

ticket, and (c) the final successful sign-on. Compared with the original protocol, ticket transparency requires only one more round of communications between the IdP and the log server, to blindly sign the ticket and record it in the logs.

We measured the network delay of the Google SSO service (https://accounts. google.com) after a user has been authenticated. Note that, in the real-world deployment, more rounds of communications are possible for one instance of the SSO protocol. In particular, the Google SSO service takes four rounds of communications between the browser and the Google SSO server, after a user has been authenticated: three to verify and update the cookie in the browser, and the last one to return the ticket (i.e., id_token of OpenID Connect). With the browser running in our laboratory at the University of Kansas, the average delay is 873.49 ms, excluding the communications between the browser and RPs. Note that, this delay includes data verifications by the browser and the Google SSO service. Therefore, we estimate that about $873.49/4 = 218.37$ ms will be introduced by one round of communications between the IdP and the log server in ticket transparency. Therefore, the total overhead introduced by ticket transparency, in terms of end-to-end processing time, is about 233.34 ms with 112-bit security or 260.66 ms with 128-bit security, about 25%–30% of the original SSO protocol.

6   Conclusion and Future Work

The SSO services are popular in the Internet. An SSO ticket issued by an IdP allows a user to sign onto numerous RPs on behalf of the account labeled in the ticket. Therefore, we argue that the online signing system of SSO services will become an attractive target of interests to adversaries so that they should not be fully trusted. So we need a new security mechanism to detect and/or prevent fraudulent SSO tickets signed by potentially compromised IdPs.

This paper proposes *ticket transparency, the first open framework in the literature to provide the public accountability of IdPs.* With ticket transparency, each IdP-signed ticket is recorded in the public logs, so that any user who suspects there are fraudulent tickets issued under his account is enabled to detect fraudulent tickets in the logs. To achieve ticket transparency while mitigate the privacy leakage by the utilization of public log, we integrate blind signatures, IBE, and Bloom filters in the design to balance transparency, privacy and efficiency in different scenarios. The preliminary performance analysis shows that ticket transparency introduces a reasonably small overhead in the SSO services.

In the future, we plan to prove the security of ticket transparency in a more formal way as [16]. Moreover, for better user privacy, the techniques of privacy-preserved transparency [20,35,45,52] will be integrated into ticket transparency, or we may re-design ticket transparency directly based on homomorphic encryption [1] and zero-knowledge proofs [22]. We will build the prototype on top of open-source SSO systems, to finish more comprehensive experiments.

References

1. Acar, A., Aksu, H., Uluagac, S., Conti, M.: A survey on homomorphic encryption schemes: theory and implementation. ACM Comput. Surv. **51**(4), 79:1–79:35 (2018)
2. Amann, J., Gasser, O., Scheitle, Q., Brent, L., Carle, G., Holz, R.: Mission accomplished? HTTPS security after DigiNotar. In: 17th Internet Measurement Conference (IMC), pp. 325–340 (2017)
3. Ateniese, G., et al.: Provable data possession at untrusted stores. In: 14th ACM Conference on Computer and Communication Security (CCS), pp. 598–610 (2007)
4. Barker, E., Barker, W., Burr, W., Polk, W., Smid, M.: SP 800-57 - Recommendation for key management - Part 1: General. Technical report, National Institute of Standards and Technology (2006)
5. Beekman, J., Manferdelli, J., Wagner, D.: Attestation transparency: building secure Internet services for legacy clients. In: 11th ACM on Asia Conference on Computer and Communications Security (AsiaCCS), pp. 687–698 (2016)
6. Bellare, M., Namprempre, C., Pointcheval, D., Semanko, M.: The one-more-RSA-inversion problems and the security of Chaum's blind signature scheme. J. Cryptol. **16**(3), 185–215 (2003)
7. Bloom, B.: Space/time trade-offs in hash coding with allowable errors. Commun. ACM **13**(7), 422–426 (1970)
8. Boneh, D., Franklin, M.: Identity-based encryption from the weil pairing. In: Kilian, J. (ed.) CRYPTO 2001. LNCS, vol. 2139, pp. 213–229. Springer, Heidelberg (2001). https://doi.org/10.1007/3-540-44647-8_13
9. Bowers, K., Juels, A., Oprea, A.: Proofs of retrievability: theory and implementation. In: ACM Workshop on Cloud Computing Security (CCSW), pp. 43–54 (2009)
10. Chase, M., Meiklejohn, S.: Transparency overlays and applications. In: 13th ACM Conference on Computer and Communications Security (CCS), pp. 168–179 (2016)
11. Chaum, D.: Blind signatures for untraceable payments. In: Chaum, D., Rivest, R.L., Sherman, A.T. (eds.) Advances in Cryptology, pp. 199–203. Springer, Boston (1983). https://doi.org/10.1007/978-1-4757-0602-4_18
12. Chow, S.S.M.: Removing escrow from identity-based encryption. In: Jarecki, S., Tsudik, G. (eds.) PKC 2009. LNCS, vol. 5443, pp. 256–276. Springer, Heidelberg (2009). https://doi.org/10.1007/978-3-642-00468-1_15

13. Comodo Group Inc.: Comodo report of incident (2011). https://www.comodo.com/Comodo-Fraud-Incident-2011-03-23.html
14. Cooper, D., Santesson, S., Farrell, S., Boeyen, S., Housley, R., Polk, W.: IETF RFC 5280: Internet X.509 public key infrastructure certificate and certificate revocation list (CRL) profile (2008)
15. Desmedt, Y.: Society and group oriented cryptography: a new concept. In: Pomerance, C. (ed.) CRYPTO 1987. LNCS, vol. 293, pp. 120–127. Springer, Heidelberg (1988). https://doi.org/10.1007/3-540-48184-2_8
16. Dowling, B., Günther, F., Herath, U., Stebila, D.: Secure logging schemes and certificate transparency. In: Askoxylakis, I., Ioannidis, S., Katsikas, S., Meadows, C. (eds.) ESORICS 2016. LNCS, vol. 9879, pp. 140–158. Springer, Cham (2016). https://doi.org/10.1007/978-3-319-45741-3_8
17. Eckersley, P.: A Syrian man-in-the-middle attack against Facebook (2011). https://www.eff.org/deeplinks/2011/05/syrian-man-middle-against-facebook
18. Elmufti, K., Weerasinghe, D., Rajarajan, M., Rakocevic, V.: Anonymous authentication for mobile single sign-on to protect user privacy. Int. J. Mob. Commun. 6(6), 760–769 (2008)
19. Erman, P., Kantarcioglu, M., Lin, Z., Ulusoy, H.: Preventing cryptographic key leakage in cloud virtual machines. In: 23rd USENIX Security Symposium (2014)
20. Eskandarian, S., Messeri, E., Bonneau, J., Boneh, D.: Certificate transparency with privacy. In: 17th International Symposium on Privacy Enhancing Technologies (PETS), pp. 329–344 (2017)
21. Gasser, O., Hof, B., Helm, M., Korczynski, M., Holz, R., Carle, G.: In log we trust: revealing poor security practices with certificate transparency logs and internet measurements. In: Beverly, R., Smaragdakis, G., Feldmann, A. (eds.) PAM 2018. LNCS, vol. 10771, pp. 173–185. Springer, Cham (2018). https://doi.org/10.1007/978-3-319-76481-8_13
22. Gennaro, R., Gentry, C., Parno, B., Raykova, M.: Quadratic span programs and succinct NIZKs without PCPs. In: Johansson, T., Nguyen, P.Q. (eds.) EUROCRYPT 2013. LNCS, vol. 7881, pp. 626–645. Springer, Heidelberg (2013). https://doi.org/10.1007/978-3-642-38348-9_37
23. Ghasemisharif, M., Ramesh, A., Checkoway, S., Kanich, C., Polakis, J.: O single sign-off, where art thou? An empirical analysis of single sign-on account hijacking and session management on the Web. In: 27th USENIX Security Symposium, pp. 1475–1492 (2018)
24. GlobalSign: Security incident report (2011). https://www.globalsign.com/resources/globalsign-security-incident-report.pdf
25. Google Inc.: Known logs (2018). http://www.certificate-transparency.org/known-logs
26. Goyal, V.: Reducing trust in the PKG in identity based cryptosystems. In: Menezes, A. (ed.) CRYPTO 2007. LNCS, vol. 4622, pp. 430–447. Springer, Heidelberg (2007). https://doi.org/10.1007/978-3-540-74143-5_24
27. Goyal, V., Lu, S., Sahai, A., Waters, B.: Black-box accountable authority identity-based encryption. In: 15th ACM Conference on Computer and Communications Security (CCS), pp. 427–436 (2008)
28. Gudgin, M., et al.: W3C Recommendation - SOAP Version 1.2 Part 1: Messaging Framework, 2nd edn. (2007)
29. Gustafsson, J., Overier, G., Arlitt, M., Carlsson, N.: A first look at the CT landscape: certificate transparency logs in practice. In: Kaafar, M.A., Uhlig, S., Amann, J. (eds.) PAM 2017. LNCS, vol. 10176, pp. 87–99. Springer, Cham (2017). https://doi.org/10.1007/978-3-319-54328-4_7

30. Han, J., Chen, L., Schneider, S., Treharne, H., Wesemeyer, S.: Anonymous single-sign-on for n designated services with traceability. In: Lopez, J., Zhou, J., Soriano, M. (eds.) ESORICS 2018. LNCS, vol. 11098, pp. 470–490. Springer, Cham (2018). https://doi.org/10.1007/978-3-319-99073-6_23
31. Han, J., Mu, Y., Susilo, W., Yan, J.: Anonymous single-sign-on for n designated services with traceability. In: 6th International Conference on Security and Privacy in Communication Networks (SecureComm), pp. 181–198 (2010)
32. Houlihan, R., Du, X., Tan, C.-C., Wu, J., Guizani, M.: Auditing cloud service level agreement on VM CPU speed. In: IEEE International Conference on Communications (ICC), pp. 799–803 (2014)
33. Jing, J., Liu, P., Feng, D., Xiang, J., Gao, N., Lin, J.: ARECA: a highly attack resilient certification authority. In: 1st ACM Workshop on Survivable and Self-Regenerative Systems (SSRS), pp. 53–63 (2003)
34. Kate, A., Goldberg, I.: Distributed private-key generators for identity-based cryptography. In: Garay, J.A., De Prisco, R. (eds.) SCN 2010. LNCS, vol. 6280, pp. 436–453. Springer, Heidelberg (2010). https://doi.org/10.1007/978-3-642-15317-4_27
35. Kubilay, M.Y., Kiraz, M.S., Mantar, H.A.: CertLedger: a new PKI model with certificate transparency based on blockchain. Comput. Secur. **85**, 333–352 (2019)
36. Langley, A.: Further improving digital certificate security (2013). https://security.googleblog.com/2013/12/further-improving-digital-certificate.html
37. Laurie, B., Kasper, E.: Revocation transparency (2012). http://sump2.links.org/files/RevocationTransparency.pdf
38. Laurie, B., Langley, A., Kasper, E.: IETF RFC 6962 - certificate transparency (2014)
39. Lee, T.-F.: Provably secure anonymous single-sign-on authentication mechanisms using extended Chebyshev Chaotic Maps for distributed computer networks. IEEE Syst. J. **12**(2), 1499–1505 (2018)
40. Li, W., Mitchell, C.J.: Analysing the security of Google's implementation of OpenID connect. In: Caballero, J., Zurutuza, U., Rodríguez, R.J. (eds.) DIMVA 2016. LNCS, vol. 9721, pp. 357–376. Springer, Cham (2016). https://doi.org/10.1007/978-3-319-40667-1_18
41. Liu, Q., Wang, G., Wu, J.: Consistency as a service: auditing cloud consistency. IEEE Trans. Netw. Serv. Manag. **11**(1), 25–35 (2014)
42. Lynn, B.: Stanford IBE library v0.7.2. https://github.com/SEI-TTG/id-based-encryption
43. Mainka, C., Mladenov, V., Schwenk, J.: Do not trust me: using malicious IdPs for analyzing and attacking single sign-on. In: 1st IEEE European Symposium on Security and Privacy (Euro S&P), pp. 321–336 (2016)
44. Matsumoto, S., Steffen, S., Perrig, A.: CASTLE: CA signing in a touch-less environment. In: 32nd Annual Computer Security Applications Conference (ACSAC), pp. 546–557 (2016)
45. Melara, M., Blankstein, A., Bonneau, J., Felten, E., Freedman, M.: CONIKS: bringing key transparency to end users. In: 24th USENIX Security Symposium, pp. 383–398 (2015)
46. Microsoft: MS01-017: Erroneous VeriSign-issued digital certificates pose spoofing hazard (2001). https://technet.microsoft.com/library/security/ms01-017
47. Morton, B.: Public announcements concerning the security advisory (2013). https://www.entrust.com/turktrust-unauthorized-ca-certificates
48. Morton, B.: More Google fraudulent certificates (2014). https://www.entrust.com/google-fraudulent-certificates/

49. Mozilla: Binary transparency (2017). https://wiki.mozilla.org/Security/Binary_Transparency
50. Nadalin, A., Kaler, C., Monzillo, R., Hallam-Baker, P.: OASIS standard - Web services security: SOAP message security 1.1 (2006)
51. Nykvist, C., Sjöström, L., Gustafsson, J., Carlsson, N.: Server-side adoption of certificate transparency. In: Beverly, R., Smaragdakis, G., Feldmann, A. (eds.) PAM 2018. LNCS, vol. 10771, pp. 186–199. Springer, Cham (2018). https://doi.org/10.1007/978-3-319-76481-8_14
52. Peeters, R., Pulls, T.: Insynd: improved privacy-preserving transparency logging. In: Askoxylakis, I., Ioannidis, S., Katsikas, S., Meadows, C. (eds.) ESORICS 2016. LNCS, vol. 9879, pp. 121–139. Springer, Cham (2016). https://doi.org/10.1007/978-3-319-45741-3_7
53. Reiner, S.: Golden SAML: Newly discovered attack technique forges authentication to cloud apps
54. RSA Laboratories: PKCS #1 v2.2: RSA cryptography standard. Technical report, EMC Corporation (2012)
55. Ryan, M.: Enhanced certificate transparency and end-to-end encrypted mail. In: 21st ISOC Network and Distributed System Security Symposium (NDSS) (2014)
56. Sakimura, N., Bradley, J., Jones, M., de Medeiros, B., Chuck, M.: OpenID Connect Core 1.0 (2014). http://openid.net/specs/openid-connect-core-1_0.html
57. Shoup, V.: Practical threshold signatures. In: Preneel, B. (ed.) EUROCRYPT 2000. LNCS, vol. 1807, pp. 207–220. Springer, Heidelberg (2000). https://doi.org/10.1007/3-540-45539-6_15
58. Singh, A., Sengupta, B., Ruj, S.: Certificate transparency with enhancements and short proofs. In: Pieprzyk, J., Suriadi, S. (eds.) ACISP 2017. LNCS, vol. 10343, pp. 381–389. Springer, Cham (2017). https://doi.org/10.1007/978-3-319-59870-3_22
59. Soghoian, C., Stamm, S.: Certified lies: detecting and defeating government interception attacks against SSL (short paper). In: Danezis, G. (ed.) FC 2011. LNCS, vol. 7035, pp. 250–259. Springer, Heidelberg (2012). https://doi.org/10.1007/978-3-642-27576-0_20
60. Somorovsky, J., Mayer, A., Schwenk, J., Kampmann, M., Jensen, M.: On breaking SAML: be whoever you want to be. In: 21st USENIX Security Symposium, pp. 397–412 (2012)
61. SSL Shopper: SSL certificate for mozilla.com issued without validation (2008). https://www.sslshopper.com/article-ssl-certificate-for-mozilla.com-issued-without-validation.html
62. Start Commercial (StartCom) Limited: Critical event report (2008). https://blog.startcom.org/wp-content/uploads/2009/01/ciritical-event-report-12-20-2008.pdf
63. Sun, S.-T., Beznosov, K.: The devil is in the (implementation) details: an empirical analysis of OAuth SSO systems. In: 19th ACM Conference on Computer and Communications Security (CCS), pp. 378–390 (2012)
64. VASCO Data Security International Inc.: DigiNotar reports security incident (2011). https://www.vasco.com/about-vasco/press/2011/news_diginotar_reports_security_incident.html
65. Walton, J.: Crypto++ library 7.0. https://cryptopp.com/
66. Wang, C., Chow, S., Wang, Q., Ren, K., Lou, W.: Privacy-preserving public auditing for secure cloud storage. IEEE Trans. Comput. 62(2), 362–375 (2013)
67. Wang, C., Wang, Q., Ren, K., Lou, W.: Privacy-preserving public auditing for data storage security in cloud computing. In: INFOCOM, pp. 525–533 (2010)

68. Wang, H., Zhang, Y., Li, J., Gu, D.: The achilles heel of OAuth: a multi-platform study of OAuth-based authentication. In: 32nd Annual Computer Security Applications Conference (ACSAC), pp. 167–176 (2016)
69. Wang, H., et al.: Vulnerability assessment of OAuth implementations in Android applications. In: 31st Annual Computer Security Applications Conference (ACSAC), pp. 61–70 (2015)
70. Wang, J., Wang, G., Susilo, W.: Anonymous single sign-on schemes transformed from group signatures. In: 5th International Conference on Intelligent Networking and Collaborative Systems (INCoS), pp. 560–567 (2013)
71. Wang, R., Chen, S., Wang, X.: Signing me onto your accounts through Facebook and Google: a traffic-guided security study of commercially deployed single-sign-on web services. In: 33rd IEEE Symposium on Security and Privacy (S&P), pp. 365–379 (2012)
72. Wang, R., Zhou, Y., Chen, S., Qadeer, S., Evans, D., Gurevich, Y.: Explicating SDKs: uncovering assumptions underlying secure authentication and authorization. In: 22nd USENIX Security Symposium, pp. 399–414 (2013)
73. Wilson, K.: Distrusting new CNNIC certificates (2015). https://blog.mozilla.org/security/2015/04/02/distrusting-new-cnnic-certificates/
74. Zhou, Y., Evans, D.: SSOScan: automated testing of web applications for single sign-on vulnerabilities. In: 23rd USENIX Security Symposium, pp. 495–510 (2014)
75. Zusman, M.: Criminal charges are not pursued: Hacking PKI (2009). https://www.defcon.org/images/defcon-17/dc-17-presentations/defcon-17-zusman-hacking_pki.pdf

Decentralized Privacy-Preserving Reputation Management for Mobile Crowdsensing

Lichuan Ma[1,2], Qingqi Pei[1,2(✉)], Youyang Qu[3], Kefeng Fan[4], and Xin Lai[5]

[1] The State Key Laboratory of Integrated Services Networks, Xidian University, Xi'an 710071, China
lcma@xidian.edu.cn, qqpei@mail.xidian.edu.cn
[2] Shaanxi Key Laboratory of Blockchain and Security Computing, Xi'an, China
[3] Deakin University, Melbourne, VIC 3125, Australia
quyo@deakin.edu.au
[4] China Electronics Standardization Institute, Beijing 100007, China
fankf@126.com
[5] Xunlei Network Technologies Limited, Shenzhen 518057, China
laixin@xunlei.com

Abstract. In mobile crowdsensing, mobile devices can be fully utilized to complete various sensing tasks without deploying thousands of static sensors. This property makes that mobile crowdsensing has been adopted by a wide range of practical applications. Since most crowdsensing platforms are open for registration, it is very possible that some participants might be motivated by financial interest or compromised by hackers to provide falsified sensing data. Further, the urgent privacy-preserving need in this scenario has brought more difficulty to deal with these malicious participants. Even though there have existed some approaches to tackle to problem of falsified sensing data while preserving the participants' privacy, these approaches rely on a centralized entity which is easy to be the bottleneck of the security of the whole system. Hence in this paper, we propose a decentralized privacy-preserving management scheme to address the problem above. At first, the system model is present based on the consortium blockchain. Then, a novel metric to evaluate the reliability degree of the sensing data efficiently and privately is designed by leveraging the Paillier crytosystem. Based on this metric, how to update reputation values is given. Extensive experiments verify the effectiveness and efficiency of the proposed scheme.

Keywords: Reputation management · Privacy-preserving · Blockchain · Mobile crowdsensing

1 Introduction

Benefiting from the sensing and communicating technologies, mobile crowdsensing (MCS) has attracted great attentions from both academia and industry. The

S. Chen et al. (Eds.): SecureComm 2019, LNICST 304, pp. 532–548, 2019.
https://doi.org/10.1007/978-3-030-37228-6_26

key idea of MCS is to fully utilize the sensing capabilities of mobile devices to undertake various sensing tasks without deploying thousands of static sensors [1] and [2]. Due to this property, MCS has been already adopted by different practical applications, like road surface alarming [3], air condition monitoring [4], smart city [5] and electronic healthcare [6].

In order to encourage more people to be enrolled in undertaking MCS tasks, most of the MCS platforms are open for registration and anyone that possesses a mobile device can contribute sensing data according to different tasks. This property of MCS makes it difficult to guarantee all the participants to be reliable. Motivated by financial interest or compromised by hackers, some participants can become malicious to provide falsified sensing data to change the final aggregating result. As stated by [7], even a single forged data can make the aggregating result very different from the original one.

When deal with malicious participants that provide falsified data, reputation management mechanisms are usually introduced and their effectiveness has been verified in different scenarios, like cognitive radio networks [8] and online social networks [9]. In these mechanisms, the reliability of sensing data is firstly evaluated. After that, a reputation value for the corresponding data provider is updated according to the degree of the sensing data reliability. By doing this, the reputation value of a malicious participant can be very low. When setting the reputation value as the weight of the according sensing data for aggregation, the influence of the sensing data from malicious participants can be constrained.

However, designing a reputation mechanism for MCS is never a simple task. The first reason is that urgent privacy-preserving needs make it difficult to update the reputation values of the MCS participants. The sensing data in MCS are usually tagged with time and location information. When directly sharing these data, a lot of private information can be inferred and this leads to high privacy leakage risks [3]. A great number of approaches have been proposed to preserve privacy for MCS participants. Generally, these approaches can be classified into two categories: anonymity-based, and encryption-based. The goal of anonymity-based approaches is to make it impossible to link particular sensing data to the related providers [10]. In encryption-based approaches, all the original sensing data are encrypted and only legitimate entities can decrypt them [11]. Without specific settings, anonymity-based approaches make it impossible link the reliability degree of the sensing data to the corresponding provider and cryptography-based approaches make it difficult to evaluate the reliability degree of the sensing data.

The second reason is that centralized reputation management mechanisms would not satisfy the requirements of MCS. Currently, most reputation management mechanisms rely on a centralized reputation manager to evaluate the reliability of the provided data and update the reputation values. As the sensing data become increasingly fine-grained and complicated, more and more data should be sensed, transmitted, and processed [3]. Meanwhile, many MCS tasks are geographically distributed and many sensing tasks might happen in a parallel manned at the same time. Only utilizing one reputation manager would lead to high delays for updating reputation values and this offers more chances for malicious participants to provide falsified sensing data. Moreover, such a centralized entity can be an obvious target of different cyber attacks and thus is the bottleneck of the whole system security [12].

Hence in this paper, we aim to work out a distributed privacy preserving reputation management scheme for MCS to conquer the above two challenges. The contributions of our work are summarized as follows.

- By adopting the concept of edge computing and the consortium blockchain, we firstly present system model for the decentralized privacy-preserving reputation management scheme.
- By leveraging the Paillier cryptosystem, we then design a novel metric to evaluate the reliability degree of the sensing data efficiently and privately. Based on that, the rule for updating reputation values are proposed.
- Extensive experiments verify that the proposed scheme are efficient and effective to deal with the malicious participants that provide falsified sensing data.

The rest of the paper is organized as follows. Related work is summarized in Sect. 2. Preliminaries utilized in this paper are introduced in Sect. 3. A simple introduction of the proposed system model is presented in Sect. 4. The distributed privacy-preserving reputation management scheme is introduced in Sect. 5. The efficiency and effectiveness of the proposed scheme are verified in Sect. 6. Section 7 concludes the paper.

2   Related Works

To motivate more owners of mobile devices to undertake MCS tasks, most MCS platforms are open for registration. This leads to that the reliability of the participants in MCS can not be guaranteed. Motivated by financial interests or compromised by hackers, some participants would become malicious to provide falsified sensing data to influence the final aggregating results. Reputation management schemes have been proved to be effective to deal with the malicious participants that provide falsified data in different scenarios, like [8] and [9].

As the sensing data are usually tagged with time and space information, directly sharing these data can bring great privacy leakage concerns among the participants. As a result, how well the privacy of the participants can be preserved determines how far MCS can go. This makes privacy preserving for MCS a hot research topic recently and a great number of approaches have been proposed. Generally, these approaches can be classified into two categories, anonymity-based and encryption-based. The goal of anonymity-based approaches is to make it impossible to link particular sensing data to the corresponding provider [10]. However, according to [13], this kind of approaches are fragile to tracing attack. With respect to the encryption-based approaches, the original data are encrypted and higher security level can be guaranteed via introducing many complex computations [11]. These two kinds of approaches have shown their high performance to preserve the privacy of MCS participants.

But without of specific settings, these approaches make it difficult to introduce reputation management schemes to deal with malicious participants. In other words, pure privacy-preserving approaches might increase the chance that the whole MCS system suffer from falsified sensing data of malicious participants.

Recently, there have been some works trying to propose reputation management schemes with privacy preserving functions. In [10], the authors propose a anonymity-based privacy-preserving reputation management scheme for crowdsensing. As the participants are kept anonymous during the process of undertaking tasks, an additional redeeming phase is utilized to update reputation values. Apart from the fact that anonymity-based approaches are vulnerable to tracking attacks, malicious participants are possible to provide falsified sensing data with high reputation values for somewhile if they refuse to go on the redeeming phase. To conquer the drawbacks in [10], our previous work [14] introduces the somewhat homomorphic encryption scheme to achieve privacy-preserving reputation management. Compared with [10], this work achieves higher security level but homomorphic encryption based sensing data aggregation and reputation values update are time-consuming. Moreover, both in [10] and [14], the reputation management schemes rely on a centralized manager. According to our previous analysis, such a centralized entity cannot satisfy the requirements of geographically distributed MCS tasks and is easy to be the bottleneck of the security of the whole system.

To eliminate the centralized reputation manager in the reputation management scheme, the blockchain technology is considered to be very promising to achieve this. As the underlying foundation of Bitcoin, blockchain is an open and distributed ledger maintained by all the entities in the network [15]. This makes blockchain to be reliable and tamper-proof. Due to its high security and reliability, blockchain has been introduced to different practical application scenarios, like mobile crowdsourcing [12], smart grid [15], IoT [16], and vehicular networks [17]. In [12], the authors design a private and anonymous crowdsourcing system based on open blockchain. The goal of this work is to guarantee the workers that undertake outsourcing tasks can really gain the payoff as claimed. The authors of [15] design a blockchain-based energy trading system for typical energy trading scenarios with moderate cost. In [16], blockchain is introduced to achieve secure distributed data storage for IoT. The above approaches in [12, 15, 16] verify the great potential for blockchain to realize distributed schemes to conquer the drawbacks of centralized ones. With respect to reputation management, the authors of [17] proposes a decentralized reputation management for vehicular networks. This work is inspiring but the privacy of the original data are not considered when updating the reputation values.

To summarize, designing a decentralized privacy-preserving reputation management scheme is of far-reaching significance for the further development of MCS. Although there have existed some works trying to solve this problem, they cannot satisfy the requirements of privacy-preserving and decentralizing goals for reputation management in MCS.

3   Preliminaries

In this section, we will simply introduce the blockchain technology and the Paillier cryptosystem that are essential to achieve our decentralized privacy-preserving reputation management scheme for MCS.

3.1   Blockchain

The definition of blockchain is first proposed in [18]. As the building foundation of Bitcoin, blockchain is a decentralized ledger maintained by all the entities in the network. As each entity stores a copy of this ledger, the blockchain would be tampered if and only if the adversaries compromise more than half of the total nodes in the whole network. This equips blockchain with high reliability and security.

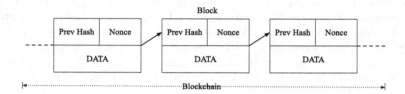

Fig. 1. The blockchain architecture

As is shown in Fig. 1, a blockchain is constructed by sequentially linked blocks. Each block stores the hash value of the previous one, the nonce value and data. Here, the data stored in a block are determined by the actual application scenario, for example, transactions data are stored in Bitcoin and the sensing data would be stored in MCS [12]. Since each block contains the hash value of its previous block, the blocks are linked in a sequential order. This setting is the origin of the tamper-proof property of blockchain. If the adversaries want to tamper a block, all the subsequent blocks should be tampered.

The nonce value is the solution of a mathematical problem and only the nodes that compute the right nonce value are selected as miners. The miners are responsible for writing data in a new block and broadcast this block across the whole network. When other nodes verify the validity of this block, it would be added to the blockchain maintained by these nodes themselves. When more than half of the total nodes add this block to its own blockchain, this block is admitted by all the nodes in the network. This process is the so-called proof-of-work (PoW).

Generally, blockchain is classified into three categories, public blockchain, private blockchain and consortium blockchain. As the participants in MCS are geographically distributed and their number can be very large, it is impossible to let each participant maintain a copy of the blockchain. For this reason, we introduce the concept of consortium blockchain where only authorized nodes are responsible for maintaining the blockchain.

3.2   Paillier Cryptosystem

To update the reputation values without revealing the original sensing data, we utilize the Paillier cryptosystem in our scheme which supports addition homomorphism. This cryptosystem is first introduced in [19] and it consist of the following three algorithms [20]:

- **Paillier.KeyGen:** this algorithm outputs the public and secret key pair (pk, sk). The detailed process is (1) randomly choose two large primes p and q such that $gcd(pq, (p-1)(q-1)) = 1$; (2) compute $N = pq$ and $\lambda = lcm(p-1, q-1)$; (3) randomly choose g from Z_{N^2} such that $\mu = (L(g^\lambda (mod N^2)))^{-1}(mod N)$, where $L(x) = (x-1)/N$. In this way, we have $pk = (N, g)$ and $sk = (\lambda, \mu)$.
- **Paillier.Enc:** this algorithm outputs the ciphertexts of any message. Given any message m in Z_N, randomly choose r and compute the ciphertext c as $c = g^m \cdot r^N (mod N^2)$.
- **Paillier.Dec:** this algorithm is used to decrypt any ciphertext via $m = L(c^\lambda (mod N^2)) \cdot \mu (mod N)$.

One important property of the Paillier cryptosystem is its support of addition homomorphism. Given any two messages m_1 and m_2, their encryptions are $E(m_1, pk) = g^{m_1} r_1^N (mod N^2)$ and $E(m_2, pk) = g^{m_2} r_2^N (mod N^2)$. Now, the following two equations hold:

$$D(E(m_1, pk) \cdot g^{m_2}) = m_1 + m_2 (mod N) \tag{1}$$

$$D(E(m_1, pk)^k) = km_1 (mod N) \tag{2}$$

4   System Model

In our MCS system, we introduce the paradigm of edge computing by deploying geographically distributed edge nodes (ENs) for collecting sensing data and maintaining the blockchain for decentralized privacy-preserving reputation management. As is shown in Fig. 2, the participants can act as both a sensing requester and the one that undertakes sensing tasks. A certificate authority (CA) is adopted to generate the public and secret key pairs for privacy-preserving goals. Here, there is no need to assume ENs following the semi-honest model and they can be considered untrusted. The data stored in a block are the parameters for updating reputation values, the encrypted sensing data and the historical reputation values of the participants.

To achieve the privacy-preserving goal, the proposed scheme is capable of defending against the following two attacks (**A1**) and (**A2**).

- **A1:** The ENs might try to infer the original sensing data from the received encryptions.
- **A2:** The ENs might collude with some participants to infer the original sensing data of the others.

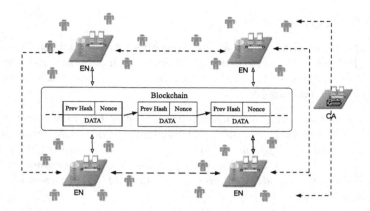

Fig. 2. The system model

To deal with the malicious participants that provide falsified sensing data, our scheme is designed to conquer the attacks of (**A3**)–(**A6**).

- **A3:** The malicious participants always provide falsified sensing data when undertaking different sensing tasks.
- **A4:** The malicious participants alternately provide falsified and original sensing data to keep their reputation values at a certain level.
- **A5:** The ENs do not aggregate the sensing data in the predefined manner.
- **A6:** The requester do not provide the actual data that are used to update the reputation values.

In the following sections, we will present the decentralized privacy-preserving reputation management scheme in detail and analyze how the proposed scheme can defend against the attacks of **A1–A6**.

5   The Decentralized Privacy-Preserving Reputation Management Scheme

In this paper, the proposed decentralized privacy-preserving reputation management scheme has two phases: completing sensing tasks and updating reputation values. Without loss of generality, how the proposed scheme works is illustrated by completing one sensing task. Before the MCS system begins to work, CA would first send each registered participant i the secret key $sk_{s,i}$ for signing sensing data and the public key $pk_{s,i}$ for verifying the data signed by i. As for any edge node EN_j, sk_{s,EN_j} and pk_{s,EN_j} are also generated by CA.

5.1   Completing the Sensing Tasks

Let q and τ denote the requester and the current sensing task respectively. The edge node near the requester q is denoted by EN_q and the one located in the target area of the sensing task is denoted by EN_τ. Further, let $\mathcal{P}_\tau$ denote the set of the participants that undertake the sensing task τ. The whole process to complete the sensing task τ is shown in Fig. 3.

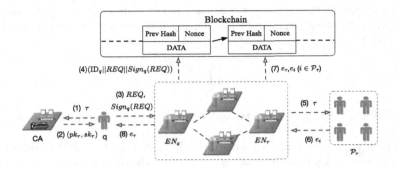

Fig. 3. The whole process to complete the sensing task τ.

Step 1: Before q publish the sensing task τ, he first request the CA to generate the public and secret key pair (sk_τ, pk_τ) for encrypting and decrypting sensing data in the Paillier cryptosystem.

Step 2: Then, the CA runs the **Paillier.KeyGen** algorithm to generate (sk_τ, pk_τ) and send it to q.

Step 3: On receiving the keys, q constructs the sensing task request as $REQ = (\tau||pk_\tau)$ and signs this request to obtain $Sign_q(REQ)$ with $sk_{s,q}$. After that, both REQ and $Sign_q(REQ)$ are sent to EN_q.

Step 4: When REQ and $Sign_q(REQ)$ are received, EN_q verifies the correctness of $Sign_q(REQ)$. If $Sign_q(REQ)$ passes verification, EN_q initiates a request to add $(ID_q||REQ||Sign_q(REQ))$ to the blockchain. After running the PoW consensus process, the miner EN_m is elected to generate a new block that stores $(ID_q||REQ||Sign_q(REQ))$ and broadcasts this newly generated block across the network. The remaining edge nodes verify the correctness of $Sign_q(REQ)$ and determine whether to accept this block. If $Sign_q(REQ)$ passes the verification of all the other edge nodes, the block is finally generated and the sensing task is formally published.

Step 5: The edge node in the target area EN_τ broadcasts REQ to the participants nearby. The ones that want to undertake the sensing task τ form the set $\mathcal{P}_\tau$.

Step 6: For $i \in \mathcal{P}_\tau$, let $\hat{s}_i$ denote its sensing data, which is an m-dimension vector. Here, $\hat{s}_i = \{s_{i,j}, j = 1, \ldots, m\}$. Since the Paillier cryptosystem only supports positive integers, we need to normalize the original sensing data to obtain $\bar{s}_i$ by:

$$\bar{s}_{i,j} = \frac{\hat{s}_{i,i} - lb_j}{ub_j - lb_j} \tag{3}$$

where, lb_j and ub_j are the lower and upper bounds of the sensing vector's jth dimension. Each element in $\bar{s}_i$ multiplies 10^ϵ and the round number of the result are the values of s_i. To preserve the privacy of the participants, s_i would be encrypted with pk_τ to obtain $e_i = \{\mathbf{Paillier.Enc}(s_{i,j}), j = 1, \ldots, m\}$. Then, e_i would be sent to EN_τ.

Step 7: After receiving the sensing data, EN_τ gets the reputation values of the participants in $\mathcal{P}_\tau$ from the blockchain. Let rep_i denote the reputation value of i. Next, EN_τ would aggregate the sensing data to get the encryption of the final result e_τ via $(j = 1, \ldots, m)$:

$$e_{\tau,j} = \prod_{i \in \mathcal{P}_\tau} e_{i,j}^{\frac{rep_i}{\sum_{i \in \mathcal{P}_\tau} rep_i}} \tag{4}$$

Then, EN_τ initiates a request to add $e_\tau = \{e_{\tau,j}, j = 1, \ldots, m\}$ and e_i to the request.

Step 8: e_τ is returned to q with the help of EN_q. After decrypting e_τ with sk_τ, q can get s_τ. By ϵ, lb_j and ub_j, q can recover the original aggregated sensing data.

Up to now, the sensing task τ is completed. In the following, we will describe how to update the reputation values of the participants in $\mathcal{P}_\tau$.

5.2 Updating Reputation Values

Since the Paillier cryptosystem only supports addition homomorphism, the reputation values cannot be updated based on the deviation from the aggregated result as in our previous work [14]. According to the fact that the sensing data from ordinary participants are very similar but very different from those of malicious participants, we design the rule for updating reputation values as is shown in Fig. 4.

Step 1: At first, the edge node in the target area EN_τ randomly generates a base vector s_b which has m dimensions (as $s_b = \{s_{b,j}, j = 1, \ldots, m\}$) such that $s_{b,j} > max\{s_{i,j} : i \in \mathcal{P}_\tau\}$. Since the values of s_i are obtained by the normalized values multiplying 10^ϵ, we can set the message space of the Paillier cryptosystem to be at least $[0, 2 \cdot 10^\epsilon]$. By this way, the values of s_b can be randomly selected from the range $[10^\epsilon + 1, 2 \cdot 10^\epsilon]$. Then, EN_τ encrypts s_b with pk_τ to get e_b.

Step 2: As EN_τ has e_i $(i \in \mathcal{P}_\tau)$, $E(d_i)$ can be computed by:

$$E(d_i) = \prod_{j=1}^{m} \frac{e_{b,j}}{e_{i,j}} \tag{5}$$

where $d_i = \sum_{j=1}^{m}(s_{b,j} - s_{i,j})$. For the reason that each elements in s_b is greater than those of the original sensing vector, the value of d_i reflects the deviation of i's sensing vector from the base vector to some extent. Since the sensing data from ordinary participants are very similar, the values computed through (5) are also very similar.

Step 3: EN_τ encrypts s_b with sk_{EN_τ} and sign the encryption to get $Sign_{EN_\tau}(E(sk_{EN_\tau}, s_b))$. Together with $E(d_i)$ $(i \in \mathcal{P}_\tau)$, EN_τ initiates a request to add them to the blockchain.

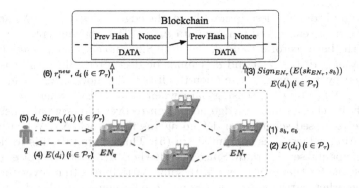

Fig. 4. The whole process to update the reputation values of the participants in $\mathcal{P}_\tau$.

Step 4: After the newly generated block is admitted by the whole network, EN_q obtains $E(d_i)$ $(i \in \mathcal{P}_\tau)$ and sends them to the requester q which has the secret key sk_τ.

Step 5: After receiving $E(d_i)$ $(i \in \mathcal{P}_\tau)$, q decrypts them to get d_i $(i \in \mathcal{P}_\tau)$ and signs the decryptions to get $Sign_q(d_i)$ $(i \in \mathcal{P}_\tau)$. Both d_is and $Sign_q(d_i)$s are sent back to EN_q.

Step 6: When obtaining d_is, EN_q classifies them into two groups by the k-means method. At this time, the group with more members is denoted by **Rew** and the other is denoted by **Pel**. According to the assumption in Sect. 4, the proportion of the malicious participants is less than a half and this make **Rew** mainly contain normal participants and their reputation values would be increased. The reputation values of the participants in **Pel** would be decreased. Hence, two parameters, α and β, are introduced to control the increase and decrease of the reputation values, respectively. As a result, the rule for updating reputation values is:

$$r_i^{new} = \begin{cases} r_i + (1 - r_i) \cdot \alpha & \text{if } i \in \textbf{\textit{Rew}} \\ r_i \cdot (1 - \beta) & \text{if } i \in \textbf{\textit{Pel}} \end{cases} \tag{6}$$

where both α and β are positive and $\beta < 1$. After getting the updated reputation values r_i^{new} $(i \in \mathcal{P}_\tau)$, EN_q would sign them and initiates a request to add d_is and signed r_i^{new}s to the blockchain. When passing all the verifications, the block containing all the updated reputation values are admitted by the network. Up to now, the phase of updating reputation values is finished.

5.3 Security Analysis

In the following, we will show how the proposed scheme can defend against the attacks of **A1–A6**.

A. When $m \geq 2$, the proposed scheme can defend agains the attacks of A1 and A2.

Analysis: From the description above, the edge nodes (both EN_q and EN_τ) can only hold the encrypted sensing data e_i $(i \in \mathcal{P}_\tau)$, the encrypted aggregated result e_τ, the base vector s_b, and d_i $(i \in \mathcal{P}_\tau)$. Since no edge nodes can obtain the private key sk_τ, e_i $(i \in \mathcal{P}_\tau)$ and e_τ cannot be decrypted. Since the base vector is generated by EN_τ and d_is are open to all the edge nodes, EN_τ can compute $s_b - d_i$ to get the original sensing data when $m = 1$. But when $m \geq 2$, there can be infinite choices and no edge nodes can recover the original sensing data. Hence, the proposed scheme can defend agains the attack **A1**. When updating the reputation values, d_i is computed via (5). This computation is irrelevant to other participants' sensing data. Since the edge nodes cannot decrypt e_i $(i \in \mathcal{P}_\tau)$, it is impossible for them to collude with some participants to recover the sensing data of the other participants. So, the proposed scheme can also defend agains the attack **A2** when $m \geq 2$.

B. When malicious participants keep providing falsified sensing data, their reputation values converge to 0.

Analysis: Assume that the ith participant in $\mathcal{P}_\tau$ is malicious and he keeps providing falsified sensing data. When updating his reputation values, the computed d_i via (5) is very different from that of normal participants. Since the proportion of malicious participants is less than a half, this participant would be classified into the group **Pel**. After being updated by (6), his new reputation value would be $r_i \cdot (1 - \beta)$. Since $1 - \beta < 1$ obviously holds, his reputation value would converge to 0 if he keeps providing falsified sensing data when undertaking the following sensing tasks. From this sense, the proposed scheme can defend against the attack of **A3**.

C. When $\frac{\alpha}{\alpha+\beta} < 0.5$, the influence of the attack A4 can be mitigated.

Analysis: Note that the attack of **A4** is known as the famous On-Off attack. As stated in [21], the influence of this attack can be mitigated when the reputation value increase for providing right sensing data is less than the decrease when providing falsified sensing data. Generally, the reputation value of the participant that launches the attack of **A4** is above a certain level (e.g. greater than 0.5). Otherwise, it is of no use for the participants with small reputation values to launch such an attack. Assume that the ith participant in $\mathcal{P}_\tau$ launches this attack and its reputation value r_i is larger than 0.5. According to (6), his new reputation value becomes $r_i + (1 - r_i) \cdot \alpha$ after providing right sensing data. Here, the increase of his reputation value is $(1 - r_i) \cdot \alpha$. When this participant provides falsified sensing data, his new reputation value changes to $r_i \cdot (1 - \beta)$ and the decrease is $r_i \cdot \beta$. If $(1 - r_i) \cdot \alpha < r_i \cdot \beta$ holds, we can get $\frac{\alpha}{\alpha+\beta} < 0.5$.

D. The proposed scheme is able to defend against the attack of A5.

Analysis: In the proposed scheme, it is required that the sensing data should be signed by the providers to prevent being tampered. In the meanwhile, s_τ should be signed EN_τ so that the aggregated results cannot be denied by EN_τ. Moreover, the encrypted sensing data and the aggregated result should be stored in the blockchain. In this way, the correctness of s_τ can be also verified. Only when more than half of the edge nodes are compromised, the attack of **A5** cannot be detected. Actually, compromising more than half of the edge nodes is almost impossible to be achieved. Thus, the proposed scheme can defend agains the attack of **A5**.

E. The attack of A6 can be traced through the data stored in the blockchain.

Analysis: When the requester decrypts $E(d_i)$ to get d_i ($i \in \mathcal{P}_\tau$), they should be signed by q. This setting avoids q denying the results of decryption. Since all the data related to $E(d_i)$s are stored in the blockchain and they are open for consulting, any participant that is not satisfied with his reputation value can initiate a request to check whether his reputation value is correctly updated. This request can be fulfilled with the help of CA who generates the keys. In this way, the attack of **A6** can be detected if it really exists.

6 Experimental Results

In this section, we will carry out extensive experiments to verify the effectiveness of the proposed scheme. At first, we show the influence of different values of α and β on updating reputation values. Then, the running time efficiency of the proposed scheme is analyzed. At the end of this section, the effectiveness to defend against malicious participants is demonstrated.

For the following experiments, we simulate the scenario of air quality monitoring. As stated by [22], a 13-dimension vector is provided by each participant that undertakes the sensing task.

6.1 Choices of α and β

According to (6), the parameter α determines the increase speed of the reputation values when providing right sensing data and β determines the decrease speed when the provided sensing data are falsified. Figures 5 and 6 show the influence of different values of α and β on updating reputation values.

In Fig. 5, the values of α are 0.02, 0.04, 0.06, 0.08, and 1. From this figure, it is obvious that α determines speed that the reputation value converges to 1 when the participant always provides right sensing data. The larger the value of α, the faster the reputation value converges to 1. However, when α is too large, the participant can obtain a high reputation value only by undertaking a small number of sensing tasks. This makes the proposed scheme fragile to the attack of **A4** (On-Off attack). Hence, α should not be too large in practical applications. In the following experiments, we set $\alpha = 0.2$.

Next, we will analyze the influence of the parameter β. As is shown in Fig. 6, the values of β are 0.1, 0.15, 0.2, 0.25, and 0.3. When the participants persistently provide falsified sensing data, the values of β determines the speed that the reputation value converges to 0. The larger β, the faster the reputation value converges to 0. In order to avoid the case that the reputation value drops too much when the participant provides falsified sensing data occasionally due to the failure of the device or affected by the environment, β should not be too large. Moreover, β should not be too small for defending against the On-Off attack. In the following experiments, we set $\beta = 0.2$.

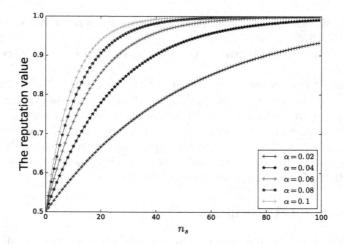

Fig. 5. The reputation value v.s. n_s where α varies from 0.02 to 0.1 with a step size of 0.02.

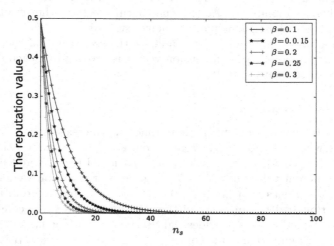

Fig. 6. The reputation value v.s. n_s where β varies from 0.1 to 0.3 with a step size of 0.05.

6.2 Running Time Analysis

In this part, we will analyze the time efficiency of the proposed scheme. According to the processes of completing sensing tasks and updating reputation values, the most time-consuming parts are the aggregation of encrypted sensing data and computation of d_i ($i \in \mathcal{P}_\tau$). Thus here, we focus on the running times of these two phase. Let t_{aggre} and t_d denote the time for aggregating encrypted sensing data and computing d_is, respectively. To achieve the Paillier cryptosystem, we use the open source Paillier Library and run this library on a virtual machine with 64-bit Ubuntu operating system, 1G memory and 20G hardware. For the Paillier cryptosystem, the bit length of the modulus is set 2048.

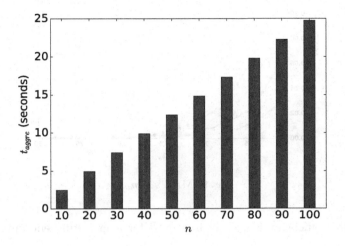

Fig. 7. t_{aggre} v.s. n.

As is shown in Fig. 7, t_{aggre} increases as n increases. Obviously, the larger n, the more encrypted sensing data would be aggregated. This leads to the increase of t_{aggre}. Since the number of multiplication and addition operations linearly increases as n increases, t_{aggre} linearly increases as n increases. When $n = 10$, t_{aggre} is approximately 2.47 s. As n reaches 100, t_{aggre} is 24.73 s. Comparing with

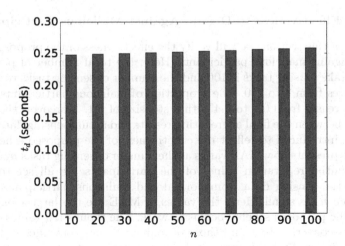

Fig. 8. t_d v.s. n.

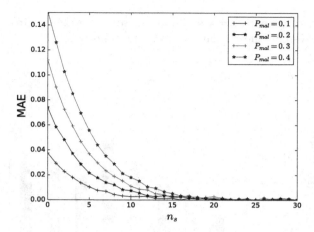

Fig. 9. MAE v.s. n_s.

[14], the time efficiency is greatly improved for aggregating encrypted sensing data.

Figure 8 presents how t_d varies as n increases. From this figure, the value of t_d keeps steady as n increases (t_d is around 0.25 s). This is because that when computing d_is through (5), we should first encrypt the base vector and then multiply related encrypted values. Here, the most operations are multiplying large numbers which can be easily and efficiently achieved by the Paillier Library. In our experiments, multiplying two large numbers costs about 0.0043 ms. Compared with the remaining operations, the running time for multiplications can be neglected.

6.3   The Effectiveness to Defend Against Malicious Participants

At the end of this section, we will verify the effectiveness of the proposed scheme to defend agains malicious participants. Here, the total number of participants that undertake sensing tasks is 100 and the number of sensing tasks to be undertake increases from 1 to 100. The proportion of malicious participants, denoted by P_{mal} increases from 0.1 to 0.4 with a stepsize of 0.1. Moreover, the absolute mean error between the final aggregating results and actual sensing data, referred as MAE, is introduced to reflect the effectiveness of the proposed scheme.

Figure 9 presents how MAE varies as the number of sensing tasks n_s increases. Since the initial reputation values of the participants are all set to 0.5, the weights of the sensing data from normal and malicious participants are very similar when n_s is small. Here, the values of MAE are the largest ones. As n_s increases, the proposed scheme begins to work. The reputation values of normal participants converges to 1 and those of malicious ones converges to 0. At this time, the weights of the sensing data from malicious participants converge to 0. This makes the values of MAE decrease and converge to 0 as n_s increases. Note that in order to more clearly present the variation of MAE, we only give the cases when $n_s \leq 30$.

7   Conclusion

In this paper, we propose a decentralized privacy-preserving reputation management scheme for MCS on the basis of blockchain. From the perspective of performance consideration, we introduce the consortium blockchain and the edge computing paradigm in our system model. The geographically distributed edge nodes are responsible for processing sensing data and maintaining the blockchain. To efficiently and privately aggregating sensing data, we design a novel rules for updating reputation values by leveraging the Paillier crytosystem. In the experiments, the cost efficiency and the effectiveness to deal with malicious participants are verified. These experimental results give a direct guidance to how the proposed scheme can be adopted by practical applications.

Acknowledgements. This work is supported by the National Key Research and Development Program of China under Grant 2016YFB0800601 and the Key Program of NSFC-Tongyong Union Foundation under Grant U1636209.

References

1. Yang, D., Xue, G., Fang, X., et al.: Incentive mechanisms for crowdsensing: crowdsourcing with smartphones. IEEE/ACM Trans. Netw. **24**(3), 1732–1744 (2016)
2. Qu, Y., Yu, S., Zhou, W., et al.: Privacy of things: emerging challenges and opportunities in wireless Internet of Things. IEEE Wirel. Commun. **25**(6), 91–97 (2016)
3. Ni, J., Zhang, A., Lin, X., et al.: Security, privacy, and fairness in fog-based vehicular crowdsensing. IEEE Commun. Mag. **55**(6), 146–152 (2017)
4. Min, M., Reddy, S., Shilton, K., et al.: PEIR, the personal environmental impact report, as a platform for participatory sensing systems research. the 7th ACM International Conference on Mobile Systems. Applications, and Services, Krakow, Poland, pp. 55–68. ACM (2009)
5. Basudan, S., Lin, X., Sankaranarayanan, K.: A privacy-preserving vehicular crowdsensing-based road surface condition monitoring system using fog computing. IEEE Internet Things J. **4**(3), 772–782 (2017)
6. Hicks, J., Ramanathan, N., Kim, D., et al. AndWellness: an open mobile system for activity and experience sampling. In: the 1st ACM SIGMOBILE International Conference on Pervasive Computing Technologies for Healthcare, Munich, Germany, pp. 34–43. ACM (2010)
7. Fan, J., Li, Q., Cao, G.: Privacy-aware and trustworthy data aggregation in mobile sensing. In: The 3rd IEEE Conference on Communications and Network Security, Florence, Italy, pp. 31–39. IEEE (2015)
8. Pei, Q., Ma, L., Li, H., et al.: Reputation-based coalitional games for spectrum allocation in distributed cognitive radio networks. In: 2015 IEEE International Conference on Communications, London, UK, pp. 7269–7274. IEEE (2015)
9. Liu, Y., Sun, Y.L.: Securing digital reputation in online social media. IEEE Signal Process. Mag. **31**(1), 149–155 (2014)

10. Wang, X.O., Cheng, W., Mohapatra, P., et al.: Enabling reputation and trust in privacy-preserving mobile sensing. IEEE Trans. Mob. Comput. **13**(12), 2777–2790 (2014)
11. Li, Q., Cao, G., La Porta, T.F.: Efficient and privacy-aware data aggregation in mobile sensing. IEEE Trans. Dependable Secur. Comput. **11**(2), 115–129 (2014)
12. Lu, Y., Tang, Q., Wang, G.: ZebraLancer: private and anonymous crowdsourcing system atop open blockchain. In: the 38th IEEE International Conference on Distributed Computing Systems, Vienna, Austria, pp. 853–865. IEEE (2018)
13. Li, H., Chen, Q., Zhu, H., et al.: Privacy leakage via de-anonymization and aggregation in heterogeneous social networks. IEEE Trans. Dependable Secur. Comput. (2017, early access)
14. Ma, L., Liu, X., Pei, Q., et al.: Privacy-preserving reputation management for edge computing enhanced mobile crowdsensing. IEEE Trans. Serv. Comput. **12**(5), 786–799 (2019)
15. Li, Z., Kang, J., Rong, Y., et al.: Consortium blockchain for secure energy trading in industrial Internet of Things. IEEE Trans. Ind. Inform. **14**(8), 3690–3700 (2018)
16. Ruinian, L., Tianyi, S., Bo, M., et al.: Blockchain for large-scale Internet of Things data storage and protection. IEEE Trans. Serv. Comput. **12**(5), 762–771 (2019)
17. Yang, Z., Yang, K., Lei, L., et al.: Blockchain-based decentralized trust management in vehicular networks. IEEE Internet Things J. **6**(2), 1495–1505 (2019)
18. Nakamoto S. Bitcoin: a peer-to-peer electronic cash system. Working paper (2008)
19. Paillier, P.: Public-Key cryptosystems based on composite degree residuosity classes. In: Stern, J. (ed.) EUROCRYPT 1999. LNCS, vol. 1592, pp. 223–238. Springer, Heidelberg (1999). https://doi.org/10.1007/3-540-48910-X_16
20. Yi, X., Bouguettaya, A., Georgakopoulos, D., et al.: Privacy protection for wireless medical sensor data. IEEE Internet Things J. **13**(3), 369–380 (2016)
21. Kang, X., Wu, Y.: A trust-based pollution attack prevention scheme in peer-to-peer streaming networks. Comput. Netw. **72**, 62–73 (2014)
22. Vito, S.D., Piga, M., Martinotto, L., et al.: On field calibration of an electronic nose for benzene estimation in an urban pollution monitoring scenario. Sens. Actuators B Chem. **143**(1), 182–191 (2009)

Location Privacy Issues in the OpenSky Network Crowdsourcing Platform

Savio Sciancalepore[✉], Saeif Alhazbi, and Roberto Di Pietro

Division of Information and Computing Technology College of Science
and Engineering (CSE) - Hamad Bin Khalifa University (HBKU), Doha, Qatar
{ssciancalepore,rdipietro}@hbku.edu.qa, salhazbi@mail.hbku.edu.qa

Abstract. OpenSky Network leverages the freely accessible data generated by the aircraft through the Automatic Dependent Surveillance -
Broadcast (ADS-B) technology to create a participatory global open-access network where individuals, industries, and academia can freely
contribute and obtain data. Indeed, avionic data are acquired through
on-ground general purpose antennas, installed and operated in adequate
locations, and later delivered to the OpenSky Network community.

To maintain operators' privacy while still keeping data value, Open-Sky Network promises not to reveal the antenna location, if the data
contributor wishes so. Thus, open data provided to the participating
entities contain neither the location of the operating receiver, nor other
location identification data.

In this work, we practically demonstrate that maintaining full location privacy in this scenario is almost unfeasible. We apply a time-based
location estimation technique that, leveraging: (i) the disclosed location
of legitimate receivers that did not opt in for location privacy; and, (ii)
data provided by commercial and military aircraft, reveals with reasonable accuracy the location of the receivers that did opt-in for location
privacy.

Results achieved by simulations and an experimental campaign over
real data provided by the OpenSky Network support our claim, further
confirming that maintaining location privacy while still contributing to
the community cannot be fully achieved in the actual setting, hence calling for further research.

Keywords: ADS-B · Location privacy · Time-based localization ·
Receiver localization

1 Introduction

Automatic Dependent Surveillance - Broadcast (ADS-B) is the next generation
wireless technology, designed to improve the safety of civil, commercial, and
military aircraft. It will become mandatory on all the civil and military aircraft
flying in Class A, B, and C airspaces starting from the year 2020, and some of the

S. Chen et al. (Eds.): SecureComm 2019, LNICST 304, pp. 549–568, 2019.
https://doi.org/10.1007/978-3-030-37228-6_27

major airlines in the world already equipped their aircraft with the necessary ADS-B capabilities, including Qatar Airways, British Airways and American Airlines [1]. In contrast with previous technologies, ADS-B enables aircraft to autonomously generate messages, without waiting for explicit polling by ground stations. In this way the ADS-B technology enables real-time communications between airplanes, and with ground stations, achieving also an improved control by the pilots over the surrounding environment [2].

ADS-B messages are delivered on the wireless communication channel in clear-text, without any native encryption mechanism [3]. While posing straightforward privacy concerns [4–6], this openness enabled the rise of spontaneous open-participation initiatives, dedicated to the provisioning of advanced services by using open, freely-available data, such as Opensky Network and FlightRadar24. In this context, OpenSky Network represents one of the widest and most promising communities [7].

OpenSky Network is a pervasive, participatory sensor network specifically built up for the air traffic research community [8]. During the years, it has involved many independent entities, including industries, academia and even autonomous hobbyists, excited by the possibility to easily access data delivered by aircraft operating in the surroundings, as well as to have access to high volumes of data for research purposes. Nowadays, the OpenSky Network includes around 1000 receivers, deployed over 70 countries worldwide. In addition, data acquired and provided to the community by the OpenSky Network have been the basis of a lot of research contributions in the avionics area [9].

The data provided by OpenSky Network mainly consist of information about the receiving sensors and the emitting airplanes, including the time-of-arrival of the messages (feasible for use in multi-lateration techniques), the Received Signal Strength Indicator (RSSI), and the content of the messages originated by the aircraft equipped with ADS-B capabilities. Furthermore, for privacy reasons, contributing receivers can decide to maintain their location *private*, activating a feature called *anonymity* by the platform. Hence, data acquired through these receivers are said to be *anonymized* by nullifying the fields dedicated to the direct identification of the receivers, such as its geographical coordinates (latitude, longitude, and altitude), and the RSSI—all data that could directly lead to the identification of a receiver's position.

Our Contribution. In this paper we discuss the location privacy issues associated with the OpenSky Network crowdsourcing platform. Indeed, we adapt and apply a time-based multi-stage location estimation technique, in a way to be able to almost spot the location of a contributing receiver in the OpenSky Network community, even if its location has been appropriately protected through the *anonymity* mechanism offered by OpenSky Network. To achieve its goal, the technique described hereby needs only three information: (i) the position of receivers other than the target *protected* one, which did not opt in for the location privacy; (ii) the time-of-arrival of messages delivered by the aircraft and received on the set of receivers including not only the target *protected* receiver, but also other receivers in the same geographical area, whose position is well-known; and, (iii) the location of emitting aircraft, embedded in the ADS-B messages. Combining these information in an approach rooted on a Least Squares (LS) estimator and further outlier elimination techniques, we are able to reveal the location of the target receiver with an accuracy of few hundred meters, even in harsh environmental conditions.

We point out that the aim of our work is not to devise a new location estimation technique. Instead, we point out an underestimated and neglected location privacy issue associated with the particular operation of the OpenSky Network crowdsourcing platform, hence calling for further protection measures.

The performance of the location estimation have been assessed via both a simulation analysis and by using real data available from the OpenSky Network, showing that full location privacy in this kind of system is actually unfeasible and thus calling for further research in the field.

We already informed the steering committee of the OpenSky Network community of our results; now, they are aware of the issue and are working toward the improvement of the system.

Roadmap. The rest of the paper is organized as follows: Sect. 2 briefly reviews the closest related work and provides the necessary background on the ADS-B communication technology and the OpenSky Network community. Section 3 introduces the system and the adversary models assumed in this work, as well as some preliminary assumptions, while Sect. 4 provides the mathematical details of the applied technique and the detailed description of its procedures. Section 5 provides the performance assessment of the solution, both via simulations and real experimentation on open data. Finally, Sect. 6 tightens conclusions and draws future research activities.

2   Background and Related Work

This section is dedicated to the introduction of the ADS-B communication technology and the OpenSky Network project. In addition, a summary of the related work is provided.

2.1   ADS-B and OpenSky Network

Despite the birth of the ADS-B technology is dated back in the late 1980s, the interest about this communication technology has started raising up only in the last years, mainly because of the upcoming deadline 2020 fixed by the International Civil Aviation Organization (ICAO) on its mandatory adoption on-board of all commercial and military aircraft flying in Class A, B, and C airspaces, in both the United States and Europe [1,10]. ADS-B leverages two dedicated equipment operating on-board of the aircraft. On the one hand, a Global Positioning System (GPS) receiver periodically acquires the position of the aircraft by using the satellites. Then, this position is transmitted wirelessly in broadcast, allowing anyone equipped with a compatible receiver to detect and decode the messages. This operational mode, namely *ADS-B OUT*, allows ground stations located in the airports to continuously monitor ongoing flights, and only its deployment is mandatory by the year 2020. In a different operational mode, namely *ADS-B IN*, the aircraft exchanges information with other equipped airplanes, essentially to provide weather information and manage self-separation. However, the mandatory support for *ADS-B IN* capabilities on all commercial and military aircraft has not been scheduled, yet, thus making its integration still an optional feature [11].

The wireless operations usually happen on the ES1090 frequency band (at the operating frequency of 1090 MHz), by using very small packets having a size of only 112 bits, as depicted in Fig. 1.

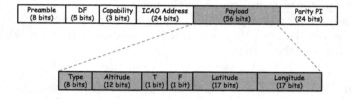

Fig. 1. The format and content of the ADS-B packet.

Within such a limited size, 24 bits are dedicated to the identification of the transmitter, through its ICAO address, assigned at the boot-up of the flight. Only 56 bits, instead, are available in the payload for real flight information, and its content varies according to the content of the type field. It can provide either the position, or the velocity, or other flight-related information about the emitting aircraft. As for the position, ADS-B adopts the Compact Position Reporting (CPR) format, requiring 34 bits for each of the two geographical coordinates, i.e., latitude and longitude. Thus, given that only 17 bits are available for each of them in the payload, two consecutive ADS-B messages are required to convey a complete position information, namely the *odd* and the *even* message.

At the physical layer, ADS-B packets are encapsulated in Mode-S frames. As such, they use Pulse-Position Modulation (PPM) and the broadcast messages are encoded by a certain number of pulses, each pulse being 1 μs long [12].

As it is evident from the previous description, all ADS-B messages are transmitted in clear text, without any encryption mechanism. On the one hand, this lack of security features has paved the way to a huge amount of research, showing potential security issues and threats that could be caused by even non-expert users, simply equipped with compatible radio equipment [1]. On the opposite hand, the openness of the system allows everyone to receive and decode the data, and to construct advanced services further elaborating the streamed data.

In this context, taking advantage of the complete openness of the data, open communities such as FlightRadar24 and Opensky Network have been established, with the aim of continuously collecting data delivered from operational airplanes equipped with the ADS-B technology [7]. Specifically, OpenSky Network, operating from 2014, consists of more than 100 receivers, deployed worldwide over more 70 countries and operated both by private and public entities [9]. In addition, OpenSky Network makes data accessible to researchers worldwide for experimentation and testing.

The data provided by the OpenSky Network consist of the following fields:

- *SensorType*, containing information about the manufacturer of the sensor receiving messages and contributing data to the community (i.e., the receiving sensor);
- *sensorSerialNumber*, uniquely identifying the receiving sensor;
- *SensorLatitude*, indicating the latitude of the receiving sensor;
- *SensorLongitude*, indicating the longitude of the receiving sensor;
- *SensorAltitude*, indicating the altitude (in feet) of the receiving sensor;
- *timeAtSensor*, indicating the time (in seconds) of the reception of the message;
- *timestamp*, indicating the hardware reception timestamp of the sensor, in nanoseconds;
- *timeAtServer*, indicating the reception time of the message on the OpenSky Network servers;
- *rawMessage*, reporting the encoded ADS-B packet, including payload information;
- *RSSIPacket*, indicating the RSSI of the message at the receiving sensor;
- *RSSIPreamble*, reporting the RSSI calculated over the 8-bit preamble of the received packet on the receiving sensor;
- *SNR*, reporting the estimation of the Signal to Noise Ratio (SNR) of the received packet on the receiving sensor.

In case a receiver would like to maintain its location private, but still contribute data to the community, Opensky Network allows to activate an *anonymity* feature (as reported by the website), through which the exact location of the receiver is hidden. The OpenSky Network community achieves such a service by nullifying the *sensorSerialNumber*, *SensorLatitude*, *SensorLongitude* and *SensorAltitude* fields, as well as the fields related to the RSSI, such as *RSSIPacket*, *RSSIPreamble* and *SNR*. Such a feature, instead, appears not to be available in other similar communities, such as FlightRadar24.

We remark that maintaining location privacy could be desirable for a variety of reasons, including legal concerns related to the country in which the sensor is operated, as well as protecting the sensor against unauthorized physical accesses. As of June 2019, 51 over 812 online receivers (6.3%) already activated the *anonymity* feature.

2.2   Related Work

The approach discussed in this contribution is very close in its nature to common localization approaches, e.g. based on multi-lateration techniques or grid-position solutions. Indeed, such approaches have been already applied in the context of avionics communications, to provide aircraft's track verification. For instance, in [13] the authors present a reliable and high precise ADS-B/MLAT data fusion surveillance framework, that uses the dynamic flight model of aircraft and the flight information system, while the authors in [14] presented a technique for performing secure location verification of position claims by measuring the time-difference of arrival (TDoA) between a fixed receiver node and a mobile one. However, it is worth noticing that our contribution tackles a scenario requiring a resolution strategy that is different from a classical localization approach, e.g. based on multi-lateration or triangulation techniques. Indeed, legacy multi-lateration and triangulation techniques strives for different objectives. For instance, the multi-lateration applied for the GPS is aimed at verifying the location of a receiving device based on signals received from dedicated satellites. Also, multi-lateration approaches envision a network of cooperative receivers that wants to localize a target device, actively contributing in the process by transmitting packets. In our case, instead, the final objective is to obtain a location estimation of a completely passive receiver, that do not transmit anything on the communication channel, while the received traces are available. Even if the problems are somehow closely related, we are not aware of any scientific contribution tackling this specific scenario. In the context of the avionics research landscape, the availability of real data provided through the OpenSky Network database daily allows for the real application and performance assessment of distributed algorithms, aimed not only at aircraft localization and track verification. Indeed, many works such as [2,13,15], and [16], already tested their solutions by using the data provided by the open-source community. In addition, such data have been used to infer meteorological parameters [5], as well as relationships between governments [17], showing their potential to be applied as a cross-verification method also in parallel research fields.

However, no previous work analyzed location privacy opportunities and limits related to the receivers participating in the sharing of ADS-B data. In addition, while related work has focused on localizing operational airplanes and verifying their track, none of them has previously reversed back the proposed technique with the aim of verifying or determining the location of the participating sensors. In this context, the present contribution improves the actual state-of-the-art by not only showing the presence of location privacy limitations in the context of such pervasive, open-participation communities, but also providing a technique useful for the verification of the receiver position in such a scenario.

3   System and Adversary Models

In this section we introduce the system model assumed throughout this work. In addition, we briefly introduce the model of the adversary.

3.1   System Model and Assumptions

The reference scenario assumed in this work is depicted in Fig. 2.

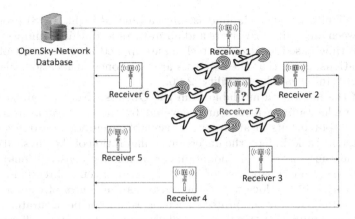

Fig. 2. Reference scenario tackled in this work. There are several ADS-B receivers exposing their position, while one receiver would like to maintain its location private.

A set of K receivers are distributed over a wide area. They are equipped with omnidirectional ADS-B antennas, able to detect and receive packets emitted by N planes located in their reception range. We assume that each aircraft delivers M messages, that are detected by the receivers and then forwarded to the OpenSky Network servers. While the positions of $K - 1$ receivers is well-known, we suppose a receiver would like to maintain its location private, thanks to the *anonymity* feature offered by the OpenSky Network site. We refer to this receiver as a *protected* receiver. Thus, even if this receiver collaborates with the system by providing data (i.e., reception timestamps of the packets delivered by the aircraft), it does not transmit anything on the wireless communication medium and its position is not revealed. The position of an emitting plane at the time instant in which it delivers the message is well-known, given that it periodically broadcasts its position and velocity within ADS-B packets. Note that the planes do not need to be altogether present in the scenario at the same time instant. Indeed, they can be located in the reception range of the receivers also in different (non overlapping) time frames.

In addition, we assume that all the receivers are time-synchronized. Indeed, this assumption is fully consistent with the actual system setting, where the receivers are always connected to the Internet.

We also assume that the measurements errors are i.i.d. with zero-mean and variance σ_e^2. These assumptions are reasonable in practical deployments with homogeneous commercial-off-the-shelf (COTS) devices, where the timing accuracy is typically limited by the ADC rate and/or clock resolution [18]. Thus, they represent a worst-case assumption in the case of specialized equipment such as the one mounted on board of ADS-B-equipped aircraft. Furthermore, if the error distribution can be assumed Gaussian, then the LS estimator used in our approach represent the optimal Maximum Likelihood (ML) estimator, as well-known in the literature [19].

We highlight that our technique assumes a Line Of Sight (LOS) propagation model between any pair of receivers and aircraft. Indeed, this assumption is very common in time-based localization techniques applied in the context of ADS-B communications, given that the receivers are positioned at locations elevated in altitude, with full clear-sky visibility [2,20].

Even if the meta-data available from the OpenSky Network already enable the rough understanding of the area covered by the *anonymous* receiver, we remark that spotting its location with reasonable accuracy is a different issue, and not a trivial task. In fact, the uncertain configuration of the physical environment around the sensors (e.g., mountains or man-made constructions) severely affects the reception capabilities of the sensors in specific directions. Thus, a trivial estimation of the location of the sensor as the *centre* of the locations of the airplanes detected by the *protected* sensor would not be accurate.

Finally, we emphasize that the so-called *anonymity* feature offered by the OpenSky Network project is a technique to protect the *location privacy* of the sensors, rather than their identity. Indeed, the two problems can be different if two or more sensors share the same area: in such a case, the technique discussed below could break the privacy in the location of each of them, without compromising their identity.

3.2   Adversary Model

The adversary assumed in our work is a global eavesdropper, that does not transmit any packet on the wireless communication channel. Indeed, it stays stealthy by simply connecting to the OpenSky Network database and gathering data about ongoing avionics communications, with the aim of spotting the location of a receiver that aims to protect the privacy of its location. The gathered data include packets received both by the receivers that did not opted-in for location privacy and the ones that activated the *anonymity* feature provided by OpenSky Network, protecting their location.

In addition, the adversary could also deploy additional ADS-B receivers, integrating them to the OpenSky Network community. This feature could be particularly useful when the *protected* receiver has few other receivers around. Using such a strategy, almost any *protected* receiver could be attacked.

4   Estimating the Location of ADS-B Receivers

This section is dedicated to the illustration of the mathematical details of our technique. Sect. 4.1 provides the details of the LS estimator, being the core building block of the applied solution. The full technique is described in Sect. 4.2. The notation used throughout this paper is summarized in Table 1, with lower-case letters denoting a scalar, and boldface lower-case letters designating vectors.

The location estimation technique described hereby is inspired by [18] and [21]. However, several modifications are provided. First, we switch from a 2-D to a 3-D approach, providing modifications in the LS estimator (see Sect. 4.1).

Table 1. Summary of the Notation.

Symbol	Description
K	Overall Number of Receivers
N	Overall Number of Packets sent by a generic aircraft
M	Overall Number of Aircraft
$K_{n(m)}$	Number of receivers receiving the m-th packet emitted by the n-th aircraft
$R_{kn(m)}$	Reception timestamp of the m-th packet sent by the n-th plane on the k-th receiver
$t_{n(m)}$	Timestamp of the m-th packet sent by the n-th aircraft
$d_{kn(m)}$	Distance between the k-th receiver and n-th aircraft at the transmission of the m-th packet
p_k	3-D position of the k-th receiver
$p_{n(m)}$	3-D position of the n-th aircraft at the transmission of the m-th packet
$e_{kn(m)}$	Random noise component on the m-th packet transmitted by the n-th aircraft and received by the k-th receiver

In addition, we do not consider any mechanism for receiver-to-receiver synchronization. Finally, the scenario is also completely different, given that entity to be localized does not emit any message, being located only thanks to the shared data.

We remark that hereby we are not providing a brand new location estimation technique. Indeed, same results (and possibly better) could be achieved also by other location estimation approaches. Instead, our aim is to investigate the limitations in the location privacy assurance that can be achieved in the present settings of the OpenSky Network community.

4.1 The Least-Squares Estimator

With the notation reported in Table 1 and the above assumptions, the reception timestamp measured at the generic k-th receiver for the m-th packet sent by the n-th aircraft can be written as in the following Eq. 1:

$$R_{kn(m)} = t_{n(m)} + \frac{d_{kn(m)}}{c} + e_{kn(m)}, \tag{1}$$

where $d_{kn(m)} = \|p_k - p_{n(m)}\|$ denotes the distance between the receiver k and the n-th aircraft at the time instant in which the m-th packet is delivered, while c is the speed of light. Note that the terms $p_{n(m)}$ are well-known, the terms p_k are known only for the $K - 1$ receivers whose position is well-known, while they are unknown for the k-th receiver that activated the *anonymity* feature.

Thanks to Eq. (1), the problem can be cast into a non-linear LS form. In order to reduce numerical errors, we recenter the timestamp data for each packet m

around the reference time $R_{1n(m)}$, and re-scale all terms by the speed of light c [22]. To this aim, we define the new terms:

$$\tilde{R}_{kn(m)} \overset{\text{def}}{=} \left(R_{kn(m)} - \overline{R}_{1n(m)} \right) \cdot c, \tag{2a}$$

$$\tilde{t}_{n(m)} \overset{\text{def}}{=} \left(t_{n(m)} - \overline{R}_{1n(m)} \right) \cdot c, \tag{2b}$$

$$\tilde{e}_{kn(m)} \overset{\text{def}}{=} e_{kn(m)} \cdot c. \tag{2c}$$

With these definitions, the Eq. (1) rewrites as in the following Eq. 3:

$$\tilde{R}_{kn(m)} = \tilde{t}_{n(m)} + d_{kn(m)} + \tilde{e}_{kn(m)}. \tag{3}$$

It is possible to further elaborate Eq. 3 as in the following Eq. 4:

$$\tilde{e}_{kn(m)} = \tilde{R}_{kn(m)} - \tilde{t}_{n(m)} - d_{kn(m)}. \tag{4}$$

It is worth noting that the terms $\tilde{R}_{kn(m)}$ can be computed directly from the input data, as well as the terms $\boldsymbol{p}_{n(m)}$.

To ease the notation, we denote all the variables of interest (i.e, the unknown variables) with the vector $\boldsymbol{z} \overset{\text{def}}{=} [\boldsymbol{p_K}] = [p_{Kx}, p_{Ky}, p_{Kz}]$

Note that the set of unknown variables that allow to minimize the estimation errors in Eq. 4 are the same set of parameters that can be obtained by extracting and applying the negative log-likelihood function to the same equation above. Given that the error terms $\tilde{e}_{kn(m)}$ are i.i.d. and Gaussian, the negative log-likelihood function can be expressed as:

$$\ell\left(\boldsymbol{z}, \boldsymbol{t}_n \right) = \frac{1}{2} \sum_{m=1}^{M} \sum_{n \in \mathcal{A}_m} \left(\tilde{t}_{n(m)} + d_{kn(m)}(\boldsymbol{z}) - \tilde{R}_{kn(m)} \right)^2. \tag{5}$$

Note that, in addition to the variables of interest for our problem, that are the 3-D coordinates of the unknown receiver, also the transmission timestamps of the aircraft are unknown. Thus, solving directly the Eq. (3) would require to estimate a total of $3 + M \cdot N$ unknown variables, that are the 3 coordinates of the unknown receiver, and the M timestamps for each of the N planes involved in the scenario.

However, it is possible to get rid of the $M \cdot N$ transmission timestamps by taking into account the pairwise differences between the reception timestamps on the receiver. Specifically, for a generic packet m sent by the aircraft n, consider the reference receiver $\overline{k}$ and another receiver $k \neq \overline{k}$, and denote the difference between their respective time-of-arrivals residuals by:

$$\xi_{kn(m)} \overset{\text{def}}{=} \tilde{e}_{kn(m)} - \tilde{e}_{\overline{k}_n(m)} =$$
$$\tilde{R}_{kn(m)} - \tilde{R}_{\overline{k}n(m)} - d_{nm}(\boldsymbol{z}) + \overline{d}_m(\boldsymbol{z}) \tag{6}$$

In the following, we select the reference receiver as $\bar{k} = K$, i.e., the reference receiver is selected as the unknown receiver. In this case, it is possible to neglect all the constant terms related to pairwise differences on the receivers with well-known positions, that would create numerical issues in the solution of the problem, and to provide only the pairwise differences related to the unknown variables of interest.

Note that this structuring of the problem introduces non-independent error terms, that must be included in the formulation of the generalized LS form through a non-diagonal covariance matrix, hereby denoted as Σ_m. For this particular case, the covariance matrix will have a simplified structure, independent of the choice of the reference receiver, with diagonal elements having a value of 2 and off-diagonal values set to 1. The interested reader can refer to [18] for more details.

In summary, our LS estimator can be expressed in the following form:

$$
\hat{z} = \arg\min_{z} \sum_{m=1}^{M} \boldsymbol{\xi}_{n(m)}^{T} \boldsymbol{\Sigma}_{n(m)}^{-1} \boldsymbol{\xi}_{n(m)} =
$$

$$
\arg\min_{z} \sum_{m=1}^{M} \left(\sum_{\substack{k \in \mathcal{A}_{n(m)} \\ k \neq \bar{k}_{n(m)}}} \xi_{kn(m)}^{2} - \frac{1}{K_{n(m)}} \left(\sum_{\substack{k \in \mathcal{A}_{n(m)} \\ k \neq \bar{k}_{n(m)}}} \xi_{kn(m)} \right)^{2} \right), \tag{7}
$$

where $K_{n(m)}$ refers to the number of receivers that successfully received the m-th packet sent by the n-th aircraft. With the formulation in Eq. (7), the dimensionality of the search space has been drastically reduced to 3, i.e., only the variables of interest for our problem.

The LS estimator discussed above, however, is only a (crucial) part of the overall technique, devised to estimate the location of the *protected* receiver. The reasons and the systematization of such an approach are discussed in the following section.

4.2 Details of the Location Estimation Technique

As discussed in previous work about wireless localization and multi-lateration, the method discussed above is able to provide very good position estimations in practice, provided that the references used for the timestamps differences are uniformly distributed around the point to be localized. However, given the very large area of the scenario and the lack of any control on the position of the planes, this cannot be achieved in practice for every run of the LS estimator.

Thus, to correctly discover the position of the unknown receiver, the LS estimator discussed in Sect. 4.1 should be executed repeatedly for a number of I runs, each time considering a different subset of the available aircraft. The pseudo-code of the resulting technique is shown in Algorithm 1.

The solution leverages the execution of the LS estimator described in Sect. 4.1 for I runs, from which a set of I solutions is obtained, consisting of the x,y, and

Input: Reception Timestamps on K receivers;
Decoded Messages from N planes;
Position of $K - 1$ receivers.

1 **for** $i=1:I$ **do**
2 | Select a group of $J < N$ planes;
3 | $pos \leftarrow LS(J)$ /* Run the Ls estimator in Eq. (7)   */
4 | $pos\_vect \leftarrow pos$ /* Store the solution in a vector   */
5 **end**

6 $P_{act} \leftarrow$ pruning(pos_vect) /* Apply the pruning algorithm in Algo. 2 */
7 $P \leftarrow$ median(P_{act},2) /* Select the median of the pruned position vector
    as the estimated point.   */

8 **Output**: estimated position P of the protected receiver.

Algorithm 1: Pseudo-code of the multi-stage location estimation algorithm.

z-coordinates of the aircraft. Even if making the I iterations independent from each other can improve the resolution time (especially when having parallel computing units), in the devised technique they are not independent from each other. Specifically, the final point estimated at the i-th iteration is used as the starting point of the estimator in the $i + 1$-th iteration, in order to improve the resolution accuracy. Of course, such an improvement is obtained at the expense of an higher resolution time—but we do not consider it an issue here, given that our scenario does not involve any real-time constraint.

As anticipated before, some of the computed solutions might be actually far from the real position of the unknown receiver, given that the geometry of the scenario is not perfect, i.e., the airplanes are not always uniformly distributed in a close proximity with respect to the target position. Thus, we apply a pruning algorithm that cuts off a given percentage of outliers. Specifically, the algorithm iteratively calculates the median of all the available solutions and, for each run, cuts off from the pool the points having the greater distance from this median point. In this way, outliers are cut off and more accurate location estimations are provided. The pseudo-code of the pruning algorithm is shown in Algorithm 2.

It is worth noting that the assumption of a uniform distribution of airplanes around the sensor applies in the majority of the cases, especially where there are no constraints in the areas that can be crossed by aircraft—e.g. absence of no-fly zones.

5 Performance Assessment

The multi-stage location estimation technique described in Sect. 4 has been implemented in Matlab© R2018b, and its performance have been first evaluated through a simulation campaign, with the aim of establishing its performance in a controlled scenario. Then, we have tested the technique with real avionics data, available by the OpenSky Network community. All the tools have been run by using a Dell XPS15 9560 laptop with 32 GB of RAM and the Linux Ubuntu

16.10 Operating System. The simulation analysis is included in Sect. 5.1, while tests over real aircraft data are discussed in Sect. 5.2.

Input: Vector P_{est} of Estimated 3-D Coordinates.

```
1  R ← size(P_est,1)*PRUNING_PERCENTAGE /* Calculate the number of
       elements to be pruned.                                          */
2  P_act = P_est /* Initialize the position vector.                   */
3  for i=1:R do
4      med_pos = median(P,2) /* Calculate the median over the columns.
          */
5      dist = P_act - med_pos /* Calculate the distance between each point
          and the median point.                                       */
6      pos_vect ← pos /* Store the solution in a vector.              */
7      [index_del, max_dist] = max(pos_vect) /* Find the element having the
          maximum distance.                                           */
8      P_act = P_act/{ P_act{index_del} } /* Eliminate the element having the
          maximum distance from the solution vector.                  */
9  end
10 Output: Vector P_act of pruned positions.
```

Algorithm 2: Pseudo-code of the pruning algorithm.

5.1 Simulation Analysis

In the following, we provide different simulation results about the performance of the location estimation technique in the scenario. In each test we varied one of the critical parameters in our technique, and we show how such a variation affects the location estimation accuracy. The tests involved both *uncontrollable parameters*, i.e. the ones depending on the physical environment underlying the scenario (such as the noise and the packet loss in the communication link, not tunable on our side), and *controllable parameters*, that is the ones depending on tuning choices of our solution, such as the number of packets to be considered for each aircraft and the number of contemporary aircraft trajectories to be analyzed. Specifically, each of the figures reports the Empirical Cumulative Distribution Function (ECDF) of the position estimate error along the x-y coordinates, computed over 1000 different seeds and different positions of the receiver to be located, while varying some specific system parameter. Note that we used the *fminsearch* tool offered by Matlab for solving the LS minimization problem formulated in Eq. 7, given that it provides the best result among the many estimators offered by Matlab.

First, we investigated the accuracy of the location estimation technique assuming different levels of the environmental noise in the underlying scenario. Results are reported in Fig. 3, by considering 10 trajectories, each of them characterized by 50 packets, all of them received by all the receivers.

Indeed, as in almost all of the localization algorithms, the accuracy of the final estimation is strictly dependent on the intensity of the noise affecting the data. Our technique, however, exhibits a good level of accuracy even with a medium

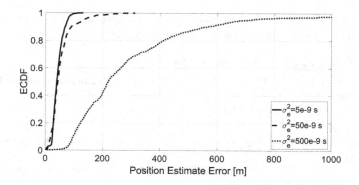

Fig. 3. Estimation accuracy while varying the variance σ_e^2 of the surrounding noise.

noise intensity, i.e., a noise with variance $\sigma_e^2 = 50$ ns. In fact, in almost 90% of the cases, the difference between the results obtained with a low level of noise (variance $\sigma_e^2 = 5$ ns) and a medium level of noise (variance $\sigma^2 = 50$ ns) is almost negligible. Overall, with a variance $\sigma_e^2 = 5$ ns, the technique always provides a solution affected by an error less than 150 m, practically compromising the privacy of the location of *protected* receiver. In more noisy scenarios (i.e., when many obstacles and mountains affect the LOS assumption in our model), the performances naturally decrease but, in the 90% of the cases, the receiver could be localized with an accuracy less than 600 m.

By considering the less noisy scenario, consistent with our system model, we also evaluate the effect of an increasing number of trajectories in the devised location estimation technique. The related results are reported in Fig. 4.

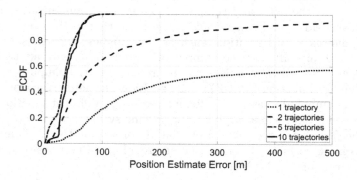

Fig. 4. Estimation accuracy with increasing number of planes trajectories.

As it can be seen from the above figure, generally speaking, increasing the number of trajectories has positive effects on the final resolution accuracy. In fact, the position estimate error when 5 trajectories are considered is lower than when 2 and 1 trajectories are considered. However, after reaching a given ECDF profile, further increasing the number of trajectories does not affect the result anymore, but only reduces the variance of the results, providing improvements mainly on the tails of the ECDF. Thus, the technique does not need to consider many trajectories (i.e., a consistent number of samples) to obtain a reasonable estimation accuracy. Indeed, good performance can be obtained also by using limited computational resources, and without requiring data covering long periods of time. As demonstrated by some recent studies [15], the ADS-B communication technology is affected by severe packet loss issues. Therefore, considering the less noisy scenario and 10 trajectories, we evaluated the effect of an increasing percentage of packet loss, as shown in Fig. 5.

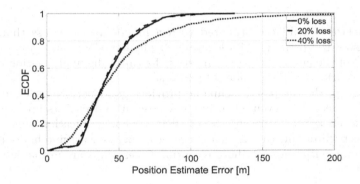

Fig. 5. Accuracy of the location estimate, while varying the packet loss percentage.

It clearly emerges that the described technique is able to obtain very good position accuracy also when a significant level of packet loss affects the communication links. In fact, the accuracy in the position estimation when the 20% of packet loss is considered is almost similar to the performance when an ideal loss-less scenario is considered. A decrease in the performances, instead, can be observed when we have a mean packet loss of the 40%, suggesting that an high level of packet loss would cause higher localization errors.

However, it is worth noting that the location estimation technique does not imply any specific real-time constraint. Indeed, because of the inherent features of the scenario (i.e., the receiver is fixed and it is not intended to be moved away) the location estimation technique can be ran even for long periods of time. Thus, it could be easily possible to gather a consistent amount of data and then filter out the packets that are not received by the majority of the receivers, thus ensuring, practically, a limited amount of packet loss. Finally, we show in Fig. 6 the accuracy in the position estimation process, considering an increasing amount of packets delivered by the aircraft in a single trajectory.

Indeed, increasing the number of packets does not affect the localization accuracy. Even by using fewer packets for each trajectory, e.g. 20 packets, the

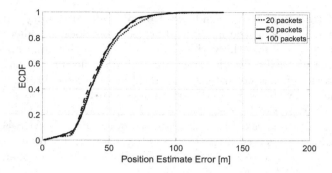

Fig. 6. Accuracy of the location estimate, varying the number of delivered packets.

receiver position could be estimated with a maximum error less than 150 m, compromising the privacy of its location. Negligible effects are only noticeable in the tails of the curves, while the most of the times the final position estimate is almost invariant to the number of packets.

To sum up, the discussed technique provides good performances in localizing *protected* receivers, even when just few aircraft and packets are considered. However, when severe packet loss issues affect the communication links, the best approach is to filter out packets that are received by the least number of receivers and work only with packets whose reception timestamps are available on many different receivers.

5.2   Experimental Performance Evaluation

The location estimation technique conceived in this contribution has been also applied on real avionics data, freely available at the following link: https://OpenSkyNetwork.org/datasets/raw/.

For our experimentation we selected the area of Switzerland, mainly due to the following reasons: (i) it is very dense of receivers participating in the OpenSky Network project, offering the possibility to avoid possible packet loss issues; (ii) it is very often crowded of airplanes, being on the route of the most commercial aircraft in the area of center Europe; and, (iii) it is covered by high mountains, possibly breaking our LOS assumption. Note that exploiting a large number of receivers is a regular condition for the attacker, rather than a best-case. As highlighted in the adversary model, an attacker could always place the desired number of receivers at a reasonable distance around the target one, and register each of these to the crowdsourcing platform, reaching the desired number of receivers. At the same time, considering a given area, the number of aircraft trajectories needed to obtain good location estimations is always compatible with the mean number of aircraft that are normally detected by an ADS-B receiver. Thus, the presence of mountains and obstacles in the chosen region makes the considered scenario as one of the harshest regions where testing location privacy limits. The map of the scenario considered in this analysis is showed in Fig. 7.

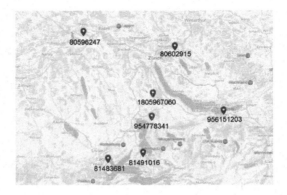

Fig. 7. Map of the receivers considered in our analysis—scale 1:500000.

Indeed, the results provided hereby only cover receivers in known positions, that did not opted in for the *anonymity* feature. This was needed to have a *control*, i.e., to establish a baseline for the performance of the technique in real environments, as well as not to break OpenSky Network terms of usage. Specifically, we assumed that the receiver having ID # *954778341* is a *protected* sensor, that opted in for the *anonymity* feature. We considered a total number of 200 position messages, delivered by a total number of 10 aircraft, further organized into 100 trajectories, and we divided them in different subsets of 5, 10, 15, and 20 packets per run. For each of them, we considered several combinations of planes. Overall, a packet loss ratio of the 13% on the data is achieved, not being an issue for the performance of our technique, as showed by results discussed in the previous subsection. Figure 8 shows the ECDF of all the results on several different combinations of planes and packets, while the following Fig. 9 shows the x-y map of the deployment tackled in the analysis, as well as the mean point of all the solutions. The location estimation technique is able to locate the *protected* receiver with a remarkable precision. Over an area of almost $60 \times 35 \,\text{km}^2$, in the

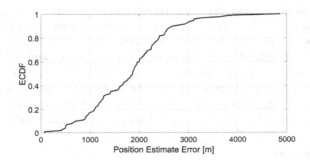

Fig. 8. Real experimentation. ECDF of the position estimate error on several different runs on real data available from OpenSky Network.

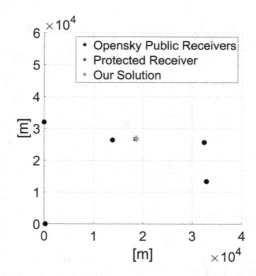

Fig. 9. Sensors in known positions (black circles), protected sensor (red square), and final determined point (green diamond). (Color figure online)

90% of the cases, we are able to locate the protected receiver with less than 2.5 km of error. In addition, by mediating all the points and taking the median value, as shown in Fig. 9, the final solution is just 392.24 m far from the real one, even assuming an unfavorable scenario as the one considered in our analysis. These results further confirms that complete location privacy in this scenario cannot be fully achieved. The gap between the real position of the sensor and its estimated one could be due to a variety of factors affecting the real scenario: (i) the position of the sensors reported by OpenSky Network could be affected by a small measurement error; (ii) the position of the airplanes could be affected by measurement errors, mainly due to the latency in the GPS communication link; (iii) the level of environmental noise affecting the scenario could be quite high; (iv) there could be shadowing and Non-Line of Sight (NLOS) effects, not accounted in our model and affecting the estimation accuracy. Further measurements in better operational conditions are part of our future work.

Nevertheless, we remark that the aim of our analysis is to analyze the location privacy limitations actually existing in the current deployment of the OpenSky Network. Indeed, even in this worst case conditions, the location of a *protected* sensor could be guessed with a small error, actually not being really *private*: the geographical area, the country and also the district where the sensor is located could be easily spotted by applying standard location estimation techniques.

6   Conclusions

In this paper we investigated the location privacy limitations affecting the popular OpenSky Network avionics crowdsourcing platform. To this aim, we applied a time-based location estimation technique, able to spot with a reasonable error the location of a receiver in the pervasive and ubiquitous OpenSky Network community, even when its location is *protected* in the disclosed data. To achieve location estimation of *protected* receivers, our technique leverages: (i) the time-of-arrival of messages delivered by ADS-B-equipped airplanes; (ii) the position of other receivers, who did not opt in for location privacy; and, (iii) the location of emitting airplanes. For a wide range of system parameters, the discussed technique can locate a supposedly *protected* receiver with an error less than 400 m, over an area of thousands of square Kilometers. Thus, maintaining full location privacy in this kind of scenario is actually difficult, and calls for further research in this domain.

Future work include the refining of our system model in the hypothesis of non uniform aircraft distribution over the sensors, its application on other sensors in other geographical areas, and the extension of our results to areas with a reduced number of public receivers. Particular attention will be also dedicated to the design of possible countermeasures to still allow the receivers to maintain their location private. All the above issues are a call for the research community for further investigations on the subject.

Acknowledgements. This publication was partially supported by awards NPRP-S-11-0109-180242, UREP23-065-1-014, and NPRP X-063-1-014 from the QNRF-Qatar National Research Fund, a member of The Qatar Foundation. The information and views set out in this publication are those of the authors and do not necessarily reflect the official opinion of the QNRF.

References

1. Strohmeier, M., Lenders, V., Martinovic, I.: On the security of the automatic dependent surveillance-broadcast protocol. IEEE Commun. Surv. Tutorials **17**(2), 1066–1087 (2015)
2. Strohmeier, M., Martinovic, I., Lenders, V.: A k-NN-based localization approach for crowdsourced air traffic communication networks. IEEE Trans. Aerosp. Electr. Systs. **54**(3), 1519–1529 (2018)
3. Kim, Y., Jo, J., Lee, S.: ADS-B vulnerabilities and a security solution with a timestamp. IEEE Aerosp. Electron. Syst. Mag. **32**(11), 52–61 (2017)
4. Strohmeier, M., Smith, M., Moser, D., et al.: Utilizing air traffic communications for OSINT on state and government aircraft. In: International Conference on Cyber Conflict (2018)
5. Trüb, R., Moser, D., Schäfer, M., et al.: Monitoring meteorological parameters with crowdsourced air traffic control data. In: International Conference on Information Processing in Sensor Network, April 2018
6. Sciancalepore, S., Di Pietro, R.: SOS - securing open skies. In: Wang, G., Chen, J., Yang, L.T. (eds.) SpaCCS 2018. LNCS, vol. 11342, pp. 15–32. Springer, Cham (2018). https://doi.org/10.1007/978-3-030-05345-1_2
7. Schäfer, M., Strohmeier, M., Lenders, V., et al.: Bringing up OpenSky: a large-scale ADS-B sensor network for research. In: Proceedings of International Symposium on Information Processing in Sensor Network, pp. 83–94, April 2014

8. Strohmeier, M., Martinovic, I., Fuchs, M., et al.: OpenSky: a swiss army knife for air traffic security research. In: Digital Avionics Systems Conference, pp. 1–14, September 2015

9. Schäfer, M., Strohmeier, M., Smith, M., et al.: OpenSky report 2018: assessing the integrity of crowdsourced mode S and ADS-B data. In: Digital Avionics Systems Conference, September 2018

10. Kacem, T., Wijesekera, D., Costa, P.C.G.: ADS-Bsec: a holistic framework to secure ADS-B. IEEE Trans. Intell. Veh. **3**, 511–521 (2018)

11. Strohmeier, M., Schäfer, M., Pinheiro, R., Lenders, V., Martinovic, I.: On perception and reality in wireless air traffic communication security. IEEE Trans. Intell. Transp. Syst. **18**(6), 1338–1357 (2017)

12. Calvo-Palomino, R., Ricciato, F., Repas, B., et al.: Nanosecond-precision time-of-arrival estimation for aircraft signals with low-cost SDR receivers. In: Proceedings of ACM/IEEE International Conference on Information Processing in Sensor Network, pp. 272–277 (2018)

13. El Marady, A.: Enhancing accuracy and security of ADS-B via MLAT assisted-flight information system. In: International Conference on Computer Engineering and Systems, pp. 182–187, December 2017

14. Baker, R., Martinovic, I.: Secure location verification with a mobile receiver. In: Proceedings of the ACM Workshop on Cyber-Physical Systems Security and Privacy, pp. 35–46 (2016)

15. Sciancalepore, S., Alhazbi, S., Di Pietro, R.: Reliability of ADS-B communications: novel insights based on an experimental assessment. In: ACM Symposium on Applied Computing, April 2019

16. Martínez-Prieto, M.A., Bregon, A., García-Miranda, I., Álvarez Esteban, P.C., Díaz, F., Scarlatti, D.: Integrating flight-related information into a (big) data lake. In: Digital Avionics Systems Conference, September 2017

17. Strohmeier, M., Smith, M., Lenders, V., Martinovic, I.: The real first class? Inferring confidential corporate mergers and government relations from air traffic communication. In: IEEE European Symposium on Security and Privacy, April 2018

18. Ricciato, F., Sciancalepore, S., Gringoli, F., et al.: Position and velocity estimation of a non-cooperative source from asynchronous packet arrival time measurements. IEEE Trans. Mob. Comput. **17**(9), 2166–2179 (2018)

19. Ogundare, O.: Understanding Least Squares Estimation and Geomatics Data Analysis. Wiley, Hoboken (2018)

20. Strohmeier, M., Lenders, V., Martinovic, I.: Lightweight location verification in air traffic surveillance networks. In: Proceedings of ACM Workshop on Cyber-Physical Systems Security, pp. 49–60 (2015)

21. Ricciato, F., Sciancalepore, S., Boggia, G.: Tracing a linearly moving node from asynchronous time-of-arrival measurements. IEEE Commun. Lett. **20**(9), 1836–1839 (2016)

22. James, G., Witten, D., Hastie, T., Tibshirani, R.: An Introduction to Statistical Learning. STS, vol. 103. Springer, New York (2013). https://doi.org/10.1007/978-1-4614-7138-7

Privacy-Preserving Genomic Data Publishing via Differentially-Private Suffix Tree

Tanya Khatri, Gaby G. Dagher$^{(\boxtimes)}$, and Yantian Hou

Department of Computer Science, Boise State University, Boise, USA
gabydagher@boisestate.edu

Abstract. Privacy-preserving data publishing is a mechanism for sharing data while ensuring that the privacy of individuals is preserved in the published data, and utility is maintained for data mining and analysis. There is a huge need for sharing genomic data to advance medical and health researches. However, since genomic data is highly sensitive and the ultimate identifier, it is a big challenge to publish genomic data while protecting the privacy of individuals in the data. In this paper, we address the aforementioned challenge by presenting an approach for privacy-preserving genomic data publishing via differentially-private suffix tree. The proposed algorithm uses a top-down approach and utilizes the Laplace mechanism to divide the raw genomic data into disjoint partitions, and then normalize the partitioning structure to ensure consistency and maintain utility. The output of our algorithm is a differentially-private suffix tree, a data structure most suitable for efficient search on genomic data. We experiment on real-life genomic data obtained from the Human Genome Privacy Challenge project, and we show that our approach is efficient, scalable, and achieves high utility with respect to genomic sequence matching count queries.

1 Introduction

In this revolutionary era of science and technology, it is much easier to access, analyze and interpret genomic data. Genomes are the most vital part of the human, as they include health and other information about the person as well as their ancestors, siblings and decedents. Since the sharing of genomic data is essential for the advancement of genomic research, it is important to ensure that sensitive information about individuals in their genomic sequences are protected in any shared data for scientific research. Maintaining the correct trade-off between utility and privacy is particularly challenging for genomic data as each individuals' DNA sequence is unique and therefore, a DNA sample can never be made truly anonymized.

Health Insurance Portability and Accountability Act (HIPAA) [2] and Genetic Information Nondiscrimination Act (GINA) [3] are frameworks provided by the government to achieve the aforementioned delicate balance. Genome Wide

S. Chen et al. (Eds.): SecureComm 2019, LNICST 304, pp. 569–584, 2019.
https://doi.org/10.1007/978-3-030-37228-6_28

Table 1. Homer's Attack: The attacker knows the genome of the victim (set of variants), the size of the mixture he's attacking and the population allele frequencies [17].

Id	Allele frequency			Distance measure $D(x) = |x-p| - |x-m|$	Inference
	Reference population(p)	Mixture(m)	Person of interest(x)		
j	0.25	0.75	1.0	0.50	Most likely to be in the Mixture
j+1	0.25	0.75	0.50	0.00	Equally likely to be in the Mixture and in the Reference Population
j+2	0.25	0.75	0.0	−0.50	Most likely to be in the Reference Population

Association Studies (GWAS) investigate genomic and biometric data with the purpose of identifying genetic variations that may be linked to diseases. The goal of GWAS is to produce aggregate statistics that are produced by examining many single nucleotide polymorphism (SNPs) locations from a group of study participants. This can be achieved by calculating *chi-squared* and *p-value* statistics. Since the aggregate statistics are taken from a sample of thousands of individuals, researchers believed that privacy was preserved by using de-identification techniques and a large sample size.

With the emergence of cloud computing, the possibility of large scale distribution of data collection from multiple resources has increased, as has the threat to privacy or information leakage. Recent work has shown, however, that the large volume of data collected from each patient exposes them to privacy breaches, even if only the aggregate statistics are reported. Homer *et al.* [17] show that a participant's information can be inferred from the allele frequencies of a large number of single-nucleotide polymorphisms (SNPs). Given the minor allele frequencies (MAFs) of both a reference population and a test population, the presence of an individual with a known genotype can be inferred using a t-test and a distance metric designed to contrast similarity between an individual and the test population. Table 1 shows an example statistics for Homer's attack, where given the genome of the victim (set of variants), the size of the mixture and the population allele frequencies, an attacker can re-identify an individual in a case group with a certain disease. by calculating the distance measure $D(x) = |x - p| - |x - m|$. If $D > 0$, it means that an individual is most likely to be in the mixture and if $D < 0$, it means that an individual is most likely to be in the reference population. $D = 0$ means equally likely to be in the mixture and in the reference population. Wang *et al.* [28] show that a participants' actual genomes can be reconstructed using correlation information about the SNPs. There are many other attacks [14,15,24] that could result in breaching the privacy of individuals.

In this paper, we address the problem of privacy-preserving genomic data publishing by proposing an approach that efficiently perturbs the raw genomic data and outputs an anonymized suffix tree that is privacy-preserving to effectively and efficiently support count queries for genomic sequence matching. To generate a privacy-preserving suffix tree, we utilize differential privacy [8], a rigorous privacy model that provides strong privacy guarantees independent of an adversary's background knowledge and computational power. Differential privacy is typically achieved through random perturbation, noise is carefully calibrated to the sensitivity. A differentially-private mechanism ensures that all outputs are insensitive to any individual's data. In other words, an individual's privacy is not at risk because of her participation in the dataset. Figure 1 illustrates a ϵ-differentially-private version of the raw data. An attacker can not infer anything about an individual by looking at ϵ-differentially-private data, regardless of any background knowledge about an individual.

1.1   Contributions

The contributions of this paper can be summarized as follows:

- We propose a novel non-interactive approach for anonymizing genomic data and releasing differentially-private suffix tree with an effective utility for genomic sequence matching. We are the first to publish differentially-private suffix tree for efficient searching on genomic data.
- We propose a top-down partitioning approach using Laplace mechanism to efficiently process datasets containing large number of genomic sequences.
- To obtain higher utility, we apply a normalization technique on the partitions to ensure consistency among genomic sequences and their suffixes.
- We implemented our approach and performed extensive experiments on real-life genomic data obtained from Human Genome Privacy Challenge [1]. The results show that our approach is efficient, scalable, and achieves high utility with respect to count queries.

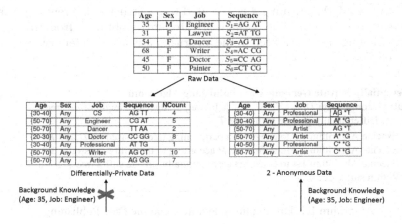

Fig. 1. Linkage attack

2   Problem Overview

Let $\mathcal{D}$ be a raw genomic data containing n sequences $\{S_1, \ldots, S_n\}$, where each sequence consists of a number of SNPs, for example, $S_1 = AGAT$. To achieve differential privacy, the principal approach is to perturb the true output by adding a random noise to it. To generate the noise according to Laplace distribution, we need to determine the privacy budget B beforehand. The suffix tree is one of the most important and widely used data structures in bio-informatics and comparative genomics. It is a special data structure, with a wide range of application, including exact matching problems, substring problems, data compression and circular strings. Suffix tree is crucially important in sequencing and investigating DNA, such as looking for the longest common substring of two DNA sequences, finding exact and inexact matchings of a sample in a long sequence. The motivation of this work is that in computational biology, molecular biology and bio informatics these problems are crucially important. In our approach, we aim to generate a differentially-private suffix tree $\mathcal{T}$ that will support count queries. Count queries, as a general data analysis task, are the building block of many data mining tasks. We denote by *user count query* any data mining's count query that attempts to answer the following question: how many times a specific pattern u occurs in the data, i.e., suffix-tree $\mathcal{T}$?

3   Proposed Solution

3.1   Differentially-Private Genomic Data Publishing

This main algorithm (Algorithm 1.1) takes as input a raw genomic data $\mathcal{D}$, a privacy budget B and user-specified height h, and returns a suffix tree $\mathcal{T}$ satisfying B-differential privacy, as shown in Algorithm 1.1. In Step 1, it calls Algorithm 1.2 to construct a noisy partitioning tree $\mathcal{P}$ based on Laplace noise and specialization threshold θ. In Step 2, Algorithm 1.3 is called, which takes as input a differentially-private partitioning tree $\mathcal{P}$, and normalize $\mathcal{P}$ based on the utility constraints to maintain the usefulness of the outputted normalized partitioning tree $\hat{\mathcal{P}}$. In Step 3, Algorithm 1.4 is executed to construct a differentially-private suffix tree $\mathcal{T}$ based on the differentially-private suffixes obtained from the normalized partitioning tree $\hat{\mathcal{P}}$. In Step 4, the algorithm outputs a differentially-private suffix tree $\mathcal{T}$.

Differentially-Private Genomic Data Publishing Algorithm
Input: Genomic Data $\mathcal{D} = \{S_1, \ldots, S_n\}$, Privacy Budget B, Height of the tree h
Output: Differentially-private suffix tree $\mathcal{T}$

1. Execute Algorithm 1.2 to construct a partitioning tree $\mathcal{P}$ based on $\mathcal{D}$ and B.
2. Execute Algorithm 1.3 to normalize $\mathcal{P}$ according to the utility constraint 3.3
3. Execute Algorithm 1.4 to construct a differentially-private suffix tree $\mathcal{T}$ from $\hat{\mathcal{P}}$.
4. Return suffix tree $\mathcal{T}$.

Algorithm 1.1: Differentially-Private Genomic Data Publishing

3.2   Partitioning Tree Generation

In this phase, our approach is to generate differentially-private suffixes, to ensure privacy-preserving data publishing. Our strategy for generating suffixes in a differentially-private manner is to use a top-down approach based on constructing disjoint partitions for multiple levels using Laplace mechanism and specialization threshold θ. Therefore, we construct a partitioning tree $\mathcal{P}$ by recursively grouping sequences in $\mathcal{D}$ into disjoint sub-datasets based on their suffixes. Given a raw genomic data $\mathcal{D} = \{S_1, \ldots, S_n\}$, privacy budget B and user specified height h, Algorithm 1.2 generates a differentially-private partitioning tree $\mathcal{P}$. Each partition contains four values: the nucleotide type, the suffix, sequences containing the suffix and the noisy count associated with it as described in Definition 3.2. In Step 1, we compute the specialization threshold $\theta = c * 2\sqrt{2k/B_l}$ (two times the standard deviation of noise) [7], where c is a constant that will be determined through experiments, k is the length of the sequence and B_l is the privacy budget per level.

Step 2 creates a virtual root partition r, where a partition is a data structure formally defined as follows.

Partition. *A partition is a tuple with four values [Nuc, UNuc, Seqs, NCount], where:*

- *Nucleotide (Nuc) is a type of bases adenine, guanine, thymine, and cytosine A, G, T, C in a strand of DNA.*
- UNuc *keeps track of the suffixes of* Seqs $= \{S_1, \ldots, S_n\}$ *for each child partition.*
- Seqs $= \{S_1, \ldots, S_n\}$ *is the set of sequences that ends with the suffix* UNuc.
- NCount *is the noisy count which is the summation of count of sequences* Seqs *and the Laplace noise.* □

All sequences in $\mathcal{D}$ are initially assigned to $r.Seqs$, $r.UNuc$ is set to *Any*, and $r.UNuc$ and $r.NCount$ are set to *Null*. In Step 3, for each nucleotide type A, G, T and C, we create child partition v for r. For each child partition v, we assign $v.Nuc$ as the nucleotide type and $v.UNuc$ as $v.Nuc \cup Parent(v).UNuc$. For each sequence we determine if $v.UNuc$ is a suffix of S, then assign it to $v.Seqs$. The variance of the Laplace noise is $2 * S(f)/(B_l - \sqrt{B_l})$, where $S(f)$ is the sensitivity and $(B_l - \sqrt{B_l})$ is the privacy budget used for partitioning. The noisy count associated with each partition is the sum of the true count and the Laplace noise. To build $\mathcal{P}$, we use uniform budget allocation scheme. We divide the total privacy budget B equally, i.e., the privacy budget used per level for constructing $\mathcal{P}$ is $B_l = B/h$. One important observation is that all partitions on the same level contain disjoint sequence sets, and therefore the privacy budget allocated to a level can be used in full for each partition in it. In Step 5, for each child partition v created in Step 3, we continue to create further child partitions if $v.Ncount \geq \theta$ for that partition and height $h > 0$. Step 6 outputs the differentially-private partitioning tree $\mathcal{P}$. Figure 2 provides an example of $\mathcal{P}$ from raw data in Fig. 1.

Differentially-Private Partitioning Tree Generation Algorithm
Input: Genomic Data $\mathcal{D} = \{S_1, \ldots, S_n\}$, Privacy Budget B, Height of the tree h
Output: Differentially-private partitioning tree $\mathcal{P}$

1. Compute the specialization threshold $\theta = c * 2\sqrt{2k/B_l}$, where k is the length of the sequence.
2. Construct a partitioning tree $\mathcal{P}$ with a virtual root partition r:
   (a) Assign all sequences in $\mathcal{D}$ to r: $r.Seqs = \{S_1, \ldots, S_n\}$
   (b) Set nucleotide $r.Nuc$ to *Any*.
   (c) Set $r.UNuc$ and noisy count $r.NCount$ to *Null*.
3. For each nucleotide type A, C, G and T, create a child partition v:
   (a) Set $v.Nuc$ to the nucleotide type.
   (b) Set $v.UNuc$ to $v.Nuc \cup Parent(v).UNuc$.
   (c) For each sequence S in $Parent(v).Seqs$, assign S to $v.Seqs$ iff $v.UNuc$ is a suffix of S.
   (d) Generate a Laplace noise $L_{noise} = Lap(2 \times k \times h/(B_l - \sqrt{B_l}))$.
   (e) Set $v.NCount$ to $|v.Seqs| + L_{noise}$, where $|v.Seqs|$ is the number of sequences assigned to partition v.
4. $h \leftarrow h - 1$.
5. While $h > 0$, for each child partition v created in Step 3, if $v.NCount \geq \theta$, then repeat Steps 3 and 4.
6. Return $\mathcal{P}$.

Algorithm 1.2: Differentially-Private Partitioning Tree Generation

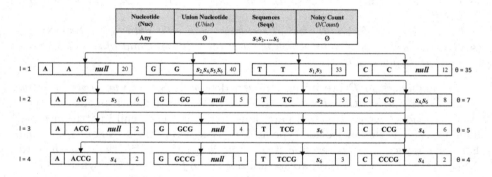

Fig. 2. Partitioning tree

Privacy Budget Allocation. B-differential privacy can be achieved by applying a differentially-private mechanism, commonly Laplace mechanism [9], that consumes a privacy budget B and calibrates noise according to the global sensitivity $S(f)$ of a function f. To address the existing utility and privacy trade-off, a geometric mechanism [12] was proposed which is a factor of an optimal mechanism $\mathcal{M}_u$ that is user-independent for every user u [6]. As in our approach we will be normalizing the generated partitioning tree $\mathcal{P}$ so that leaf nodes would be least noisy, therefore, to construct partitions at each level, we employ a uniform budget allocation scheme. That is, the privacy budget allocated to each level l is $B_l = B/h$, which is used for constructing partitions at level l in $\mathcal{P}$, as well as to compute the specialization threshold θ.

3.3 Bottom-Up Normalization

To ensure utility (usefulness) and consistency of the data, a bottom-up approach is proposed to normalize the partitioning tree based on the following utility constraint.

Utility Constraint. The noisy count $NCount$ of any node v in the partitioning tree $\mathcal{P}$ should be greater or equal to the total sum of its children's noisy counts. That is:

$$\forall v \in \mathcal{P}, \; v.NCount \geq \sum_{u \in child(v)} u.NCount$$

$\square$

Algorithm 1.3 takes the differentially-private partitioning tree $\mathcal{P}$ as an input and updates the noisy count $NCount$ of partitions from leaf to root to generate a normalized partitioning tree $\hat{\mathcal{P}}$. Following the bottom-up approach, we start with level $l = h - 1$, where h is the height of the differentially-private partitioning tree $\mathcal{P}$. The algorithm ensures that for each non-leaf node in $\mathcal{P}$, the utility constraint holds true.

Bottom-Up Normalization Algorithm
Input: Differentially-private partitioning tree $\mathcal{P}$
Output: Normalized partitioning tree $\hat{\mathcal{P}}$
Apply a bottom-up approach on $\mathcal{P}$ to obtain a normalize partitioning tree $\hat{\mathcal{P}}$:
1. $l \leftarrow h - 1$, where h is the height of $\mathcal{P}$.
2. For each non-leaf node v in $\mathcal{P}$ at level l, if the utility constraint 3.3 is not satisfied, then update the noisy count of v:
   $v.NCount \leftarrow \sum_{u \in child(v)} u.NCount$.
3. $l \leftarrow l - 1$.
4. While $l > 0$, repeat Steps 2 and 3.
5. Return $\hat{\mathcal{P}}$.

Algorithm 1.3: Bottom-Up Normalization

If the utility constraint 3.3 is not satisfied, that is, the noisy count of the parent is less than the sum of the noisy count of its children, then the parent's noisy count is updated to be the sum of the noisy count of all its children, as described in Step 2. We keep normalizing based on the utility constraint until we reach the root partition of the tree. In Step 5, a differentially-private normalized partitioning tree $\hat{\mathcal{P}}$ is produced as an output.

3.4 Suffix Tree Generation

This algorithm (Algorithm 1.4) takes as an input the normalized partitioning tree $\hat{\mathcal{P}}$, and based on a top-down approach it outputs the B-differentially-private suffix tree T. In the normalized partitioning tree, $U.Nuc$ represents suffix and $NCount$ represents the normalized noise count. We traverse the normalized partitioning tree level-wise and create a branch in the suffix tree for each suffix present in $\hat{P}$. Starting with level 1, for each partition v in a normalized tree $\hat{P}$, we use the suffix presents in $v.UNuc$ and its corresponding $v.NCount$ to create a tree branch in the suffix tree T, as shown in Fig. 3, and add the associated noisy count at the end. For each added branch, we append the dollar sign \$ equal to the noisy count $v.NCount$. Every path from the root to the square node represents a suffix. Because the tree is normalized, there is no violation of utility constraint when we take the parent suffix and add it to the suffix tree i.e., following a top-down approach. Since, the noisy count of the parent partition is always grater than or equal to the noisy count of its children, the suffixes maintain consistency. Step 5 outputs the differentially-private suffix tree T that support count queries for genomic sequence matching and maintains data utility.

4   Algorithm Analysis

4.1   Privacy Analysis

We use the composition properties of differential privacy to guarantee that the proposed algorithm satisfies B-differential privacy as a whole. Any sequence of computations that each provides differential privacy in isolation also provides differential privacy in sequence, which is known as *sequential composition*.

Suffix Tree Generation Algorithm
Input: Normalized partitioning tree $\hat{P}$
Output: Differentially-private suffix tree T
Apply a top-down approach on $\hat{P}$ to obtain a differentially-private suffix tree T:
  1. Set the initial level: $l \leftarrow 1$.
  2. For each node v in $\hat{P}$ at level l:
    (a) Use $v.UNuc$ sequence to create a tree branch in T.
    (b) Append $v.NCount$ dollar signs \$ to the added branch.
  3. $l \leftarrow l + 1$.
  4. While $l \leq h$, where h is the height of $\hat{P}$, then repeat Steps 2 and 3.
  5. Return T.

Algorithm 1.4: Suffix Tree Generation

Sequential composition [22]. Let each A_i provide B_i-differential privacy. A sequence of $A_i(\mathcal{D})$ over the dataset $\mathcal{D}$ provides $(\sum_i B_i)$-differential privacy.   □

However, if the sequence of computations is conducted on disjoint datasets, the privacy cost does not accumulate but depends only on the worst guarantee of all compositions. This is known as *parallel composition*.

Parallel composition [22]. Let each A_i provide B_i-differential privacy. A sequence of $A_i(\mathcal{D})$ over a set of disjoint datasets $\mathcal{D}$ provides B_i-differential privacy.   □

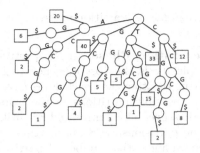

Fig. 3. Differentially-Private Suffix Tree generated from the normalized version of partitioning tree $\hat{\mathcal{P}}$ shown in Fig. 2.

Given a privacy budget B, our algorithm generates B-differentially-private genomic suffix tree. *Proof:* Our proposed algorithm consists of three phases - *partitioning tree generation, bottom-up normalization* and *suffix tree generation*. We have a fanout $f = 4$. According to Lemma 4.1, we can use the same privacy budget for each partition at the same level. Therefore, if we can prove that the summation of the privacy budget used in each partitioning level is less than or equal to B, we get the conclusion that our approach satisfies B-differential privacy.

In the partitioning tree generation step of our algorithm, the allocation of privacy budget per level is $B_l = B/h$, where h is the height of the partitioning tree $\mathcal{P}$. The privacy budget needed for computing the specialization threshold θ is $\sqrt{B_l}$. As all the partitions on the same level in the partitioning contain disjoint sets of sequences, according to Lemma 4.1, the total privacy budget for each partition to build the noisy partitioning tree $\mathcal{P}$ is $B_l - \sqrt{B_l}$. The only time we refer to the original data is when we compute total count of the sequences in each partition and as we mention above for each partition we compute $B_l - \sqrt{B_l}$ privacy budget. For the bottom-up normalization and suffix tree generation phase, no privacy budget is consumed as we are not utilizing the original data. Therefore, the total privacy budget consumed can be formulated as:

$$\sum_{l=1}^{h} \underbrace{(B_l - \sqrt{B_l})}_{\text{partition}} + \underbrace{\sqrt{B_l}}_{\text{threshold}} = h \times B_l \leq B$$

As proven by Hay *et al.* [16], a post-processing of differentially-private results remains differential private. Therefore, our approach satisfies B-differential privacy. □

4.2 Complexity Analysis

(Complexity). The overall complexity of our proposed approach in the average case is $\mathcal{O}(h^2 \times n)$. *Proof.* We can determine the time complexity of the proposed approach in terms of three phases: Partitioning tree generation, Normalization and Suffix tree generation.

Partitioning Tree Generation Phase. In the partitioning tree generation phase, the runtime complexity is the cost of generating each partition times the number of partition in the tree. For each level l of the partitioning tree, the maximum number of possible partitions in the worst case is 4^l, and the total number is $\sum_{l=1}^{h} 4^l$. However, since threshold θ is utilized, that restricts the exponential growth of the partitions, as θ fluctuates according to the Laplace noise distribution, which balances the number of partitions [10]. Therefore, in the average case, the number of partitions per level is $P_l \approx 4 \times l \ll 4^l$, and the total number of partitions is:

$$\sum_{l=1}^{h} 4 \times l = 2 \times h^2$$

Given that we process n sequences per level, the total cost of constructing a partitioning tree in an average case is $\mathcal{O}(n \times h^2)$, where, n is the number of sequences and h is the height of the partitioning tree.

Normalization Phase. In the normalization phase, we traverse the partitioning tree once. Therefore, the total cost to construct a normalized partitioning tree in an average case is: $\sum_{l=1}^{h} 4 \times l = 2 \times h^2 = \mathcal{O}(h^2)$.

Suffix Tree Generation Phase. In the suffix tree generation phase, the runtime complexity is the time taken to insert a full sequence times the number of sequences generated. As stated by [13,27,30], a string of length h can be inserted in $\mathcal{O}(h)$. In the average case, the number of full sequences to be generated from the partitioning tree is $\mathcal{O}(h)$, where these full sequences will account for all the trimmed sequences (short inbuilt suffixes). Therefore, the average computational cost to build a suffix tree is $\mathcal{O}(h \times h) = \mathcal{O}(h^2)$.

Therefore, the overall complexity of our proposed approach in the average case is: $\mathcal{O}(h^2 \times n + h^2 + h^2) = \mathcal{O}(h^2 \times n)$. $\qquad\square$

Given that $h \ll n$, we show in our experiment that our algorithm scales linearly w.r.t. a linear increase of n.

5   Performance Evaluation

5.1   Implementation Setup and Dataset

We implemented our algorithm in Java, and our experiments were conducted on a machine equipped with an Intel(R) Core(TM) i7-6700 CPU @ 3.40 GHz processor and 32.0 GB RAM, running Windows 10 64-bit operating system.

The humane SNPs were obtained from the Human Genome Privacy Challenge [1]. The chr2 and chr10 datasets contain 311 SNPs and 610 SNPs respectively. The length of the sequences is 200. The information of datasets is provided in Table 2.

Table 2. Properties of Experimental Datasets

Dataset	# of SNP Sequences	Length of Sequence
chr2	311 (29504091-30044866)	200
chr10	610 (55127312-56292137)	200

5.2   Experimental Results

In this section, our objective is to study the impact of enforcing differential privacy on the data quality in terms of determining optimal value of constant c, scalability, efficiency and utility.

Determining Optimal Value of Constant c. Recall that $\theta = c * 2\sqrt{2k/B_l}$. To determine the optimal value of constant c for the specialization threshold θ, we randomly generate queries of varying length from the suffix tree and experiment data utility for different c values. We started experimenting with a $0.25 < c$, and noticed that θ was too big and the condition to partition further was never satisfied. Therefore, we experimented on c values from the range $[0, 0.25]$. As shown in Fig. 4, the best results in terms of average relative error is for $c = 0.15$.

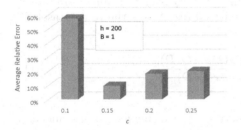

Fig. 4. Determining the optimal value of c for threshold θ

Fig. 5. Comparative evaluation of our proposed algorithm with [29]

Scalability. The objective is to measure the runtime of each construction phase to ensure its capability to scale up in terms of record size. We measure the runtime of our proposed algorithm with respect to the linear increase in the number of sequences. We set the privacy budget B to 1, height of the tree to 200 and the value of c as 0.15. Figure 6 illustrates the runtime of our algorithm w.r.t. a linear increase in the number of sequences in the randomized dataset (200k, 400k, 600k, 800k and 1000k records). The x-axis represents the number of sequences and the y-axis shows the runtime in minutes. We observe that the growth in total runtime is linear when the data records increase linearly. We also observe that the partitioning tree construction phase is the most dominant phase in the algorithm, but they all scale linearly w.r.t. the number of sequences.

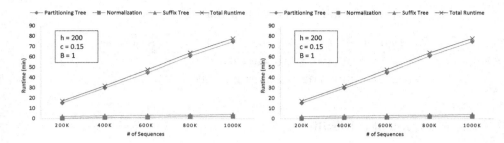

Fig. 6. Scalability w.r.t # of sequences   **Fig. 7.** Efficiency w.r.t budget B

Efficiency. We evaluate the efficiency of our proposed approach on the chr2 and chr10 dataset with respect to the privacy budget B varying from 0.5 to 1.25 at an interval of 0.25. The x-axis represents privacy budget B and the y-axis represents the runtime in milliseconds as shown in Fig. 7. We observe that for chr2 dataset the runtime is between 200–300 milliseconds and for chr10 dataset the runtime is between 600–700 milliseconds. However, the runtime is consistent with the increase in B for both datasets.

Utility. We measure the utility of a count query Q over the sanitized dataset $\tilde{\mathcal{D}}$ by its *relative error* with respect to the actual result over the raw dataset $\mathcal{D}$. The relative error is computed as:

$$Relative\ Error = \frac{|Q(\tilde{\mathcal{D}}) - Q(\mathcal{D})|}{max(Q(\mathcal{D}), s)}, \tag{1}$$

where s is a sanity bound that is set to 1.

We randomly generate 500 counting queries with varying length of sequences. We divide the query set into five subsets such that the query length of the i-th subset is uniformly distributed in $[1, \frac{i}{5}\sqrt{|S|}]$ and each query is drawn randomly, where $|S| = 200$ is the length of the sequence. All relative error will be computed based on the average of 10 runs. The experimental results are generated using both datasets: chr2 and chr10. With 500 random queries of length $l \in [1, 14]$, since $i = 5$ in our experiments. The query length of the first subset for 20% of query length will be $[1, \frac{1}{5}\sqrt{200}]$, which is equal to [1,3]. Similarly, the five

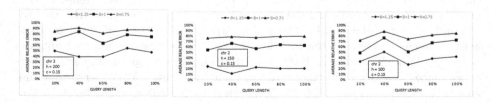

Fig. 8. Average relative error with respect to query length percentage for chr2 dataset

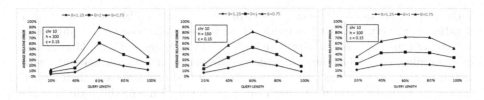

Fig. 9. Average relative error with respect to query length percentage for chr10 dataset

uniformly distributed subsets for 20%, 40%, 60%, 80% and 100% of query length
are $[1, 3], [1, 6], [1, 8], [1, 11], [1, 14]$ respectively. We select five random queries for
each sampling and the relative error is the average of 10 runs.

Figures 8 and 9 depict the average relative error as the value of privacy budget
B grows from 0.75 to 1.25 at an interval 0.25, and height is set to 100, 150 and
200 with $c = 0.15$. The x-axis represent the maximum query length of each subset
in terms of the percentage of $\sqrt{|S|}$ and the y-axis represent the average relative
error. We observe that the average relative error decreases with the increase of
B with respect to both datasets, and the best data utility is obtained for privacy
budget $B = 1.25$. This observation remains true irrespective of the height h of
the tree, as shown in both figures for $h \in \{100, 150, 200\}$. This is due to the
fact that as we increase the privacy budget, we are decreasing the noise that is
being added and hence the data utility will be more. Also, we observe that in
chr2 dataset (the smaller dataset), the average relative error is almost constant
for each B and h, regardless of the query length. On the other hand, in chr10
dataset, the average relative error is variable depending on the query length.
This is due to the fact in a larger dataset, the size of the data grows, and more
noise is added to ensure privacy since the noisy count of more partitions will
surpass threshold θ.

We also compare the performance of our proposed algorithm with the
research work done by Wang et al. [29] for the differentially-private genome
data dissemination through top-down specialization. We use the same dataset
as in [29], and make the experimental settings as close as possible. We set the
privacy budget $B = 1$, and determine the accuracy of our algorithm as follows:

$$Accuracy = 1 - Average\ Relative\ Error, \qquad (2)$$

where the relative error is computed using Eq. 1. Figure 5 illustrates that for
both datasets chr2 and ch10, our proposed algorithm provides higher accuracy
than [29]. That is, for $B = 1$, both algorithms achieves better accuracy on larger
dataset (chr10), while our solution achieves higher accuracy with up to 70%.

6   Related Work

Genome-Wide Association Studies (GWAS) is used for analysis of sets of DNA
sequences to discover and identify the genetic basis of disease. Although these

statistics that are published as the result of GWAS can possibly be used for identification of the participating individuals. This has led to research on publishing GWAS data in a differentially-private manner. The papers [4,11,18,23,26,29,31] list a number of mechanisms to achieve differential privacy on genomic data. Akgün et al. [4] have categorized previously identified problems and their respective solutions introduced in research prior to theirs. Some of the problems and their solution techniques discussed by [4] are discussed in the following paragraphs in this section. Wang et al. [29] introduce an approach to disseminate differentially-private genomic data using top-down specialization. This method assumes a data owner has a data table $\mathcal{D}(A^i, A^{snp})$ where A^i are explicit identifiers and A^{snp} a set of SNPs. The algorithm aims to satisfy ϵ-differential privacy while retaining data utility with a high sensitivity and generates an anonymized data table $\hat{D}$ that can be released to the public. Uhler et al. [26] introduce methods that focus on releasing differentially-private minor allele frequencies, p-values, and χ^2 statistics for the M most relevant SNPs regardless of arbitrary external information. They also apply penalized logical regression technique while maintaining differential privacy guarantee to locate genome-wide associations in the data. Finally, for testing the approach, the proposed techniques are compared both on simulation data and on real canine hair length genomic data. This approach is an adaptation of Bhaskar et al. [5] to genome wide association studies. Yu et al. [31] extend the work of Uhler et al. [26] by allowing for an arbitrary number of cases and controls and performance of a risk-utility analysis. Next, the methods proposed are compared to the differentially-private publishing mechanism proposed by Johnson and Shmatikov [20]. The work of Li et al. [21] introduces the compressive mechanism which uses a probabilistic compression procedure that generates a synopsis, adds Laplace noise to the compressed data, and then decodes the results. Compared to other synopsis proposals, the compressive sensing mechanism provides more accurate statistical query results while using less noise under certain conditions. Building upon this work, Roozgard et al. [25] presents a compressed sensing based, differentially-private genomic data dissemination algorithm that takes sequences of genomic nucleotides from multiple subjects, and transforms the frequencies of SNPs into a sparse vector representation. Laplace noise is then added to all elements of the sparse vector. Jiang et al. [19] suggests a method for releasing the top-K most significant SNPs across the genome when K is small.

7   Conclusion

When publishing genomic data, achieving the right balance between privacy and utility is challenging since each person's DNA sequence is unique (with the exception of identical twins) and a DNA sample therefore can never be made truly anonymized. In this paper, we propose an algorithm for privacy-preserving genomic data publishing via differentially-private suffix tree that is scalable, efficient and support count queries. We perform the privacy and complexity analysis of our approach and show that our approach preserves privacy and is scalable even with respect to large datasets. We also evaluate the performance of our algorithm and present the experimental to determine the scalability, efficiency and utility of our solution. The experiments demonstrated that our approach is scalable, efficient and maintains high utility to answer count queries.

Acknowledgement. This research was partially supported by Forsta, Inc (www. forsta.io).

References

1. Human genome privacy protection challenge
2. Health insurance portability and accountability act (hipaa) (1996)
3. Genetic information nondiscrimination act (gena) (2008)
4. Akgün, M., Bayrak, A.O., Ozer, B., Sağıroğlu, M.Ş.: Privacy preserving processing of genomic data: a survey. J. Biomed. Inform. **56**, 103–111 (2015)
5. Bhaskar, R., Laxman, S., Smith, A., Thakurta, A.: Discovering frequent patterns in sensitive data. In: Proceedings of the 16th ACM SIGKDD International Conference on Knowledge Discovery and Data Mining, pp. 503–512. ACM (2010)
6. Bonomi, L., Xiong, L.: A two-phase algorithm for mining sequential patterns with differential privacy. In: Proceedings of the 22Nd ACM CIKM, pp. 269–278 (2013)
7. Chen, R., Fung, B.C.M., Desai, B.C., Sossou, N.M.: Differentially private transit data publication: a case study on the montreal transportation system. In: Proceedings of the 18th ACM SIGKDD on KDD, pp. 213–221 (2012)
8. Dwork, C.: Differential privacy. In ICALP, pp. 1–12 (2006)
9. Dwork, C., McSherry, F., Nissim, K., Smith, A.: Calibrating noise to sensitivity in private data analysis. In TCC (2006)
10. Dwork, C., Roth, A.: The algorithmic foundations of differential privacy. Found. Trends Theor. Comput. Sci. **9**(3–4), 211–407 (2014)
11. Fienberg, S.E., Slavkovic, A., Uhler, C.: Privacy preserving GWAS data sharing. In: IEEE International Conference on Data Mining Workshops, pp. 628–635 (2011)
12. Ghosh, A., Roughgarden, T., Sundararajan, M.: Universally utility-maximizing privacy mechanisms. SIAM J. Comput. **41**(6), 1673–1693 (2012)
13. Giegerich, R., Kurtz, S.: From ukkonen to mccreight and weiner: a unifying view of linear-time suffix tree construction. Algorithmica **19**(3), 331–353 (1997)
14. Goodrich, M.T.: The mastermind attack on genomic data (2009)
15. Gymrek, M., McGuire, A.L., Golan, D., Halperin, E., Erlich, Y.: Identifying personal genomes by surname inference. Science **339**, 321–324 (2013)
16. Hay, M., Rastogi, V., Miklau, G., Suciu, D.: Boosting the accuracy of differentially private histograms through consistency. Proc. VLDB Endow. **3**, 1021–1032 (2010)
17. Homer, N., et al.: Resolving individuals contributing trace amounts of DNA to highly complex mixtures using high-density SNP genotyping microarrays (2006)
18. Huang, Z.: Privacy preserving algorithms for genomic data
19. Jiang, X., et al.: A community assessment of privacy preserving techniques for human genomes. BMC Med. Inform. Decis. Making **14**(Suppl 1), S1 (2014)
20. Johnson, A., Shmatikov, V.: Privacy-preserving data exploration in genome-wide association studies. In: Proceedings of ACM SIGKDD International Conference on Knowledge Discovery and Data Mining, pp. 1079–1087 (2013)
21. Li, Y.D., Zhang, Z., Winslett, M., Yang, Y.: Compressive mechanism: utilizing sparse representation in differential privacy. In: Proceedings of the 10th Annual ACM Workshop on Privacy in the Electronic Society, pp. 177–182 (2011)

22. Frank D. McSherry. Privacy integrated queries: an extensible platform for privacy-preserving data analysis. In: Proceedings of the SIGMOD 2009, pp. 19–30 (2009)
23. Naveed, M., et al.: Privacy in the genomic era. ACM Comput. Surv. 48(1), 6:1–6:44 (2015)
24. Rodriguez, L.L., Brooks, L.D., Greenberg, J.H., Green, E.D.: The complexities of genomic identifiability
25. Roozgard, A., Barzigar, N., Verma, P.K., Cheng, S.: Genomic data privacy protection using compressed sensing. Trans. Data Privacy 9(1)–13 (2016)
26. Uhlerop, C., Slavković, A., Fienberg, S.E.: Privacy-preserving data sharing for genome-wide association studies. J. Priv. Confidentiality 5(1), 137 (2013)
27. Ukkonen, E.: On-line construction of suffix trees. Algorithmica 14(3), 249–260 (1995)
28. Wang, R., Li, Y.F., Wang, X.F., Tang, H., Zhou, X.: Learning your identity and disease from research papers: information leaks in genome wide association study (2009)
29. Wang, S., Mohammed, N., Chen, R.: Differentially private genome data dissemination through top-down specialization. BMC Med. Inform. Decis. Making 14(1), S2 (2014)
30. Weiner, P.: Linear pattern matching algorithms. In: SWAT 1973, pp. 1–11 (1973)
31. Yu, F., Fienberg, S.E., Slavković, A.B., Uhler, C.: Scalable privacy-preserving data sharing methodology for genome-wide association studies. J. Biomed. Inform. 50, 133–141 (2014)

Author Index